*The Harvard Medical School Guide
to Suicide Assessment and Intervention*

The Harvard Medical School Guide to Suicide Assessment and Intervention

Douglas G. Jacobs, M.D., Editor

Foreword by Joseph T. Coyle, M.D.

Sponsored by Harvard Medical School

Jossey-Bass Publishers
San Francisco

Jossey-Bass books and products are available through most
bookstores. To contact Jossey-Bass directly, call (888) 378-2537,
fax to (800) 605-2665, or visit our website at www.josseybass.com.

Substantial discounts on bulk quantities of Jossey-Bass books
are available to corporations, professional associations, and
other organizations. For details and discount information,
contact the special sales department at Jossey-Bass.

 Manufactured in the United States of America on Lyons Falls Turin
Book. This paper is acid-free and 100 percent totally chlorine-free.

Library of Congress Cataloging-in-Publication Data

The Harvard Medical School guide to suicide assessment and
intervention / Douglas G. Jacobs, editor.
p. cm.
ISBN 0-7879-4303-7 (cloth: alk. paper)
1. Suicide. 2. Suicide—Prevention. I. Jacobs, Douglas G.
II. Harvard Medical School.
RC569.H37   1998
616.85'8445—ddc21

98-25332

FIRST EDITION
HC Printing
10 9 8 7 6 5 4 3

CONTENTS

FOREWORD

In the current environment of managed behavioral health care, suicidality represents one of the diminishing number of criteria for justifying the psychiatric hospitalization of patients. As humane succor and the restorative effects of asylum are eliminated from the lexicon of psychiatric care, it must be emphasized that psychiatric illness has a substantial risk of lethality, primarily through suicide. Thus, a simplistic dichotomous decision based primarily on a patient's self-report of the presence or absence of suicidal thinking must be replaced by a more nuanced appreciation of risk and protective factors.

Suicide Assessment and Intervention evolved out of a two-day conference on the issue that brought together Harvard faculty and outside experts. The intent is to be comprehensive in addressing issues of assessment and intervention and in recognizing special issues, such as age. For example, suicide is a leading cause of death for youth, and assisted suicide is an important matter for the elderly, who have concerns about the quality of the end of life. It is hoped that the book strikes a useful balance between evidence-based and practical state-of-the-art approaches to the serious clinical problem of suicide.

Cambridge, Massachusetts JOSEPH T. COYLE, M.D.
September 1998

For my loving family
Mary, Carolyn, and Deborah
and
those others who have supported me

PREFACE

This book is designed to help clinicians in their assessment and treatment of the suicidal patient. Each chapter ends with a section entitled "Implications for the Clinician," which condenses the chapter to highlights that would be relevant in clinical practice. I have reviewed each chapter and, wherever possible, have tried to minimize redundancy. There is an overlap among several of the chapters, however, which will allow the reader to appreciate that the same subject can be viewed from different perspectives by acknowledged experts.

Contributors were selected on the basis of their career interest and expertise in the field of suicide or in specific related issues, such as psychopharmacology or child and adolescent psychiatry. Given that suicide is a multidimensional, complex clinical problem, there is no one correct method of assessment and treatment, and this book reflects the different approaches of acknowledged experts in the field. It allows the reader to select the approach that best fits the specific problems presented by an individual patient and that complements the already established patient-clinician relationship. It is not meant to be construed as the standard of care, however.

The majority of chapters are original manuscripts written specifically for this book and designed to provide the reader with practical, clinically relevant information that will help the clinician work better with the suicidal patient.

ACKNOWLEDGMENTS

I would like to thank Dr. Joseph Coyle and the Harvard Department of Psychiatry Executive Committee for supporting the concept of this book and for encouraging participation from faculty members.

The contributors to this book, many of whom are members of the Harvard faculty, have generously given their time and expertise in writing their respective chapters.

I acknowledge the Department of Psychiatry at the Cambridge Hospital, particularly its Continuing Education Division, for collaborating on the 1997 Harvard Suicide Conference that served as a stimulus for many of the chapters in this book. Moreover, I have an ongoing intellectual debt to the Cambridge Hospital, where I was a member of the faculty from 1975 to 1985. The Cambridge Hospital served as the foundation for my clinical and academic experience in the field of suicide, particularly John Mack and Leston Havens, my two mentors in the field of suicide, who have had meaningful impacts on my professional career.

Appreciation goes to my colleagues at McLean Hospital, where I am currently affiliated. In particular, Ross Baldessarini supported the overall project and provided meaningful editorial comments on my own chapter.

Thanks go to Anthony Komoroff and the staff of the Harvard Medical Publications for their coordination of this project.

The staff of the National Mental Illness Screening Project—Barbara Kopans, Joelle Meszler Reizes, Laura Stoll, and Nicole Rutkowski—were involved with multiple phases of this project and provided administrative assistance and research, which allowed this project to proceed on time. In particular, Nancy Deutsch and Allison Make worked diligently on several of the chapters and other aspects of the project to facilitate its conclusion. Marci Klein-Benheim made meaningful contributions. Margaret Brewer was a steady hand in the overall project in terms of writing, researching, and providing editorial assistance.

I want to acknowledge Alan Rinzler for his thoughtful participation and insight and all the editors at Jossey-Bass Publishers for their hard work and dedication.

Finally, I want to acknowledge the invaluable contribution of my assistant, Shelley Truett, who has been with me for more than twelve years and who has allowed this project to become a reality.

Wellesley Hills, Massachusetts   DOUGLAS G. JACOBS, M.D.
September 1998

The Harvard Medical School Guide
to Suicide Assessment and Intervention

PART ONE

ASSESSMENT

CHAPTER ONE

Suicide Assessment

An Overview and Recommended Protocol

Douglas G. Jacobs, M.D.
Margaret Brewer, R.N., M.B.A.
Marci Klein-Benheim, Ph.D.

This chapter presents an overview of the clinical considerations involved in suicide assessment. We review what is known about risk factors associated with suicide and highlight both their clinical utility and limitations. The chapter presents our version of a suicide assessment protocol that is intended as a suggested guideline; it is not a standard of care but an approach to the clinical problem of suicide. A guiding principle is that suicide is a multi-determined phenomenon that requires a multidimensional approach. Each element of the protocol is reviewed and case examples are cited to demonstrate how the protocol can be used clinically. A purpose of the chapter is to provide clinicians methods of assessing patients' degree of suicide risk. It also demonstrates why reliable prediction of individual suicide at a specific time is impossible.

Suicide is the ninth leading cause of death in the United States, accounting for more than thirty thousand deaths per year, and the third leading cause of death for Americans aged fifteen to twenty-four (Mościcki, 1997). Moreover, these rates are almost certainly underreported because of the social stigma associated with suicide (Mościcki, 1995a).

Despite these statistics, suicide continues to have a very low base rate in the general U.S. population, with an annual incidence of 11.2 suicides for every 100,000 persons, or 0.011 percent (Mościcki, 1997). This low incidence contributes

We acknowledge Dr. Ross Baldessarini, who reviewed this chapter and provided meaningful comments.

to the difficulty of developing accurate clinical instruments to identify individuals at risk. There is no psychological test, clinical technique, or biological marker sufficiently sensitive and specific to support accurate short-term prediction of suicide in an individual person (Goldstein, Black, Nasrallah, and Winokur, 1991). Furthermore, efforts to improve the sensitivity of available risk-prediction measures result only in more false positives: individuals identified for further evaluation but who do not in the near future try to commit suicide. In contrast, efforts to improve the specificity of such measures result in more false negatives, or the overlooking of some individuals who are actually at risk. MacKinnon and Farberow (1975) pointed out the difficulties in identifying specific cases because of the low base rates and the error rate of all proposed predictive measures. They found that even if one used an imaginary instrument with an idealistically low false-positive and false-negative rate of 1 percent, only 20 percent of the suicide predictions would be accurate (true positives).

Researchers have identified several factors associated with increased individual lifetime risk of suicide. These risk factors can be divided into sociodemographic and clinical measures (Table 1.1). Sociological factors include being male, aged sixty years or older, living alone and being unmarried, white or Native American, not having young children in the home, and financial problems. Clinical risk factors include manic-depressive disorder, major depressive disorder, schizophrenia, substance abuse, history of suicide attempts, suicidal ideation, comorbid panic attacks, severe anhedonia, and recent humiliation (Hirschfeld, 1996; Hirschfeld and Russell, 1997). Although these risk factors apply to most completed suicides, most persons with one or more of these risk factors do not complete or attempt suicide in any given year.

A study by Pokorny (1983) illustrates how a method to predict suicide based on recognized risk factors will not only lead to an overidentification of those at risk, but also to a high number of missed or undetected cases. In this study, Pokorny attempted to identify which of 4,800 consecutive patients at a Veterans Administration hospital would commit suicide. On the basis of twenty-one known suicide risk factors, he identified a subsample of 803 patients as having increased risk of suicide. Only 30 of the 803 (3.74 percent) patients so identified actually committed suicide during a five-year follow-up period (0.922 percent per year). Furthermore, of the 67 suicide victims, 37 were not identified, producing more false negatives than true positives. (See Table 1.2.)

Although this study may have been too short, it leads to an important question: If suicide is not predictable in individual patients, what is the value of assessing individuals for suicide risk? The answer to this question about any clinical assessment is the need to inform a clinician as to what to do next. In order for clinicians to plan their interventions, a useful way to begin is with an idea of where a patient is along a suicide risk continuum and what possible substrates of suicidality are in the individual being assessed. Thus, the goal of a

Table 1.1. Risk Factors for Suicide in Adolescents and Adults.

Factor	Adults	Adolescents
Demographic	Males more than females	Males more than females
	People who are widowed, divorced, single	Married people more than unmarried people
Psychosocial	Lack of social supports	History of perinatal distress
	Unemployment	Status of being unwed and pregnant
	Drop in social or economic status	Parental absence, abuse
		Academic problems
Psychiatric and medical	Presence of a psychiatric diagnosis, especially major affective disorder	Affective illness, especially bipolar
	Comorbidity	Substance abuse, attention deficit hyperactivity disorder, epilepsy
	Physical illness	Conduct disorders, impulsivity, explosiveness
	Family history	Family history
	Psychological turmoil	Disciplinary crisis, humiliation
	Previous attempts	Previous attempts
Miscellaneous	Alcohol use or abuse	Exposure to suicide
	Presence of firearms	Presence of firearms and alcohol

Source: Adapted from GL Klerman, Clinical epidemiology of suicide, *The Journal of Clinical Psychiatry.* 48[12, Suppl]:33–38, 1987. Copyright 1987, Physicians Postgraduate Press. Reprinted by permission.

Table 1.2. Pokorny's Results on Predicted Versus Actual Suicides.

Predicted Suicides	Actual Suicides		
	Yes	No	Total
Yes	30 (true positives)	773 (false positives)	803
No	37 (false negatives)	3,960 (true negatives)	3,997
Total	67 suicides	4,733 nonsuicides	4,800

suicide assessment is not to predict suicide, but rather to place a person along a putative risk continuum, to appreciate the bases for the suicidality, and to allow for a more informed intervention.

Our comprehensive protocol for suicide risk assessment in clinical settings is set out in Exhibit 1.1. The chapter concludes with two case examples that illustrate how this protocol can be used in clinical practice.

CONSIDERING AXIS I DISORDERS AS PREDISPOSING FACTORS

Although there are many public misconceptions about suicide, the widely held belief that one must be mentally ill to commit suicide is not one of them. Psychological autopsy studies have consistently shown that 90 to 93 percent of completed suicides satisfy the criteria for one or more axis I disorders (Clark and Fawcett, 1992b; Goodwin and Runck, 1992). This strong association of psychiatric illness and suicide suggests that a reasonable place to begin a suicide assessment is to identify the presence or absence of axis I diagnoses and to consider them as predisposing factors for suicide. Other authors have described the presence of a psychiatric illness as a necessary but not sufficient condition for suicide (Goodwin and Runck, 1992) or as a distal risk factor for suicide (Mościcki, 1997).

As Table 1.3 indicates, the three most common axis I diagnoses associated with suicide are major affective disorders (bipolar disorder and major depressive disorder), alcoholism, and schizophrenia (Murphy, 1984).

Affective Disorders

Not surprisingly, major affective disorders, primarily in depressive phases, are the diagnoses most often found in suicide victims. Indeed, a primary diagnosis of major depression has been found in as many as 70 percent of completed suicides

---

Exhibit 1.1. Suicide Assessment Protocol.

Step 1. Identify or detect predisposing factors.

Step 2. Elucidate potentiating factors.

Step 3. Conduct a specific suicide inquiry.

Step 4. Determine the level of intervention:

      A. Estimate the acuteness or chronicity of the patient's suicidality.

      B. Evaluate competence, impulsivity, and acting out.

      C. Assess the therapeutic alliance.

      D. Plan the nature and frequency of reassessments.

Step 5. Document the assessments.

Table 1.3. Relationship Between Specific Axis I Diagnoses and Suicide.

Diagnosis	Lifetime Risk	Percentage of Suicides	High-Risk Profile
Affective disorders	15 percent	50–70 percent	Anxiety or panic symptoms Moderate alcohol abuse
Schizophrenia	10 percent	10–15 percent	Formerly high-functioning person Depressive symptoms
Alcoholism and substance abuse	2–3 percent	15–25 percent	Interpersonal loss Comorbid depression

(Barraclough, Bunch, Nelson, and Sainsbury, 1974), although the mean from many studies is about 50 percent (Murphy, 1984). The significance of bipolar disorder and its relationship to suicide is discussed in more detail in Chapters Fourteen and Twenty.

Study after study has confirmed that the presence of a major affective disorder is a significant risk factor for suicide. However, it is important to place this risk in perspective by considering the annual suicide rate in the population of persons with affective disorder. It is known that in the general U.S. population, with an annual incidence of 30,000 suicides, or 11.2 per 100,000, that 99.989 percent of persons at risk in any year do not commit suicide. If one assumes that 50 percent of completed suicides have an affective disorder, then there are approximately 15,000 suicides with a diagnosis of an affective disorder. Given that the annual prevalence for affective disorders is approximately 18 million (Blazer et al., 1994; Kessler et al., 1994), the annual suicide rate in this population would be approximately 83.3 suicides per 100,000 depressive persons. This rate is approximately eight times that found in the general population. However, this means that approximately 99.92 percent of persons with affective disorders *do not* commit suicide in any given year. Thus, the clinical challenge is in recognizing which depressed patients are at a higher risk for suicide.

In order to aid clinicians, researchers have reported on factors associated with an increased risk of suicide in patients with major depressive disorders. For instance, the more severe the clinical depression is, the more acute the danger is. Hagnell and Rorsman (1979) found that every suicide in their study occurred within the group of patients designated as having moderate or severe depression, and no suicides occurred within the group of patients designated as having mild depression. Researchers have also found that suicide is more likely to occur when there is more than one psychiatric diagnosis, the co-occurrence of psychiatric and substance abuse disorder, or high levels of other psychiatric symptoms in addition to a primary diagnosis (Shafii et al., 1985; Rich, Young, and Fowler, 1986c; Brent, Perper, Goldstein, et al., 1988; Rich and Runeson, 1992; Henriksson et al., 1993; Mościcki, 1997). Given that manic-depressive illness carries a high risk of suicide, it is critical for clinicians to consider this diagnosis when evaluating patients who seem to present with only a depressive disorder. There is some controversy as to whether the risk for suicide is actually greater in delusional than nondelusional depression (Black, Winokur, and Nasrallah, 1988).

Certain points in the course of an affective illness, and in the course of a single episode, also convey an increased risk of suicide. For example, suicidality tends to occur early in the course of unipolar depressive illness before diagnosis and treatment, and it is intensified by increasing agitation and worsening melancholic symptoms (Himmelhoch, 1987). Baldessarini and Tondo in Chapter Twenty in this book also find this phenomenon in bipolar disorder patients. Furthermore, as Jamison (Chapter Fourteen) points out, the recovery period and the period following hospitalization are particularly high-risk times for both unipolar and bipolar patients.

The work of Fawcett and colleagues (Fawcett, 1988; Fawcett, Clark, and Busch, 1993) has identified clinical correlates of suicide in depressive disorders to aid clinicians in the assessment of suicidal risk. In their prospective studies, patients were divided into early (within one year) versus late (after one year) suicide. Patients with affective disorders in the early suicide group were more likely to have panic attacks, severe psychic anxiety, diminished concentration, global insomnia, moderate alcohol abuse, and severe loss of interest or pleasure, whereas patients in the later suicide group were more likely to have severe hopelessness, suicidal ideation, and a history of suicide attempts.

Fawcett's observations are significant for clinicians in planning interventions, since they suggest that anxiety may contribute to eventual suicide in patients with affective disorders. Hirschfeld (1996) hypothesized that the coupling of depressed feelings, such as worthlessness and hopelessness, with affects generated by anxiety, such as anxious worrying and agitated distress, were energizing and increasingly intolerable. To patients with such feelings, suicide may appear as the only way out (Hirschfeld, 1996). However, it should be noted that greater severity of depression, as indicated by coexisting anxiety symptoms, may be the important variable (Coryell, Noyes, and House, 1986; Noyes, 1991).

These findings suggest that clinicians should note and ask about symptoms of anxiety and agitation as well as depression in their suicide assessments. One risk factor for early suicide, psychic anxiety, defined as "subjective feelings of anxiety, fearfulness, or apprehension, whether or not focused on specific concerns" (Spitzer and Endicott, 1978), is often hidden and may not be obvious to the clinician. In addition, as Fawcett, Clark, and Busch (1993) point out, anxiety is a potentially modifiable risk factor. Based on this hypothesis, it would not be unreasonable to prescribe antianxiety medications as an adjunct in the acute phase of depression, as long as clinicians are aware of the potential adverse effects of these medications.

Finally, depression among suicide victims has been frequently found to be undiagnosed, untreated, or undertreated (Murphy, 1984; Rihmer, Barsi, Arato, and Demeter, 1990a). In addition, several studies indicate that the treatment provided was insufficient (Rihmer, Barsi, Arato, and Demeter, 1990a). Roy (1982a) found that only 29 percent of the suicide victims in his study who were depressed were receiving adequate antidepressant or lithium treatment at the time of the suicide. Such findings have led several authors to state that undiagnosed affective disorders are found in series of completed suicides (Khuri and Akiskal, 1983; Rihmer, Barsi, Arato, and Demeter, 1990a). Thus, early identification and aggressive treatment of depression (as well as mania and anxiety) in affectively ill patients is a useful first step in addressing the clinical problem of suicide.

Alcoholism

Psychological autopsy studies indicate that approximately 25 percent of suicides suffer from an alcohol use disorder (Murphy, Wetzel, Robins, and McEvoy, 1992). In addition, as many as 50 percent of suicide victims were drinking at or near the time of their death (Frances, Franklin, and Flavin, 1987), and 89 percent of alcoholics were drinking at the time of their suicide (Dorpat and Ripley, 1960). Thus, alcohol appears to increase the risk of suicide for both alcoholic and nonalcoholic populations (Frances, Franklin, and Flavin, 1987).

There is yet no unifying theory that adequately explains the mechanism whereby the abuse of alcohol increases suicide risk. Some researchers have suggested that the predisposition to substance abuse and certain personality disorder symptoms (for example, impulsivity, affective instability, and dependency) derive from a common but as yet unidentified biological or psychological substrate (Frances, Franklin, and Flavin, 1987; Marzuk and Mann, 1988). Other researchers have hypothesized that substance abusers are "self-medicating" their major mental disorders such as depression or psychosis (Chapter Seventeen in this book; Weiss, Najavits, and Mirin, 1998). It is also thought that alcohol and certain drugs may increase the risk of suicide by altering brain neurochemistry directly (Marzuk and Mann, 1988). Still others posit that substance abuse may turn an ambivalently conceived self-destructive act into a completed act either by decreasing inhibition or impairing judgment or that intoxication may increase risk taking (Marzuk and Mann, 1988).

Several factors have been specifically linked to suicide in alcoholic patients. First, as expected, comorbidity with a depressive disorder is a significant finding of suicide among alcoholics. Indeed, studies found major depressive episodes in half to three-fourths of alcoholic suicides (Murphy and Robins, 1967; Beskow, 1979; Rich, Young, and Fowler, 1986c). In addition, alcoholics who suffer from depressive episodes are more likely to commit suicide than persons with major depression or alcoholism alone (Fawcett, Clark, and Busch, 1993).

Murphy, Wetzel, Robins, and McEvoy (1992) found several other factors to be closely linked to suicide in alcoholics: continued drinking, communication of suicidal intent, poor social support, serious medical illness, unemployment, and living alone. Loss or disruption of a close interpersonal relationship was also found to heighten the risk of suicide in alcoholics (Murphy and Robins, 1967; Murphy et al., 1979; Rich, Fowler, Fogarty, and Young, 1988a). Murphy, Wetzel, Robins, and McEvoy (1992) also found that the likelihood of a suicidal outcome increased with the total number of risk factors, which clinicians can quantify as part of their risk assessment. It should be stressed that some factors identified were not characteristically acute. For instance, communication of suicidal intent was usually of several years' duration, and health, economic, and social functioning had deteriorated gradually. In fact, in contrast to suicide in depressed patients, suicide in alcoholics appears to be a relatively late sequela of the disease (Hirschfeld and Russell, 1997).

There are several clinical implications of these findings. First, clinicians might consider systematically ruling out the presence of a comorbid depressive disorder in alcoholic patients and not assume that depressive symptoms are the typical sequelae of alcoholism or substance abuse (Fawcett, Clark, and Busch, 1993; Chapter Seventeen in this book; Weiss, Najavits, and Mirin, 1998). Second, the status of a patient's current and recent relationships can also be important to determine insofar as interpersonal losses can be associated with suicidal crises in alcoholic patients (Fawcett, Clark, and Busch, 1993). Finally, although the assessment of suicide risk in alcoholic patients generally proceeds in the same way as that for patients with other psychiatric disorders, clinicians might ask alcoholic patients specifically about a history of drug overdoses, legal and financial difficulties, and escalating patterns of substance abuse, crime, debt, social losses, and similar other difficulties (Marzuk and Mann, 1988). In such patients, it may be helpful to corroborate the history by interviewing family members or friends.

Schizophrenia

Suicide accounts for the majority of premature deaths among patients with schizophrenia (Tsuang, Woolson, and Fleming, 1980b; Chapter Sixteen in this book; Black, Warrack, and Winokur, 1985; Allebeck, 1989; Fenton et al., 1997). Miles (1977) estimated that individuals with schizophrenia have a lifetime risk of suicide of 10 percent.

Several researchers have found an association between the type of schizophrenia and the extent of suicide risk (Fenton, McGlashan, Victor, and Blyler, 1997). For example, Fenton and McGlashan (1991b) found a greater suicide risk among patients with paranoid schizophrenia and a lower risk of suicide among patients with negative or deficit subtypes of schizophrenia. Indeed, the paranoid subtype of schizophrenia, which emphasizes positive symptoms and the absence of negative symptoms, was associated with a threefold greater suicide risk than the nonparanoid subtypes and an eightfold greater suicide risk than the deficit subtype (Fenton, McGlashan, Victor, and Blyler, 1997). Patients with the nondeficit subtype of schizophrenia, or the absence of enduring negative symptoms, were found to have a sixfold greater risk of suicide than patients with the deficit subtype (Fenton, McGlashan, Victor, and Blyler, 1997).

Although relatively little is known about the causes of suicide in schizophrenia, Fenton, McGlashan, Victor, and Blyler (1997) hypothesized that "the progressive loss of social drive, the diminished capacity to experience affect, and the indifference toward the future associated with deficit symptoms, although often markedly debilitating, may preclude the painful self-awareness associated with suicide. . . . [In contrast,] the good premorbid functioning, late illness onset, preservation of affect and cognitive capacities, and intermittent course associated with nondeficit and paranoid subtypes of schizophrenia encompass many of the preconditions for the emergence of dysphoric and hopeless states" (p. 203). Others researchers have similarly noted that suicide in schizophrenics is due to the overwhelming culmination of feelings of hopelessness, fatigue, and awareness of the deterioration of abilities (Fenton and McGlashan, 1991a; Fenton, McGlashan, Victor, and Blyler, 1997; Nyman and Jonsson, 1986) and despair and dissatisfaction with the limited results of treatment (Fenton, McGlashan, Victor, and Blyler, 1997; Virkkunen, 1976a).

In addition to the type of schizophrenia, researchers have identified other factors associated with an increased risk of suicide in patients with schizophrenia (see Exhibit 1.2). These factors have also been identified for other psychotic disorders such as manic-depressive illness. For instance, suicide in schizophrenic patients is more likely to occur during periods of improvement after relapse or during periods of depressed mood and hopelessness rather than during florid psychotic exacerbations (Westermeyer, Harrow, and Marengo, 1991; Fawcett, Clark, and Busch, 1993). Moreover, Robins (1986) found that only 20 percent of suicide victims were psychotic at the time of their death.

Exhibit 1.2. Risk Factors for Suicide in Psychotic Patients (Schizophrenic or Manic-Depressive Illness).

Young age
Early stage of illness
Good premorbid history (school or work progress)
Good intellectual functioning
Frequent exacerbations and remissions
Painful awareness of the discrepancies between the "normal" future once
    envisioned and the likely degree of chronic disability in the future
Periods of clinical improvement following relapse
Supervention of a depressive episode and increased hopelessness
Communication of suicide intent

Source: Adapted from *Suicide: Guidelines for Assessment, Management, and Treatment,* edited by Bruce Bongar, p. 40. Copyright © 1992 by Oxford University Press, Inc. Used by permission of Oxford University Press, Inc.

Additional short-term risk factors for suicide in schizophrenia include being young and male, having a relapsing illness, having been depressed in the past, being currently depressed, having been admitted in the last period of psychiatric contact with accompanying depressive symptoms or suicidal ideas, having recently changed from inpatient to outpatient care, and being socially isolated (Drake, Gates, Whitaker, and Cotton, 1985; Roy, 1986). Because schizophrenic patients can develop depressions, these patients may be mistakenly diagnosed as affective disorders with psychotic features.

In sum, we suggest that clinicians be alert to risk factors for suicide in schizophrenic patients, especially since such patients are less likely than others to communicate their suicidal intent in a clear way (Fenton, McGlashan, and Victor, and Blyler, 1997). In addition to the diagnostic subtype and course of illness risk factors, the presence of comorbid depressive disorder or substance abuse greatly increases the risk of suicide in schizophrenic patients.

It is important for clinicians to consider the diagnosis of panic disorder when assessing suicide risk. In the late 1980s and early 1990s, there were initial reports of an increased association between panic disorder and suicidal behavior and completed suicide (Noyes, 1991; Weissman, Klerman, and Johnson, 1992). However, a reanalysis of this proposal has concluded that the association between panic disorder and suicide is due mainly to the comorbid presence of an affective disorder (Hornig and McNally, 1995). Therefore, clinicians should have a heightened sense of awareness when treating patients with panic disorder who have comorbid depression or bipolar diagnoses.

In summary, we suggest that clinicians consider the following aspects of axis I disorders when assessing for suicide risk:

- Diagnostic-specific risk factors (for example, psychic anxiety in affective illness)
- The presence of comorbidity (for example, substance abuse)
- The severity and nature of symptoms
- Where the person is in the time course of his or her illness (for example, early versus late)

DETECTING POTENTIATING FACTORS

It has been said that clinicians do not treat disorders but rather persons suffering from disorders (Michels, personal communication). Nowhere is this dictum more relevant than in the assessment of suicide risk. As Motto has emphasized in this book (see Chapter Twelve) and in other writings (1979), we must appreciate the unique aspects of a person in conjunction with known risk factors to help decide degree of suicide risk. Suicide almost always results from a combination of predisposing factors and potentiating factors (see Figure 1.1). The category described here as "potentiating factors" has also been called "sufficient conditions" (Goodwin and Runck, 1992) and "proximal risk factors" (Mościcki, 1997). Potentiating factors include family and social milieu, personality variables, physical illness, life stress, previous suicidal behavior, presence of firearms, and other such factors. Almost always, the interaction of predisposing factors and potentiating factors accounts for crossing an imaginary suicidal threshold. Clinicians might consider a schematic model of a suicide threshold in assessing suicide risk (see Figure 1.1). This model is designed to convey that it is the combination of predisposing factors (axis I diagnosis) and potentiating factors that lead to a suicidal crisis or threshold. Even within that group of vulnerable persons, fortunately very few cross the suicidal threshold to complete suicide. It may be helpful to think of the threshold as those factors (or barriers) that protect against suicide, such as supportive relationships, religious beliefs, and responsibility for children.

Family History and the Social Milieu

While taking a social history, it is useful to ascertain whether there is a family history of suicide, mental illness, or substance abuse. Suicides are more likely in patients with a family history of suicidal behavior and mood or substance abuse disorder (Shafii et al., 1985; Shaffer et al., 1988; Brent et al., 1993b; Lesage et al., 1994; Mościcki, 1997; Wagner, 1997). The effects of family history are presumably mediated through both shared genetics and shared environment (Goodwin and Runck, 1992; Mościcki, 1997).

Figure 1.1. A Model of Suicide: Three Elements.

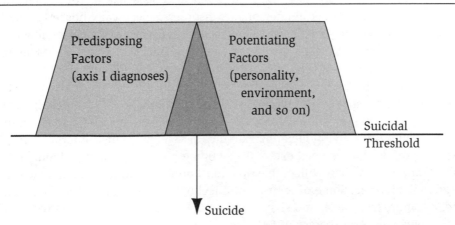

Clinicians should not assume, however, that an affectively disordered patient is at lower risk of suicide than other patients just because there is no family history of suicide. Sheftner et al. (1988), for example, did not find family history to be a useful indicator of suicide potential in affectively disordered probands, perhaps because a positive family history for affective disorder, but not necessarily of suicide, was common to most subjects in their study. Thus, it is suggested that clinicians consider that a positive family history increases suicide risk, but the absence of a family history does not decrease risk.

Finally, it should be noted, not surprisingly, that suicides are more likely to come from dysfunctional families where there is a history of parental separation, divorce, or widowhood; family conflict or stress; or parental legal troubles (Smith, Mercy, and Conn, 1988; Brent et al., 1993b; Mościcki, 1997; Wagner, 1997). Family violence and abuse, both physical and sexual, have also been associated with attempted and completed suicide among young people (Shafii et al., 1985; Briere and Zaidi, 1989; de Wilde et al., 1991; Brent and Perper, 1995; Mościcki, 1997; Wagner, 1997). Similarly, van der Kolk et al. (1991) found histories of childhood physical and sexual abuse, as well as parental neglect and separations, to be strongly correlated with a variety of self-destructive behaviors in adulthood. Thus, clinicians are advised to be alert for signs of family violence and abuse and to consider asking about them in suicide risk assessments. Indeed, as Mościcki (1997) has pointed out, family violence and abuse can act as both proximal and distal risk factors for suicide.

Personality Disorders

Axis II disorders are included in the category of potentiating factors because suicide can occur in a personality-disordered individual who does not have a comorbid Axis I diagnosis, such as affective disorder or substance abuse (Jacobs, 1992). In fact, the diagnosis of personality disorder follows depression, alcoholism, and schizophrenia in order of importance as a risk factor for suicide (Soloff et al., 1994a). Certain personality disorders, specifically borderline personality disorder, antisocial personality disorder, and narcissistic personality disorder, have been particularly associated with both suicide attempts and fatalities (Perry, Cooper, and Michels, 1987; Goldsmith, Fyer, and Frances, 1990).

From a psychodynamic perspective, suicide-vulnerable individuals lack self-regulatory capacities due to pathological ego development. These people have difficulty maintaining an adequate sense of self-worth, keeping a sense of internal composure, and moderating extremes of rage. Since their internal control is compromised, they need external sustaining resources (such as family or a clinician) and are more vulnerable than most others to painful affects or loss of external supports. Some of their painful feelings (such as aloneness, self-contempt, murderous rage, and shame and panic) are closely associated with suicidal behavior (Maltsberger, 1988).

Borderline Personality Disorder. Gunderson (1988) defined the essential feature of borderline personality disorder as fear and intolerance of being alone and describes that fear as leading to the behavioral markers associated with the disorder: repetitive self-destructiveness, substance abuse, promiscuity, and other desperate impulsive actions. Borderline personality disorder is the only personality disorder diagnosis for which self-injurious or suicidal behavior is given as a criterion for diagnosis. Suicide attempts and self-mutilation are common in this disorder.

Akiskal et al. (1985) found a 4 percent rate of suicide in a six- to thirty-six-month follow-up study of borderline patients. Pope et al. (1983) found a 7.4 percent rate of suicide in a four- to seven-year follow-up study of borderline patients. Stone (1987) found a 9.5 percent rate of suicide in a fifteen-year follow-up study. An important question that arises in this patient population is the impact of comorbid disorders on the suicide rate.

Some follow-up and psychological autopsy studies suggest that it is comorbidity (either affective disorders or substance use disorders) that increases the risk for suicide among patients with borderline personality (Friedman et al., 1982, 1983; Goldsmith, Fyer, and Frances, 1990; Isometsä et al., 1996b). For example, McGlashan's (1986) follow-up study indicated a 3 percent overall suicide rate for patients with pure borderline personality disorder, an 8 percent rate for patients with pure unipolar depression, and a 16 percent rate for patients with combined personality disorder and depression (Soloff et al., 1994a). Stone's study (1987) found similar findings, with the additional observation that there was a 45 percent rate for suicide in patients with borderline personality disorder and comorbidity for two disorders: major depression and substance abuse. Furthermore, Stone also suggested that persistent alcohol abuse doubles the suicide rate in borderline patients (Soloff et al., 1994a).

Several studies have found a history of attempted suicide, particularly severe or multiple attempts, to be more common in borderline suicide victims than in living persons diagnosed with borderline personality (Kullgren, 1988; Paris, Nowlis, and Brown, 1989; Kjelsberg-Eikeseth and Dahl, 1991; Isometsä et al., 1996b). Soloff et al. (1994a) found that borderline patients at highest risk for suicidal behavior were older and had a history of impulsive actions, antisocial behavior, depressive moods, or prior suicide attempts. Brodsky et al. (1997) found that impulsivity was the only characteristic of this patient population that was associated with a higher number of previous suicide attempts after controlling for lifetime diagnosis of depression and substance abuse.

Wagner and Linehan (1994) found that women with borderline personality disorder and a history of childhood sexual abuse engaged in more self-injurious behavior than women with the same personality disorder but without such a history. The association between childhood sexual abuse and increased lethality of parasuicide such as cutting or other self-destructive behavior without suicidal intent is consistent with research on the long-term effects of childhood sexual abuse. Browne and Finkelhor (1986b), for instance, found increased rates of depression, parasuicidal behavior, and completed suicide in borderline patients with a sexual abuse history. Thus, it must be emphasized strongly that a knowledge about history of abuse can assist the clinician in assessing suicide risk in borderline patients.

Antisocial Personality Disorder. Antisocial personality disorder "is a pattern of socially irresponsible, exploitative, and guiltless behavior, evidenced in the tendency to fail to conform to the law, to fail to sustain consistent employment, to exploit and manipulate others for personal gain, to deceive, and to fail to develop stable relationships" (Goldsmith, Fyer, and Frances, 1990, p. 161). This disorder is often associated with externally directed violence. The fact that it is also associated with internally directed violence or suicide is less well known (Goldsmith, Fyer, and Frances, 1990).

Miles (1977) estimated that 5 percent of antisocial patients eventually die by suicide. However, three psychological autopsy studies of young adults found that most suicide victims with antisocial personality disorder also fulfilled criteria for borderline personality disorder (Rich, Young, and Fowler, 1986c; Runeson, 1989; Rich and Runeson, 1992). Thus, the risk of suicide associated specifically with antisocial personality disorder is unknown. The 5 percent rate of completed suicides cited may include persons who have concurrent Axis I depressive syndromes, substance use disorders, or other personality disorders that themselves increase the risk for suicide (Goldsmith, Fyer, and Frances, 1990).

Narcissistic Personality Disorder. Narcissistic personality disorder has occasionally been observed in men who commit murder-suicide, albeit an extremely rare event (Perry, 1989). (A more detailed discussion of murder-suicide is found in Chapter Ten in this book.) A common scenario involves attachment syndrome, whereby a young man is having unbearable difficulty with separation or divorce and is unable to tolerate the separation. He perceives a deep narcissistic injury when he is left and is moved to violence.

There has not been a great deal of research on the relationship between narcissistic personality disorder and suicide, though, as Perry (1989) has noted, "The extreme vulnerability to loss of self-esteem coupled with dysphoria in response to failure, scandal, criticism, and humiliation should put these individuals at high risk for suicide attempts" (p. 159). On the other hand, as with antisocial patients, it is possible that the overlap between narcissistic and borderline personality disorders may explain the increased risk of suicide, especially among males (Perry, 1989).

Recent psychological autopsy studies have reported that approximately one-third of suicide victims met the criteria for a diagnosis of a personality disorder

(Bronisch, 1996). Isometsä et al. (1996b) found that factors most clearly differentiating suicide victims with a personality disorder from those without such disorders were a higher prevalence of comorbidity, often including abuse of multiple psychoactive substances, but not medical disorders, and a history of nonfatal suicide attempts. The particular challenge in assessing patients with personality disorders is to differentiate between self-destructive behavior that is nonsuicidal and self-soothing and behavior with suicidal intent. Chapters Eight, Eighteen, and Nineteen in this book address this issue more closely.

In assessing new or emergency room patients with borderline personality disorder, it is important to take a careful history of their responses to previous treatment efforts. Suicidality in borderline patients often occurs in the context of, and sometimes is a complication of, ongoing treatment (such as acting out in the transference). Hence, the patient's current therapist should be consulted whenever possible to assist in the assessment of suicide risk. It is also important to take a history of past suicide attempts and the patient's subsequent treatment since borderline patients commonly use self-destructive behavior as a means of gaining hospital admission. The decision not to hospitalize has risks, such as encouraging more acting out, and these risks must be carefully considered and compared with alternatives that make sense to both the patient and clinician (Goldsmith, Fyer, and Frances, 1990).

Life Stressors

Recent severe, stressful life events have been associated with suicide in vulnerable individuals (Mościcki, 1997). The most frequently identified stressors in young persons who complete suicide are interpersonal loss or conflict, economic problems, legal problems, and moving (Brent et al., 1993b; Lesage et al., 1994; Rich, Fowler, Fogarty, and Young, 1988a; Mościcki, 1997). Humiliating events, such as financial ruin associated with scandal, being arrested, or being fired, have also been found to precede suicide in vulnerable individuals (Hirschfeld and Davidson, 1988).

Consequently, clinicians can learn valuable information by asking about patients' recent life stressors. It is important to cover financial, marital, legal, and occupational factors. A few simple questions will suffice—for example, "How are things going in your marriage? Your family? At home? At work?" (Hirschfeld and Russell, 1997). Whether it is the total number of recent stressors rather than the specific nature of the stress that might increase the risk for suicide has received attention in the literature (Brent et al., 1993b; Lesage et al., 1994; Mościcki, 1997).

In the assessment of current life stressors, it sometimes seems that a patient's depressive illness is a "natural reaction" to adverse life events; however, regardless of whether a precipitating cause is identified, depression as an illness needs to be treated. The fact that a depression seems "appropriate" within the context of a person's life does not mean that the depression does not need specific treatment. As Fawcett, Clark, and Busch (1993, p. 251) have stated, "The presence of a 'reason' for depression does not constitute a reason for ignoring its presence."

Physical Illness

Clinicians assessing suicidality should ask about the presence of a severe, debilitating, or terminal illness. Medical illnesses with pain, disfigurement, restricted function, and fear of dependence can diminish a person's will to live and may thereby increase the risk of suicide in vulnerable individuals (Mackenzie and Popkin, 1990). Furthermore, according to Blumenthal (1990), medical illnesses may contribute to suicidal behavior by precipitating or exacerbating severe depression and other psychiatric illnesses and by producing an organic mental disorder (such as delirium) that leads to perceptual, cognitive, and mood changes that may predispose to impaired judgment, impulsivity, and suicidal behavior.

Harris and Barraclough (1994) identified several medical disorders associated with an increased risk for suicide. These included Huntington's disease, malignant neoplasms, multiple sclerosis, peptic ulcer, renal disease, spinal cord injuries, and systemic lupus erythematosus. Epilepsy is also associated with a fourfold increase in suicide (Blumenthal, 1990) and is, in fact, the only medical diagnosis found to have a documented increase in suicide in children and adolescents (Brent and Kolko, 1990). It should be stressed that most of these diseases are associated with psychiatric disorders. It is not clear whether these medical disorders (aside from epilepsy) are independent risk factors for suicide in the absence of depression and substance abuse (Mościcki, 1997).

Mackenzie and Popkin (1990) also identified factors that can increase the risk of suicide in patients with medical illnesses: advancing age, male gender, a painful terminal illness, dyspnea, depression, psychosis, organic mental disorder, alcoholism, demanding and complaining behavior, poor interpersonal relations, access to lethal means, AIDS, cancer, peptic ulcer, spinal cord injury, head injury, inadequate sedation, a weak patient-physician bond, and failure to monitor the patient's state. Clinicians should be alert to the presence of these factors when assessing physically compromised individuals.

The connection between AIDS and suicide was first documented with epidemiologic evidence by Marzuk et al. (1988). They found that men aged twenty to fifty-nine years of age with a diagnosis of AIDS were about thirty-six times more likely to commit suicide as matched controls in the general population of New York City (Marzuk et al., 1997). Moreover, it is likely that these results underestimate the true AIDS-related suicide rate, given the difficulties of establishing both AIDS and suicide in official AIDS statistics. Suicide deaths of AIDS patients are usually considered as AIDS-caused deaths in official statistics (Glass, 1988). It is interesting that the increased risk of suicide is not found in those patients who are HIV positive.

Glass (1988) also proposed two periods during the course of AIDS that may be especially associated with suicide. Suicide risk may be high shortly after the diagnosis is made because of the psychologically devastating effect of an AIDS diagnosis, with powerful feelings of panic, guilt, depression, and helplessness and hopelessness. Later in the course of the illness, there may be another period of high suicide risk related more to biologic factors due to the development of delirium or dementia as central nervous system (CNS) complications. Although there is little research to verify these proposed risk periods for AIDS, it is clear that persons treating AIDS patients should have a high index of suspicion for suicide risk in these patients and inquire about it routinely, particularly if there are indications of depressive symptoms or CNS complications. Suicide in AIDS patients usually occurs as a manifestation of a comorbid psychiatric disorder rather than a "rational" choice (Glass, 1988).

Clinicians should routinely discuss with medically ill individuals the potential impact of their illness on their lives. It is particularly useful to determine how the patient perceives the future. Does the patient believe that death is inevitable or does he or she maintain some hope? Is the patient future oriented? What is the patient's concept of death? How much more can the patient tolerate? According to Mackenzie and Popkin (1990), ascertaining how much strength a patient has left will help gauge how the patient will respond to changes in his or her condition.

Access to Lethal Means of Suicide

Firearms are an increasingly common means of suicide and account for the highest proportion of suicides in the United States (Sloan et al., 1990). Indeed, studies have shown that 57 percent of suicides in the United States involve firearms (Baker, 1984; Sloan et al., 1990). Moreover, the proportion of suicides by firearms has increased most recently among persons under age twenty-five (O'Carroll et al., 1994; Price, Everett, Bedell, and Telljohann, 1997).

Firearms are the preferred method of suicide for both men and women, followed by poisoning for women and hanging for men (Mościcki, 1995a). Firearms are also the most lethal method of suicide. Card (1974) reported, for example, that 92 percent of suicide attempts by firearms were successful compared to 78 percent for both carbon monoxide and hanging, 67 percent by drowning, 23 percent by poisoning, 9 percent by gases other than carbon monoxide, and 4 percent by cutting.

Studies have also shown that keeping one or more guns in the home increases the risk of suicide for both genders, even after other risk factors, such as depression and alcohol abuse, are taken into account (Brent et al., 1988, 1991; Kellerman et al., 1992; Mościcki, 1995a). Brent et al. (1991), for example, found that guns were twice as likely to be found in homes where an adolescent had committed suicide compared with homes in which an adolescent had only attempted suicide. No difference was found in the level of risk with respect to the type of firearm used or whether the weapon and ammunition were stored in separate locations. Sloan et al. (1990) did find an association between gun control and lower rates of suicide in the age group fifteen to twenty-four years. Their findings suggest that for this age group, suicides are more likely to be impulsive acts, so restricting access to handguns may have some benefit.

Clinicians should ask about availability of weapons when they are assessing a patient who acknowledges suicidal intent with a specific and plausible plan. The clinician then needs to determine whether to recommend to the family that the firearms be removed. If the patient is assessed to be at imminent risk for suicide, removal of guns may not be enough. Unfortunately, almost anything can be used as a suicide method (medications, knives, plastic bags, and cars, to name just a few). With patients who are assessed at imminent risk of suicide, hospitalization may be the only reasonable choice.

Clinicians may believe that families would not listen to their advice about removing guns; however, a recent study indicates otherwise. Haught, Grossman, and Connell (1995) studied adults' perceptions of physicians' advice with regard to not keeping guns in the home and found that 47 percent claimed that they would follow the advice and an additional 37 percent would think over the advice of a physician. Only 6 percent claimed they would ignore or be offended by such advice.

CONDUCTING SPECIFIC SUICIDE INQUIRIES

A suicide assessment should include questions about suicidal thoughts, plans, and behavior. This section of the protocol presents approaches to conducting a specific suicide inquiry.

Determining Presence of Suicidal Ideation

Anyone who has worked with psychiatric patients knows that suicidal ideation is commonly expressed. It has been estimated that over five million people in the United States have suicidal ideation each year (Mościcki, 1989), and yet only about thirty thousand people a year die by suicide (Mościcki, 1997). We are using the narrow definition of suicidal ideation, which encompasses more than just thoughts of death and includes a person's active consideration of taking his or her own life, with or without a specific plan. Thus suicidal ideation with this narrower definition is not a robust indicator of impending suicide. However, psychological autopsy studies indicate that nearly 70 percent of suicide victims have communicated their thoughts about suicide shortly before their death (Robins et al., 1959a; Dorpat and Ripley, 1960; Barraclough, Bunch, Nelson, and Sainsbury, 1974; Beskow, 1979; Hagnell and Rorsman, 1979; Rich, Young, and

Fowler, 1986c). Given these observations, clinicians need to elicit patients' suicidal ideation and appreciate its range of seriousness.

Clinicians can begin their inquiry about suicidal ideation with a broad question such as, "Have you had thoughts about harming yourself?" If the patient responds that he or she has had suicidal thoughts, the clinician can probe for more information by asking questions like the following:

- What are the thoughts?
- Are they active or passive?
- When did they begin?
- How frequent are they?
- How persistent are they?
- Are they obsessive?
- Can you control them? (See Appendix.)
- Are there command hallucinations?

The purpose of such questioning is to gauge the severity of the suicidal ideation. The Scale for Suicidal Ideation (Beck, Kovacs, and Weisman, 1979), which has been used in research, includes additional questions that can be asked, such as the wish to live or die, wishes or reasons for living or dying, deterrents, and capability of carrying out the suicidal act.

Having suicidal thoughts is deeply disturbing and frightening to most people. Patients who have lived with depression and intermittent suicidal ideation for years usually develop some coping strategies and support systems to help them through stressful periods. However, the first time a person has suicidal ideation, he or she has no past experience on which to draw and is therefore potentially at higher risk than the ideation might otherwise indicate. Thus, according to Table 1.4, a depressed patient who says, for the first time, that he has been thinking he might be better off dead would be categorized as low risk, because he is having passive or nonsuicidal thoughts of death (Clark and Fawcett, 1992b). However, because it is the patient's first experience of suicidality, the clinician might assign an elevated risk and plan the intervention accordingly until the risk is thoroughly determined or the episode has passed.

Table 1.4. Risk Model Related to Suicidal Ideation.

Lowest risk	No thoughts of death
Low risk	Nonsuicidal thoughts of death
Elevated risk	Suicidal thoughts without specific method
Highest risk	Suicidal thoughts with specific method

In addition, patients are not always forthcoming to clinicians about suicidal ideation. In such cases, it may be helpful to obtain the patient's permission to talk with family members or friends, especially if the patient seems to be at risk because of other factors. For example, Fawcett (1988) found that more than half of suicide victims denied suicidal ideas or admitted to only vague thoughts of suicide when asked about suicidal ideation by an experienced interviewer.

Assessing Content of Suicidal Ideation

The content of the suicidal ideation is relevant in suicide risk assessments. It may be helpful to explore indications of ambivalence, psychological pain, and hopelessness, since such feelings have been associated with suicide.

Ambivalence. Thoughts of suicide usually imply a mental conflict between a wish to die and a wish to live (Barraclough, Bunch, Nelson, and Sainsbury, 1974) or for rescue and intervention (Shneidman, 1989). Ambivalence about suicide is almost always present in suicidal persons (Shneidman, 1989). This ambivalence is not uncertainty, but rather the collision of two opposing but equally strong forces. The resulting cognitive dissonance increases anxiety and agitation, which itself can increase suicide risk. However, on the positive side, ambivalence also offers the clinician a chance to intervene and to ally with the side of the patient that wants to live.

Paradoxically, if a patient's agitation suddenly decreases, it may be a signal that the patient has made a resolution to commit suicide. A misleading reduction of anxious or depressed affect can occur in some patients who have resolved their ambivalence by deciding to commit suicide (see Appendix). A patient who has made the decision to die may appear at peace and not show signs of an inner struggle. In addition, as Sylvia Plath illustrated in her book *The Bell Jar*, individuals about to commit suicide may perceive death as a peaceful refuge (Maltsberger and Buie, 1989; Lifton, 1989). Thus, it is suggested that clinicians ask patients who seem to be getting better but still seem emotionally removed or display constricted affect whether they are still having suicidal thoughts. The recovery periods and the postrecovery periods are particularly high-risk times for suicide in certain patients.

Psychological Pain. According to Shneidman (1989), "The common stimulus in suicide is psychological pain" (p. 17). In other words, suicide is "a movement away from intolerable emotion, unendurable pain, unacceptable anguish" (p. 17). The psychological pain is conceptualized as related to frustrated, blocked, or thwarted psychological needs, such as the need for achievement, autonomy, recognition, succorance, avoidance of humiliation, shame, or pain. (Chapter Five in this book contains a fuller discussion on this subject.) Thus, another avenue for exploring the patient's suicidal ideation is to take a psychological pain history (Buie, 1981; Jacobs, 1992). What is the degree of disintegration? Is the person feeling disconnected, empty, invalid, or worthless? Is the person unable to tolerate any more pain? Is there evidence of depressive turmoil or perturbation? Statements such as, "I feel like Humpty Dumpty about to crack" or "I can't take the pain anymore," can be important warning signs in some patients.

Hopelessness. Hopelessness is defined as the degree to which a person holds negative expectations about the future (Beck et al., 1990) or the "emotion of active, impotent, ennui" (Shneidman, 1989, p. 18). There is a growing body of evidence suggesting that hopelessness is directly related to suicidal ideation and intent (Beck et al., 1990). In fact, hopelessness may be more directly related to suicide intent than depression alone (Drake and Cotton, 1986; Beck et al., 1990).

Why does hopelessness serve as a relevant factor in suicide assessment? Beck et al. (1990) hypothesized that the intensity of a person's hopelessness is similar in recurrent periods of depression. Young et al. (1996) further argue that there is a trait component to hopelessness that is stable over time and therefore can be associated with suicidal behavior over long periods. In other words, there is a hopelessness trait that influences both hopelessness and suicidal behavior across long periods of time in some patients (Young et al., 1996). In fact, Young et al. (1996) found that suicide attempts and subsequent depression were especially related to a trait level (baseline) of hopelessness that was still present when the depression had remitted.

Clinical implications of these findings include the need to assess the level of hopelessness in patients with Axis I disorders. Some sample questions can be suggested:

- Have you been discouraged or felt hopeless?
- What kind of future do you see for yourself?
- Can you see yourself or your situation getting any better?

Not only will such inquiries help clinicians to identify severity of risk, but they can be used in conjunction with other factors to determine the indicated intervention, which may include hospitalization, involuntary commitment, or the need for a caretaker or constant observation.

Finally, hopelessness is important in suicide risk assessments because, in contrast to demographic and other predictors, it can often be modified by clinical intervention (Beck, 1990). For instance, there is evidence that an individual's hopelessness increases with increased severity of depression (Young et al., 1996). Thus, one way for clinicians to reduce hopelessness is to treat depression, usually with a combination of somatic therapy and cognitive therapy; the cognitive therapy can be specifically aimed at reducing hopelessness (Rush et al., 1982; Young et al., 1996).

Determining Suicidal Intent

Intent is one component of suicide risk or potential, which includes elements such as the lethality of methods, knowledge and skill concerning their use, and the absence of protective intervening persons and circumstances. Beck, Kovacs, and Weisman (1979) define intent as the seriousness or intensity of one's suicidal wish. They continue, "The concept of suicidal intention encompasses such factors as the intensity, pervasiveness, and duration of the individual's wish to die, the degree to which the individual's wish to die outweighs the wish to live, and the degree to which the individual has transformed a 'free-floating' wish to die into a concrete formulation or plan to kill him-or herself" (p. 344). Shneidman (Chapter Five in this book) refers to this concept as "lethality."

In general, the clearer a person's intent to attempt suicide (regardless of the level of damage that is actually done), the greater the risk of suicide. For example, some patients can take six aspirin tablets and be at high risk for future suicide if they thought they would kill themselves with this dosage. Other patients can take fifty pills as a way to manipulate others and not have had suicide in mind, even though they may have died because of miscalculation not intending to kill themselves.

When examining suicidal wishes, clinicians should explore the dynamic meanings and motivations for suicide. For instance, what form does the patient's wish for suicide take? Is there a wish to die, to hurt someone else, to escape, or to punish oneself? In addition, what does suicide mean to the patient? Is there a wish for rebirth or reunion? Is there an identification with a significant other? Does death have a positive meaning to the patient (Maltsberger and Buie, 1989)? (For a more in-depth discussion of the principal purposes and fantasies expressed in suicide, see Maltsberger and Buie, 1980.)

The method chosen may also be an important clue to the psychodynamics of suicide and the personality of the suicidal person. However, as Lester and Beck (1980–1981) have noted, choice of method for suicide seems to be unrelated to most biographical and personality variables studied. In fact, only the demographic variables of sex, age, and rural location have been found to be correlated with choice of method for suicide (Lester and Beck, 1980–1981). Males usually make suicide attempts with more lethal methods than do females; older people use more lethal methods than younger people; and rural people use more lethal methods than urban people (Lester and Beck, 1980–1981).

Identifying Suicide Plans

After learning that a patient has suicidal ideation and intent, the clinician should ask if the patient has ever considered a particular method of suicide or a plan. Although it is not uncommon to see in a medical record that a patient has a plan, the details of the plan are often lacking. Factors to consider include these:

What is the plan? When will it happen? Does the patient have access to the method? How much planning has taken place? Has the patient rehearsed the suicide? Including these details in a note has obvious risk management benefits and can make for a more informed clinical assessment.

In general, the more detail that is evident about the plan, the more serious the suicidality is. Particular attention should be paid to violent, irreversible methods, such as shooting, jumping, or car wrecks, which carry a greater risk of death. There are also other indicators of the severity of suicidal intent, such as suicide notes, final acts in preparation for death (making a will, giving away possessions), and deception (Dorpat and Boswell, 1963; Tuckman and Young-man, 1968; Resnik and Hawthorne, 1972; Beck, Morris, and Lester, 1974; Beck, Kovacs, and Weisman, 1979; Hirschfeld, 1996). If the patient states that he has not considered a specific plan, clinicians should then ask whether the patient intends to follow through with the suicidal ideas by implementing them in the near future. Clark and Fawcett (1992b) believe that it is very important to listen carefully to the reasons that patients give as to why suicide is unlikely. They note that patients often list such factors as the responsibility for dependent children, fear of self-injury or pain, reluctance to expose family members to a suicide, or the wish to be present at some future event as reasons that they would not actually commit suicide. Assessing a person's religious beliefs and ideas sometimes can be useful. These inhibitory mechanisms, or protective factors, should be weighed into the clinician's estimate of suicide risk. Studies have shown that the presence of a child under age eighteen in the home can be a deterrent to suicide (Young, Fogg, Scheftner, and Fawcett, 1994).

Changes in the nature, method, or lethality of suicidal thoughts and plans can have clinical significance. A change to a more lethal method or plan clearly warrants more detailed exploration. However, a switch to a less lethal method may also have clinical significance, such as pill taking. For example, is the patient giving up something that has sustained him, such as the fantasy of a violent death?

Categorizing Suicide Attempts and Self-Destructive Behavior

Finally, clinicians should ask about past suicidal behaviors. The rate of suicide among previous attempters is five to six times greater than that for the general population: between 18 percent and 38 percent of persons who commit suicide have made previous attempts (Clark and Fawcett, 1992a). Nevertheless, although "prior suicide attempts may be the best single predictor of completed suicide" (Mościcki, 1995a), the majority of suicides (at least 60 percent) have never made a prior attempt.

As with other singular predictors of suicide, a history of suicide attempts is not clinically reliable to predict individuals at immediate risk for suicide since it will generate a large proportion of false positives and false negatives (Mościcki, 1997). At least 90 percent of attempters do not go on to complete suicide, and only 7 percent of past attempters eventually kill themselves (Clark and Fawcett, 1992a). In addition, the risk factors for suicide attempts differ in some ways from the risk factors for suicide (Hirschfeld and Davidson, 1988). For instance, although the risk factors for suicide attempters and completers are similar for marital status, employment status, and psychiatric diagnosis, they differ considerably for age and sex. Fourth-fifths of suicides are committed by men, whereas approximately two-thirds of attempts are committed by women. In addition, more suicides occur in those over age fifty, while more suicide attempts occur before that age (Hirschfeld and Davidson, 1988). The peak period for suicide attempts is between ages twenty and twenty-four (Hirschfeld and Davidson, 1988).

Clinicians frequently characterize suicidal acts as either gestures, meaning not serious attempts, or serious attempts, even though there are many suicidal attempts of intermediate lethality. This common practice is a problem because it oversimplifies assessment and minimizes behavior that has significance in a suicide assessment. Jacobs (Jacobs and Brown, 1989; Jacobs, 1992) has long argued for abandoning the term *gesture* and focusing instead on lethality and intent. Other authors have identified the same problem; as a result, quantitative methods for assessing the lethality of suicide attempts have been proposed. Beck, Weisman, Lester, and Trexler (1976), for example, found four dimensions important to the assessment of suicidal attempts: expectancies and attitudes, degree of premeditation, precautions taken or not taken against being discovered, and the type and clarity of oral communications of suicidal intent to friends or relatives.

Weisman and Worden (1972) devised a method of assessing the lethality of suicide attempts. The hypothesis underlying their "risk/rescue rating system" was that the lethality of the method of suicide, defined as the probability of inflicting irreversible damage, may be expressed as a ratio of factors influencing "risk" and "rescue." Weisman and Worden rate risk by the method used and the actual damage sustained during an attempt. Factors considered in assessing risk include the means used, whether there is impaired consciousness, the extent of tissue damage sustained, the degree of reversibility, and the level of medical treatment required. They define rescue as the observable circumstances and available resources present at the time of the attempt. Factors needed to assess rescue include location, the person initiating the rescue, the probability of discovery by any rescuer, the accessibility to rescue, and the delay until recovery.

In our proposed protocol, a relatively simple model (Table 1.5) is used to categorize the risk of suicide associated with self-destructive behavior (Clark and Fawcett, 1992b). In this model, risk is based on both estimated suicidal intent and the lethality of the behavior. Obviously the absence of past suicide attempts or self-destructive behavior does not eliminate the risk of current or future suicide attempts.

Table 1.5. Risk Model Related to Self-Destructive Behavior.

Lowest risk	Absence of self-destructive behavior
Low risk	Behavior without suicidal intent and with minimal lethality
Moderate risk	Behavior without suicidal intent but with moderate to high lethality *or* behavior with suicidal intent but with minimal lethality
Severe risk	Behavior with suicidal intent and moderate to high lethality *or* any self-destructive behavior with ongoing suicidal intent

While discussing suicide attempts, clinicians can also inquire about a history of self-mutilation. Although such acts as wrist cutting may often represent attempts at self-soothing rather than attempts to die, patients who self-mutilate do sometimes commit suicide. (See Chapter Eight for an extensive discussion of this complex issue.)

Considering Murder-Suicide

Although frequently covered with much fanfare in mass media, combined murder-suicide has not received nearly as much attention in the scientific literature as either homicide or suicide alone. Only a few case studies have been completed on the topic since 1923, when Cavan conducted an early systematic study of murder-suicides in the Chicago area (see Chapter Ten in this book). There is still no standard definition of murder-suicide, although Marzuk, Tardiff, and Hirsch (1992b) maintain that a murder-suicide has occurred when, on the basis of medical examiner review, a person has committed a homicide and then commits suicide within one week or less of the homicide.

Despite the dearth of research in this area, 1.5 to 4 percent of all suicides and 5 percent of all homicides in the United States occur in the context of murder-suicide (Wolfgang, 1958a; Rosenbaum, 1990; Clark and Fawcett, 1992b; Chapter Ten in this book). This rate translates into one thousand to fifteen hundred deaths resulting from murder-suicide annually in the United States. Thus, although murder-suicide is exceedingly infrequent, certain patient profiles might suggest further exploration of the possibility and eventual intervention.

Although rates of murder-suicide tend to be relatively stable across nations, sociocultural differences do lead to varying characteristics of such acts. For example, most murder-suicides in the United States are perpetrated by men against a spouse or lover and occur in the context of domestic violence (see the section in this chapter on attachment syndrome discussed in narcissistic personality disorder). However, other types of murder-suicide do occur, such as women who first kill their children (particularly in the postpartum period), elderly individuals who first kill their mates, and disgruntled employees who first kill those who "wronged" them and others who may be present at the time.

The assessment of a potential risk for murder-suicide should include a diagnostic interview, particularly for signs and symptoms of depression or psychosis, an exploration of motives, and an evaluation of risk for violence and suicide. Clues to potential for murder-suicide are pronounced feelings of hopelessness and ruminative or psychotic preoccupations that involve jealousy, paranoia, and fantasies of reunion or deliverance and salvation during episodes of major depression, postpartum depression, or psychosis (often bipolar). The presence of alcohol or substance use is likely to increase the risk of murder-suicide when other conditions co-occur. Indeed, alcohol can lead to disinhibition and depression, whereas cocaine and amphetamines can increase impulsivity, volatility, paranoia, and grandiosity (Marzuk and Mann, 1988). Clark and Fawcett (1992b) state that "severely depressed persons are often surprised and relieved to find that the interviewer inquires about the degree to which suicidal thinking has also implicated other persons or family members and generally discuss the vicissitudes of their homicidal ideas in a forthright manner" (p. 24). Clinicians may be reluctant to inquire about violence in their patients, but should appreciate both its diagnostic and therapeutic value. A history of abusive behavior toward a spouse, past or current impulsivity, stalking behaviors, or exhibition of anger, desperation, obsessive preoccupation, or hostility should heighten the clinician's concern about the possibility of murder-suicide.

Two final points need to be made. First, the assessment that a patient is at high risk of violence implies the need for notification of potential victims. This "duty to warn" standard originated in 1969 in the case of *Tarasoff* v. *Regents of California.* In many state statutes, a warning to the potential victim is appropriate when the patient "has made a specific threat of violence" or where the patient has communicated a "serious threat of physical violence against a reasonably identifiable victims or victims" (Callahan, 1996, pp. 205–206). Second, clinicians should be aware that most individuals who fit the profile of a murder-suicide perpetrator do not die by murder-suicide. Thus, clinicians should be aware that their attempts to predict murder-suicide based on risk factors will almost certainly overpredict mortality.

DETERMINING THE LEVEL OF INTERVENTION

After the risk factors related to underlying diagnosis, life situation, and suicidal ideation and plans have been assessed, the clinician is faced with deciding how to care for the patient. It may help to think about the source of the patient's suicidality. Is the suicidality primarily based in the axis I disorder or in the person's personality and persistent view of the world? Most of the time a combination of factors is involved, just as we described in the combination of predisposing and potentiating factors. As Exhibit 1.3 indicates, what we refer to as disorder-based suicidality is primarily a function of the patient's axis I illness and is characterized by a depressed or dysphoric mood with tension, anxiety, or anger. Prominent feelings include anguish, pain, and a wish to escape. For instance, the patient may say, "I can't take the pain anymore" or "My family would be better off without me." In disorder-based suicidality, the risk of suicide tends to be more acute than chronic. There is a compulsive or driven quality to the suicidality.

Distinguishing Disorder-Based Suicidality from Personality-Based Suicidality

Disorder-based suicidality implies that the patient's capacity to take control of his life is reduced; therefore, the clinician must assume more control. Options for the clinician may include working with the family or other available supports to address the patient's safety until the episode has passed. Other treatment options are hospitalization, psychological support, medication, and electroconvulsive treatment (ECT).

Such patients will need reassurance that there is hope and that they will indeed feel better. They also need to be educated about the uneven nature of recovery, oscillating between periods when they feel better and others when they feel worse again, but with a trend toward feeling better. This information should be offered again and again because, as Jamison notes in Chapter Fourteen, a downturn after feeling better can be devastating to some patients.

Exhibit 1.3. Disorder-Based Suicidality.

Description
- Suicidality related to Axis I diagnosis (predisposing factors)
- Prominent feelings of anguish or pain and a wish to escape
- Risk that tends to be more acute
- More compulsive, driven quality to the suicidality

Treatment Focus
- An attempt to keep patient safe until the suicidal state diminishes or abates
- Options:
  Medication
  Environmental controls (such as hospitalization)
  Supportive psychotherapy
  Electroconvulsive therapy
  Relatively more clinician responsibility and control

Personality-based suicidality is related to the patient's personality and persistent worldview. As indicated in Exhibit 1.4, prominent feelings are anger, aggression, and vengeance. The risk of suicide in personality-based suicidality tends to be more chronic than acute and tends to occur more in reaction to an external circumstance, including transference problems and crises, rather than in the course of an illness. There is an impulsive quality to the suicidality.

Managing this type of suicidality in personality disorders has been the subject of countless articles, chapters, and books and cannot be addressed thoroughly in this paragraph; however, general guidelines can be offered. When a patient is suicidal primarily because of personality-based issues, the responsibility for treatment planning and decision making can be shared with the patient rather than solely taken by the clinician. The amount of control the clinician assumes varies, but in general it is less than with disorder-based suicidality. The assignment of responsibility is not easily done and can often become a power struggle, a subject discussed further in Chapter Eighteen. Clinicians are advised to consider assessment of the therapeutic alliance in relation to personality-based suicidality. Both limit-setting techniques and consultation can be invaluable in managing these patients.

As Figure 1.2 indicates, many patients can have elements of both disorder-based and personality-based suicidality. Determining which predominates at a particular time can help to clarify the type of intervention needed. For instance, a patient with borderline personality disorder will frequently present with personality-

---

Exhibit 1.4. Personality-Based Suicidality.

Description
- Suicidality related to personality and environmental factors (the potentiating condition)
- Prominent feelings of anger, aggression, vengeance
- Risk that tends to be more chronic
- Suicidality that has impulsive quality

Treatment Focus
- An attempt to teach the patient to work within the therapeutic alliance to keep himself or herself safe
- Options:
    Assessment of the therapeutic relationship
    Consultation
    Limit setting
    Behavioral techniques
    Relatively more patient responsibility

---

based suicidality, but during a depressive episode, that same patient may have more disorder-based suicidality and require a different type of intervention. It is suggested that a clinician treating a patient with primarily personality-based suicidality reassess that patient's ability to assume responsibility each time suicidality is evident.

Assessing the Therapeutic Alliance

It is generally believed that the presence of an ongoing meaningful relationship will be protective against suicide. As Simon (1992a) writes, "Patients who maintain their personal relationships and have a working alliance with their therapist, combined with a strong religious and cultural conviction against suicide, present a diminished risk for suicide" (pp. 270–271). Many studies conclude that social support is protective against depression (Lin et al., 1979; Colletta, 1983; Compas et al., 1986) and suicide.

The therapeutic alliance is defined as "the conscious task-oriented collaboration between therapist and patient in which the therapist's aim is to form an alliance with the patient for the purpose of mutual exploration of the patient's problems" (Karasu, 1989). According to Simon (1992a), the very presence of a therapeutic alliance is "one of the most important nonverbal statements indicating a

Figure 1.2. Determining Level of Intervention from Basis of Suicidality.

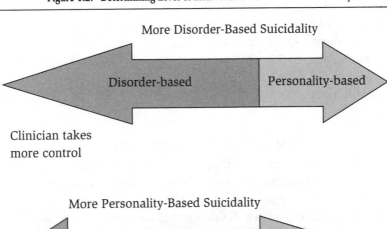

desire to live" because it indicates that the patient "is willing to seek help and sustenance during serious emotional crises" (p. 271). Thus, it is suggested that clinicians assess not only whether a therapeutic alliance versus hostile dependency exists, but also the strength and reliability of that alliance. It should be noted that suicidal behavior can be an indication of problems in the therapeutic alliance. Obviously difficulties can also arise for the clinician when there is overinvolvement. It is suggested that clinicians be prepared to be tested and use psychodynamic principles by interpreting responses in the context of a therapeutic alliance.

Inherent in the concept of alliance is the implication of two-way communication; when working with a suicidal patient, that communication should include the topic of suicidal thoughts. Indeed, the clinician needs to find out from the patient whether he or she is willing or able to communicate suicidal or self-destructive thoughts, and the patient should be informed that the clinician expects and needs to hear these thoughts. The better the clinician and patient understand each other, the more protection that understanding offers against suicide.

Certain types of patients may be at increased risk for suicide because of their inability to form or sustain a working alliance. This includes patients with borderline, narcissistic, or antisocial personality disorders, who can fluctuate in and out of a working alliance; schizoid patients, who may have difficulty reaching out to anyone; and paranoid patients, who may avoid close relationships due to extreme fear (Simon, 1992a). However, even these patients can usually maintain a modicum of a relationship with someone else. Thus, it is important to find out about these relationships and foster them because they can be crucial to getting such patients through suicidal crises (Simon, 1992a). Patients with hopeless feelings may also have difficulty maintaining a therapeutic alliance and may terminate treatment because they do not believe that the therapist can relieve their pain.

Using No-Suicide Contracts

A no-suicide contract is a written or verbal agreement between the patient and clinician in which the patient agrees to a certain course of action other than suicide should he or she become suicidal (Callahan, 1996). The no-suicide contract was first espoused by Drye, Goulding, and Goulding (1973), and has been used extensively in clinical practice over the years. Some clinicians feel that no-suicide contracts can be a way to reaffirm the therapeutic alliance and can communicate that the clinician cares what happens to the patient (Davidson, Wagner, and Range, 1995). Others feels that they can gauge the patient's suicidal intent by the patient's willingness or unwillingness to formalize the alliance into a contract (Simon, 1992a).

Although the use of no-suicide contracts is common, it is also controversial. As Motto (1979) has pointed out, such agreements are meaningless even if there is an established relationship. Clinicians are also cautioned about depending on no-suicide contracts when dealing with adolescents, patients with poor impulse control, certain psychotic patients, and patients with histories of drug or alcohol use, even if there is a strong therapeutic alliance (Davidson, Wagner, and Range, 1995; Motto, 1979). (Chapter Twenty-Six in this book reviews the advantages and limitations of no-suicide contracts.)

Evaluating Competence

If a patient is being treated involuntarily because of imminent suicidal behavior, the legal need for periodic suicide assessments is obvious. The word *competence* has a specific legal meaning as it pertains to suicidal patients and commitment standards (Black, Nolan, and Connolly, 1979; Gutheil, Bursztajn, and Brodsky, 1986). However, the word *competence* also has a broader clinical sense. Evaluating a person's competence means assessing the extent to which a patient's judgment and self-control are impaired by their illness.

This broader view of competence is similar to that of Gutheil, Bursztajn, and Brodsky (1986), who developed a multidimensional model for assessing the dangerousness of patients in relation to their ability to engage in informative dialogue with clinicians. They mean: Can the patient weigh the risks and benefits of his or her actions? Is the patient capable of giving informed consent? In this sense, both informed consent and the therapeutic alliance assume and require some level of patient competence.

At some point near the end of the assessment, the clinician should make an informed decision about the patient's judgment, ability to control impulses, and ability to understand and comply with the treatment plan. Impulsivity is significantly associated with suicide and suicide attempts in certain patient populations (Jameison and Wall, 1933; Reich and Kelly, 1976; Myers and Neal, 1978). In fact, Brodsky et al. (1997) found that the trait of impulsivity was associated with a greater number of previous suicide attempts among inpatients with borderline personality disorder, even after controlling for the lifetime prevalence of major depression, substance abuse, and the global severity of the borderline disorder.

In sum, clinicians who are conducting suicide assessments should attempt to evaluate a patient's competence to assist in the overall determination of risk. The evaluation of competence is especially important because it can help the clinician determine the amount of control the patient can assume. That is, the less competent the patient is, the more control the clinician must take.

Planning the Frequency of Reassessments

A scheduled reassessment for suicide can be a useful part of the treatment plan. The frequency of assessments is determined clinically. A low-risk outpatient, for example, might be assessed at monthly consultations, while a high-risk inpatient might be assessed several times per twenty-four hours by nursing staff and at each meeting with a psychiatrist or other responsible clinician.

PROVIDING DOCUMENTATION

Documentation of the suicide assessment is invaluable. It can help clinicians provide good care and intervention by clarifying the treatment plan and communicating to other caregivers. Also, it can be useful in the event of a bad outcome.

As Exhibit 1.5 indicates, suicide risk should be assessed and documented at the first psychiatric assessment and upon admission to a hospital, as should the occurrence of any new suicidal behavior or ideation and when there is any noteworthy clinical change. In addition, for inpatients in whom suicidality is a concern, suicidal risk should be assessed and documented before the patient receives passes or any increase in privileges, as well as before discharge. Documentation should be timely, thorough, and clear (legible and understandable) but can be brief. Exhibit 1.6 indicates suggested elements to be included in each note.

Exhibit 1.5. Times to Assess and Document Suicide Risk.

Assess and document suicide risk
    Upon first psychiatric assessment or upon admission
    With the occurrence of any suicidal behavior or ideation
    Whenever there is any noteworthy clinical change
    Whenever suicidality is an issue for an inpatient
    Before increasing privileges or giving passes
    Before discharging a patient

Exhibit 1.6. Elements of Suicide Risk Documentation.

Assessment
Degree of risk: Low, moderate, severe
Objective data
Subjective data

Diagnosis
Working or differential diagnosis

Treatment Plan for Addressing/Managing Suicide Risk
Risk-benefit analysis of proposed treatment
Basis for clinical judgment and decision making
Relevant medications (for example, antidepressant, antianxiety)
Tests ordered (such as psychological testing)
Consultation ordered (for example, neurological or second opinion on suicidality)
Precautions and privileges
Reassessment of suicidality

EXAMINING SAMPLE CASES

The following case examples illustrate the steps to consider when assessing suicidality.

Case 1: Disorder-Based Suicidality

A fifty-two-year-old married, white male is admitted to the hospital after being found in his house, threatening to shoot himself with a rifle.

Step 1. Identify or Detect Predisposing Factors. He is diagnosed as having major depression with vegetative symptoms, severe, but without psychotic features, first episode, and evidences significant psychic anxiety. He has recently started drinking alcohol to excess.

Step 2. Elucidate Potentiating Factors. Axis II diagnosis is deferred, but personality issues do not seem prominent. He has recently been laid off from his job and is worried about his financial situation. His father committed suicide. There is a family history of alcoholism. His wife seems supportive but passive and not insightful about psychiatric illness. He has two adult children. He is a hunter and has an extensive gun collection.

Step 3. Conduct a Specific Suicide Inquiry. He admits to wanting to kill himself. He says he is sorry he did not shoot himself before his son pulled the gun out of his hands. He feels his family would be better off without him because he has an insurance policy. He says he just cannot bear this agony anymore and would like to "finish the job."

Step 4. Determine the Level of Intervention.

- *Estimate the acuteness or chronicity of the patient's suicidality*: His suicidality is almost entirely disorder based. He is in the midst of a major depressive episode and has received no treatment for it. The patient is unable to assume any control at this time. The intervention is to hospitalize and conduct appropriate searches and institute one-on-one observations.

- *Evaluate competence, impulsivity, and acting out.* The patient is not obviously psychotic, although there is an exaggerated quality to his financial worries, and his judgment is severely impaired. His suicide attempt was impulsive according to his family.

- *Assess the therapeutic alliance.* This is a new patient, unknown to staff or psychiatrist. Although he seemed somewhat relieved to talk about his problems, his risk is increased because he is not known and has no firm alliance.

- *Plan the nature and frequency of reassessments.* This patient will be assessed every shift by the nursing staff and reassessed by his psychiatrist daily until his depression begins to respond to treatment. At that point, the frequency of reassessments can be reevaluated. The patient has been started on medication.

Step 5. Document the Assessments. An assessment of suicide risk should appear in each shift's nursing note, for example, "Mr. X continues to feel suicidal although he says he is not thinking about it constantly since he slept better last night and feels somewhat calmer after taking antianxiety medications. 1:1 observations maintained throughout shift." A more detailed assessment of his psychological state and a revised treatment plan should appear in his psychiatrist's notes, for example, "Mr. X reports feeling intense suicidal thoughts twice today; he was able to talk with the nurse only once, but asked for extra antianxiety medication both times. He reported the suicidality decreased after these were given. I discussed again with him the fact that his antidepressant medication would take some time to work and that when it did the progress would be uneven. I encouraged him to continue talking to staff and to ask for the PRNs when needed. I will continue his suicide precautions, 1:1 observations and unit restriction for the time being and consider changing observations to 15 minutes checks when his anxiety and suicidality decrease."

Case 2: Personality-Based Suicidality

A twenty-one-year-old single, white, female college student is admitted to the hospital after cutting her arms and abdomen.

Step 1. Identify or Detect Predisposing Factors. This is the third admission at this facility and one of many lifetime admissions for this young woman, who was previously diagnosed as having dysthymia, a history of polysubstance abuse, and borderline personality disorder. Her comorbid diagnoses increase the risk.

Step 2. Elucidate Potentiating Factors. Axis II diagnosis of borderline personality disorder is prominent. She has been under more stress at school and is required to complete several papers before receiving credit for last semester's work. She has also been fighting with her most recent boyfriend, an alleged drug dealer who is facing legal charges. Her parents are divorced and live out of town but have been in touch with the social worker and are familiar with this unit. Her mother expressed some frustration at this most recent difficulty and is concerned about continued insurance coverage. Her therapist of several years is on vacation.

Step 3. Conduct a Specific Suicide Inquiry. She says she wanted to die when she cut herself recently, but also says it relieved the tension she was experiencing and made her "feel real." She says she does not feel like dying at the moment but that she is frequently overwhelmed by suicidal thoughts.

Step 4. Determine the Level of Intervention.

- *Estimate the acuteness or chronicity of the patient's suicidality.* Her suicidality is largely personality based, although there are times when disorder-based suicidality becomes an issue. Twice in the past she has made near-lethal suicide attempts by overdoses on multiple drugs, both prescribed and illicit. Her cutting behavior is usually associated with tension release rather than with suicidal intent. It seems that her current suicidality is more personality based than disorder based and that she has the capacity to take some control.

- *Evaluate competence, impulsivity, and acting out.* She is not psychotic. Her cutting was precipitated by the combination of her academic adviser's issuing a warning about her work and her boyfriend's being unavailable. Her long-term therapist is on vacation. She can be quite impulsive when she is feeling stressed and has acted out angry feelings, usually by cutting.

- *Assess the therapeutic alliance.* This patient has been admitted to this unit twice before and is well known to most staff members. She has a good alliance with her therapist, who will return in two days.

- *Plan the nature and frequency of reassessments.* This patient will be assessed every shift by the nursing staff and assessed by her therapist upon his return from vacation. Nursing staff will also ask her about her suicidal feelings any time she isolates herself.

Step 5. Document the Assessments. An assessment of her suicide risk should appear in each shift's nursing note. A more detailed assessment of her psychological state and a revised treatment plan should appear in her psychiatrist's notes, for example, "Ms. X reports having fleeting suicidal thoughts three times today but she was able to talk with the nurse and stayed in the activity room where she was with staff and other patients. She reported the suicidality decreased after working on a craft project and one time after taking a PRN dose of perphenazine (2 mg)."

IMPLICATIONS FOR THE CLINICIAN

This chapter presents an overview of the complex issues involved in the assessment of suicide risk in clinical settings. There can be no formula or reductionist approach to suicide risk assessment because of the complexity and

Exhibit 1.7. Suicide Assessment Protocol Guidelines.

Consider Predisposing Factors: Axis I Diagnosis
Affective illness: 15 percent lifetime risk of suicide, 60 percent of suicides
   Risk related to severity
   Risk highest in depressive states
   Anxiety or panic as modifiable risk factor
Schizophrenia: 10 percent lifetime risk of suicide, 10 percent of suicides
   Higher risk for paranoid type
   Risk usually higher after recovery from psychotic phase
   High correlation between depression or depressive symptoms and suicide
Alcohol and other substance abuse: 3–5 percent lifetime risk of suicide,
25 percent of suicides
   Alcohol use very prevalent in suicides
   Interpersonal loss important as precipitant
   Mechanism unclear (increased impulsivity?)
Evaluation of category of disorder, time course of illness, clinical features; and
comorbidity

Detect Potentiating Factors
Family and social milieu
   Biological vulnerability
   Interpersonal dynamics and family construct
Personality disorders and traits
   Borderline personality disorder
      Clinician differentiates between self-mutilation and suicide attempts
      Clinician inquires into intent
   Antisocial personality disorder (males)
   Narcissistic personality disorder
      Extreme narcissistic injury as stimulus
      Correlation with attachment syndrome in murder-suicide
Physical illness
Life stress or crisis
Firearms and other available methods

Conduct a Specific Suicide Inquiry
Determination made of suicidal ideation and intent
Assessment of suicide plans and attempts

Determine the Level of Intervention
More control taken by clinician when patient has disorder-based suicidality
More control given to patient who has personality-based suicidality
Assessment made of patient's competence (judgment, level of compliance, ability
to understand treatment)
Assessment made of therapeutic alliance
Reassessment of suicidality scheduled

Document the Assessments

---

interrelationship of many factors. The goal of the assessment is to determine the severity of risk at a point in time, acknowledging possible shifts in the risk and the need for repeat evaluations. The assessments can then help determine the level and type of intervention. Because there is neither a test nor a technique to determine the level of risk objectively, we recommend that the clinician consider multiple factors and clinical elements in arriving at a clinical judgment (see Exhibit 1.7).

CHAPTER TWO

Epidemiology of Suicide

Eve K. Mościcki, Sc.D., M.P.H.

T he field of suicide research has made great advances since Emil Durkheim's study of suicides in France a century ago (Durkheim, [1897] 1951). This chapter reviews the epidemiology of suicide in the United States by presenting incidence data on completed suicides and prevalence data on attempted suicides, describing the occurrence of completed and attempted suicides by sociodemographic correlates, and discussing distal and proximal risk factors for completed and attempted suicides. Knowledge of the epidemiology of suicide complements clinical research to provide useful information for suicide intervention efforts in clinical settings.

COMPLETED SUICIDES

The primary source of data on suicide mortality in the United States is death certificate information reported by each state to the National Center for Health Statistics. It is generally recognized that suicides are underestimated in official statistics, but the extent of the undercount is believed to be modest. Operational criteria for the classification of suicide were developed and published in 1988

This chapter is adapted from Mościcki, 1997, and is supported in part by the National Institute of Mental Health (NIMH) Epidemiologic Catchment Area Program (U01 MH34224, U01 MH33870, U01 MH33883, U01 MH35386).

(Rosenberg et al., 1988). Although their application has not been uniform, due in part to the range of reporting practices among local jurisdictions, officially reported suicide mortality data are considered reliable and useful for the study of selected risk factors and correlates of suicide (Monk, 1987; O'Carroll, 1989; Sainsbury and Jenkins, 1982).

An additional, powerful tool in the study of completed suicides has been the emergence, in the last decade or so, of population-based psychological autopsy studies (Brent et al., 1993b; Beskow et al., 1990). These are postmortem studies of consecutive suicide deaths within a defined geographic area such as a county. Psychological autopsy studies permit the examination of suicide deaths in considerable detail, and, if conducted using appropriately selected control or comparison groups, produce findings that can be generalized beyond the study.

In 1995, the most recent year for which national suicide data are available, suicide was the ninth leading cause of death in the United States. It was recently displaced from its decades-long rank of eighth leading cause by deaths from human immunodeficiency virus (HIV) infection (Anderson et al., 1997). In 1995, there were 31,284 deaths from suicide, compared with 2,313,132 deaths from all causes. The age-adjusted suicide rate was 11.2 per 100,000, unchanged from 1994 (Anderson et al., 1997). This rate is much lower than the age-adjusted death rate from diseases of the heart, the leading cause of death at 138.3 per 100,000. Deaths by suicide vary from state to state. For example, in 1995, the unadjusted death rate ranged from 7.3 per 100,000 in New Jersey to 25.8 per 100,000 in Nevada.

Suicide rates vary by age, gender, and race. Rates increase with age, although suicide is not a leading cause of death in the elderly. The highest rates are among elderly white men. Men consistently have higher rates than do women, with a gender ratio of 4.6 in 1995. In 1995, the overall age-adjusted rate for men was 18.6 per 100,000, ranging from rates near 0 in boys five to nine to 63.1 per 100,000 in men eighty-five years and older. The comparable rates for women were much lower. The overall age-adjusted rate was 4.1 per 100,000, with a range of 0.0 per 100,000 in girls five to nine to 6.9 per 100,000 in women aged forty to forty-four. Figure 2.1 shows that suicide rates among blacks are lower than those for whites, although a recent increase in the suicide rate for young black men has been noted (Shaffer, Gould, and Hicks, 1994; Centers for Disease Control, 1998). Gender differences are similar by race: the 1995 age-adjusted rate for black men was 12.4 per 100,000, compared with 19.7 per 100,000 for white men; for black women the rate was 2.0 per 100,000, compared with 4.4 per 100,000 for white women (National Center for Health Statistics, unpublished data). Unlike the rates by sex, the age distribution differs by race. In black men, the distribution of suicide rates by age resembles the age distribution seen among American Indians and Alaska Natives (Indian Health Service, 1996a, 1996b). In both groups, the highest rates occur among young men ages twenty to twenty-nine, with a decline in the later years of life.

Figure 2.1. Suicide Rates by Age, Race, and Gender, United States, 1995.

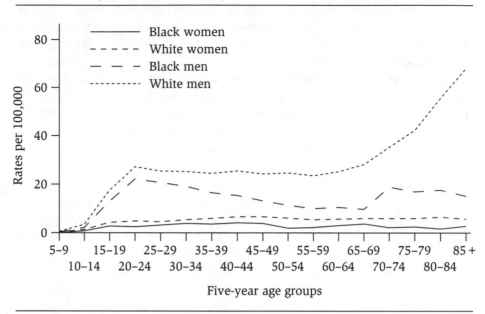

Source: National Center for Health Statistics, unpublished data.

In the United States, firearms are the primary method of suicide death for both men and women across all age groups. Each year, approximately 60 percent of all suicide deaths are by means of firearms. The second most common method for men is hanging; for women, the second most common method of death is self-poisoning. The increase in rates from the 1950s to the 1970s can be largely attributed to increases in deaths from firearm suicides (Boyd, 1983; Boyd and Mościcki, 1986).

ATTEMPTED SUICIDES

Unlike information on suicide mortality, there is no single primary data source for information on suicide morbidity. Systematic research on attempted suicide faces two important challenges. First is the lack of an agreed-upon, standardized nomenclature that can be used reliably and consistently to describe attempted suicide events. This, in turn, hinders collection of reliable data at the national level and limits the nature of the clinical, public health, and policy decisions that can be made to address suicide morbidity.

A nomenclature for suicidal behaviors has recently been proposed (O'Carroll et al., 1996), in which a suicide attempt is defined as "a potentially self-injurious action with a nonfatal outcome for which there is evidence, either explicit or implicit, that the individual intended to kill himself or herself." An important innovation of the proposed nomenclature is that it takes into account both lethality and intent of a suicidal behavior. *Lethality* refers to the potential for death associated with the means used to attempt suicide. For example, ingesting ten acetaminophen tablets would be considered less lethal than losing consciousness after deliberately locking oneself in the garage with the car engine running. *Intent* refers to the individual's desire to die and expectation that death would result from action. Lethality and intent are independent indicators of severity, although they are significantly correlated (Andrews and Lewinsohn, 1992). Both need to be taken into account in the clinical management of suicide attempters (Beautrais et al., 1996; Brent, 1987; Lewinsohn et al., 1996; O'Carroll et al., 1996; Pedinielli et al., 1989).

Although there are no national data on attempted suicide, several epidemiologic surveys have been conducted that have yielded population-based lifetime and twelve-month estimates of prevalence. Estimates of lifetime prevalence among adults range from 1.1 to 4.3 per 100; twelve-month prevalence estimates range from 0.3 to 0.8 per 100 (Mościcki et al., 1988, 1989; Paykel et al., 1974; Ramsay and Bagley, 1985; Schwab et al., 1972). Among representative samples of adolescents, lifetime prevalence estimates increase to over 7 per 100 (Andrews and Lewinsohn, 1992). When lethality and intent are taken into account, however, the range decreases to 1.6 to 2.6 per 100 (Andrews and Lewinsohn, 1992; Garrison et al., 1993; Meehan et al., 1992). Twelve-month prevalence estimates of attempted suicide among adolescents range from 0.2 to 2.6 per 100 (Andrews and Lewinsohn, 1992; Garrison et al., 1993).

Few population-based, prospective studies of attempted suicide exist. Information on incidence rates, that is, occurrences of new cases within a given time period, is therefore difficult to ascertain. From the available data, incidence of attempted suicide is estimated to range from 0.2 to 2.2 per 100, with the higher rate representing younger age groups (Andrews and Lewinsohn, 1992; Petronis et al., 1990).

Lifetime data on attempted suicide in both adults and adolescents indicate that women report higher rates than do men (Andrews and Lewinsohn, 1992; Garrison et al., 1993; Mościcki et al., 1988). However, these findings are not supported by data on incident attempts, which show no significant differences between men and women (Andrews and Lewinsohn, 1992; Beautrais et al., 1996; Petronis et al., 1990). The gender differences in the lifetime data can be partially explained by the fact that women tend to be better reporters of their health history than do men; this is not a complete explanation, however, and the reasons merit further study.

Cross-sectional, population-based data on attempted suicide from various sources have consistently found that rates are higher among younger than older persons (Mościcki et al., 1988; Andrus et al., 1991; Beautrais et al., 1996). Data on ethnicity and attempted suicide are infrequently reported. In most studies, it was found that whites tend to report attempted suicide more frequently than do nonwhites. Both Garrison et al. (1993) and Mościcki et al. (1988) found that risk of attempted suicide was higher among whites than among nonwhites. A recent study conducted in a large sample of Hawaiian high school students (Yuen et al., 1996), however, found a six-month prevalence rate of 4.3 per 100. This rate is higher than twelve-month rates reported for white adolescents, which are less than 3 per 100 (Andrus et al., 1991; Garrison et al., 1993; Meehan et al., 1992).

There is little information available from representative samples of suicide attempters on the method of attempt. Retrospective data, largely from hospital surveys, consistently report that self-poisoning by ingestion is the most common method used, which accounts for about 70 percent of all attempts, regardless of the nature of the sample (Andrus et al., 1991; Beautrais et al., 1996; Schmidtke et al., 1996; Weissman, 1974). The second most common method used by suicide attempters is reported to be cutting or stabbing, and carbon monoxide poisoning (Andrews and Lewinsohn, 1992; Beautrais et al., 1996). Self-poisoning, the premier method used in attempted suicide, is the second most common method used in completed suicides.

RISK FACTORS

Suicide is a complex event that has been associated with so many correlates, antecedents, and risk factors, that making appropriate clinical or policy decisions regarding preventive or treatment interventions can be difficult. It is helpful, therefore, to organize knowledge of suicide risk factors into a framework that distinguishes between *distal* and *proximal* risk factors. A *risk factor,* as opposed to a correlate, is a measurable characteristic, variable, or hazard that increases the likelihood of development of an adverse outcome (Last, 1983). The critical feature of a risk factor that distinguishes it from a correlate or other characteristic indicating an association between two variables, is that a risk factor precedes the outcome in time (Kraemer et al., 1997).

Distal risk factors may be thought of as the foundation for attempted and completed suicides. Distal risk factors may not obviously occur immediately antecedent to the suicidal event itself. They are necessary, but not sufficient, for suicide. *Proximal risk factors,* on the other hand, are closely associated with the suicide event, and can be thought of as precipitants or "triggers" for suicidal behavior. Unlike distal risk factors, proximal risk factors are neither necessary nor sufficient for suicide in and of themselves.

Risk factors rarely act individually to increase risk. Indeed, many persons may have one or more risk factors and not be suicidal. How, then, do distal and proximal risk factors increase risk for suicide? It is their co-occurrence and interaction among a variety of risk factors that can result in the necessary and sufficient conditions for attempted or completed suicide. For the purposes of discussion in this paper, risk factors will be presented individually or in clusters. It should be kept in mind, however, that it is the cumulative and interactive effects of co-occurring risk factors that result in increased risk for suicide.

Psychopathology

The strongest known risk factor and primary context for completed and attempted suicide is the presence of mental or addictive disorders. Psychopathology is necessary for serious suicidal behaviors to occur (Rich et al., 1986b; Shaffer et al., 1988). Psychological autopsy studies have consistently found that over 90 percent of all completed suicides in all age groups are associated with psychopathology (Brent et al., 1987; Henriksson et al., 1993; Martunnen et al., 1991; Rich and Runeson, 1992; Rich et al., 1986b; Runeson, 1989; Shaffer et al., 1996). The most frequently reported diagnoses are mood disorders, found in both men and women, followed by substance abuse (predominantly alcohol abuse/dependence), and conduct disorder or antisocial personality (Brent et al., 1988, 1993a; Conwell and Brent, 1995; Henriksson et al., 1993; Lesage et al., 1994; Martunnen et al., 1991; Rich et al., 1986b; Shaffer et al., 1988, 1996; Shafii et al., 1988). There are differences in the age and sex distributions of these disorders. Mood disorders are more frequently identified among elderly suicides and the small numbers of women who commit suicide (Barraclough, 1971; Rich et al., 1986b; Henriksson et al., 1995); substance abuse and behavioral disorders are found in greater proportions among adolescent and young adult suicides, especially in men (Brent et al., 1988, 1993a; Conwell and Brent, 1995; Henriksson et al., 1993; Lesage et al., 1994; Martunnen et al., 1991; Rich et al., 1986b; Shaffer et al., 1988, 1996; Shafii et al., 1988).

Rigorous studies of suicide attempters have also found significant, independent associations between serious suicidal behavior and mental and addictive disorders. They have been found in the large majority of medically injurious attempted suicides (Andrews and Lewinsohn, 1992; Beautrais et al., 1996; Brent et al., 1993b; Garrison et al., 1993; Lewinsohn et al., 1996; Petronis et al., 1990). As with completed suicides, the strongest risk is associated with mood, substance abuse, and personality disorders. These findings have been reported from studies conducted in both the clinic and the community.

There is substantial evidence that severity of psychopathology greatly increases suicide risk. For example, comorbid disorders have been identified in 70 to 80 percent of all completed suicides (Brent et al., 1988; Henriksson et al., 1993; Rich and Runeson, 1992; Rich et al., 1986b; Shaffer et al., 1988, 1996; Shafii et al., 1985, 1988), and in a large proportion of attempted suicides (Lewinsohn et al., 1996; Mościcki, 1995b; Beautrais, 1996). Both Beautrais (1996) and

Mościcki (1995b), in studies done ten years apart and on widely differing geographic populations, reported a fivefold increase in risk of attempted suicide associated with more than one diagnosis. The diagnoses can be comorbid mental disorders, mental and addictive disorders, or mental disorders with physical illness. Mood and addictive disorders, and mood and personality disorders appear to be particularly lethal combinations (Beautrais, 1996; Rich et al., 1986b; Shaffer et al., 1988, 1996; Henriksson et al., 1993, 1995). Despite the strong evidence that comorbidity greatly contributes to suicide risk, it is not clear whether comorbidity is a necessary condition for suicide to occur.

A word of caution is in order on the role of panic disorder as a risk factor for suicide. Some early reports in the literature suggested that panic disorder was associated with an increased risk for attempted suicide (Weissman et al., 1989). Other reports disputed this finding (Beck et al., 1991), and it was rarely identified in studies of completed suicide. Recent studies have demonstrated that an association of panic disorder with attempted and completed suicide appears to be indirect, and that panic disorder is not an independent risk factor (Beck et al., 1991; Henriksson et al., 1996; Johnson et al., 1990). Panic disorder can occur comorbidly with other psychopathology, usually a mood or substance abuse disorder, to increase suicide risk.

A history of suicide attempts as a risk factor for completed suicide has consistently appeared in the literature (Robins et al., 1959b; Rosenberg et al., 1988; Shaffer et al., 1988, 1996). These reports are based on retrospective studies, however, and a history of attempts may not be a clinically reliable, independent predictor of imminent suicide risk in most cases (Pokorny, 1993). In conjunction with other indicators such as a current severe mood disorder, hopelessness (Beck et al., 1985, 1990; Lewinsohn et al., 1996), or other strong characteristics, it may be very valuable in identifying high risk patients. A history of previous suicide attempts may be more reliable in identifying elderly, rather than younger, persons at increased risk for suicide. Lower ratios of attempts to completions have been reported for older than younger persons in both clinical and population-based studies (Maris, 1992; Mościcki, 1995b). Clinical and sociodemographic characteristics of elderly suicide attempters closely resemble those found in elderly suicide completers (Merrill and Owens, 1990; Frierson, 1991). The expectation is that elderly persons presenting with a history of attempted suicide are at greater risk for death and require immediate intervention.

Substance Abuse

A substance abuse disorder, or intoxication with a substance of abuse, has frequently been identified as a potent risk factor for both completed and attempted suicide (Andrews and Lewinsohn, 1992, Beautrais et al., 1996; Brent et al., 1987, 1988; Garrison et al., 1993; Henriksson et al., 1993; Kienhorst et al., 1990; Lesage et al., 1994, Lewinsohn et al., 1996; Martunnen et al., 1991; Petronis et al., 1990; Rich et al., 1986b; Shaffer et al., 1988, 1996; Shafii et al., 1985, 1988). Alcohol is the most common single drug of abuse across all age groups, including the elderly (Rich et al., 1986b; Henriksson et al., 1995) and is also the most common substance of abuse found in suicides diagnosed with multiple substance abuse (Fowler et al., 1986; Garrison et al., 1993; Lesage et al., 1994; Remafedi, Farrow, and Deisher, 1991). In addition, alcohol intoxication at the time of death is a highly significant correlate of suicide and has been found in approximately half of youthful suicides (Fowler et al., 1986; Hlady and Middaugh, 1988; Rich et al., 1986b; Shaffer et al., 1988). Cocaine abuse has also been identified as a significant contributor to completed suicides (Marzuk et al., 1992c) and as an independent risk factor for attempted suicide (Petronis et al., 1990). Substance abuse is associated with greater frequency and repetitiveness of suicide attempts, more medically lethal attempts, more serious suicidal intent, and higher levels of suicidal ideation (Lewinsohn et al., 1996; Crumley, 1990).

Neurochemical Risk Factors

One of the most consistent findings in the suicide literature, reported both in post mortem studies of suicide completers and in clinical studies of suicide attempters, has been evidence of decreased brain stem levels of serotonin (5-HT) or its principal cerebral spinal fluid metabolite (CSF 5-HIAA) (Mann, 1995; Mann et al., 1986; Brown and Goodwin, 1986; Stanley and Stanley, 1989). The reduced levels appear to be independent of psychiatric diagnosis. Until recently, it was believed that serotonin abnormalities were associated with impulsive and violent suicides (Arango et al., 1990; Coccaro et al., 1989). It has now been shown that reduced serotonergic activity may actually be linked to a history of planned, nonimpulsive attempts, especially more medically lethal attempts (Stoff and Mann, 1997). Since CSF 5HIAA levels are stable, they may be a biochemical trait indicative of potential suicidal behavior in high-risk individuals (Mann, 1995). See Chapter Six for a further discussion of this topic.

Recent reports have appeared in the literature suggesting a link between lowered levels of total plasma cholesterol and increased risk for suicide (Freedman et al., 1995; Jacobs et al., 1995). It has been proposed that this relationship may be mediated by changes in serotonergic activity, termed the *cholesterol-serotonin hypothesis* (Kaplan et al., 1997). There is evidence from animal studies that supports the plausibility of this hypothesis, although the clinical implications of this finding are not entirely clear. One cautious interpretation may be that lowering cholesterol for some individuals may have adverse effects under some circumstances (Kaplan et al., 1997).

Familial Risk Factors

The clustering of risk represented by familial risk factors is mediated through shared biological vulnerability and shared environment. Without intervention, a negative environment will have adverse effects on persons with potential biological vulnerability, and increase the likelihood of intergenerational transmission of psychopathology or suicidal behavior. Family history of psychopathology and/or suicidal behavior has been found in numerous studies of suicide completers and attempters (Brent et al., 1996; Egeland and Sussex, 1985; Lesage et al., 1994; Roy, 1989a; Roy et al., 1991; Shaffer et al., 1988; Shafii et al., 1985; Wagner, 1997). Disrupted family environments as indicated by divorce, separation, or widowhood can contribute to suicidal outcomes (Brent et al., 1995; Smith et al., 1988; Wagner, 1997). Such environments are characterized by family conflict, stress, parental legal troubles, and separation from parents or other parental absence (Wagner, 1997). There is consistent evidence from studies of youth suicide that negative parenting and physical and sexual abuse are associated with later adolescent suicide attempts (Briere and Zaidi, 1989; de Wilde et al., 1991; Wagner, 1997), and these risk factors appear to be associated with completed suicides as well (Brent et al., 1996; Shafii et al., 1985).

Suicide and Sexual Orientation

A sensitive area that merits further investigation is the hypothesized relationship between sexual orientation and suicide (Muehrer, 1995; Working Groups, 1995). To date, there is no evidence from unbiased, population-based studies that nonheterosexual orientation is an independent risk factor for completed or attempted suicide outside the context of mental or addictive disorders. Rigorous research in this area is extremely difficult to do, complicated by the lack of information on the true rate of homosexuality in the population and the reluctance of sexual minorities to self-identify. Only two population-based studies, published a decade apart, have examined sexual orientation in suicide completers. Both found that there were no differences in suicide risk between gay and nongay suicides (Rich et al., 1986a; Shaffer et al., 1995). Both studies also found high rates of mental and substance abuse disorders among all the suicides. Findings from reports of self-selected samples suggest that sexual orientation may increase risk for attempted suicide (Remafedi, Farrow, and Deisher, 1991; Harry, 1989). As with completed suicide, however, the key issue of independence has not been addressed in unbiased samples, and further careful investigation is needed.

Proximal Risk Factors

In and of themselves, proximal risk factors are unlikely to contribute to risk for suicide. However, their clustering with distal risk factors, such as a past or current psychiatric disorder, may result in the necessary and sufficient conditions for attempted or completed suicide. One of the strongest of the proximal risk factors is a firearm in the home. Access to a firearm, regardless of the type of weapon or storage practices, independently increases risk for suicide for both men and women across all age groups (Brent et al., 1991, 1988; M. S. Kaplan et al., 1994; Kellerman and Reay, 1986; Kellerman et al., 1992). A particularly lethal combination is a mental or substance abuse disorder, intoxication (most frequently with alcohol), and a firearm in the home (Brent et al, 1987).

Severe, stressful life events, in conjunction with an underlying mental disorder, can precipitate a suicide event in vulnerable individuals. The three most common groups of life stressors that have been identified in completed suicides are conflict-separation-rejection, economic difficulties, and physical illness. These vary in their impact according to age and gender (Rich et al., 1991). Stressors most frequently associated with completed suicides in youth and young adults include interpersonal conflict, separation or rejection, and legal problems such as arrest and incarceration (Brent et al., 1993b; Hayes, 1989; Kerkhof et al., 1990; Lesage et al., 1994; Rich et al., 1988a, 1991). Economic difficulties such as job loss or financial strain are important stressors in midlife, particularly in men (Rich et al., 1991). Medical illness is the dominant stressor in older adult suicides (Henriksson et al., 1995; Rich et al., 1991). A recent study of natural disasters found that suicide rates were significantly increased for both sexes and all age groups following severe earthquakes, floods, and hurricanes (Krug et al., 1998). It is likely that the number of stressors, rather than the specific type of stressor, may lead to suicide, as has been noted by some investigators (Brent et al., 1993b; Lesage et al., 1994).

Contagion, which is defined here as exposure to suicidal behavior of others through the media, peer group, or family, has been shown to increase suicide risk in some vulnerable youth (Davidson et al., 1989; Brent et al., 1989; Gould and Shaffer, 1986; Wagner, 1997). The potential role played by the print or broadcast media is somewhat controversial, but young people appear to be at greater risk from contagion than do adults (Schmidtke and Hafner, 1988; Gould et al., 1990a, 1990b). Studies of suicide clusters, which rarely occur in the United States, have found that nearly all clusters occur in adolescents and young adults (Gould et al., 1990a, 1990b).

Physical illness has been hypothesized to be a major risk factor in suicides, particularly among the elderly. It is not clear, however, whether it is an independent risk factor outside the context of depression or substance abuse (Marzuk, 1994). For example, of the physical illnesses believed to have an increased risk for suicide, most are associated with psychiatric diagnoses (Harris and Barraclough, 1994). Although positive HIV status was previously shown to have an greatly elevated suicide risk (Marzuk et al., 1988), recent work has demonstrated that persons who are most at risk for HIV infection are also at increased risk for other factors associated with both suicide and HIV infection, including drug abuse (Marzuk et al., 1997). The independent contribution of HIV infections to suicide risk is now considered to be modest at best.

The role that prescription medications play in completed and attempted suicide needs further examination. Drugs and medicaments, especially antidepressant medications, are the second most common method of completed suicide among women (Mościcki, 1995b) and the method of choice in attempted suicide (Meehan et al., 1992; Weissman, 1974). The likelihood of death appears to be significantly greater from an overdose of the older antidepressant medications, such as desipramine, nortriptyline, amitriptyline, and imipramine, than from newer antidepressants such as trazodone or fluoxetine (Kapur et al., 1992). On the other hand, depression may be an unintended outcome of a poorly coordinated medication regimen, especially among elderly patients (Sorenson, 1991), and caution is needed in prescribing practices (Marzuk et al., 1992a).

IMPLICATIONS FOR THE CLINICIAN

A great deal is known about suicide and suicide risk, both from epidemiologic and clinical research. The evidence has shown, clearly and consistently, that suicide has multiple, interacting causes arising from psychopathological processes that produce individual vulnerability. Suicidal acts in a vulnerable individual can be precipitated by a variety of proximal risk factors. Despite our greatly increased knowledge, however, accurate prediction of which patients are likely to attempt or complete suicide continues to be as much an art as it is a science (Pokorny, 1993). Some principles have emerged that can provide guidance in making clinical decisions.

- The best hope for prevention of suicide lies in recognizing the critical role of mental and addictive disorders. Identification and appropriate and timely treatment of psychopathology, especially of comorbid conditions, has the greatest potential for saving lives.

- Risk factors are cumulative and interact with each other to produce lethal outcomes. Many persons may suffer from psychiatric disorders, or have one or two other risk factors, and not be suicidal. However, the greater the number of risk factors, the higher the risk for suicidal outcomes.

- Comorbidity, especially of mood disorders with other illnesses, greatly increases risk for attempted or completed suicide in both sexes across all age groups. Comorbid substance abuse and personality disorders are more common in young people; comorbid depressive disorders and physical illness are more common among the elderly.

- A history of physical or sexual abuse in an already vulnerable young person is an important indicator of increased suicide risk.

- Even though the contribution of sexual orientation to suicide is unclear, individuals in distress, especially young people, should be treated with sensitivity and dignity regardless of sexual orientation.

- Clinicians are advised to assess overall psychopathology in patients presenting with panic disorder to identify those who may be at high risk for suicide.

- Because of the potential lethality associated with some antidepressant medications if taken in overdose, a safer practice for depressed patients may be to prescribe newer medications such as the selective serotonin reuptake inhibitors (SSRIs).

- The prescription of multiple medications for physical and mental disorders needs to be carefully monitored to avoid the development of depression as an unintentional outcome, especially in the elderly.

- Because of the potential increased risk for suicide associated with co-morbid depression and physical illness, diagnosis of a terminal illness, especially in an elderly person, should be accompanied by an assessment of mental health to rule out an underlying mood disorder.

- Because of the low ratio of attempts to completions among the elderly, older persons presenting with attempted suicide should be regarded as being at great risk for imminent death.

- The clinician needs to be alert to, inquire about, and remove any potential means of suicide from the home of the suicidal patient, especially firearms and prescription medications. The particularly lethal combination of a mood disorder, comorbid substance abuse or intoxication, and a firearm in the home requires immediate intervention.

- The complexity of suicide requires complex interventions for effective prevention. The best method is likely to be one that includes a long-term approach designed to address the major distal risk factors in an integrated manner—prevention and appropriate treatment of mental and addictive disorders at the clinical level, and increased restrictions on access to the most lethal means of suicide at the public health and policy levels.

CHAPTER THREE

A Community Psychiatry Approach to Preventing Suicide

Robert A. Dorwart, M.D., M.P.H.
Michael J. Ostacher, M.D., M.P.H.

In this chapter we view suicide from a public health perspective. First, we describe a general approach to prevention of mental disorders. Then, we elaborate the approach with examples from the literature in suicide prevention. Next, we describe a community psychiatry approach in which an organized community mental health center (CMHC) provides a broad strategy for intervening with suicidal patients. We develop this model in some detail because it has proven to be a feasible and effective one that can be adapted to most hospitals and community mental health centers (Dorwart and Epstein, 1993; Dorwart and Chartock, 1989). We describe the evolution and transformation of one center in Cambridge, Massachusetts, in order to illustrate an advanced stage of the CMHC model. Next, we illustrate the public health approach and community psychiatry strategies in action with the following two cases: a community consultation after a tragic homicide of a ten-year-old boy, and a suicidal patient in a family context complicated with substance abuse. Finally, we conclude with some general observations and principles applicable to community psychiatry programs today, which are also useful for community hospitals and CMHCs seeking to improve their capacity to treat suicidal patients and other community-based emergencies.

NEW PUBLIC HEALTH PREVENTION STRATEGIES

In the past few decades we have seen enormous advances in the theory and practice of public health strategies for prevention of and intervention in acute and chronic illnesses. This progress permits a reconceptualization of the theory of prevention as applied to mental disorders. The traditional system of classifying prevention strategies in public health, and until recently mental disorders as well, was to use the terms *primary, secondary,* and *tertiary* prevention. Recently, the Committee on Prevention of Mental Disorders (1994) proposed a new classification for the study of prevention of mental disorders that is more complex and specific than the traditional schemes. These approaches represent a new paradigm in public mental health policy; namely, a move toward truly effective primary prevention strategies—sometimes called *pre-intervention* strategies—and an increased recognition of the importance of interventions that include treatment and health status maintenance (formerly called secondary and tertiary prevention). These distinctions do not represent simply a more "medical model" approach to prevention; rather, they represent more sophisticated and targeted strategies for both medical pre-interventions and postillness psychosocial prevention strategies.

An important distinction made by the Committee on Prevention of Mental Disorders report concerns a scheme of classification for interventions developed by Gordon (1987). He identified three types of interventions that are population based: *universal* preventative interventions, *selective* preventative interventions, and *indicated* preventative interventions.

Universal interventions may be undertaken without knowledge of specific individual risk factors and may be safely directed at an entire population thought to be at risk for developing mental disorders in the future. For example, public education campaigns to inform the general public about the dangers of substance abuse or early warning signs of depression would be classified as universal. *Selective* measures refer to those targeted at a subgroup with a shared risk factor. Examples might include children of parents with manic depressive illness or children who are victims of physical or sexual abuse. Such individuals may or may not have signs and symptoms of mental disorder but, based on current research, they may be at higher risk for developing personality disorders, depression, or other recognizable and treatable conditions in the future. *Indicated* measures refer to approaches employed with people who already have early signs and symptoms of a mental disorder, such as anxiety, sleep disturbance, early patterns of eating disorder, "flashbacks," or repeated self-injurious behaviors. All three types of measures represent subtypes of *primary* prevention. More traditional forms of treatment, health status maintenance and aftercare (including rehabilitation), may be distinguished from these three types of primary prevention, according to Gordon's taxonomy. Altogether, this approach is referred to as the "mental health intervention spectrum for mental disorders." Figure 3.1 depicts this spectrum.

It is necessary and desirable to rethink public health prevention of mental disorders for a number of reasons. One reason is that we now have the possibility of truly preventative interventions. We have medications, for example,

Figure 3.1. The Mental Health Intervention Spectrum for Mental Disorders.

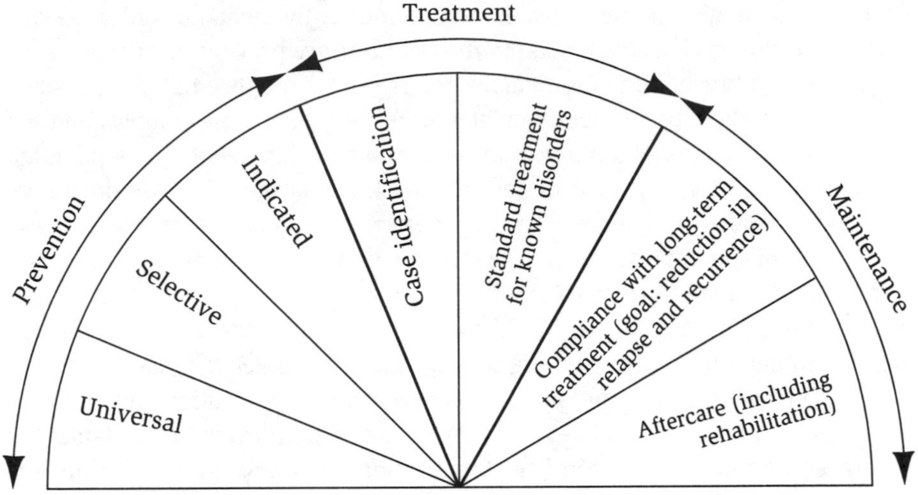

Source: Reprinted with permission from *Reducing risks for mental disorders: Frontiers for preventive intervention research.* Copyright 1994 by the National Academy of Sciences. Courtesy of the National Academy Press, Washington, D.C.

that could be used in the prodromal stages of illness to prevent full-blown, diagnosable mental disorders—an analogy in the medical area would be the use of cholesterol-lowering agents to reduce the risk of later development of atherosclerosis. Similarly, an antianxiety or antipanic agent might be used in combination with psychotherapy to treat a person who is a victim of, or witness to, violent behavior, such as a homicide, suicide, or traumatic accident. This approach might well prevent the development of diagnosable post-traumatic stress syndrome or delayed grief reaction and a major depressive episode if not yet present. One reason that this more elaborate and more specific schema is now appropriate is the greatly expanded pharmacopoeia. In addition, our growing understanding from neuroscientific, biological, and genetic research into the etiology of mental disorders will probably permit targeting of individuals at high risk in the future. For example, Mann notes that low levels of the neurotransmitter serotonin in the brain may point to an increased risk of suicide. He believes this may someday provide a routine means for detecting patients at high risk for suicide. As discussed in Chapter Six, Mann (1997) posits that newer serotonin reuptake inhibitors have "the potential for reducing suicide rates."

A second reason for employing this new schema is the prevalence of serious and persistent mental illness, in contrast to acute, time-limited episodic disorders. These psychiatric conditions require an appreciation for ongoing, supportive, and rehabilitative treatment. In particular, the rehabilitative aspects of treatment of long-term disorders are now seen as the sine qua non of comprehensive community-based mental health services today. Patients whose social functioning is improved may suffer fewer relapses than those who receive treatment only of acute symptoms (Group for the Advancement of Psychiatry Report, 1992). Moreover, recent research has indicated that even for patients with severe and potentially lifelong illnesses (for example, schizophrenia), the acuity of the illness may vary through the life cycle (Adler, 1995). In other words, interventions that may be appropriate and necessary for patients in their twenties or thirties may be very different from those for patients in their fifties or sixties.

In sum, what is called for increasingly is a model of public health prevention and intervention strategies that takes into account the evolving state of knowledge with regard to biological as well as psychological and psychosocial preventions of mental disorders and their treatment. The practice of psychiatry has evolved dramatically over the past decade from predominantly solo office-based practices to organized systems of care (Dorwart et al., 1992). This means that primary prevention programs and postdiagnosis interventions may be multimodal and involve a variety of forms of organized social and environmental intervention as well as specific treatment of individual patients. We give some examples of these approaches later in this chapter.

Most important, then, in thinking programmatically about the assessment and intervention for patients at risk for suicide is the availability of a variety of interventions beyond the psychotherapeutic and psychopharmacologic ones. For example, it is useful to have a twenty-four-hour emergency and crisis response service, staffed with mental health professionals, available by telephone and in person and accessible to the individuals during periods of highest risk. Whereas this may seem obvious, it is not always considered adequately within the domain of traditional outpatient mental health services. As organizational changes and trends in mental health policy presage reduced emphasis on hospitalization, decreased use of involuntary commitment, greater reliance on patient choice and self-determination, and constraints on effective (insured) demand for services, it is necessary for mental health providers to anticipate the need for bearing greater risk with patients who are potentially suicidal. This balancing of factors may create ethical and clinical dilemmas for the clinician. A key organization component of the mental health services system relevant to suicide prevention assessment or intervention is the community mental health (CMHC) model itself.

PRE-INTERVENTION STRATEGIES

To address adequately the problem of how to plan public health interventions to reduce suicide, examining what efforts have been made to study interventions to date is a helpful first step. Multiple efforts have been made to study the effects of broad public health measures to reduce suicide. The primary problem in using data from such studies as a basis for planning community and population interventions to reduce suicide is that methodological problems are legion in designing studies (Gunnell and Frankel, 1994). All of these efforts have been limited by problems in design, primarily the defining of an adequate control group, thus limiting the generalizability of the results. The generalization of the results of given efforts in reducing suicide is also troublesome because the place and time of such efforts in the context of confounding factors (economic conditions, for instance) may be changeable.

Few national efforts have been made at suicide prevention; most have been done on a state or local level. The "primary prevention" programs aimed at preventing suicide in previously unidentified populations have been studied in terms of their impact on suicide. The three "primary prevention" programs most studied in the United States (and elsewhere) are school-based suicide prevention programs (a universal preventive intervention), so-called "suicide prevention centers" (selective preventive intervention), and the effects of the Samaritans (indicated preventive intervention) and the reduction in specific means of suicide.

After the emergence of several clusters of suicides in school-aged children, the Centers for Disease Control (1992) issued recommendations for establishing specific suicide prevention programs in schools. The recommended components of such a program include community (including parental) and school (teacher) training, student and peer-support training, access to suicide hotlines, means reduction (for example, reducing access to guns), and postvention. These principles to a greater or lesser extent are a part of most such programs studied to date (Hazell and King, 1996).

School-based prevention programs generally do not target at-risk student populations directly. Instead, an effort is made to engage others—parents, students, teachers, and administrators—in identifying at-risk students (Hazell and King, 1996). One-third to one-half of adolescent suicides communicate in some way their intent to confidants (Mulder, Methorst, and Diekstra, 1989). The arguments for peer education are that adolescents can be trained to help identify suicidal peers and that disturbed teens are more likely to confide in other teens than in adults (Kalafat and Elias, 1994; Kalafat, Elias, and Gara, 1993). The data regarding peer identification, however, suggest that few peers subsequently confide in adults about their troubled friends and that male students sometimes respond to distressed peers in unhelpful ways (Vieland, Whittle, Garland, Hick, and Shaffer, 1991).

School-based prevention programs have been difficult to assess. Perhaps paradoxically, in the United States, the states with the highest proportion of students in specific school-based prevention programs have seen a rise in the rate of youth suicide (Lester, 1992). Whether this is a result of the programs themselves is not known, but as a fact it is sobering. It may well be that these programs have reduced the rate of rise of suicide rates, but without adequate control groups, conclusions are difficult to draw.

The effectiveness of suicide prevention centers and the Samaritans in preventing suicide is in dispute. Few studies that have found a preventive effect have shown a statistically significant one. Dorwart and Chartock (1989) found no benefit from suicide prevention centers. Lester (1997), however, performed a meta-analysis of fourteen of these studies and found that, on average, they might have a small but statistically significant preventive effect. Of course, methodological problems abound, especially in assigning an adequate control group. In contained populations, such as prisons, video has led to a reduction of suicide, thus suggesting that some high-risk populations may be helped by specific interventions (Smialek and Spitz, 1978).

An interesting attempt to prevent suicide by public health measures involves the reduction or elimination of specific means of committing suicide. Given that the most common cause of death by overdose in the 1980s was from tricyclic antidepressants, we must wait and see whether the reduction in the use of those medications in favor of newer, safer antidepressants will have an effect on overall suicide rates. The lowering of the maximum amount of tricyclic antidepressant per pill probably had some preventive effect; Gunnell and Frankel (1994) estimate that it might reduce the overall suicide rate by 4 percent. They go on to suggest that significant suicide reduction can be obtained through government and industry action; for example, by reducing the toxicity of car exhaust (which has been estimated to cause 22 percent of suicides in England [Wagg and Aylwin, 1993]) with catalytic converters. Other such measures might be more effective gun control (Kellerman et al., 1992), reduction of the lethality of acetaminophen, or monitoring of frequent suicide venues (for example, the Golden Gate Bridge in San Francisco), although some assert that the elimination of certain means of suicide will simply increase the rate of others in a compensatory way (Rich, Young, Fowler, Wagner, and Black, 1990).

The role of the media in preventing suicide is much debated. Prohibitions against reporting of certain suicides (difficult to accomplish in the United States, due to First Amendment issues, but for which guidelines exist in the United Kingdom) may be responsible for a reduction in a specific method for suicide. After the Austrian government limited the reporting of subway station suicides, the rate of suicides by that method dropped considerably (but without measurable effect on the overall rate) (Etzerdorfer, Sonneck, and Nagel-Keuss, 1992).

Some have proposed that suicide clusters in adolescents may be due in part to a "copycat" effect from suicides among peers and in part to a desire to have others see an account of the suicide on television (Davidson, Rosenberg, Mercy, Franklin, and Simmons, 1989). Lester (1990) suggests that by using the media to publicize the less sensational side of suicide—liver failure from acetaminophen overdose, gun injuries that maim but do not cause death—some impact could be made from a public education perspective.

To be effective and efficient, public health approaches to reduce the incidence of suicide must target the populations most at risk of suicide. Understanding the epidemiology of suicide (discussed in depth in Chapter Two) and the sub-populations most at risk is necessary in recommending specific public health approaches and should inform the design of prevention plans. For instance, approaches to clinical populations and to general populations (or subpopulations) may have different means for accomplishing the goal of suicide reduction. Programs to educate school-aged youth or the elderly about their own risk of suicide and how to prevent it will have an impact different from, say, education aimed at increasing health care providers' recognition of the signs of potential suicides.

Population-Based Prevention

The decision to design population-based prevention programs is traditionally the providence of federal, state, and local policymakers. Clinically based prevention, on the other hand, can become the standard practice of health care organizations and can be implemented with perhaps less cost (and perhaps greater efficiency). Although widespread intervention by government and industry might ultimately lead to powerful preventive effects, interventions for high-risk clinical populations may also prove valuable.

The population most at risk of suicide comprises the mentally ill as a group, especially those recently acutely ill. Retrospective reviews of suicide suggest that over 90 percent of all suicides are committed by people with major mental illness. Remarkably, many of those mentally ill are overlooked: only one-third to one-half of suicides are committed by current or former psychiatric patients (Gunnell and Frankel, 1994). The risk of suicide for psychiatric patients within a month after their discharge, compared to the general population, is estimated as two hundred times greater for men and one hundred times greater for women (Goldacre, Seagrott, and Hawton, 1993). Having ever been a psychiatric patient (inpatient or outpatient) increases the risk tenfold and accounts in Britain, for example, for 50 percent of all suicides (Gunnell and Frankel, 1994). To be effective, any attempt to reduce suicide in this group should probably take place in the context of their psychiatric treatment.

Unfortunately, few studies have shown any suicide reduction through psychiatric treatment of any kind. To quote Lester (1990), "The effectiveness of individual psychiatric and psychotherapeutic treatment remains unproven for suicide prevention." Black, Winokur, Mohandoss, Woolson, and Nasrallah (1989) did not find significant evidence that somatic treatment for depression reduced the risk of suicide. In Hungary—the country with the world's highest suicide rate—there is some evidence to the contrary: the rate of suicide is inversely correlated with the rate of inpatient and outpatient treatment for depression in different regions, perhaps suggesting that access to treatment may reduce suicide (Rihmer, Barsi, Veg, and Katona, 1990b). The dearth of evidence in support of psychiatric treatment for the reduction of suicide due to mental illness stems largely from the methodological problems involved in such studies.

The problems in documenting that psychiatric treatment can reduce suicide risk should not discourage efforts to prevent suicide but instead call forth a redoubling of our efforts to do so. The limitations of specific treatment interventions—medications, for example—do not capture how whole treatment systems can approach the problem of treating potentially suicidal patients. If these were to be studied, we would probably find that they have significant effects on the outcomes for such patients.

The presence of alcohol and substance use disorders (with or without comorbid mental illness), discussed in detail in Chapter Seventeen, increases risk of suicide by a factor of twenty. Such cases represent 15 to 20 percent of completed suicides. A recent study confirms the positive relationship between alcohol dependence and suicidal ideation in depressed subjects (Pages, Russo, Roy-Byrne, Ries, and Cowley, 1997). Many substance abuse disorders escape clinical detection and intervention. Pre-intervention strategies such as public health measures to decrease substance abuse disorders would probably reduce suicide related to these disorders.

Prevention in Primary Care

The ability to screen earlier for mental illness in the primary care setting and the increasing frequency with which primary care providers treat primary, uncomplicated mental disorders such as anxiety and depression, provides an opportunity for broad suicide prevention interventions in the primary care setting. Again, the effects of such interventions remain to be studied in terms of effect on overall suicide rates; nonetheless, such interventions, given recent advances in screening tools and psychopharmacology, are likely to have an impact on suicide prevention. The role of primary care as a setting for public health interventions—pre-interventional as well as treatment and health status maintenance types—is likely to grow as the importance of primary care in managed care environments grows in this country.

The presence of a psychiatric illness, as has been stated, is the greatest general risk factor in suicide, although many psychosocial stressors are also statistically associated with suicide. One of the most powerful of these is medical illness. Medical illness appears to be an especially significant risk factor for suicide for older persons (Carney, Rich, Burke, and Fowler, 1994). Since the risk of serious medical illness increases with age, the proportion of suicides that occur in the context of medical illness increases with age. Aging, itself, is a risk factor for suicide, as the suicide rate in general increases with age. The identification of potential suicidal persons in the primary care setting may allow for significant helpful intervention, and failure to do so (and to act accordingly) may have serious consequences (Carney, Rich, Burke, and Fowler, 1994; Kirmayer et al., 1993).

Several reports show that a high percentage of persons who committed suicide had had a recent visit with a primary care provider (Vassilas and Morgan,

1993). A British study in the 1970s found that 60 percent of suicides had contact with their physicians within a month of their deaths, at which time they often revealed suicidal thoughts (Barraclough, Bunch, Nelson, and Sainsbury, 1974). In the San Diego study, suicides over sixty years of age were significantly more likely than younger subjects to have seen a health professional within the past thirty days (57 versus 30 percent), but a substantial proportion of both groups had visits within a month of suicide (Carney, Rich, Burke, and Fowler, 1994). In those over sixty years of age, an astonishing 94 percent of suicides had a physical complaint. Other studies have shown that nearly all elderly patients committing suicide have a diagnosable mental disorder (greater than 90 percent) and that those with depression are often undertreated (Carney, Rich, Burke, and Fowler, 1994; Frierson, 1991; Draper, 1994, 1995).

Whereas visits to primary care physicians are more common in older patients, a retrospective study of suicides in people under age thirty-five in Manchester, England, suggests that (for those subjects who did visit their physician) visits to general practitioners increased in the three months prior to death and that 60 percent of those visits were for psychological reasons (Appleby, Amos, Doyle, Tomenson, and Woodman, 1996). Although it is often difficult for primary care physicians to diagnose depression in patients with primarily somatic complaints, they may undertreat it even when the diagnosis of depression is made (Kirmayer et al., 1993).

The primary care setting must play an essential role in the detection and treatment of mental disorders if the early treatment and detection of depressive and substance abuse disorders is to lead to suicide prevention (see Chapter Twenty-Nine). According to Rihmer et al., specific training of primary care providers can directly lead to a reduction in suicide rate and psychiatric hospitalization in the area served by the trained providers (Rihmer, Rutz, and Pihlgren, 1995). The underdetection of depression in men, however, continues to be a problem, thus suggesting that training programs need to specifically address this issue (Rutz, von Knorring, Pihlgren, Rihmer, and Walinder, 1995). It appears that improving detection and providing access to treatment and psychiatric consultation may lead to suicide reduction though primary care treatment.

THE EVOLUTION OF COMMUNITY HEALTH CENTERS

In the 1960s, Congress passed the National Community Mental Health Centers (CMHC) Act, which led to the establishment of over 700 federally funded community mental health centers throughout the United States (Foley, 1975). Initially, these centers were required to offer a basic set of services, including inpatient, outpatient, emergency, day-treatment, and community consultation and education services (Dorwart and Epstein, 1993). It was understood that these centers would be available to treat everybody who sought help for a mental disorder from the defined community and also would engage in public mental health activities such as prevention, consultation, and education. The funding of the centers was initially with construction and staffing grants that were to be phased out over a period of several years. During this initial funding period, the centers were expected to become self-supporting. What actually happened to the CMHCs in practice was more complicated. The evolution and reconfiguration of CMHCs have implications for public mental health theory and practice today.

Because of their open mandate to treat "everybody" in need in the community, that is, to provide unrestricted access on demand to all who sought their help, the CMHCs often were overwhelmed with requests for services. One unintended consequence of this open-door policy was that there were often fewer resources available to be devoted to providing for individuals with severe mental illnesses, many of whom were long-term residents of state and county mental hospitals and many of whom were uninsured. As deinstitutionalization proceeded in different states, the CMHCs often were unable to keep up with the needs of patients being discharged rapidly from large mental hospitals. As the federal support for the CMHCs dwindled, centers tended to divide into two groups: those which served primarily severely and persistently mentally ill individuals and received grants from state and county government for this purpose; and those which diversified their funding base to treat patients who had insurance or other means to pay for their care. The patients of this latter group were often not as severely ill as the uninsured patients leaving the mental hospitals, but they tended to use up the available capacity of CMHCs.

With the needs for services greatly outstripping the available resources, many CMHCs went bankrupt or had to be reorganized. Those that did survive had to rely on fee-for-service practices and had little or no surplus capacity to engage in nonremunerative activities such as consultation and public education. More recently, CMHCs have developed into "multi-service organizations," with average annual revenues of $1 to $2 million a year. They are providing a wider range of services ranging from clinic-based to residential and rehabilitative programs in their communities. The remaining centers often work in partnership with other community agencies or community hospitals to be able to provide a continuum of services for patients in their local communities. Increasingly, federal, state, and local grants support activities such as crisis intervention, community crisis response teams, and twenty-four-hour emergency psychiatric services and consultation to schools, employers, court clinics, and social service agencies. Though the effectiveness of specific suicide prevention programs has been difficult to measure (Dorwart and Chartock, 1989), it is likely that rapid, proximate, interpersonal interventions by trained mental health professionals in crisis situations in communities will reduce the risk of morbidity and mortality in these patients. This service may include a crisis-response team that goes to a patient's home or institutional setting. Another example would be the intervention in schools by mental health professionals as consultants and counselors when there has been a suicide of a student or sometimes several suicides in succession in the same school. An analogous situation to the intervention in the face of completed suicides would be community mental health interventions to prevent other forms of violence, such as youth violence, domestic violence, or a sequence of traumatic events in the community such as rape, accidents, or murder.

We next describe the evolution of a model community mental health center in Cambridge, Massachusetts, and illustrate the general CMHC approach with responses to specific events and cases.

The Cambridge-Somerville Community Mental Health Center (CSCMHC) was established as a federally funded CMHC in 1968 with five basic services: inpatient, outpatient, emergency, day treatment, and consultation-education. Over subsequent years, the Department of Psychiatry at the Cambridge Hospital, founded at about the same time, grew to incorporate these basic services and much more. It expanded the scope of its mission to function as a modern model of an academic community mental health center. The dramatic growth of services—more than threefold in the past decade alone—means that many more severely ill and suicidal patients are treated.

The Department of Psychiatry at the Cambridge Hospital recently celebrated its twenty-fifth anniversary. The long-term goals of the department's founders to provide community-integrated mental health services in an academic milieu depended upon a tripartite partnership of the city, the commonwealth, and the Harvard Medical School—a partnership that has thrived. Although the Cambridge Hospital had been cited in the early 1960s as one of the worst municipal hospitals in the country, by the 1990s it was winning national awards for organizing an outstanding community health network.

Both the CSCMHC and the Cambridge Hospital Department of Psychiatry were thus developed in an era infused both with the idealism of the community mental health center movement and the intellectual excitement of psychoanalysis. The Cambridge Hospital Department of Psychiatry has grown and developed so that today it carries out a mix of medical, psychodynamic, psychosocial, and humanistic approaches practiced in the acute care general hospital and in several neighborhood health centers. Beyond treating individual patients with competence and compassion, the department pursues the additional public health mission of creating a "healthier community." The transformations occasioned by these changes in clinical practices in psychiatry and in public health care policy make practicing psychiatry at Cambridge Hospital continuously challenging.

The community mental health service system in Cambridge has grown gradually over the years. Following its merger with the Somerville Hospital's Department of Psychiatry, the Cambridge Hospital's Department of Psychiatry has roughly 100 beds for adult, child, and addictions treatment. Ambulatory visits, including a busy emergency service, are approaching 100,000 annually. There are two dozen subspecialty clinic programs. Among the more innovative of these are the multilingual clinics (for example, Haitian, Latino, and Portuguese), a Victims of Violence Program, a mobile crisis consultation team, a school consultation program in the local high school, and a behavioral medicine program. Affiliated programs provide drug treatment (North Charles Foundation), roughly 150 beds for residential care (CASCAP), and day treatment. Taken together, the services fulfill the founders' goal of a comprehensive community-based system of mental health and addictions services.

Perhaps the greatest asset of the Cambridge Hospital Department of Psychiatry is its teaching faculty, which represents a range of disciplines, interests, and subspecialties. In a typical year, there are also twenty-five psychiatry residents treating adults, ten child and adolescent fellows, twenty psychology interns, and numerous social work and nursing trainees.

In 1996, the Cambridge Public Health Commission was established and a new mission for mental health and additions was articulated. One aim of the Cambridge Public Health Commission, together with the Cambridge Hospital Department of Psychiatry and its affiliates, is to improve the health and mental health status of the community. It seeks to provide, create, and coordinate a communitywide network of services. It provides leadership to ensure that the elements of this system function as an innovative and integrated mental health and addictions service continuum that provides high-quality, cost-effective treatment for all patients seeking services. These elements include an excellent Harvard-affiliated training and education program; a services-based research program that contributes to improvement of care locally and nationally; a network of community affiliates who provide a continuum of community-based care for ambulatory, rehabilitative, and preventative services; and a faculty and staff who participate in academic, professional, hospital, and network affiliations to improve services, teaching, and knowledge. The metaphor of a braided three-stranded rope might optimally represent the relationship among services, training, and research.

In pursuing this mission, a critical short- and long-term strategy is the integration of various divisions of the service system. These divisions include services and training; primary care in medicine, psychiatry, and the addictions; hospital and community care; psychosocial and biosocial interventions; public and private resources and programs; service provisions and quality improvement; treatment, prevention, and rehabilitation; hospital and community providers; research and teaching; local services and regional (Boston hospital network) systems; community and academic resources; and sources of funding (Department of Mental Health; Division of Medical Assistance; Department of Medical Security; Medicare; health maintenance organizations [HMOs]; and commercial).

THE PREVENTION PROCESS: A CASE STUDY

When an event occurs in a community, especially a reasonably tight-knit neighborhood or a small bounded community (sometimes referred to as a *catchment area*), it is imperative that the reaction of potential mental health consultants or interveners be swift, focused, and clinically sensitive. The event may be a suicide, a series of suicides, a trauma such as a school bus accident, a fire, or a drowning incident, or it may be a kidnapping or shooting at a local school. In all such types of incidents it is important, not only for the consultants to become visible and available, but also to act in such a way as to mobilize the community's social strength and psychological resilience in the service of supportive and preventive activities. To illustrate this process, we choose the example of a recent incident in Cambridge, Massachusetts.

In fall 1997, a ten-year-old boy was kidnapped and brutally molested and murdered by two young adults in the neighborhood of mid-Cambridge. Cambridge is a city of approximately 100,000 people, but it lies in close proximity to the larger city of Boston, with its ample media outlets and regional news networks. The city of Cambridge is known for its civic activism as well as its social consciousness and intellectual and socioeconomic diversity. As it happens, the young boy was of Irish descent from a well-established family, with a father who was a member of the local fire department. Within hours, the news of the kidnapping and subsequent events were broadcast on local radio, television, and newspapers. It was imperative to have a coordinated response, not only from the criminal justice system to search for the boy and to apprehend his alleged abusers, but also from the public health community. In this instance, leadership was provided by the Department of Psychiatry of the Cambridge Hospital and the Cambridge Public Health Commission. Trained and experienced in community crisis response, the department quickly mobilized a number of teams and individuals within the hospital and within the mental health community to provide consultation, support, and advice for the public schools, public officials, the police department, and other agencies. In particular, the skills and expertise of child psychiatrists and psychologists were called upon. We briefly review some of these activities in order to illustrate the workings of one example of a response to such situations.

First, child psychiatrists, psychologists, and social workers contacted the superintendent of schools and offered to help at the elementary school where the boy had been enrolled. During the weekdays, the mental health staff went to the school and met with the principal and groups of teachers to talk about how to respond to the anxieties and concerns of students and parents. On the weekend, the school was open for groups of students or parents to meet with teachers, or to consult with the mental health professionals about recent events and for advice about what to tell their children. As the story unfolded and more information became available, these gatherings served to reduce the distortion of rumors and to provide information-based counseling to anxious parents and children. Soon a "town meeting" was organized at the school, which was attended by several hundred people. Leaders of the community, including the commissioner of the public health commission, the superintendent of schools, and members of the city council, attended to hear from concerned members of the community and to respond with information, advice, and reassurance. These forums provided an opportunity for abreaction by some distressed members of the community and an occasion to vent their feelings of fear, anger, and grief publicly. The meeting took on the tone of a psychodrama, with cameras, microphones, speeches, and outpouring of emotion, including criticism of public officials for allowing such events to take place in the community. The large forum also served to demonstrate the active leadership of community leaders and offered a venue for them to provide information and to describe plans for improving public safety. The leader of the discussion was a child psychiatrist.

At the same time, family therapists (a social worker and a psychologist) made increased use of their ongoing local community cable television call-in show, sponsored by the Couples and Family Center, to discuss issues of terror, loss, grieving, betrayal, shock, and sadness at the events surrounding the occurrence. Six extra hours of airtime were offered by the Cambridge cable television station to provide more access for crisis intervention. Since one of the alleged perpetrators was a well-known neighbor himself, the atmosphere of fear was particularly heightened. The co-hosts of the program afforded the opportunity for the expression and clarification of emotions on the part of family members, friends, relatives, acquaintances, neighbors, and schoolmates of the deceased. A guest mental health counselor who works in consulting with the schools was invited to convey information he had described in a book on grief for children. The program also offered a way for individuals to call to express their views or to ask questions that might be more relevant to themselves than to the family of reference. Not only did leaders of the community and adults call in, many children and classmates of the victim also called the program to express their concerns and ask questions.

This general public education approach, though seemingly novel, might be considered a standard technique of intervention in situations of this sort. It might also provide information about resources for referral and help to other individuals in the community grappling with similar or related problems. The salience of such efforts is greatly heightened by the affects surrounding the tragedy.

At the same time, clinical administrators in the Department of Psychiatry were meeting with hospital officials and leaders of the city's public health department. A strategy for disseminating information, organizing focus groups in the community, and coordinating inquiries and requests for consultation and information through the twenty-four-hour staffed psychiatric emergency room and crisis response teams was organized. Drawing on a pool of experienced community psychiatrists, it was possible to inform decisions that needed to be made by school personnel, public safety officials, and Department of Public Health Administrators, so that their actions would be in a psychologically sound direction with a tailored orientation to the different phases of what was widely viewed as a "community crisis." For example, it was felt desirable to organize visits by the children from the local school to the wake at the funeral home of the deceased child. Transportation was offered for children and parents to attend funeral proceedings and, where appropriate, to be accompanied by teachers, counselors, or mental health professionals. Discussion groups were held in the schools in which children could talk with one another, share their own experiences, ask questions, and express their feelings about the events. The clinical material in these sessions was often remarkable and reflected the level of development of the students according to age, social class, and religious belief. For example, many students denied the reality of the death of the young boy and suggested that he had merely run away and that he would be returning soon to their midst. Rumors abounded and clarification was essential. In one version of the story of the murder trauma, the child had been killed by a relative. In another version, the child had befriended an older man. In another version of the story, the alleged assailants were strangers who lured the child with gifts. In actuality, the facts of the case were stark, shocking, and repulsive. We purposely are not relaying the specifics of this case here for a variety of reasons, including a concern that attention ought to be paid primarily to the process of consultation rather than to the specifics of the individual case.

The essence of the successful community crisis team response is having a group of skilled clinicians who are organized in their approach, resourceful, and flexible working along with members of the community and other leaders in the community. In addition, of course, the traditional pathways to help seeking in the form of clinic visits to therapists should be made available on a walk-in basis to members of the community, and special efforts should be made to see people promptly (ideally the same day), shortly after the incident has occurred. Again, the exact nature of the traumatic event may vary widely, but the idea of an organized, systemic response with active outreach and engagement of mental health professionals working within a public health model and framework should be considered essential to promoting health and preventing further psychopathology in such circumstances.

We now turn to a vignette about a suicidal psychiatric patient and how the organized systems function, or sometimes malfunction, under stressful and risk-filled clinical circumstances.

PUBLIC HEALTH PLANNING: A CASE STUDY

Case studies can be useful tools to examine how epidemiological data and systems of care can be understood and used to inform public health recommendations on suicide prevention. Certainly not all suicides can be prevented; nonetheless, understanding how suicides unfold may shape future planning in effective suicide prevention.

A previously unknown forty-seven-year-old woman came to the psychiatric emergency department of a community hospital complaining of increasing anxiety and depression in caring for her three school-aged children. She was somewhat guarded during the interview with the crisis worker, but admitted that her stress had increased since the state Department of Social Services (DSS) began investigating her for neglect of her eight-year-old girl after the child began acting bizarrely at school. She mentioned feeling "unfairly attacked" but did not appear to have any overt delusions. She was well groomed, dressed in business attire. She denied any suicidal ideation or intent, and denied doing anything to harm her children but refused to give any information regarding any past treatment. She stated that she has been a single mother "for years" and that she lives alone with her children. Her medical problems included ammenorrhea and hot flashes, and she had been seen multiple times in a primary care clinic at the same institution for pelvic pain of unknown etiology. Toxic screening and general lab work were unremarkable. Because she did not appear to be in danger of harming herself and apparently wanted help, and because of the impression made by her good grooming and hygiene, inpatient hospitalization was not considered. However, because she was unknown to the staff at the emergency department and because of her suspiciousness and the outside investigation of neglect, she was referred to an intensive outpatient program for further evaluation and treatment.

In the outpatient program her suspiciousness became more apparent. She initially allowed contact with a therapist of five years prior who saw the patient as "mostly borderline personality disorder" but had never seen the patient as psychotic or suicidal. The staff provided support during her continuing investigation by the DSS and noted that during her contacts with her three children she appeared attentive and interested. Although members of her church community, on their own, contacted the staff regarding their concerns about the patient, most comments were about her poor appetite and her being "distant" during church activities.

The patient remained anxious and guarded, however, about the staff speaking to outside caregivers and the DSS. Although the DSS had a release for information because of their ongoing investigation of the client, the patient did not allow the DSS to speak with the staff about their own findings. She refused to allow any further contact with previous caregivers.

Over several weeks, the patient's paranoia became more severe. Though agreeing to antidepressant treatment, she became angry when her psychiatrist prescribed an antipsychotic medication for her and, after filling the prescription, refused to take it. She refused to allow the staff to communicate anything to anyone in her life. The staff considered hospitalizing her against her will but concluded, since she denied any wish to harm herself or others and was able to care for herself, that she did not satisfy criteria for involuntary hospitalization. Believing that the staff were "out to get" her, she demanded that she be allowed to read her medical record. The staff allowed this, but during this time the patient revealed her wish to change her insurance carrier and thus her treaters, feeling she could no longer be helped by her current staff.

The next day, after a hearing with the DSS, the patient called the program to state that she had changed insurance and that she would no longer be attending the program. (In Massachusetts, a number of different managed care plans insure the Medicaid population; built into the program is the ability to change HMOs easily.) The DSS was called and would give no information about the patient and how she responded to the hearing. The patient reported that the hearing went well—she was allowed to keep custody of her children—and that she and her children were at her apartment. She told the clinician who spoke with her on the phone that she was "fine" and that she had set up her treatment with appointments for the following day in another treatment system. Four hours later, she was found hanged in her apartment, having sent her children to play with friends for the evening.

Postvention was performed for several weeks by the psychiatric emergency services staff in concert with the children, the children's schools, and the religious community of which she was a part. During that time it was revealed that in the several days prior to her death she had confided in several church members that she wanted to end her life, but they did not report this to staff. It was also revealed that she had had a psychiatric hospitalization after a suicide attempt by overdose and alcohol in her early twenties and that the patient was a recovering alcoholic who had been attending Alcoholics Anonymous for nearly fifteen years. She had been divorced after the birth of her first child, a teenager, and had another child with a man she never married.

A discussion of this tragic case provides a rich opportunity to address public health issues in suicide prevention. Certainly the patient had characteristics of high suicide risks: a prior suicide attempt, current psychiatric illness and treatment, recent medical care with chronic physical complaints, financial distress, and divorce. Evidence suggests—mitigating our surprise that she killed herself— that these are frequently the characteristics of completed suicides (although even among the population with these characteristics, suicide remains a rare event).

Could her death have been prevented? This is a difficult question to answer. She was in current treatment, yet, as has been discussed above, evidence is lacking that psychiatric treatment by itself actually prevents suicide. There are points in her care in which intervention could have been made that, even just temporarily, may have prevented her death. First, the people closest to her apparently knew of her despair and her wish to end her life, yet they did not know to communicate this to her treaters. Second, the DSS would not communicate with staff about the patient's response to their investigation; after her hearing she was not seen again by her outpatient treaters. Third, the patient was able to switch, in a very short time, her insurance status to a new HMO; the current staff would no longer be paid—even if they had convinced her to return—for her care. Fourth, the patient did not allow the staff to know the full extent of her own history, leaving them frustrated in their attempts to assess her risk adequately. If any of these factors had been different, the patient may have had a different outcome.

Perhaps the core purpose of public education regarding suicide should be the education of the general public in recognizing the signs of potential suicide; specifically, social service agencies and health care provider agencies need to educate those not in the field of mental health who may encounter at-risk persons. Another issue is the structure of the health care system, with its focus on consumer choice, and how such a system serves the mentally ill. Finally, the largest issue may be that of patient confidentiality. Certainly it is important to protect, but that protection in itself carries risks.

IMPLICATIONS FOR THE CLINICIAN

In distinguishing between the goals of mental health programs and psychiatry, Sartorius argues convincingly, "Mental health programmes thus have a vastly different set of responsibilities and interests and must involve a variety of other social sectors, such as education, welfare and justice, in implementing their tasks" (1991). A remarkable consensus has emerged among numerous sources of opinion based on a growing knowledge concerning how to organize mental health services. We can summarize these general recommendations as follows:

1. Every effort should be made to *integrate* mental health services provision with the existing health and social service systems, especially primary care providers (for example, physicians, nurses, clinics, and general hospitals). This will require training of nonspecialist health care providers in the assessment and basic care of mental disorders.

2. Direct services should be provided through a *decentralized, coordinated* network at a local level that emphasizes a continuum of care with outreach, assessment, aftercare, community support, and more intensive treatments when necessary. This means a reduced reliance on large mental hospitals that historically have formed the basis of care systems and instead planning for a balanced system comprised of many elements and levels of care.

3. *Cost-effective* methods of treatment should be introduced and disseminated. This means selective use of *medical* and *psychosocial* treatment strategies, including pharmacotherapy, psychoeducational family therapy, and alternatives to hospitalization such as day treatment, home visits, self-help support groups, and the judicious use of traditional healers.

4. Prevention and educational efforts by government and individuals, especially in relation to categories of neuropsychiatric disorders with known psychosocial and environmental risk factors, should be promoted. This means reducing exposure to neurotoxins, supporting prenatal and nutritional programs, contributing to public health education about the risks of substance abuse and sexually transmitted diseases, and consulting about general educational activities concerning the nature of mental disorders and their treatment.

In conclusion, there are basically two ways to achieve the sort of integration and balance that we propose. The first is explicitly to alter the allocation of resources in a more balanced fashion through national policies, central budgeting, managerial guidelines, and local planning for the configuration of services. The second is to foster integration of services and programs through national policy together with financial incentives, decentralized coordination of local services, and professional education. Whereas the first way focuses on adjusting current resources by gathering and disseminating outside resources to alter the current system, the second way concentrates on maximizing the efficiency of already existing networks by combining current resources. Either approach may move mental health systems in the direction of a more balanced and integrated system of services, depending on the local circumstances, including the quantity and quality of existing networks and the availability of additional funds and resources. In either case, clear national policies are important to stimulate mental health initiatives that promote primary care, acute psychiatric intervention, and coordination with rehabilitative and social services. For suicidal patients not in a hospital, relying on a complex organized system of care providers may be crucial to survival. Likewise, all clinicians must not only be aware of what the service systems have to offer but also be ready and able to intervene on behalf of their patients effectively.

1. Clinicians should be familiar with the epidemiology of suicide and have a working knowledge of risk factors such as psychiatric illness, substance abuse, and availability of means of suicide.

2. Clinicians should be aware that the concepts of primary, secondary, and tertiary prevention have been recast into universal, selective, and indicated preventative interventions.

3. Clinicians should make themselves available to schools and communities to serve as resources when there are suicides in the school and should be familiar with the effects of dramatic news reporting on teen suicide.

4. The role of the clinician in pre-interventional strategies may be developed and the clinician's usefulness broadened to include becoming a resource for community agencies (especially as health care systems integrate and evolve).

5. Clinicians should be prepared to serve as consultants and resources in the primary care setting or other medical setting to colleagues who are likely to encounter the suicidal or potentially suicidal patient.

6. Clinicians should investigate effective models of the community mental health center and how they can best function to serve the potentially suicidal patient.

CHAPTER FOUR

The Psychodynamic
Understanding of Suicide

John T. Maltsberger, M.D.

That suicide is the turning of murder against the self was evident long before psychoanalysts took the subject up, for, after all, the German word for it, *Selbstmord,* "self-murder," says as much. But the psychological operation of this extraordinary phenomenon, whatever its neurochemical matrix may be, is far from obvious. In suicide the powerful forces for survival and self-preservation are overpowered by something else. Suicide does not occur in any other species. It is a uniquely human occurrence; it appears to require a capacity for conscious thought. Certainly it puzzled Freud.

Another obvious but often overlooked point is that psychic pain drives suicide (Shneidman, 1993; Chapter Five in this book). There is plenty of evidence that suicide has many secondary motives, such as the wish to take flight, to be reborn, to punish those left behind, some of which will be discussed later in this chapter. But they do not ordinarily impel with much force in the absence of anguish, the prime mover of suicide.

At the 1910 meeting when the Vienna Psychoanalytic Society took the subject up, Freud was uncharacteristically reticent, hardly going further than to warn against reaching premature conclusions on the subject. He suggested that the study of melancholia might be the right place to start (Friedman, 1967). Freud continued to think about the subject for the rest of his career, and in my opinion, never felt he fully understood it. His most important paper on the subject, "Mourning and Melancholia," was written five years after the 1910 meeting, and introduced the subject of confusion between oneself and another person into the literature as the core mental phenomenon of suicide (Freud, 1917). Accordingly I have chosen to begin this chapter with object loss and identification of parts of the self with the lost person. Many of the other suicide determiners to be discussed here depend on subjective blurring of the sense of separateness of the self from someone else to work their influences.

The experience of loss is strongly connected to suicide, just as it is strongly connected to mental anguish. It is a clinical commonplace that many suicides are precipitated by the loss of someone without whom the patient feels he cannot carry on, someone whose absence occasions excruciating suffering. Other suicides are triggered by the loss of some valued personal capacity or association (Maltsberger, 1986). Though Barraclough (1987) showed that the loss of a parent in childhood was no more frequent among a sample of actual suicides than it was in a control group, he nevertheless found that the recent death of a parent or spouse was significantly more frequent among suicides than among controls.

MURDER TURNED AGAINST THE SELF

At the heart of the matter lies an unconscious identification of the self with another person who is both loved and hated. Thus it becomes possible to treat oneself, or some part of oneself (typically one's disavowed body), as an alien and an enemy. The following passage of Freud's has been so much quoted that it has nearly become a mantra: "Thus the shadow of the object fell upon the ego, and the latter could henceforth be judged by a special agency, as though it were an object, the forsaken object. In this way an object-loss was transformed into an ego-loss and the conflict between the ego and loved [and now hated] person into a cleavage between the critical activity of the ego and the ego as altered by identification" (Freud, 1917, p. 249).

This much repeated formulation will nevertheless bear some clarifying. We now understand that "special agency" has come to mean *superego*, or conscience, the critical faculty the mind. Furthermore, the term *ego* may confuse us. Without going much into the history of how the term *ego* has evolved, the reader may understand ego here to mean "self." In turn, understand "self" to comprise the total of the physical and mental attributes of a person. Freud's formulation holds that in melancholia an identification between the self and a lost person who was once loved takes place. Since he penned it, clinical experience has shown over and over that it is correct. But we can make more sense of Freud's statement in examining suicidal phenomena if we stipulate which part or parts of the self become identified with someone else.

Foremost the body takes on the identification of the other, and thereafter it bears the thrust of the attack by the superego. The body is experienced as "not me." Further, certain mental experiences, particularly fantasies highly colored with sexual or sadistic feeling, are assigned to the alienated body, and to the genitalia especially, as their evil nest of origin. Certain thoughts or feelings are treated as the body's responsibility; the body is blamed for them. So it comes about, once the body has been objectified, that it can be experienced as a loathsome source of mental trouble and even persecution.

Psychologically speaking this kind of self-body alienation is not likely to occur before adolescence, at which time the smooth small body of the latency child begins to undergo the changes of puberty and to exhibit sexual characteristics that may be both unwelcome and frightening. Puberty can be experienced as a taking over of oneself from within by an unwelcome intruder, a parent, perhaps, who seizes the flesh of the child and begins to shape it into something vile.

Furthermore, because the prepubertal child commonly experiences the body as mother's or father's thing, or possession, the physical and emotional changes that accompany adolescence are likely to be experienced as forcing the developing child away from the mother. This is one among several adolescent phenomena that make maturation a forced experience of separation and loss, a matter that can be psychologically disastrous for adolescents who have not laid down the necessary psychological groundwork to make such a growing-away a tenable maturational enterprise.

The incapacity to accept the changes of adolescence with relative comfort is probably related to the fact that suicide is extremely unusual before the changes of puberty assert themselves. Laufer argues that adolescent suicide is an aggressive attack on the internalized parent, and simultaneously an attack on the alienated body-self, which at the time is not experienced as belonging to oneself. It is as though "puberty had suddenly changed the body into an enemy" (Laufer, 1968, p. 126; Laufer and Laufer, 1984; Laufer, 1995).

Not adolescents only but many adults as well are not at home in their bodies. Indeed, it seems probable that the body-self alienation that begins in puberty is a sine qua non for suicide, an uneasiness in one's own flesh that overshadows the rest of adult life. The body may be experienced as a prison, a cage, or even as a haunted, crowded tenement populated by hostile hallucinatory voices. The alienated body may be experienced as troublesome in less disturbed patients (hypochondria, body dysmorphic disorder), as unreal, empty, or otherwise defective in others, as possessed by alien presences in psychosis, and as divisible, in certain dissociative states. All these conditions have in common the nonintegration of the body-self with the mental-self of the person. Such patients do not feel their bodies are essential to the sense of "me" as a self. Suicide suggests itself to them as a means of escape when the body-cage finally becomes intolerable (Maltsberger, 1993).

Although I agree with Shneidman (1993) that the most proximate cause of suicide is intolerable anguish, the door to killing the body is further forced open when a patient believes that physical self-destruction is not mental self-destruction. Many are convinced that the mental self will escape from the flesh, transformed and freed from suffering. My experience suggests that such convictions of resurgence are virtually universal in suicide, though they may not be entirely conscious, lurking only at the edge of awareness. Laufer and Laufer (1984) even assert that every suicide attempt must be viewed as a psychotic episode. "A suicide attempt, however minor, always represents a temporary loss of the ability to maintain the link to external reality and must be viewed as an acute psychotic episode. However sane the adolescent [or adult patient] believes he was at the time of the attempt, there is no objective reality attached to the idea of his own death. Instead the action is totally determined by a fantasy that excludes any awareness of the reality of his death" (p. 112).

DIFFICULTIES IN THE INTERNAL MANAGEMENT OF HATE EXPERIENCES

We can define the introjection of hostile or persecutory objects as taking hate inside and organizing it around the image of another person.

We do not know whether the extraordinary aggressiveness of suicide-vulnerable persons arises primarily from neurochemical inheritance or from formative morbid experiences across childhood and adolescent development. Probably there is an interaction between the two; it is likely that some children are more genetically vulnerable to psychological traumatization, and that others, because of their temperaments, invite more of it in the developmental milieu (Nordström, Schalling, and Åsberg, 1995b).

As psychoanalysis has understood it, love and hate in the developing child are the raw materials from which the structures of the mind (ego and superego) are built up, after they have undergone a process of "neutralization." The other persons in the child's life, most particularly the parents, come to be represented in the mind by the taking in and consolidation of experiences, memories, and fantasies as introjects.[1] Introjects are emotionally colored with mixtures of love and hate. Mental development organizes the mind's passions around inner representations of the parents, the mother first of all.

We have come to speak of the "good" internal mother (introject) and the "bad" (introject), for these earliest object representations, precursors of the ego and superego systems, appear to be organized according to the little child's experiences of pleasure and pain (Klein, 1958). Ordinarily these earliest introjects are reworked, influenced by experiences of development, and consolidated. When there is too much aggression in the system, this consolidation may fail or be lost, with the result that a patient may too much rely on "splitting" as a defense, as in borderline disorders (Kernberg, 1992).

In the course of ordinary development, reshaped and transmuted, introjects take up their places in the ego (where "neutralization" is most complete) and superego. (Here I am using ego and superego to refer to the faculties of mental function as in Freud's structural theory [1923].) The introjective origins of the superego are always betrayed by its quality of watchful otherness; it is built up from internalized parental experiences of censure and approval. Structurally it is the seat of conscience.

Persons successful in development achieve adulthood with more or less loving and reasonable consciences, an indication that the superego has been built up out of a good proportion of loving experiences (libidinal energy) and not too many aggressive ones, and that it has been open to amelioration by good corrective experiences through the course of development (Freud, 1923; Schafer, 1960).

Less fortunate are those children whose development is overcharged with feelings of hate and anxiety. These cannot develop normally. Certain vital functions of the ego fail to consolidate, and in the matter of identity and character formation, the ego itself tends to break into compartments. Vulnerability to psychosis and suicide are thus built in (Freud, 1940, especially pp. 201–204; Kernberg, 1966; Fairbairn, 1952). Introjects of an intensely hostile nature take their places in the mind, and the minds of such patients are structurally fragile. Whereas the superego-ego systems of the mentally well remain more or less stably integrated through adulthood, very aggressive introjects are difficult to neutralize and bind down into one structure or another. They tend to be structurally itinerant, in the sense that at one moment they appear to assert themselves in the superego system, at another to dominate in projection-susceptible object-representations. At still other moments, hostile introjects tend to become entangled with the self-representation, especially the body-representation. This makes the patient's body loathsome to him and causes it to feel alien. When the body is experienced in this way and identified as a source of suffering and torment, suicidal self-attack can occur. Sometimes the hostile introjects seem to dominate both the conscience and large proportions of the self-representation.

Under the influence of hostile introjects the conscience is aggressive, uncompromising, unrealistic, and severe. Suicidal patients fear the full awakening of the rageful conscience, so intense may be its flagellation. Thoughts and fantasies, even dreams, are subject to the same cruel judgment as actions. There is little middle ground for thinking, feeling, or living. One patient said his conscience had a motto: "Everything not compulsory is forbidden." The conscience is typically perfectionistic, and whatever is not perfect or "nice" is dismissed as ridiculously inadequate and "bad." It offers no self-approval short of achievement of the impossible. The conscience in these cases has no kindly, protective quality—it is cold, implacable, omnipotent in its demands, and it never sleeps. When operating with force it directs so much hostility against the self that intolerable states of anguish may be generated.

Untamed, hate-charged introjects can be reprojected out onto other people. This makes others seem unfriendly or hostile to the patient, even though there may be much in reality to contradict such a view of them. In therapeutic relationships the hostile introject will sooner or later manifest itself in the transference. The patient may then devalue the well-intentioned physician who attempts to find the right psychopharmacological regimen for him and react to whatever is prescribed as though he were being offered a poison. "Side effects" will be experienced. If the psychopharmacologist shows signs of impatience, the patient will take it as evidence that the doctor is hostile.

In psychotherapy, the patient, projecting his hostile inner presences (introjects) onto the therapist, may become convinced that the therapist wants to get rid of him, or that he even harbors the secret wish the patient would go ahead and kill himself (Orgel, 1974; Maltsberger and Buie, 1974, 1994; Asch, 1980; Maltsberger, 1998).

SUICIDE-INVITING FAILURES IN EGO FUNCTIONING

D. H. Buie (personal communication, 1993) has observed that in the absence of certain ego-capacities, patients are vulnerable to fall into psychotic or suicidal crises. Successful adult functioning requires more or less autonomous capacity to bear and master anxiety, depression, and rage; to feel worthwhile; to feel real; and to maintain a reasonably stable sense of personal identity, even when under stress. I would add that the capacity to tell the difference between what one imagines about the exterior world and the truth about that world (reality testing) is also essential.

Anxiety Mastery

The psychoanalytic theory of anxiety and the capacity to bear it distinguishes between primary anxiety and signal anxiety. *Signal anxiety,* Freud argued, is a useful alerting function of the ego that sends an alarm signal to the self of some threat or danger, and makes possible adaptational shifts toward the real world in the service of mastering a difficulty. He believed that the capacity for signal anxiety was built up over time, and required that the developing child should not be subjected to excessive, overwhelming anxious experiences along the way. Overwhelming anxiety of paralyzing proportions injures development, he believed. When anxiety is overwhelming and incapacitating, he labeled it *traumatic anxiety* (Freud, 1926). Taken in smaller doses, it fosters independence and mastery.

Empirical research has now demonstrated that borderline personality disorder patients, especially, but also patients with major depressive illness, have a high incidence of childhood traumatization that expectably would provoke considerable anxious horror; namely, mental illness of a parent, childhood family separations, and physical and sexual abuse (Ogata et al., 1990).

Suicide-vulnerable persons are well known to suffer from intolerable levels of mental suffering in which both anxiety and depression are commingled. That Kraepelin (1921, pp. 31, 95) reported a high incidence of anxiety and panic in his depressed manic-depressive patients is sometimes forgotten. The anxious and depressive experiences of suicide-vulnerable persons are extreme, unmodulated, and likely in themselves to be experienced as traumatic. Affective experiences that are so overwhelming correspond to early childhood, primitive traumatic, or primary anxiety as Freud described it—these experiences are so incapacitating that patients are often rendered helpless.

Some patients simply do not have the capacity to moderate and regulate painful affects. When the painful feelings are severe enough, no adaptation is possible and breakdown occurs (Rosenberg, 1949; Zetzel, 1965; Krystal, 1998). Shneidman (1993), as we have seen, believes that unmodulated painful affect is the central driving force to suicide.

Fawcett (1997) has shown how commonly unmodulated anxiety is associated with suicide. The severity of psychic anxiety and the presence of panic attacks are significantly correlated with suicide within the first year of follow-up in his cases. Furthermore, preliminary review (a "non-blinded" analysis) of some seventy-five inpatient suicide records showed clear evidence of severe anxiety-agitation in 78 percent of the cases in the week before suicide.

Depression Mastery

While signal anxiety in mentally healthy people may be regarded as a healthy adaptational tool, some degree of depression is inevitable from time to time as normal persons come to terms with life's inevitable losses, disappointments, and narcissistic injuries. Psychic integrity requires the toleration of the passive experience of suffering as the patient comes to terms with his inability to modify a painful existing reality. (It is one of the saddest rules of life that painful things that cannot be changed must be endured.)

Perhaps while still somewhat depressed, patients must be able to move toward those areas of gratification and achievement that remain available to them. Patients need not only to bear up under depressive pain, but take preliminary steps to reinvest their energies and capacities in new directions even when the suffering has not entirely abated.

Depression becomes pathological under certain circumstances. For instance, the tendency toward all-or-nothing thinking in more disturbed individuals makes it both difficult for them to tolerate depressive pain (sinking into hopelessness, they believe their suffering will last forever), and to summon the courage to reach out to life and rebuild a future.

Zetzel (1965) makes not only these points, but further shows that a good capacity for object relationships is critical for containing depression. She writes, "The capacity to renounce an omnipotent self-image, and acceptance of the limitations of reality appear to be decisive areas. Persons whose object relations have been highly ambivalent, whose self-esteem has been dependent either on successful performance or on excessive gratification, appear, on the other hand, to be highly vulnerable. Psychotic depression thus is the outcome of a failure to experience and master the depression inevitable in developmental crises" (p. 88).

Obviously persons whose childhoods have been filled with experiences of helplessness, hopelessness, and traumatic experiences of anxiety and depression will have difficulty in trusting others. Their object relations will be ambivalent and their self-esteem unstable.

The Capacity to Feel Real and Continuous Across Time

Experiences of depersonalization, derealization, and self-fragmentation are characteristic of suicidal states and reflect the incapacity of the ego to organize memories, affects, and images of the self as experienced across time into a coherent self-representation. The self-representation is excessively fluid in these patients, and tends to break up, fragments of it sometimes becoming confused with object representations. Subjectively this means that patients may experience parts of themselves as belonging to others—certainly this is true of feelings, but it is even true of body parts in psychotic states. One patient declared that her body was a fake, an imitation, foisted off on her by some obscure malignant force, and she attacked it repeatedly with a knife in order to put a stop to what she experienced as a persecution from within her own flesh (Maltsberger 1993, 1998).

ECDYTIC DEATH FANTASIES

The combination of body-self disavowal, intense mental suffering, and regressive surrender of reality testing provides fertile ground for the elaboration of escape, repudiation, and rebirth fantasies.

In the examination of suicidal patients the question "What do you think it would be like to be dead?" will sometimes elicit a conscious metamorphic fantasy, but commonly patients will reply that death would mean "nothingness." When pressed such persons are likely to say that "nothingness" is a dreamless sleep, peaceful and forever. The examiner will immediately recognize that dreamless sleep is not a condition of death at all but a condition of the living. The patient may not recognize it, but his suicidal wish has at its heart the equation of sleep and death. An argument can be made that the longing for such a nirvanalike state bespeaks the forgotten memory of the untroubled rest of earliest childhood contentment (Rado, 1933; Friedlander, 1940; Lewin, 1950; Shneidman, 1967).

Fantasies of reunion through suicide are perhaps the commonest frank ecdytic formations one is likely to encounter in clinical practice. Over and over patients will affirm that death is a passage through which they expect to be reunited with a dead parent, relative, or even sometimes a pet.

> A fifty-seven-year-old unmarried veterinarian's assistant suffering from bipolar disorder, depressed phase, developed the delusion that by self-phlebotomy she could purify herself of the filthy blood that had filled her veins since her childhood incest, and rise in purity to reunion with a beloved sister who had died a year before [Maltsberger, 1997].

This case example shows that multiple wishes are sometimes expressed in suicidal fantasies. This patient not only expected to rejoin her sister in death, but at the same time to rid herself of her bad blood, linked to her abusive father, not experienced as an essential part of herself, and to undergo a purificatory rebirth.

Others imagine themselves infested with a persecutor that they identify with their bodies and attempt suicide in order to escape it. They become, as it were, paranoid against themselves. From time to time patients express the conviction that aliens or other obscure enemies have tampered with their bodies, or parts thereof, causing them to think or feel intolerable things. I have encountered one woman who located something like an "influencing machine" in her head (Tausk, 1933).

> A twenty-three-year-old office worker developed a delusional conviction a malignant intruder had taken up residence in her head in order to torment her and to take control of her thoughts and feelings, forcing her to experience the vilest of impulses. She killed herself in order to get rid of the intruder [Maltsberger and Buie, 1980].

Other patients blame their bodies for life's disappointments and carry grudges against them for years. One such patient conceived the idea that life was not worth living unless she achieved an Olympic gold medal for championship swimming. She believed that having been born female was a terrible and unmerited handicap because it limited her strength. In spite of the most arduous training possible, she never qualified for Olympic competition. Never at peace in her body—she hated it from puberty if not before—she now turned against it and blamed it for her failure.

> A thirty-year-old athlete decided to kill herself to get rid of her detested female body when she failed to qualify for the Olympic team. She said she would return in another life as an Apollonian male, perfect in skill and muscle. She imagined death in orgiastic terms, comparing it to the moment of winning a gold medal, thinking of the roar of the crowd and ecstatic excitement as she died to achieve apotheosis [Maltsberger, 1997].

The mental structural weaknesses in suicide-vulnerable persons—for example, comparative incapacity to modulate anxiety and depression, difficulty in reality testing, instability of the self and object representations within the mind, and overreliance on projection, distortion, and denial—make these patients especially reliant on other people to compensate for their own functional and developmental failures. The patient who cannot modulate his own anxiety must seek soothing from someone else; another patient who cannot escape the scornful denunciation of his own conscience turns to others for reassurance and forgiveness. Frequently these patients must rely on others to set them right about the difference between what actually transpires in the external world, and what they fear is transpiring, or is about to. In short, these patients are unusually reliant on others to do for them emotionally what they are unable to do for themselves. To the extent that others are used in this way, as narcissistic supports and stabilizers, they serve as "self-objects" (Kohut, 1971).

Overreliance on self-objects has particular bearing on the matter of suicide risk in a number of respects. First of all, it explains the vulnerability to crises of anguish when important supportive others are lost, whether through death, separation, rejection, imagined rejection, or other means. Without the necessary external support the patient may expectably experience some degree of ego-collapse (regression) with expectable emotional dysregulation. Panic, despair, turning against the self, paranoid crises, or the like, effloresce. The horror of abandonment lies at the heart of borderline personality disorder and in the hearts of many other patients who are suicide prone.

Second, self-object dependency is relevant to the way in which patients sometimes seek to resolve their ambivalence about living and dying. Many suicide attempts have some quality of leaving the outcome of the attempt to "chance." The conscious or unconscious ambivalence of the attempter shapes the odds for survival as against death. Attempted suicide is often a test to discover whether another person (a self-object) cares enough to intervene in a life-saving way. In almost all instances, a warning is given before deadly action. Stengel (1964) observed that within every suicide attempt lies an appeal to someone else, sometimes to God, or to fate, to choose what the outcome will be. Close study of attempts and of successful suicides shows that there is often a fantasy of rescue built in to the behavior (Jensen and Petty, 1958).

Third, reliance on self-objects is essential in understanding scapegoating phenomena. Because suicide-vulnerable persons are primed to believe that dying is perhaps the better choice, they are uniquely sensitive to expressed or tacit murderous wishes of those to whom they are close, such as other family members. There is a gruesome but apposite aphorism, "In cases of suicide, ask who wanted the patient dead." From time to time, suicide supervenes when families are exhausted by the worry and trouble a suicidal adolescent imposes on them and give up. Sabbath has discussed the phenomenon and gives a number of illustrative cases (1969). Richman has explored the role of hostility in the family as a suicide-promoting factor. The phenomenon in question can be understood in terms of whether a self-object counterbalances the deadly force of a murderous introject, or through rejection, gives suicide the additional necessary impetus (Richman and Rosenbaum, 1970; Richman, 1986).

> A woman reported to her husband that she had just swallowed twenty sleeping pills. He responded with jocular disbelief. When unable to rouse her the next morning (she was in a coma), he left for work [Maddison and Mackey, 1966].

IMPLICATIONS FOR THE CLINICIAN

The following statements epitomize this discussion, and are generally true in suicide:

- Suicide is inextricably connected to object loss.
- The primary cause of suicide is intolerable mental anguish.
- Confusion through misidentification of parts of the self with others is a common underlying process in suicide.
- The changes of puberty tend to alienate suicide-vulnerable adolescents from their bodies, which are then sometimes experienced as alien and persecutory.
- Fantasies of resurgence into a new life are nearly universal in suicide.
- Untamed aggressive impulses organized around inner derivatives of early relationships (hostile introjects) tend to break down and prevent the development of mental cohesion and the capacity to modulate affects.
- Suicide-vulnerable people cannot regulate themselves well and for this reason are unusually dependent on "self-objects" to hold themselves together.
- Many suicidal patients are driven by fantasies of metamorphosis (ecdysis), imagining they will emerge from death into a new and better world.
- Overdependency on others to hold them together (self-object dependency) makes suicide-vulnerable persons subject to crises of anguish when faced with loss, relates to ambivalent suicide attempts, and accounts for why they are so endangered by scapegoating.

Note

1. An *introject* is a part of a person's mind, having been formed when part or parts of the mental images of someone else were internalized and imbued with love, hate, or other qualities, and more or less assimilated into the mental representation of the self, or a part thereof (Meissner, 1981).

CHAPTER FIVE

Perturbation and Lethality

A Psychological Approach to Assessment and Intervention

Edwin Shneidman, Ph.D.

Hug the shore, naught new is seen; and "Land ho!" at last was sung when a new world was sought. . . . It is the world of mind, wherein the wanderer may gaze round with more of wonder than Balboa's band roving through the golden Aztec glades.
—Herman Melville, *Mardi (Chapter 169)*

I have chosen to begin this chapter with an overview of the implications of my point of view so that, from the outset, readers might know the idiosyncratic features of this chapter that lie ahead. The principal assertions of this chapter and the chief implications for the clinician are as follows:

1. The psychological dimensions of almost every case of committed suicide (or serious contemplation of it) can be understood in terms of intensely felt psychological pain (called *psychache*), coupled with the idea of death (surcease, cessation, nothingness, oblivion) as the best solution to the problem of unremitting and intolerable psychache.

2. The unendurable psychache itself is generated by frustrated or thwarted psychological needs. The pattern of needs may be idiosyncratic for that individual (Murray, 1938).

3. The theoretical implication of this formulation is that if the psychache is mollified (by means of addressing the pressing psychological needs), then the suicidality (or lethality) of the person will be sufficiently reduced so that the reason for suicide will no longer exist. This approach focuses on the psychological sector of the complex suicidal drama, a drama that admittedly has concomitant biological, biochemical, sociocultural, epidemiological-demographic, diagnostic-classificatory (Kraepelinian-*DSM*ical), psychodynamic, and philosophic components.

4. The clinical implications would seem to be obvious. There are (at least) two. The first is that the therapist should early on make an assessment of the patient's weightings of psychological needs. This is in addition to case history, differential diagnosis, psychodynamic formulations, biochemical assay, demographic understanding, or anything else. For most clinicians, it will be a new template with which to think of their patients in terms of their disposition of psychological needs. The second main clinical implication—and the main point of this chapter—flows from the first: that the talk therapy then reflects the therapist's understanding of the patient's thwarted or blocked psychological needs in that suicidal scene. This focus should be coupled with practical ways to address and mollify the patient's psychological pain, including contacts with significant others and key persons in the patient's larger life. The goal of psychologically oriented therapy is to reduce the psychache so that the patient can choose to endure, bearing what was previously thought to be unbearable by changing the perception of that burden and making it more realistically endurable.

CONCEPTS BASIC TO THE PSYCHOLOGICAL APPROACH

Being competent in any profession is dependent on mastering the terminology and nomenclature of that discipline. To master the special vocabulary that defines a specialty is a large part of being that kind of specialist, and suicidology is no different. In the editions of the *Encyclopaedia Britannica* that have appeared in the nineteenth and twentieth centuries, multiple books about suicide (written by a single author and available in English) are cited: by A. Alvarez, R. S. Cavan, J. Choron, J. D. Douglas, L. I. Dublin, E. Durkheim, K. Menninger, E. Shneidman, and E. Stengel. An examination of their contents reveals the common key words that make up the language of suicide study. (A grand concordance of these books would yield the vocabulary of the basic texts of self-inflicted death.)

There are, of course, several legitimate approaches to the study of suicide. About a dozen can be listed (Shneidman, 1992):

- Literary and personal document approach, focusing on suicide notes, diaries, and anamnestic reports
- Philosophic and religious approaches, focusing on the meaning of life and man's relation to the god he believes in
- Demographic approach that looks for constancies in the flux of numbers
- Sociocultural approach that seeks to relate suicide rates and practices to different cultures

- Sociological approach that relates suicidal man to the strength of his ties with the larger society

- Dyadic and familial approach that views suicide primarily as a small-group event

- Psychodynamic approach that explains suicide in terms of unconscious irresolutions

- Psychiatric or mental illness approach that relates suicide to Kraepelinian or *DSM* nosological categories

- Constitutional or genetic approach that places suicidal events in the genealogical tree

- Biological approach that seeks out biochemical markers (in blood, spinal fluid, endocrine flow) of suicide

- Legal and ethical approaches that discuss and explicate thorny issues like assisted death

- Psychological approach that focuses on psychological pain and frustrated psychological needs

All of these approaches may be present in the close analysis of any single case of suicide.

My central belief is that in the distillation of each suicidal event, its essential element is a psychological one; that is, each suicidal drama occurs in the mind of a unique individual. Suicide is purposeful. Its purpose is to respond to or redress certain psychological needs. There are many pointless deaths, but there is never a needless suicide. Suicide is a concatenated, multidimensional, conscious, and unconscious "choice" of the best possible practical solution to a perceived problem, dilemma, impulse, crisis, or desperation.

To use an arboreal image, the psychological component in suicide is the trunk of it. An individual's biochemical states are the roots. The method of suicide, the contents of the suicide note, the calculated effects on the survivors, and so on are the branching limbs, the flawed fruit, and the camouflaging leaves. But the psychological component, the lethal problem-solving choice—the best solution to the perceived problem—is the main trunk.

Some of the key words in this psychologically-oriented suicidology follow.

Perturbation refers to being upset, mentally disturbed, perturbed. It exists in every individual, ratable from, say, 1 to 9. A rating of 8 or 9 indicates that an individual is very disturbed: hypermanic, inert, frenzied, bereft. Such an individual may be diagnosed (for managed care purposes) as schizophrenic, or catatonic, or depressed, or rageful, or something else, but *perturbation* refers to that continuum from being serene, contented, and well adjusted to being out-of-this-world and possibly dangerous to oneself and others. Everyone is ratable. No one we know is a 1; sociopaths may be 3s or 4s; postgraduate students normally range from 5 to 7; hospitalized mental patients are 6 and up; 8s and 9s should be watched carefully.

In a study of thirty high-IQ men in the Terman Study of the Gifted (begun in 1921 and continuing to this day), the detailed, longitudinal life histories of the five men who subsequently committed suicide contained discernible indexes of heightened childhood perturbation (Shneidman, 1971). There were prodramata in the life history, years before the suicidal event.

Lethality refers to the probability that a specific individual will be dead, by suicide, within the next several days—in other words, that the individual will "do" something about his perturbation. *Lethality* is a synonym for *suicidality.* It is not synonymous with *perturbation.* There is no heightened lethality without heightened perturbation, but there is, thank goodness, plenty of elevated perturbation without elevated lethality. Lethality is fueled by perturbation. Of course, we take away the suicidal patient's gun, the sharps, the pills, and the belt, and we secure the window, addressing the lethality directly, but we recognize that the most effective treatment of high lethality is to diminish the perturbation that drives it. We use psychotherapy, milieu management, medication, and even electricity to mollify the individual's sense of perturbation. Very high lethality, say an 8 or a 9, cannot usually be sustained for more than a few days before either an affect or a bullet is discharged. In general, 8s and 9s belong in a sanctuaried space, like a hospital ward.

Constriction refers to the honing in, the tightening down of the diaphragm of the mind. There is dichotomous thinking, a fixation on a single pain-free solution *or* death. Choices seem limited to two or one. The most dangerous word that one can hear from a potentially suicidal person is the quietly said *only,* as in, "It's the only thing I can do." Constriction accounts for the fact that most suicide notes turn out to be rather pedestrian and banal (Shneidman, 1973); a person who could write a full and pscyhodynamically informative note would not likely commit suicide in the first place.

In nineteenth-century England, *anodyne* was a frequently used word. It referred to a substance, such as morphine or laudanum, that relieved pain. By extension, it can also refer to an agent (a person) who can do the same. Some psychiatrists believe that their principal function is to treat mental disease; others recognize that a proper principal function of a psychiatric service is to be anodynic, that is, to assuage the psychache that drove the patient through the doors. (In Chapter Eleven, Leston Havens discusses this aspect of clinical intervention from a related perspective: the use of analgesics in psychiatry.) When all is said and done, the main goal of psychotherapy is anodynic, to reduce mental pain. The great literary work on this topic is Thomas De Quincy's unforgettable *Confessions of an English Opium Eater* (1821).

Psychache (pronounced sīk-āk) is the hurt, anguish, or ache that takes hold of the mind. It is intrinsically psychological; it is the introspectively felt mental pain of negative emotions, such as guilt, shame, anguish, fear, panic, angst, loneliness, helplessness. It is not the somatic pain of a toothache, an earache, or a headache; psychache is autonomously mental. It is "in" the mind; it is the pain of selfhood. When we feel it, its introspective reality is undeniable. Psychache is the introspective recognition of perturbation. Suicide occurs when the psychache is deemed to be unbearable and when death is actively sought in order to stop the unceasing flow of intolerable consciousness.

The primary goal of suicide is to effect the cessation of painful mental life. Suicide is primarily a drama in the mind. In this view, suicide stems from heightened unbearable psychache. To understand suicide, we must understand suffering and psychological pain and various idiosyncratic (and culturally bound) thresholds for enduring it. To treat suicidal people (and to intervene against suicide), we must address and then soften the psychache that drives it. The key question is, "Where do you hurt?" No psychache, no suicide. The major implication of this view would seem to be obvious: reduce the pain, and the raison d'être for suicide will disappear.

In general, the sources (or causes) of psychache are frustrated, blocked, or thwarted *psychological needs*. An explication of these needs is given to use prepackaged and ready-made in Murray's *Explorations in Personality* (1938), one of the half-dozen most important books in American psychology. In that book are formulated the needs we spend our lifetimes pursuing. Murray asks, "For what is suicide but an action to put an end to intolerable emotions?" Murray leisurely presents, defines, discusses, and illustrates a score of these psychodynamic elements of personality. He defines a need as "a force in the brain which organizes perception and intellection in such a way as to appease or satisfy the organism" (See Table 5.1.) Each of us has an idiosyncratic disposition made up of our own constellation and weighting of psychological needs. Indeed, the relative weightings that we give these various needs is a window into our personality. It reflects who we are and what makes us tick—and what makes us vulnerable to suicide, each of us in our own idiosyncratic way.

In general, two different constellations of psychological needs can be identified for any individual: (1) needs that characterize the everyday functioning, ongoing personality, the person's usual disposition of needs, the needs the person lives with, the *modal* needs; and (2) needs that the individual focuses on when he or she is under duress, suffering heightened inner tension, and is in considerable mental pain. These are the needs, the frustration of which the person is willing to die for, the suicidal needs, the *vital* needs. Indeed, being suicidal is a state of heightened psychache stimulated by a shift (and increased intensity) of certain psychological needs.

With twenty needs, one might think that there might be twenty "kinds" of suicide. In practice, as few as a half-dozen needs are typically implicated in suicide. For practical purposes, most suicides tend to fall into one of five clusters, reflecting different kinds of psychological pain:

Table 5.1. Murray's Psychological Needs.

Need	Definition
Abasement	Submitting passively to external force; accepting criticism; surrendering; blaming or belittling the self; seeking and enjoying pain, illness, and misfortune
Achievement	Manipulating objects, humans, or ideas; overcoming obstacles; rivaling and surpassing others; increasing self-regard by successfully exercising talent
Affiliation	Drawing near to and enjoyably cooperating with an allied person; pleasing and winning affection of the admired person; adhering and remaining loyal to a friend
Aggression	Overcoming opposition; fighting, attacking, or injuring another; opposing another forcefully; belittling, censuring, ridiculing, slandering; being angry, combative
Autonomy	Shaking off restraint or breaking out of social confinement; resisting coercion and constriction; acting according to desire; defying convention
Counteraction	Mastering or making up for failure; obliterating past humiliation through resumed action; overcoming weakness; suppressing fear; making preemptive strikes
Defendance	Defending the self against assault, criticism, blame; concealing or justifying a misdeed, failure, or humiliation; vindicating the ego
Deference	Praising, honoring, or eulogizing another; yielding eagerly to the influence of another; emulating an exemplar; conforming to custom
Dominance	Controlling one's human environment; influencing or directing the behavior of others through suggestion, seduction, or command; dissuading or prohibiting
Exhibition	Making an impression; being seen and heard; exciting, amazing, fascinating, entertaining, shocking, intriguing, amusing, or enticing others
Harm avoidance	Avoiding pain, physical injury, illness, and death; escaping from a dangerous situation; taking reasonable precautionary measures
Inviolacy	Remaining separate; resisting attempts by others to intrude on or invade one's own psychological space; being isolated, immune from criticism

Table 5.1. Murray's Psychological Needs, cont'd.

Need	Definition
Nurturance	Giving sympathy and gratifying the needs of another person, especially someone who is weak; supporting, consoling, protecting, nursing, or healing (compare Succorance)
Order	Putting things or ideas in order; arranging, organizing, tidying, and working for precision among things in the outer world or ideas in the inner world of the mind
Play	Acting for "fun," without further purpose; laughing and making jokes; relaxing; participating in pleasurable activities for their own sake
Rejection	Separating oneself from negatively viewed persons; excluding, abandoning, expelling, or remaining indifferent to an inferior person; snubbing or jilting another
Sentience	Seeking sensuous experience; enjoying good food and wine, silk sheets, fine clothes; emphasizing the look and feel of things
Shame avoidance	Avoiding humiliation and embarrassment; avoiding scorn, derision, or indifference of others; refraining from action because of fear of failure
Succorance	Receiving support, help, and love; having one's needs gratified by the sympathetic aid of another; being sustained, protected, indulged, taken care of
Understanding	Asking and answering questions; speculating, formulating, analyzing, and generalizing; wanting to know the answers to general questions; theorizing; philosophizing

Source: Adapted from *Explorations in Personality* by Henry A. Murray. Copyright 1938, renewed 1966 by Henry A. Murray. Used by permission of Oxford University Press, Inc.

1. Thwarted love, acceptance, and belonging—related to frustrated needs for succorance and affiliation

2. Fractured control, predictability, and arrangement—related to frustrated needs for achievement, autonomy, order, and understanding

3. Assaulted self-image and avoidance of shame, defeat, humiliation, and disgrace—related to frustrated needs for affiliation, defendance, and shame-avoidance

4. Ruptured key relationships and attendant grief and bereftness—related to frustrated needs for affiliation and nurturance

5. Excessive anger, rage, and hostility—related to frustrated needs for dominance, aggression, and counteraction

But there are more than five kinds of suicide, and each sad case should be assessed and understood in terms of its own idiosyncratic details.

THE STORY OF BEATRICE

Beatrice Bessen is a comely young woman, age twenty-two, of average height, conspicuously thin, noticeably well groomed, blond, attractive, well spoken, and bright. The following are selected verbatim portions from her written anamnestic account.

My childhood was fine, growing up in the suburbs, which were relatively safe then. I had self-confidence like most children do. My memory becomes rather intense at the age of ten. I remember knowing, somehow, that my parents were going to divorce someday, so I began to read books about children of divorce. When I told my mother how I felt, she said they had no plans of divorce. Three years later my mom moved out of the house.

At the age of ten I sort of "woke up" to the horrors of the world. I came out of my childhood innocence and dove headfirst into the dark side of life. Recognizing that I was vulnerable to severe pain, and predicting that my household was breaking up, I began to pull away from my parents. By the time my mom and pop came out of their denial, I had distanced myself enough so that their separation didn't affect me. I submerged myself in my friends, having discounted my family's ability to support me.

I had secretly wanted to live with my father, but couldn't hurt my mother's feelings. Unfortunately, my father leaned on me too strongly and confessed to me his thoughts of suicide and his increasing abuse of alcohol. I listened, thinking he was doing me a favor by confiding in me, and carried around an impossible load of guilt and sadness for my father's state of mind.

High school had its highlights, but it wasn't enough to distract me from my growing self-hate. At age fifteen I was struggling with my feelings and did not understand what was happening to me. I remember trying to explain it to my friends, who shook their heads in disbelief at my descriptions of falling in a black hole and my declarations that life was meaningless, but they simply could not relate to my morbid ideations.

Once I realized I was alone in my thoughts, I stopped talking about them. I was terrified that I was insane and didn't want anyone to find out, so I continued to mimic the behaviors of my "normal" friends and put on a smile everywhere I went. That same year my brother moved out and went out of the state to college, leaving me with the fragmented mess known as our family. I still resent his narrow escape from the family hell that followed in his absence. I heard everything.

At this point, although I was rarely at either parent's house, I needed something to distract myself from the burden of their bickering. The answer was handed to me by a teenage boy I was dating and thought I "loved." He told me that I needed to lose five pounds. I believed him, anxious to find a reason why I was so unhappy. At 5 feet 6 and 120 pounds, I went on a diet. The diet gave me many of the things I craved: attention, control, self-confidence, and order. Little did I know that I would end up with an eating disorder that haunts me to this day.

The boyfriend who began my descent into anorexia chose the following week to break up with me. He abruptly broke up with me. I could not handle the overflowing waves of pain that washed though my body immediately after the breakup. I had never felt such intense pain, and I could not handle it. I was alone at home and ran desperately around, panicked over the flood of emotions that was traveling through my body. I ended up taking the kitchen knife into my room and cutting myself, slashes all along my arms. The physical pain let me pull my attention off the emotional agony, and I just concentrated on not letting the blood spill over onto the carpet. That day I clearly remember wanting to die.

In retrospect, that day was a catalyst for a speedy downward spiral that engulfed the rest of my adolescence. I was able to maintain a "false self" at school and in my activities. For the next two years no one, not even my close friends, knew how I felt inside. Every night, before fading off to sleep, I imagined committing suicide. I became obsessed with death. I rehearsed my own funeral over and over, adding careful details each time. I listened to a genre of music known as "gothic," which had dark, murky tunes to accompany tragic lyrics of loss and death. I began to write poetry questioning existence, God, human intentions, and philosophy. But nothing gave me relief. I became more and more cynical about the daily task of living, and distanced myself further from my emotions. After awhile, I was completely numb.

I used my excessive discipline to deprive myself of food and comfort. I felt I needed to "suffer" in order to "deserve" the right to walk down the street. I used drugs, ditched school, and slept overnight in my car (telling whichever parent that I was at a friend's house). I managed to maintain an impossibly low weight for the summer before my senior year of high school. The bad mood had taken over. I described it then as a monster that was bigger than I was. I was tired, very tired, and I gave in to it.

Though I had considered suicide for a long time, I had not made a serious attempt yet. After working on a plan for three months, I tried to kill myself a week before my seventeenth birthday. In my beloved car, at 2 A.M. on a rainy night, I slit my wrists with a newly purchased, large Exacto knife. I had already prepared an audiotape (I felt that a suicide note was too commonplace and wanted to be original), and I left copies of it at the door of two close friends. I was ready to die.

I know now that slitting my wrists was not as poetic or as easy as I had imagined. Due to blood clotting and fainting, it is actually difficult to die from such wounds. The evening dragged on with me busy reopening the stubborn veins that insisted on clotting up. I was patient and persistent, thinking of myself for over an hour. The battle with my body to die was unexpected, and after waging a good fight, I passed out.

Someone looked into the car. I was sure I was going to be sent to jail. Instead, a few phone calls were made, and I was taken to a mental hospital.

I spent three and a half months locked indoors on an adolescent psychiatric unit. I met other kids who felt the way I did. I was introduced to a million therapies. And I attempted suicide again in my tiny room after smashing a light bulb and using glass to slice my veins open. Yet the overall experience was a positive one. I was removed from my "family" environment long enough to gain some perspective on my situation, and I connected with others who felt as desperate as I did. However, I was not "cured." I was released from the hospital AMA [against medical advice] because my father was fed up with the high costs and the pop psychology suggestions of the institution. The day after I was out, I went on my first real eating binge, devouring my father's kitchen contents after months of hospital food. The following day I resolved to diet once again.

Although I was feeling better, the underlying causes of my unhappiness had yet to be tackled. I no longer spent my evenings planning my funeral; instead I prepared the following day's menu and exercise regimen. I spent the last semester of my senior year (having kept up with my classmates by using the hospital's school program) alternately dieting and bingeing. I lost and gained the same fifteen pounds a hundred times.

Going away to college at age eighteen was a wise choice for me. Escaping from the chaos of my home life, as well as the confusion of a big city, helped me quite a bit. I slowly made new friends. Of course, it wasn't perfect. My eating disorder took on new shapes, resulting in heavy laxative abuse and bingeing during my first two years of college and strict dieting and severe weight loss during my final two years. I attended a support group for bulimia and anorexia, but never entered one-on-one therapy, having feared no real solution after my experience with intensive therapy in the hospital.

During my fairly peaceful college years, suicide still played a role. Most obvious was my eating disorder, which on some level was an attempt to slowly end my life. Less obvious was my disturbingly dark poetry, and my instant thought of suicide each time a difficult problem would arise. I simply kept suicide in the back of my mind as an option. It made me feel safer. My sick logic hadn't changed since adolescence.

My final year of college was the best one. My anorexia was manageable and my spirits lifted enough to enjoy life. I even allowed myself a few months thinking I was "cured" and that the pain of the past decade was finally over. But as graduation approached, I started sleeping more and eating less. I was definitely coming down from a yearlong high.

I have now graduated from college. I moved back home, am living with my father, and was rehired at last year's summer job for the whole year. I have been accepted into graduate school, but I am deferring that for a year. I do not want to spend the rest of my life sliding up and down the scale of mental illness. I need to address things that were not dealt with in the hospital.

My anorexia has grown much worse since I've been home, and I know my health is in danger. For me, restricting my food intake is not about being fashionably thin; it's about my death wish that actually never left me.

Psychological Test Data

Two psychological tests, both designed to pull thematic threads in the person's inner interpersonal life, were administered: the Thematic Apperception Test (TAT) and the Make-A-Picture-Story (MAPS) test. The TAT (Murray, 1943) consists entirely of a set of reproduced photographs, typically of two people, in which the social-psychological situation is not quite clear. The subject's task is to tell a story, relating what the characters in the picture are thinking, feeling, and doing; what is going on; and how the whole thing turns out. Murray has said (1943) that the TAT "is based on the well-recognized fact that when someone attempts to interpret a complex social situation he is apt to tell as much about himself as he is about the phenomena on which he is focused. . . . Wishes, fears, as well as conscious and unconscious expressions of his experiences and fantasies."

Here is Beatrice's response to a TAT card in which a young boy is contemplating a violin which rests on a table in front of him:

> It's a picture of a little boy. And it seems like he's missing something. Like he's being reminded of something about this violin. He's being reminded looking at this violin in front of him. Maybe he's missing the person who used to play the violin. A friend, or teacher, or parents, or another sibling. He just is looking at the violin and missing the player of it and eventually he'll get up and go about his day. It is a reminder of somebody, because they are no longer playing the music.

Another TAT card shows a young man sitting opposite an older man who looks as though he were emphasizing some point in an argument. Here is what Beatrice said:

> Two men are listening to a story that is being told to them by someone who is not in the picture. The younger man is looking intently at the person who is telling the story, listening very hard, and the older man is looking at him, looking for his facial reaction. Perhaps he already knows the story. Maybe it's this man's wife and he knows what she is going to say, and he's looking for the young man's reaction.

The MAPS test, a first cousin of the TAT, consists of twenty unpopulated background pictures and sixty-seven separate figures. The subject's task is to select one or more of the figures, put them in a background as they might be in real life, and then tell a story to the situation thus created (Shneidman, 1951).

Here are a few of Beatrice's MAPS test responses. For the living room background, Beatrice selected the figure of Superman and the figure of a small dog:

> Okay. We have here an old-fashioned setting of a man, a man in a costume, and he comes bursting through the door. He's strong, big and handsome, and he has this stylish outfit on. And he comes through the door and there's the dog, sitting

by the couch. The dog is feeling bored and is not impressed by the owner dressing up. . . . He lives there with his sister and mother but they're not home. He thought they might be home. He isn't doing this for the dog.

For the cemetery background, she chose a single figure: a young woman slightly bending forward:

> This is a cemetery and this woman has been wandering. She has no destination. And she's been going wherever her steps would take her. And she ended up in the graveyard, just the local graveyard, and she's wandering among the gravestones, and for some reason this certain grave with the sort of interesting mark on top appealed to her and she decided to approach it, and she thought she could hear something, and she looked around, and there was no one around, in the sunny afternoon in the graveyard. And she reads the name on the place, and she doesn't know the person, it is not anybody she knows, but she feels drawn to it, and she leans in almost to pick up on what she thinks might actually be somebody saying something. She knows it's somewhat strange and she keeps looking around to make sure that people aren't looking at her, but she really thinks there is something she can hear. So she's leaning in to listen to the grave. She's not scared though; she's just curious.

For the stage background, she selected two African American figures, a man and a woman. Here is her story:

> This is a theater. They are on the stage, two people. This is an audition. And the man is just reading his lines. The play has not been cast. And she is saying her lines; she is really auditioning. She is very into the character and very serious and trying to be passionate about the character, but he is just reading the lines and not trying to act. But she is trying to concentrate and she's nervous because it's a serious audition. It's a modern play about singles and their relations.

Reflections and Applications of the Psychological Approach

In Herman Melville's murky but exciting offbeat novel *The Confidence Man*, there is a three-page chapter about Charlemont, a French merchant living in nineteenth-century St. Louis. He is a young bachelor possessed of "sterling and captivating kindliness," a genial host and a bountiful friend, who, on becoming suddenly bankrupt, withdraws from society and eventually from the city. Some years later he returns, "gay, polite, humane, companionable"; "he was himself again." But the question remained: Why had he withdrawn, not asked his friends for help, and kept his troubles to himself? At last, one late evening at the close of a dinner party, one friend dared to ask him "to explain the one enigma of his life." After some hesitation, Charlemont spoke slowly: "If ever, in days to come, you shall see ruin at hand, and thinking you understand mankind, shall tremble for your friendships, and tremble for your pride; and partly through love for the one and fear for the other, shall resolve to be beforehand with the world, and save it from a sin by prospectively taking that sin to yourself, then you will do as one I now dream of once did, and like him will you suffer" (Melville, 1857).

From the beginning, I thought of Beatrice in terms of her bondage to her need for counteraction—"to be beforehand with the world"—coupled with her second-tier needs for autonomy, inviolacy, succorance, and understanding. Any attempts to help her would be more effective if the form and the shape (as well as the contents) of those efforts reflected her particular (and somewhat unusual) constellation of psychological needs.

Never mind for the moment whether we think her difficulties reflect a transference neurosis or a narcissistic neurosis (or a combination of them); her main difficulty is her inability to trust other people, to make them significant in her life, indeed to see them in the scene at all. In my decades of experience with the TAT and the MAPS test, I have never heard a record that so emphasized the people offstage, out of reach, "dead to the world." This arid theme is made explicit in almost every one of her stories. Her psychache is the pain of loss, of despair, of identity confusion, of self-generated orphanhood, and for the search for what has been lost, including the possible nurturing others whom she has denied herself. She thinks that she is onstage, when she is, in fact, "in the wings" of her own life; it is the people offstage who are central to her drama. She is *contra mundi* without the strength to stand indifferent to the world.

Two additional short points about Melville's story of Charlemont are relevant here. The title is "The Story of the Gentleman-Madman." Certainly Beatrice— well groomed, well mannered, genteel, college trained, her father well placed in society—is a young gentlewoman, and she is, in Melville's sense of the word, also mad. This is seen in her mistrust of others, her undigested rage at her parents, her conversion of a genuine domestic tragedy into a fruitless existential search for trustworthy Truth, a dichotomization of thinking (with very little of the large in-between gray area where much of life is practically lived in the hurly-burly of compromise and of acceptance of less than perfection in oneself and others).

The last line of Melville's story is, "When the guest went away it was with the persuasion that some taint of Charlemont's old malady survived, and that it was not well for friends to touch one dangerous string." Nevertheless, keeping all of the above in mind, the key to her rescue lies in involving her (admittedly limited) capacity for positive transference. She currently gets along with adults very well—up to a point. But a psychotherapist would have to be very mindful of Beatrice's need to be first in any maneuver that smacked of rejection, such as the therapist's illnesses, crises, changes of appointments, vacations, comments, interpretations. This does not mean that the therapist would want to agree with Beatrice's formulations about the clear-cut nastiness of life and the beguilements of suicide. On the contrary, disagreement (not disapproval) from almost the beginning with her life-diminishing and suicide-enhancing agenda should be the therapist's constant position.

But sight of the therapist's principal anodynic function should not be lost for a moment: support, approval, reinforcement. There should be constant monitoring of her levels of perturbation and lethality. Any sudden increases should be the signal for reassessment and possible action: extra sessions, consultations, contact with one or both parents, hospitalization. None of these precludes the recognition (by both parties) of the difficult nature of her climb to a more tranquil state of mind. The climb is to a better place, but it is an uphill path almost all the way, as witnessed by this recorded exchange:

ES: Tell me more about your pain.

BB: All my pain has been more mental than anything else. I have always had a hard time crying or being emotional or throwing myself about. But I have spent time thinking and analyzing myself to the point where I feel insane. I can talk myself into a trap in my head. I think my doubts come from whether or not people can change. Change fundamental things. I myself have changed after going through college, as opposed to the person I was in high school. But I feel there are fundamental things that I have never been able to change, but wanted to. So I have some doubts about the whole theory that you can just change these opinions that people have of the world.

ES: Could you describe one of those fundamental things which you don't think can change?

BB: Fully trusting anybody. Totally trusting yourself. [Lengthy pause]

ES: What are you thinking about?

BB: I'm thinking about extremes. And how my tendency is to go for all or nothing. And I don't feel that my past is really gone, or that it's a time behind me. I feel like it's here all the time, that it's present. I mean I recognize that it's past, but it doesn't feel that way.

ES: Is it possible for you to see the past in any slightly different way?

BB: Sure, I think it is, logically. I've logically talked myself out of any kind of destruction, but it doesn't stay. Because when the trauma happened, when you were eight years old or whatever, at the time it felt like life or death. I definitely understand that I was scared when I was younger, even though it isn't rational as an adult. But now I need to keep a control on it because I just can't live like that every day. I just can't live in such extreme fear, am I going to die or am I going to live? State of mind. It's too hard. But unfortunately I have picked controls that are eventually deadly.

ES: Can you say what they are?

BB: For me currently it's dieting. But it's been other things. I think it's addictions. I've used drugs. I've fantasized about suicide obsessively, all the time. And I wasn't going to die from thinking, but I believe that was an eventual destruction because the goal was to fulfill those fantasies.

ES: And how was that?

BB: Various ways. It was over a period of three or four years when I was fantasizing every night before I went to bed. One example was to bleed to death; bleeding was poetic and tragic and somehow romantic. I was very immersed in gothic songs and poems I was writing. It was a control thing, because I was using all that mind energy, that obsessing, to avoid what was really going on. It was an addiction. I think that ends up being destructive in and of itself. Like adopting tranquilizers when you go to surgery and then every time you get nervous and every time you feel scared, to be dependent on them, and on people.

ES: And why is that so bad?

BB: I agree with you that people need to be dependent, but I'm talking about something severe. I would use another person the way I use dieting now. As a way to keep fear at bay. I would use them to a point where it wasn't humanly, nicely dependent. I couldn't see the line between him and me, where we were different people. I don't think it was healthy at all. I'm talking about not letting go. Ever. Being afraid of not using the tranquilizers, being afraid of letting go of the other person. That's what I'm talking about. I'm only comfortable living in the extremes.

ES: Do you want to change that?

BB: Yes, of course, because I've discovered that living in the extremes is dangerous. I don't believe that when you die you become null, nonexistent. I believe that energy changes form, but doesn't die. That's a whole other big issue. It's interesting to consider what people who try to commit suicide think about death.

ES: Isn't suicide a way of throwing your life away?

BB: So?

ES: What do you mean, so?

BB: Well, if a person really wants to commit suicide, I don't think it would matter, that you can't do it just in order to keep your status with other people. I think that if you were in position to really kill yourself, you wouldn't care. Actually, people might take you more seriously, thinking that you had some insight.

ES: Do you think you'll believe this ten years from now?

BB: I don't think I'll make it to then if I'm still thinking this way. I don't think I'd bother.

CHAPTER SIX

The Neurobiology
of Suicidal Behavior

J. John Mann, M.D.
Victoria Arango, Ph.D.

A consideration of the neurobiology of suicide requires recognition that suicide is the outcome of a complex set of factors. The neurobiological changes may reflect any or all risk factors that include a psychiatric disorder in over 90 percent of suicides, as well as predisposing personality traits such as aggression and impulsivity, social stressors such as unemployment and bereavement, male gender, substance or alcohol abuse, and familial and genetic transmission of much of the preceding. Finally, in postmortem studies, it is critical to consider the effects of medications, drugs of abuse, and the degradative effects of postmortem delay. Another challenge is to distinguish between biological effects that are consequences of the suicidal act and not related to risk factors for the act. Such biological consequences can result from the effects of ingested substances, medications, or drugs used in an overdose; medical injuries; the postattempt medical treatment or agonal effects where death is not rapid. An example of problems is the head injury resulting from the suicide when the method involves jumping from height or a gunshot wound to the head. This matter is complicated by the fact that the incidence of past head injury is elevated in suicide attempters compared to psychiatric controls. Head injuries can alter serotonergic function as well as that of other monoaminergic systems.

Support for the work reported in this chapter was provided by MH40210, AA09004, and MH46745. Parts of this material were modified and updated from a paper published in 1996 by Mann, Underwood, and Arango.

This chapter reviews neurobiological correlates of suicidal behavior and is organized by neurotransmitter system. Within the discussion of each system, the findings relevant to the above issues will be discussed. Data are drawn from studies of completed suicides and suicide attempters, which appear to be on a continuum depending partly on the degree of medical damage inflicted.

GENETICS OF SUICIDE

A considerable body of evidence indicates that there is transmission of familial and genetic factors that contribute to the risk for suicidal behavior. Major psychiatric illness such as mood disorders, schizophrenia, alcoholism and substance abuse, and cluster B personality disorders are found in association with most suicides. All of these conditions have a genetic component in their etiology. It is therefore critical to determine whether the genetic transmission of suicide risk is explained by the transmission of psychiatric illness associated with suicide. Several studies have found that genetic and familial transmission of suicide risk is independent of the transmission of psychiatric syndromes (Brent, Bridge, Johnson, and Connolly, 1996; Schulsinger, Kety, Rosenthal, and Wender, 1979). Because there is genetic transmission of part of the risk for suicidal behavior, it is an indication that this predisposition has a neurobiological component and potentially a behavioral trait or traits that can be measured.

SEROTONERGIC SYSTEM IN SUICIDE VICTIMS AND ATTEMPTERS

We will address serotonergic neuron activity, serotonin receptors, and neuroendocrine studies of the serotonergic system in suicide attempters.

Serotonergic Neuron Activity

The serotonergic system is complex. Major cortical and subcortical projections arise from the median and dorsal raphe nuclei. Each serotonin neuron innervates several thousand cortical neurons, mostly, but not exclusively, GABAergic interneurons. There are thick and thin ascending fiber systems with few to numerous varicosities. The dorsal raphe nuclei have six subnuclear groups in human brain. Finally, there are over one dozen serotonin receptors, including at least two autoreceptor populations at the somatodendritic level, the 5-HT_{1A} and $5\text{-HT}_{1D/B}$ subtypes. Table 6.1 summarizes results from postmortem studies in suicide victims, although not all studies are in agreement with the conclusions shown.

Table 6.1. Neurobiology of the Serotonergic System in Suicide at the Synaptic Level.

Presynaptic/Brainstem	Postsynaptic/Nerve Terminal
Serotonin decreased	5-HT_{1A} increased
5-HIAA decreased	5-HT_{2A} increased
SERT decreased	5-HT_{2C} remained the same
SERTlike decreased	5-HT_3 remained the same
5-HT_{1D} ?	G-proteins decreased
	Signal transduction cyclic AMP ?
	PI decreased

The first studies of the serotonergic system in suicide victims span a period from the late 1960s to the mid-1980s and reported modest reductions in brainstem serotonin and/or its metabolite 5-hydroxyindoleacetic acid (5-HIAA). A major methodological caveat is that these postmortem assays cannot distinguish intrasynaptic transmitter, readily releasable transmitter in the fast turnover pool, and slow turnover pool transmitter that may be less available for release and of less functional importance. Another consideration is the rapidity with which serotonin and 5-HIAA levels drop after death. There is about a 70 percent loss of serotonin prior to assay in most studies. This means that group differences must be detected in the residual 30 percent of the serotonin or metabolite, a more difficult objective. Nevertheless, five of seven studies found reductions in either brainstem serotonin or 5-HIAA. In contrast, only three out of nine studies found a reduction in prefrontal cortex 5-HIAA levels, and no study found a reduction in serotonin (see Table 6.2). Four of six studies of other brain regions reported reductions in serotonin or 5-HIAA (not shown in Table 6.2). The evidence for a reduction in serotonin or serotonin turnover therefore appears most consistent in the brainstem. This may be a function of the sensitivity of the assay methodology, since the brainstem contains the serotonin synthesizing neurons and the highest concentrations of serotonin and 5-HIAA. Alternatively, there may be a regional localization of changes in serotonin levels or turnover, such that serotonin and 5-HIAA in the terminal fields are altered in some areas and not others.

We previously reported that the degree of reduction in serotonin or 5-HIAA in the brainstem of suicide victims has no relationship to diagnostic category (Mann et al., 1989a). The degree of reduction was similar in depressed patients, schizophrenics, personality disorders, and alcoholics. The proportion of suicide victims suffering from a major depressive illness with decreased serotonin or 5-HIAA was not different from suicide victims with other psychiatric disorders (Mann et al., 1989a). This is a critical point because it indicates that the reduction in serotonergic activity is related to suicide independent of psychiatric diagnosis. It has frequently been asserted that reduced serotonergic activity is associated with

Table 6.2. Serotonin and 5-HIAA in the Brainstem of Suicide Victims Versus Controls.

Study	Brainstem		Cerebral Cortex	
	Serotonin	5-HIAA	Serotonin	5-HIAA
Shaw, Camps, and Eccleston (1967)	less than 19 percent*	—	—	—
Bourne et al. (1968)	NC	less than 28 percent*	—	—
Paré, Yeung, Price, and Stacey (1969)	less than 11 percent*	NC	—	—
Lloyd, Farley, Deck, and Hornykiewicz (1974)	less than 30 percent*	NC	—	—
Beskow, Gottfries, Roos, and Winblad (1976)	NC	less than 30 percent*	—	less than 43 percent*
Cochran, Robins, and Grote (1976)	NC	—	NC	—
Owen et al. (1983)	—	—	—	less than 71 percent
Crow et al. (1984)	—	—	—	less than 25 percent
Korpi et al. (1986)	NC	NC	NC	NC
Owen et al. (1986)	—	—	—	—
Arató, Tekes, Palkovits, Demeter, and Falus (1987)	—	—	NC	NC
Cheetham, et al. (1989)	—	—	NC	NC
Ohmori, Arora, and Meltzer (1992)	—	—	—	NC
Mann et al. (1996)	—	—	NC	NC
Arranz, Blennow, Eriksson, Mansson, and Marcusson (1997)	—	—	NC	NC

Note: * = Statistically significant difference. NC = No change was detected between groups.

violent suicide. However, there is no convincing evidence to support this contention (Arango and Mann, 1992; Mann et al., 1989b). Therefore, the method of suicide appears to be unrelated to the biochemical findings. These analyses did not extend to an examination of specific drugs that may have been used in a suicide attempt or the antemortem drug treatment history of the subjects.

Although postmortem interval is considered critical in the quantification of indoleamines, differences in postmortem interval do not appear to explain discrepancies in the literature (Arango and Mann, 1992), probably because most of the decline in indoleamine levels occurs in the first two hours postmortem, and virtually all cases have a longer postmortem delay.

In summary, there is evidence for a modest reduction in levels of 5-hydroxytryptamine (5-HT) and 5-HIAA in the brainstem of suicide victims. It is an open question as to whether serotonin and 5-HIAA are altered in the prefrontal cortex or other brain regions.

Consistent with these findings in the brainstem of suicide victims, lower cerebrospinal fluid (CSF) 5-HIAA has been reported by most studies in depressed patients, schizophrenics, or those with personality disorders with a history of a suicide attempt, compared to control groups with the same psychiatric diagnosis. The degree of medical damage sustained in either the most recent or most lethal past suicide attempt correlates inversely with CSF 5-HIAA. Future suicide and attempted suicide are associated with low CSF 5-HIAA. Thus, low CSF 5-HIAA predicts a higher rate of past and future suicidal acts, as well as the maximal seriousness of suicidal acts in the past lifetime of the individual. CSF 5-HIAA as an index of serotonergic activity is under significant genetic regulation and stable unless perturbed by medications or medical illness. Thus, serotonergic activity represents a mechanism whereby genes can influence behaviors such as suicide. We and others have reported that the lifetime history of impulsive behaviors, including externally directed aggression, is more severe in suicide attempters with major depression or schizophrenia compared to nonattempters matched for psychiatric diagnosis. As shown in Table 6.3, there have been at least twenty-two studies of CSF 5-HIAA and suicidal behavior in mood disorders. Some involve overlapping study populations. Overall, sixteen of the twenty-two studies find evidence for a relationship between lower levels of CSF 5-HIAA and suicidal behavior. The significance of this finding and that it is consistent with reports of reduced serotonin or 5-HIAA in the brainstem of suicide victims means that regardless of receptor changes, at least part of the pathology related to suicidal behavior is reduced serotonin turnover or serotonergic neuron activity.

A possible reason for some of the negative reports (see Table 6.3) may be the type of affective disorder included in the study population. Three of the five studies that did not find reduced CSF 5-HIAA levels had included a significant number with bipolar disorder (Roy-Byrne et al., 1983; Secunda et al., 1986; Vestergaard et al., 1978). Closer examination reveals that it is not clear whether

Table 6.3. CSF 5-HIAA and Suicidal Behavior in Major Depression.

Study	Findings
Åsberg, Träskman, and Thorén (1976)	Low CSF 5-HIAA predicted 22 percent suicide rate in one year
Åsberg, Thorén, Träskman, Bertilsson, and Ringberger (1976)	Less than 40 percent of attempters had low CSF 5-HIAA versus 15 percent of nonattempters
Vestergaard et al. (1978)	No difference
Ågren (1980)	Seriousness of intent of worst suicide attempt; negative correlation with CSF 5-HIAA in unipolar but not bipolar depression
Träskman, Åsberg, Bertilsson, and Sjöstrand (1981)	CSF 5-HIAA decreased in violent attempters and decreased in nonviolent attempters
Banki and Arató (1983)	Decreased in attempters; less than 37 percent in violent versus nonviolent attempters and violent attempters versus nonattempters
Palaniappan, Ramachandran, and Somasundaram (1983)	CSF 5-HIAA decreased in attempters
Roy-Byrne et al. (1983)	No difference
Ågren and Niklasson (1986)	CSF 5-HIAA less than 12 percent in attempters ($p = 0.07$)
Edman, Åsberg, Levander, and Schalling (1986)	CSF 5-HIAA decreased in attempters
Secunda et al. (1986)	No difference
van Praag (1986)	CSF 5-HIAA decreased (probenecid) in attempters
Peabody et al. (1987)	CSF 5-HIAA correlated with HAM-D
Nordin (1988)	No correlation with suicidal thoughts
Westenberg and Verhoeven (1988)	No difference
Jones et al. (1990)	CSF 5-HIAA decreased in attempters
Lopez-Ibor, Lana, and Saiz-Ruiz (1990)	Low CSF 5-HIAA group had more attempters
Roy et al. (1990)	CSF 5-HIAA 22 percent decreased in attempters versus nonattempters but nonsignificant
Nordström et al. (1994)	Low CSF 5-HIAA predicted future suicide
Mann et al. (1992)	Only high planned suicide attempts associated with lower CSF 5-HIAA
Mann et al. (1996)	Reduced in higher lethality attempters
Mann et al. (1996)	Negative correlation with most lethal lifetime attempt

bipolar disorder is associated with lower serotonergic activity in suicide attempters; whereas one study found lower CSF 5-HIAA levels in association with suicidal behavior in unipolar but not in bipolar depressed patients (Ågren, 1980), a second study, where the depressed study group comprised about 50 percent bipolar cases, did find reduced CSF 5-HIAA in the attempters (Banki and Arató, 1983). Clearly there are other reasons that may explain why not all suicide attempter patients have low CSF 5-HIAA. Moreover, disagreement is not limited to studies of depression because it also occurs in studies of schizophrenia, where about two-thirds of all studies find low CSF 5-HIAA in attempters.

The type of suicidal act may relate to low CSF 5-HIAA, the degree of impulsivity, or the degree of medical damage inflicted. We found that more lethal suicide attempts were associated with lower CSF 5-HIAA (Malone, Corbitt, Li, and Mann, 1996). We also found that more lethal attempts are more carefully planned (Mann and Malone, 1997). Planning and impulsivity are not mutually exclusive. The decision to act on a careful plan may be impulsive. Studies of externally directed aggression suggest that it is impulsive, and not planned or predatory, aggression that correlates with low CSF 5-HIAA (Lidberg, Tuck, Åsberg, Scalia Tomba, and Bertilsson, 1985; Linnoila et al., 1983; Virkkunen et al., 1989b; Virkkunen, De Jong, Bartko, and Linnoila, 1989a; Virkkunen, Nuutila, Goodwin, and Linnoila, 1987). On that basis, it may be presumed that impulsivity plays a role in suicide attempters; if so, impulsivity would be hypothesized to be negatively correlated with CSF 5-HIAA. We have found that suicide attempters have greater lifetime aggression and impulsivity compared to depressed suicide nonattempters (Mann, Waternaux, Haas, and Malone, 1998).

As with completed suicide (Arango and Mann, 1992), it has been hypothesized that the dimension of the suicidal behavior related to low CSF 5-HIAA is the degree of violence of the attempt as opposed to some other aspect of suicidal behavior, such as suicidal intent. However, this hypothesis is not supported by the data because only three of nine studies with available data report that violent suicide attempts are associated with lower levels of CSF 5-HIAA (see Table 6.1). Since availability of method is a major factor determining choice of suicide method (Marzuk et al., 1992b), selection of a violent method for suicide is probably not directly biologically determined, but instead is dependent on the degree of intent and the availability of a specific method.

Serotonin Receptors

The most studied serotonin receptor in suicidal behavior is the serotonin transporter (SERT). There have been at least eighteen published studies of SERT binding in suicide victims (see Table 6.4). Six of ten studies reported a decrease in imipramine binding in suicide victims. In contrast, a majority of the studies that used ligands other than imipramine, or used imipramine without using desipramine as the displacing agent, did not find a reduction in binding. Three studies, however, did find decreases in binding in suicide victims: Laruelle et al. (1993) used ^{3}H-paroxetine combined with clomipramine as a displacing agent; Lawrence et al. (1990a) found a decrease in ^{3}H-paroxetine binding in the putamen; and a study from our laboratory (Arango, Underwood, Gubbi, and Mann, 1995) examined ^{3}H-cyanoimipramine binding by autoradiography.

We have found that ^{3}H-paroxetine binds with comparable affinity to two high-affinity binding sites (Mann et al., 1996a). One site corresponds to the SERT, and the binding is sodium chloride dependent. Binding to the other site is sodium chloride independent, and that site appears to be a related but nontransporter presynaptic binding site. Binding to the sodium chloride–dependent SERT site was not reduced in homogenates from prefrontal cortex of suicide victims compared to controls. Interestingly, this transporter binding site is the same site as that displaced by citalopram, the competition drug used in the studies by Andersson, Eriksson, and Marcusson (1992) and Lawrence, De Paermentier, Cheetham, Crompton, Katona, and Horton (1990a, 1990b), who also found no change in SERT binding in prefrontal cortex in suicide victims. In contrast, the sodium-independent binding site, for which sertraline has lower affinity, was reduced in number in suicides compared to controls, indicating that this site may be the one that accounts for previous reports of reduced ^{3}H-imipramine binding. A recent report by Rosel et al. (1997) that ^{3}H-imipramine binding, but not ^{3}H-paroxetine binding, was reduced in the hypothalamus of suicide victims supports this conclusion. Reductions in apparent SERT binding in the dorsal PFC reported in earlier studies may in fact have involved a binding site other than the physiologically relevant transporter site. Nevertheless, this site may still be an index of serotonergic innervation, and if it is demonstrated to be such, it may be a guide to serotonin innervation.

Another factor to consider is the brain region being studied. Gross-Isseroff et al. (1989) and Ikeda, Noda, and Sugita (1989) found regions of unchanged, increased, and decreased ^{3}H-imipramine binding in suicide victims. A reduction in ^{3}H-cyanoimipramine binding to the SERT appears to be confined to ventrolateral prefrontal cortex. This suggests that the reduction in SERT binding appears to be localized to ventrolateral prefrontal cortex (PFC), whereas most previous studies have examined dorsal PFC. Reduced ^{3}H-imipramine binding in the dorsal prefrontal cortex of suicide victims may reflect fewer non-SERT sites. Studies of other brain regions are limited, but a critical area is the brainstem, where the dorsal and median raphe are located. A preliminary report indicates no change in brainstem SERT binding or messenger RNA (mRNA) (Little et al., 1997).

A major postsynaptic serotonin receptor is the 5-HT$_{2A}$ receptor. We initially reported a 44 percent increase in ^{3}H-spiroperidol binding to the postsynaptic 5-HT$_{2A}$ receptor as defined by mianserine in prefrontal cortex of suicide victims (Stanley and Mann, 1983). We subsequently replicated this finding in two further series of brains (Arango et al., 1990; Mann, Stanley, McBride, and McEwen, 1986). Arora and Meltzer (1989a), Laruelle et al. (1993), and Hrdina, Demeter,

Table 6.4. SERT-Binding Studies in Suicide Victims.

Study	Frontal Cortex	Other Regions
Meyerson et al. (1982)	Increase of 25%[a]	—
Stanley, Virgilio, and Gershon (1982)	Decrease of 44%[a]	—
Crow et al. (1984)	Decrease of 19%[a]	—
Paul, Rehavi, Skolnick, and Goodwin (1984)	—	Decrease of 30%[a]
Owen et al. (1986)	NC	NC
Arató, Tekes, Palkovits, Demeter, and Falus (1987)	Decrease of 48%[a]	NC
Arora and Meltzer (1989)	NC	—
Gross-Isseroff, Israeli, and Biegon (1989)	NC	Decrease,[a] Increase[a]
Lawrence et al. (1990a)	NC	NC, decrease[a]
Lawrence et al. (1990b)	NC	NC
Arató et al. (1991)	Decrease of 53%[a]	—
Arora and Meltzer (1991)	NC	—
Andersson, Eriksson, and Marcusson (1992)	NC	NC
Hrdina, Demeter, Vu, Sótónyi, and Palkovits (1993)	NC	NC
Joyce et al. (1993)	—	Decrease[a,c]
Laruelle et al. (1993)	Decrease of 31%[a]	NC
Arango, Underwood, Gubbi, and Mann (1995)	Decrease of 10–20%	—
Mann et al. (1996)	Decrease[b]	NC
Little et al. (1997)	NC	NC
Rosel et al. (1997)	NC	Decrease

Note: NC = No change was detected between groups.

[a]Indicates a statistically significant difference.

[b]Decrease only due to non-SERT site.

[c]Temporal and entorhinal cortex.

Vu, Sótónyi, and Palkovits (1993) also replicated this finding using different ligands. Seven published studies have reported no alteration in 5-HT$_{2A}$ binding (Arranz, Eriksson, Mellerup, Plenge, and Marcusson, 1994; Cheetham, Crompton, Katona, and Horton, 1988; Crow et al., 1984; Gross-Isseroff, Salama, Israeli, and Biegon, 1990; Lowther, De Paermentier, Crompton, Katona, and Horton, 1994; Owen et al., 1986; Owen et al., 1983), but three of these studies came from a single research group.

Laruelle et al. (1993) and Hrdina, Demeter, Vu, Sótónyi, and Palkovits (1993) used the more selective ligand, ^{3}H-ketanserin, and found increased binding in suicide victims. The degree of difference between the suicides and the controls appears to be greater in prefrontal cortex than in temporal cortex (Arango et al., 1990), suggesting regional differences in the suicide effect. Further work is needed to map the distribution of change in 5-HT$_{2A}$ receptors in suicide victims throughout the prefrontal cortex as well as in other cortical brain regions.

The six studies that found an increase in 5-HT$_{2A}$ receptor binding in suicide victims had a higher proportion of subjects' committing suicide using violent methods than the studies that did not find an increase in 5-HT$_{2A}$ receptor binding. Yates et al. (1990) reported lower levels of 5-HT$_{2A}$ receptor binding sites in depressed subjects who had recently been treated with antidepressants. Therefore, it is conceivable that those depressed subjects who took neuroleptics or antidepressants antemortem may have undergone downregulation of 5-HT$_{2A}$ receptors, and such an effect would potentially obscure or reverse the upregulation related to suicide. The presence or absence of a depressive illness may also be relevant. Yates et al. (1990) found an increase in 5-HT$_{2A}$ receptor number in depressed patients who died of causes other than suicide. Therefore, an increase in 5-HT$_{2A}$ receptor number may be associated with the presence of a depressive illness independent of suicide risk.

Another major cortical postsynaptic SERT is the 5-HT$_{1A}$ receptor. There have been at least six published studies of 5-HT$_{1A}$ receptors in suicide victims (see Table 6.5). Two studies reported an increase in 5-HT$_{1A}$ binding in suicide victims (Arango, Underwood, Gubbi, and Mann, 1995; Joyce et al., 1993), and four did not (Cheetham, Crompton, Katona, and Horton, 1990; Dillon, Gross-Isseroff, Israeli, and Biegon, 1991; Matsubara, Arora, and Meltzer, 1991; Stockmeier et al., 1997). Arango, Underwood, Gubbi, and Mann (1995), and Joyce et al. (1993) found the increase in 5-HT$_{1A}$ binding to be confined to discrete brain regions. Corticosteroids can mediate stress effects via mineralocorticoid receptors (MR) and glucocorticoid receptors (GR) on 5-HT$_{1A}$ receptors in the hippocampus (López, Chalmers, Little, and Watson, 1998). Stress results elevated glucocorticoid levels and downregulation of hippocampal 5-HT$_{1A}$ receptors in rodents. Suicide victims have lower levels of MR and 5-HT$_{1A}$ mRNA in hippocampus, effects consistent with stress (López, Chalmers, Little, and Watson, 1998). Therefore, techniques such as autoradiography, which can identify regional differences, are more likely to show 5-HT$_{1A}$ receptor binding changes that are highly localized.

Other receptor subtypes have barely begun to be investigated, and few studies are published of 5-HT$_{1B,}$ 5-HT$_{2C,}$ and 5-HT$_{1D}$ (Arranz, Eriksson, Mellerup, Plenge, and Marcusson, 1994) receptors in suicide victims. Lowther, Katona, Crompton, and Horton (1997) reported an increase in 5-HT$_{1D}$ binding in globus pallidus but not in putamen, parietal, or prefrontal cortex of violent suicide victims. Overall, the preponderance of data suggests that there are alterations in the serotonin system in suicide, and the use of techniques such as autoradiography coupled with gene expression studies will help to clarify the range and extent of the receptor and transmitter changes, as well as identifying where in the brain these changes are most pronounced.

Table 6.5. 5-HT$_{1A}$ Receptor Binding in Suicide.

Study	Prefrontal Cortex	Other Regions
Cheetham, Crompton, Katona, and Horton (1990)[a]	NC	NC, decrease
Dillon, Gross-Isseroff, Israeli, and Biegon (1991)	NC	NC
Matsubara, Arora, and Meltzer (1991)	NC	—
Joyce et al. (1993)	—	Increase[b,c]
Arranz, Eriksson, Mellerup, Plenge, and Marcusson (1994)	NC	NC
Arango, Underwood, Gubbi, and Mann (1995)	Increase of 28 percent	NC
Stockmeier et al. (1997)	—	NC

Note: NC = No change was detected between groups.

[a]Only depressed suicides were included in the study.

[b]Indicates a statistically significant difference.

[c]Temporal and entorhinal cortex.

Neuroendocrine Studies of the Serotonergic System in Suicide Attempters

The most common method of study of the serotonergic system in suicide attempters using the neuroendocrine technique is to measure the prolactin response to fenfluramine, which causes the release of serotonin and inhibits its reuptake. There are at least sixteen published studies of the effects of fenfluramine challenges on prolactin or cortisol in depressed and personality-disordered patients (see Table 6.6; see also Asnis et al., 1988; Coccaro et al., 1989; Kasper, Vieira, Schmidt, and Richter, 1990; Lichtenberg et al., 1992; Lopez-Ibor, Lana, and Saiz-Ruiz, 1990; Lopez-Ibor, Saiz-Ruiz, and Iglesias, 1988; Maes, Jacobs, Suy, Minner, and Raus, 1989; Mitchell and Smythe, 1990; Mitchell et al., 1990; Muhlbauer and Müller-Oerlinghausen, 1985; O'Keane and Dinan, 1991; Siever, Murphy, Slater, de la Vega, and Lipper, 1984; Targum, 1990; Weizman et al., 1988). Seven out of fourteen studies found a blunted prolactin response to fenfluramine in major depression (see Table 6.6). Three out of four studies found a blunted prolactin response in association with a history of a suicide attempt. Most studies (ten out of fourteen) lack a placebo control. A placebo challenge can determine whether differential stress responses distinguish the groups or if depression is associated with a reduction in dopaminergic activity, hypothesized to be present in major depression (Kapur and Mann, 1992).

Table 6.6. The Fenfluramine Challenge Test in Depressed and Suicidal Patients.

Study	Findings
Siever, Murphy, Slater, de la Vega, and Lipper (1984)	PRL decreased in major depression
Muhlbauer and Muller-Oerlinghausen (1985)	Cortisol responses were unaltered in untreated depressed patients
Asnis et al. (1988)	No difference
Lopez-Ibor, Saiz-Ruiz, and Iglesias (1988)	PRL response correlated with subtype of depression or suicidal behavior
Weizman, Mark, Gil-Ad, Tyano, and Laron (1988)	No difference
Coccaro et al. (1989)	PRL decreased in patients with major depression and in suicide attempters
Maes, Jacobs, Suy, Minner, and Raus (1989)	PRL increased in major versus minor depression
Kasper, Vieira, Schmidt, and Richter (1990)	PRL before treatment correlates with PRL after treatment
Lopez-Ibor, Lana, and Saiz-Ruiz (1990)	PRL and cortisol decreased in comparison with controls
Mitchell and Smythe (1990)	PRL decreased in melancholia
Targum (1990)	PRL increased in personality disorders with or without major depression
O'Keane and Dinan (1991)	PRL decreased in comparison with controls (no correlation with severity of depression but with anxiety)
Lichtenberg et al. (1992)	
Mann, McBride, Malone, DeMeo, and Keilp (1995)	PRL decreased in major depression and in suicide attempters
Malone, Corbitt, Li, and Mann (1996)	PRL decreased in more lethal attempters

Note: PRL = prolactin.

Lopez-Ibor, Saiz-Ruiz, and Iglesias (1988) and Coccaro et al. (1989) found a blunted prolactin response in patients with a personality disorder characterized by suicidal acts, but not in major depression, compared to similar patients without a history of suicide attempts. These results are consistent with our findings (Mann et al., 1995) in the sense that we found that 78 percent of the younger depression cases with a blunted prolactin response had comorbid borderline personality disorders, compared to only 29 percent of the older group (p = 0.0375). O'Keane et al. (1992) found blunted prolactin responses compared to placebo in antisocial personality disorder. We found that a blunted prolactin response was associated with a past suicide attempt, comorbid borderline personality disorder, and lifetime aggressive behavior. These effects are partially additive.

Studies using serotonergically mediated neuroendocrine responses to other agents have generated results that support the indoleamine deficiency hypothesis of depression, but there are virtually no studies of suicidal behavior. A diminished prolactin response to intravenous tryptophan is found in depressed patients compared to matched controls (Cowen, McCance, Gelder, and Grahame-Smith, 1990; Deakin, Pennell, Upadhyaya, and Lofthouse, 1990; Heninger, Charney, and Sternberg, 1984; Koyama, Lowy, and Meltzer, 1987; Price, Charney, Delgado, and Heninger, 1991). In 1991, Upadhyaya, Pennell, Cowen, and Deakin found a blunted growth hormone and prolactin to tryptophan in depression. Intravenous clomipramine generates a blunted prolactin response in depressed patients (Anderson, Ware, Da Roza Davis, and Cowen, 1992; Golden et al., 1992). Increased cortisol responses to 5-hydroxytryptophan in depressed and manic patients have been attributed to increased serotonin receptor sensitivity (Meltzer, Perline, Tricou, Lowy, and Robertson, 1984). Studies of the 5-HT$_{1A}$ receptor in depressed patients have generated conflicting results (Cowen, Power, Ware, and Anderson, 1994; Lesch, 1991; Meltzer and Maes, 1994). Pitchot et al. (1995) used the 5-HT$_{1A}$ drug flesinoxan and found differences in responses in suicide attempters.

There is evidence that the fenfluramine-stimulated increase in prolactin levels appears to be primarily mediated by serotonin rather than other neurotransmitter systems (Coccaro, Kavoussi, and Hauger, 1993; Fuller, Snoddy, and Robertson, 1988; Mann et al., 1992; Meyendorff, Jain, Träskman-Bendz, Stanley, and Stanley, 1986). However, differential levels of endogenous dopaminergic activity may potentially modulate prolactin responses to fenfluramine. Since decreased dopaminergic activity has been associated with depression (Kapur and Mann, 1992), such a change may be associated with elevated prolactin levels. We found no evidence of elevated prolactin levels during the placebo day in the depressed patients, suggesting that endogenous dopaminergic tonic regulation of prolactin release in depressed patients did not differ from the healthy controls.

No difference in prolactin responses to thyroid releasing hormone has been found in depressed patients (Anderson, Ware, Da Roza Davis, and Cowen, 1992; Golden et al., 1992; Heninger, Charney, and Sternberg, 1984; Kjellman, Ljunggren,

Beck-Friis, and Wetterberg, 1983) indicating that lactotroph function is not compromised in depression and does not explain the blunted prolactin response to fenfluramine.

THE NORADRENERGIC SYSTEM IN SUICIDE VICTIMS AND ATTEMPTERS

Along with compromised serotonergic function in suicidal behavior, a growing body of evidence has accumulated implicating altered brain noradrenergic transmission. Postmortem studies performed to date have sought to examine the noradrenergic system in the brain by measuring the concentration of norepinephrine (NE) or its metabolites in brain tissue, morphometric studies of noradrenergic neurons, measurement of tyrosine hydroxylase (the rate-limiting enzyme for NE synthesis), and assaying NE receptor subtypes. Each measure addresses a different aspect of noradrenergic function and has its own advantages and limitations, particularly in human postmortem brain. By and large, studies of suicide attempters are consistent with postmortem findings. From these varied approaches, despite methodological differences and technical limitations, a picture of altered noradrenergic neurotransmission in suicide is starting to emerge.

Alterations in noradrenergic neurotransmission in suicide are suggested based on a variety of findings, including changes in neurotransmitter indexes in postmortem brain tissue (Table 6.7) and comparable findings in vivo. Noradrenergic innervation of the mammalian cerebral cortex is derived nearly exclusively from pigmented neurons of the locus ceruleus (LC) (Dahlström and Fuxe, 1964; Freedman, Foote, and Bloom, 1975; Jones and Moore, 1977; Levitt and Moore, 1978; Porrino and Goldman-Rakic, 1982). Much like the serotonergic neurons of the dorsal raphe nuclei, these noradrenergic neurons provide widespread innervation throughout the neuraxis, including the limbic system.

We found fewer 23 percent noradrenergic LC neurons in the brain of completed suicides (Arango, Underwood, and Mann, 1996). Widdowson, Ordway, and Halaris (1992) reported less neuropeptide Y in the LC of suicide victims. Klimek

Table 6.7. Neurobiology of the Noradrenergic System in Suicide at the Synaptic Level.

Presynaptic	Postsynaptic
NE decreased	NE increased
NET decreased	α_1 decreased
α_2 decreased	α_2 decreased
Tyrosine hydroxylase increased	β_1 decreased
Cell number decreased	

Note: NE = norepinephrine; NET = norepinephrine transporter et al. (1997) found fewer NE transporter sites in the LC. Ordway, Widdowson, Smith, and Halaris (1994) reported increased binding to α_2-adrenergic receptors and increased tyrosine hydroxylase protein (Ordway, Smith, and Haycock, 1994) in the LC of suicide victims, but no difference between groups in the number of LC neurons (Ordway, Smith, and Haycock, 1994) and reduced concentration of NE in the LC (Ordway, Widdowson, Smith, and Halaris, 1994). The latter two observations are consistent with animal studies of stress-induced reductions in NE levels in the LC due to release and compensatory increases in tyrosine hydroxylase activity. Our finding of fewer noradrenergic neurons may reflect reduced functional reserve and a greater susceptibility to depletion of NE by stress-induced release. Arango, Ernsberger, Sved, and Mann (1993) and Manchon et al. (1987) found increased NE in cortex and hippocampus, respectively. A stress effect on 5-HT_{1A} receptors in hippocampus reported in rats also resembles findings in suicide victims (López, Chalmers, Little, and Watson, 1998).

Evidence from neurotransmitter or metabolite concentrations in the CSF is less convincing, with only a minority (Ågren, 1980, 1982) of studies finding reduced concentrations of the norepinephrine metabolite 3-methoxy, 4-hydroxyphenyl glycol (MHPG) in suicide attempters (Brown et al., 1982; Pickar et al., 1986; Roy et al., 1985; Roy, Pickar, De Jong, Karoum, and Linnoila, 1989; Secunda et al., 1986; Träskman, Åsberg, Bertilsson, and Sjöstrand, 1981). Reduced urinary excretion of the metabolite MHPG in suicide attempters provides some further indirect evidence (Ågren, 1980, 1982). Increased binding to β-adrenergic receptors in the cerebral cortex in suicide victims compared to controls has been reported by some investigators (Arango et al., 1990; Biegon and Israeli, 1988; Mann, Stanley, McBride, and McEwen, 1986) but not by others (De Paermentier, Cheetham, Crompton, Katona, and Horton, 1990; Little, Clark, Ranc, and Duncan, 1993; Stockmeier and Meltzer, 1991). α_1-adrenergic and/or α_2-adrenergic receptor binding in suicide victims in cerebral cortex have been reported to be increased (Arango, Ernsberger, Sved, and Mann, 1993; Callado et al., 1998; González et al., 1994; Meana and García-Sevilla, 1987) or decreased (Gross-Isseroff, Dillon, Fieldust, and Biegon, 1990). These receptor changes are difficult to interpret. Taken together, these studies suggest that altered noradrenergic neurotransmission is associated with suicidal behavior.

OTHER NEUROCHEMICAL FINDINGS IN SUICIDE

Cholinergic receptor binding (^{3}H-ZNB) appears unaltered (Stanley, 1984). μ-Opioid receptor binding appears increased in PFC and caudate but not thalamus (Gabilondo, Meana, and García-Sevilla, 1995). Corticotropin binding to PFC is reduced (Nemeroff, Owens, Bissette, Andorn, and Stanley, 1988). $GABA_B$ sites in the prefrontal cortex, temporal cortex, and hippocampus are reported to be unchanged (Cross, Cheetham, Crompton, Katona, and Horton, 1988), whereas benzodiazepine binding is increased in suicides (Manchon et al., 1987). We reported no change in the NMDA receptor (Palmer, Burns, Arango, and Mann, 1994), but Nowak, Ordway, and Paul (1995) found altered NMDA binding in the prefrontal cortex, as indicated by a decrease in high-affinity ^{3}H-CGP-39653 binding.

Several studies have evaluated postreceptor indexes, such as G-proteins and signal transducers. Cowburn, Marcusson, Eriksson, Wiehager, and O'Neill (1994) reported lower basal, GTPγS, and forskolin-stimulated adenylyl cyclase activity in the PRF of suicide victims. Levels of $G_{s\alpha\text{-}s}$ were reduced, whereas $G_{s\alpha}$ and $G_{i\alpha}$ were not different in suicides. Pacheco et al. (1996) reported GTPγS stimulation of PI hydrolysis to be reduced by 30 percent in suicides, and levels of $G_{\alpha12}$ were increased 21 percent in PFC. Pandey et al. (1997) found reduced protein kinase C binding of ^{3}H-phorbol dibutyrate in prefrontal cortex of teenage suicides. It appears that G-protein coupling and signal transduction are impaired, though it remains to be determined if this involves only selected receptors.

IMPLICATIONS FOR THE CLINICIAN

Although opiate, GABA, and other systems have been studied, the data are too few to formulate any conclusions, so interested readers are encouraged to monitor the emerging literature.

Reduced serotonergic and noradrenergic function in the brains of suicide victims is suggested (see Tables 6.1 and 6.7). Complementary findings have been made in the serotonergic system of suicide attempters and completers. Studies of the noradrenergic system of suicide attempters have generated inconsistent findings, partly reflected in the lack of indexes of brain noradrenergic activity in vivo.

Most postmortem studies have focused on the prefrontal cortex because of its hypothesized role in behavioral restraint. It is in the prefrontal cortex that there is the greatest consensus regarding receptor binding changes in suicide victims. With respect to the serotonergic system, postsynaptic serotonin 5-HT$_{2A}$ and 5-HT$_{1A}$ receptors may be increased, and the SERT binding (or to a related binding site) is decreased. 5-HT$_{2C}$ sites are present only in very low concentrations in prefrontal cortex and are more abundant, but appear unaltered, in the hippocampus of suicide victims. Since 5-HT$_{2A}$ and 5-HT$_{1A}$ receptors are located predominantly on cortical neurons and the SERT is located on the presynaptic axon terminal of serotonergic neurons that innervate the cortex, the most parsimonious conclusion is that there is reduced serotonergic innervation and a consequent upregulation of postsynaptic receptor sites in suicide victims. However, lesion studies in rodents have largely failed to demonstrate such upregulation, so the precise mechanism in suicide victims is unclear. In the brainstem of suicides, serotonin and 5-HIAA levels appear to be lower. It remains to be determined whether this reduction is because of fewer serotonin-synthesizing neurons in the dorsal and median raphe or whether there is reduced capacity for serotonin synthesis.

The ventral PFC is involved in mediating inhibition. Injuries to this brain region can result in behavioral disinhibition. If the preliminary suggestion that serotonergic input to the ventral PFC is compromised is correct, then it may explain why it plays a role in inhibition of behaviors such as suicidal and aggressive acts.

The picture for norepinephrine is less clear than for serotonin (see Table 6.7). In the cerebral cortex, α_1-, α_2-, and β-adrenergic receptors, although there is not complete agreement, appear to be altered. In the brainstem, NE and MHPG concentrations seem to be reduced, there are fewer pigmented noradrenergic neurons, and activity of the NE biosynthetic enzyme tyrosine hydroxylase is increased. The conclusion that best fits the bulk of the findings is that there is a period of noradrenergic overactivity prior to suicide, and this, together with fewer noradrenergic neurons in the LC, results in NE depletion and a compensatory increase in synthesis. This noradrenergic overactivity may have been a stress response and therefore state dependent. In contrast, serotonergic activity is generally relatively stable or traitlike and under considerable genetic control. Therefore, there may be a serotonergic trait marker that will identify the person at risk for suicide. Identification of the brain systems most affected, or predictive, of suicide may then provide the opportunity for effective pharmacological intervention. Much remains to be learned through further systematic postmortem neurochemical studies of tissue from individuals where clinical information is available and in vivo studies of high-risk patients.

CHAPTER SEVEN

Profiles of Completed Suicides

Jan Fawcett, M.D.

Suicide is the ninth leading cause of death in the United States. Only about half of the 30,000 suicides that occur annually were in treatment at the time of suicide or had seen a mental health professional at some time prior to suicide (Fawcett, Clark, and Scheftner, 1991). Although there are standard clinical correlates of suicide established in the literature, these correlates are based on uncontrolled, retrospective studies (Robins et al., 1959b; Dorpat and Ripley, 1960; Barraclough et al., 1974). Uncontrolled studies, though they may highlight behavior features common to patients who committed suicide, do not compare the frequency of these behaviors with depressed patients who did not commit suicide, and therefore do not indicate whether the correlate behavioral features noted in patients who committed suicide are common to depression or specifically to suicide. Moreover, the classic retrospective studies do not address the question of whether specific correlates of suicide (for example, suicidal ideation) are associated with imminent suicide or suicide a year or more later. Whether a putative correlate of suicide is a warning sign of acute risk or chronic risk is important clinically in terms of decisions as to what clinical interventions to initiate in a specific clinical situation.

This chapter reviews studies of suicide that suggest both time-related correlates and common "clinical profiles" of patients who committed suicide. These data are summarized from the National Institute of Mental Health (NIMH) Collaborative Program on the Psychobiology of Depression of thirty-four suicides occurring over ten years of follow-up in a sample of 954 patients with major affective disorders, a review of fourteen records of inpatients who committed suicide, and a review of thirty records of outpatient suicides who were in active treatment at the time of their suicide (Fawcett et al., 1987).

In the NIMH collaborative program, clinical correlates of suicide within a year of clinical assessment, and those associated with suicide over a period of one to ten years after assessment, were determined by statistical comparisons with the symptom severity of these correlates in the majority of depressed patients who survived. This chapter analyzes the separate inpatient and outpatient sample of suicide records mentioned above and discusses them as a partial replication of findings of the prospective NIMH collaborative study and a source of common clinical profiles of suicide.

ACUTE VERSUS CHRONIC SUICIDE CORRELATES

The NIMH Collaborative Study of Depression is a long-term follow-up study of the outcome of 954 patients entered in a naturalistic long-term outcome sample from 1978 to 1982 and followed every six months for the first five years and yearly thereafter. The follow-up is still occurring and is in its twentieth year. Over 80 percent of patients enrolled in the study were inpatients and all suffered from major affective disorders, including major depression, bipolar disorder (type I and II), and schizoaffective disorder as diagnosed by Research Diagnostic Criteria from the Schedule for Affective Disorders and Schizophrenia (SADS) by trained and certified clinical interviewers. Treatment was not administered or controlled but recorded on follow-up interviews. Thirteen suicides had occurred in the sample by the first year, twenty-five by the fifth year, and thirty-four by the tenth year of follow-up. The first, most obvious finding was the high rate of suicide in the six months ($n = 8$) to year ($n = 13$) after discharge from the hospital compared to high subsequent years of follow-up, thus suggesting a very high risk of suicide in the six months to year after hospital discharge.

A major new finding of the NIMH collaborative study was the association of severe anxiety symptoms (severe psychic anxiety, such as worry and fear, and panic attacks) that statistically significantly differentiated patients who committed suicide within one year of assessment from the majority of depressed patients who survived the one-year follow-up period (Fawcett et al., 1990). This outcome was particularly striking in the context that "standard risk factors" such as expressed suicidal ideation or intent and prior suicide attempts were not associated with suicide within one year of assessment, but were associated with suicide between two to five years of follow-up. These "standard suicide risk factors" determined from retrospective studies of suicide were thus associated with a chronic high risk of suicide but not an acute high risk in this prospective study.

These findings agree somewhat with the clinical observations of Shneidman, who describes "perturbation" as a precursor of suicide and not related to clinical depression (see Chapter Five), but to frustrated psychological needs per se. A number of studies have shown that the frequency of moderate-severe anxiety symptoms in depression is about 65 to 70 percent—even though anxiety is not considered a criterion symptom for the diagnosis (Fawcett and Kravitz, 1983). Several studies have found that treatment outcomes in patients with depression with significant comorbid anxiety and comorbid anxiety disorder diagnoses (panic disorder, obsessive-compulsive disorder) are relatively poor and require more intensive or complex pharmacological treatments (Clayton et al., 1991).

Since anxiety is a common comorbid symptom, the crucial question becomes at which point does the anxiety become severe enough to become a suicide risk indicator for a specific patient. Such clinical quantification is difficult across individual patients, and like so many clinical assessments, it probably varies from patient to patient. However, this finding points to the importance of assessing and monitoring the presence and severity of anxiety symptoms as experienced by the patient as a useful risk indicator of immediate suicide. A further discussion of the severity and types of anxiety associated with suicide in these studies follows. The rating criteria for the severity of anxiety (and other symptoms) used in training calibrating clinical raters via the SADS emphasized the patient's experience of the severity of the anxiety, as well as the proportion of the patient's day consumed by the symptom. Examples of anxiety preceding suicide are given in the clinical profiles of suicide to follow.

Inpatient records of patients who complete suicide while in the hospital are a source of prospective studies of suicide, since the inpatient staff of psychiatrists, nurses, social workers, and occupational therapists record patient behaviors prior to a suicide without anticipating the outcome of finding the patient dead from (almost always unexpected) suicide. We initially reported a study of fourteen inpatient suicide records, and have expanded the number of records to seventy-six from all across the United States (Busch et al., 1993). In our pilot study, we found that although 65 percent of patients who subsequently committed suicide denied suicidal intent as their last recorded communication, 86 percent of this group were rated to have severe anxiety/agitation associated with depression in the week prior to their suicide (Busch et al., 1993). This finding tends to replicate the initial finding of the NIMH collaborative study concerning severe anxiety symptoms as acute risk factors for suicide. As shown in the clinical profiles further on, the severity of anxiety/agitation is usually more severe and obvious in inpatients, though it is often overlooked, whereas evidence in outpatients is generally more subtle, possibly because there is less day-to-day surveillance and the patient's clinical state is filtered and attenuated by what the patient presents to the psychiatrist or therapist, which is then documented in a clinical record available for study.

There is no single pathway to suicide. We have reviewed evidence that suggests that there are several.

Anxiety or Agitation

The clinical interpretation of anxiety, based on an individual patient's description, is that anxiety is a psychic form of pain (all pain is assigned a level of severity by the brain). Unremitting pain in the presence of depression, which also carries with it hopelessness and anhedonia as core symptoms, means that a patient suffering the "psychic pain" of severe depression-related anxiety also believes the pain they feel will not remit. This is analogous to a person being held captive and being tortured every day with no hope of escape. Suicide may seem a "rational" consideration at this point. Of course the hopelessness concerning recovery during a depression may lead to similar assumptions even though depression is usually reversible with the right treatment for the individual patient.

Low Brain Serotonin Function and Low Serum Cholesterol

Other putative pathways to suicide have been posited based on research into suicide. In 1976, Åsberg, Träskman, and Thorén showed that young patients with depression that had measured decreased amounts of the final metabolite of serotonin (5HT), 5 hydroxy-indole-acetic acid (5HIAA), compared to normal levels, had a high rate of death by violent suicide on follow-up (Åsberg, Träskman, and Thorén, 1976). Subsequent replication studies have tended to confirm a relationship between low 5HIAA levels and impulsive, aggressive, and sometimes violent suicidal behavior in patients with depression in addition to this feature associated with impulsive behavior (see Chapter Six for a complete review of this topic). A vulnerability to act impulsively under pressure or in the presence of depression may constitute another pathway to suicide. Recently, a number of studies have suggested that individuals with low-fat diets, cholesterol-lowering medication, and low serum cholesterol levels may be prone to impulsive behavior, violent behavior, and death by violence, accidents, and suicide (Muldoon et al., 1990, 1993). A study of the effects of low-fat diets sustained over six months in chimpanzees showed violent fighting behaviors after five months (Muldoon et al., 1992; J. R. Kaplan et al., 1994). When cerebrospinal fluid from these animals was analyzed, low 5HIAA levels were found, thus indicating a decreased turnover of serotonin in the brain.

A number of studies have shown correlations of suicidal behavior with low serum cholesterol levels. We have studied cholesterol levels measured in forty-nine patients who committed suicide while inpatients. Their serum cholesterol levels were significantly lower than two community samples and a sample of depressed psychiatric inpatients (Glueck et al., 1994). Murphy has reported that depressed alcoholic patients have a high frequency of suicide within six months of a major interpersonal loss (Murphy et al., 1979). Many alcohol-abusing patients show profiles of impulsive, sometimes violent, behavior. There may be an overlap of these biological and behavioral traits that results in increased suicide risk in vulnerable patients under certain circumstances such as an interpersonal loss.

Based on experience reviewing the cases of suicide in the samples described above, several scenarios seem to present. Although these may be only a portion of common scenarios, they seem repetitive enough in the three samples studied to be described as profiles of suicide.

CLINICAL PROFILES OF SUICIDE

These examples are presented in the hope that they may aid in the recognition of patients at risk of immediate suicide, but not with any claim that they encompass even the majority of scenarios leading to suicide. Each of the following profiles represents a composite of three or more cases.

Profile One: Agitation, Severe Anxiety, Associated with Psychosis in an Inpatient

A thirty-seven-year-old white male was admitted because of recurrent panic attacks, which continued to worsen despite outpatient treatment, including medication and psychotherapy. The patient expressed hopelessness but denied suicidal intent stating, "I would be afraid to do such a thing. . . . It would be against my religion." The patient would pace up and down the hallways, relating little to other patients and looking preoccupied. At night he would be up frequently, sometimes complaining of chest pain. EKG and cardiac workup were negative. It was noted that although he expressed relief after receiving alprazolam, 1.0 mg, that he would also often calm down if talked to by the nurse. He seemed very motivated for and accepting of help from the staff. After he expressed fear of seeing a stranger in the nursing station with a large knife, antipsychotic medications were added to the antidepressant medications he was given. The patient's complaints persisted and he was allowed to pace the hall when he could not sleep. One night, on his seventh day of admission, he thanked the nurse and said he was feeling better and would try to sleep. Ten minutes later, the patient was found hanging by a sheet thrown over his bathroom door and tied around his neck.

This patient had sustained severe anxiety, panic attacks, and agitation, which required aggressive treatment. There is also clear evidence of psychosis in his fearful visual hallucinations that he reported to staff. He became more agitated, anxious, and psychotic as his condition persisted, inadequately treated.

Profile Two: Partial Response with Recurrent Symptoms of Anxiety and Undiagnosed Depression

A police officer was seen by his primary care physician for recurrent anxiety related to his concern that he had endangered his career by violating a regulation. He gave a history of increasing financial anxieties over the past year. During that time he had received several commendations, but never felt he was doing well enough. He had stopped pursuing his hobby of bowling with fellow officers about six months before, but continued to teach a Sunday school class for high school–aged boys. He was treated with psychotherapy and antidepressant medications. He initially reported feeling improvement, but every six to eight weeks he would complain of negative ruminations about whether he was doing his job well enough and raise questions about whether he had the right "makeup" to be a good police officer. He denied suicidal ideation, saying it would be an "unpardonable sin" and "against the Bible." The antidepressant would be changed and he would be given prn alprazolam with relief, but stop taking it in a week or two. His wife called expressing concern about his waking at night with fears that he would lose his job. Recently he expressed concern that he had violated a police regulation, and wondered whether he could be criminally prosecuted for this. He most recently stated that he was worried "a lot" about the future of his job.

His medications were changed and it was noted that he was again bothered by "obsessive negative thoughts and worries," despite evidence that he was highly respected by his peers and his captain. He was found slumped over in his police cruiser, having shot himself in the head. He had written a lesson for his next Sunday School meeting. The theme was "If you've lost Jesus in your life, you've ended your life."

This patient, while functioning responsibly and at a high level, had intermittent improvement, only to be plagued by recurrent anxious and guilty ruminations. Prior to his suicide, he developed a depressive delusion of thinking he had violated a police regulation. This concern grew to the point of his fearing he had violated the law, thus suggesting he had become delusional. This was not detected based on the treatment records, but is often difficult to discern in high-functioning individuals. The patient became increasingly suicidal as his depression recurred with increasingly intense anxiety symptoms. More aggressive treatment of his depression and anxiety, combined with addressing the delusional symptoms, might have averted a suicide.

Profile Three: Suicidal Acting Out in Borderline Disorder, Associated with Anxiety and Anticipated Loss

This scenario generally involves a young woman with a history of rejection sensitivity, inability to tolerate being alone, difficulty in relationships, and a history of angry outbursts and, not uncommonly, prior suicide gestures, often dramatic in type. The diagnosis is usually borderline features or disorder, and depression.

The patient, a twenty-three-year-old secretary, sought treatment for depression with anxiety. She was unhappy with her job and her relationships. She didn't like her job and, particularly, had trouble with her supervisor, having tried on one occasion to complain to the managing partner of the law firm over her supervisor's head. Her boyfriend was described as insensitive. She initially did well until one day she came to her appointment with an obvious abrasion on her neck. When questioned she said her boyfriend was late and she choked herself to deal with the pain of rejection. She admitted she had cut her arm or wrist in the past. Hospitalization was discussed, but the patient pointed out that she was "OK" now, and she felt more understood by her boyfriend. Subsequently, the patient appeared with a crease on her neck, saying she had become fearful she would be fired after a disagreement with her supervisor and had gone home and wrapped the phone cord around her neck. She said she did not intend suicide, but felt relief of her anxiety. Since she had not been fired, she felt better now. She did complain of depression over her boyfriend's apparent lack of interest in her. She asked for a refill of a headache medication that contained a small amount of barbiturates. She had used up her one-month supply in several days. She was told this medication could not be safely taken in such large quantities and could not be refilled. The patient reacted violently, accusing the psychiatrist of not being understanding and treating her just as her boyfriend and supervisor had. The patient stormed out of the office, inconsolable, convinced that the psychiatrist intended to drop her. When the patient did not make her next appointment, calls were made, with the resulting news that the patient had been found by her parents at home, dead, asphyxiated with a phone cord around her neck.

It is difficult to know whether suicide was the intent in this case. The patient, with depressive features, had moved from self-cutting to self-asphyxiation as a manner of coping with feelings of rejection and fears of abandonment. This patient seemed also to be dealing with anxiety, but this was experienced by the patient as a disintegration. Cutting or self-asphyxiation seemed a relief mechanism. Treatment with a low dose of antipsychotic medication, perhaps one of the atypical antipsychotics such as resperidone or olanzepine, may relieve this reaction and decrease the need for such dangerous and ineffective behaviors.

Profile Four: Interpersonal Loss in Depression, Associated with a History of Drug or Alcohol Abuse and Impulsive Behavior

A mathematics professor in his late thirties had a history of binge drinking. His marriage deteriorated, especially after it became clear to his wife that he was having an affair with a graduate student. She separated from him. Subsequently he was given psychiatric care after being admitted to an emergency room with an overdose of antidepressants prescribed by his primary care physician. He had called his wife while drunk, telling her of the overdose. She had driven him to the emergency room when he refused any other manner of help. She refused his pleading that she move back home but agreed to joint counseling. He continued to threaten both suicide and violence in vague terms if she would not agree to reestablish their marital relationship. His depression improved over several months and he seemed capable of less intimidation, helped by his suspension of bingeing with alcohol. During the separation, his wife met another man and asked for a divorce. The patient seemed to handle this well, though he managed to keep in touch through various pretexts often related to shared property that had to be sold. One year after the divorce was final, she told her ex-husband that she was getting married. He became depressed but assured his psychiatrist he could handle it. He called his ex-wife congratulating her but conveyed depression. She asked some mutual friends to check on him. He thanked them, stating he was fine. He did not show up for class the next morning and was found at home dead from a self-inflicted gunshot wound.

These cases are particularly difficult. It is difficult to ascertain just when the patient feels the separation has occurred. For the professor in Profile Four, it was not the divorce proceeding but his ex-wife's remarriage that he experienced as the final separation. Such patients often show periods of improvement, and function well, only to relapse rapidly with depression in the face of ultimate separation. Very close follow-up may help to detect the changes and respond, but these patients often do not cooperate with frequent follow-up visits, especially when there is improvement in the acute crises.

Profiles One and Two are probably easier to identify and treat to prevent a suicide. The severe anxiety, ruminations, panic attacks, and agitation are all there to observe. One has to recognize the possible significance of the symptoms, however, and treat them with a combination of short-acting benzodiazepines, olanzepine, divalproex, and perhaps gabapentin, until the symptoms are relieved.

Profile Three is difficult because the period of high risk is hard to predict, since it may hinge on unpredictable outside events. As mentioned, detecting the use of cutting or choking for self-soothing, and using atypical antipsychotics, perhaps with divalproex or neurontin if anxiety is particularly severe, is the best prevention. Benzodiazepines may be useful, but care must be taken since they may promote dyscontrol in these patients. Special care during periods of impending "abandonment" or loss is important. Events can occur too rapidly to monitor if the patient doesn't have some help in controlling their responses.

Profile Four is perhaps the most difficult, since the impulsive behavior is trait-like, often brought out by a separation precipitated by the patient. These patients are difficult to monitor closely. Adequate antidepressant treatment, with a consideration for lithium or divalproex, might be useful. Compliance can be a problem, especially if the patient is bingeing. Substance abuse treatment may help over time to reduce the impulsive behavior and increase self-awareness.

This initial profile of high-risk suicide cases, based on a review of large numbers of cases, aims to increase levels of awareness to high-risk patients and situations. At least two dimensions of the pathways to suicide, severe anxiety and impulsiveness, have been identified (Fawcett et al., 1997). Other important traits may be hopelessness and anhedonia (Clark and Fawcett, 1992a), but these traits may be of more long-term importance than for making an immediate intervention after an assessment suggests acute or immediate risk. We can hope that continued research with larger numbers of cases will increase, refine, and more accurately specify these profiles.

IMPLICATIONS FOR THE CLINICIAN

The following summarizes important implications for the clinician:

- Recent studies found severe anxiety symptoms to be acute risk factors for suicide.
- The NIMH Collaborative Study of Depression has indicated that there is a very high risk of suicide in the six months to year after hospital discharge. In addition, severe anxiety symptoms statistically significantly differentiated patients who committed suicide within one year of assessment from those who survived the year follow-up period. Standard suicide risk factors, such as suicidal ideation or intent and prior suicide attempts, were not associated with suicide within one year of assessment but were associated with suicide between two to five years of follow-up.
- Findings suggest that it is important to monitor the presence and severity of anxiety symptoms experienced by the patient as a useful risk indicator of immediate suicide.
- Two pathways to suicide have been proposed. There are certainly more to be identified. The two proposed pathways are anxiety/agitation and impulsive self-aggression, possibly related to low brain serontonin function and low serum cholesterol.
- Four clinical profiles of suicide and treatment recommendations are as follows:
  - Agitation, severe anxiety associated with psychosis in an inpatient: aggressive treatment is needed. The clinician must recognize the

possible significance of the observable anxiety, agitation, and psychosis and possibly treat with short-acting benzodiazepines, olanzepine, divalproex, and gabapentin.

- Partial response with recurrent symptoms of anxiety and undiagnosed depression: requires aggressive treatment of the anxiety and depression. Clinician must also address delusional symptoms. As with Profile One, the significance of the symptoms must be assessed and possibly treated with short-acting benzodiazepines, olanzepine, divalproex, and gabapentin.

- Suicidal acting out in borderline disorder associated with anxiety and anticipated loss: treatment with a low dose of antipsychotic medication may decrease the patient's need for suicidal behavior. Special care must be given during periods of impending abandonment or loss.

- Interpersonal loss in depression associated with a history of drug/alcohol abuse and impulsive behavior: these patients often show periods of improvement with relapses of depression in the face of ultimate separation. Very close follow-up may help to pick up the changes and respond, but these patients often do not cooperate with frequent follow-up visits, especially when there is improvement in the acute crises. Adequate antidepressant treatment and substance abuse treatment over time may help.

- A review of a large number of cases has indicated that anxiety and impulsiveness suggest an acute, immediate risk for suicide. Hopelessness and anhedonia may be long-term risk factors.

CHAPTER EIGHT

Self-Mutilation

Armando R. Favazza, M.D., M.P.H.

The difference between self-mutilation and suicide is simple yet profound: it is a difference between life and death. Suicide is an exit; suicidal persons want to stop all feelings and to terminate their existence. Self-mutilation is a morbid form of self-help; self-mutilators want to rid themselves of troublesome thoughts and feelings and to continue living. In fact, self-mutilation is defined as the direct and deliberate destruction or alteration of body tissue *without* conscious suicidal intent. Behaviors such as self-starvation, chronic alcohol ingestion, premature termination of renal dialysis, and overdosing on pills are self-injurious or parasuicidal acts but do not constitute self-mutilation. Behaviors such as trimming fingernails and cutting hair may be self-mutilation technically, but they are not clinically relevant.

CULTURALLY SANCTIONED SELF-MUTILATION

There are many culturally sanctioned rituals and practices in which persons either mutilate themselves or willingly allow others to mutilate them. Aboriginal rites of passage, for example, often involve brutal practices such as slicing open the penis along the length of the urethra, knocking teeth loose, and scarifying large areas of skin. Adolescent participants must endure pain, overcome fear, and surrender part of their autonomy by allowing themselves to be mutilated. It is the price they must pay in order to be transformed into adults with a new status and new responsibilities.

125

In Western culture, earlobe piercing to display jewelry is commonplace, and the piercing of other body parts—tongue, nose, eyebrows, nipples, navel, genitalia—is not uncommon. Tattoos are trendy, as is skin branding. More often than not, these practices serve as sexual enticements, attempts to shock others and obtain a unique or personalized characteristic, and aesthetic indulgences (beauty being in the eye of the beholder). Occasionally these practices have spiritual and therapeutic importance, such as obtaining a piercing as a way of reclaiming control over one's body following a rape. Except in the most bizarre cases (extensive mutilation of the male genitalia), body piercing, even when multiple, does not necessarily indicate mental illness, although, when surveyed in large numbers, persons with body piercing probably would demonstrate more psychopathology than would a control group. In a descriptive study of 292 men and 70 women with multiple piercings, more than half had at least a college education and were homosexual; for most, their nipples became more eroticized after the piercings (Moser, Lee, and Christensen, 1993).

PATHOLOGICAL SELF-MUTILATION

Self-mutilation that is the product of mental or neurological illness affects many areas of the body. Head banging is the most common form of self-injury to the skull, although mild head banging of a limited nature may occur in up to 6 percent of normal children, mostly boys, often coinciding with tooth eruption and the change from sitting to crawling. Head banging past the age of four years is almost always pathological, is usually found in psychotic or mentally retarded children, and may be associated with head punching and slapping, recurrent vomiting, and self-induced seizures.

Eyes

Eye mutilation in its more severe forms—enucleation and destruction of the eyeball by finger poking—is most commonly encountered in psychotically depressed or schizophrenic males in their midtwenties, especially while imprisoned. This is demonstrated by a twenty-four-year-old man who had been imprisoned for arson, rape, and other crimes. He said that after being sodomized by an inmate, he had cut his wrists and blinded one eye in order to get transferred to a psychiatric hospital. He was hospitalized because he had slashed his remaining eye with a razor in the belief that his blindness would eliminate his anxiety about looking at people and would allow him to be a successful musical entertainer. On the ward he claimed that he was Jesus, and he was preoccupied with the size of his penis (Crowder, Gross, and Heiser, 1979). In another case, a fifty-year-old man became depressed and paranoid following the death of his mother. He claimed that he saw the devil and that he had to atone for the sin of incest. He then took out an eye with his fingers (Harrer and Urban, 1950).

Patients with factitious disorder may injure their eyes for reasons that are not readily understandable other than a need to assume a patient role, have contacts with physicians, and undergo diagnostic tests and operations. A thirty-two-year-old nursing aide who seemed to be a happy, well-adjusted person claimed that a glass fragment struck her right eye when she dropped a glass into a sink. On ten occasions over three months she had glass fragments removed from her eye (Wilson, 1955). Epidemics of self-inflicted eye injuries have been reported among malingering soldiers who desired to avoid an unpleasant assignment and among personality-disordered prisoners. In one report twenty-two young, antisocial male prisoners put ground-up pencil lead, lime, and ground glass into the conjunctival sac. Sometimes they stuck a lighted cigarette into their open eyes. As a rule they injured themselves on Saturday afternoons to delay detection; some inflicted their injuries within a few weeks of their scheduled discharge from prison (Segal and Mizyglod, 1963). Occasionally personality-disordered persons may deliberately injure their eyes; an eighteen-year-old youth who was hospitalized for inexplicable stealing, fainting fits, and subjective "attacks" cut his eyelid, conjunctiva, and cornea with a razor in order to demonstrate his suffering to hospital staff. These episodes often were related to active planning for discharge from the hospital and attempts to discuss his relationship problems (Griffin, Webb, and Parker, 1982).

Self-mutilation of the mouth, particularly lips and tongue biting, is seen in children with relatively rare disorders such as the syndromes of Lesch-Nyhan, of de Lange, and of Tourette, autism, and neuroacanthosis.

Appendages

Arms, legs, hands, feet, toes, and especially fingers are well suited anatomically for self-amputation. A finger joint, for example, may be amputated rapidly and accurately with little blood loss, minimal loss of functions for many tasks, and good wound healing. Further, the deformed finger stump is readily available for public display. Self-mutilation of the hands and feet may be associated with sensory deficit disorders such as sensory radicular neuropathy and congenital indifference to pain (Landwirth, 1964; Dubovsky, 1978). Religious delusions in depressed and schizophrenic patients are prominent in all reported cases of hand self-amputation; for example, an eighteen-year-old schizophrenic college student who felt guilty about his interest in homosexuality declared himself to be an evangelist and as a special mission for God sawed off his right hand with a hacksaw and removed an eye with a screwdriver (Goldenberg and Sata, 1978). Self-injury of lower limbs has been described in men with a paraphilia in which an amputated leg stump is the object of a sexual obsession. One man whose central erotic fantasy was of himself as an amputee sought a surgical amputation when he deliberately injured himself by hammering a steel pin into his left tibia and repeatedly attempted to infect the wound by introducing pus and nasal and anal mucosa into it (Money, Jobsris, and Furth, 1977).

Skin

There are many reasons that the skin is the most common target of self-mutilation. It is easily accessible, bleeds easily, heals well, and leaves scars, which, like blood, often have symbolic significance. It is a psychologically and socially complex organ whose color may determine much of a person's fate. It forms the border between the environment and the personal self. It also is a message center of sorts in that rage may be displayed by flushing, embarrassment or shame by blushing, and fear by blanching. Compulsive types of skin mutilation are severe scratching and gouging in pursuit of imaginary parasites. Perhaps the most clinically vexing types of self-mutilation are skin cutting, burning, and carving. These behaviors are present in a wide range of conditions, including anxiety, dissociative, eating, impulse-control, personality, and mood disorders.

Genitals

Female genital self-mutilation mainly involves superficial cuts, which may result from dissatisfaction with femininity, anger over feeling valued only as a sexual object, or during masturbation with sharp objects. Male genitalia are more suited to mutilation than are women's since men have a greater tendency to localize their sexual feelings onto their protruding genitalia. Removal of testicles is somewhat more common than removal of the penis, which in turn is more common than removal of both organs. Self-castrators tend to be psychotic and suffering from schizophrenia or major depression. Their average age is thirty-two years. Alcohol ingestion is a factor in about 25 percent of cases. In one report, a twenty-six-year-old schizophrenic with a history of repeated failures in traditional male roles became intoxicated with alcohol and drugs and then cut off the tip of his penis (Englesman, Polito, and Perley, 1974). In another case a thirty-five-year-old depressed man with a history of concerns that his gentleness would cause people to regard him as homosexual developed sudden, deep religious feelings. He dwelled on the Bible, especially the words of Matthew about men who become eunuchs for heaven's sake, and on outer space. He castrated himself, believing that his act of purification would qualify him to serve as the pilot of a spaceship who would transport the godly to heaven (Kushner, 1967).

Nonpsychotic genital self-mutilators tend to be character-disordered men who act impulsively or transsexuals who have premeditated their actions and castrate themselves in a controlled fashion with a minimum of blood loss and unnecessary trauma. A thirty-five-year-old transsexual prepared for his self-castration by obtaining employment as a practical nurse in a urology department, where he familiarized himself with the surgical instruments and procedure. He cut off his testicles, flushed them down the toilet, and went to an emergency room where he stated that he had lost about fifty cubic centimeters of blood during the castration and that this was "the usual amount of blood lost by a woman during menstruation" (Lowry and Kilivakis, 1971).

CLASSIFICATION OF SELF-INJURIOUS BEHAVIORS

Although clinicians have long been aware of self-mutilative behaviors, the first attempt to classify them was by Karl Menninger. A chapter of his popular book *Man Against Himself* (1938) divided self-mutilation into four categories: neurotic, psychotic, organic, and religious. This classification was ahead of its time and never really caught on. More attention was paid to Menninger's assertions that self-castration is the prototype of all self-mutilation, self-mutilated organs symbolize the wounded genital, and self-mutilation is a form of partial suicide to avert total suicide. We now know that the first assertion is false, whereas the second and third are true only in exceedingly rare cases.

It was not until 1983 that another classification was offered. In that year Pattison and Kahan (1983) developed a differential division of self-injurious behaviors based on three variables. The direct-indirect variable, based on Farberow's work (1980), considers time and awareness. Direct self-injury takes place in a brief time span, and there is both a conscious intent to harm oneself and an awareness of the effects of the behavior; indirect self-injury takes place over a long time span, and there is a both a lack of conscious intent to harm oneself and of awareness of the harmful effects. The lethality variable, based on Litman's work (1980), assesses the degree of possibility that the self-harm will result in death. The repetition variable, based on Farmer's work (1980), refers to the number of times the self-harm behavior occurs. Thus, a bullet to the head would be classified as a direct, high-lethality, single episode. Multiple skin cutting would be classified as a direct, low-lethality, multiple episode; chronic alcoholism is a similar but indirect behavior.

Winchel and Stanley's 1991 classification categorized self-mutilation by the clinical contexts in which it mainly occurs: mental retardation, psychosis, penal institutionalization, and character disorders, especially borderline personality disorders. A more useful classification, and the one that is widely accepted, was reported in 1990 by Favazza and Rosenthal, elaborated in 1993, further modified by Favazza and Simeon in 1995, and most fully described in 1996 in Favazza's *Bodies Under Siege*. In this classification, pathological self-mutilation is divided into three major categories based on the rate and pattern of the behavior, as well as degree of tissue destruction. The categories are major, stereotypic, and superficial-to-moderate. The last category has three subtypes: compulsive, episodic, and repetitive. This phenomenological classification is comprehensive and atheoretical and disregards etiology. It is useful clinically because each type of self-mutilation is usually more prevalent in certain mental disorders as either a central diagnostic or an associated feature.

Major Self-Mutilation

The category of major self-mutilation comprises infrequent acts, such as eye enucleation, self-blinding, and amputation of body parts such as fingers, hands, feet, limbs, and genitalia. These acts, with the exception of carefully planned transsexual self-castration, tend to occur suddenly, with a great deal of tissue damage and bleeding, and fainting afterward. They are not essential symptoms of any disorder but may appear as associated features of psychosis (acute psychotic episodes, schizophrenia, depression, mania) and acute intoxication.

Some patients are unable to explain their behavior and even seem indifferent to it. A hospitalized teenage girl who was found holding her right eyeball in her hand simply told the nurse that it had spontaneously and painlessly fallen out of her head while she was sleeping (Goodhart and Savitsky, 1933). Idiosyncratic explanations that challenge understanding may be offered: a twenty-nine-year-old man who castrated himself while wading in the ocean gave his severed testicles to his mother with the intention of giving back to her the life she had given him at birth (Pabis, Mirla, and Tozmans, 1980). In many cases, however, patients' explanations have religious or sexual themes, or both.

The biblical rule of Christian comportment found in Mark 9:47–48 and Matthew 5:28–29 can have a devastating impact on some psychotic, depressed persons who, taking the words at face value, enucleate their eyes. Some patients claim an identification with the tortured, crucified Christ. A paranoid sailor, fearful of being tortured and killed by his shipmates, cooked his index finger and ate it in emulation of Christ who overcame adversity by enduring the torments of his captors (Mintz, 1964). Personal requirements for atonement, purification, and punishment for sins may be satisfied by self-mutilation. Other religious themes include godly commands, hallucinations (Crowder, Gross, and Heiser, 1979), and the influence of the devil (Rosen, 1972).

The most common sexual theme is the desire to be a female. A man sliced open his urethra to make himself "more like a woman" and several years later castrated himself, saying, "I resented the penis because I had been born wrong and then blamed for it" (Blacker and Wong, 1963). Some men are so distraught over their homosexual feelings that they cut off their penis, thinking that this will prevent them from indulging in sodomy. A mentally retarded schizophrenic was afraid that he would lose his girlfriend because of his incessant sexual demands, so he drank some beer and castrated himself. He claimed that a voice told him, "Now you can't control yourself. Go ahead and cut it off" (Favazza, 1996). Repudiation of one's genitals is another theme. An elderly man with longstanding sexual guilt castrated himself after becoming impotent secondary to his diabetes, saying that his genitals "had let me down and now were no good to me" (Hemphill, 1951). In another case, a forty-two-year-old manic man cut off his penis after his wife filed for divorce, saying, "I knew my divorce was coming up, and I would have no further use for it" (Lennon, 1963).

Acts of major self-mutilation are often tragic. Enucleated eyes are irretrievably damaged, and it may be impossible to repair or reattach body parts surgically. After their self-mutilation, many patients exhibit a calmness that suggests a resolution of unconscious conflicts. In most cases the tranquility is brief, and the self-harm behavior returns with a vengeance, but some patients may come to peace with themselves and be realistically resigned to the fact that what is done is done. The realization of having lost a body part while intoxicated may be painfully sobering when there is a clearing of consciousness.

Stereotypic Self-Mutilation

Stereotypic acts of self-mutilation tend to be monotonously repetitive, even rhythmic, and are often performed in the presence of onlookers. Stereotypic self-mutilators seem to be driven by a primarily biological imperative to harm themselves and evince neither shame nor guilt. Typically any symbolic meaning, thought content, or associated affect associated with the behaviors cannot be ascertained.

A survey of ten thousand institutionalized mentally retarded persons found a 13.6 percent prevalence of behaviors such as head banging and hitting, self-biting, orifice digging, arm hitting, throat and eye gouging, severe scratching, and hair pulling (Griffin, Williams, and Stark, 1985). Not all self-mutilation in this population, however, is stereotypic nor are these behaviors uniquely associated with mental retardation. The prevalence of mental retardation in the general population is about 1 percent; about 5 percent of cases involve severe or profound mental retardation and are at particular risk for self-injurious behavior. Autism is often associated with moderate mental retardation; head banging as well as biting of the wrist, hand, and fingers may be present. Excessive fearfulness and a high pain threshold facilitate these behaviors in some autistic persons.

Patients with Lesch-Nyhan syndrome, a rare inborn error of purine metabolism that affects only males, severely mutilate themselves by biting their lip tissue and may bite off parts of their tongue or fingers. The awesome rapidity of these mutilations is remarkable. Upon release from restraints, a child's hand may instantaneously go into his mouth, where it is bitten, accompanied by screams of pain (Christie, Bay, and Kaufman, 1982). Persons with this disorder often plead to be kept in restraints. At least a third of patients with Tourette's syndrome demonstrate self-injurious behaviors such as head banging, self-hitting, tooth extraction, sticking objects in eyeballs, joint dislocation, and biting of the lips, cheek, and tongue. The onset of this disorder is usually in childhood or early adolescence. One patient bit his mouth and tongue starting at the age of four years. At age eighteen he repeatedly punched himself in the eye, head, neck, chest, shoulder, and genitals, with resultant bruising. He also shook his head so violently on one occasion that he collapsed and died due to bleeding within his skull (Robertson, Trimbale, and Lees, 1989). Neither the disorder itself nor the self-mutilation is associated with mental retardation. Other disorders in which stereotypic self-injury may be present include de Lange syndrome, Rett's syndrome, neuroacanthosis, acute psychosis, and schizophrenia.

Superficial-to-Moderate Self-Mutilation

This classification of self-mutilation is epitomized by skin cutting and burning and by trichotillomania. It is the most common form of self-harm and has been the recent focus of much media attention. A popular biography of Princess Diana revealed that she cut her wrists, chest, and thighs (Morton, 1993); excerpts about these episodes were published in the June 27, 1992, issue of *People* magazine. The cover article of the July 27, 1997, issue of the *New York Times Magazine* dealt with a female college student who repeatedly cut herself (J. Egan, 1997).

Compulsive Type. The compulsive type of superficial-to-moderate self-mutilation involves repetitive and ritualistic behaviors that occur many times daily. Most persons with relatively mild symptoms forgo professional help, while those with more severe problems are seen primarily by dermatologists and family physicians. Persons with delusions of parasitosis injure their skin by attempting to dig out the offending organisms and to destroy them with toxic substances such as lye. Since the delusion is often an encapsulated false belief, some patients may function relatively well and not experience psychological deterioration; others may be quite disabled by their delusion, which may preoccupy them constantly and drive their family members to exhaustion. Among the causes of tactile hallucinations that need to be considered are abuse of drugs such as amphetamine and methylphenidate (Ritalin), delirium tremens, multiple sclerosis, pernicious anemia, pellagra, diabetes mellitus, hypothyroidism, and polycythemia vera.

Some perfectionist persons, usually between the ages of thirty and forty years, excoriate their skin by squeezing, scratching, and picking in compulsive attempts to remove actual or imaginary skin blemishes (Koo, 1989). Some persons are unaware of their behaviors but will admit to them when confronted, while others will steadfastly deny creating lesions by burning their skin with cigarettes and matches and by applying phenol, acids, silver nitrate, and other chemicals (dermatitis factitia or artefacta).

Hair pulling is the best-studied compulsive type of self-mutilation, and the syndrome of trichotillomania is classified as a disorder of impulse control. In this disorder, body hair, especially from the scalp, eyebrows, and eyelashes, is pulled out. Childhood-onset cases occur equally in boys and girls, have a brief and benign course, and do not necessarily imply intrapsychic or familial psychopathology (Winchel, 1992). Later-onset cases typically begin at age thirteen, mostly in females, and may have a severe chronic course, with a high rate of comorbid nail biting, skin scratching, alcohol abuse, and anxiety, obsessive-compulsive, mood, and body dysmorphic disorders. Persons with the disorder may select a hair perceived to be too kinky, crooked, or straight, then pluck it out, briefly examine it, and discard or swallow it. Hundreds of hairs may be pulled out either continuously over several hours or in brief, repetitive episodes. In focused, ritualistic hair pulling, patients are distracted from their usual tasks and experience rising tension before pulling or when attempting to resist pulling; relief follows the act. In automatic hair pulling (about 75 percent of cases) patients do not experience the urge to pluck out their hairs but do so anyway without thinking about it, especially when their attention is on a task such as driving a car or reading. Among the complications of hair pulling are scars; skin infections; muscle strain with consequent chronic back, neck, and arm pain; carpal tunnel syndrome; and trichobezoars that may result in anemia, bowel obstruction, abdominal pain, gastric bleeding, nausea, vomiting, and perforation of the bowel or stomach (Mueller, 1990).

Episodic Type. This type involves occasional behaviors such as skin cutting and burning; skin carving of words, designs, and symbols; interference with wound healing; breaking of foot and hand bone; self-punching; and needle sticking. These behaviors may have symbolic referents and often require the use of implements such as razors and matches in a complex sequence of events. Persons clearly state that the behaviors make them feel better, provide rapid relief from distressing thoughts and emotions, and help in reestablishing a sense of self-control. Such results usually last for a few hours, although they sometimes endure for a few days and, less commonly, for a few weeks. People episodically self-injure for many reasons. Favazza (1989) has provided a list of common themes:

- Mounting anxiety and unbearable tension are released. "It's like popping a balloon."
- A sense of normalcy returns to persons who report emotional dampening, estrangement from the environment, and altered perceptions of time. "I feel real again."
- Self-control is reestablished. "When I feel hyper my mind races and I can't sleep. I hit myself with a hammer, and then I'm calm again."
- A sense of security and uniqueness is provided. "Cutting, burning, and poking needles into my arms is a security for me because I know that if all else fails and leaves me feeling emotionless and empty, the pain and blood will be there for me." "I cut myself because I need to be special. I

was always taken for granted, invisible. Now, although I rarely expose my scars, I feel a smug pride. I'm not eager to give it up. Take it away from me, and I'm like everyone else."

- People may be easily manipulated to provide love or caring or a better situation. "I cut my wrist—it wasn't a suicide attempt—and told my boyfriend who was very late for our date, 'This is how deeply you have hurt me.'" "I figured that if I cut myself enough the prison guards would let me transfer to the cell where my lover lives."

- Self-hatred may be indulged. "My father tried to have sex with me when I was 22 years old, and I felt like a frightened child. I cut myself because I feel so much hate for myself."

- Pressure from multiple personalities may be relieved. "The personalities punish one another. They sometimes use IV needles to get the blood running. Occasionally you wonder why for a brief moment, but the why isn't important. You first have to do it. Stick pins and needles in your skin. Hit your hand with a hair brush. Scrape your vagina with a fish scaler. Sara [a personality] cut my foot. She couldn't hurt my stepfather, so she hurt me. She just gets angry, and I get hurt. . . . She cut my wrist with a big knife to punish me because I'm weak."

- Sexual feelings may be enhanced or diminished, "When I stick open scissors up my vagina, the cold hard steel gives me an explosive orgasm. And the blood makes it even more exciting." "Sometimes my mind churns up awful sexual visions, and I get rid of these bad pictures by cutting myself."

- Euphoria and titillation may be experienced. "When I cut myself, I get such a high feeling. It feels so good, and I feel deprived when I can't do it. I have never found a substitute for this high feeling." "Self-mutilation allows me to live on the edge. It is titillating to see just how far I can go and how much real pain I can endure. Too often I equivocate and am afraid to make choices. Here I can be swept away on a tidal wave of feeling."

- Anger can be vented. "I get my anger out when I hurt myself. It could not be expressed in my family; you always had to smile. Also with my religion it is a sin to be angry. Cutting gives me a way to vent my anger."

- Alienation may be relieved. "When 'it' strikes, self-mutilation is the only thing that provides relief, 'it' being a frantic, desperate, profound sense of alienation from the rest of the world, primarily loved ones. Sometimes I think a dose of the good things—loving, hugging—would do it, but it's simpler to reach for a razor blade."

These representative themes do not exhaust all the reasons given by patients for harming themselves. Each person has a unique story to tell. Examination of the themes, however, points to a host of mental disorders in which superficial-to-moderate self-mutilation may be present as a symptom or associated feature.

This type of self-harm is encountered in disorders in which anxiety is an essential symptom, such as generalized anxiety disorder and post-traumatic stress disorder (PTSD). It has been reported in PTSD after combat (Pitman, 1990) and rape. After being violently raped several times by the same man and threatened with death if she ever told anyone, a nineteen-year-old woman entered therapy for severe anxiety, recurrent nightmares, a bathing compulsion, and periods of memory loss; a few months later, she started cutting her wrists, forearms, and thighs: "The secrecy that surrounded her behavior seemed to parallel the silence she felt she must maintain about the rapes. She said that cutting her arm provided a release for the unbearable tension that built up as a part of a rape-isolated flashback" (Greenspan and Samuel, 1989). The behavior also may occur when anxiety is present as an associated feature of disorders such as schizophrenia, bulimia nervosa, and the use of or withdrawal from alcohol, stimulants, cannabis, cocaine, hallucinogens, inhalants, and sedatives. Anxiety may be present in many medical disorders such as hypothyroidism, hyperthyroidism, heart arrhythmias, congestive heart failure, hyperventilation, porphyria, chronic obstructive lung disease, and vitamin B_{12} deficiency. A woman cut herself to relieve the anxiety caused by benign cranial hypertension (Ballard, 1989). Another gouged pieces of skin from her limbs secondary to adrenocortical insufficiency (Addison's disease); treatment with steroids resolved the behavior in a week (Rajathurai, Chazan, and Jeans, 1983). The most typical scenario is that self-injury swiftly relieves high anxiety, although the mechanism of this process is unclear.

Cutting and burning are effective methods of terminating states of acute depersonalization. One patient who experienced his life as a series of discontinuities because of innumerable dissociative episodes claimed that he could recount the circumstances and time of each bodily mutilation; thus, "he preserved in the flash, in a dramatic and conspicuous manner, the history of events he could not integrate into the fabric of his personality" (Miller and Bashkin, 1974). In a study of one hundred patients with dissociative identity disorder (multiple personality) self-mutilation was inflicted as a punishment by one personality on another in thirty-four cases (Putnam et al., 1986).

Some persons with depressive disorders or disorders in which depression is a symptom, such as obsessive-compulsive disorder, personality disorders, adjustment disorders, and substance-induced disorders (cocaine, heroin, alcohol, digitalis, steroids, neuroleptics, barbiturates), find that self-injury may provide temporary respite from their misery. The "punishment" of self-mutilation, for example, may alleviate guilt.

Superficial-to-moderate episodic self-mutilation is common in persons with antisocial, borderline, and mixed personality disorders. The highest rate of this behavior is found in prisons and detention centers, where it is valued as a method of defying authority and outwitting rules. About 75 percent of inmates are psychopaths who may self-mutilate as a method of forcing authorities to transfer them to a preferred cell block or work assignment (Franklin, 1988). Psychopathy is associated with poor performance in monotonous tasks, with slow-wave electroencephalogram abnormalities that probably indicate cortical arousal with avoidance of drugs that reduce arousal and with a preference for novel and complex stimulation. Self-mutilation provides stimulation and even euphoria in times of boredom, as well as relief from the anxiety and depression that psychopaths experience when they are prevented from roaming free and indulging their impulsive lifestyle (Johnson and Britt, 1967; Virkkunen, 1976b). The behavior also may be a genuine, desperate cry for attention, a maneuver to instill guilt in others, such as in a relationship that is threatening to end or a simple statement of psychological bankruptcy by inmates who perceive themselves as "inescapably relegated to the junk heap of life" (Toch, 1975). Psychopaths who self-injure outside of prison usually explain away their scars and burn marks as resulting from fights.

Although self-mutilation is one of the nine diagnostic criteria for borderline personality disorder (at least five criteria must be present to make the diagnosis), the behavior is *not* synonymous with this disorder, and clinicians should not automatically make the diagnosis just because a patient cuts or burns. Among the borderline symptoms that may be temporarily assuaged by self-mutilation are mounting anxiety, depression, rapidly fluctuating emotions, anger, troublesome sexual feelings, emptiness, and alienation. The behavior provides a sense of security ("It's my best friend") and uniqueness, and is effective both in scaring people away and manipulating them to show attention and offer nurturance.

The personality problems of many persons do not fall neatly into recognized diagnostic categories. In addition to borderline and antisocial, other traits that are favorable for the emergence of self-mutilative behavior are narcissism, dependency, perfectionism, paranoia, eccentricity, and especially a histrionic flair for attention seeking.

Repetitive Syndrome. A dramatic change occurs in those persons whose episodes of self-mutilation become repetitive. There is no precise moment when this switch occurs; for some it comes after ten episodes, for others after twenty or more. Repetitive self-mutilators become overwhelmingly preoccupied with their self-harm behavior, which seems to assume an autonomous course. Although it is not listed in *DSM-IV*, many clinicians and researchers recognize a repetitive self-mutilation syndrome and code it as an impulse-control disorder not otherwise specified (312.30). Intermittent explosive disorder, kleptomania, pyromania, pathological gambling, and trichotillomania are other disorders in this class.

The essential feature of this syndrome is recurrent failure to resist impulses to harm one's body physically without conscious suicidal intent. The most common act of self-harm is skin cutting, although most persons with the disorder use multiple methods. These methods and the reasons given for self-harm are the same as for episodic self-mutilation.

Although failure to resist an impulse results in self-harm, repetitive self-mutilators brood about harming themselves for hours and even days. They may engage in rituals such as tracing areas of their skin and compulsively placing their self-harm paraphernalia in a special order. The acts of self-harm are usually performed in private. Behaviors such as drinking one's blood or saving it in small vials are strange but not psychotic. Repetitive self-mutilators often describe their condition as an addiction and may experience "withdrawal" symptoms when prevented from indulging their need to harm themselves.

Concurrent disorders often associated with the syndrome include antisocial, borderline, and histrionic disorders; PTSD; depression; and multiple personality disorder. Some persons demonstrate pathological personality traits, but these traits may subside or disappear when the syndrome remits. A particular feature of the syndrome is the presence of protean impulsive symptoms such as anorexia or bulimia nervosa, episodic alcohol or other substance abuse, and kleptomania that usually alternate with but also may exist simultaneously with self-mutilation. There is no particular order to the emergence of these symptoms. Kleptomania appears to be the most evanescent symptom. Patients recount that of the remaining symptoms, alcohol and other substance abuse is the easiest behavior to overcome and that self-mutilation is the most difficult.

The syndrome is more common in females than males, possibly by a three-to-one ratio. Its usual onset is in late childhood and early adolescence. In many patients, the disorder waxes and wanes for about fifteen years and then gradually remits, although isolated episodes of the behavior may persist. A seventy-year-old women who had not self-injured for four decades briefly returned to cutting at the time of her husband's death: "The cutting was an old friend and it made me feel better and not so alone." It is not rare for patients who have injured themselves intensely for many years to stop the behavior suddenly and permanently: "I decided that enough was enough. I needed to respect my body. I just decided to stop hurting myself and it was over."

Scars and wound infections may cause physical disfigurement that results in social rejection and isolation. Some people are so embarrassed by their appearance that they rarely appear in public. Others avoid short-sleeved shirts, revealing clothes, or bathing suits. Ten percent of patients admit to deliberate bone fractures and to tricking physicians and dentists into performing unnecessary surgery. The emergence of kleptomania often results in arrests. Bulimia may be a savagely persistent problem. The most serious complication is bona fide suicide attempts, almost always by overdoses, in persons who are demoralized over their inability to control their acts of self-mutilation. In one study, 57 percent of repetitive self-mutilators reported overdosing on drugs; half of these had overdosed four or more times (Favazza, 1989).

The onset of the syndrome is linked to stressful situations. Predisposing factors are childhood physical or sexual abuse (in about 60 percent of cases), childhood history of surgical procedures or illness, parental alcoholism or depression, residence in a total-care institution, accident proneness, perfectionist tendencies, dissatisfaction with body shape or sexual organs, inability to express and to modulate emotional expressions normally, feeling empty inside, few friends, fear of growing up and accepting adult responsibilities, a sense of not being understood by anyone, and a history of an eating disorder (Favazza, 1989). Repetitive self-mutilators do not harm others physically, although at the height of the disorder they may share razors and engage in self-cutting with other self-mutilators. The prevalence of the syndrome is unknown, but it is likely that combined episodic and repetitive self-mutilation affects 1,400 persons per 100,000 population yearly.

Although persons with the syndrome often try to hide their behavior, they become avid users of medical and mental health services once their parents and others know about it. They may first come to professional attention during the eating disorder or alcohol or substance abuse phase of their illness. A study of multi-impulsive bulimics (Fichter, Quadflieg, and Rief, 1994), for example, reported histories of self-mutilation (75 percent), shoplifting (78 percent), alcohol dependence (34 percent), and drug abuse (22 percent).

The repetitive self-mutilation syndrome contains all the essential features of an Axis I impulse-control disorder: failure to resist an impulse, drive, or temptation to perform a harmful act; an increasing sense of tension or arousal prior to the act; and an experience of pleasure, gratification, or release at the time of the act. Immediately afterward there may or may not be genuine regret, self-reproach, or guilt. An objection to the syndrome is that impulsivity and self-mutilation are elements of borderline personality disorder (BPD). However, many Axis I disorders coexist with BPD: panic disorder, substance abuse, gender identity disorder, factitious disorder, disorders of impulse control, attention deficit disorder, and eating disorders (Gunderson and Zanarini, 1987). Since BPD includes symptoms of all these disorders, the existence of a concurrent disorder often depends on the quantity of the symptoms in question. Occasional binge eating or shoplifting episodes, for example, fall within the BPD construct, but a pattern of uncontrolled, repetitive episodes warrants the additional diagnosis of bulimia nervosa and kleptomania. The same argument holds true for self-mutilation.

TREATMENT

Self-mutilators are not happy persons, and their acts of self-harm challenge the equanimity of everyone whom their lives touch. Many persons regard self-mutilation as a senseless, repugnant, frightening, mysterious behavior. Even most mental health professionals have a difficult time with their countertransference when dealing with self-injurers, as Frances (1987) clearly stated: "Of all disturbing patient behaviors, self-mutilation is the most difficult to understand and to treat. . . . The typical clinician (myself included) treating a patient who self-mutilates is often left feeling a combination of helpless, horrified, guilty, furious, betrayed, disgusted, and sad." Unlike suicide, where the victim is dead, self-mutilators remain very much alive and continue to haunt us in the flesh. Favazza has conjectured that self-mutilation may elicit such negative reactions in others because it touches upon the turbulent bloody space of the sacred (Favazza, 1996, pp. 26–29). Whatever the reasons, self-mutilators seem to threaten the sense of mental and physical integrity of those around them. Even surgeons accustomed to treating mangled accident victims may use unusually poor judgment, such as making only a halfhearted (or no) attempt to reattach a self-mutilated body part. Some chronic cutters will falsely admit to a suicide attempt in order to facilitate a warmer reception from emergency room personnel. When self-mutilators reject the care offered by caregivers, whether professional or personal, the feelings of the caregiver are hurt and, according to Tantam and Whittaker (1992), these negative feelings may lead to justification of "either harsh or indifferent treatment." This combination of factors means that the treatment of self-mutilators demands more equanimity on the part of the therapist than is needed with other patients. Generally, two cutters and burners are the maximum that most therapists should handle intensively at one time.

The different types of self-mutilation are treated with various forms of psychological or social and biological treatment methods. Different methods are preferable for different types of self-mutilators.

Major Self-Mutilation

Preventing acts of major self-mutilation is extremely difficult. These acts are most likely to be committed by psychotic schizophrenic, depressed, and manic persons, as well as by intoxicated persons, but the rate of the acts is so exceedingly low that most textbooks do not even mention them. The index of suspicion should rise when such patients are preoccupied with sexual or religious thoughts, or both, but even such patients rarely self-enucleate themselves or amputate a body part. The probability of self-mutilation increases when these patients drastically change their appearance, for example, by shaving their head or by severe hair plucking (Sweeney and Zamecnik, 1981). When psychotic or intoxicated persons seem to be fascinated by their genitals or by their eyes and start to rub or poke them, self-mutilation may occur. Only when the patient states that he plans to commit a specific act, however, can one be reasonably sure that it is likely to occur. Vague comments such as, "I think I may hurt myself," usually are not particularly ominous unless they are spoken by an agitated patient with a great deal of intensity and sincerity. Attempts should be made to elicit the patient's specific plan.

Since the rate of major self-mutilation is so low, specific preventive steps are not warranted except when a patient's behavior increases the possibility of self-injury. One-to-one nursing where an attendant is constantly at a patient's elbow may exacerbate the situation by failing to give a psychotic patient enough personal space. Such a nursing approach may prevent self-castration or a total eye enucleation (the optic nerve is quite tough, and it would probably take a determined person almost a minute to pull an eyeball totally free), but it would not prevent self-blinding, which can be impulsively completed in a few seconds by a single, hard probe with a finger. High doses of neuroleptics can be used in a perceived high-risk situation to aid in the prevention of major self-mutilation. Physical restraints may be necessary until medications take effect.

Past history is an excellent indicator of potential future self-injury. If a patient has committed one act of major self-mutilation, then it is reasonable to expect a second act during episodes of psychosis or intoxication. (A history of suicide attempts, however, seems to have little bearing on the likelihood of major self-mutilation.) The more recent the first act of self-harm is, the more likely it is that a second act will follow. A person should be considered at high risk, however, even if the first act occurred many years in the past. A person who has performed a partial self-castration as a first act may attempt to complete the castration or to attack his eyes, while a total self-castrator is likely to injure his eyes. A person who has injured an eye may injure the other one or move on to castration, and a bilateral self-enucleator or self-blinder is likely to injure his genitals.

Stereotypic Self-Mutilation

Mild cases of stereotypic self-mutilation in patients who live at home can be treated with medications (discussed below) and with simple behavioral techniques such as withholding attention when self-injury occurs. Most problematic cases, however, occur in persons who are institutionalized or live in some other supervised setting. Medications, involving rational polypharmacy, are necessary since no single drug or combination of drugs will work in all patients. Helpful medications include high-dose thioridazine (500 mg), low-dose Fluphenazine (1–5 mg), beta blockers (40–300 mg propanolol), mood stabilizers (lithium 1200 mg, carbamazapine 800 mg, valproate 1250 mg), benzodiazepines (clonazepam 4 mg, lorazepam 1–6 mg), buspirone (30 mg), and naltrexone

(50 mg). The judicious use of all these medications requires a great deal of input from the staff members that work with a patient in regard to the patient's current behaviors and psychological state. The goal should be to use the lowest effective dosage of a medication for the shortest period of time, although some patients will require years of medication. Since many patients in this population cannot articulate their needs clearly, especially when in pain, analgesics such as 200 to 800 mg ibuprofen should be used liberally. Perceptive staff may recognize behaviors that precede an episode of self-harm and may forestall it by using medication such as an anxiolytic and an analgesia as needed. Behavioral approaches such as shaping (Schaefer, 1970), positive reinforcement (Ragain and Anson, 1976), reinforcement of other behaviors (Repp and Deitz, 1974), counterconditioning (Ernst, 1973), and punishment and aversive conditioning (Ball, Sebback, and Jones, 1975) have been used with stereotypic self-mutilators for decades with some success (Lucero and Fireman, 1976; Corte, Wolff, and Locke, 1971). Medication may improve the ability of patients to respond to behavioral therapy.

Episodic Superficial-to-Moderate Self-Mutilation

The treatment of episodic superficial-to-moderate self-mutilation should focus on the basic disorder of which self-harm is an occasional symptom, although patients should be educated about and warned against an escalation in the rate of cutting and burning. They should be told that it can become an addictionlike behavior that may develop into a syndrome that will make their lives miserable for many years.

Individual psychodynamic psychotherapy is the most used long-term treatment for these patients, with expressive therapy being the form about which the most is written. The patient's current situation and behaviors are dealt with first, with childhood roots of the behaviors being dealt with later in the process. Limits are set to control acting out, and environmental support is provided by auxiliary therapists or structured social settings. Crabtree (1967) warns against both an initial introspective approach, with a focus on fantasy and feelings, because it can foster regression and lead to increased self-mutilation, and also against being too nurturant, which could increase the patient's need for self-punishment. Psychodynamically oriented supportive therapy, however, which does not emphasize insightful interpretations of transference or of unconscious conflicts but focuses on supportive techniques in which the therapist offers advice, encourages the patient to make his or her own decisions, and accentuates the positive, is more widely used than expressive therapy. Although many medications have been used to treat superficial-to-moderate self-mutilations, none, with the exception of lithium for hair pulling (Christensen, Popkin, Mackenzie, and Realmuto, 1991), has truly been proven to work.

Repetitive Cutters and Burners

Repetitive cutters and burners are very difficult patients to treat, and it is usual for multiple therapists to be involved either sequentially or concurrently over the course of an illness. The use of SSRIs has proven quite effective in dampening the impulsivity of uncontrolled cutting, although they do not selectively treat self-mutilation. High doses such as 80 to 120 mg fluoxetine, may need to be administered to patients whose impulsivity is running rampant. Many clinicians have noted, however, that cutting behaviors often returned, though at a lower rate, after several months of treatment with an SSRI. The short-term (one month) use of anxiolytics may be helpful as the patient "withdraws" from the desire to self-injure. Hospitalization, if necessary, should be brief; in five to ten days, a patient's impulsivity usually can come under adequate control.

The high-dose SSRI should be slowly reduced to an average normal dose (20 mg of fluoxetine) after a few weeks, and a mood stabilizer should be started. Medications such as neuroleptics and naltrexone are not helpful. The arduous work of psychotherapy may take many years and many turns. A psychodynamic approach may be helpful but should be supportive in nature at first. This includes such techniques as a therapeutic alliance, education, encouragement, advice, limit setting, and environmental intervention (Rockland, 1987). Cognitive therapy is used to replace thoughts about the acceptability of self-mutilation and the repulsiveness of the patient's body with thoughts such as, "I really want to be stable. I want to have relationships that don't revolve around hurting myself. I will like myself and my life better once I stop mutilating" (Walsh and Rosen, 1988). The four main categories of thoughts that lead to self-mutilation have been identified by Walsh and Rosen (1988): self-mutilation is acceptable; one's body and self are disgusting and deserving of punishment; action is needed to reduce unpleasant feelings; and overt action is necessary to communicate feelings to others.

Behavioral therapy for self-mutilation is most often written about with regard to mentally retarded patients. The self-mutilation behaviors are viewed as learned and maintained by positive social reinforcement. Therapy focuses on removal of positive reinforcement and can include counterconditioning and desensitization. It may be possible to use behavioral therapy with repetitive self-mutilators to change the usual sequence of events by using either negative consequences or thought-stopping techniques, although there are no reports that these methods have been tried. Dialectical behavior therapy (DBT) is a form of treatment currently being developed that appears quite successful and is specifically designed to deal with patients who engage in parasuicidal behaviors, including self-mutilation (Linehan, 1993a). It views self-harm as faulty problem-solving behaviors in people with low distress tolerance, inadequate coping skills, and expectancies of self-harm. DBT is a comprehensive group and individual treatment that requires great commitment by patients and extensive training for therapists. See Chapter Nine for a further description.

Favazza (1996) has suggested an approach in which a steadfast psychiatrist manages the patient's therapy by helping to find a psychotherapist, a group therapist, and another psychiatrist to prescribe medication. The psychiatrist manager meets with the patient every few months, provides overall guidance, and is always accepting of the patient (a task made possible by not having to respond with the frustrations of regular interaction). Tantam and Whittaker (1992) suggest the following treatment principles for use in therapy with self-mutilators: making and maintaining a relationship, breaking the habit, and maintaining change. Hawton also emphasizes the need for the following actions: analyzing the events that precipitate acts of self-mutilation; noting where the acts occur and what the goals, benefits, and negative consequences of the act are; gaining control over the behavior; examining underlying problems once the behavior is under control; and keeping inpatient treatment brief with written contracts and clear policies about treatment approach and restrictions for staff (Hawton, 1990). Because nurses tend to have the most contact with hospitalized self-mutilators, it is important that the nurse coordinator collaborates with the patient in developing a care plan and that a "shift associate" is assigned to the patient for each work shift. Nursing staff should help patients use self-soothing techniques, can teach anger management skills, and should collaborate with patients to identify high-risk times for self-mutilation (Pawlicki and Gaumer, 1993). Favazza (1996) has suggested referring patients for vocational rehabilitation and encouraging socialization with "normal" people.

Closing Notes on Treatment

Patients who self-mutilate as a result of a medical disorder need to receive specific treatment for that disorder but may also need adjunctive tranquilizers to help control the self-mutilation. A note should also be made about reports that indicate that psychosurgery can be effective with self-mutilation. In almost all of the patients studied, the surgery improved or removed episodes of aggression, hostility, and destructiveness. However, due to the distrust with which psychosurgery is viewed by both the public and many professionals, it is unlikely it will be used as a treatment for self-mutilation (Favazza, 1996).

Flexibility is essential in treating repetitive self-mutilators who too often become demoralized by therapists who misconstrue deliberate self-injury as suicide attempts, prescribe neuroleptics, falsely believe that every cutter has been sexually abused, and rashly suggest the presence of multiple personalities. Suicide by overdose is a distinct possibility in demoralized repetitive self-mutilators. A very helpful resource for both patients and their parents and friends is the "secret shame" site on the Internet (http://crystal.palace.net/ ~ llama/psych/injury). This site offers a great deal of useful information about self-mutilation and provides coping tips, quotes from personal stories, tips for parents and friends, and references. The site also contains a "bodies under siege" mailing list that allows self-mutilators to communicate with each other (the messages are scrutinized by the counselor who started the site, and no one can obtain a list of the persons who are on the mailing list).

IMPLICATIONS FOR THE CLINICIAN

There are various forms of self-mutilation, ranging from culturally sanctioned to pathological. Self-mutilation can affect virtually all parts of the body, from eyes to appendages to skin to genitals. Self-mutilators can pose a challenge to treatment providers and are often misdiagnosed as suicide attempters.

- Self-mutilation is best regarded as a morbid form of self-help that is antithetical to suicide. Self-mutilators want to live.

- Self-mutilation temporarily reduces a broad range of troublesome psychological symptoms such as mounting anxiety, depersonalization, guilt, and racing thoughts.

- Major self-mutilation such as self-blinding and amputation of body parts is a rare, private behavior that is most often, but not exclusively, associated with psychosis, intoxications, and transsexualism. Risk factors include a prior history of the behavior, a declaration of intent to engage in the behavior, a psychotic preoccupation with religion or sexuality, command hallucinations, and a dramatic change in appearance, such as head shaving.

- Stereotypic self-mutilation such as head banging, head slapping, and hand biting is most often, but not exclusively, associated with moderate to severe mental retardation, autism, and Tourette's syndrome. The behavior may be rhythmic, usually lacks symbolic content, and is performed openly, with neither guile nor shame.

- The compulsive type of superficial-to-moderate self-mutilation includes such behaviors as trichotillomania and excoriation of the skin.

- The episodic type of superficial-to-moderate self-mutilation includes behaviors such as cutting, burning, and carving of the skin. It is most often, but not exclusively, associated with antisocial, borderline, and mixed or histrionic personality disorders, anxiety disorders, and dissociative disorders.

- The repetitive type of superficial-to-moderate self-mutilation is a distinct syndrome characterized by onset of skin cutting in late childhood or early adolescence, peak occurrence in females fifteen to twenty-five years old, self-identity as a "cutter" or "burner," preoccupation with acts of self-harm, cravings to self-mutilate and withdrawal-like symptoms when prevented from indulging these cravings, often a fifteen-year course with sustained periods of other impulsive behaviors such as eating disorders, alcohol or substance abuse, and kleptomania. The syndrome may be coded 312.30 (Impulse-Control Disorder Not Otherwise Specified).

- Repetitive self-mutilators who become demoralized and depressed over an inability to control their self-harm are at high risk for suicide attempts by overdose.

- Pharmacotherapy for major self-mutilation consists of neuroleptics, antidepressants, and benzodiazepines, used to control the patient's psychosis, depression, or mania. For stereotypic self-mutilation, rational polypharmacy is usually needed, including a combination of neuroleptics, beta blockers, mood stabilizers, antianxiety agents, and analgesics. For superficial-to-moderate self-mutilation, the SSRIs in high dosages may be helpful in controlling impulsive cutting and burning.

- Psychodynamic insight psychotherapy can be helpful but is best preceded by supportive therapy. Dialectical behavior therapy has been reported to be helpful. Psychiatrists may have to assume the role of manager in coordinating the psychosocial intervention of these complicated patients.

- The "secret shame" site on the Internet with its "bodies under siege" billboard and mailing list is a useful source of information and support for patients and their family members.

- The most comprehensive source to date on the topic of self-mutilation is Favazza's *Bodies Under Siege* (second edition, 1996).

CHAPTER NINE

Standard Protocol for Assessing and Treating Suicidal Behaviors for Patients in Treatment

Marsha M. Linehan, Ph.D.

Most psychotherapists at one time or another are faced with the possibility of a patient's committing or attempting suicide. Studies of stress among psychotherapists indicate that the two most extreme stresses are patient suicide attempts and threats of suicide attempts (Hellman et al., 1986; Roswell, 1988). The likelihood of suicidal behavior during the course of therapy is especially high among seriously disturbed patients. Although suicidal behavior has traditionally been associated with specific axis I disorders, such as major affective disorder, bipolar disorder, and schizophrenia (Tanney, 1992; Chapters Fourteen and Sixteen in this book), it is also a major concern when treating patients with axis II disorders (Frances, 1986; Chapter Eighteen in this book).

In this chapter I describe a general treatment model for the suicidal patient and several psychosocial treatment protocols designed specifically to manage and treat the suicidal behaviors of patients in psychotherapy. The general model was developed as a framework for treating the chronically or severely suicidal individual. The protocols were designed both for general application to patients with axis I or axis II mental disorders and for application within a context of any individual treatment approach. However, the protocols have been evaluated empirically only within the context of a cognitive-behavior therapy for chronically suicidal women meeting criteria for borderline personality disorder (Barley et al., 1993; Linehan et al., 1991, 1993). Consistent with a cognitive-behavioral framework, the treatment protocols were constructed to treat suicidal behaviors directly.

DIALECTICAL BEHAVIOR THERAPY

In reviewing the literature on suicidal behavior, one cannot help but be struck by the similarities between the characteristics attributed to individuals who attempt suicide and those attributed to individuals meeting criteria for borderline personality disorder (BPD). Indeed, the presence of suicidal acts is one of the criteria for the disorder. Gunderson (1984) has described suicidal acts as the behavioral specialty of the borderline individual. It is thus no surprise that suicidal acts are particularly prevalent among individuals meeting criteria for BPD (Clarkin et al., 1983; Cowdry et al., 1985; Crumley, 1979; Graff and Mallin, 1967; Grunebaum and Klerman, 1967). Suicide attempt rates of 69 to 75 percent have been reported (Clarkin et al., 1983; Cowdry et al., 1985). Although much of the suicidal behavior of BPD individuals is without lethal intent, it is a mistake to view all suicidal behavior in this population as being without lethal risk. The suicide rate among all individuals meeting criteria for BPD (including those with no history of suicide attempts) has been estimated at 10 percent (Stone, 1987), a rate comparable to the rates for other disorders associated with suicidal behaviors. The suicide rate for borderline patients who have self-injured or attempted suicide is twice that of those with no history of suicide acts (Stone, 1987).

Dialectical behavior therapy (DBT) was developed specifically for the chronically suicidal patient. By *chronically suicidal,* I mean the patient who is unremittingly high in suicidal ideation, frequently threatens suicide or talks about taking his or her own life, has difficulty articulating any reasons for living or staying alive, and may attempt suicide or self-injure on multiple occasions. Although the treatment manuals describing DBT (Linehan, 1993a, 1993b) label it as a treatment for borderline personality disorder, in fact the first version of the manual never even mentioned BPD. The treatment and theoretical underpinnings were originally developed to apply to the suicidal individual. The metamorphosis of the treatment into one aimed at BPD was due almost entirely to the substantial overlap between BPD and suicidal behavior described above.

Theoretical Perspective

DBT was developed from a combined motivational and capability deficit model of suicidal behavior. The idea was twofold: (1) suicidal individuals lack important interpersonal, self-regulation (including emotional regulation) and distress tolerance skills and capabilities, and (2) personal and environmental factors inhibit the use of behavioral skills the individual does have, interfere with the development of new skills and capacities, and often reinforce inappropriate and suicidal behaviors. The emphasis on capability enhancement is similar to the focus on behavioral skills training, stress management, and relapse prevention among various behavioral therapies. It is compatible with supportive psychodynamic psychotherapies. Interestingly, it is also similar to the emphasis by pharmacotherapists on changing individual capacities. The emphasis on changing motivational factors is similar to behavioral treatments emphasizing exposure (for example, desensitization, flooding, cue exposure) and to models based on principles of operant conditioning (that is, reinforcement, extinction, and aversive contingencies). It is also compatible with cognitive therapies and expressive psychodynamic psychotherapies.

DBT presumes that attention to both skill acquisition and behavioral motivation is essential. In developing the treatment, however, it quickly became apparent that (1) focusing on patient change, either by motivation or by enhancing skills, is experienced as invalidating by chronically suicidal individuals and precipitates withdrawal, noncompliance, and, at times, early dropout from treatment; (2) skills training to the extent believed necessary is extraordinarily difficult if not impossible within the context of a therapy oriented to reducing the motivation to die or act in a suicidal fashion; (3) sufficient attention to motivational issues cannot be given in a treatment with the rigorous control of therapy agenda needed for skills training; (4) new behavioral coping skills are extraordinarily difficult to remember and apply when one is in a state of crisis, making generalization of skills to suicidogenic situations extraordinarily difficult without additional help; and (5) suicidal individuals often unwittingly reinforce therapists for iatrogenic treatment and punish them for effective treatment strategies.

Three modifications in standard behavior therapy were made to take these factors into account. First, strategies that better reflect radical acceptance and validation of patients' current capacities and behavioral functioning were gathered and added to the treatment. The dialectical emphasis of the treatment insures the balance of acceptance and change within the treatment as a whole and within each individual interaction. Second, the therapy was split into three components: one that focuses primarily on skill acquisition, one that focuses primarily on motivational issues and skill strengthening, and one designed explicitly to foster generalization of skills to everyday life outside the treatment context. Third, a consultation or team meeting with specific guidelines for keeping the therapist within the treatment frame was added as a fourth treatment component. The four modes in standard outpatient DBT are structured psychosocial individual or group therapy (for skills training), individual psychotherapy (addressing motivational and skills strengthening), telephone coaching with the individual therapist (addressing generalization), and peer consultation or supervision meetings (to treat the therapist). On a psychiatric inpatient or day-treatment unit, the coaching might be done by the milieu; in community mental health settings it might be done by after-hours teams or crisis phone workers. Within each treatment mode, DBT is characterized by a philosophy of dialectics, a biosocial theoretical perspective, a hierarchy of treatment targets specific to the mode, and a set of treatment strategy groups. Space here is too brief to give a detailed description of each component of the treatment. The interested reader is referred to the treatment manual and associated updates (Linehan, 1993a, 1993b).

A Biosocial Model

The emotional picture of the suicidal individual is one of chronic, aversive emotional dysregulation. Those individuals who suicide are characterized by extreme dysphoria, often combined with high anxiety and panic (Fawcett et al., 1990). Suicide attempters appear to be more angry, hostile, and irritable (Crook et al., 1975; Lester, 1968; Nelson et al., 1977; Paykel and Dienelt, 1971; Richman and Charles, 1976; Weissman et al., 1973) than nonsuicidal psychiatric and nonpsychiatric individuals and more depressed than both suicide completers (Maris, 1981) and other psychiatric and nonpsychiatric groups (Weissman, 1974).

Generally, suicidal individuals are unlikely to have the ability to ameliorate or tolerate the emotional, interpersonal, and behavioral stresses in their lives. Cognitive difficulties found in studies of suicide attempters consist of cognitive rigidity (Levenson, 1973; Neuringer, 1964; Patsiokas et al., 1979; Vinoda, 1966), dichotomous thinking (Neuringer, 1961), and poor abstract and interpersonal problem solving (Goodstein, 1982; Levenson and Neuringer, 1971; Schotte and Clum, 1982). Impairments in problem solving may be related to deficits in specific (as compared to general) episodic memory capabilities (Williams, 1992), which have been found to characterize suicide attempters when compared to other psychiatric patients. In my own work, we found that suicide attempters exhibit a more passive (or dependent) interpersonal problem-solving style (Linehan et al., 1987). Hopelessness is a strong predictor of both suicide attempts and eventual suicide (see Weishaar and Beck, 1992, for a review of this literature). Those who suicide are further characterized as indecisive and as having difficulties concentrating (Fawcett et al., 1990).

From a biosocial perspective, suicidal behaviors are viewed as problem-solving behaviors that function to remediate negative emotional arousal and distress directly (for example, by ending all life, and presumably pain, by putting the individual to sleep or distracting from emotional stimuli) or indirectly (for example, by expectations of insurance money for one's children or by eliciting help from the environment), or are viewed as inevitable outcomes of unregulated and uncontrollable negative emotions. Although suicidal behaviors are not logically inevitable outcomes, paradigms of escape conditioning suggest that strong urges to escape or actual escape behaviors can be learned so completely that they are automatic for some individuals when faced with extreme and uncontrollable physical or emotional pain. Suicide, of course, is the ultimate escape from problems in this life.

Among those who are *chronically* suicidal or who frequently attempt suicide, I have further hypothesized that this pattern of dysregulated emotion and behavior is a result of an initial temperamental or biological disposition to emotionality or inadequate modulation, combined with an invalidating rearing environment (Linehan, 1993a). Such an environment is characterized by a tendency to disregard emotional experiences, especially negative ones, to oversimplify the ease of solving difficult problems, and to put a high value on positive thinking. Although such attitudes are certainly beneficial for some, if not most, this type of environment invalidates the experiences of vulnerable individuals and does not take their communications seriously, especially when such communications have to do with nonpublic events and with difficulties meeting social expectations. Invalidating environments, especially neglectful and physically or sexually abusive families, contribute to the development of emotion dysregulation, as well as fail to teach the child how to label and regulate arousal, how to tolerate emotional distress, and when to trust one's own emotional responses as reflections of valid interpretations of events (see Wagner and Linehan, 1994, and Wagner and Linehan, 1998, for a review of the relationship between childhood abuse and subsequent suicidal behavior).

It is not unreasonable to suppose that vulnerable individuals exposed to such environments may eventually adopt the characteristics of the invalidating environment. They may invalidate their own affective experiences, look to others for accurate reflections of external reality, and oversimplify the ease of solving life's problems. This oversimplification leads inevitably to unrealistic goals, an inability to use reward instead of punishment for small steps toward final goals, and self-hate following failure to achieve these goals. Suicidal behavior in these individuals may function to punish or attack the self. It is not uncommon for chronically suicidal persons to say that they deserve to be hurt or to die. Intense shame, as well as exacerbation of intense emotionality, may also be a natural result of a social environment that "shames" those who express emotional vulnerability.

As noted above, suicidal behaviors can be very effective at ending unbearable emotions: by ending life itself, by distraction, by directly reregulating (for example, by sleep) the biological or emotional system, or by changing environmental characteristics precipitating the emotional distress. In addition, for the vulnerable but invalidated individual, suicidal behavior can communicate both to the suicidal individual himself or herself and to the environment. "Things are as bad as I say they are" is the message. These two polar extremes, vulnerability versus invalidation, represent the central dialectical dilemma of the chronically suicidal patient and his or her therapist.

Dialectics

DBT flows from a dialectical philosophical position. *Dialectics* is used here in two contexts, that of persuasive dialogue and relationship, and that of the fundamental nature of reality. From the point of view of dialogue and relationship, it refers to change by persuasion and by making use of the oppositions inherent in the therapeutic relationship, rather than by formal impersonal logic. Similar to cognitive constructionist theories, dialectics does not seek absolute truth but instead attempts to facilitate the construction or evolution of truth over time. As a world view, dialectics conveys the coexisting multiple tensions that must be addressed within the therapeutic relationship, as well as the emphases in DBT on (1) fostering a systems perspective (asking always "What is being left out of our understanding here?"); (2) searching for synthesis and balance (to replace the rigid, often extreme, and dichotomous response characteristics of both suicidal patients and their therapists); and (3) enhancing comfort with ambiguity and change, which are viewed as inevitable aspects of life. The overriding dialectic for the therapist is the necessity of acceptance of the patient as he or she is within the context of simultaneously trying to produce change. Treatment strategies are polarized into those most related to acceptance and those most related to change, although it is this very polarization that is the root of many therapeutic failures. DBT requires that the therapist balance use of these two types of strategies within each treatment interaction.

Treatment Targets

With suicidal patients, treatment targets for individual DBT therapy and for DBT as a whole are the same and are hierarchically arranged as follows: (1) reducing high-risk suicidal behaviors (intentional self-injury, including suicide attempts, high-risk suicidal ideation, plans, and threats); (2) reducing therapy interfering behaviors, that is, all responses or behaviors of both the patient and the therapist that make therapy progress or continuation difficult (for example, missing, coming late to sessions, or avoiding topics during sessions, phoning at unreasonable hours or otherwise pushing a therapist's limits, noncompliance, invalidating the other, not returning phone calls or otherwise pushing a patient's limits); (3) reducing behavioral patterns serious enough to interfere substantially with any chance of a reasonable quality of life, including patterns that put one in a high-risk group for suicidal behaviors (severe depression and other severe axis I disorders would qualify here, also homelessness, chronic losing relationships or jobs); (4) acquiring sufficient behavioral skills to meet patient goals (skills in emotion regulation, interpersonal effectiveness, distress tolerance, self-management, as well as mindfulness); (5) reducing post-traumatic stress responses related to previous traumatic events (that is, exposure based or psychodynamic "uncovering," treatment of sequelae of childhood abuse); (6) increasing self-respect; and (7) other goals of the patient. With respect to each target, the task of the therapist is first (and many times thereafter) to elicit the patient's collaboration in working on the target behavior, then to apply the relevant treatment strategies described below. Attention to each target within individual therapy, ordinarily involving direct and focused work on the behaviors relevant to the target, is jointly determined by the hierarchical list above and by the behaviors and problems that have surfaced since the last session or during the current session. Thus, treatment is oriented to current behaviors, with self-injury, suicide attempts, and life-threatening suicidal ideation, planning, and urges taking precedence over all other behavioral topics. Therapy is somewhat circular in that target focal points revolve over time. Note that DBT combines treating suicidal behaviors directly with a subsequent focus on treating the associated disorders.

Treatment Strategies

DBT addresses all problematic patient behaviors and therapy situations in a systematic, problem-solving manner that interweaves conducting a collaborative behavioral analysis, formulating hypotheses about possible variables influencing the problem, generating possible changes (behavioral solutions), and trying out and evaluating the solutions. The context for these analyses and this solution-oriented approach is that of validation of each patient's experiences, especially as they relate to the individual's vulnerabilities and sense of desperation. In contrast to many behavioral approaches, at least as described in print, DBT places great emphasis on the therapeutic relationship. In times of crisis, when all else fails, it is the relationship itself that may hold the patient in this life.

There are five very detailed groups of treatment strategies that are combined to deal with suicidal behaviors and other problematic situations. Not all strategies are necessary or appropriate for a given session; the pertinent combination may change over time and the emphasis on particular strategies varies depending on mode of treatment. These are more fully described in the treatment manual (Linehan, 1993a, 1993b).

Dialectical Strategies. Dialectical strategies are woven throughout all treatment interactions. The primary dialectical strategy is the balanced therapeutic stance described above. The constant attention to combining acceptance with change is thus the essence of the dialectical strategy. The goal is to bring out the opposites, both in therapy and the patient's life, and to provide conditions for syntheses. The key idea guiding the therapist's behavior is that for any point, an opposite position can be held. Synthesis and growth require a continuous search for what is being left out in both the therapist's and patient's current ordering of reality, and then assisting the patient to create new orderings that embrace and include what was previously excluded. The therapist helps the patient move from "either-or" to "both-and." Strategies include extensive use of stories, metaphor, myth, and paradox; the therapeutic use of ambiguity; drawing of the patient's attention to the fact of reality as constant change as well as the unavoidance of change in the therapeutic conditions; cognitive challenging and restructuring techniques; and reinforcement for use of intuitive, nonrational knowledge bases. Dialectical strategies, especially a dialectical framework on the part of the therapist, are essential in every interaction with the patient and also inform the treatment supervision and staff meetings.

Core Strategies. Core strategies consist of the balanced application of validation and problem solving. Validation requires the therapist to search for, recognize, and reflect the current validity, or sensibility, of the individual's response. With respect to suicidal behavior, in particular, it is important that the therapist recognize how life, indeed, may not be not worth living unless substantial changes are made (the assumption that needed changes can be made, of course, is what often differentiates the therapist from the patient). Pointing out how a response was functional in the past but is not functional in the present is invalidating, not validating. Nor is validating simply building up self-esteem— although cheerleading, focusing on the strengths of the individual, and believing in the individual no matter what, is an important part of validation.

Problem solving is a two-stage process involving, first, an analysis and acceptance of the problem at hand and, second, an attempt to generate, evaluate, and implement alternative solutions that might have been made or could be made in the future in similar problematic situations. Behavioral analyses and interpretive strategies require a very detailed chain analysis of the events and situational factors leading up to and following the particular problematic response at hand. Over time, the chains of events are examined for patterns and clues to information about factors influencing the problematic responses. The behavior analysis strategy is repeated for every instance of targeted problem behaviors (for example, suicide attempts, serious suicide threats, increase in suicidal ideation) until the patient achieves an understanding of the response patterns involved. The second stage, which is actually interwoven with the first, requires the generation of alternate response chains (that is, adaptive solutions to the problem), as well as an analysis of the individual's response capabilities. At each link in the chain leading from a precipitating situation to a suicidal response, the therapist engages the patient in looking for an alternate, more adaptive response that might have been made. This process often leads into brief skills acquisition strategies (for example, modeling, suggesting, or advising) or work on motivation and strengthening of skills the individual already has via attention to reinforcement contingencies, therapeutic exposure to reduce emotions inhibiting functional behavior, and changing cognitions that lead to dysfunctional behaviors.

Case Management Strategies. There are three case management strategies designed to guide each therapist during interactions with individuals outside the therapy dyad. The consultation or supervision strategy requires that each DBT therapist meet regularly with a supervisor or consultation team. The idea here is that severely suicidal individuals should not be treated alone. The extreme stress and anxiety inherent in such treatments can interfere with the most finely honed therapeutic skills. Therapists in these meetings apply many of the DBT strategies to each other, both validating each other and the problem-solving cases presented. The consultant-to-the-patient strategy is a simple concept but very hard to carry out. The strategy is the application of the principle that the DBT therapist teaches the patient how to interact effectively with the patient's environment, rather than teaching the environment how to interact with the patient. This strategy represents a point of view that looks at adversity and "bad" treatment of the patient by the environment (including other professional helpers) as an opportunity for practice and learning. From another perspective, it views the role of the therapist as teaching the patient to live in the world as it is, with all its problems and inequities.

The exception to the consultant strategy is in the following circumstance: The patient does not have the requisite capability (or sometimes willingness) to influence the environment, the immediate outcome is more important than the patient's long-term learning, and the therapist can influence the outcome. In this instance, the therapist works to affect immediate changes that are essential and that the patient cannot yet produce. Environmental intervention strategies can be particularly important for the suicidal patient when the therapist may need to intervene directly and immediately to save the patient's life or prevent serious harm.

Communication Strategies. In DBT, the therapist balances two communication strategies that represent rather different interactional styles. The modal style is the reciprocal strategy, which includes responsiveness to the patient's agenda and wishes, warmth, and self-disclosure of both personal information that might be useful to the patient and immediate reactions to the patient's behavior. Reciprocity is balanced by an irreverent communication style that is characterized by a matter-of-fact attitude wherein the therapist takes the patient's underlying assumptions or unnoticed implications of the patient's behavior and maximizes or minimizes them, in either an unemotional or overemotional manner, to make a point the patient might not have considered before. The essence of the strategy is that it "jumps track," so to speak, from the patient's current pattern of response, thought, or emotion.

Structural Strategies. A set of structural strategies specify for the therapist how to start and end therapy, how to set an agenda and organize time during sessions, and how to terminate DBT. For example, DBT uses a number of strategies drawn from social psychology to create and enhance commitment to living, therapy, and change. There are, as well, a number of integrative strategies covering crisis management, suicidal behavior, compliance and relationship issues, medication, and use of ancillary treatments. The suicidal behavior strategies are described next.

The task of the therapist in responding to suicidal behavior is twofold. First, therapists must respond actively enough to block patients from actually killing or seriously harming themselves. Second, therapists must respond in a fashion that minimizes reinforcement of suicidal behavior. Requirements of these two tasks often conflict. Therapy with suicidal patients is similar to walking a tightrope stretched over the Grand Canyon. Bending one direction, the therapist must act to keep the patient alive in the present. Bending the other direction, the therapist must be careful not to respond in a manner that increases the likelihood of future suicide. The tension arises between demands to keep a patient alive versus demands to teach the patient behavioral patterns that will make staying alive worthwhile. Complicating all of this are the fears almost all therapists have of falling off the tightrope with the patient and of being held responsible for a patient's death if a misstep is taken and balance is lost.

How therapists respond to any single instance of suicidal behavior or threat will always be mitigated by characteristics of the individual patient, the situation, and the relationship between patient and therapist. The protocols presented here are designed to provide the therapist with general guidelines for responding to suicidal behavior, including chronic and frequent suicidal ideation, threats, and suicide attempts, as well as a crisis-oriented protocol for responding to specific threats of suicide. The first protocol has to do with planning interventions aimed directly at reducing suicidal behaviors. The second has to do with responding to situations where the patient is at imminent risk of attempted suicide or suicide.

Keep in mind that the protocols described here are designed to fit within a larger context of psychotherapy. Although they have been evaluated empirically only within the larger framework of dialectical behavior therapy, they are meant as general guidelines to be used within any therapeutic approach. The reader who does not share a behavioral theoretical orientation will need to do some translating of technical terms, but many of the ideas, if not the terms, are general ones expressed by therapists of many different orientations.

PROTOCOL ONE

A number of specific steps can assist in the treatment planning of suicidal patients. A detailed protocol is presented below.

Assess the Long-Term Risk of Attempted Suicide or Suicide

Treatment planning with suicidal patients requires that therapists have a reasonably good idea of how much actual risk of attempted suicide or suicide is actually present. Two types of assessment are important: short-term or imminent risk and long-term risk, which are outlined in Table 9.1 and Exhibit 9.1. (For a further discussion of short-versus long-term risks for suicide, see Chapters One, Two, and Seven.) Therapists must have these risk factors firmly committed to memory so they are available to recall at a moment's notice. It is not possible to look up risk factors in the middle of a crisis.

Table 9.1. Factors Associated with Long-Term Risk for Attempted Suicide or Suicide.

	Attempted Suicide	Suicide
Environmental characteristics		
Life changes/negative events	Losses (particularly interpersonal)[a]	Losses (particularly interpersonal)
	Sexual abuse history	Sexual abuse history
	Major upsetting events	—
	Uncontrolled events	—
	Jailed	Jailed
Social support		
Work	Absent	Absent
Marital rates	Unmarried > married	Unmarried > married
Marital frequency	Married > unmarried	Married > unmarried
Family	Hostile	Less available
Interpersonal contact	Low/has no confidant	Low/lives alone
Church membership	—	Absent
Models	Socially linked to other parasuicides	Family suicide rate higher
Method availability	Available	Available
Demographic characteristics		
Sex	Female > male	Male > female[b]
Age	Decreases with age	Increases with age[c]
Race	Nonwhites overrepresented	White > nonwhite
Behavioral characteristics		
Overt motor		
Interpersonal	Low social involvement	Low social involvement
	Less likely to ask for help	Less likely to ask for support or attention
	High friction and conflict	—[d]

	20 percent–55 percent previous parasuicide	20 percent–65 percent previous parasuicide
Styles	Alcohol and drug abuse	Alcohol and drug abuse
	—	Criminal behavior (young men)
	Unemployed	Unemployed or retired
Cognitive		
Style	Rigid	—
	Possibly impulsive	—
	Passive problem solvers	—
Content	Possibly hopeless	Hopeless
	Powerless	—
	Negative self-concept	—
Physiological/affective		
Affective	Angry, hostile	Apathetic, anhedonia
	Depressed	Depressed
	Dissatisfied with treatment	Indifferent to treatment
	High preference for affiliation and affection	Possibly dependent, dissatisfied
	Uncomfortable with people	Psychic anxiety, panic attacks
	Possibly poor health	Poor health (increases with age)
		Insomnia
Somatic	—	Low pain tolerance
	Low frustration tolerance	
Genetic/biochemical	—[e]	Suicide in biological relatives; low CSF 5-HIAA levels

[a]For children, conflict with parents also increases risk.

[b]The risk is almost equal among male and female psychiatric patients.

[c]For blacks, the risk decreases with age.

[d]Data are mixed on friction and conflict; some find increased risk with lower conflict.

[e]Risk of violent parasuicide increases if CSF 5-HIAA levels are low.

Source: Linehan, 1993a.

Exhibit 9.1. Factors Associated with Imminent Risk for Attempted Suicide or Suicide.

Direct indexes of imminent risk for suicide or attempted suicide
1. Suicide threats
2. Suicide planning or preparation
3. Suicide attempt in the last year, especially if suicide intent expressed at time
4. Suicide ideation

Indirect indexes of imminent risk for suicide or attempted suicide
5. Patient's shift into suicide or attempted suicide risk population
6. Recent disruption or loss of interpersonal relationship; negative environmental changes in past month
7. Indifference to or dissatisfaction with therapy; elopements and early pass return by hospitalized patients
8. Current hopelessness or anger or both; increased psychological perturbation
9. Recent medical care
10. Indirect references to own death; arrangements for death

Circumstances associated with suicide or attempted suicide in the next several hours or days
11. Major depression with
    a. Severe agitation, psychic anxiety, panic attacks; severe obsessive ruminating or compulsive behaviors
    b. Global insomnia
    c. Severe anhedonia
    d. Diminished concentration, indecision
12. Alcohol consumption
13. Suicide note written or in progress
14. Methods available or easily obtained
15. Isolation
16. Precautions against discovery or intervention; deception or concealment about timing, place, and so forth
17. First twenty-four hours of jail incarceration
18. Recent media publicity about a suicide

Source: Linehan, 1993a.

Conduct Comprehensive Analysis of Suicidal Behaviors

Changing behavior requires, at a minimum, a good understanding of the behaviors in need of change. A thorough description of problematic behaviors is a good starting point. Because verbal labels, such as "depressed" or "suicide attempt," often mean different things to different people, it is essential to get a precise definition of what a specific patient means by the terms he or she uses. It is also important to understand the function of the problem behaviors in the patient's life and what other patient responses or events are associated with those behaviors. The chain analysis focuses on the function and context of behavior.

Information on suicidal behaviors is gathered at two points in therapy. During intake sessions, the therapist should take a comprehensive history of all previous suicidal behaviors, including suicidal ideation or wanting to be dead, planning or threatening suicide, and all suicidal acts, even if there was no intent to die. Thereafter, all changes in suicidal ideation, suicide crisis behavior, and instances of self-injury and suicide attempts should be individually assessed and analyzed. When taking a history, it is important to inquire about past suicidal behaviors even for patients who do not appear to be currently suicidal. Patients should be asked about suicidal behaviors per se as well as about times when they intentionally harmed or injured themselves with no thought of committing suicide. Behavioral analyses of suicidal behaviors include several steps as follows.

Describe Suicidal Behaviors in Detail. The frequency and emotional intensity of suicidal ideation and urges to suicide in the past (for intake assessments), currently, and since the last contact should be described. Although continued suicidal ideation and urges to self-injure do not always need to be discussed in detail in every therapy session, significant changes, either increases or decreases, should be explored even if only briefly. Periodically, the therapist should assess whether the patient has made plans to attempt suicide and has the means available to carry out a suicide attempt. Similar information regarding urges to self-injure should also be obtained. Current suicidal ideation may be communicated spontaneously and directly or may only be hinted at and require considerable probing by the therapist. With some patients, the only hint of suicidal ideation may be the presence of an event known to be a frequent precipitant of suicidal ideation. At other times, the only hint may be behaviors frequently found in individuals considering suicide, such as statements that life is not worth living or giving gifts to others of important belongings.

Suicide crisis behaviors, that is, behaviors that make someone think suicide is imminent (such as suicide threats), may have occurred in interactions with the therapist or they may have occurred in interactions with other individuals, such as family or inpatient staff, and be communicated to the therapist by these third parties. Frequency of these behaviors in the past should be determined during intake assessments. When these behaviors occur during ongoing therapy, they should be reviewed during therapy sessions to be sure there is agreement on just what the behaviors were, including what was said, how it was said, and any other activities engaged in, such as writing a suicide note, obtaining lethal means, and so forth. If the suicide threat was made to other mental health professionals, family, or friends who then informed the therapist, the story received from these others should be discussed with the patient to obtain a fuller description of exactly what was said and done, how it was said and done, and under what circumstances. With the chronically suicidal patient, it is particularly important to keep up on whether or not the patient is obtaining and keeping suicide implements (buying or keeping guns, ropes, or poisons; hoarding drugs; carrying razors around; and so forth).

With respect to suicide attempts in the immediate or distant past, the therapist should assess the exact nature of the self-injurious behavior (for example, where and how deep was the cut, exactly which and what quantities of chemicals or drugs were ingested), the environmental context (for example, alone, with others), the physical effects, any medical attention obtained, the presence of accompanying suicidal ideation, communications to others, and conscious intent. Therapists often find it extremely difficult to focus on obtaining this material, but it is important nonetheless.

Monitor Ongoing Behavior. In ongoing psychotherapy, it is important that the therapist know about suicidal behaviors that occur between sessions. Certainly, the therapist can ask about suicidal behaviors. However, in my experience, once suicidal behaviors have not occurred for a number of weeks, it gets increasingly difficult for the therapist to ask about the behavior. Therapists often are reluctant to ask about suicidal ideation or suicide attempts every week if they have not occurred for the last six months. Nonetheless, in my experience, increases in suicidality are unlikely to be spontaneously reported. Suicide attempts may or may not be reported depending on whether the function of the act is communication to the therapist. Events that have historically precipitated suicidal behaviors may be reported only after the suicidal behavior occurs. The often reported increase in suicide risk as patients improve from a depression may be due to the neglect of suicidality rather than its absence.

The easiest solution to these difficulties is to have the patient fill out a diary card or some other record form each and every week, where information is obtained on a daily basis about relevant behaviors. If diaries are being kept on other behaviors, such as daily activities and thoughts in cognitive therapy, spaces for recording suicidal behaviors and their precipitants can be incorporated into those forms. Or if some form of weekly in-session monitoring is used, such as giving patients a depression inventory before each psychotherapy session, questions about suicidal responses can be inserted. Information can be obtained about types and amounts of prescription, over-the-counter, and illicit drugs taken (which keeps the therapist aware of the "lethal means" available to the patient), degree of suicidal ideation, urges to suicide, degree of misery (or *perturbation* in Shneidman's terms, see Chapter Five), known precipitants of suicidal behaviors, and whether any suicidal acts have occurred.

Generally, any suicidal behaviors that are typical for the specific patient should be monitored, although a case could be made for monitoring suicidal ideation and urges to suicide as well as degree of misery or perturbation among all suicidal patients. If very high suicidal ideation or urges to self-injure are reported, they should, of course, be assessed to determine whether the patient is a high risk for suicide or attempted suicide. Intentional self-injury—especially when dealing with chronically suicidal or self-injurious patients for whom self-mutilation, overdosing on drugs, or other suicidal acts are frequent—should be assessed and discussed, never ignored. Failure to take prescribed drugs may be a risk factor both because the symptoms the drugs target may increase, thereby precipitating suicidal behavior, and also because it may signal hoarding of lethal doses of medications.

Conduct Moment-to-Moment Chain Analyses of Environmental and Behavioral Events Linked to Suicidal Behavior. Once a fairly good description of the patient's suicidal behaviors is obtained, the next step is to solicit information about the precipitants of the behavior and the consequences. During the first several therapy sessions, this information should be obtained about previous suicidal behaviors. A detailed chain analysis should be carried out in excruciating, moment-to-moment detail. The therapist should elicit enough detail to clarify the environmental events, emotional and cognitive responses, and overt actions that sequentially led up to the suicidal response as well as the consequences of the suicidal behavior (and thus the functions it served). The starting point of the analysis is the moment the patient identifies as the beginning of the suicidal crisis, or the moment of the first thought or urge to commit suicide, threaten suicide, or intentionally self-injure. One indirect (but intended) consequence of such a detailed and specific assessment is that the questions themselves highlight that (contrary to the patient's beliefs) suicidal responses are not necessary responses to the moment under discussion.

It is of critical importance to determine whether suicidal behavior is primarily respondent behavior, operant behavior, or both. Behavior is respondent when it is automatically elicited by a situation or specific stimulus event. The behavior is under the control of the preceding events; often it is impulsive. With respect to suicidal behavior, the behavioral paradigm here is that of escape learning. That is, suicidal responses are viewed as escape behaviors elicited by aversive conditions, such as traumatic events or physical or emotional pain.

When Shneidman proposes that the universal precipitant of suicidal behavior is unbearable perturbation, he is proposing that suicidal behavior should be conceived of as respondent. Suicidal ideation and urges elicited by extreme panic or by explosive anger are examples.

When the suicidal behavior is operant, it is under the control of the consequences. Operant behaviors function to affect the environment. When suicide, suicide attempts, and suicidal ideation and threats function to reunite one with dead loved ones or to elicit care or guilt, get others to take one seriously, get into a hospital, and so on (assuming these outcomes are not neutral), the behavior is functionally operant. The notion of suicidal behavior as a "cry for help," popularized by Shneidman and Farberow (1957), is an example of suicidal behavior as operant.

It is extremely important that the therapist not *assume* suicidal behavior is operant or respondent. Assessment is crucial. Neither theory nor the patient's diagnosis can answer this question; only careful observation can. Much of the time, suicidal behaviors, especially chronic suicide attempts and suicide threats, are simultaneously respondent and operant. Hopelessness, despair, and the unbearableness of life elicit the behavior. The community response (for example, giving help, taking the person seriously, taking the person out of difficult situations, taking responsibility for the person, and providing care for the person) reinforces the behavior.

Connect Suicidal Behaviors to Overall Behavioral Patterns. The therapist should help the patient see patterns of suicidal behavior that are occurring. Generally, this will involve pointing out regularities, such as usual precipitants and consequences, together with an analysis of the importance of these regularities. Once such patterns become clear, the therapist and patient can focus more attention on learning how to handle problematic situations more effectively or on how to generate desired outcomes in nonsuicidal ways.

Conduct Comprehensive Solutions Analysis

Suicidal behaviors always occur within a matrix of precipitating problematic events and expected or real consequences that reduce or solve the precipitating problems. Whether one views the problematic events as fundamentally environmental, biological, or psychological (that is, as caused by intrapsychic conflict, emotional dysregulation, dysfunctional cognitive processes, mental or physical disease, or some other characteristic of the individual's psychosocial world) depends primarily on one's theoretical point of view. However, no matter what one's theoretical view is, an important focus of treatment with the suicidal person must, of necessity, be the amelioration of the problems setting off suicidal behaviors as well as the replacement of suicidal responses with nonsuicidal, skillful responses to problematic events. Solutions analysis is the phase of treatment wherein patient and therapist analyze the problem from this perspective: What solutions other than suicidal behaviors could be applied to the problem at hand?

Identify Ways to Prevent or Reduce Precipitants to Suicidal Behaviors or Replace Suicidal Responses with More Skillful and Adaptive Responses to Precipitating Events. Although suicidal individuals often see no way out of their problems except suicide or parasuicide, there are, of course, any number of other ways to solve problematic situations, even ones accompanied by seemingly unendurable pain. If it were not so, the suicide rate would be far higher than it is. In analyzing various solutions, the therapist and (optimally) the patient must address several questions.

The first question has to do with whether the individual has the capacity to modify problematic precipitating events. Can the individual prevent problematic precipitating events from occurring again or resolve them once they start? Does the individual have the requisite capabilities to engage in more adaptive responses to problematic events? Does the individual have the capacity to construct or reconstruct a life worth living? The exact questions necessary here will be mostly a function of one's theories about what the individual's core problems actually are. If the problems are viewed as primarily environmental or interpersonal, then the questions must address whether the individual has the necessary skills to change the environment or improve interpersonal relationships. If not, what new capabilities does the individual need? If the problems are emotional or physical, does the individual have the ability to change or improve his or her own emotional and physical functioning? Can the person regulate his or her own emotional and physical responses to events? If not, what new capacities are needed? Psychodynamic therapists might ask whether the individual has the capacity for insight or analysis and resolution of intrapsychic conflicts. Does the individual have the necessary capacity to regulate cognitive processes, such as attention, or reduce unwanted cognitive interference, such as hallucinations? If not, what new cognitive capabilities are needed? Cognitive therapists might ask whether or not the individual needs to learn new schemas or information-processing strategies. Is the individual capable, even, of learning new information processing strategies? If the answer to these questions is "no," a focus on skills training procedures is appropriate. If capacities can be restored with medication, a somatic intervention may also be called for.

The second question has to do with whether capacities that the patient actually has are being used. Careful analyses of factors inhibiting or interfering with implementation of the solution is a very important part of problem solving. Generally, these analyses will focus on motivational factors. There are, of course, a number of motivational models used in psychotherapy. Where one searches for motivational problems will depend largely on the therapist's theories. Several hypotheses can usefully be examined. Conditioned, negative emotional responses, such as fear or shame, may inhibit many responses. Patients may be too afraid or ashamed to engage in the necessary problem-solving behaviors. Or emotional responses such as rage or panic may interfere with the patient's ability to think or may disrupt capable behaviors. Exposure-based procedures (for example, formal desensitization, emotionally expressive procedures) may be useful. Inhibition can also be due to maladaptive beliefs, self-statements, and expectations. Hopelessness, the belief that nothing will help, is characteristic among suicidal patients and is a belief that clearly inhibits active coping strategies; therefore, formal or informal cognitive interventions may be useful.

Skillful response can also be precluded by the prior emission of incompatible behaviors. This is most likely when inappropriate, incompatible behaviors are higher in the individual's response hierarchy (usually because of a stronger history of reinforcement) than appropriate, effective responses. Suicidal ideation and rumination, similar to excessive worry, may be avoidance behaviors that successfully keep the patient from encountering the actual source of problems (see Borkovec, 1990, for a further discussion of this theoretical point). Contingencies operating in the patient's current environment may favor ineffective over effective behavior. In invalidating environments, in particular, people often listen more carefully and respond more caringly when an individual threatens or attempts suicide. Suicidal behavior often "wakes up" the environment and elicits behaviors from others that nothing short of suicidal behavior could elicit.

It can be extremely difficult to withhold reinforcement from an individual when the consequence for such restraint is that the individual may end up dead. It is essential, however, that the therapist be vigilant to reinforce nonsuicidal behaviors that represent clinical progress. In addition, contingent relationships between suicidal behaviors and reinforcing outcomes must be broken. Although clinicians often believe the only way to do this is by withholding reinforcers or by pairing them with aversive consequences, the other way to break a contingency is to make reinforcers easily obtainable by many other responses. For example, in DBT, patients may call their therapist between sessions when they are suicidal. But they can also call to hear the therapist's voice (that is, for contact), for coaching in noncrisis situations, and to repair the relationship. The only time they cannot call their therapist is the twenty-four hours following a nonfatal suicidal act. In analyzing solutions to a particular problem situation or life pattern, the therapist must be careful to assess adequately the variables influencing the patient's suicidal behavior in that particular area rather than blindly applying a preformulated theory. Once the therapist and patient have figured out what is interfering with use of effective problem-solving behaviors, they can jointly consider how to proceed.

Discuss Alternative Solutions Versus Tolerance. Not all problems can be solved immediately. At times, solving one problem can create other, more serious problems. Although behavior therapy has historically emphasized solving problems by changing one's self or the environment, it is also important for the therapist to suggest that one solution to the problem is to simply tolerate the painful consequences, including negative affect, which the situation has generated. The Alcoholics Anonymous prayer is relevant here: the therapist must often teach the patient to accept what cannot be changed.

Develop Commitment to Nonsuicidal Behavioral Responses. The final step is eliciting and maintaining a commitment from the patient to stay alive, avoid suicidal behavior, and use the problem-solving strategies just developed. An enormous amount of evidence indicates that the commitment to behave in a particular way, particularly when the commitment is made publicly instead of privately, is strongly related to future performance (for example, Hall et al., 1990; Wang and Katzev, 1990). Whether these commitments should be written or not is matter of personal preference. Frequently, the suicidal patient will maintain that there is no solution to the problem except suicidal behavior. Two responses are possible. First, the therapist can review with the patient the previous commitment to try to avoid suicidal behavior. Second, the therapist can generate other alternative behaviors and elicit a commitment from the patient to try such behaviors on an experimental basis. One alternative behavior is for the patient to call for help before engaging in suicidal behaviors.

Have a Definite Stance on Suicide. Although many, if not most, therapists would agree that obtaining a commitment to stay alive is important in treating suicidal patients, some therapists argue that a patient's rights to self-determination and the need to validate the individual patient's ability to make life-and-death choices should be considered more important. Nor do all therapists believe that obtaining a commitment to reduce or avoid intentional self-injury is important. When treating patients who have experienced extremely abusive or controlling environments, in particular, some therapists believe it is important to allow patients greater behavioral choice without pressure to stop nonfatal suicidal behavior. Although such positions are clearly matters of individual values and ethics, it is essential that therapists be very clear on their positions vis-à-vis these issues.

Among some individuals the desire to be dead is often reasonable in that it is based on a life that currently is not "livable." Although many biological and psychological theories suggest that such a position is inevitably due to some sort of mood or cognitive disorder, at times the problem is not one of distorting positive situations into negative situations. Instead, the problem is that the patient simply has too many life crises, environmental stressors, problematic interpersonal relationships, difficult employment situations or physical problems to enjoy life or find meaning in it. In addition, the patient may have habitual dysfunctional behavior patterns that create their own stress as well as interfere with any chance of creating a life of quality. In sum, some individuals have good reasons for wanting to be dead.

Although some therapists can be quite effective in helping competent individuals decide whether suicide is a reasonable life option, most therapists cannot oscillate back and forth between the role of neutral confidant or advisor and advocate of "life under any circumstances." Thus, at the very beginning of therapy (or with all patients), the therapist must decide whether or not the goal of therapy is to help the individual decide whether to live or die, or whether the goal is to help the individual create a life that is worth living. In the latter case, therapists, even when confronted by lives of incalculable pain, must always be on the side of life over death by suicide. Reasons for this stance against suicide are as follows. First, the agenda of many suicidal patients seems at times to be to convince the therapist that life is indeed not worth living. Such arguments may have many different functions. The patient may assume that if the therapist agrees, he or she will intervene directly (magically, perhaps) and change the quality of the patient's life. Or the patient may be trying to work up courage to commit suicide. Or the patient may be using the process of arguing with the therapist to elicit reasons for hope and reassurance. Whatever the reason, a therapist can easily become convinced by patients that they are right. Not only does the patient's life seem unlivable, but the therapist may see no way out for the patient. Then both patient and therapist may be hopeless (see Chapter Nineteen).

A therapist's hopeless beliefs about a particular patient, however, are no better as a guide to reading the future than are the patient's hopeless beliefs. That is, a therapist may feel hopeless about a patient who subsequently improves the quality of his or her life dramatically. This is not a particular deficit on the therapist's part. Feelings of hopelessness by the therapist, at least with patients in intense and unremitting pain, are common. But current life events of the therapist, the state of the therapeutic relationship, and transitory moods of both therapist and patient influence these feeling of hopelessness certainly as much as factors actually predictive of future progress.

Although a therapist might believe that any quality of life is worth living, lives of many individuals come perilously near the edge. Whether the suffering is due to their own behavior or uncontrollable environmental events is irrelevant. Indeed, one can make the case that keeping a patient alive within an untenable life is no admirable feat. Thus, therapy must be more than a suicide prevention program. It must be a life improvement program as well. The desire to suicide, however, has at its base a belief that life cannot or will not improve. Although that may be true in some instances, it is not true in all instances. Death, however, unequivocally rules out hope. We do not have any data that people who are dead lead better lives.

Some individuals at times make informed and rational decisions to commit suicide. This phenomenon is certainly not limited to those not in psychiatric or psychological treatment. Nor are patients with mental disorders incapable of making an informed decision about whether to commit suicide. However, beliefs in individual liberty do not mean that the therapist must agree with any person that suicide is a good, or even an acceptable, choice. In the face of persistent attempts on the part of some patients to convince the therapist that suicide is a good idea as well as their occasional success in such attempts, the therapist is well served by a predetermined, nonnegotiable position on suicide. It cannot be a debatable option lest the patient lose. Although one can value those whose therapeutic task from the very initiation of treatment is to help patients choose whether to live or die, allowing such a possibility when treating suicidal patients insures, it seems to me, that some of the time the therapist will encourage suicide for an individual who, if he or she lives, will not regret living. Knowing that some who live may regret that choice, the therapist who takes the stance of life must also accept the responsibility of giving every help possible to assist the individual create a life that is worth living. There is an old saying that he who saves a life is then responsible for that life.

A strong case can be made against ignoring self-injurious and suicidal acts, even in the short term and even when there is no lethal intent and no medical risk of substantial harm or death. First, self-injurious and suicidal behaviors are linked to subsequent suicide. Parasuicide (including both types of behavior), for example, is the best predictor of suicide (see Maris et al., 1992, for a review of this literature). Second, self-injury damages the body, often irrevocably. Cutting and burning, for example, cannot be undone. Scars are permanent. Other forms of nonfatal suicide acts not only damage the body but hold out the possibility of accidental death. Third, actions based on the intent to harm one's self are simply incompatible with every other goal of any therapy. The effectiveness of all voluntary psychotherapy is based, at least to some extent, on developing an intent to help one's self rather than harm one's self. Thus, treatment of suicidal behavior goes to the heart of the therapeutic task. Fourth, it is quite difficult for the therapist to credibly communicate caring for the patient if the therapist does not react to the patient's deliberate self-harm or attempt to die. Responding to a suicide attempt by insisting that it must stop, and devoting the full resources of therapy to preventing it, is a communication with compassion and care at its very core.

Reinforce Nonsuicidal, Adaptive Responses. It may go without saying, but it is essential nonetheless, that therapists reinforce patients for coping with problematic situations in ways other than suicide crisis behaviors or suicide attempts. Reinforcers may include increased therapist warmth, a more ambient therapeutic session, and control over the use of session time. Attention and positive feedback are generally effective here, but the therapist must be very careful that praise not be interpreted by the patient as lack of concern about the patient's continued emotional distress. A patient's reports of high misery, but low suicidal ideation or self-injurious urges, should be met with as much care and concern as high suicidal ideation. If the patient has to continue suicidal behavior to elicit concern and active therapeutic help, one can be assured that suicidal behaviors will continue. Also, the therapist should be alert to the need to reassure the patient that therapy is not going to end just because suicidal behavior is improving.

Focus on Negative Effects of Suicidal Behavior. The therapist should enumerate or elicit from the patient the actual or potential negative effects of the suicidal behavior. It is important that the patient begin to see the negative interpersonal consequences of both suicide crisis behaviors and suicide attempts. Suicidal patients may need considerable help in understanding the emotional impact of their behavior on others and how suicidal behavior is interpreted by others. Giving the patient feedback on any negative impact of the suicidal behaviors, on the therapeutic relationship, and on the therapist's feelings and attitudes toward the patient can be very useful.

If the behavior was conducted in private and no negative environmental effects are immediately obvious, the therapist can point out that over the long run, suicidal behavior is not going to work as a means to resolve problems, even if it does temporarily alleviate painful affective states or obtain needed help from the environment. The negative effects of the suicidal behavior on the patient's self-esteem can be discussed. The therapist must be careful not to fall into the trap of agreeing with the patient that suicidal behavior was a good, or the only, solution to the problem. In the case of suicidal ideation, the therapist should address the fact that thinking about suicide in response to problems-in-living serves only to divert attention from ways of solving the problem to ways of escaping the problem.

Maintain a Strong Relationship

A strong, positive relationship with a suicidal patient is absolutely essential. Although some other types of therapies may be effective with certain individuals or may target complaints without such a relationship, or with a considerably diluted relationship, this is not true of work with suicidal patients. Indeed, the strength of the relationship is what keeps the patient, and often the therapist, in the therapy. The effectiveness of many treatment strategies relies upon the presence of a positive relationship between patient and therapist. There are also times when the positive relationship will help the therapist maintain a working alliance with the patient or prevent her or him from responding with hostility, frustration, or other countertherapeutic behaviors.

Validate Suicidal Feelings

No matter how unreasonable the suicidal behavior may appear to be, the therapist must always be careful to express understanding of the feelings of unbearable psychological pain that led the patient to consider suicide. It is quite easy to get carried away with invalidating suicidal behavior as a solution to problems and to neglect to validate the feelings that led up to the behavior. The patient who feels invalidated by the therapist may feel forced to suicide as a means of self-validation.

PROTOCOL TWO

An active therapeutic response is called for when a patient communicates directly or indirectly an intent to commit suicide or to engage in a nonlethal suicidal act. Communications can occur in a crisis situation, and then the therapist is faced with determining the immediate risk, possibly at an inconvenient time and over the telephone. In other instances, the patient may directly or indirectly communicate an intent to commit suicide or to engage in other intentional self-injurious behavior (such as self-mutilation) during a scheduled treatment session with the threatened suicidal behavior either to take place very soon (for example, that night) or only if some future event occurs (such as an anticipated rejection or failure of the therapy).

The recommended treatment protocol is a blend of crisis intervention and rehabilitation medicine models: whenever possible, therapists keep individuals in their stressful environments and go in themselves and help the individuals learn to cope with life as it is. Patients are strengthened *in the situation* (even when the situation is best described as an emotional or mood state), not out of the situation. The philosophy is that "now is the time to learn new behavior." The notion is to "strike while the iron is hot." The limiting caveat is that the risk of imminent suicide must be of paramount importance and the therapist's sense of liability cannot be ignored completely. The following protocol is designed to address threats of imminent attempted suicide and suicide.

Assess Risk of Immediate Suicide or Attempted Suicide

Persons who commit suicide as well as those who engage in nonlethal suicide attempts frequently communicate their intent ahead of time. Patients who habitually self-injure, for example, may report urges to mutilate themselves or put themselves to sleep for a week. These individuals may be very clear that they have no intent to commit suicide. For example, persons planning to cut their wrists sometimes say that they are cutting (or "have to cut") to relieve unbearable tension. Similarly, individuals planning suicide may be very direct about their plan to die.

Patients often think about or plan suicidal behavior without directly informing the therapist. A question, then, is whether one ought to ask about suicidal ideation if the patient has not brought up the topic. Several events might cue the therapist to probe for suicidal ideation. Most important, the occurrence of any event known to have been a precipitant of a prior suicide attempt, a suicide crisis, or serious suicidal ideation should prompt such questioning. In particular, the therapist should be very alert to specific, almost identical events that have been associated with previous suicidal behavior or intent. Past behavior in context is the best predictor of future behavior in the same context. Especially for the patient who repeatedly attempts suicide, the events that have previously precipitated near-lethal behavior (in contrast to similar but not identical events that precipitate much less lethal behavior) may precipitate suicide in the present. The therapist should not expect the patient to be particularly forthcoming about this and instead should assume that the patient may downplay lethal intent if questioned. In addition, statements by individuals that they can't stand it any longer, wish they were dead, believe others would be better off without them, and so forth, should alert the therapist to probe further.

Once it is clear that the patient is considering suicide, the next task is to assess the immediate risk factors outlined in Exhibit 9.1. Questions should be asked about the intended method and whether the implements for such a method are currently available or can be easily obtained. In the case of a proposed drug overdose, the therapist must ask for the name of every drug that the patient has, together with the number of pills left and their dosage levels. In addition, the therapist should determine whether the patient has written a suicide note, has any plans for being alone or isolated, or has taken any precautions against discovery or intervention. It is also important to assess how available other people are to the patient now and how available they will be over the next several days. The therapist should be alert to signs of severe or deepening depressive affect and of emerging panic attacks. If the risk assessment takes place over the phone, the therapist should ask where the patient is at the moment, how available other people are at the moment, and whether the patient has been drinking or taking nonprescribed drugs. In the case of intoxication, it is very important that the therapist not downplay the risk simply because the person does not sound or act obviously intoxicated.

The response to the patient's threatening suicide, however, will depend on the therapist's estimate of the actual risk of death or substantial harm. Therefore, it is important that the therapist make some attempt to ascertain the lethality of the drugs the patient has ingested or threatened to ingest. There are a number of aids and procedures. First, the therapist should have close at hand information about all the prescription and nonprescription drugs the patient is known to possess or take, together with information about dosage levels, the prescribing physician, and the patient's weight in kilos. Second, unless medically qualified, the therapist should always check his or her assessment of lethality immediately with a medically qualified person. If usual medical consultation is not available, the best place to call is a local public hospital emergency room. This is the place least likely to want unnecessary hospitalizations and thus most likely to want to help the therapist. Patients may threaten suicide by means other than a drug overdose. The therapist must know the likely lethality of various methods of suicide. Obviously, the threat to jump from a height of three feet is less potentially lethal than the threat to jump from a height of fifty feet. Common methods in order of decreasing lethality are (1) firearms and explosives, (2) jumping from high places, (3) cutting and piercing vital organs, (4) hanging, (5) drowning (cannot swim), (6) poisoning (solids and liquids), (7) cutting and piercing nonvital organs, (8) drowning (can swim), (9) poisoning (gases), and (10) ingestion of analgesic and soporific substances (Schultz, 1982).

Explore the Problem Now

During crisis and under high emotional arousal, individuals quite often lose track of the event that precipitated the emotional response in the first place. The tendency is to attend not only to the precipitating event, but to all similar events that have occurred either in the patient's life or in the past several weeks. One event may have set off the crisis, but the patient may rapidly switch from one topic to another in trying to communicate what is happening to her or him. The therapist should continuously help the patient focus on what exactly has happened since the last contact and not be drawn into a discussion of all the negative events in the patient's life.

Identify Key Events That Have Set Off Current Emotional Response. Frequently, a very minor event will set off an overwhelming crisis response. In these instances, it is critical that the therapist help the patient identify that precipitating event. Often, the patient will list a whole series of unmanageable events and life conditions. The therapist should listen and respond selectively. That is, the therapist responds only to workable material and ignores irrelevant or unmanageable aspects of the story. The patient should be asked to be both concrete and specific in describing events. The therapist should select some portion of the patient's crisis response, such as feeling overwhelmed, hopeless, desperate, suicidal, and so on, and ask the patient to pinpoint just exactly when that response first began, when it increased or decreased, and so on. The idea is to constantly link a specific patient crisis response (or set of responses) to a specific event or series of events.

Formulate and Summarize the Problem Situation with Patient. Problem formulation and summary may be needed repeatedly during a crisis session. The therapist should focus on arriving at an agreement on a definition of the problem's main elements. Quite often, the patient will focus on solutions to the problem without adequately defining the precipitating problem. Of course, a main solution often put forward by the patient is suicidal behavior. In crisis intervention, it is very easy to get diverted by overfocusing on the proposed solution to a problem (that is, suicidal behavior) while completely neglecting the actual problematic event precipitating the suicidal response. Generally, overfocus on aspects of the suicidal response is the result of the therapist's anxiety that the patient will attempt suicide before an intervention can be completed. Suicidal behavior, of course, is a problem—especially to the therapist who is trying to prevent it. However, the task here is to balance attention to suicidal behavior as a problem itself with attention to the problem it is purportedly solving.

Focusing on the problem situation rather than on the planned suicidal behavior is also useful because undue emphasis on the latter will divert attention from finding alternative solutions. Some problems may be so complex that the therapist, too, may be unable to arrive at alternatives likely to reduce the scope of the problem. In these instances, the therapist should simply state that just because neither can think of a nonsuicidal solution at the moment does not prove there is no recourse but suicide. The finality of suicide as a solution can then be discussed and the possibility of holding off on suicide can be presented.

Address High-Risk Environmental Factors

As can be seen in Exhibit 9.1, there are a number of environmental factors that increase the risk of suicidal behaviors. One crisis intervention strategy is to focus on each risk factor in turn and try to create some change.

Remove or Convince the Patient to Remove Lethal Items. Once it is determined that the patient is suicidal and possesses lethal means, the next focus of attention should be on convincing the patient to remove or dispose of the lethal items. During telephone conversations, this can be done by instructing the patient to throw potentially lethal drugs down the toilet or give them to another individual in the house. If the patient is both drinking and planning to take drugs, also have the patient dispose of any available liquor. Razor blades and cutting instruments, matches, poisons, and so on, should be thrown in a trash bin outside the home. A gun, or the ammunition, can be locked in the trunk of a car or in a locker and the key can be given to someone else. The general idea is to put distance and effort between the patient and the means. The therapist may need to be creative here. During sessions, patients may be asked to hand over whatever lethal means they have with them for safekeeping. These instructions should be given to the patient in a matter-of-fact way, communicating a positive expectancy that the patient will in fact carry out instructions. On the phone, the therapist can simply tell patients what they are to do and wait while patients dispose of lethal items. If the suicidal threat occurs during a regular session, patients can be instructed to bring the lethal items to the next session, or if immediate danger exists, patients may be instructed to go home and bring the items in immediately.

It is important that the therapist not be diverted from the task of removing lethal items. Possession of lethal means is often perceived by the patient as a safety factor. The patient may become very anxious at the prospect of removing any possibility of committing suicide. A useful rationale for removing lethal items is that the presence of such items may lead to an accidental suicide, even if in retrospective analysis of the situation, the patient would probably not have decided to kill himself or herself. The therapist can also emphasize that the patient can always stock up on lethal items again at a future point. The removal of lethal items should be presented as a technique to give the patient more time to think rather than an absolute ruling out of any suicidal behavior in the future.

It is also important not to overfocus on the task when it becomes clear that the patient is simply not going to comply. The power struggle that ensues may be very hard to win. It is important to avoid getting painted into a corner here. If the patient refuses, the therapist can back off and bring it up another day. Persistence at opportune times will usually be successful. The therapist should neither underestimate the importance of bringing in lethal items or throwing them away nor underestimate the panic at loss of control that may prevent the patient from complying with the therapist's wishes. The therapist must balance these two competing concerns in a manner that can eventually lead to a solution for both individuals.

Maintain Contact When Suicide Risk Is Imminent and High. Perhaps the most difficult treatment situation encountered by the therapist is the patient who convincingly threatens suicide, is alone, and the therapist is unable to resolve the crisis. The general rule is to stay in contact with the patient, either in person or by phone, until the therapist is convinced that the patient will be safe (from suicide or serious harm) once contact is broken off. If possible, therapy sessions or phone calls should be extended during a crises until a satisfactory plan is developed with the patient. A home visit may be called for if the therapist is clear that such a visit will not inadvertently reinforce the suicide communication. In periods of high stress or when suicidal ideation and urges are intense, the therapist should work out with the patient some manner of easy phone access by planning regular phone calls, being available on a beeper or other paging system, or giving out multiple phone numbers and times at each number. When traveling, it may be important to call the suicidal patient periodically, send postcards, and so on. Although emergency backup should always be available, suicidal patients generally find it extremely difficult to ask for and get help from strangers.

Communicate with Patient's Network. If the therapist is unable to stay in contact with the patient personally during a high-risk crisis, help can be elicited from significant others, family members, or other treatment personnel such as case managers or house counselors if the patient lives in residential housing, or temporary hospitalization can be suggested. If the patient is willing, he or she can be referred to area emergency services, such as an emergency room. The threat of imminent suicide is not the time for confidentiality. The patient who threatens suicide or engages in potentially lethal suicidal behaviors, however, often requests that the therapist keep such behavior confidential. The therapist should not agree to absolute confidentiality if a believable threat to the patient's life is made. (This point, of course, should be made very clear to patients at the beginning of therapy.) The rule of thumb is to select the least intrusive intervention necessary.

Meeting with a patient's interpersonal network (even if it is minimal, including only other mental health professionals) can be very helpful both before and during crises. During these meetings, plans can be made for who the patient can or should call during a crisis, how people might respond, and where the patient might go for additional support. Therapists can also make very clear their likely responses to threats of suicidal behavior and parasuicidal behavior. Agreements can be made about how the network will be informed of imminent risk of suicidality. When necessary, the therapist can instruct the network in principles of reinforcement, helping the network develop a response that is immediately helpful and not simultaneously likely to increase future suicidality. If the support system is minimal, therapists should strategize with patients how to increase social support, at least during a crisis. Area churches, synagogues, and volunteer organizations are possibilities. Several meetings might be necessary so that all people who can assist during a crisis are included. One important side benefit of these meetings is that patients are often surprised to find that people care so much whether they engage in suicidal behavior. It also can be very helpful for the patient to check out ahead of time how people are going to respond to various requests for help. Whether to make these meetings with the network optional or compulsory is a clinical decision. With adolescents and children, of course, it is essential that their families be well informed of the patient's suicide risk. With adults, such meetings might be required only when the patient is at serious risk for suicide and other, more acceptable means of reducing risk are unavailable.

Intervene to Stop Ongoing Traumatic Events. Two factors are important in treatment planning and deciding on how active to be in responding to a suicidal crisis. The first factor is the short-term risk of suicide if the therapist does not actively intervene. The second factor is the long-term risk of suicide, or a life not worth living, if the therapist does actively intervene. The therapist's response to the patient requires a good knowledge of current risk factors and of the functions of suicidal behavior for this particular patient. Because a therapist will be much less clear about risk factors and the functions of suicidal behavior in the case of new patients, treatment should be more conservative in the early stages of therapy.

Risk factors have been described in Table 9.1 and Exhibit 9.1. The general rule is that the higher the risk, the more active the therapist's response should be. Mitigating this, however, is the function of the behavior and the likely long-term consequences of various courses of action. Although in the short run a particular therapeutic response may decrease the probability of suicide, the same response may actually increase the likelihood of future suicide. A useful analysis that can be made is whether in the specific instance the patient's suicidal ideation, suicide preparations, and communications are best considered automatic escape behaviors or operant behaviors, that is, those controlled by positive reinforcement. Suicidal ideation and urges are automatic escape behaviors when the primary function of the behavior is to stop or escape from unbearable events or stop unendurable painful emotions. Suicidal behaviors elicited by major losses, extreme hopelessness, or severe, melancholic depression might be examples of respondent behavior. In these instances, suicidal behavior functions as escape behavior elicited automatically by painful and unbearable events. The behavior is negatively reinforced, that is, the reinforcer for the behavior is getting out of the unendurable situation or reducing or ending unbearable emotional pain. When suicidal behavior is negatively reinforced or functions as escape behavior, therapists do not have to be as wary that they will accidentally reinforce it by intervening.

When suicidal behavior is positively reinforced, it is functioning to bring about some positive change in the individual or the immediate environment. Often, the behavior functions to get help or assistance from others. In these instances, the therapist must be wary of inadvertently reinforcing the very behavior, the high-risk suicidal behaviors, that the therapist is trying to stop. The difficult tightrope one walks here is that if the therapist withholds active involvement, the patient can always escalate to a point where the therapist does intervene. At that point, the therapist has just reinforced more lethal behavior than was happening previously. In this way, the lethal quality of the suicidal behavior can escalate.

Much of the time, suicidal behaviors, especially chronic suicide attempts and suicide threats, are simultaneously respondent and operant. Hopelessness, despair, and the unbearableness of life elicit the behavior. The community response—giving help, taking the person seriously, taking the person out of difficult situations, taking responsibility for and providing care for the person—reinforces the behavior. The best response here is one that both reduces the eliciting factors and minimally reinforces the behavior. When intervening actively, the therapist should try to find a way to do it that requires some improved patient behavior first and keeps the patient safe.

The therapist must be flexible in the number of response options considered. The therapist should figure out the function of the behavior and then be active, but not in a manner that keeps the behavior functional. There are many ways to keep a patient alive. For example, if the behavior functions to get time and attention, insisting that the problem is obviously so serious that the patient must get to the hospital right away—talking to the therapist can wait until later—maintains safety without reinforcement when going into the hospital is not what the patient wants. However, the therapist must remember not to give the patient extra time once the patient is in the hospital. When the functional value of the behavior is to get into a hospital, then the response should, of course, be different. Here the therapist may need to give far more attention and active support outside of the hospital, or line up sufficient community resources to keep the patient safe outside of a hospital. Or the therapist may suggest that perhaps involuntary hospitalization should be considered (assuming that is not a preferred option). It is always a good idea to have area hospitals ordered in terms of patient preference. For patients who become suicidal to gain admission, the therapist should try to get them into the least preferred place.

In summary, for operant suicidal behavior, the plan is to design a response that is natural instead of arbitrary, somewhat aversive (but not so aversive that you only temporarily suppress the behavior or drive it into secrecy), and is not the preferred therapeutic response. For respondent suicidal behavior, the plan is to design a therapeutic response that both stops the eliciting events and teaches the patient how to prevent them in the future. The therapist should reinforce alternative (to suicidal behaviors) problem-solving behaviors. For combined operant and respondent suicidal behaviors, the therapist ought to combine the strategies.

Two points are important here. First, the therapist should not assume suicidal behavior is operant or respondent. Assessment is crucial. Neither theory nor the patient's diagnosis can answer this question—only careful observation can. Second, in working with chronically suicidal individuals there will be times when reasonably high risks must be taken. It is very difficult to feel secure when a patient is directly or indirectly threatening suicide. Difficulty formulating the best response is most likely when suicidal behavior is both respondent and operant and has been on an intermittent reinforcement schedule previously.

Recommend or Consider Hospitalization. To date there are no empirical data to suggest that acute, inpatient hospitalization is effective in reducing suicide risk, even when the individual is considered a high suicide risk. Nor does available evidence suggest that hospitalization is the treatment of choice for the chronically suicidal patient, particularly when that patient meets criteria for borderline personality disorder. These data not withstanding, there are some situations in which the therapist should consider recommending brief, inpatient hospitalizations. These situations are listed in Exhibit 9.2. The therapist's policy on hospitalization should be discussed with the patient at the beginning of therapy.

**Exhibit 9.2. Situations in Which Brief Inpatient Psychiatric Hospitalization
Should Be Recommended or Considered.**

Situations in Which to Recommend Hospitalization
1. The patient is in a psychotic state and is threatening suicide, unless there is convincing evidence to suggest that the patient is not at high risk.
2. The risk of suicide outweighs the risk of inappropriate hospitalization (see the sections called "Protocol One" and "Protocol Two" for further discussion).
3. Operant suicide threats are escalating, and the hospitalization is aversive (see the sections called "Protocol One" and "Protocol Two" for further discussion; see Chapter Eighteen for alternate strategy).
4. The relationship between the patient and therapist is seriously strained; the strain is creating a suicide risk or unmanageable crisis for the patient, and outside consultation seems necessary. Inpatient staff can be very helpful in counseling both parties and helping to repair the relationship. A joint meeting with the therapist, the patient, and inpatient staff should be considered.
5. The patient is on psychotropic medications, has a history of serious medication overdose, and is having problems that necessitate close monitoring of medication or dose.
6. The patient needs protection during the early stages of exposure treatment of post-traumatic stress or during later stages that are particularly taxing. This should be arranged at a full conference of the inpatient staff. (Many inpatient staff members are afraid of patient "regression" and do not want to or are unable to treat patients going through exposure treatment.)

Situations in Which to Consider Hospitalization
1. The suicidal patient is not responding to outpatient therapy, and there is severe depression or disabling anxiety.
2. The patient is in an overwhelming crisis and cannot cope with it alone without risk of serious harm to himself or herself, and no other safe environment can be found. The risk to a life worth living outweighs the risk of inappropriate hospitalization. (This reason should be used *very* sparingly.)
3. There is emergent psychosis for the first time; there is emergent psychosis thereafter, the patient cannot easily cope with such a state, the patient has little or no social support, and the patient is suicidal.

Source: Adapted from Linehan, 1993a.

Consider Involuntary Intervention When Necessary. Given the absence of empirical data that involuntary intervention actually decreases suicide risk in any way, one would think that involuntary commitment of suicidal individuals to inpatient treatment would be more controversial than it is. Certainly, some therapists are more willing than others to use this option, and opinions differ as to its ethics and efficacy. The most important point in therapy is that therapists should absolutely know where they stand on this issue before the patient becomes suicidal. The middle of a suicide crisis is no time to be figuring this out. Patients also should be clearly informed of the therapist's views on hospitalization, involuntary interventions, and, particularly, involuntary commitment to a hospital. Just exactly what will precipitate therapist attempts to exert involuntary control and what a patient has to do to avert such control should be absolutely clear to the suicidal patient. Taking a patient's liberty away without prior warning, even when life is at stake, is a use of power that, though it keeps the patient alive in the moment, may have extremely serious, negative repercussions both for the patient's therapy and for his or her life. Also, therapists must know the applicable legal guidelines, procedures, and legal precedents in their own state for involuntary commitment. A crisis is no time to learn these laws and procedures.

It is important to be direct and clear about the reasons for interventions against the wishes of the patient. Often therapists act in their own best interest (because of fear or exhaustion) rather than in the interest of the patient. In any case, when intervention is involuntary, the therapist's view of the patient's interests conflicts with the patient's view of his or her own interests. Fortunately or unfortunately, in our legal system, when a person threatens suicide in a credible manner, he or she gives up power to mental health professionals and loses some individual rights of freedom.

In such cases, when the therapist's self-interest is at issue, this should be clearly communicated to the patient. For example, a therapist may involuntarily commit a suicidal patient to avoid the threat of being sued if the patient suicides. The therapist may be aware that hospitalizing reinforces the behavior but is afraid to take the risk of suicide if the patient is not hospitalized. Some therapists are willing to take many fewer risks than others. There is no need to explain all active interventions as designed to protect the welfare of patient, independent of the therapist's own welfare. If the patient has frightened the therapist, this should be pointed out and the therapist's right to maintain a comfortable existence should be highlighted. When the therapist's self-interest is not at issue, usually when suicide risk is judged as very high and the individual is incapable of acting in his or her own best interest, this should be made clear also. For example, although I am generally opposed to involuntary commitment, I would not hesitate to commit an actively suicidal individual in the middle of a psychotic episode. An important focus in working with suicidal patients is on helping the patient appreciate the motivations of individuals in the community who must respond to suicidal behavior.

The therapist's position on involuntary commitment and how one is likely to respond to threats of imminent suicide should be made very clear to patients at the beginning of therapy. I tell my patients that if they ever convince me that they are going to commit suicide, I will most likely actively intervene to stop them. Although I believe in the individual's right of self-determination, including the rights of patients in therapy due to mental disorders, I have no intentions of having my professional life and treatment program threatened by a lawsuit due to a patient committing suicide when I could have stopped it. I go on to express my personal philosophy on involuntary commitment, but am clear that I might violate that if necessary.

Follow Specific Policy if Patient Insists on Hospitalization but Therapist Opposes It. The chronically suicidal patient may want to be hospitalized when the therapist does not believe it is indicated. The patient may be in the midst of a crisis she or he wishes to escape from and report feeling suicidal, wanting the therapist to facilitate a hospital admission. It can be extremely difficult in some situations to assess the person's actual risk and need for hospitalization. In these situations, the following policy can be used.

1. *Maintain one's own position.* The therapist does not have to agree with the patient about everything. Just because a patient feels he or she cannot cope outside of a hospital without committing suicide does not mean that the therapist has to agree. The therapist may believe that the patient is capable of coping and surviving, at least with the therapist's help.

2. *Validate the patient's rights to maintain his or her own position.* Just because the therapist thinks a patient can cope does not mean the patient can. Therapists must recognize that they could be wrong. It is very important for them to be honest with themselves and to be humble. A spirit of willingness is what is needed. The therapist should encourage the patient to evaluate both positions and support the patient's ability to maintain a position independent of the therapist. If the therapist pretends to agree with the patient when he or she doesn't actually agree, the therapist robs the patient of the opportunity to learn from the divergent opinions.

3. *Insist that the patient take care of himself or herself.* The therapist should tell patients that in this situation, they have to do what they think is best. Even if the therapist disagrees, patients should pursue hospitalization if they believe it is important. At this point, the therapist ought to tell patients that they must act in their own best interest, even if others do not give them permission to do so. The message is that patients are ultimately responsible for their own lives

and they must take care of them. The therapist should encourage self-reliance and autonomy.

4. *Assist patients in getting themselves admitted.* In these situations, therapists should teach patients how to get themselves admitted to an inpatient, acute care hospital unit without the therapist. This is almost always possible, of course, if the patient goes to an emergency room and says he or she is going to commit suicide. However, there are a number of less drastic options available to the patient. The idea is to teach the patient how to consult another professional for a second opinion and for assistance in achieving the patient's goals—in this case getting into a hospital for inpatient care. Consult with the patient on how to carry this out.

5. *Do not punish the patient who gets admitted to a hospital against therapeutic advice.* It is absolutely essential that the therapist not punish patients if they get themselves admitted to a hospital against the therapist's advice. The only important thing to consider is whether the patient is acting in accord with his or her own best judgment, weighing all the facts, rather than acting according to transient, crisis-related emotions and a rigid construction of events.

Remove or Counteract Modeling of Suicidal Behaviors. Exposure to other individuals engaging in suicidal behavior can increase the probability of a patient committing or attempting suicide or engaging in other parasuicidal behavior. The therapist should be particularly alert to the risk of suicide whenever a suicide is prominent in the media, when individuals the patient knows (often other patients) suicide or attempt suicide, and on or near the anniversary of a relative's or friend's suicide. Although the patient cannot be protected from such exposure, the impact should be assessed immediately. The patient should be advised to stay away from novels, autobiographies, movies, TV shows, and songs about individuals who suicide. Therapy groups where suicidal behavior of other members is routinely discussed should ordinarily not be recommended. The contagion of suicidal behavior is a particular problem with adolescent patients. A suicide on an inpatient unit is, by definition, a crisis for this population.

Address Behavioral High-Risk Factors

As with environmental factors, another crisis intervention strategy is to focus on each of the behavioral factors listed in Exhibit 9.1 that are associated with a high risk of suicide and attempted suicide.

Pay Attention to Affect Rather Than Content. Attention to the patient's affect rather than to speech content is especially important when the patient is highly aroused emotionally. The therapist should identify the patient's feelings, communicate to the patient the validity of his or her feelings, provide an opportunity for emotional ventilation, verbally reflect to the patient the therapist's own emotional responses to the patient's feelings, and offer reflective statements.

Immediately following traumatic events, one of the most important tasks for the individual is to describe and talk about the trauma, over and over and over. The task here is for the patient to process the traumatic event emotionally in the context of repeatedly being exposed to cues associated with the traumatic event. Such verbal processing (together with the concomitant grieving) has been called the "remembrance and mourning" phase of treating trauma by Judith Herman (1992). It is compatible with the exposure-based procedures advocated by cognitive and behavioral therapists. The effectiveness of exposure-based treatment has been attributed to processes of extinction, habituation, biological toughening up, and emotional processing that lead to integration of new corrective information incompatible with existing threat-related cognitive structures. Whatever the reason, the simple act of relating the facts of a traumatic event to another person can be soothing and should be encouraged by the therapist. Thus, even in very high-risk crises, where the therapist is also stressed and anxious to "solve" the crisis, time must be allowed for the patient to tell his or her story—more than once.

Focus on Affect Tolerance. Generally, the patient will communicate to the therapist an inability to tolerate the crisis situation. Not only is the situation overwhelming, but the patient can't stand it. While validating the patient's pain, the therapist must also directly confront the patient with the necessity of tolerating the negative affect. The therapist should not expect the patient to empathize with this point of view at earlier stages of therapy. However, this should not deter the therapist from making these statements repeatedly throughout the crisis.

Consider Short-Term Somatic Treatment. Crises are often accompanied by incapacitating anxiety, panic, or transient psychosis. Brief pharmacotherapy, on an emergency basis and up to several weeks, may be helpful. At times, severe insomnia can itself precipitate a crisis. In these situations, four or five days of sedatives or hypnotics may be useful to break the cycle of sleeplessness. As said above, lethal drugs should not be given to lethal people. During crises, it can also be useful to insist (or at least strongly recommend) that the patient stop drinking alcohol and other drugs that might disinhibit behavior.

Generate Hope and Reasons for Living. In some crisis situations, the best thing a therapist can do is generate as many solutions as he or she can think of and hope that one of the solutions will help the patient acknowledge the possibility that other solutions to the problem exist. If one doesn't "catch," the therapist can propose another. The therapist can also be helpful by refocusing the patient's attention on aspects of his or her environment that are acceptable or positive to balance the current focus on the crisis situation. The role of the therapist here is to provide balance. To avoid oversimplifying the patient's problems, however, it is essential that the therapist combine hopeful statements with frequent validation of the patient's intense despair and hopelessness.

Focus on Problem Solving

During a crisis, suicidal patients often communicate a pervasive hopelessness that any problem solution other than suicide is possible. Even when solutions are possible, patients may say that they are simply too tired to do the work necessary to solve the problem. Other patients will communicate an intense desire to "make everything OK right now," explicitly or implicitly demanding that either something must get better this minute or suicide is inevitable. In these situations, the therapist must help the patient reduce the painful negative emotions while helping the patient see that the ability to put up with some of the current emotional pain is necessary if the problem is to be solved.

If problem-solving techniques are used here, it is almost always essential to select some *small area* of the current crisis for attention. The patient is already overwhelmed with affect and the therapist must be careful not to aggravate the situation by requiring large or complex problem-solving efforts beyond the patient's capability. On the other hand, it is equally important to elicit some active or improved problem-solving behavior from the patient. The therapist must get the patient moving toward a solution. The therapist should model the breaking down of a problem into small parts and dealing with one aspect at a time. In problem solving during a crisis, the following procedure should be followed in addition to standard problem-solving techniques.

Emphatically Instruct Patient Not to Commit Suicide. Often, it is helpful to simply tell the patient emphatically not to suicide or attempt suicide. Once again, the therapist can tell the patient that refraining from suicidal behavior now does not prevent her or him from doing it in the future.

Persist with Statements That Suicide Is Not a Good Solution, That a Better One Can Be Found. Suicidal patients often try to get therapists to agree that suicide is the only way out, seemingly so they can go ahead and kill themselves. It is essential that the therapist not give such permission. Therapists should never instruct patients to go ahead and kill themselves under a mistaken assumption that such statements may arouse sufficient anger and inhibit any suicidal behavior (that is, do not use paradoxical instruction). Nor should therapists "bait" patients with statements implying that the patient will never carry out a suicide threat. Such statements may force patients to prove to you that they are actually serious. Rather, validate the emotional pain that has led to suicidal ideation and at the same time refuse to validate suicidal behavior as an appropriate solution.

Predict Future Consequences of Various Plans of Action. Suicidal patients often focus on short-term gain and ignore long-term consequences of their behavioral choices. Continuously urge the patient to focus on long-term consequences of her or his behavior. Help the patient examine the pros and cons of various action alternatives from the points of view of their effectiveness at achieving objectives, maintaining interpersonal relationships, and helping the patient respect and feel better about herself or himself.

Confront the Patient's Ideas or Behavior Directly. In the midst of a crisis and high emotional arousal, it is unusual that the patient can calmly examine the pros and cons of various action plans. In these instances, when the therapist believes that a given course of action will have detrimental effects, confront the patient directly about the outcomes of her or his behavioral choices. Frequently, such behavioral choices will be linked to unrealistic beliefs on the part of the patient. In these instances, the patient's beliefs must also be confronted. When the therapist confronts a patient who is in a state of intense emotional arousal, the patient will frequently respond with statements indicating that the therapist does not really understand the patient's situation. In these instances, it is helpful to immediately make a statement expressing understanding and validation of the pain the patient is experiencing and follow such a statement with one indicating a belief that, even though painful, an alternate action choice would be preferable in the long term.

Give Advice and Make Direct Suggestions. Although it is preferable to adopt a consulting role, helping the patient generate and then choose from among several response alternatives, there are times when the patient simply does not know what to do or how to handle a given situation. In these instances, it is appropriate for the therapist to give the patient concrete advice and make direct suggestions about possible action plans. This is especially important in dealing with the person who verbally reports great distress and difficulty but nonverbally seems far less distressed. When dealing with these "apparently competent" persons, it is very common for therapists to assume that patients actually could figure out what to do but simply lack confidence in their own ability to do so. In these situations, it is easy to make the mistake of refusing to give the patient advice under the mistaken theory that the patient does not need the advice. It is therefore important to assess patients' capabilities carefully and respect patients' knowledge about their own capabilities. It is essential that patient passivity not be unilaterally interpreted as lack of motivation, as resistance, or lack of confidence, and so on. Many times passivity is a simple function of inadequate knowledge and skills.

Offer Solutions from the Perspective of the Other Skills That Patient Is Learning in Therapy. All problems can be solved in more than one way. It depends on one's perspective. The ability to approach a crisis from the perspective of the current focus of treatment, applying the life skills one is teaching the patient to any problematic situation, is at once important and very difficult. Therapists must themselves know the skills they are teaching inside and out and be able to think quickly within a crisis.

Clarify and Reinforce Adaptive Responses on the Part of Patient, Especially Adaptive Problem-Solving Ideas or Prior Adaptive Responses in Similar Situations. As a patient begins to learn adaptive cognitive and behavioral responses, it is important to reinforce these responses. During a crisis, carefully attending to any adaptive responses or ideas generated and helping to clarify and then reinforce these responses are often beneficial. At other times, the therapist can refer back to other occasions when the patient has dealt with similar situations adaptively and praise such behaviors.

Identify Factors Interfering with Productive Plans of Action. Once the patient and therapist have identified a plan of action that appears productive, the therapist must then help the patient identify factors that might interfere with such a plan of action. If this step is neglected, the patient is likely to experience failure in carrying out the plan. Such failure might then precipitate further or more serious suicidal behavior. At a minimum, problem solving in the future will be more difficult. The identification of factors interfering with productive plans should be followed, of course, by further discussion of how these problems can be solved.

Commit to a Plan of Action

The therapist should make every effort to develop with the patient a plan of action that specifies what the patient will do and what the therapist will do between now and the next contact. An explicit, time-limited contract should be negotiated with concrete demands or requirements on the patient before the next contact. In other words, the therapist should communicate to the patient that he or she is expected to take the agreed upon steps to begin to resolve his or her current crisis.

Reassess Suicide Potential. Despite the therapist's best efforts, the patient may continue to maintain that suicide or intentional self-injury is the only solution to his or her problems, even after an extensive interaction. The therapist should check to see whether the crisis has been alleviated enough so that the patient believes he or she can refrain from committing suicide between this interaction and the next contact. If the patient cannot agree to this, the therapist should remain in close contact with the patient or arrange for some alternative form of crisis intervention until the crisis is alleviated.

Anticipate a Recurrence of the Crisis Response. Together, patient and therapist will often formulate an action plan that promises to reduce the patient's current feelings of being overwhelmed. Although these plans may in fact be quite helpful, the patient will commonly experience a resurgence of the overwhelming affect (after a short period of time). The patient and therapist should therefore plan or structure the patient's time during the crisis period between the current contact and the next contact. The patient should be warned that the aversive feelings very likely will reoccur and several strategies for coping with such feelings should be planned.

IMPLICATIONS FOR THE CLINICIAN

Dialectical behavior therapy was developed specifically for the chronically suicidal patient from a combined motivational and capability deficit model of suicidal behavior. It is based on the ideas that

- Suicidal individuals lack important interpersonal, self-regulation, and distress tolerance skills and capabilities
- Personal and environmental factors inhibit the use of behavioral skills the individual does have, interfere with the development of new skills and capabilities, and often reinforce inappropriate and suicidal behaviors

Treatment targets for therapy are

- Reducing high-risk suicidal behaviors
- Reducing behaviors that interfere with therapy
- Reducing behavioral patterns serious enough to substantially interfere with any chance of a reasonable quality of life
- Acquiring sufficient behavioral skills to meet patient goals
- Reducing post-traumatic stress responses related to previous traumatic events
- Increasing self-respect
- Increasing other goals for the patient

There are five treatment strategies in DBT:

1. Dialectical (bringing out the opposites both in therapy and in the patient's life and providing conditions for synthesis—moving from "either-or" to "both-and")
2. Core (applying a balance of validation and problem solving)
3. Case management (including three strategies)
   - Consultation or supervision, which requires that each therapist meet with a supervisor or consultation team regularly
   - Consultation-to-the-patient, in which the therapist teaches the patient how to interact effectively with the patient's environment, rather than vice versa
   - Environmental intervention, in which the therapist intervenes directly to enact change in the patient's environment that the patient is not yet able to enact but that is necessary to save the patient's life or to prevent serious harm
4. Communication (applying a balance of two different interactional styles, reciprocal and irreverent)
5. Structural (specifying how to start and end therapy, how to set an agenda and organize time during sessions, and how to terminate therapy)

Two tasks of the therapist in responding to suicidal behavior are to respond actively enough to block patients from killing or seriously harming themselves and to respond in a fashion that minimizes reinforcement of suicidal behavior. Two protocols for treating suicidal behaviors are as follows:

Treatment Planning with the Suicidal Patient
- Assess long-term risk of suicide or attempted suicide (see Table 9.1)
- Conduct comprehensive analysis of suicidal behaviors
  - Describe suicidal behaviors in detail
  - Monitor behavior of patient
  - Conduct moment-to-moment chain analysis of environmental and behavioral events linked to suicidal behavior
  - Connect suicidal behaviors to overall behavioral patterns
- Conduct comprehensive solutions analysis
  - Identify ways to prevent or reduce precipitants to suicidal behaviors or replace suicidal responses with more skillful and adaptive responses to precipitating events
  - Discuss alternative solutions versus tolerance

- • Develop commitment to nonsuicidal behavioral responses
- • Have a definite stance on suicide
- • Reinforce nonsuicidal, adaptive responses
- • Focus on negative effects of suicidal behavior
- • Maintain a strong relationship
- • Validate suicidal feelings

Management of Acute Suicidal Behaviors and Crisis Intervention

- • Assess risk of immediate suicide or parasuicide (see Exhibit 9.1)
- • Explore the problem now
  - • Identify key events that have set off current emotional response
  - • Formulate and summarize the problem situation with patient
- • Address high-risk environmental factors
  - • Remove or convince the patient to remove lethal items
  - • Maintain contact when suicide risk is imminent and high
  - • Communicate with patient's network
  - • Intervene to stop ongoing traumatic events
  - • Recommend or consider hospitalization (see Exhibit 9.2)
  - • Remove or counteract modeling of suicidal behaviors
- • Address behavioral high-risk factors
  - • Pay attention to affect rather than content
  - • Focus on affect tolerance
  - • Consider short-term somatic treatment
  - • Generate hope and reasons for living
- • Focus on problem solving
  - • Emphatically instruct patient not to commit suicide
  - • Persist with statements that suicide is not a good solution, that a better one can be found
  - • Predict future consequences of various plans of action
  - • Confront the patient's ideas or behavior directly
  - • Give advice and make direct suggestions
  - • Offer solutions from the perspective of the other skills that patient is learning in therapy
  - • Clarify and reinforce adaptive responses on the part of patient, especially adaptive problem-solving ideas or prior adaptive responses in similar situations
  - • Identify factors interfering with productive plans of action
- • Commit to a plan of action
  - • Reassess suicide potential
  - • Anticipate a recurrence of the crisis response

CHAPTER TEN

Murder-Suicide

Phenomenology and Clinical Implications

Matthew K. Nock
Peter M. Marzuk, M.D.

The relationship between violence and suicide has always interested social scientists. Freud (1957), for example, stated that the self-hatred observed in depression originated in anger toward a love object that the individual turned back on himself. He believed that suicide, the extreme outcome of such a process, reflected the repressed desire to kill someone else.

Andrew Henry and James Short (1954) later postulated that there was an inverse relationship between homicide and suicide. Homicide was thought to be the result of the tendency of those of lower social classes to blame others, because of "external restraints," when facing frustrating circumstances. Suicide, on the contrary, was thought to be the upper social class's self-blaming reaction to frustration. Evidence for this inverse socioeconomic relationship is lacking. Although subsequent studies have shown that homicide is seen more frequently in the lower end of the socioeconomic scale (Smith and Parker, 1980), suicide is seen in all socioeconomic groups and is more directly related to loss of social status and downward mobility (Breed, 1963; Maris, 1975). Moreover, the aggressive acts of homicide and suicide seem, in some individuals, to involve separate, but overlapping motives. It has been estimated, for example, that at least 30 percent of violent persons have a history of self-destructive behavior, whereas nearly 20 percent of suicidal persons have a history of violence

This work was supported by a grant from the Dewitt Wallace Reader's Digest Foundation/ New York Community Trust.

directed at others (van Praag, Plutchik, and Apter, 1990). Nowhere is the link between these two behaviors more evident than in the case of murder-suicide, a dramatic behavioral phenomenon in which an individual kills one or more persons and shortly thereafter kills himself.

Murder-suicide was first systematically studied by Ruth Cavan (1928), who examined thirty-nine murder-suicides that occurred in the Chicago area in 1923. It has not received nearly as much attention in the scientific literature as simple homicide or simple suicide; only a handful of case studies have been conducted since Cavan's first investigation (Wolfgang, 1958b; Dorpat, 1966; West, 1967; Selkin, 1976; Berman, 1979; Palmer and Humphrey, 1980; Allen, 1983; Coid, 1983; Daly and Wilson, 1988; Rosenbaum, 1990; Currens et al., 1991; Cooper and Eaves, 1996). Although murder-suicide occurs much less frequently than either simple suicide or homicide, it can affect a large number of people, sometimes entire families. The event has a profound effect on surviving family members, friends, and members of the local community. The limited research on this topic elucidates the difficulties inherent in both predicting and preventing these events. Murder-suicides often occur suddenly; all parties directly involved are dead; there is little, if any, prior clinical documentation; and often the possibilities for psychiatric intervention are limited.

DEFINITION OF MURDER-SUICIDE

There is no standardized operational definition of murder-suicide. Indeed, the research literature differs in what constitutes a murder-suicide: whether an individual had to have committed homicide or merely attempted homicide prior to suicide, and in the time elapsed between homicide and suicide. For instance, the few studies that have specified time intervals between homicide and suicide reported a range from one day to three months (Palmer and Humphrey, 1980; Allen, 1983; Currens et al., 1991). We believe the defining aspect of murder-suicide is the intrinsic linkage of the two acts in the motivation of the perpetrator; it is thus necessary for the two acts to occur in close temporal proximity—in most cases, the suicide occurring within seconds or minutes of the homicide. If the two acts are not a unitary event, a murder-suicide has not occurred.

We will follow the definition of murder-suicide outlined by Marzuk, Tardiff, and Hirsch (1992b): a murder-suicide has occurred when, on the basis of medical examiner review, a person has committed a homicide (codes E960–969 of the *International Classification of Diseases*, Ninth Revision [ICD-9]) (World Health Organization, 1977) and subsequently commits suicide (ICD-9 codes E950–959) within one week of the homicide. We use the term *murder-suicide,* which is used most often in the literature, although we acknowledge that the term *homicide-suicide* may be more appropriate. Murder is a degree of homicide defined by legal statute in the United States. It is not necessary, of course, for a person to be convicted of murder prior to his or her suicide; these cases never come to trial because the perpetrator is dead. In addition, the period of one week is used to distinguish the linked murder-suicide incident from a larger group of individuals who die by suicide and who, by history, have committed homicide in the remote past. Two types of situations, which are very similar clinically to murder-suicide, are not included in the definition: those involving individuals who commit homicide and subsequently attempt, but do not complete suicide, and individuals who unsuccessfully attempt to murder someone and later commit suicide.

Cultural variations of murder-suicide also exist. Although not included in the clinical typologies of murder-suicide that we discuss here, they are worth noting. One such phenomenon is the suicidal variant of *amok,* which is most frequently observed in Malaysia, and similar syndromes such as *wihtiko psychosis* among the Cree Indians, *jumping Frenchman* in Canada, and *imu* in Japan (Cooper, 1934). *Amok* is defined as "an acute outburst of unrestrained violence associated with homicidal attacks, preceded by a period of brooding, and ending with exhaustion and amnesia" (Yap, 1951, p. 319). The perpetrator of *amok,* known as a *pengamok,* is typically a middle-aged man who has a history of impulsive and irresponsible behavior and has recently experienced shame and humiliation (Gaw and Bernstein, 1992). Such bouts of rage most often end when the perpetrator is killed by others who are trying to stop the episode, is safely captured and jailed, or commits suicide. *Amok* was long thought by the Malaysians to be an appropriate response by an individual to stressful and embarrassing circumstances. Some have hypothesized that since the Malay are of the Muslim religion, which strictly prohibits suicide, some Malaysians consider *amok* to be an acceptable way to commit suicide. This explanation, however, is dubious. After 1893, when the Malaysian government passed a law sentencing those who commit *amok* to be hanged, the incidence of *amok* declined markedly (Teoh, 1972). Gaw and Bernstein (1992) argued that *amok* resembles the now-removed *DSM-III* diagnosis of isolated explosive disorder, which is "a single, discrete episode of failure to resist an impulse that led to a single, violent, externally directed act, which had a catastrophic impact on others and for which the available information does not justify the diagnosis of schizophrenia, antisocial personality disorder, or conduct disorder. An example would be an individual who for no apparent reason suddenly began shooting at strangers in a fit of rage and then shot himself" (American Psychiatric Association, 1980, p. 297).

Because there is no operational national surveillance system for tracking murder-suicides, the annual incidence of these events in the United States is difficult to determine. The manner and cause of death, determined by the medical examiner, is listed on an individual's death certificate, and records do not necessarily link related deaths. Nonetheless, a 1989 *Time* magazine survey of all deaths by firearms during a one-week period in the United States reported eleven incidents of firearm-related murder-suicide, which resulted in twenty-two deaths (Leviton and Riley, 1989). If this period is representative of an average week in the United States, there are 572 firearm-related suicides of this type per year and more than an equal number of homicides (some perpetrators kill more than one victim before committing suicide). This translates into one thousand to fifteen hundred deaths resulting from murder-suicide annually.

Coid reviewed seventeen studies from ten nations spanning the period 1900–1979 and concluded that murder-suicide occurred at a remarkably constant rate, averaging 0.20 to 0.30 per 100,000 (ranging from 0.04 in Scotland to 0.40 among Israeli Western Jews), although the countries studied showed marked variation in their overall simple homicide and simple suicide rates (Coid, 1983). Thus, murder-suicide as a percentage of all homicides and suicides differs markedly among countries. For example, Philadelphia had an extremely high homicide rate from 1948 to 1952, and Denmark had a remarkably low homicide rate from 1958 to 1960; however, both had virtually identical murder-suicide rates (0.21 and 0.22 per 100,000, respectively). During this period, only 3.6 percent of all murderers in Philadelphia subsequently committed suicide, whereas 42 percent of those in Denmark who committed murder later committed suicide (Wolfgang, 1958b; West, 1967). A recent replication of Coid's study yielded similar findings, with slightly more variation in rates, ranging from 0.05 in Scotland to 0.55 in Miami (Milroy, 1995). In 1995, the most recent year for which figures are available, the overall homicide rate in the United States was 8.6 per 100,000, accounting for 22,552 total deaths; for suicide, it was 11.9 per 100,000, resulting in 31,284 deaths (Anderson, Kochanek, and Murphy, 1997). Thus, it is likely that roughly 1.5 percent of all suicides and 5.0 percent of all homicides in the United States occur in the context of murder-suicide.

Although the rates of murder-suicide appear to be relatively stable across nations, sociocultural influences lead to varying characteristics of murder-suicide. For example, most murder-suicides in the United States are perpetrated by men against their spouse or lover, whereas in Japan the highest percentage of murder-suicide perpetrators are mothers who kill their children and subsequently commit suicide.

CLINICAL TYPOLOGIES

Clinical typologies of murder-suicide provide a useful means for clinicians and researchers to conceptualize and classify these events. The victim-perpetrator relationship observed in murder-suicide is typically restricted to family members compared with simple homicide, which involves disputes among strangers and acquaintances, drug dealing, and robbery. For instance, in two recent studies, only 1 to 2 percent of murder-suicide incidents involved victims who were not known by the perpetrator, compared with 22 percent of simple homicides (Palmer and Humphrey, 1980; Milroy, 1995).

Marzuk, Tardiff, and Hirsch (1992b) have proposed a comprehensive classification system that categorizes murder-suicide by type of victim-perpetrator relationships and by class of common precipitants or motives (see Table 10.1). Our discussion of this typology may be useful to the many clinicians who will encounter the potential murder-suicide perpetrator, including psychiatrists, emergency physicians, psychologists, family practitioners, marital counselors, and internists, in assessing the risk of this type of violence. Those discussed include *spousal murder-suicide* as the result of either amorous jealousy or declining health; *filicide-suicide*, which usually involves the parental killing of children; *familicide-suicide*, in which entire families are destroyed; and *extrafamilial murder-suicide*, which includes the uncommon, yet highly publicized, incidents of mass murder and suicidal bombings. A fictitious case report precedes each section to illustrate each prototypical incident.

Spousal-Amorous Jealousy

Michael and Samantha were high school sweethearts who married two years after graduation. Michael took a job in a local contracting business, while Samantha worked as an office assistant. The two enjoyed a relatively satisfying relationship for the first five years. Trouble started after Samantha was promoted to office manager. Michael accused her of having an affair because she was working longer hours and dressing more attractively. Samantha was unhappy that Michael had started to drink heavily and use cocaine. The two fought verbally almost daily, which soon escalated to frequent physical confrontations. Samantha grew frustrated and unsatisfied with the relationship and moved back to her parents' home. Michael, who became very depressed after his wife's departure, threatened her, to no avail, demanding that she move back into their apartment or "she would be sorry." Exactly three months after Samantha moved out, Michael went to her office and shot her once in the chest, killing her instantly. He then shot himself in the head.

Murder-suicide between spouses or lovers represents one-half to three-fourths of all murder-suicides in the United States (Dorpat, 1966; Palmer and Humphrey, 1980; Allen, 1983; Currens et al., 1991). It is most frequently the culmination of a chaotic, abusive relationship marked by amorous jealousy, which is also referred to in the literature as *psychotic* or *morbid jealousy* (Selkin, 1976; Berman, 1979; Shepherd, 1961). The suspected infidelity may be real or imagined and thus ranges from ruminative or obsessional to psychotic. Although the murder-suicide sometimes occurs at the onset of this morbidly jealous state, typically it occurs after a prolonged, bitter conflict, marked by verbal abuse and sublethal violence (Dorpat, 1966; Berman, 1979; Allen, 1983). The precipitating event is

**Table 10.1. Proposed Clinical Classification of Murder-Suicide
Based on Victim-Offender Relationship (Type) and Principal Motive or Precipitant (Class).**

Type of Relationship

I. Spousal or Consortial[a]

   Perpetrator
   1. Spouse
   2. Consort

   Type of Homicide
   i. Uxoncidal (spouse-killing)
   ii. Consortial (murder of lover)

II. Familial[b]

   Perpetrator
   1. Mother
   2. Father
   3. Child (under 16 years)
   4. Other adult family member (over 16 years)

   Type of Homicide
   i.   Neonaticide (child < 24 hours)
   ii. Infanticide (child > 1 day, < 1 year)
   iii. Pedicide (child 1 through 16 years)
   iv. Adult family member (> 16 years)

III. Extrafamilial[c]

Class

A. Amorous jealousy
B. "Mercy killing" (because of declining health of victim or offender)
C. "Altruistic or extended suicides" (includes salvation fantasies of rescue and escape from problems)
D. Family financial or social stressors
E. Retaliation
F. Other
G. Unspecified

Note: Classification of murder-suicides is specified by type (Roman numeral) with subtype of perpetrator (number) and subtype of homicide (lowercase Roman numeral), as well as by letters to denote principal motives or precipitants. This classification can include mixed types of victims and multiple motives of offenders. Examples using the typology, including a "mixed type," are as follows: (1) A husband who killed his wife out of suspicions of infidelity would be coded type I(1)i-A. (2) A mother would killed her two-year-old son (maternal filicide) to "rescue" him from a perceived ruinous world would be coded type II(1)iii-C. (3) An adult who kills his adult brother for unknown motives would be coded type II(4)iv-G. (4) A man who kills his wife and six-year-old son and two-year-old daughter because he suspects his wife of infidelity and is under severe financial pressures represents a mixed category and would be coded type I(1)i/II(2)ii,iii/A,D.

[a]Principal victim-offender relationship is spouse or lover.

[b]Principal victim-offender relationship is consanguineal (blood relative) or other familial, nonmarital relationship.

[c]Principal victim-offender relationship is not marital, consortial, or familial and includes friends, acquaintances, and strangers.

Source: PM Marzuk, K Tardiff, CS Hirsch. The epidemiology of murder-suicide. *Journal of the American Medical Association* 1992;267:3179–3183. Copyright 1992, American Medical Association.

often the victim's decision to end the relationship and her subsequent attempt to separate from the perpetrator. Shortly after this occurs, the perpetrator, typically a man, murders his girlfriend, fiancé, or spouse and subsequently commits suicide, usually using a firearm. A "triadic death" has also been described in which the perpetrator kills the spouse, the rival lover, and then himself (Selkin, 1976).

In the United States, 57 percent of simple spousal homicides are committed by men and 43 percent are committed by women (Mercy and Saltzman, 1989). In contrast, men are responsible for over 90 percent of spousal murder-suicides. A review of the literature found that from 19 to 26 percent of male spouse murderers commit suicide, compared with only 0 to 3 percent of females (Marzuk, Tardiff, and Hirsch, 1992b). Thus, women who kill their husbands are much less likely to commit suicide afterward. A possible explanation is that most wife-perpetrated homicides are preceded by a history of violence by the husband, and the murderous act is often unintentional or in self-defense (Cooper and Eaves, 1996; Mercy and Saltzman, 1989). Men who kill their female partners, on the other hand, usually do so in response to the woman's attempt to leave the abusive relationship (Browne, 1987; Wilbanks, 1983). Cooper and Eaves (1996) found that separation was a factor in more than 57 percent of male-perpetrated domestic murder-suicides and only 36 percent of male-perpetrated domestic homicides.

Easteal (1994) examined coroner reports and court documents of murderers in Australia from 1989 to 1991 and found that 21.3 percent of perpetrators who killed a sexual intimate subsequently committed suicide, whereas only 3.6 percent of those who killed a nonintimate committed suicide. In addition, compared with sexually intimate murderers who did not commit suicide, those who did were more likely to be older males who were estranged from the victim, used more violent means for homicide, and were much less likely to have used alcohol. Couples who die by murder-suicide also tend to be older and to have been married for a longer period of time than those couples in which simple homicide occurs. Rosenbaum (1990) reported that 75 percent of couples involved in murder-suicide were married (an average of fifteen years) compared to 25 percent (an average of six years) of those involved in simple homicide. Moreover, the percentage of sexually intimate murderers who subsequently commit suicide rises significantly with age, from less than 10 percent among those aged eighteen to twenty-nine years to nearly 50 percent in those over sixty years (Easteal, 1994).

Spousal Declining Health

Joe, age seventy-eight, and Edna, age seventy-four, had been married for fifty-four years when it was discovered that Edna had developed cancer. Her doctor said she had a few years to live if she opted for treatment and one year without any treatment. Edna decided to undergo chemotherapy and remain at home so that she and Joe could spend "quality time" together. Joe was happy that Edna was able to stay with him while he cared for her. He preferred this situation to uncomfortable hospital visits. This changed, however, when Edna's condition soon worsened, and Joe became visibly bothered by her rapid weight loss, decreased functioning, and increased depression. Joe was frustrated that neither he nor the doctors could do more to help her recover. Six months after Edna was originally diagnosed with cancer, Joe fed her a massive amount of barbiturates and subsequently committed suicide by hanging himself.

The typical perpetrator of this type is an elderly man who either has an ailing spouse or is medically ill himself who kills his partner and then commits suicide (West, 1967; Currens et al., 1991; Fishbain, Goldberg, Rosomoff, and Rosomoff, 1989). The perpetrator, who acts as the caretaker and is usually several years older than the victim (Copeland, 1985), comes to see the victim as being too dependent on him for care. Financial pressures on the couple or the deteriorating medical conditions of either the victim or the perpetrator often serve as the precipitant. Typically, the perpetrator experiences feelings of impotence and frustration and sees himself as unable to continue his role as a provider. Murder-suicides of this type seem to fit the "extended suicide" model outlined by several authors (Berman, 1979; Palermo, 1994). In such cases, the primary motive for murder is the "altruistic" desire to "protect" the victim from life without the caretaker after his suicide. The murder is thus viewed by the perpetrator as a mercy killing.

The line between murder-suicides of this type and suicide pacts is often blurred. Cases that are considered to be double suicides, or suicide pacts, often consist of an individual who is the aggressor and is depressed and suicidal, and another who is coerced into participation or is killed by the aggressor (Rosenbaum, 1983). Most individuals who die in suicide pacts are not impulsive young lovers like Romeo and Juliet but codependent couples over the age of fifty who have carefully planned their deaths. Double suicides are often motivated by the couples' fear of separation due to serious physical illness or their fantasies of reunion after their deaths (Rosen, 1981). A comparison of perpetrators of "noncriminal" murder, murder-suicide, and suicide pact instigators (Rosenbaum, 1983) showed they were similar in the presence of both a psychiatric illness, most often depression, and a previous suicide attempt.

Filicide-Suicide

Mrs. A. was twenty-four years old when she married. She gave birth to her first child, a boy, at the age of thirty-one and her first girl one year later. Mrs. A. had worked as an attorney in a small law firm, but decided to take time off after the birth of her son. Shortly after the birth of her daughter, Mrs. A. developed signs of fatigue, agitation, depressed mood, and back pains. Her condition rapidly worsened. Her husband asked her to see a psychiatrist after noticing her frequent crying spells and overpossessiveness with their two children. The psychiatrist diagnosed depression and prescribed an antidepressant. Two weeks later, Mr. A. came home to find that his two children had been suffocated by his wife, who had subsequently committed suicide using a handgun they had in the home for protection.

In the United States, at least half of all pedicides (murder of a child aged one through sixteen) and infanticides (children under the age of one year) are perpetrated by a parent, most often the mother (Adelson, 1991; Myers, 1970; Resnick, 1969). Strangers who kill children usually do so in connection with a sexual crime (Harder, 1967). Although the percentage of strangers who commit suicide after murdering a child is very low, 16 percent to 29 percent of mothers and 40 percent to 60 percent of fathers commit suicide after murdering their own children (Adelson, 1991; Myers, 1970; Rodenburg, 1971; Wilkey, Pearn, Petric, and Nixon, 1982; d'Orbán, 1979). This percentage falls to 2.3 percent of mothers and 10.5 percent of fathers when one considers only infanticide-suicides (Daly and Wilson, 1988). Thus, among filicide-suicides, the most commonly encountered subtypes are maternally and paternally perpetrated murders of children between one and sixteen years of age. The most common methods of murder employed by mothers are drowning, suffocating, gassing, beating, and defenestration, whereas fathers tend to use firearms, stabbing, beating, and kicking (Adelson, 1991; Myers, 1970; Resnick, 1969; Rodenburg, 1971; Marks and Kumar, 1995).

The most dangerous period for victims of simple filicide is the first six months of life. When filicide-suicide occurs in the first six months, it is probably due to the presence of postpartum depression and psychosis in the maternal perpetrator (Resnick, 1969; Marks and Lovestone, 1995). Schizophrenia has also been associated with filicide-suicide and often involves delusions of salvation (West, 1967; Resnick, 1969; Browne and Palmer, 1975). In studies of mothers who killed their children, the motives of those who committed filicide-suicide were most often "altruistic"—"there would be no one to care for the children"—and delusional—"to save them from a violent world" (Resnick, 1969; d'Orbán, 1979). The younger the child is, the more likely the mother is to think of him as an extension of herself.

Neonaticide-suicides, defined as the killing of a newborn within the first twenty-four hours after birth followed by the perpetrator's suicide, are much less common than infanticide-suicide or pedicide-suicide. Compared to mothers who murder older children, mothers who commit simple neonaticide tend to be younger, unmarried, and not mentally ill. The motive for neonaticide is most often the disposal of unwanted children, not salvation or deluded "altruism";

thus there is a lower percentage of neonaticide-suicides than filicide-suicides (Resnick, 1970).

Murder-suicides of older children also occur less frequently then pedicide-suicides. Fink and Roth (1979) reported a case of a twenty-four-year-old female described as depressed, paranoid, anxious, and voicing suicidal ideation who had pleaded with her father to "put her out of her misery." Her father, who had assumed responsibility of his daughter after she was discharged from a psychiatric hospital a few weeks earlier, later shot her and then turned the gun on himself. He kept a journal that described feelings of hopelessness about his daughter's illness.

Familicide-Suicide

Harold, a forty-four-year-old bus driver, was married for twenty years and had three young children living at home. Harold had been experiencing heart problems for the past two years. Although his doctor informed him that the problem was not life threatening, Harold feared the worst and became quite depressed. His depression worsened, and he soon began missing days of work. After two months of unsatisfactory work performance, Harold was fired. Harold's wife was unsupportive, warning that if he did not find work soon, they would lose their home and could no longer afford to feed and clothe their children. After a few weeks, Harold's wife indicated that she wanted a divorce because she "needed to be with someone who could care for her and her children." Harold was still unable to find work and soon could no longer afford to see his doctor. One night while Harold's family was sleeping, he took his pistol from his closet, shot his children and wife while they slept, and then shot himself.

Familicide-suicide occurs when one member of the family (and on a few occasions two family members in conjunction) kills all other members of the household, including spouse, children, parents, other relatives, and even pets, and subsequently commits suicide. Sometimes the house is set afire. The perpetrator of this type closely resembles Dietz's "family annihilator," who is most typically "the senior man of the house who is depressed, paranoid, intoxicated, or a combination of the three" (Dietz, 1986, p. 482). A mother tends to kill only her children and herself (Daly and Wilson, 1988), whereas a father who kills his children is more likely to kill his entire family, including his spouse (Rodenburg, 1971).

Familicide-suicide is less common then either the spousal amorous-jealousy, filicide-suicide, or declining-health types but frequently combines features of all of them. Malmquist (1981) interviewed paternal perpetrators of simple familicide, some of whom subsequently attempted suicide, and found two common elements among them. The first was a chronic depressive state. The second was a persistent pattern of disturbance in their marital lives, which often included violent arguments about infidelity and financial difficulties. The perpetrators felt distanced from their spouse but were incapable of either improving or leaving the relationships. The children may be seen as an extension of the mother, in which case killing them would represent the complete destruction of the relationship between the mother and father. Notes left by those who murdered their families before committing suicide have suggested that the murderers often see themselves as "altruistically" delivering the family from continued hardships or from shame and humiliation (Selkin, 1976; Daly and Wilson, 1988). Sometimes the perpetrator's health is declining or members of his family are ill, and he feels hopeless about the prognosis. Often there are multiple precipitants converging at once: marital instability, financial difficulties, and poor health.

Extrafamilial Murder-Suicide

Derek was a twenty-four-year-old security guard at a major department store. Although he was working at an entry-level position, he took his job seriously and had hopes of someday working in law enforcement. However, he did not communicate well with his coworkers and had received warnings from his supervisor on several occasions for becoming overly aggressive with customers. His work performance was rated as slightly below average. Derek confronted his supervisor in a verbally abusive and physically aggressive manner when he learned that he had once again been passed over for promotion. His supervisor then suspended him for two weeks without pay. The next day Derek returned to the store in uniform, went into the security office, and shot his supervisor and three other coworkers before turning the handgun on himself.

Most murder-suicides occur in the context of the family, and incidents in which the perpetrator and victim are unrelated are rare. However, extrafamilial murder-suicides tend to affect more people per incident, including friends, employers, police officers, and innocent bystanders caught in the cross fire. Perpetrators comprising this type resemble Dietz's "pseudocommando" category, who are "preoccupied by firearms and commit their raids after long deliberation" (Dietz, 1986, p. 482). Extrafamilial murder-suicide perpetrators typically include disgruntled individuals who probably have paranoid and narcissistic traits who believe they have been slighted in some way (Copeland, 1985). The act is often precipitated by some form of perceived rejection or humiliation, such as being passed over for promotion or deprived of appropriate recognition. The act of violence is a form of vindication in which they strike against those who have "wronged" them, as well as others who may be present at the time. The act is ended with the perpetrator's turning the weapon, most often a firearm, on himself after the target of his aggression has been killed or when he is cornered and capture is imminent. In other variations, which are technically not murder-suicides, the perpetrator is killed by police officers or others who intervene. In some instances, the perpetrator provokes the police into killing him as a form of indirect suicide. Individuals who kill police officers also have a high risk for subsequent suicide (Lester, 1987).

Those who participate in suicidal terrorist bombings are included in the category of extrafamilial murder-suicide. These events should probably be conceptualized differently from other types of murder-suicides. Although such events are murder-suicides, the perpetrator probably does not regard his own death as a suicide, but as a necessary outcome of the successful completion of his mission. Terrorists often consider their actions a form of "service" to their state or religion with the subsequent chance for honor as martyrs (Taylor and Ryan, 1988). The Japanese kamikaze pilots who flew airplanes heavily armed with explosives into enemy ships in World War II can also be considered in this group.

ETIOLOGY OF MURDER-SUICIDE

One central theme seen in all types of murder-suicide is the perpetrator's overvalued attachment to a relationship that, when threatened by dissolution, leads him to destroy the relationship. This theme is seen most clearly, and has been most thoroughly studied, in incidents of spousal amorous jealousy. Easteal (1994), for instance, found that spousal murderers are more than twice as likely to commit suicide when the victim was recently estranged (35 percent) rather than living in the home (15 percent). This fear of separation is also evident in the familicide-suicide perpetrator, the elderly caretaker of a partner who has declining health, the suicidal parent who "altruistically" kills his or her child, and the disgruntled worker who feels he has been separated from his job or deprived of recognition to which he believes he is entitled. To elucidate the etiology of murder-suicide further, we believe it is useful to look for common elements in demographics, diagnosis, and intent.

Demographics

In a review of existing studies that examined murder-suicide in the United States, Marzuk, Tardiff, and Hirsch (1992b) found that the average age of perpetrators is 39.6 years, that 93 percent to 97 percent of perpetrators are male, and that 50 to 86 percent are white (Wolfgang, 1958b; Selkin, 1976; Berman, 1979; Allen, 1983; Currens et al., 1991; Copeland, 1985). In contrast to the male predominance of perpetrators, over 85 percent of all victims are female. Perpetrators and victims are usually of the same race (Wolfgang, 1958b; Hanzlick and Koponen, 1994).

Almost 90 percent of all murder-suicide incidents involve only one victim (Selkin, 1976; Berman, 1979; Allen, 1983; Currens et al., 1991). The principal method of both homicide and suicide is firearms, which are used in 80 percent to 94 percent of all cases (Currens et al., 1991; Copeland, 1985), but all means, including aircraft, have been described (Lew, 1988; Marcikic, 1990; Goldney, 1983; Hendin, 1994).

The demographic characteristics of perpetrators and victims are different in other countries. For example, in the United States, filicide-suicides account for only 6 percent to 16 percent of all murder-suicide incidents (Palmer and Humphrey, 1980; Allen, 1983; Hanzlick and Koponen, 1994), whereas filicide-suicides account for 40 percent of murder-suicides in Sweden (Lindqvist, 1986), 48 percent in England (West, 1967), and 70 percent in Japan (Sakuta, 1995).

Mental Illness and Substance Abuse

It is difficult to imagine circumstances that would lead a person to murder his spouse and children and subsequently take his own life. Some have described the homicide of nonrelatives in terms of evolutionary psychology (Daly and Wilson, 1988). That is, simple murder occurs as part of the natural competition for resources to ensure the survival of one's genes (such as murder of a sexual or territorial rival or a threat to safety). The killing of one's natural child or sexual intimate, or oneself, however, results in a decreased likelihood of passing on one's own genes and runs counter to Darwinian processes. One explanation is that an individual who would nullify his chances for gene survival by killing his offspring, his mate, or himself must be mentally ill. In support of this theory, Cooper and Eaves (1996) found that the killing of a natural child is more likely to be followed by suicide (58 percent of incidents) than the killing of a stepchild (11 percent of incidents).

Psychological autopsy studies of simple suicide have established that 90 to 95 percent of those who commit suicide have a diagnosable mental illness (Robins et al., 1959b; Dorpat and Ripley, 1960; Rich, Young, and Fowler, 1986c; Barraclough et al., 1974). In a study of murderers, West (1967) reported that only one out of thirty-four "criminal" perpetrators in his sample (3 percent) was found to be "insane," compared with fifty-nine of the remaining 104 "domestic" perpetrators (57 percent). In contrast, psychological autopsy studies of murder-suicide incidents are difficult because those who are most familiar with the perpetrator are often themselves dead. Nonetheless, investigators who reviewed medical examiner, police, and any mental health files reported that 30 to 75 percent of murder-suicide perpetrators have a diagnosable mental illness (West, 1967; Rosenbaum, 1990; Cooper and Eaves, 1996; Lindqvist, 1986). It is possible that suicidal and violent behaviors are correlated because they are independent features of certain mental disorders or because they arise from a common neurobiologic substrate in those illnesses (Marzuk, 1998).

Individuals who commit suicide are most likely to have a diagnosis of a mood disorder (Robins et al., 1959b; Barraclough et al., 1974). Although the link between depressive illness and simple homicide has not been thoroughly explored, in many cases of simple spousal homicide, the perpetrator suffers from a depressive illness at the time of the crime (Rosenbaum, 1983; Hirose, 1979; Parker, 1979; Frazier, 1974). Not surprisingly, many studies also emphasize the role of depression in murder-suicide (Hansen and Bjarnason, 1974; Fishbain, Rao, and Aldrich, 1985). Using the psychological autopsy method, Rosenbaum (1990) reported that nine of twelve (75 percent) murder-suicide perpetrators had a diagnosis of depression at the time of the incident compared to none of twenty-four of the simple homicide perpetrators in his sample. The perpetrators' depression seems to be precipitated or exacerbated by the breakup of the relationship, usually when the woman tells her lover she is leaving.

Most of these suicides follow immediately after the homicide has occurred, which suggests they are the result of uncontrollable impulses or premeditation; they usually do not occur after hours or days of guilt and remorse. Many of these incidents are planned; occasionally the perpetrator leaves a note outlining the motives for committing both the murder and subsequent suicide; and in some cases the victim has been stalked repeatedly before their death.

The presence of psychosis, especially schizophrenia, has also been reported as a potential motivational factor leading to murder-suicide. Case reports have focused most specifically on the presence of delusions of jealousy in spousal murder-suicide (Dorpat, 1966; Shepherd, 1961) and of rescue or salvation in maternal filicide-suicide (Selkin, 1976; Myers, 1970; Browne and Palmer, 1975).

The use of drugs and alcohol should be considered a risk factor for murder-suicide, acting not as a direct cause of the event but as a facilitator by disinhibiting behaviors, impairing judgment, inducing paranoia, or exacerbating depression. In several studies 12 to 55 percent of perpetrators (Wolfgang, 1958b; Selkin, 1976; Berman, 1979; Allen, 1983; Currens et al., 1991; Milroy, 1995; Lindqvist, 1986; Somander and Rammer, 1991; Wallace, 1986) and 14 to 29 percent of victims (Allen, 1983; Copeland, 1985) had alcohol detectable in their blood at autopsy. However, substance abuse may actually play less of a role in murder-suicide than in either simple homicide or simple suicide. For instance, studies that have compared alcohol use in murder-suicide perpetrators and simple murderers have found that 50 to 70 percent of murderers but only 30 to 55 percent of murder-suicide perpetrators had alcohol detectable in their blood at autopsy, while 37 percent of murder victims and 0 percent of murder-suicide victims tested positive for alcohol upon autopsy (Wolfgang, 1958b; Rosenbaum, 1990; Wallace, 1986). Cooper and Eaves (1996) found that at least 10 percent of perpetrators of murder-suicide and 7 percent of victims had been using illicit drugs. These figures are probably lower than those found in many simple homicides.

Since most individuals who experience depression, substance abuse, or interpersonal difficulties do not commit murder-suicide, the presence of these elements alone is insufficient to explain murder-suicide. Therefore, investigators have postulated the presence of a suicidal and violent propensity, an amalgam of maladaptive psychological traits best conceived as impulsiveness, which may also be the result of a deficit in serotonergic functioning (Marzuk, Tardiff, and Hirsch, 1992b; Mann and Stanley, 1986). Low cerebrospinal fluid (CSF) levels of the serotonin metabolite 5-hydroxyindoleacetic acid (5-HIAA) have been associated with impulsive acts such as arson (Virkkunen, Nuutila, Goodwin, and Linnoila, 1987), unpremeditated homicide (Linnoila et al., 1983), and suicide attempts and completions (Åsberg, Schalling, Träskman-Bendz, and Wägner, 1987), as well as depression (Åsberg, Träskman, and Thorén, 1976), schizophrenia (van Praag, 1983), and certain personality disorders (Brown et al., 1979). Further study has shown that homicide perpetrators who had killed someone with whom they had had a sexual relationship had lower CSF 5-HIAA concentrations than other murderers (Lidberg, Tuck, Åsberg, Scalia-Tomba, and Bertilsson, 1985). Lidberg, Winborg, and Åsberg (1992) documented the first case of low CSF 5-HIAA in murder-suicide in which the perpetrator had killed his two sons, attempted to kill his estranged lover, and subsequently committed suicide—albeit two months after admission to a psychiatric hospital. (For a further discussion of the neurobiology of suicide, see Chapter Six.)

The Question of Intent

There is considerable overlap between violent and suicidal behavior. There has been debate in the literature as to whether the intent of the perpetrator more closely resembles that of murderers or suicide victims. Are these perpetrators murderous individuals who also commit suicide, or are they suicidal individuals who kill others in the process of their own death? Marzuk, Tardiff, and Hirsch (1992b) have proposed that murder-suicide occupies a distinct domain that overlaps with simple suicide, domestic homicide, and mass murder. The intent of perpetrators spans a spectrum, which seems to vary by typology, from predominantly homicidal to predominantly suicidal. Incidents examined through psychological autopsy and by review of notes left by the perpetrators have shown some cases where suicide is the stronger motive and some where a homicidal drive predominates. The killing of blood relatives seen in filicide-suicide and familicide-suicide seems to stem from a suicidal motivation and is best conceptualized as an extended suicide. The mercy killing of an ailing spouse is also of a predominantly suicidal motivation. Murder-suicides of the spousal-amorous jealousy type and extrafamilial murder-suicides seem to involve murderous intent, motivated, respectively, by jealousy and revenge. Wolfgang (1958b) found that murder-suicide perpetrators used more acts of violence than necessary to kill their victim (such as shooting five times instead of one) and significantly more than in simple homicide. This may signify that the perpetrator was experiencing uncontrollable rage, which was not assuaged by simply killing the person with one blow and was not completely satisfied until suicide had occurred.

Whatever the principal motive, in every incident of murder-suicide the perpe-trator holds the desire to murder and the urge to commit suicide to some degree. Lindqvist and Gustafsson found that ten of sixteen (63 percent) perpetrators showed homicidal behavior or ideation before committing murder-suicide, and eleven of sixteen (69 percent) displayed suicidal behavior prior to the event, four of whom had made serious suicide attempts (Lindqvist and Gustafsson, 1995). In a similar finding Buteau, Lesage, and Kiely (1993) noted that in their study of murder-suicide perpetrators in Quebec from 1988 to 1990, 23 percent of perpetrators had made a recent suicide attempt or threat.

ASSESSMENT OF MURDER-SUICIDE

Most patients seen in a psychiatric emergency room or outpatient setting are as-sessed for suicidal and homicidal ideation separately. Few clinicians, however, link the two behaviors and realize that there can be significant overlap between them. Skodol and Karasu reported that 17 percent of all patients seen in the psy-chiatric emergency room are outwardly violent, 17 percent are suicidal, and 30 percent of the violent patients also display suicidal tendencies (Skodol and Karasu, 1978). Therefore, all patients who present with a recent suicide attempt, have a plan for suicide, or voice suicidal ideation should be carefully evaluated for risk of violent or homicidal behavior. Similarly, those who present with re-cent violent behavior or voice homicidal ideation should be extensively assessed for risk of suicidal behavior. Although the assessment of violence and suicidal-ity is done separately, the clinician should think of the simultaneous occurrence of both in a single individual. Perhaps the most important consideration in the assessment of murder-suicide is the consideration of murder-suicide at all.

As with attempts to predict simple suicide and homicide, any evaluation of murder-suicide risk is likely to overpredict mortality (Marzuk, Tardiff, and Hirsch, 1992b; Hughes, 1996). Most individuals who fit the profile of one of the above types will never die in a murder-suicide event. For instance, as many as four million women receive severe or life-threatening injuries inflicted by a male partner each year (Koss et al., 1994), yet there are only one thousand to fifteen hundred deaths attributable to murder-suicide annually (Marzuk, Tardiff, and Hirsch, 1992b). Nonetheless, it is useful to consider both the types of settings where potential perpetrators or victims of murder-suicide present for evaluation as well as the behavioral patterns or life circumstances associated with a higher-than-normal risk for murder-suicide. In assessing risk, the clinician may need to work in conjunction with other health care and legal professionals to iden-tify the potential murder-suicide perpetrator, the potential victim, or both.

The presence of obsessional or delusional jealousy, especially when comor-bid with depression in an individual with a history of domestic abuse, should always raise concerns about the possibility of murder-suicide. Victims in the amorous-jealousy and familicide-suicide types have usually been exposed to prolonged domestic abuse, are thus more aware of the potentially dangerous situation they are in, and are more likely to seek help than victims of any other type. Potential victims, many of whom have lacerations or bruises inflicted by a spouse or lover, may be identified during a domestic violence call to police or in an emergency room or primary care setting. The potential amorous-jealousy or familicide-suicide perpetrator is most likely to be encountered in a hospital or clinic setting either alone (with personal injuries resulting from a fight) or with his spouse (with physical signs of abuse) and either in an emergency room or during marital therapy. These perpetrators are also likely to be seen at home by police on a domestic violence call or in a courtroom, usually during proceedings for a divorce, separation, or an order of restraint. Stawar reported that in a county in Florida, female petitioners for protection had a homicide rate that was eleven times that of the general rate in the county, and male respondents had a suicide rate thirteen times that of the overall county rate (Stawar, 1996).

In cases in which the domestic violence is less severe, clinicians may encounter potential perpetrators or victims, or both, in a psychotherapeutic setting, where the clients present with depressive symptoms stemming from a chaotic and abusive relationship.

Identification of persons at risk for the declining-health type of murder-suicide typically occurs in a medical unit where a couple has learned that one partner's medical condition has deteriorated, which may lead to increased responsibility for the healthier partner, or separation of the couple due to the necessity of inpatient or nursing home care. Assessment for murder-suicide risk is indicated if such an individual shows signs of depression and dependency, exhibited by such statements as, "I can't go on without her," or "I can't take care of her anymore, and I can't see her in a nursing home." Clinicians should be especially aware of the pressure put on overwhelmed families to have their medically ill, hospitalized family members discharged and cared for at home or placed permanently in a nursing home.

In consideration of potential filicide-suicide, clinicians are more likely to encounter the potential perpetrator than the victim. Potential filicide-suicide perpetrators may bring their child or toddler to a primary care physician's or pediatrician's office or present in a mental health care setting to complain of being overwhelmed or depressed. Parents, especially mothers, may also compensate for murderous feelings by displaying overpossessiveness or concern about their child's being harmed by the spouse, baby-sitter, or others.

Potential perpetrators of extrafamilial murder-suicide are least likely to be identified in clinical settings. If identification does occur, it will probably be in an employee assistance program where the employee is referred for poor job performance and seems markedly disgruntled, angry, and paranoid.

Assessment of the potential murder-suicide perpetrator should begin with an interview that assesses both the diagnosis and motives presented by the potential perpetrator. The presence of an episode of major depression or post-partum depression accompanied by pronounced feelings of hopelessness, particularly with ruminative or psychotic preoccupations that involve jealousy, paranoia, and fantasies of reunion or deliverance or salvation, should alert the clinician to the risk of murder-suicide. As in simple suicide or homicide, the presence of alcohol or substance abuse or dependence probably magnifies risk. The use of cocaine or amphetamines can increase the potential perpetrator's impulsivity, volatility, paranoia, and grandiosity; the use of alcohol may augment disinhibition and depression (Marzuk and Mann, 1988).

The assessment of suicide risk in the perpetrator should follow the usual pattern of assessment: a history of past attempts, a plan or ideation, access to means, and so forth. The assessment of homicide risk should involve exploration of past violence, which includes the time of onset of violent behavior, circumstances leading to each violent episode, the frequency and target of violent behaviors, and the degree of injury resulting from each episode (Tardiff, 1992). Violent ideation can be assessed analogously to that of suicide: severity, intensity, presence of a specific plan, access to lethal weapons or means of inflicting injury, specific target, intent to injure or die, presence of psychosis, alcohol or substance abuse, and history of compliance with treatment (Tardiff, 1996). Clinicians should remember that the risk for suicide is greater in single or divorced people who have no children, whereas the risk of murder-suicide is greater among individuals who are married or recently estranged, and many have children. A history of abusive behavior toward a spouse, past or current impulsivity, stalking behaviors, or exhibition of anger, desperation, and hostility should heighten the clinician's concern. The clinician should be especially concerned by a history of aborted or failed murder-suicide attempts: incidents in which the individual had attempted suicide or exhibited self-destructive behavior following violent behavior directed at another person, usually a spouse or family member. Although there are no studies of this phenomenon, it is likely that this behavior portends ominously.

Unlike the assessment of the risk of simple suicide or homicide, the clinician assessing murder-suicide risk may first encounter the potential victim, not the person potentially initiating the act. If the potential victim is the identified patient presenting for examination, the clinician should consider asking the victim about symptoms she may have observed in the potential perpetrator, such as motives, history of suicidal or assaultive behavior by the perpetrator, or prior aborted murder-suicide incidents. If at all possible, the clinician should try to arrange for the potential perpetrator to agree to be seen for a psychiatric evaluation and murder-suicide assessment.

INTERVENTION

There are no systematic studies that outline the most effective approaches for intervening in murder-suicide events. As with assessment, intervention of a potential murder-suicide is complicated because the perpetrator may not be the identified patient, and it may not be possible to contact him or get him into treatment. This makes intervention in many such incidents virtually impossible. Conversely, many potential murder-suicide scenarios may be complicated by the involvement of entire families as targets, making intervention and treatment extremely problematic.

In cases where the potential perpetrator has been identified and evaluated and is considered to be at risk for committing murder-suicide, the general principles of treating simple suicidal and simple homicidal behavior are probably most effective. Therefore, hospitalization of the perpetrator is indicated if he or she is acutely suicidal, homicidal, or both. If hospitalization is not warranted, the immediate goal of intervention is to protect the target of the perpetrator's violence while diffusing the intensity of the victim-perpetrator relationship. For example, in the case of the disgruntled employee who is making threats to his supervisor, there should be immediate security measures to protect the potential victim, assessment of the potential perpetrator if possible, and active participation of the employing institution to take responsibility for mediating all communication with the aggressor and deflecting any perceived blame directed at the supervisor. Furthermore, it may be appropriate for the clinician to warn the victim. The clinician should be familiar with the principles of the *Tarasoff*-type rulings, which have to do with the duty to warn, particularly when there is an identifiable victim and threat (*Tarasoff* v. *Regents of the University of California*, 1976; Appelbaum, 1985). Because of the complexity of this issue, clinicians are advised to seek consultation (Simon, 1992a).

Diffusing the Intensity of the Victim-Perpetrator Relationship

The diffusion of the intensity of the victim-perpetrator relationship should focus on exploring the motives for the aggressive behavior and restoring the perspective that is frequently lost by individuals who see murder-suicide or suicide as the only solution to their intolerable situation (Levenson and Neuringer, 1971; Neuringer, 1964). Clinicians should assess on a case-by-case basis whether diffusing the intensity of the victim-perpetrator relationship is best achieved through marital therapy, individual therapy, or group counseling for the perpetrator with other physically abusive spouses; and whether separation of the potential victim and perpetrator is indicated. Some have reported that psychoeducational group therapy has proved to be the best option for treating battering behavior (Edleson and Syers, 1991). Some authors have suggested that couples counseling, which may uncover issues that anger the male, may serve only to escalate physical abuse and is thus "emphatically not recommended" (Mintz and Cornett, 1997). Others, however, report that marital therapy may be indicated as long as the spouse's safety can be ensured (Tardiff, 1992). Although diffusing the intensity of the victim-perpetrator relationship may buy time to allow the perpetrator to engage in intensive treatment, serious thought should be given to separating the potential perpetrator from the victim until outpatient treatment is effective in decreasing the likelihood of violence. Separation of the potential victim and perpetrator is sometimes not possible since the victim may be reluctant to leave for financial or emotional reasons. It is further complicated because separation itself is often the precipitating event in murder-suicide incidents (Cooper and Eaves, 1996; Milroy, 1995). Until studies are conducted, it is not possible to give definite advice about how to handle separation issues.

Treating Mental Illness

Although each potential murder-suicide scenario is different, there are some common specific principles of intervention that can be considered in all cases. Perhaps most important is the intensive treatment of underlying psychiatric disorders, most often depression or psychosis, in the potential perpetrator. This can be done with standard antidepressants and neuroleptics, psychotherapy, or both. Intense behavioral psychotherapy and pharmacotherapy are also effective treatments for nonsuicidal aggressive patients (Corrigan, Yudofsky, and Silver, 1993).

Removing Firearms

Another key intervention factor in all potential murder-suicide scenarios is the removal of lethal means, especially firearms, from the home. The removal of firearms is often complicated since many of the perpetrators are estranged, and it is thus difficult to know if they have access to a firearm, and, if so, to have it removed from their possession. A case was recently reported in which a restraining order was filed against the perpetrator, his gun permit was canceled, and all of his guns were confiscated. He still managed to obtain a shotgun to commit the crime (Easteal, 1994).

The responsibility of the clinician in the process of removing firearms is extremely complicated. It can range from notifying significant others to notifying the police. Furthermore, it is useful for clinicians to obtain consultation from another colleague or a risk management representative in a hospital setting to review appropriate steps when the presence of a firearm has been determined.

Providing Support

Provisions should be made for social service assistance in all scenarios identified as potential murder-suicide incidents. Dvoskin and Steadman (1994) reported that twenty-four-hour availability of case management and access to mental health services in one community reduced violence by mentally ill persons in that community. As a possible means to avert a murder-suicide, social workers should be made available to provide assistance to individuals who have been abused or separated from their spouse or lover or to families experiencing financial difficulties; health care workers should be available to families who have a member with declining health and who is being discharged; postpartum counseling and parenting classes should be offered for new mothers experiencing difficulties; and employee assistance programs workers should keep in contact with workers identified as "troubled" or "disgruntled."

In the unfortunate case in which murder-suicide does occur, psychiatric services should be immediately extended to survivors of the event, particularly young children who lose both parents in a murder-suicide event and especially to those who witness the incident. Immediate counseling may reduce the likelihood of the development of post-traumatic stress disorder in survivors.

IMPLICATIONS FOR THE CLINICIAN

The authors define *murder-suicide* as having taken place when a person commits a murder and subsequently commits suicide within one week of the homicide. Murder-suicides typically involve family members and can be broken down into four types: (1) spousal murder-suicide (generally the result of amorous jealousy or declining health), (2) filicide-suicide (usually parental killing of children), (3) familicide-suicide (in which entire families are destroyed), and (4) extra familial murder-suicide (which includes mass murder and suicide bombings). The common theme among all types is the perpetrator's overvalued attachment to a relationship that, when threatened by dissolution, leads him to destroy the relationship. There is considerable overlap between violent and suicidal behavior and certain risk factors can help clinicians assess potential perpetrators.

- Clinicians should assess for risk of violence and suicide in all patients, especially when there is a history of ideation or either behavior. The two can occur simultaneously.

- Clinicians should assess for risk of murder-suicide when presented with depressed individuals involved in domestic violence accompanied by amorous jealousy; couples with declining health; depressed mothers expressing overpossessiveness or "altruistic" fantasies; families with financial, marital, or health problems; or persons expressing a sense of disgruntlement or desperation at work.

- Assessment of potential murder-suicide perpetrator should include a diagnostic interview, particularly for signs and symptoms of depression or psychosis, an exploration of motives, and an evaluation of risk for violence and suicide.

- Intervention in potential murder-suicide incidents should include intensive treatment of underlying mental illness when appropriate, diffusion of intensity of relationship between potential perpetrator and victim, removal of lethal means, and provision of social support.

- When murder-suicide does occur, services should be extended to survivors, especially those who may have witnessed the event.

Excerpts from an Academic Conference and Recognition of Suicidal Risks Through the Psychological Examination

Leston L. Havens, M.D.

EDITOR'S NOTE: Les Havens has been a supervisor, mentor, and friend to me since my residency years at the Massachusetts Mental Health Center. This chapter contains material from the writings of Dr. Havens and a speech made at the 1997 Harvard Suicide Conference, where he was a presenter. This material touches on the core of working with suicidal patients—to be able to appreciate their despair and understand how to use empathic skills to allow the patients to share and reduce their emotional burden at a particular point in time.

The first section, excerpts from the 1997 Cambridge Hospital Harvard Medical School Suicide Conference, provides suggestions for how clinicians can intervene once they have recognized suicide risk. The second section is a paper that was published in the 1960s and still has relevance today as it highlights the complexity of detecting the patient at risk for suicide as we attempt to recognize suicide risk (Havens, 1967). The article aids clinicians by informing them of a variety of methods for appreciating suicide risk. The methods are not laboratory or other tests but rather methods of observation and skills at interviewing—unfortunately, skills that are underused.

EXCERPTS FROM THE CONFERENCE

So, our psychiatry remains the way surgery was before anesthesia. Remember how they used to do operations before anesthesia. You got four big people to hold a person down. You gave them the biggest slug of whiskey you could get into them without killing them. And you still only had—you know how long you had for an appendectomy. The masters were measured in fifty to sixty seconds. A hernia repair was a little quicker. That's all the time you had.

We can't use anesthetics because we generally need our patients to be awake. But there are psychological analgesics. I suggest to you there are three.

The first analgesic in our work is the protection of self-esteem. We owe that emphasis to the great Harry Stack Sullivan. How do you make sure that every moment in your relationship with the patient, you have that uppermost in your mind? Humans dissemble, they self-deceive, they lie, they hide under any circumstances. But when their self-esteem is threatened, they do it in spades. So that's exactly like cutting the abdomen open and hoping they'll stay still.

And some of you, I'm sure, are geniuses at that, probably much better at it than I am. But one thing that I have found that can make a significant difference in the protection of a person's self-esteem is the willingness to admire the patient. And that the first effort at any connection with the patient must be to find the ground that you can enjoy in the other person, that you can celebrate in the other person.

The second analgesic in psychiatry and psychology is understanding. I don't mean understanding in the sense of figuring out what's wrong with the person or deciding that they have this or that illness. Because that's generally terrifying to patients. By understanding, I mean, can we see the patient's experience from their point of view? Do we get it? Not what we think, but what they think.

When you feel understood, you feel immediately comforted. A great part of what's meant by friendship is the sense that when you are with your friend, you are understood. Maybe you even think your point of view crazy—but it's understood by this person.

And the third and perhaps most vital is providing a future. You have to provide the sense that the world can be different. The sense that the world can be made better for you. Don't forget, patients come to us generally as a last resort. They've exhausted their families, friends, the clergy, other doctors. There's nobody else. So, most patients, in my experience, are in significant despair by the time they get to us.

Need for Psychological Analgesia

The comparison between interviewing patients and performing surgery is perhaps not immediately obvious, because sensitivity does not have the same status in our minds as physical sensitivity. The standard medical interview provides examples of psychological insensitivity breathtaking in their prevalence. Shy people are routinely queried about their sexual experiences. Intimate personal happenings are discussed as if the topic were baseball. Patients are asked about fathers and mothers, perhaps the most extended and complex relationships most people have, as if they could be summoned up and characterized in a sentence.

"How do you feel about your mother?" the clinician asks and then hurries on to the next question. Even tactful workers blunder into one crisis of shame after another. It is no wonder Sullivan called our records "wonderful works of clinical fiction." These abrupt intrusions are excused by medical necessity. Yet this often valid excuse does not undo the pain, distortion, and sometimes unnoticed defensiveness that result.

There are specific interview techniques and stances available to the clinician which can make the probing less painful to the patient. They are, in effect, psychological analgesics. They serve to stabilize the clinical field so that investigation and treatment can proceed relatively undisturbed by disruptions in the relations with the caregiver. Their importance springs from the primacy of wounds to self-esteem, feeling misunderstood, and uncertainty about the future as signals of danger to self, to the relationship with immediate others, and to continued existence.

Protection of Self-Esteem

The protection of self-esteem proceeds on two fronts: what clinicians do with themselves and what they do to forestall or repair what the patients do. It is not enough to avoid insults; one must also prevent patients' developing themes which undermine forward movement.

It is much more difficult to avoid insulting people than is generally understood. Our language is full of sexist and racist expressions, and prejudices abound concerning height, weight, work states, being unmarried, divorced, adopted, poor, rich—the list is almost inexhaustible. Much derogation of others proceeds from categorization of them: social, economic, diagnostic, and so forth. It is therefore best to carry any categories we discern lightly, skeptically, and tentatively, which is to practice the existential "reduction," the attempt to concentrate on what is human, what is in common or unique.

As a general interviewing rule, the clinician can protect the patient's self-esteem by finding something to admire or celebrate in the patient and by sharing that admiration with the patient in a nonthreatening way. It may be necessary to point out to the patient that they are loved and appreciated by others in their life.

It is no easier to forestall or repair what the patient does to undermine self-esteem. Patients can "set themselves up" in the quietest, most routine and ordinary ways, to be diminished or hurt by others, as if they were accustomed to lighting a fuse in their pockets. It is not wise to highlight these habits, unmasking the patient's limitations. A fresh awareness will only be added to other shames. Instead, concentrate on not playing the game so the patient can have a new sort of relationship and a better sense of self. When the patient is strong enough, he or she will notice what has been happening.

Need for Understanding

The second element for reducing a patient's pain and sensitivity is called understanding. By this is meant some intellectual grasp of the other's feelings and situation with an acceptance, and evidence of like-mindedness, toward those feelings and situation. It is something we recognize in an instant and are warmed by. Especially if we are deeply troubled or confused and heartsick, it affects us like a superlative tonic, reducing pain and increasing morale. It also acts to loosen tongues. A famous description is Hawthorne's from *The Scarlet Letter* (1850, pp. 130–131):

> A man burdened with a secret should especially avoid the intimacy of his physician. If the latter possesses native sagacity, and a nameless something more,—let us call it intuition; if he shows no intrusive egotism, nor disagreeable prominent characteristics of his own; if he have the power, which must be born with him, to bring his mind into such affinity with his patient's, that this last shall unawares have spoken what he imagines himself only to have thought; if such revelations be received without tumult, and acknowledged not so often by an uttered sympathy as by silence, and inarticulate breath, and here and there a word, to indicate that all is understood; if to these qualifications of a confidant be joined the advantages afforded by his recognized character as a physician,— then, at some inevitable moment, will the soul of the sufferer be dissolved, and flow forth in a dark, but transparent stream, bringing all its mysteries into the daylight.

Actions so powerful must be deeply rooted in our natures. A patient with a troubled or secret-bearing perspective is, often unwittingly, in search of a like-minded outlook onto which it can place its burden. Recognition of the burden by the clinician, signaling a willingness to share it, then finding the mix of words and feeling-expressions to signal like-mindedness allows the understanding to take place, lets the patient feel understood. If the patient feels understood, the clinician can then, from a position of understanding, credibly offer another, more hopeful view of the patient's future.

Anticipation of a More Livable Future

Just as patients with cancer wonder whether they will live, so a person in the grip of psychological distress wonders whether he or she can survive. Thoughts of suicide occur, sometimes with even minor distress, and doubts about whether existence is bearable or if one's mind will go. So, in addition to protection of self-esteem and understanding the clinician can offer an attitude and remarks that balance the imminent terror and despair with a viable future and intact mind. The patient needs to feel the clinician has been here before, knows what to do and can see a way to bring the patient out on the other side of the troubles. Each clinician cultivates an individual style in these matters which reflects one's experience and temperament.

It is best not to contradict a patient's uncertainty or despair. These must be fully acknowledged, even deepened, while the burden of hope is carried by the clinician alone. "Of course you can't believe things will change; how could you believe until they do?" Expect to be shaken by successive revelations. In part the clinician is being tested as a patient uncovers his or her history of hurts and failures. Do not reassure; do not try to offset the bad news with sunny thoughts. Just let it come. Perhaps nod as the stream discharges itself: "How have you stood it?" And expect the worse may still lie in wait. Above all, do not hurry; test the bottom with a possibility still more disheartening, "Perhaps he wanted you to die." Try to exceed whatever horrors have been faced. Then the patient may offer reassurance.

Relevant Readings

Havens LL. The anatomy of suicide. *N Engl J Med* 1965;272:401–406.

Havens LL. Diagnosis of suicidal intent. *Ann Rev Med* 1969;20:419–424.

Havens LL. Explorations in the uses of language in psychotherapy: Counterprojective statements. *Contemp Psychoanal* 1980;16:53–67.

Havens LL. Explorations in the uses of language in psychotherapy: Counterintrojective statements (performatives). *Contemp Psychoanal* 1984;20:385–399.

Havens LL. The need for tests of normal functioning in the psychiatric interview. *Am J Psychiatry* 1984;141:1208–1211.

Havens LL. *Making contact: Uses of language in psychotherapy*. Cambridge, MA: Harvard University Press 1986.

Havens LL. *Clinical interview with a suicidal patient*. Madison, CT: International Universities Press 1989.

Havens LL. *A safe place: Laying the groundwork of psychotherapy*. Cambridge, MA: Harvard University Press 1989.

RECOGNITION OF SUICIDAL RISKS THROUGH THE PSYCHOLOGICAL EXAMINATION

The vast bulk of suicidal efforts spring from despair and helplessness before one or another of life's crises.[1] By itself this is of little help medically; psychiatry enters and psychiatric knowledge is useful because of an altogether separate fact: many people fail to express despair openly or respond to helplessness in ways that make their desperation unrecognizable. The diagnosis of despair can be as difficult and elusive as the most difficult diagnostic problems that general medicine presents.

During the development of medicine superbly systematic methods of locating and identifying physical disease accumulated. The history, physical examination, laboratory procedures, and possible environmental agents are all now routinely searched through whenever the patient presents any but trifling diagnostic problems. The result is some degree of mastery of *differential diagnosis*: a range of appropriate responses to most of the clues the patient's environment, physical state, history, and laboratory findings can offer.

Training in psychiatry seldom equips the physician so well. The training itself is abbreviated, the problems mysterious, and the whole field largely without the quantitative measures and distinctions that are the glory of general medicine. It is no wonder that we too despair. Confronted by a multitude of obscure human problems, with no firm guidelines between the normal and the abnormal or between sickness and sin, we turn back to the challenges of physical diagnosis with relief and confidence. As a result psychiatric problems, which require, if anything, *more* system, completeness, and attention, receive perfunctory efforts, shallow reassurances, and unsystematic groping.

This dismal picture will not be corrected by the paragraphs that follow. I will present, however, the principal elements of the psychological examination that should be held in mind as suicidal risks are weighed. Most should be part of *any* workup when diagnostic problems cannot be immediately resolved. Any one may be the starting point of investigations much more detailed than are described here. *All* should be as much a part of the physician's available methods as inquiries about headache, constipation, or change in appetite are part of the review of systems. I must restrict myself to those factors apparent in the *psychological examination*; there will be little chance to discuss historical and environmental factors. Even the psychological examination will not be exhausted by these remarks; like discussions of physical diagnosis short of a volume or two, this account of psychological diagnosis must be incomplete—the merest sampling.

The restriction to the psychological examination should not lead physicians to think that they can work with it alone. *Any one group of facts by themselves may entirely mislead.* The patient's appearance may be reassuring. Perhaps nothing suggestive is given historically; however, one learns from a family member that events of catastrophic importance to the patient have transpired. Medicine has taught physicians to *compound their methods of inquiry,* and seldom to trust a negative finding alone. The same is true of psychiatry. There is an old legal rule, *caveat emptor*: "Let the buyer beware." In the recognition of suicide let the doctor beware of depending on any one (or two) method of inquiry. The pathologic processes that lead to suicide are no more self-evident than those that lead to cancer. In fact it is the obscurity, the essential secrecy of each, that makes them both so deadly a threat.

Procedure of the Psychiatric Examination

The psychological examination in psychiatry itself and medicine at large has become a mechanical affair, largely ignored in practice and out of touch with recent developments in the field. Appearance and behavior, mood, mental content, insight, and judgment make up several of the familiar categories that were intended to identify significant symptoms and signs and lead to a firm diagnostic appraisal. That they seldom do so by themselves, even in the hands of experienced psychiatrists working with symptomatic conditions, can be demonstrated by a review of the records of any of our leading institutions.

One reason for this failure is that the psychological examination has gradually come to include four large areas of investigation not always part of the routine teaching of medical students and often not systematically written out even by psychiatrists. In the nineteenth century, diagnosis depended chiefly on face-to-face interviews during which the *most prominent symptoms and signs* were elicited (many symptoms were first defined in that period) and the patients reinterviewed at intervals of a few months or years to determine the *course* of the signs. Emphasis was on objective phenomena, particularly motor phenomena such as catatonic signs; histories were sketchy, and the social environment not routinely investigated. (These general remarks are not true of all nineteenth-century psychiatry but represent the prevailing trends.)

As the modern period opened, psychiatric interests and methods began to change remarkably. There was, first, a gathering effort to strike behind symptoms and signs to *pathologic processes*. In schizophrenia, for example, various splitting processes, partly modeled on observations of aphasia, were described. Psychoanalysis pointed out a host of special mechanisms, repression, projection, reaction formation, denial, and many others. A tendency to replace symptoms and sign descriptions with these shorthand terms for the pathologic events believed to lie beneath the surface phenomena—to refer, for example, to hallucinations as projections—gradually crept into the practice of psychiatry.

Further, psychiatrists and psychologists began to collect in great detail patients' accounts of their subjective experiences—the sense of time, space, or color, for example, in the various states of illness. The result was *phenomenology*: the knowledge of pathologic psychic life from within. Of the four developments that I am briefly sketching, phenomenology has had the smallest impact on the general psychiatric scene, although recently there have been signs of a greater influence.

Thirdly, the systematic investigation of social, institutional, and family contributions to disturbed mental life also began in the early twentieth century, under the stimulus of psychoanalysis, Adolf Meyer and the social-work movement; in the last twenty years it has gathered impressive momentum. The methods include all the techniques of psychiatry but applied beyond the patient to his surrounding figures. The epidemiology and ecology of mental illness, family dynamics, and the impact of hospital life on patients—in short, the sociology of psychiatry—illuminate what can be termed the *environmental envelope* of psychic life, the conditions and interactions that shape individual psychologies from without. The modern psychiatrist is as obliged to understand his patient's family, class, and social experience as a modern internist is to know his patient's dietary habits and environmental hazards.

Such facts are part of the *history* or of the direct study of the family or employers and not of the psychological examination. In one vital respect, however, they impinge on it, for the patient offers, in the psychological examination, *a specimen of his social interactions.* He will, within certain limits, treat the physician as he does many others in his environment; in addition, the physician's reactions to him should give important clues to the way in which others feel about and treat him. Of course, I state "within certain limits" because he will not treat us just as he does everyone else, and our reaction will not be exactly that of many others. But, for all our specialness as individuals and as doctors, his treatment of us and our reactions to him, can provide leads to much that is occurring elsewhere in his life.

Physicians must keep as careful track of *their* response to the patient as they do of his to them. The patient may not look depressed; indeed, he may state that he is happy and content. But we notice a lagging of our own mood in his presence, a little despair or turning away. Perhaps it is late in the afternoon, or perhaps we are running behind in our appointments, but perhaps it is none of these things. Feelings are contagious. The clue of our own response may be the only clue to depression and should be enough to energize the search in other areas, and to review more carefully the patient's recent experience, the state of his relationships, or disappointments in life and work. We may not be sure that the strange cell was a lupus cell. But it might have been; so there are other things to do. The point is that physicians have an instrument in themselves with which to sense concealed despair.

Finally, psychiatry has been enormously enriched by the free associative method of psychoanalysis. Mental content that comes to light relatively free to self-editing, social conventions, and censorships of many kinds has provided connecting links that make intelligible a great body of material hitherto obscure. The impact of this on the psychological examination has been immense. Medicine has learned the value of listening more and talking less, of concentrating attention on lapses, puzzling details, jumps of logic, dreams, slips and jokes, misunderstandings of all kinds, any of which may lead to underlying themes, ideas, and aspirations of the greatest importance. The value of "listening with a third ear" should be no surprise to the physician. The tracking down of physical disease has always required the finest sensitivity and intuition, the willingness to follow up what seems hardly present at all, an openness not only to the loud and obvious but to the obscure and apparently insignificant as well. Medicine is like detective work or safe cracking; it requires fine fingers.

In summary, an adequate psychological examination necessitates that the patient be observed, as of old—his speech, expression, movement, dress, the fullest range of outer signs. It also requires that we learn as much as possible of the inner experience of the patient, one of the most difficult depths to plumb. The examination, further, demands self-examination: how the patient makes us feel—what personal responses, on the one hand, reflect the patient's mood or, on the other, undermine, through contagious sadness or annoyance, the physician's most complete and objective professional attention. Through all this we must *listen* for anything that does not fit or for things that fit too well. Finally, and while still conducting the examination, we must compare the information being obtained from the various sources and decide what psychological processes are at work. We may note, for instance, that the patient shuts out every unpleasant topic just as he or she approaches it and replaces the unpleasantness with something cheerful and misleading; this smiling on the outside while crying on the inside is called the manic defense. We then have to press a little to see how sturdy the defense is and what lies behind it.

Applications

Such are the present methods of the psychological examination. They constitute a formidable armory. Even the newest intern has more of them at his command than he generally realizes, which experience and practice can sharpen to a fine point. The chief trouble is that few of us use them self-consciously and systematically. We despair of acquiring psychiatric skills and do not render even our basic equipment serviceable and automatic. We should not be content with this.

The application of the psychological examination to the problem of recognizing suicidal risks may now be taken up directly. Because the examination is a type of interview that, in turn, is a type of personal encounter, it is well to begin using such terms as *interview* or *encounter* in addition to the very scientific sounding but misleading term *examination*. One *enters* an interview as much as one *makes* an examination—that is, we do not stand outside the interview but are constantly within its field of force, influencing the "object" of examination and being influenced by it. And most people seriously intending suicide are powerful radiators of influence; they shape the interview, its content and emotive coloring, its exclusions and its inclusions as much as the physician ever does.

We must take note throughout the interview of the feelings present. What are the principal ones? Do they change as the doctor and patient come in closer contact, or are they flexible and appropriate, or fixed and independent? Specifically, do they respond to changes in the subjects under discussion and over what range? *Are any feelings present at all?* We decide this by looking at the patient, his face, mannerisms, and movements, listening to his voice, noting his account of his inner state (does he describe being empty of feelings, the stoppage of time, the dulling of colors?), and then recording our own response to him. If the only response is bewilderment or uneasiness, it may be that no clear emotive signals are coming across. If all the evidence agrees, he will *look* flat, blank, and without expressive mobility, *describe* inner emptiness, and *leave the listener* unfeeling. From this it cannot be concluded that no feelings are present anywhere; it is safer to suppose that they are deeply buried. The point is that no emotive clues *one way or the other* are given for the determination of the suicidal risk. The patient is going it secretly, alone, and such patients have, many times, killed themselves. The obvious inference is that we must look elsewhere—for example, in the history of the environment—and, above all, realize that we are operating in the dark.

I will not describe the psychological findings that accompany anger or depression: the typical expressions and preoccupations; the changes in the sense of time, space, and color; or the effects on the physician that accompany these states of mind. I must give a warning, however, that bitterness, especially if it is semisecret, has a way of irritating most listeners to the point where they may argue with the patient, lecture him, and probably make him more bitter than before. (The secrecy, also, can extend to our own feelings—it may take a colleague's comment to give a reminder, both of how irritating the patient is and of how angry we have become.) We must expect to be annoyed or saddened by being in the presence of angry and depressed people, and appreciate that our own reactions are merely part of the clinical picture. Knowing this will sometimes make it a little more difficult to dismiss or avoid an irritating patient who nevertheless needs help.

Beware, too, of depressed people who recover suddenly, without obvious reason, and who assume a calm and settled purposefulness. Not a few have decided to die. There is an old story about the recruit who suddenly appeared less bedraggled toward the end of his basic training. He was asked why, and he said it had just struck him that there was only a week to go.

Neither anger nor depression presents the problem that flatness does, or the closely allied *pseudocheerfulness* that so often leads us astray. Everyone knows, socially as well as clinically, *people who never complain.* Through thick and thin, they bear immense inner burdens, taking pride in garnering praise for never whimpering, blaming, or shedding a tear. "How well she took her husband's death," one says, or, "Nothing ever gets him down." So secret do some keep their troubles, and what they feel about them, that if the person destroys himself, everyone is astonished and cannot imagine the cause. Actually, one cause is this very secrecy. Sometimes, the independence, the brave front arise from fear and pride; the person is trapped inside his cheerful, courageous mask, behind which accumulate unspoken convictions of not being understood or the burdens appreciated. The physician cannot "get through" to the person within; we may not even think we need to. These secret resentments are like enormous tubercles; the active material is protected by layer on layer of defensive tissue.

The psychological examination by itself is helpless under such circumstances; it is in fact misleading. We must determine and weigh *what has actually happened*, placing the historical and environmental events *beside* the impressions of the interview. The physician cannot let the patient reassure him, or reassure himself or the patient. He must restrict himself to considering how an average organism could be expected to respond to the loss of a spouse, the death of friends, difficulties at work, or financial problems. *Then* he can come back to the cheerfulness. Does it not seem strange? Oh yes, it is heroic, but we are doctors, not epic poets. We are paid to understand, not to admire or pass judgment. If a patient has been bitten by a rabid dog, the physician is not reassured because the physical examination reveals nothing but a pair of tooth marks; he knows that the destructive material may at this moment be silently ascending the nerve. There are emergency situations in medicine that can be as quiet and reassuring as a day in June.

Now the clinical value of the idea of defenses makes itself felt. Once the patient is seen as a playground of forces, new ones impinging, old ones passing out of sight, fences and boundary lines being erected, standing firm, or collapsing, the physician will set himself the task of gauging the powers at work (especially the power of anger, on the one hand, and the punitiveness of conscience and the patient's ideals, on the other), the means by which they are managed, the strength and type of defenses, and the extent of danger that infective elements will break their bonds and be seeded everywhere. To do these things successfully, we need the historical and environmental information while we examine psychologically; each must be used to throw light on the other. We should be like the radiologist, who does not want to interpret an X-ray film without some history.

Because psychological judgment is part of everyday social and work life, we all grow accustomed to thinking we understand people. On the basis of a glance, a snatch of conversation, we apply the rough categories of popular diagnosis: smart or dumb; brave or cowardly; good or bad; normal or abnormal. Every man is a psychiatrist; he practices to improve or preserve himself and those close to him. If his methods and ideas are ancient ones, they still inspire trust, partly because of their age.

One result is that the psychiatric interview is subject to the restrictions and assumptions prevalent in social life. Such restrictions and assumptions seldom affect the *physical* examination; we are not so shy about palpating an abdomen or doing a pelvic examination as about asking many psychological and social questions. Physicians often hesitate to ask the patient if he or she is contemplating suicide. The whole subject is abhorrent, and we draw back from approaching it; we know it will be a tender area to palpate. Nevertheless, we must ask the question, gently, and listen after, not only for the words but for the music that follows. Suicidal thoughts are not at all unusual in the general population; a flat denial of them is more likely to be defensive and protective than it is honest. And we must continue to listen after the patient has apparently closed out the subject for good. Interviewing is like reaching for something underwater. If we move too fast, the current from our hands may remove the object further. Therefore, the physician should go slowly, keep in mind the refractive error the surface introduces, and look for distant reverberations of his touch. (The fact is that we work through the medium of another person's mind.) The patient may deny suicidal thoughts and intentions, seemingly change the subject, but change it to bridges, cliffs, knives, or pills—or to a lost person of great importance. Something has floated to the surface of the interview. Again, we should not grab; we use fine fingers. We should sense, feel, and trust our hunches. All this is listening with the third ear.

Sooner or later, if a conviction of the patient's wanting to die persists, we must take courage and ask, *is his life now worth living?* This is not the kind of question one drops into a friendly chat over cocktails before dinner. Nor is it the kind of question doctors like to ask. Our lives are so much given up to preserving life that we cannot acknowledge easily that there are people who want to die. Confronted by such a person, we are likely to be unbelieving or indignant, and to break off the relationship. But we must ask the question to ourselves, and we may ask it out loud to the patient. Perhaps all that gave sparkle and value to life has gone from the patient's world—the son or daughter, husband, wife, home, job, or ambition that lit up every day and made burdens light. The money, position, or acquaintances that the patient lists as reassurance may be only obligations and sources of guilt. The physician *must know.* He must find out what the patient has valued, and watch for signs of animation when "the best things" are touched on (noting especially the patient's eyes) and determine independently if they are still available. Then we will say, "Life must not seem worth living anymore." Let the lesion leap into view, the sadness, desires to die, the real heartbreak and the fury. The physician must hold on while this floods over him, repeating what he has just said—a surgeon does not stop operating if there is blood in the field. Clarify; do not reassure, criticize, or abbreviate the interview; keep the feelings and troubles in view. Only then will the doctor and the patient be ready to consider what to do.

In this discussion of the psychological examination of the suicidal risk, I have centered attention on the examiner, the interviewer, perhaps to a surprising extent. My goals have been to systematize an approach to the suicidal patient and to enlarge the conception of the materials that can be used in assessment. Attention will remain on the interviewer as we take up one last and particularly sensitive matter.

The question just considered—whether the patient can find life worth living—has a counterpart for the environment of friends and family. Here again, the relatives may need to be interviewed if the history is not altogether convincing, but the question I have in mind can in part be answered from within oneself and hence from the psychological examination: *Does anyone want the patient to live?* This is not a matter that doctors are taught to consider; it is not an item that appears among the causes of death in textbooks of medicine and surgery. But many recent observations suggest its importance. The cry for help may be ignored, danger signals overlooked, and gestures made toward patients that in retrospect seem like invitations to suicide.

The diagnostic problem is to pierce the veil of convention that will cover most answers to the question. Murderous impulses, especially toward those close to a person, are not easily confessed; the extent of murderousness in the whole human race is not readily acknowledged, despite the facts of widespread war, homicide, and suicide. The hidden attitude of the relatives will have to be gauged with as much care as those of the patient. Accidents are often a sign of unconscious destructive processes at work. *Dreams* may signal with surprising clarity the unspoken desires of patients or relatives. Withdrawal and silence are frequently the ways in which "civilized" people express their rage toward one another. But what of the physician's own responses to the patient?

We should candidly ask ourselves, as the interview proceeds, if we, married to the patient or his father or son, would want him alive. It is granted that everyone entertains if only fleetingly such thoughts on occasion. We should try to allow for any special chemistry that may have "fitted" the patient with husband or wife in their beginnings. But the physician must tot up the ledger as best he can and determine if the weight of evidence comes down on the side of life or death.

The value of knowing—one can as a rule only guess—is obvious. Remarkably active, although unconscious and subtle, efforts may be on foot to rid the world of this person. The physician may unwittingly assist them. Or there may be only one person in the patient's world who stands between him and the desire to die. What if that person is lost, moves away, or has a falling out with the patient? The individual under examination will be as much deprived of vital nutrients as if he had stopped eating. The discovery of such conditions sometimes requires active intervention, often with psychiatric consultation, and an attempt to grasp the main forces at work in the case and turn them into fresh and more hopeful courses. But first of all diagnosis is crucial: the physician must discover, test and weigh, over the whole broad range of psychiatrically significant phenomena. He should have as clearly in mind the succession of questions that he must answer about the suicidal patient as he does the series of steps in a physical examination. Then treatment, at least in its emergency elements, will not be a great puzzle.

I close with a passage that must at first seem wildly irrelevant. It is about an old man who did *not* commit suicide but the very opposite. He lived *more* and *more* as he lived longer, not less and less as is the way with most people. Perhaps the contrast of the description with the problem I have been discussing will provide a touchstone, a standard, to carry into the psychiatric interview. The passage is from an essay by Robert Louis Stevenson (1988, p. 24) on John Knox, the reformer, and the whole piece closes in this way:

> Let us bear in mind always that the period I have gone over begins when the Reformer was already beyond the middle age, and already broken in bodily health: it has been the story of an old man's friendships. This it is that makes Knox enviable. Unknown until past forty, he had then before him five-and-thirty years of splendid and influential life, passed through uncommon hardships to an uncommon degree of power, lived in his own country as a sort of king, and did what he would with the sound of his voice out of the pulpit. And besides all this, such a following of faithful women! One would take the first forty years gladly, if one could be sure of the last thirty. Most of us, even if, by reason of great strength and the dignity of gray hairs, we retain some degree of public respect in the latter days of our existence, will find a falling away of friends, and a solitude making itself round about us day by day, until we are left alone with the hired sick-nurse. For the attraction of a man's character is apt to be outlived, like the attraction of his body; and the power to love grows feeble in its turn, as well as the power to inspire love in others. It is only with a few rare natures that friendship is added to friendship, love to love, and the man keeps growing richer in affection—richer, I mean, as a bank may be said to grow richer, both giving and receiving more—after his head is white and his back weary, and he prepares to go down into the dust of death.

The calculations that Stevenson made in his judgment of Knox's happiness are ones that must be made in medicine, and especially in the estimation of suicidal risks.

Note

1. I am indebted to John D. Merrifield, M.D., for helpful comments.

CHAPTER TWELVE

Critical Points in the Assessment and Management of Suicide Risk

Jerome A. Motto, M.D.

T he recognition, assessment, management, and treatment of persons at risk for suicide continues to be a major issue in the delivery of health care. Preparation for this task is included in the instruction of health care professionals and supplemented by ongoing reports in the literature of each discipline and by workshops and training exercises in a variety of ongoing educational programs.

Observation and research have generated a large body of information about suicide that usually provides the content of the teaching and training of persons in these programs. I refer to this information as "traditional," suggesting that there has been general agreement among experienced clinicians and investigators as to the validity of the concepts involved. For example, the nature of various "risk factors" and the significance of specific demographic characteristics have long been recognized as established observations, basic to an understanding of the field (for example, Goldstein et al., 1991).

CRITICAL POINTS

The present discussion is one clinician's view of where traditional information might fall short, thus providing misleading or insufficient guidance for addressing the enormous variety of circumstances suicidal persons can present. I identify a number of such circumstances as "critical points" in assessment and management, as they are seen as common sources of potential difficulty. Though some points are supported by formal investigation, they are offered here only as clinical observations.

The Recognition That We Are All Patients

Though professionals are prone to refer observations to "patients" or "clients," it is important to remember that no one is invulnerable. Colleagues, relatives, friends, acquaintances, patients, and collaterals all deserve attention when under high or protracted stress.

Example 1. A small child was admitted for severe burns suffered when he was left momentarily in a bathtub and managed to turn the hot water on. While the staff gathered to assess the severity of the injury, the child's guilt-ridden mother jumped from the fifth floor pediatric ward.

Example 2. A veteran staff member of a mental health outpatient clinic was known to be having some marital conflict, but he did not speak of it spontaneously, and because it had no apparent effect on his work, the staff "respected his privacy." When his suicide was made known, a mixture of grief and guilt feelings led to intensive discussion among the staff, with mutual agreement that subsequent inquiry about each other's well-being would not be regarded as intrusive.

Basic Point. From a suicide prevention point of view, we must realize that in a sense we are all patients, and that no one is invulnerable to suicide.

Diagnosis

It is a refinement of the preceding point that one of the misleading aspects of traditional information about suicide is the frequent coupling of the act with a psychiatric disorder, especially depression (Robins, 1981). Hence the comment, so often expressed after a suicide, "Oh, I didn't know he was depressed." Of course the presence of depression (or any other psychiatric disorder) requires assessment regarding suicide risk. The problem is in the implication that the *absence* of depressive signs or symptoms indicates little or no risk, whether or not other psychopathology is present. The overemphasis on associating suicidality with a specific diagnosis is encouraged by contemporary patterns of health care that require documentation of "acuteness" to justify the hospitalization of a patient, resulting in the use of diagnostic labels to assure third party approval of continued inpatient care. For some managed care systems, for example, the diagnosis of "adjustment disorder with depressed mood" is allowed fewer hospital days than the more serious sounding "major depressive disorder."

Underlying this observation is the concept that many suicides are not caused by illness, but by psychic pain or anticipation of pain that exceeds an individual's threshold of pain tolerance. This may be due to a mood disorder, a thought disorder (psychosis), or an anxiety disorder, for example, but may also be inflicted by stressful life circumstances that do not constitute a disorder at all. Characterological patterns with intense commitment to specific values such as independence or an unblemished reputation for integrity may generate unbearable pain if those values become compromised.

Example. Chief of Naval Operations Admiral Jeremy Boorda committed suicide in May 1996 when a question arose as to whether he had worn an unearned military decoration.

Basic Point. A diagnosable psychiatric disorder is important to consider as a significant risk factor, but the *absence* of such disorder, especially depression, does not necessarily mean that the risk is low.

Limitations of Risk Factor Scales

Continuing efforts to improve our understanding and prevention of suicide over the past one hundred fifty years have generated a large number of "risk factors" to help the clinician recognize and assess the degree of risk in a given individual. Starting with demographic characteristics (for example, age, sex, race, occupation, marital status) and going on to clinical features (for example, severity of emotional disturbance, family history of suicide, history of prior suicide attempts, availability of contemplated method), there is now a long list of such items that deserve attention. Some of the best known are feelings of hopelessness, degree of detail in the suicide plan, and strength of the support system. Most of these have been retrospectively derived from large samples and constitute valid epidemiological data.

The limitation is that *in a given individual,* a risk factor may have no significance at all, or may have the opposite effect postulated. For example, a person hospitalized for a serious suicide attempt reported two years later that he no longer had suicidal ideas because he had finally gotten a divorce. Yet numerous studies indicate that divorced persons are at higher risk than married persons. Similarly, a high-functioning individual with a strong and extensive support system found a way to suicide because his sense of guilt over being a burden to those whom he felt close to and had previously taken care of was unbearable to him. For this individual, what would generally be regarded as a deterrent to suicide served as a precipitant. Such exceptions to the significance of "high risk factors" are numerous (Motto, 1985).

Basic Point. Every person is unique. Getting well acquainted with an individual's uniqueness can provide a better understanding of his or her suicidality than adding up "risk factors" presented as a scale for estimating suicide risk. It is probably for this reason that no scale has been widely accepted by the clinical community. Though a scale should not be ignored, its applicability to a given individual cannot be taken for granted, even though its epidemiological basis is valid. This point has been made in the literature, with insufficient emphasis, by the statement that every suicide is "a unique event" (Simon, 1992b, p. 8).

The Role of Alcohol

One of the most consistent of the traditional markers of increased suicide risk is the abuse of alcohol. Alcohol is certainly the most common drug of abuse, and its destructive potential is well known. Also well known, but less often acknowledged, are its sedative, euphoriant, and anesthetic effects that have led to the expression "feeling no pain" as a synonym for alcohol intoxication.

For some persons, the use of alcohol enables them to cope with levels of psychic pain or anxiety that would otherwise be unendurable. Whether intermittent ("binge drinker") or chronic ("chronic heavy drinker"), alcohol use can thus have a transient stabilizing effect for such persons. The problem is that whereas the short-term effect may have benefits, the long-term effect is to increase the level of psychic pain by a familiar sequence of losses: job, friends, family support, community acceptance, health, and self-respect. When these become too painful to tolerate, a sense of futility and despair can trigger a suicide, often during an alcohol-free period of clarity. Thus a past history of alcohol abuse deserves serious attention, as well as the disinhibiting effect of current abuse (Motto, 1974, p. 290; Murphy, 1992).

Basic Point. If a person is persuaded or coerced (Wife: "Next time I'm leaving with the children") to stop drinking as a suicide prevention measure, the risk of suicide can paradoxically escalate. It is therefore essential to increase the individual's support system as much as possible without delay (AA, support group, hospitalization, counseling, family encouragement, religious resources).

For further discussion of alcohol and its relationship to suicide, see Chapter Seventeen.

The Problem of Schizophrenia

Psychotic disorders have a recognized place among the risk factors for suicide, primarily because of the unpredictability of behavior associated with them. During acute episodes the person's earnest reassurance that no thoughts of suicide are present may be followed by sudden impulses or command hallucinations that prove irresistible. This traditional risk factor can mislead us by suggesting that when the psychotic disorder is effectively treated and is in remission, the risk of suicide is correspondingly diminished. In many instances that is the case, but in a significant subgroup it is not, and suicide risk may even be increased.

This seeming paradox has been observed primarily in young persons with schizophrenia whose illness developed after several years of normal emotional development and function. With characteristic youthful resistance to accepting any chronic disorder, each period of remission is interpreted as freedom from illness, a perception that is dashed by a subsequent acute episode. Frequently the acute recurrence is precipitated by the person feeling so confident they are no longer ill that they discontinue their antipsychotic medication.

High risk is triggered when, in remission, it is finally clearly seen that the disorder is not going to go away, and that it will have to be coped with indefinitely. At that point, when the person appears clinically at their best, a suicide attempt is likely to occur (Roy, 1982b; Drake et al., 1984; Drake and Cotten, 1986).

Basic Point. Persons with recurrent episodes of severe psychotic disorder deserve close monitoring regarding suicide risk during periods of remission as well as during acute episodes, especially young people with a preceding period of normal development.

For further discussion of psychosis and suicide, see Chapter Sixteen.

The Problem of Emotional Exhaustion

Everyone carries an emotional burden of stressful feelings—uncertainty, anxiety, fear, guilt, anger, despair, frustration, and so forth—in an amount and combination unique to each individual. For those with known emotional disorders, at least a portion of this burden is made apparent to others by the presence of signs and symptoms. The weight of the burden tends to fluctuate, as does the amount of effort required to carry it, and the availability of psychic energy to make that effort.

The pertinence of this concept to suicide risk assessment is the generally accepted view that persons in a suicidal state will, in almost all instances, communicate their consideration of suicide before they engage in a self-destructive act. This has been widely observed and verified. Yet with disturbing frequency we encounter suicides by persons who have consistently denied active suicidal thoughts, who were working in an effective way daily, and whose family, friends, and colleagues state that they were acting "just like their usual selves" until the time of their suicide.

In such instances, we are sometimes informed by a suicide note, often with an apologetic tone, that the person was just too tired to go on any longer. It was as though they had simply and inexplicably run out of energy, as a gas tank runs dry without warning. Attempts to identify a triggering event are usually unproductive, though a seemingly minor issue may be found that could have provided the "last straw." The unpredictability of the point at which emotional exhaustion might occur produces an inherent vulnerability to an unexpected suicide if the person is unable to inform others of their inability to carry the burden any longer. It is likely that many unexpected and seemingly inexplicable suicides can be accounted for by this mechanism.

Example. A fifty-year-old female laboratory research assistant with a long history of treatment-resistant dysphoria was monitored over a two-year period for depressed mood and intermittent suicidal ideas. She consistently maintained her home life with her family and functioned at a "superior" level at work. She assured her therapist, with whom she had a very good relationship, that though her despondency continued, she had no thoughts of suicide. Two days later she died of an overdose, indicating in a suicide note that she was sorry that she was "so tired" and no longer had the strength to go on. The only added stressor that could be found was a routine mammogram that she feared would reveal a malignancy. Her therapist, coworkers, and family members had seen no significant changes in her behavior or other indications of an impending suicide.

Basic Point. In monitoring chronic dysphoric states, we need to go beyond checking the current level of functioning to inquire whether the person feels able to *continue* to function, with explicit agreement as to what to do if that should change. Ideally, family members are cautioned about the risk of an unpredictable suicidal act.

The Role of Personality

The significance of traditional risk factors is tempered by the uniqueness of each individual's personality, which can influence risk assessment and management more than any other one consideration. This does not necessarily imply a personality *disorder*, such as the dilemma of risk in borderline personality disorder, which includes recurrent suicidal behavior as one of its diagnostic criteria.

Example 1. A fifty-year-old male with extreme dependent needs was free of suicidal behavior as long as he could gain admission to a hospital on request, even though his symptoms were not always deemed serious. When he encountered a managed care system and was denied admission for his complaint of "feeling nervous," he returned home and impulsively jumped out a window, though he had assured the hospital staff that he had no intent to harm himself. The severity of his characterological need to be taken care of was not evident in his brief emergency room examination.

Example 2. A forty-eight-year-old female on a medical ward following a serious overdose refused to be seen by a psychiatric consultant until she had completed elaborate preparation of her hair, makeup, and clothing. When transfer to a psychiatric unit was discussed with her, she adamantly refused. After a close family member advised the consultant that admission to a psychiatric ward would do such violence to her narcissism that the likelihood of a subsequent suicide would be high, consideration of an involuntary procedure was dropped. An alternative supervised setting that the patient found acceptable was devised using family members. The plan included daily telephone sessions with the consultant for a two-week period after discharge.

A rule of thumb in psychiatric consultation is that anyone seen on a medical or surgical ward for a serious suicide attempt should be transferred to a psychiatric unit unless there is an overriding reason to do otherwise. This is an example of such a reason.

Example 3. A forty-five-year-old man was hospitalized on an acute psychiatric ward after spending three days in a secluded area with a gun intending to shoot himself. The consultant for suicide risk was impressed by the extreme rigidity of the patient's thinking, in that he adhered to his views with remarkable tenacity. Though the circumstances appeared ominous, the patient reiterated that the experience of the prior three days had absolutely convinced him that he was unable to commit suicide, and he was ready to go on with his life. In view of his rigid personality structure and his conviction that suicide was out of the question, he was discharged at an early date to a follow-up program.

Example 4. A thirty-nine-year-old woman with a history of several years of psychotherapy and several suicide attempts by overdose presented herself for outpatient care, still contemplating suicide and distrustful of the mental health system. She immediately stated that she would only accept treatment on the condition that she be given absolute control over the issue of suicide, in the form of a prescription for one hundred sleeping pills, to be kept in her safe deposit box. It became clear that an intense need for a feeling of control pervaded all aspects of her life, and in its absence her stability was seriously compromised. The therapist knew her well, and sensed that in spite of the obvious risk, not to give her that control and not to convey the message "I trust you" would constitute an even greater risk. The pills were still unused at thirty-nine-year follow-up.

Basic Point. Personality structure, as well as personality *disorder*, is a major consideration in assessment and management of suicidal persons as well as in the evaluation of risk factors. Some elements, such as impulsiveness or histrionic behavior, are readily identified. Others may be more subtle and difficult to determine in a brief interview. In any case, it is important to recognize the importance of personality in determining outcome.

Suicide as a Power Mechanism

Individuals who threaten suicide unless some condition is met can create understandable tension in those who feel responsible for their well being. At least two responses deserve consideration when this is encountered.

The first is to give careful consideration to the demand made, even if it was expressed in an abrasive way. Too often an immediate reaction is resistance to "manipulative behavior," sometimes tinged with irritation due to feeling pressured (Hayes, 1995, p. 109). Though it may be manipulative, we know that some persons grow up in a subculture that believes no one will provide for your needs unless you coerce them. If the demand is feasible (for example, increase meds, allow visitors), consider meeting it and using the situation therapeutically by exploring the reality of the person's attitude about helping and being helped. Even if an element of manipulation is present, that should not preclude a positive response. A degree of harmless manipulation is acceptable as long as one knows and understands what is going on.

The second response to consider, when the demand is not possible to grant, is to make clear why it cannot be met, and as regards the threat of suicide to simply acknowledge, "I can't stop you. If you suicide, it will be your decision." This is not an artificial maneuver, but an acceptance of the reality that in any power struggle over suicide, eventually the patient has the greater power. It also conveys the message, "If you suicide, I will be sad, but I won't feel guilty." This addresses a basic motivation for the threat of suicide, that is, the induction of guilt as a coercive force.

Basic Point. If faced with the threat of suicide to force a concession, concede what is within reason and use the episode as a therapeutic tool ("Do you really think your needs would not be met unless you threatened us?"). If no concession is possible, explain why that is, seek an alternative solution, and acknowledge that you cannot control the person's behavior beyond a certain limit. Most important, avoid being provoked into a power struggle with the person as to whether you can preclude his or her suicide, as the person will eventually be able to prevail, and may feel a need to demonstrate that (Hayes, 1993).

The Problem of High-Functioning Persons

A frequent and difficult challenge, even for the most experienced clinician, is in the high-functioning individuals who make a serious suicide attempt and shortly after hospitalization insist on discharge because there are no longer any thoughts of suicide, and unless they are permitted to meet their occupational obligations they fear their state of mind will become progressively worse. Such persons may have no significant history of emotional problems and display no evidence of a thought or mood disorder. The suicidal episode is characterized as a transient aberration, sometimes influenced by the disinhibiting effects of alcohol. They are usually able to persuade a judge or hearing officer that a legal hold beyond seventy-two hours is not warranted. Their strengths and social skills seem to effectively screen whatever emotional vulnerabilities they may have.

Yet discharging persons to their own care shortly after a serious suicide attempt is discomforting under any circumstance. The following measures can be considered in this situation:

- The chart should reflect that a thorough inquiry was made regarding past history, the presence of stressors, mental status in general, and suicidal ideas, impulses, plans, and intent in particular.

- The spouse or other family members should be interviewed for their view of the episode and the results documented. If the patient refuses to allow an interview with family, document that.

- Have a consultant see the person and enter a note in the record regarding suicide risk.

- Arrange for outpatient follow-up. If this is refused, inform the family and indicate the limitations involved. Advise the family what to do if questions arise after discharge. Document these steps. If possible, have the outpatient therapist-to-be see the patient while still in the hospital, and discharge the patient to a firm outpatient appointment.

- If a high level of uncertainty remains, skip the preceding step, request an extended legal hold, and let the court procedure mandate the discharge or continued evaluation and treatment.

Another dilemma with high-functioning persons arises when hospitalization is indicated but is refused on the basis of social or professional stigma.

Example 1. A twenty-eight-year-old single female attorney was brought by friends to a psychiatric clinic after a second suicide attempt by overdose. She was very cooperative, as it frightened her that the second attempt was "so easy." When hospitalization was recommended, however, she flatly refused, pointing out that she had recently joined a law firm and that a psychiatric hospitalization for a serious suicidal state would surely compromise her entire career. Though an involuntary hold was feasible, to support her cooperativeness and her desire to be helped, an arrangement was made for admission to a general hospital under the care of her gynecologist. The continued psychiatric evaluation and preparation for discharge to outpatient care was carried out at the bedside in this substitute setting. She was stable and functioning well during a three-month follow-up.

Example 2. A forty-one-year-old anesthesiologist with suicidal ideas due to severe marital conflict was recognized by his internist as being at risk for suicide. Consultation by a psychologist led to recommendation for hospitalization, as did a second consultation by a psychiatrist. Both recommendations were refused by the patient with the contention that he would be rendered unemployable by entering a psychiatric hospital. Both examiners agreed that he did not meet criteria for an involuntary hold, as he had no defined mental illness, denied any intent to act on his earlier suicidal thoughts, accepted the addition of marital counseling, and functioned well in his highly skilled professional role. When his wife unexpectedly informed him she was leaving, he abruptly suicided. In subsequent litigation, all his professional caretakers were found to have acted appropriately, in spite of the adverse outcome.

Basic Point. High-functioning persons in responsible positions can pose management dilemmas that our social and professional resources do not provide for. If such persons are judged to be at high risk for suicide, we should use every legal means available to us to treat them in a protected setting, even at the risk of alienating the person or exposing them to the hazard of social or professional stigma. In the presence of considerable personality strengths, equivocal situations are common, and we are obliged to follow our intuitive judgement with careful documentation of observations and rationale. Cases in which we take obvious risks (for example, deferring hospitalization or allowing access to potentially lethal means), the rationale is usually that in our judgment, available alternatives to the measures taken would have posed an even greater risk.

The Use of Contracts

The practice of contracting with patients for no self-harm has become widespread. Such contracts range from formal written and signed documents to informal verbal agreements, stipulating the extent and duration of the contract; for example, no self-harm while on the inpatient unit, or no self-harm before the next outpatient appointment.

The limitations of this procedure seem quite evident, but one point deserves emphasis; specifically, the degree to which one can rely on a contract depends not only on the amount of control the person has but, most important, on the presence of a strong and mutually trusting relationship with the person. An assessment in the emergency room, in a consultation setting, or even on an acute treatment ward provide less basis for a contract than a long-term therapy relationship. The potential usefulness and problems associated with using clinical contracts in the management of suicidal patients is still a subject of systematic study (for example, M. P. Egan, 1997; Davidson, Wagner, and Range, 1995).

Clinicians often utilize a form of contract without using that term, as in asking "Can you manage OK until our next appointment?" or "Will you call me if things get to be too much for you to cope with?" Even the acceptance of a future appointment can serve in this way.

Example. A therapist who habitually opened his office door for patients after a session, did so for one with a long history of suicidal episodes, saying, "I'll see you next week." When the patient rose to leave without responding, the therapist closed the door, and asked, "Am I going to see you next week?" There was a long silence. Finally the patient said very softly, "Yes" and the door was again opened. The first words spoken in the next week's session were, "If I hadn't told you I'd be here today, I don't think I'd have made it through the week."

Basic Point. Although the use of contracts is a frequent practice, the strength of this device as a deterrent to suicide varies widely. When used, estimating that strength becomes part of the assessment process.

Legal Considerations

Legal concerns must not dictate clinical practice, but the prominence of suicide in malpractice litigation and the old adage that the best legal defense is good clinical care suggest that the issue deserves close attention. This is especially true in view of changes in health care that diffuse clinical responsibility and hence diminish control. That is, the actions of any one clinician on the treatment team can have a legal impact on every team member.

From the psychiatric point of view there are at least five critical elements regarding suicide risk that should be reflected in the record:

1. Evidence that an assessment of risk was carried out. What constitutes "an assessment of risk" depends to a large extent on the circumstances of each case. The more uncertainty encountered, the more extensive and detailed the inquiry needs to be. Ideally, the record reflects attention to suicidal ideas, impulses, plans, intent, and behaviors, both current and past, in the subject and in the family. It also reflects awareness of both short-term and long-term predictors and deterrents of suicidal acts. Detailed discussions of these issues are readily found (for example, Simon, 1992b; Maris et al., 1992; Chapters One and Eight in this book). In practice, a clinician usually obtains enough information to form an opinion with reasonable certainty as to the level of risk.

2. A plan appropriate to manage the estimated level of risk was formulated, with the rationale for any risks inherent in the plan.

3. The plan was implemented in a timely manner.

4. Pertinent family members were consulted, when indicated, for their input regarding risk and to inform them of the clinician's estimate of risk if it was clinically significant.

5. If there are ambiguous or conflicting data, or any circumstances that create uncertainty regarding the level of risk or its management, a consultation was obtained and integrated into the patient's care.

If these five measures are documented, clinicians will deserve the undying gratitude of their liability insurers and the risk management office of their institutions, as it will be amply demonstrated that no negligence was involved regarding suicide risk. An important element in the documentation is explicit reference to the unpredictability of a recurrence of suicidal impulses and behavior during and after the acute treatment period. Professionals in health care are not required to demonstrate perfection in judgment or foresight. Even though errors may occur and an adverse outcome result, if those errors are not due to negligence, carelessness, or incompetence, a finding of legal liability is very unlikely. Our goal, and the most likely outcome in such cases, is that litigation will not be initiated at all because a knowledgeable attorney will recognize that the record clearly shows the absence of negligence (Simon, 1992b).

The importance of working closely with the family is often underestimated. Family members frequently suffer as much or more than the patient during the course of treatment, and can be very sensitive to how seriously their input is regarded. Ideally, they are included as important members of the treatment team. Some patients refuse to permit this, and some families are resistant to it, but the record should reflect that an effort was made to bring it about. Family members who have felt excluded or ignored have been known to contact an attorney within hours of a suicide. Those who have felt included and supported by the therapist tend under those circumstances to respond as to a fellow survivor, embracing and thanking him or her for having done what they could.

If such an adverse outcome occurs, the family must become the primary concern. Though each family is unique, the therapist or treatment team should immediately make counseling available to deal with the feelings of grief, guilt, and anger that so frequently ensue, especially if there are surviving children. Though presented here in the context of legal considerations, this is simply optimal clinical care, which, it bears repeating, is one's best defense against legal action.

Basic Point. Protection from legal liability arising from the treatment of suicidal patients requires documentation that the risk was recognized, assessed, and managed in a nonnegligent manner. That can be achieved by well-established clinical procedures, though increased time and effort is required to assure that the medical record is detailed and clear in this regard. Forming a close working relationship with family members can be critical. The process is entirely consistent with optimal clinical care and record keeping.

For further discussion of suicide and legal liability, see Chapter Thirty-One.

The Problem of Chronic Suicidality

As used here, the term *chronically suicidal* characterizes individuals whose best level of adjustment is not far from an acute suicidal state. That is, when at baseline and functioning optimally, any severe stress can abruptly precipitate suicidal thoughts, impulses, and behaviors. Thus, persons who are chronically suicidal tend to have a history of multiple suicidal episodes, triggered by stressors such as perceived personal rejection, job loss, eviction, or other painful emotional experience. This pattern is often accompanied by a diagnosis of substance abuse, chronic mood disorder, thought disorder, or anxiety disorder, or it may exist as a personality disorder with the periods between episodes free of visible pathology. In the latter case, the category of borderline personality disorder is often used for lack of a more specific diagnosis (Soloff, 1994).

Chronically suicidal persons pose a special dilemma for mental health care providers because of the treatment-resistant nature of the disorder and the unpredictability of recurrent acute suicidal episodes. When persons with schizophrenia or depression suffer a relapse, they can be readmitted and treated, but when suicidal impulses abruptly and unpredictably arise, the person does not always survive long enough to reenter a protective setting.

The clinician is thus faced with a philosophical challenge: Is it better to keep such persons in a safe environment (the hospital) even when symptoms have resolved, or to discharge them to their home setting even though there is a significant risk that a suicidal state will recur at an unpredictable time due to circumstances that are unforeseeable and uncontrollable? In other words, which is the greater value, safety of life, or quality of life? One's humane impulse (and statutes requiring that the "least restrictive environment" be used) incline us toward the latter, but it is not an easy choice.

The contemporary solution is to discharge the person when symptom-free and attempt to develop a strong enough support system outside the hospital to respond promptly when danger recurs. This exercise in clinical creativity takes the form of family resources when available, ongoing monitoring by a mental health clinician, medication as needed, support groups, telephone safety checks, church-related activities, twelve-step programs, and ready availability of emergency and inpatient facilities. In spite of the potential for abuse, a useful support element is to assure the person that they can be readmitted to the hospital on request, thus removing one potential barrier to this rejection-sensitive subgroup. If an individual has few personal resources and is unable to effectively utilize community support, long-term partial hospitalization or inpatient care can be used.

Basic Point. Chronically suicidal persons pose a severe challenge to clinicians and health care systems because there is no way to be free of risk without seriously compromising quality of life. It is important to make this known to family members as early as possible to enlist their support and to reduce the number of legal actions resulting from unrealistic expectations of mental health clinicians and facilities. Nowhere is it more true that if we are not prepared to lose the patient we are not prepared to treat them. It is equally important that health care personnel appreciate the nature of their chronic pattern in order to respond to every new episode with appropriate concern and compassion.

IMPLICATIONS FOR THE CLINICIAN

Although the primary focus of the health care worker is to treat the underlying disorder that generates a suicidal state, other persons also have the means to reduce the potential risk of suicide in a very simple way—specifically, to repair the sense of alienation, isolation, and lack of connectedness that can be unbearably painful to a person in despair. Often a short note, a brief telephone call, or an expression of caring may have a powerful impact on an individual at a vulnerable time. Such an influence may be inadvertent. One young person who jumped from the Golden Gate Bridge left a note behind reading, "If one person smiles at me on the way to the bridge, I will not jump." Though suicide prevention efforts at the professional level can be complex, demanding, time consuming, and filled with uncertainty, that must not mask the reality that essentially all persons with the desire and motivation to reduce the frequency of suicide may have it in their power to do so.

Each of the twelve preceding points constitutes a caution to the clinician, which can be restated as follows:

- Apply suicide prevention principles to everyone under stress, not only to patients.
- A high risk for suicide can be present with any psychiatric diagnosis, or with no psychiatric diagnosis.
- Every person is unique. Traditional "risk factors" have statistical validity, but for a given individual a risk factor may not apply to all or may exert an influence opposite to that attributed to it. Each factor deserves exploration with this in mind.
- The use of alcohol or other drugs can exert a short-term suicide *prevention* influence, which must be taken into account when such use is discontinued.
- Remission of a schizophrenic disorder may paradoxically increase the risk of suicide, especially in young persons with a prior period of high

function, hence continued close monitoring is indicated even when symptoms improve.

- Abrupt and unpredictable exhaustion of energy can result in unexpected suicide with no premonitory indications when chronic low-grade pathology gives the appearance of stability.

- Characterological issues that may be difficult to detect in a brief interview (for example dependent needs, need for control) can be the most important determinants of effective management.

- If the threat of suicide is used as a coercive measure, try to find a positive response, use manipulative behavior therapeutically, and avoid a power struggle over control of suicidal behavior.

- High-functioning persons who appear symptom-free very soon after a suicidal episode can raise unanswerable questions as to ongoing risk. An approach as conservative as circumstances allow is called for, using intuitive judgments based on available facts and documenting the rationale for the measures taken.

- The deterrent value of a no self-harm contract is determined largely by the strength of the relationship with the therapist.

- Legal vulnerability is minimized by documentation that affirms that the following steps were taken.
  - The risk of suicide was assessed.
  - A plan commensurate with the estimated risk was made.
  - The plan was implemented.
  - Family members were included to the extent feasible.
  - A consultation was obtained.

- Chronically suicidal patients are a major challenge to the clinician to create and depend on a support system that is sufficiently extensive and sensitive to facilitate immediate access to care whenever a suicidal crisis occurs. It is also no small challenge to those in the mental health system to maintain a positive and supportive feeling toward those patients who make repeated emergent demands on it.

CHAPTER THIRTEEN

Can Suicide Ever Be Eradicated?

A Professional Journey

Pamela Cantor, Ph.D.

Ihave been writing papers on adolescent suicide for many years, and it is the first time I have had difficulty. The topic, "Understanding Adolescent Suicide?" has caused some soul searching, and with my highly honed talent for procrastination I have had plenty of time to reflect on my thirty years of study of self-destructive behaviors. I have examined some basic questions and must reluctantly admit a few hard facts.

Can we ever understand suicide? Yes, in some cases. No, in many others. Can we accept the self-inflicted death of a young person? Not in my experience. Can we prevent suicide? Sometimes, if we get the chance. Can we predict suicide? Occasionally. Can we reduce the overall number of suicide attempts or deaths? A cautious maybe. Do we understand more about suicide today than we did more than a quarter of a century ago when I first began the study of self-inflicted death? A little, perhaps.

In what follows, I synthesize my thirty years of study. (When I finish, you, too, may conclude that I might have been better off following my desire to work on a fashion magazine, or even pursuing a career as a heavyweight boxer, as I probably have as much chance of winning the title from Mike Tyson as I have of understanding suicide.)

I first became familiar with this topic through the suicide attempt of one of my closest friends. She was, and still is, the most adventuresome female I have ever known. She embraced every opportunity to explore and shied away from nothing. She experimented with LSD in weekly therapy sessions while in high school before LSD became a fashionable route to the unconscious mind. She took off to live, love, and swim at nude beaches with an expatriate fisherman on a lush Australian island while the rest of her girlfriends back home on Long Island were having pajama parties and pondering life-altering questions such as whether we would ever let any boy touch our breasts. My friend went to college and then became the manager for an infamous comedy group and traveled around the world flushing their cocaine down the toilet. After her stint with show business (or should I call it "snow" business) she went into business for herself and became a sought-after public speaker who dressed in purple velvet slacks and reveled in shocking audiences by discussing topics considered taboo in our society. She lived life on the roller coaster and always avoided the merry-go-round. She had fun, probably with a capital "F." She also made a serious suicide attempt while in college.

At the same time, two of my college instructors committed suicide the semester after I had them in class. Both were young males.

Soon after college graduation, my ninth grade boyfriend shot himself and died. He was my first steady, probably my first love, and I wore his ring around my neck with pride until he betrayed me by asking one of my best friends out. I gave him his ring back the next day in social studies class but, somehow, we remained friends until he died.

In graduate school I volunteered to work in the children's division of a hospital. I was assigned to tutor a thirteen-year-old boy who later stabbed his brother with a steak knife and then turned the knife on himself. He kept trying to seduce me as we sat side by side on his bed in the crowded psychiatric ward and went over math problems, but, at least for the time I knew him, he stayed alive and did not murder his brother.

While in graduate school I had to do a paper for child psychopathology class. I chose to write on self-destructive behaviors in children and adolescents because I had become intrigued with my seductive, suicidal tutee with murderous rage. I later milked this topic for an anthropology class. By expanding it to include anthropological literature, such as the prevalence of suicide among the Trobiand Islanders, I could ace this paper with little extra work. Then for an analytic study for personality class I chose to examine the life of Jack London, a famous adventurer who lived by violence and died by suicide.

While I was in graduate school I was asked out by the son of a West Coast entrepreneur. I think I said "yes," but never got to meet this young man because he jumped off the balcony of his Park Avenue apartment before our intended date. (There are easier ways to break a date.)

Soon after, another close friend from college married and moved to California. Within the year she was dead. Neither her parents nor her husband would ever tell me how she died. Rumor had it that she had an adverse reaction to birth control pills. I believe differently.

As my graduate career in psychology moved from its original focus of educational, to developmental, then clinical psychology, I was looking for a way to blend my varied interests. At this time, Johns Hopkins Medical School and the National Institute of Mental Health were posting an invitation for applicants for a fellowship in the study of suicide and self-destructive behaviors, and I applied.

I went for my interview in Baltimore and was greeted by two of the best-looking men I had seen in a long time. (Of course, I had been hanging out in the bowels of Columbia University, so that was not saying much, but they were handsome.) One asked me whether I would like to remove my coat—only it was my dress (in the popular Jackie Kennedy Onassis coatdress style of the 1960s), and I was sold. (Once again seduction and suicide were entwined. It may be of more than passing interest that many of the early suicide researchers dropped the death field to study sex, and in this we might find support for Freud's claim that love, work, and sex keep us alive.)

I spent the next year commuting between Baltimore and New York. Suicide fascinated me because it encompassed psychology, pharmacology, toxicology, pathology, anthropology, sociology, theology (I never knew there were so many "ologies"), psychiatry, pedagogy, history, literature, public health, preventive medicine, and of, course, violence. My fear of violence, and perhaps a need to master it, could be one primary reason I study suicide. I have always abhorred violence and I remember, as a child, I could not read Nancy Drew stories because even these juvenile mysteries were too graphic. In more recent years I asked my psychoanalytically schooled insightful brother whether he had any idea why I was so fascinated with violence. He looked at me for a moment before he held up the newly published book he had been working on for twelve years, which had rested on the car seat between us, *The Death of Che Guevara*, a fictional biography of the famous Latin American revolutionary, who lived and died by violence. His first book involved an analysis of the Patty Hearst case and his third was about two flat one-dimensional comic strip characters, Krazy Kat and Ignatz Mouse, who evolved into fully rounded complex human beings through the discovery of violence, sex, and psychoanalysis. We, however, still puzzle over the answer to our mutual fascination with violence.

While I was in Baltimore, I learned that the sister of a friend of mine, a first-year graduate student, jumped off the roof of her dormitory and died.

I completed my fellowship, did my doctoral dissertation on the personality characteristics of adolescent female suicide attempters, and continued to study suicide while teaching at Boston University. There I had the privilege of working with a young graduate student from another university who had come to collaborate with me for her dissertation research. Not too long after, I learned she had jumped out of a window of her dorm and would never walk again.

Somewhere during that time I appeared on the *Phil Donahue Show*. Shortly after I got home I received a letter from a young man I had known when we were in junior high school. He was my back-fence neighbor and he used to carry my pink, leather, zippered three-ring notebook up the hill from the bus stop for me every day after school. He wrote to tell me he had gotten my number from the television network and he was in the hospital in New Haven because he had jumped from a building. He said this was not his first suicide attempt and he asked me to contact him. I was afraid to call him and, true to my personality style, I procrastinated. When I called, I could not reach him. I am still trying to find him and I am haunted by the fear that he is not alive.

I would like to tell you that my many associations with suicide gave me some clarity, some profound insight, but they did not. With the additional personal exposure that my clinical work with suicidal individuals has given me over the years and with all my education, I still do not know why my friends, students, or teachers committed suicide or attempted it, but I do know there was not one reason; rather, suicide is multidetermined. I can try to explain their acts with the following reasons, but none of them are particularly erudite nor illuminating.

My fish-loving, sexually unrepressed friend attempted suicide because her heart was broken by a subsequent lover. She was not then and is not now mentally ill, although one might say that when one suffers from a broken heart one is depressed.

My professors were both homosexual males. It was the 1960s and the climate was not welcoming for homosexuality. It was considered a perversion by the mental health, social, and religious communities. I would guess that there was some relationship between the two men but I will never know. I doubt they were mentally ill, but they were socially "unacceptable." Perhaps one was a rejected lover. It was all very "hush-hush" then; no one talked about homosexuality or suicide.

My steady boyfriend was a bit of a rebel, a James Dean type, beautiful, gently masculine, and quietly rebellious. He might have suffered some emotional difficulties as many brilliant young men do, but these factors do not necessarily predict a suicide by gunshot.

My thirteen-year-old tutee was angry and frustrated and had no parental support and no money. I will never know what turned his rage into homicidal and suicidal impulses. It could have been an emotional illness or it could have been an inability to appropriately channel his anger.

My friend's sister probably committed suicide because of an inherited vulnerability to depression, which was untreated, and parents who, in spite of her beauty and brains, neglected her in favor of their prized firstborn.

My junior high school neighbor will remain an enigma and a source of guilt because my not phoning him may have been another "nail in his coffin," but it is unfair to both of us to speculate.

My graduate student assistant, with whom I worked for months, appeared as sane and stable as anyone I knew. I have no idea what caused her to jump and I was too devastated, and probably too cowardly, to try to find out.

I believe the entrepreneur's son had access to too many designer drugs, and his death may have been a tragic misadventure.

My college friend was a joyful person—we laughed our way through travels and travails. I saw her daily for months and even lived with her. I had no knowledge of her ever being depressed or ill. I am troubled by her sudden death because no one was willing to talk about it. It could have been accidental, but I suspect otherwise. I miss her and her death must still be very painful to me because I could not even think about including her in this paper until two days ago.

After all my years of education and exposure, and after examining the many losses I have experienced, I have come to believe people commit suicide because of pain, sadness, hopelessness, and helplessness.

Often the most profound statements are the simplest. We do not need to be very complex or convoluted about it.

So here is my E=MC squared. I would like to change the word *suicide,* which means "self-murder," to *suisad,* which would mean "self-sad." I would like to add this word to the lexicon of suicidology because I think it may be more illuminating than saying someone has murdered himself. I would like to say people do not commit *suicide,* they commit *suisad* because people really do not want to murder themselves. They want to save themselves but "murder" the sadness. A depression can create a psychic pain that is as unbearable as any physical pain, and the person wants to get rid of it.

What else have I learned in thirty years that could add to our understanding of suicide?

Self-destructive behaviors among young people are a growing problem. These behaviors include, but are not limited to, alcohol and drug abuse, smoking, self-mutilation, eating disorders, dangerous or demeaning sexual practices, and suicide. All of these behaviors are self-defeating and some can lead to death.

Suicide is not a disease. It is a symptom of other problems, physical or emotional, which can be caused by disease, disability, or a difficult situation. These problems are often temporary. Suicide, however, as Shneidman says, is "a permanent solution to a temporary problem." It is an act that terminates life.

The purpose of understanding suicide is to prevent it. To prevent it effectively we would like to know why it happens. Unfortunately, "the authorities" do not agree on the causes of suicide.

Experts in sociology, anthropology, and theology believe the reasons for self-inflicted deaths reside in society—in the tolerance of violence, the rampant use of drugs, the abuse of alcohol, the stratification of social classes, the deprivations of poverty, the demise of organized religion, the increase in working mothers, and the dissolution of the family.

Epidemiologists and public health officials believe suicides are the result of the availability of lethal weapons such as handguns and rifles or pills.

Psychologists state the cause of self-destructive behavior is psychological pain—or to use Shneidman's newest term, it is "psychache," the emotional pain caused by profound unhappiness coupled with a hopeless attitude about the possibility of changing the future.

Psychiatrists believe the root cause of suicide is mental illness, and most will make the claim that a mental illness is almost always present in the history of a suicidal individual. Some will even say it is present 100 percent of the time. Yet, in a recent speech, when Dr. Joseph Coyle, psychiatrist, neuroscientist, and chairman of the consolidated department of psychiatry at Harvard Medical School, was asked whether there are biological factors that affect the risk for suicide, his answer was a very cautious yes. "Since 1950 the rate of adolescent suicide has increased fourfold and this suggests social factors. Affective disorders are also increasing, but it is foolish," he said, "to equate suicide with affective disorders."

The continued arguments among the experts seem to me to obfuscate the obvious, that a person who takes his life is deeply miserable, that this profound unhappiness may have different "roots" or "triggers," and that if we wish to "understand" suicide we cannot attribute all suicides to one "root" cause or "precipitating factor" such as mental illness or poverty or a lethal weapon. Further, we cannot eradicate suicide with psychological therapy or with a medicine or a change in society or an elimination of a risk factor; we can only hope to reduce its occurrence. If the cause of the desire to die is a mental illness, then medication might be the perfect thing to preserve a life. If the cause is unfortunate events conspiring to "hit" a person when he does not have the ability to cope, then the suicide could be the result of what appears to be limited options combined with the proximity of a lethal weapon and destructive impulses, where help comes too late.

Whether we understand suicide or not, if our goal is to prevent suicide, we want to be able to predict it. Yet suicide is an infrequent event that is difficult to predict.

Here is what is known about the prediction of suicide.

1. A person is at risk if he has made a suicide attempt or has a specific plan to end his life. This means we are using suicidal behavior to predict suicidal behavior, which is akin to using old age to predict longevity by saying if a person lives to age ninety with no physical illness he has a good chance of living to ninety-five. This is hardly a revelation and certainly is associative, not causative.

According to the Suicide Assessment Protocols produced by Dr. Douglas Jacobs, somewhere between 18 and 38 percent of those who die by suicide have made a prior attempt. Yet 90 percent of those who attempt suicide do not go on to complete suicide. The question then becomes: What saves those 90 percent who are at high risk for suicide? Is it that someone provided effective intervention? If we did absolutely nothing would the same 90 percent still survive?

2. A person is at risk if he is impulsive, anguished, or agitated. This does not imply mental illness but rather a compromised state of mind.

3. A person is at risk if he is unable to see any solution to his problems. This, again, is a state of mind. A "suicidal state of mind" can be caused by mental illness or by hitting a period when one does not think clearly and feels too overwhelmed to be rational or hopeful about contending with life.

4. A person is at risk for suicide if he has access to a lethal weapon. A popular method of committing suicide in England was asphyxiation with home heating gas. Just by changing the highly lethal coke gas to a less lethal natural gas, the English reduced the suicide rate in their country by 33 percent. In other words, by eliminating access to a lethal weapon the English suicide rate was decreased because suicidal individuals did not switch to another means. This provides support for the epidemiological approach of limiting access to lethal weapons and taking them out of the hands of impulsive teenagers. We know the gas did not cause suicide, it was a means to suicide, but removing the means saved lives.

5. A person is at risk if he is depressed. William Styron, the Pulitzer Prize–winning author who shared his struggle with deep depression in a recent HBO television documentary, said it is misleading to think of this profound misery as "depression." "*Depression* is a wimp of a word. It implies a declivity in the ground. You are not depressed. You are insane. . . . *Melancholia*," he said, "has much more of an impact." His description of depression brings these five words to my mind: impenetrable, interminable, intolerable, unrelenting torture. This is a mental illness.

Depression carries a lifetime risk for suicide of 15 percent.

6. The suicide rate for panic disorders, although less frequently discussed in the suicide literature, is a significant issue (see Appendix).

7. Schizophrenia carries a lifetime risk of suicide of 10 percent.

8. Borderline personality disorder carries a 7 percent risk.

9. Alcoholism carries a 3 percent lifetime risk.

10. A person is at risk if he has identified with or witnessed someone who has committed suicide. Thus, we see an increase in suicidal behaviors in mental hospitals after a patient has committed suicide, in schools or communities after a student has committed suicide, or in the general public after a celebrity has committed suicide. This is called the *copycat phenomenon*. These "copiers" do not necessarily have a *DSM* diagnosis, although a case could be made that these individuals are suffering from post-traumatic stress disorder, but a case also could be made that "copycat" suicides among young people are committed by those who believe they have an opportunity to find fame and glory in death.

11. Post-traumatic stress disorder also carries a risk.

12. A person is at high risk if he or she has been abusing alcohol or drugs.

In sum, a person is at risk if he has no strength to cope with problems, cannot envision a brighter future, and is convinced that suicide is the best way to end his misery. He could be angry or frustrated or have hit a snag he cannot handle. He could be clinically depressed, anxious, or suffering from another emotional illness. He could be physically ill or disabled. He is at greatest risk if he has a history of suicidal behaviors, or a family history of suicide or violence, has witnessed a suicide or violent death, and has access to a lethal weapon such as a car, a gun, drugs, or, as my personal accounts portray, access to a balcony, window, or roof.

The most significant research finding that has shed light on the issue of suicide in the last thirty years, in my opinion, is the discovery of the role of a low serotonin metabolite 5-hydroxy-indole-acetic acid (5-HIAA) and homovanillac acid (HVA) in the cerebrospinal fluid of suicides. The discovery of a low serotonin level in violent and aggressive individuals, in depression and in obsessive-compulsive disorder, in migraine headache, and in premenstrual syndrome has revolutionized the treatment of these problems. I accept that our knowledge of the biology and biochemistry of the brain is in its infancy, and I understand that the major inroads in the treatment of mental illness will come from the research in this vital field. I most gratefully applaud the chemical treatment of brain dysfunction and certainly acknowledge the brain as an organ susceptible to attack by viruses and toxins and effected by nutrition and chemistry. Although I personally would award the Nobel Prize to Marie Åsberg in Sweden for her research into serotonin and to Judith Rapaport at NIMH for her research into the application of serotonergic drugs on obsessive-compulsive disorder and although I clearly support basic biochemical research, I do fear the now popular view that all suicides are a result of a mental illness, and I lament the movement toward the "biologizing" of suicide. Depression, for example, is arguably not the only cause of suicide, and even if it were, the advent of highly effective antidepressant medications has not reduced the numbers of suicides one whit in recent decades.

A. Alvarez (1970, pp. 283–284) puts it beautifully in the last paragraph of his personal exploration of suicide, *The Savage God*, published a year or so after I started my own explorations. He writes, "As for suicide: the sociologists and psychologists who talk of it as a disease puzzle me now as much as the Catholics and Muslims who call it the most deadly of mortal sins. It seems to me to be somehow as much beyond social or psychic prophylaxis as it is beyond morality, a terrible natural reaction to the strained, narrow, unnatural necessities we sometimes create for ourselves."

A more contemporary writer, Louis de Bernieres, author of *Legends of the Fall*, reached the same conclusion almost thirty years after Alvarez. He writes about a scenic cliff called Beachy Head, the most famous suicide spot in England. In his effort to understand why, for centuries, people have leapt to their death here he inquired of the local coroner, Michael Davey.

> It seems that long ago Davey gave up any elaborate theories about who jumps off Beachy Head and why. He told me that, in his opinion, people kill themselves because they are very unhappy, that about twelve per annum do so on the Head, though it has been as many as twenty-eight. . . . No particular kind of person does it; the age range runs from sixteen to ninety. Davey used to think it was mainly men, especially young men who could not bear the pangs of dispriz'd love, but there are in fact, very few teenagers. More prevalent are menopausal women in their forties. . . .
>
> Yes, some of the victims have a history of mental illness. No, it has not become any worse since the government changed the system of health care for the mentally ill. Davey used to think that spring was the worst time of year, but now it seems to have evened out. Suicides occur in batches, possibly because potential jumpers read reports in the papers about the most recent casualty. A quarter of them visit Beachy Head in advance of their attempt in order to reconnoiter. . . .
>
> Most interestingly, Davey believes that the Beachy Headers do not commit suicide "while the balance of mind is disturbed" but that it is a rational decision often carefully planned [pp.40–42].

If these two authors are correct, to prevent suicide we must prevent unhappiness. Since this is impossible, and "—it happens," we must try to help kids understand that the happiest people are not those with the fewest problems, but those with the best coping skills. We need to tell kids that stressful times are inevitable, that they can recognize problems in each other and must never keep the secret of someone's plans for self-harm because help is available. Another method that could reduce suicide is the limitation of lethal weapons. Sixty-five percent of all teen suicides are committed with guns. Every time a gun is used to prevent a crime it is used 67 times as often in an accidental or suicidal death. We must get guns out of the houses where there are young people. And we need to urge physicians and pharmacists to provide emetics with prescription medications. If a teen overdoses and changes his mind, he can take an emetic and reverse the process. This resource has been available for many years in Israel but rarely is made available in the United States.

Screening for mental illness and providing treatments, both biological and psychological, can also help, if we can then get treatment to the kids who need it.

And, of course, we must continue to support vital research into the chemistry and biology of the brain. This is where the real inroads will be made into the prevention of mental illness— even though it may have little impact on the numbers of suicides.

Which brings us back to the original question: Can we understand it when a young person takes his life? Adolescents commit suicide for the same reasons adults do—I just have a very hard time accepting it as a rational choice for someone who is twelve, or fifteen, or twenty. Although I may never be able to understand the depths of a young person's despair because I have not walked in his shoes, and I may never be able to predict suicide accurately because it could take a lifetime to create a suicidal adolescent—or only twenty minutes—I will continue to treat adolescents who are unhappy, or feel unloved or trapped or anxious or pressured, or suffer with emotional illness, and I will continue to talk with students and parents and teachers to help them recognize the warning signs of trouble in themselves or their friends. Thinking about this question has shown me that I may be wise to give up trying to further my understanding of suicide, accept the belief that suicide really is "suisad," and keep concentrating on what I can do to alleviate unhappiness and keep kids alive.

Will we ever eradicate or completely prevent suicide? Not a chance. Not on your life. On this point, I can no longer deceive myself. The years of professional "turf wars" and ego battles with few significant advances in understanding have convinced me that mankind is no closer to solving the problems of self-destruction than we were centuries ago. In fact, I fear, with the escalation of violence, the apparent disregard for human life, and an increase in the murder and suicide rates, we are closer to self-destruction than ever before.

This dour observation should mark the end of my discourse; however, I do not want to stop on a pessimistic note, so I will leave the reader with this humorous story about experts discussing professional opinions. It is a tale about four religious leaders who frequently argued their theories. Invariably the same one person always had a point of view that was different from the other three. During one heated conversation, this individual looked up to the sky for divine intervention and said, "God, please give these three a sign, show them that I am correct." Immediately there was an enormous clap of thunder and flash of lightning. He looked at the other three and said, "See, I am right. There is the sign." But the other three dismissed this as a coincidence. So he looked back up to the sky and said, "God, give me another sign." At which point there were thunder and lightning, followed by rain, a rainbow, and an immense snowfall. He looked at the other three and said, "There, now you have a sign. I am correct." Once again, they dismissed him. He looked up at the sky and said "God, please help me." And then there came an enormous voice saying, "Listen he's right, already, he's right." With only a moment's hesitation the other three looked at him and said, "OK, now it's three against two."

I expect you understand that I believe I am right, even though it may be three against two.

PART TWO

INTERVENTION

CHAPTER FOURTEEN

Suicide and Manic-Depressive Illness

An Overview and Personal Account

Kay Redfield Jamison, Ph.D.

Suicide accounts for up to 20 percent of deaths in severe bipolar illness; at least one in four people with severe bipolar illness will attempt suicide at least once (Goodwin and Jamison, 1990). Patients with depressive and manic-depressive illnesses are far more likely to commit suicide than individuals in any other psychiatric or medical group (Guze and Robins, 1970; Fawcett et al., 1987; Goodwin and Jamison, 1990). The mortality rate for untreated manic-depressive patients is higher than it is for many types of heart disease and cancer (Goodwin and Jamison, 1990).

Although many researchers have noted the strikingly high rate of suicide in patients with manic-depressive illness, relatively few have written articles or books dealing specifically with the clinical problems or correlates of suicidal behavior in such patients. This dearth of information is unfortunate, as more precise determination of which individuals are most likely to commit suicide, and when they are most likely to do so, would permit the initiation of more timely and aggressive clinical intervention. Studies that have examined clinical correlates of suicide in bipolar patients have found, for example, that there are risk periods for

The extracted portions in this chapter are taken from *An Unquiet Mind* by Kay Redfield Jamison (1995). Copyright © 1995 by Kay Redfield Jamison. Reprinted by permission of Alfred A. Knopf, Inc. The author would like to acknowledge the assistance of Marci Klein-Benheim in the preparation of this chapter.

suicide specific to this population. They have also found that certain genetic factors and clinical states correlate strongly with suicide risk (Goodwin and Jamison, 1990; Roy et al., 1997a).

Current research also provides evidence that lithium significantly decreases the suicide rate in manic-depressive patients (see Chapter Twenty). Other studies, however, show that nearly half of all bipolar patients discontinue taking their lithium at least once, against medical advice (Jamison et al., 1979; Jamison and Akiskal, 1983); unfortunately those patients at highest risk for suicide and those most likely to respond well to lithium are often the patients least likely to take lithium on a consistent basis. The noncompliance issue is further compounded by the fact that lithium can be hoarded and then used for a suicidal overdose. Despite such critical findings, very few of the thousands of articles written about lithium deal with noncompliance in a substantive way. Even fewer have examined the ability of the anticonvulsant medications to lower suicide rates, even though such medications are increasingly being used as an alternative to lithium.

The first section of this chapter provides an overview of suicide in manic-depressive illness. Specific attention is devoted to the rates of attempted and completed suicide, clinical correlates of suicide, and treatment issues such as medication noncompliance. The second section recounts a personal experience with manic-depressive illness, my own, and the factors leading up to a nearly lethal suicide attempt.

RATES OF ATTEMPTED AND COMPLETED SUICIDE

Early studies demonstrated that manic-depressive patients far exceed the mortality rate expected for the same age group in a normal population (Guze and Robins, 1970); more recent studies have indicated a less striking, but still considerable increase in mortality (Goodwin and Jamison, 1990; Blair-West et al., 1997; Harris and Barraclough, 1997; Inskip et al., 1998). Differences between the older and the more recent studies are attributed not only to differences in severity of illness and in how manic-depressive patients were classified, but also to probable improvements made in treatment of this psychiatric illness over time.

Methodological problems, in particular diagnostic classification, largely account for the variability across studies (Goodwin and Jamison, 1990). In early studies, for example, researchers often did not differentiate bipolar from unipolar patients. The early European, British, and American studies used the term *manic-depressive illness* in the Kraepelinian sense to refer to both recurrent unipolar and bipolar disorders.

Suicide is by far the most important factor contributing to increased mortality among bipolar patients (Goodwin and Jamison, 1990). Guze and Robins (1970) were the first to review and systematically document the extent of suicide risk in bipolar patients. They found the suicide rate in patients with primary affective disorders to be in the range of 15 percent. In no study that they reviewed was the rate less than 12 percent. For our text *Manic-Depressive Illness,* Goodwin and I (1990) reviewed more than thirty studies of completed suicide in manic-depressive patients. We found a range of 9 to 60 percent of deaths due to suicide, with a mean of 19 percent. Robins and coworkers (1959b) examined this question from a different perspective; they found that nearly half (46 percent) of the individuals who commit suicide suffered from manic-depressive illness.

Hagnell and colleagues (1981), who conducted a longitudinal study of correlates of suicide in rural Sweden, combined patients with bipolar and unipolar depressive disorders into a single depressive syndrome group. They found that the risk for suicide among men with "depressive syndrome" increased seventy-nine times when compared with those with no psychiatric disorder. This is consistent with studies showing that as many as nine out of ten individuals who commit suicide suffer from a major psychiatric illness at the time of their death, and that nearly five out of the ten have primary depression (Clark and Fawcett, 1992a).

Furthermore, Hagnell and associates (1981) found that every one of the suicides in their study occurred within the "medium" and "severe" depression subgroups. In other words, the men who met diagnostic criteria for depression, but who did not have serious depressive illness, did not commit suicide. This suggests that it is the *severity of the depressive illness* and not depression alone that correlates with suicide. This finding is important because researchers tend to report the lifetime incidence of suicide among patients with primary affective disorder as 15 percent, an annual rate 3.5 to 4.5 times higher than that of other psychiatric diagnostic groups, and twenty-two to thirty-nine times higher than the general population rate (for example, Fawcett et al., 1987; Guze and Robins, 1970; Miles, 1977; Murphy, 1986; Pokorny, 1964; Temoche et al., 1964). However, the studies that arrived at the 15 percent figure were based on earlier studies of hospitalized patients with severe and recurrent depressions. One would estimate a lower rate if researchers included depressed outpatients, or all individuals who met the *DSM-IV* diagnostic criteria for depressive disorder (Harris and Barraclough, 1997; Inskip, 1998).

Studies that have compared unipolar to bipolar patients in terms of suicide risk report inconsistent results; some find unipolar patients to have increased rates (Dunner et al., 1976; Morrison, 1982), some find decreased rates (McGlashan, 1984; Martin et al., 1985b), and others find similar rates (Perris and D'Elia, 1966; Tsuang, 1978; Weeke and Vaeth, 1986). Studies that further divide bipolar patients into subgroups, such as bipolar I or bipolar II, suggest that patients with *bipolar II disorder* may be at increased risk for suicide (Dunner et al., 1976; Stallone et al., 1980). Rihmer and colleagues (1990a), for example, studied a hundred consecutive suicides in patients with mood disorders and found that 46 percent had bipolar II disorder, 1 percent had bipolar I disorder, and 53 percent had nonbipolar major depression.

One possible explanation for the increased risk of suicide among bipolar II patients is that they are more likely to have comorbid problems, including alcoholism and personality disorders (Endicott et al., 1985; Rihmer et al., 1990). They are also likely to lead chaotic lives, to have inadequate or unpredictable support systems, and to comply poorly with medication (Goodwin and Jamison, 1990). Although their mood swings are less severe and less dramatically disruptive than patients with bipolar I illness, the overall treatment outcome may be limited by these associated features.

Studies show that between one-quarter to one-half of bipolar patients have attempted suicide at least once. In comparison, Mościcki and colleagues (1988) reported that 2.9 percent of the 18,571 respondents in the National Institute of Mental Health (NIMH) Epidemiologic Catchment Area (ECA) study said that they had attempted suicide during their lifetime; the rate varied from 1.5 percent at the Piedmont, North Carolina, site to 4.3 percent at the Los Angeles site. This figure is consistent with other community surveys, none of which showed a lifetime rate of attempted suicide higher than 5 percent (Mościcki et al., 1988). Individuals with manic-depressive illness thus appear to be at least five to ten times more likely to attempt suicide during their lifetime than individuals in the general population, and at least twenty times more likely to attempt suicide than individuals with no history of psychiatric illness (Regier et al., 1988a).

In summary, manic-depressive patients seem to be at high risk for both attempted and completed suicide. Furthermore, certain factors place some manic-depressive patients at an even greater risk for completed suicide. These factors include the *severity of the depressive illness* and, perhaps, the *type of bipolar illness* the person manifests. It should be noted that populations of attempters and completers, although overlapping, exhibit some significant differences (Miles, 1977). Females with manic-depressive illness appear to be at greater risk than males for suicide attempts.

Finally, although suicide is the most important factor contributing to the increased premature mortality among bipolar patients, other causes of death contribute as well. Individuals with manic-depressive illness have an elevated risk of early death through cardiovascular disease (Weeke, 1979; Weeke and Vaeth, 1986), and the indirect consequences of psychotic behavior during untreated manic-depressive episodes (for example, malnutrition, substance abuse, stress, sleep deprivation, exposure, and exhaustion) may also lead to increased mortality by compromising general health (Goodwin and Jamison, 1990).

CORRELATES OF SUICIDE

The following are significant correlates of suicide.

Family History of Suicide

Manic-depressive illness is clearly genetic, although no specific genes have yet been identified (MacKinnon et al., 1977). There is strong evidence that suicide runs in families, and that the predisposition to suicide may be genetically transmitted (Kallman and Anastasio, 1947; Haberlandt, 1965, 1967; Roy et al., 1991, 1997a). Haberlandt (1967) examined data from 149 sets of twins in which at least one twin had committed suicide. He found that in sets of identical twins, the other twin had committed suicide in 18 percent of the pairs; the other twin had attempted, though not completed, suicide in another 10 percent of the pairs. There were no fraternal twin pairs in which both twins had committed suicide.

Suicide was also found to be disproportionately high among the biological relatives of seventy-one adoptees with a personal history of affective disorder and suicide in Denmark (Wender et al., 1986). Indeed, 3.7 percent of biological relatives of these adoptees committed suicide compared with 0.3 percent of the adoptive relatives of these adoptees. There were no significant differences between the biological and adopting relatives of the control group, which was composed of adoptees with affective disorder who had not committed suicide. This may suggest that inheritance (or prenatal or perinatal events) is sufficient to predispose a person to suicide, as opposed to later familial environmental events.

Family members of a suicide victim may be at greater risk for suicide because a genetic predisposition for specific psychiatric disorders (for example, mood disorders) occurs in families (Pitts and Winokur, 1964; Clark and Fawcett, 1992a; Roy et al., 1997a). This position is supported by studies finding that the majority of patients with a family history of suicide also have a history of affective disorder. It is also supported by studies finding that the association between familial and patient suicide disappears largely when a background of affective disorder is common to all subjects (Clark and Fawcett, 1992a).

However, the fact that suicide occurred in some families with bipolar disorder and not in other families with bipolar disorder suggests that a vulnerability to suicide may be inherited independent of a depressive diathesis. Roy (1983), for example, examined the charts of 243 Canadian psychiatric inpatients with a family history of suicide. He compared these charts to the charts of 5602 psychiatric inpatients at the same hospital who had no history of suicide. Attempted suicide occurred in 37.9 percent of the bipolar patients where a first or second degree relative had committed suicide and in only 13.9 percent of the bipolar patients who had no family history of suicide. Schulsinger and colleagues (1979) also hypothesized that suicidal behavior is genetically transmitted independent of other disorders, possibly through a biochemical predisposition that manifests itself at times of stress.

A *family history of suicide* is thus found in many individuals who commit suicide. In all likelihood, psychological, environmental, and genetic factors operate together to increase risk for suicide (Roy et al., 1997a).

Alcohol Abuse

Morrison (1975) found that bipolar patients who were alcoholic had a higher rate of suicide in their family histories than bipolar patients who were not alcoholic. Other researchers have found a similar association between *alcohol abuse* and suicide. Rich and associates (1988), for example, found that, in addition to mood disorders, alcoholism was the most frequent diagnosis among their sample of 204 completed suicides. Fawcett and colleagues (1987), in their study of 954 bipolar and unipolar patients, found moderate alcohol abuse to be a significant risk factor for early suicide, especially in males.

The relationship between suicide and substance abuse may be attributed, in part, to increased impulsivity and aggressiveness (Goodwin and Jamison, 1990). It should be stressed, however, that the relationship between suicide and *increased impulsivity and aggressiveness* goes well beyond an association with substance abuse (Goodwin and Jamison, 1990). Violence, anger, irritability, impulsivity, and other such features have long been associated with suicide and self-destructive behavior (Jameison and Wall, 1933; Reich and Kelly, 1976; Myers and Neil, 1978). These same features are also common aspects of mania and mixed states.

Risk Periods for Suicide

There appears to be an elevated risk of suicide *early in the course of manic-depressive illness* (Guze and Robins, 1970; Johnson and Hunt, 1979; Roy-Byrne et al., 1988; Weeke, 1979). This is particularly unfortunate because the denial of the illness is most substantial during and after the first episode, as is the tendency not to comply with medication. In addition, there appears to be an increased risk of suicide in *mixed states,* in the *depressive phase,* in the *recovery period,* and in the *period following psychiatric hospitalizations.*

Mixed states are among the most dangerous clinical phases for suicide risk (Kraepelin, 1921; Jameison, 1936; Goodwin and Jamison, 1990). In his study of a hundred suicides, Jameison (1936) noted that the combination of depressive symptoms, mental alertness, and tense, apprehensive, and restless behavior was particularly lethal. He felt that "the retardation of thought and action that paralyzes the acting out of this wish for death in the average depressed patient is entirely absent in these persons" (p. 4).

In his 1921 text, *Manic Depressive Insanity and Paranoia*, Kraepelin described in painstaking detail the desperation, pain, and violence that manic-depressive patients can experience: "The patients, therefore, often try to starve themselves, to hang themselves, to cut their arteries. They beg that they may be burned, buried alive, driven out into the woods, and there allowed to die. One of my patients struck his neck so often on the edge of a chisel fixed on the ground that all of the soft parts were cut through to the vertebrae" (1921, p. 25). The combination of very depressive, morbid thought with high energy and agitation is dangerously uncomfortable. Impulsive and violent agitations, during which an individual can feel like putting his hand through a glass window or jumping from a car, are not uncommon in mixed states.

Studies have also shown that insomnia and excessive concern about sleep disturbance are correlated with suicide (Jameison and Wall, 1933; Barraclough et al., 1974; Motto, 1975).

The *depressive phase* of bipolar illness is associated with a greatly disproportionate rate of suicide. Winokur and coworkers (1969), for example, found no suicide attempts during mania, although suicidal ideation did occur during 7 percent of manic episodes. Likewise, Robins and associates (1959b) found that none of their suicide victims had committed suicide in the manic phase; all were depressed at the time of death. Weeke (1979) also found that more than half (58 percent) of the patients who committed suicide were in a constant, or worsening, depressive state at the time of death.

What is even more interesting, however, is Weeke's (1979) finding that nearly one-third (30 percent) of the suicide victims were classified as being in a "depressive state, recovering" at the time of death. The increased risk of suicide in the *recovery period* and in the *period following hospitalization* has been observed by others (Jameison and Wall, 1933; Keith-Spiegel and Spiegel, 1967). The beginning of medication response is often cited as a dangerous period, because the patient is experiencing some return of energy and motivation, but is still feeling hopeless and depressed (Goodwin and Jamison, 1990). However, the causal relationship between a drug response and increased suicide risk has been questioned by others (see Chapter Twenty-One).

There are several hypotheses that may account for the counterintuitive observation that many individuals kill themselves not when they are in the depth of their depression but when they seem to be getting better. The apparent improvement may simply reflect the resolution of ambivalence once a decision to die has been made; it may represent a genuine calm before the storm brought about by biological changes, or a transition from one phase of the illness into another; or, the "improvement" may be a deliberate deception of physicians, hospital staff, and family in order to carry out a suicide plan (Goodwin and Jamison, 1990).

The improvement may also reflect actual clinical improvement, with a concomitant level of hopelessness and despair if symptoms recur. Schweizer and colleagues (1988), for example, found *rapidly cycling mood* to be a suicide risk factor. Mood disorders are frequently cyclic, and recurrence can be a devastating experience. It is extremely demoralizing to a patient who thinks that he or she is getting better to suddenly plummet back down into depression. It can be helpful in treating bipolar patients to stress that the recovery period is often extremely rocky and very difficult. Predicting mood lability can sometimes lessen the sense of hopelessness.

Under managed care, patients with acute mania are frequently hospitalized for very short periods. This can create potentially dangerous clinical situations. Approximately one-half of patients with acute mania will have a very severe post manic depression (Goodwin and Jamison, 1990); several authors have found suicide to be at a higher than expected rate in the depressive episodes following mania (Winokur et al., 1969), as well as in the first six to twelve months following hospital discharge (Roy, 1982a; Fawcett et al., 1987). Thus, in effect, many patients are being released out into the community at a time of maximum risk for suicide. It is critical to implement careful intervention plans during these high-risk recovery and postrecovery periods.

TREATMENT ISSUES

The points that follow should be considered when treating suicidal manic-depressive patients.

Lithium

There is strong evidence that lithium decreases suicide rates (see Chapter Twenty). This is, in part, because there is a high rate of suicide in patients with mood disorders, and lithium is often very effective in treating these illnesses. But there is also evidence from the human and animal literature that lithium may exert an antisuicide effect independent of the prevention of depression. In addition to having a mood-stabilizing effect and, ideally, preventing recurrences of the illness, it may have an anti-impulsivity effect, as well. The decrease in the suicidality appears to be most pronounced when lithium has been taken for at least two years (Chapter Twenty).

Problematically, however, rates of lithium noncompliance are high.[1] It is estimated that up to one-half of bipolar patients stop taking their lithium against medical advice at least once during their lives, and that approximately one-third of these patients are noncompliant two or more times (Jamison et al, 1979; Jamison and Akiskal, 1983). As noted below, patients who fail to comply are usually young, male, early in their illness, reluctant to give up their highs, and/or prone to elevated moods or delusions:

Risk Factors for Medication Noncompliance

- First year of treatment
- History of noncompliance
- Younger
- Male
- Fewer episodes
- History of grandiose, euphoric manias
- Elevated mood
- Complaints of missing highs

Reasons cited for noncompliance vary. Medication side effects, such as weight gain, emotional dulling, and cognitive impairment, are major reasons given for stopping lithium against medical advice. These side effects are often dose related and can, in many instances, be minimized by carefully lowering the dose.

It is particularly disheartening that lithium noncompliance rates tend to be highest in those patients most at risk for suicide—that is, young males early in their illness. Moreover, it is ironic that lithium may be most effective for those people who are least likely to take it, that is, patients with a history of grandiose, expansive, and euphoric manias. This has led some researchers (for example, Lenzi et al., 1989) to suggest that compliance with prophylactic therapy may be more successful if lithium is started after a depressive episode or after a dysphoric psychotic episode rather than after a euphoric manic episode.

The consequences of lithium noncompliance can be profound and life threatening. Not only does noncompliance lead to relapses and possible intensification of affective episodes, but the psychiatrist can also be misled into believing the drug in question is ineffective (Blackwell, 1976; Lenzi et al., 1989). The consequences of noncompliance include interpersonal chaos, substance abuse, financial crisis, marital failure, family disruption, psychiatric hospitalization, violence, and, most significantly, suicide (Goodwin and Jamison, 1990). Indeed, pills not taken are often hoarded and used for suicidal overdose (Blackwell, 1976; Lenzi et al., 1989). The consequences of lithium noncompliance are thus clinically equivalent to those of untreated or inadequately treated manic-depressive illness.

Anticonvulsants

The use of anticonvulsant drugs (for example, carbamazepine and valproic acid) to treat manic episodes dates back to the 1970s (Okuma et al., 1973). Anticonvulsants may be the treatment of choice for patients with rapid cycles or a prior history of lithium failure or intolerance to it. Whether the anticonvulsants are preferable for patients with mixed states remains to be seen (Goodwin and Jamison, 1990, Chapter Twenty; see also Chapters Twenty-One and Twenty-Three).

There is, to date, little evidence that the anticonvulsant medications decrease suicide rates. This does not mean that they do not. They probably do. There is some research, for example, suggesting that carbamazepine may be beneficial because of its antiaggressive properties, especially if the suicidal behavior is part of a mixed state. However, at present, we do not have data demonstrating that the anticonvulsants lower suicide rate (see Chapter Twenty).

Despite this, prescriptions for the anticonvulsants have been increasing at a rapid rate and the prescriptions for lithium decreasing (Fenn et al., 1996). This may or may not be a good thing. On the one hand, lithium carries with it a very high noncompliance rate; clearly, it is of limited value to have a drug available that people do not take. Although there has been less extensive research on the use of anticonvulsants in the treatment of bipolar illness, the clinical impression of many physicians and researchers is that anticonvulsants tend to have fewer problematic side effects, and greater compliance, than lithium. Obviously, it is tremendously important to have these alternatives available for people who do not respond to, or have adverse reactions to, lithium. On the other hand, it is also important to be circumspect about replacing lithium, which has a demonstrated capacity to decrease suicide rates in high-risk populations, with anticonvulsants, which do not. Given the importance of this clinical problem, it is surprising that so little research has examined combined lithium-anticonvulsant therapy.

Psychotherapy

Because manic depression has clear biological roots, there has been a tendency to dismiss or minimize the importance of psychotherapy. Moreover, with managed care, there has been a tendency to view psychotherapy as a luxury rather than a necessity. There is now, however, a growing body of evidence showing that psychotherapy, in combination with mood-stabilizing medications, is more effective than mood-stabilizing agents alone (Cochran, 1984; Frank et al., 1985; Glick et al., 1985; Miklowitz et al., 1988).

Although no one psychotherapeutic technique has been proven to be clearly superior to others in the treatment of manic-depressive patients, clinicians have had success with adjunctive individual and family therapy. Miklowitz and colleagues (1988), for example, compared patients who received lithium alone with patients who received lithium and behavioral family treatment (including education, communication training, and problem solving). They found that 70 percent of the lithium alone group relapsed compared with 13 percent of the behavioral therapy and lithium group. Cochran (1982) had shown earlier that patients treated with cognitive therapy more often took their lithium as prescribed than patients who did not receive cognitive therapy; they had fewer recurrences of their illness and fewer hospitalizations, as well. In general, psychotherapy seems to help manic-depressive individuals come to terms with the repercussions of past episodes, reconcile themselves to having to take medication, and comprehend the practical and existential implications of having the illness.

Hospitalization

Most bipolar depressed patients can be treated in an outpatient setting. However, hospitalization may be advisable for some patients to reduce the risk of suicide and to enhance treatment efficacy. For instance, inpatients on occasion respond to medications they had not responded to as outpatients (Kotin et al., 1973), perhaps because of increased compliance.

Hospitalization, though it decreases the risk of suicide, does not eliminate it completely. Robins and coworkers (1959b), for example, found that 7 percent of the patients in their sample committed suicide while in a psychiatric hospital. Weeke (1979) reported an even higher rate: 27 percent of the manic-depressive patients who committed suicide in his sample did so while under hospital care, although half were on a pass from the hospital or had absconded.

The Impact of Inadequate or Lack of Treatment

Unfortunately, most people who have manic-depressive illness are not being treated. A study carried out in Finland, for example, found that the overwhelming majority of individuals who committed suicide were depressed at the time of suicide, although only 33 percent were on antidepressants at the time of death, and only 3 percent at an adequate level (Isometsä et al., 1994a). These findings are consistent with Rihmer and colleagues (1990) in Hungary and Keller et al. (1982) in the United States. Roy (1982a) found that only 19 percent of suicide victims who were depressed during their last episode were receiving adequate antidepressant treatment or mood-stabilizing drugs at the time of their suicide.

A PERSONAL ACCOUNT OF MANIC-DEPRESSIVE ILLNESS AND ATTEMPTED SUICIDE

I decided, several years ago, to write a book about my own experiences with manic-depressive illness and suicide. One of the major reasons was that it was clear to me that most people did not have much of a sense of the manic side of manic-depressive illness; depression, on the other hand, was better understood. Most individuals did not really understand how addictive euphoric mania could be, not just on a psychological level, but almost certainly on a deep biological level as well.

Approximately 50 percent of the people who get manic have these euphoric or grandiose manias; the other 50 percent have very mixed, or paranoid and highly irritable, dysphoric manias (Goodwin and Jamison, 1990). For those who do have euphoric or grandiose manias, the experience can be seductive, compelling, and addictive. They can have, in effect, a dual diagnosis, a secondary addiction, although it does not get labeled as such. This has very real treatment implications; indeed, for some people, the manic experience is exceedingly difficult to give up.

I was brought up in a very conservative, traditional world. My father was a scientist as well as a pilot and an Air Force officer. He also had manic-depressive illness, as did many other members of my family. But nobody talked about it. No one said anything and, as a result, I had no preparation for it. When I became psychotic for the first time at around age sixteen or seventeen, I, like many others with this illness, had absolutely no idea what was going on.

During my childhood, I had never thought about suicide. Had you told me that people actually thought about trying to kill themselves and wanting to die, it would have been inconceivable to me. I loved life. I was an enthusiast. I was full of energy. I couldn't wait to get up in the morning, couldn't wait to see my friends, couldn't wait to get to school. And then, all of a sudden, when I was sixteen or seventeen years old and in my senior year in high school, I started thinking about suicide most of the time. I started thinking about dying and death. Yet, I had no real concept of what it all meant. Fortunately, after four months of a psychotic depression that had followed upon a mild mania, I got well, as one is likely to do. One of the few good things about having a mood disorder is that you do tend to move on—if you don't kill yourself first.

I went to college and graduate school. It was a totally tumultuous period in my life, although I had no diagnostic label or understanding for it yet. When I joined the medical school faculty as a young assistant professor at UCLA, after a brief period of intoxicating hypomania, I became delusional and psychotically manic. It was very clear that it was a medical emergency and that I didn't have any choice but to see a psychiatrist. Fortunately, I received excellent medical care, started taking lithium, and responded very well. Then, like so many others with manic depression, I stopped taking my medication.

This is what I want to address in the remainder of this chapter. Why do people stop taking their medication? What are the medical consequences of doing so? How can this result in an attempt to take one's own life? Clearly, stopping medication against medical advice is unnecessary and unwise. It is, however, very understandable and very human.

I was first prescribed lithium in the fall of 1974; by the early spring of 1975, against medical advice, I had stopped taking it. Once my initial mania had cleared and I had recovered from the terrible depression that followed in its wake, an army of reason had gathered in my mind to form a strong line of resistance to taking medication. Some of the reasons were psychological in nature. Others were related to the side effects that I experienced from the high blood levels of lithium that were required, at least initially, to keep my illness in check. (In 1974 the standard medical practice was to maintain patients at considerably higher blood levels of lithium than is now the case. I have been taking a lower dose of lithium for many years, and virtually all of the problems I experienced earlier in the course of my treatment have disappeared. The side effects I had for the first ten years were very difficult to handle. In a small minority of patients, including myself, the therapeutic level of lithium, the level at which it works, is perilously close to the toxic level.)

There was never any question that lithium worked very well for me—my form of manic-depressive illness is a textbook case of the clinical features related to good lithium response: I have grandiose and expansive manias, a strong family history of manic-depressive illness, and my manias precede my depressions, rather than the other way around—but the drug strongly affected my mental life. I found myself beholden to medication that also caused severe nausea and vomiting many times a month. . . .

Nausea and vomiting and occasional toxicity, while upsetting and embarrassing at times, were far less important to me than lithium's effect on my ability to read, comprehend, and remember what I read. In rare instances, lithium causes problems of visual accommodation which can, in turn, lead to a form of blurred vision. It also can impair concentration and attention span and affect memory. Reading, which had been at the heart of my intellectual and emotional existence, was suddenly beyond my grasp. I was used to reading three or four books a week; now, it was impossible. I did not read a serious work of literature or non-fiction, cover to cover, for more than 10 years. . . . I found that children's books, which, in addition to being shorter than books written for adults, also had larger print, were relatively accessible to me, and I read over and over again the classics of childhood. . . .

But of all the children's books, I returned most often to *The Wind in the Willows*. I found myself occasionally totally overwhelmed by it. Once, I remember, I broke down entirely at a particular passage describing Mole and his house. I cried and cried and could not stop.

Recently, I pulled down my copy of *The Wind in the Willows*. . . . After a brief search I found the passage I had been looking for. Mole, who had been away from his underground home for a very long time exploring the world of light and adventure with his friend Ratty, one winter evening is walking along and suddenly and powerfully, with "recollection in fullest flood," smells his old home. Desperate to revisit it, he struggles to persuade the Rat to accompany him: "Please stop, Ratty!" pleaded the poor Mole, in anguish of heart. "You don't understand! It's my home, my old home! I've just come across the smell of it, and it's close by here, really quite close. And I must go to it, I must, I must! O, come back Ratty! Please, please come back!"

The Rat, initially preoccupied and reluctant to take the time to do so, finally does visit Mole in his home. Later, after Christmas carols and a night cap of mulled ale in front of the fire, Mole reflects on how much he has missed the warmth and security of what he once had known, all of those "friendly things which had long been unconsciously a part of him."

At this point in my rereading, I remembered exactly, and with visceral force, what I had felt reading it not long after I had started taking lithium: I missed my home, my mind, my life of books and "friendly things," my world where most things were in their place and where nothing awful could come in to wreck havoc. Now I had no choice but to live in the broken world that my mind had forced upon me. I longed for the days that I had known before madness and medication had insinuated their way into every aspect of my existence [pp. 92–97].

Before I was diagnosed with manic-depressive illness, I had had little interest in the study or treatment of mood disorders. I had had some interest in drugs, but not in prescribed ones. As soon as I recovered from my mania, however, I became single-mindedly interested in manic-depressive illness and, within a short time, two of my colleagues and I started the Affective Disorders Clinic at the University of California at Los Angeles. It soon became clear to us that the residents and the psychology interns training in the clinic did not seem to have much of a clue about the subjective experience of manic-depressive illness. To supplement their medical readings, I wrote (anonymously) very brief descriptions of mania and described what it was like to take lithium. The following "Rules for the Gracious Acceptance of Lithium into Your Life" were written to give the residents and interns a sense of why not every patient is wildly enthusiastic about taking medication:

> *Rules for the Gracious Acceptance of Lithium into Your Life*
> 1. Clear out the medicine cabinet before guests arrive for dinner or new lovers stay the night.
>
> 2. Remember to put the lithium back into the cabinet the next day.
>
> 3. Don't be too embarrassed by your lack of coordination or your inability to do well the sports you once did with ease.
>
> 4. Learn to laugh about spilling coffee, having the palsied signature of an eighty-year-old, and being unable to put on cuff links in less than ten minutes.
>
> 5. Smile when people joke about how they think they "need to be on lithium."
>
> 6. Nod intelligently, and with conviction, when your physician explains to you the many advantages of lithium in leveling out the chaos in your life.
>
> 7. Be patient when waiting for this leveling off. Very patient. Reread the Book of Job. Continue being patient. Contemplate the similarity between the phrases "being patient" and "being a patient."
>
> 8. Try not to let the fact that you can't read without effort annoy you. Be philosophical. Even if you could read, you probably wouldn't remember most of it anyway.
>
> 9. Accommodate a certain lack of enthusiasm and bounce that you once had. Try not to think about all the wild nights you once had. Probably best not to have had those nights anyway.

10. Always keep in perspective how much better you are. Everyone else certainly points it out often enough, and, annoyingly enough, it's probably true.

11. Be appreciative. Don't even consider stopping your lithium.

12. When you do stop, get manic, get depressed, expect to hear two basic themes from your family, friends, and healers: But you were doing so much better, I just don't understand it; I told you this would happen.

13. Restock your medicine cabinet.

Psychological issues ultimately proved far more important than side effects in my prolonged resistance to lithium. I simply did not want to believe that I needed to take medication. I had become addicted to my high moods; I had become dependent upon their intensity, euphoria, assuredness, and their infectious ability to induce high moods and enthusiasms in other people. Like gamblers who sacrifice everything for the fleeting but ecstatic moments of winning, or cocaine addicts who risk their families, careers, and lives for brief interludes of high energy and mood, I found my milder manic states powerfully inebriating and very conducive to productivity. I couldn't give them up. More fundamentally, I genuinely believed—courtesy of strong-willed parents, my own stubbornness, and a WASP military upbringing—that I ought to be able to handle whatever difficulties came my way without having to rely upon crutches such as medication [pp. 97–99]. . . .

Part of my stubbornness can be put down to human nature. It is hard for anyone with any illness, chronic or acute, to take medications absolutely as prescribed. Once the symptoms of an illness improve or go away, it becomes even more difficult. In my case, once I felt well again I had neither the desire nor incentive to continue taking my medication. I didn't want to take it to begin with; the side effects were hard for me to adjust to; I missed my highs; and, once I felt normal again, it was very easy for me to deny that I had an illness that would come back. Somehow I was convinced that I was an exception to the extensive research literature, which clearly showed not only that manic-depressive illness comes back, but that it often comes back in a more severe and frequent form.

It was not that I ever thought lithium was an ineffective drug. Far from it. The evidence for its efficacy and safety was compelling. Not only that, I knew it worked for me. It certainly was not that I had any moral arguments against psychiatric medications. . . . I believe, without doubt, that manic-depressive illness is a medical illness; I also believe that, with rare exception, it is malpractice to treat it without medication. All these beliefs aside, however, I still somehow thought that I ought to be able to carry on without drugs, that I ought to be able to continue to do things my own way.

My psychiatrist, who took all of these complaints very seriously—existential qualms, side effects, matters of value from my upbringing—never wavered in his conviction that I needed to take lithium. He refused, thank God, to get drawn into my convoluted and impassioned web of reasoning about why I should try, just one more time, to survive without taking medication. He always kept the basic choice in perspective: The issue was not whether lithium was a problematic drug; it was not whether I missed my highs; it was not whether taking medication was consistent with some idealized notion of my family background. The underlying issue was whether or not I would choose to use lithium only intermittently, and thereby ensure a return of my manias and depressions. The choice, as he saw it—and as is now painfully clear to me—was between madness and sanity, and between life and death. . . . In fact, underneath it all, I was actually secretly terrified that lithium might not work: What if I took it and I still got sick? If, on the other hand, I didn't take it, I wouldn't have to see my worst fears realized [pp. 101–102].

The consequences of my refusal to take lithium on a consistent basis were predictable. I again became floridly psychotic; this, in turn, was followed by a suicidal depression that lasted for more than a year and a half.

From the time I woke up in the morning until the time I went to bed at night, I was unbearably miserable and seemingly incapable of any kind of joy or enthusiasm. Everything—every thought, word, movement—was an effort. Everything that once was sparkling now was flat. I seemed to myself to be dull, boring, inadequate, thick brained, unlit, unresponsive, chill skinned, bloodless, and sparrow drab. I doubted, completely, my ability to do anything well. It seemed as though my mind had slowed down and burned out to the point of being virtually useless. The wretched, convoluted, and pathetically confused mass of gray worked only well enough to torment me with a dreary litany of my inadequacies and shortcomings in character, and to taunt me with the total, the desperate, hopelessness of it all. What is the point in going on like this? I would ask myself. Others would say to me, "It is only temporary, it will pass, you will get over it," but of course they had no idea how I felt, although they were certain that they did. Over and over and over I would say to myself, If I can't feel, if I can't move, if I can't think, and I can't care, then what conceivable point is there in living?

The morbidity of my mind was astonishing: Death and its kin were constant companions. I saw Death everywhere, and I saw winding sheets and toe tags and body bags in my mind's eye. Everything was a reminder that everything ended at the charnel house. My memory always took the black line of the mind's underground system; thoughts would go from one tormented moment of my past to the next. Each stop along the way was worse than the preceding one. And, always, everything was an effort. Washing my hair took hours to do, and it drained me for hours afterward; filling the ice-cube tray was beyond my capacity, and I occasionally slept in the same clothes I had worn during the day because I was too exhausted to undress. . . .

My psychiatrist repeatedly tried to persuade me to go into a psychiatric hospital, but I refused. I was horrified at the thought of being locked up; being away from familiar surroundings; having to attend group therapy meetings; and having to put up with all of the indignities and invasions of privacy that go into being on a psychiatric ward. I was working on a locked ward at the time, and I didn't relish the idea of not having the key. Mostly, however, I was concerned that if it became public knowledge that I had been hospitalized, my clinical work and privileges at best would be suspended; at worst, they would be revoked on a permanent basis. . . .

At the time, nothing seemed to be working, despite excellent medical care, and I simply wanted to die and be done with it. I resolved to kill myself. I was coldbloodedly determined not to give any indication of my plans or the state of my mind; I was successful. The only note made by my psychiatrist on the day before I attempted suicide was: "Severely depressed. Very quiet." . . .

Within psychiatric circles, if you kill yourself, you earn the right to be considered a "successful" suicide. This is a success one can live without. Suicidal depression, I decided in the midst of my indescribably awful, eighteen-month bout of it, is God's way of keeping manics in their place. . . . There is an assumption, in attaching Puritan concepts such as "successful" and "unsuccessful" to the awful, final act of suicide, that those who "fail" at killing themselves not only are weak, but incompetent, incapable even of getting their dying quite right. Suicide, however, is almost always an irrational act and seldom is it accompanied by the kind of rigorous intellect that goes with one's better days. . . .

I, for example, thought I had covered every contingency. I could not stand the pain any longer, could not abide the bone-weary and tiresome person I had become, and felt that I could not continue to be responsible for the turmoil I was inflicting upon my friends and family. . . . I was doing the only fair thing for the people I cared about; it was also the only sensible thing to do for myself. One would put an animal to death for far less suffering [pp.110–115].

Suicide, because it is often impulsive, is not necessarily undertaken in the manner in which one originally plans. I knew, for example, that the major problem with killing oneself with lithium is that lithium has an acute effect on the gut. Thus, in order to prevent vomiting from what I knew to be a lethal dose of lithium, I made certain to take antiemetic medications as well. I also took other precautions. For instance, I made sure that the telephone was far away from me. However, when my brother fortuitously called from Paris, I got down on my hands and knees, in a semiconscious state and went over to the phone and picked it up. My brother heard my terribly slurred voice and called my doctor. When I later emerged from my coma, and eventually recovered, I made a definite decision to stay on my lithium. And I have ever since.

I want to end on a note of appreciation to my psychiatrist, who is a superb doctor. I think that it is very easy for surgeons and internists to get credit for saving lives. Psychiatrists, psychologists, social workers, and others involved in treating mental illness do not get the same kind of credit, even though what they do is often far more difficult.

The debt I owe my psychiatrist is beyond description. I remember sitting in his office a hundred times during those grim months and each time thinking, What on earth can he say that will make me feel better or keep me alive? Well, there never was anything he could say, that's the funny thing. It was all the stupid, desperately optimistic, condescending things he didn't say that kept me alive; all the compassion and warmth I felt from him that could not have been said; all the intelligence, competence, and time he put into it; and his granite belief that mine was a life worth living. He was terribly direct, which was terribly important, and he was willing to admit the limits of his understanding and treatments and when he was wrong. Most difficult to put into words, but in many ways, the essence of everything: he taught me that the road from suicide to life is cold and colder and colder still, but—with steely effort, the grace of God, and an inevitable break in the weather—that I could make it [p. 118].

IMPLICATIONS FOR THE CLINICIAN

- Suicide is the major cause of premature death in bipolar illness. Significant risk factors for suicide in manic-depressive illness include:

  History of previous suicide attempt
  Family history of suicide
  Increased severity of depressive or manic-depressive illness

- Treatment of the underlying illness is the most effective way to reduce the risk of suicide in manic-depressive patients. Treatment should be pursued aggressively at all times, but especially in those phases of the illness during which suicide is most likely to occur: in the depressive phase, early in the illness, during mixed states, in the recovery period, and in the period following hospitalization.

- Clinicians should be apprised that the determination of suicide risk involves assessment of family history of suicide, personal history of suicide attempts or violence, substance abuse, current psychiatric status, psychological assets and liabilities, and treatment history.

- Treatment entails, first and foremost, keeping the patient safe. Hospitalization or close monitoring may be required. Different medications, or altered dosages of those already prescribed, may be necessary. In some cases, electroconvulsive therapy may be required. Additional medication, such as anxiolytics or neuroleptics, may be needed for symptoms that can increase the risk for suicide—for example, delusions, agitation, severe anxiety, and sleep disorders.

- Noncompliance complicates the treatment of manic-depressive illness. Lithium has been shown to decrease suicide rates in manic-depressive patients, and may have additional "antisuicide" effects beyond mood stabilization. Unfortunately, the people at highest risk for suicide (young males, early in the illness) and those for whom lithium is likely to be most helpful (individuals with expansive, euphoric manias) are also those who are less likely to comply with the medication.

- Anticonvulsants are being prescribed more frequently, whereas the use of lithium is decreasing. It is important to have alternatives for those who do not benefit from lithium or for those who cannot or will not take it, but it is also important to be aware that the anticonvulsants, unlike lithium, have not yet demonstrated efficacy in preventing suicide.

- Psychotherapy, in conjunction with mood stabilizers, has been shown to be more effective than mood stabilizers alone and may increase compliance with medication.

- Clinicians should be acutely aware that the intense desperation and psychological pain that patients with manic-depressive illness suffer, particularly during depression and mixed states, can lead to suicide. Suicide assessment should be repeated frequently during these vulnerable periods. Clinical contact should be frequent, families and friends should be kept involved, as appropriate, and the uneven and difficult nature of the recovery process should be discussed with the patient.

Note

1. It should be noted, however, that Frank and coworkers (1985) found that the rate of noncompliance for tricyclic antidepressants is even higher than that for lithium. Indeed, in their review, 32 to 76 percent of patients given tricyclics alone were noncompliant.

CHAPTER FIFTEEN

Lifetime Risk of Suicide
in Major Affective Disorders

David C. Clark, Ph.D.
Ann E. Goebel-Fabbri, Ph.D.

Me miserable! Which way shall I fly
Infinite wrath, and infinite despair?
Which way I fly is hell; myself am hell;
And in the lowest deep a lower deep,
Still threat'ning to devour me, opens wide,
To which the hell I suffer seems a heaven.
—John Milton, *Paradise Lost*

Public education campaigns about depression typically claim that "15 percent of *untreated* depressed patients eventually die by suicide over the course of their lifetimes," implying that proper treatment lowers this figure down to the vicinity of 0 percent. Reviews of lifetime mortality associated with depression or other mood disorders, however, contradict this claim at two points. First, the great majority of long-term mortality follow-up studies contributing to our knowledge about lifetime risk for suicide in major depression are based on groups of patients *in treatment,* usually patients receiving inpatient care. Although the same studies rarely document whether the same patients were still in treatment, or recently in treatment, at the point when they die years or decades after the initial treatment contact when they were enrolled into the study, virtually all were in treatment for periods earlier in their lifetimes.

Second, there are no systematic data about the degree to which mental health treatment reduces lifetime risk for death by suicide among patients with mood disorders, unless one refers to lithium clinic studies. The lithium studies tend to show a significant reduction in suicide rates for patients who remain in treatment over time, but since no outcome study of lithium therapy has ever randomly assigned patients to lithium therapy versus a comparison condition, the effects of lithium action and treatment compliance are hopelessly intertwined in all available studies, undermining our ability to claim that lithium therapy is the cause of any observed drop in suicide rates. (See Chapters Fourteen and Twenty for a fuller discussion of this subject, with references to specific studies addressing the question of whether lithium therapy may be responsible for reducing the suicide risk.)

An often cited review of lifetime risk of suicide in mood disorders was published almost thirty years ago (Guze and Robins, 1970). In this chapter we summarize this review and critically examine the original tabulations; we then summarize U.S. epidemiological trends for depression and suicide over this century and all the recent long-term follow-up mortality studies of patients with major depressive disorder published in English or German between 1970 and 1998.

A REEXAMINATION OF THE 1970 STUDY BY GUZE AND ROBINS

Guze and Robins (1970) reviewed seventeen published studies on the course and outcome of patients with depressive disorders. They found that suicide accounted for 12 percent to 60 percent of all deaths in these studies, and they demonstrated that the most fruitful way to examine suicide trends over time was to plot the percentage of all deaths that were suicides against the percentage of all subjects dead. This approach led them to two conclusions:

1. The percentage of all deaths that were suicides approached an asymptote of 15 percent as the percentage of all deaths approached 100 percent.

2. Early in the course of major depressive disorders, before other types of deaths (such as by natural causes) have come fully into play, the percentage of all deaths that were suicides is much higher than 15 percent.

Although the core findings of Guze and Robins (1970) seem robust, a reexamination of the studies and data they cited indicates the need for some corrections. In Table 15.1, summary data for five of the cited studies are followed by corrected data as gleaned from the original studies. Note in particular that for the Stenstedt (1952) and Lundquist (1945) studies, some data were transposed. These corrections do not alter the general findings of Guze and Robins in any significant way, as portrayed in Figure 15.1, a graph of the corrected data.

U.S. EPIDEMIOLOGICAL TRENDS SINCE 1970

Because long-term follow-up mortality studies are reported infrequently, changes (secular trends) in U.S. suicide rates over time might make it difficult to compare the results of mortality studies undertaken in different decades. Aggregate

Table 15.1. Early Studies of Suicides in Mood Disorders.

| Investigator | Sample Size | Follow-Up (years) | All Deaths | | Suicides or All Deaths (percent) |
			N	Percentage of Sample	
Helgason (1964)	103	—	47	23	51
(Corrected)	93	47	34	37	53
Hastings (1958)	238	6–12	35	15	35
(Corrected)	238	6–12	37	15	24
Watts (1956)	368	5	31	8	19
(Corrected)	341	5	25	7	24
Stenstedt (1952)	319	20	119	37	14
(Corrected)	216	15	42	19	14
Lundquist (1945)	216	2–20	42	19	14
(Corrected)	319	9–28	119	37	14

Source: Guze and Robins, 1970, Table 1, with corrections included.

Figure 15.1. General Findings of Guze and Robins (1970).

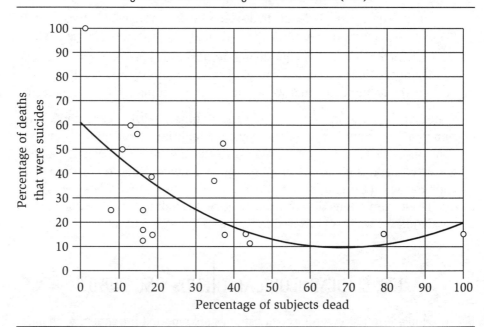

Source: Guze and Robins, 1970, Figure 1.

Note: Each circle represents data from one of seventeen studies.

U.S. annual suicide rates are available from 1933, when uniform state reports were mandated. Suicide rates were somewhat higher during the period 1933 through 1940, the years of the Great Depression (15 per 100,000 persons annually), and dropped during the World War II period, 1940 through 1945 (to 10 per 100,000 in 1943–1944). Since 1945, U.S. suicide rates have ranged from 10 to 13 per 100,000 annually. This aggregate stability, however, masks dramatic changes by age over time: elderly rates declined threefold between the late 1930s and 1990, and youth rates increased threefold between 1956 and 1977, for example. Yet the net change in U.S. suicide rate for persons of all ages combined since 1945 has been minimal—neither up nor down.

Nevertheless, a large national epidemiologic study has suggested important changes in U.S. rates of major depressive disorder over the course of this century. Klerman and Weissman (1989) showed that each generation in this century (particularly for those born following World War II) has evidenced higher depression rates, earlier age at first onset of depression, and a narrowing of the gap between male and female depression rates. Since psychological autopsy studies of completed suicide (Clark and Horton-Deutsch, 1992) have consistently documented that major depressive disorder is implicated as one pivotal factor in 40 to 60 percent of all completed suicides by adults, it is curious that U.S. suicide rates have remained stable while depression rates have been climbing. It is possible that suicide rates would have increased even more after 1945 if better access to mental health services, antidepressants, and mood stabilizers had not appeared, but neither clinical nor epidemiological studies can confirm this possibility at present.

FOLLOW-UP MORTALITY STUDIES OF MOOD DISORDERS

Table 15.2 identifies fifty-seven long-term follow-up mortality studies of patients with mood disorders (including those originally identified by Guze and Robins). These studies were identified by computer searches for English- or German-language scientific journal publications on suicide mortality in mood disorders. To qualify for inclusion, reports had to be explicit about the psychiatric diagnostic criteria they employed. The diagnoses were depression, simple depression, endogenous depression, periodic endogenous depression, periodic melancholia, neurotic depression, depressive neurosis, puerperal depression, involutional melancholia, involutional psychosis, involutional psychotic reaction, affective disorder, primary affective disorder, major affective disorder, affective psychosis, psychotic depression, unclassified depressive psychosis, reactive psychosis, manic-depressive illness, manic-depressive psychosis, manic-depressive reaction, bipolar affective disorder, periodic depression or mania, cyclothymic depression, cyclothymic melancholia, schizoaffective disorder, and affective

Table 15.2. Follow-Up Mortality Studies of Major Mood Disorders.

Study	Follow-Up Interval (years)	Number of Subjects	Percentage of Subjects Dead	Percentage of Subjects Dead by Suicide	Of Dead Subjects, Percentage Dead by Suicide	Country
Carlson, Kotin, Davenport, and Adland (1974)	1–9	49	4	4	100	United States
Seager (1959)	?	105	2	2	100	United Kingdom
Huston and Locher (1948a, 1948b)	1–4	135	2	1	67	United States
Murphy, Woodruff, Herjanic, and Super (1974)	3–6	38	8	5	67	United States
Buchholtz-Hansen, Wang, Kragh-Sørensen, and the Danish University Antidepressant Group (1993)	2–10	219	11	7	64	Denmark
Seager (1958)	1–3	356	4	2	57	United Kingdom
Lehmann et al. (1988)	11	93	22	12	55	Canada
Fremming (1951)	52–56	45	22	11	50	Denmark
Ziskind, Somerfeld-Ziskind, and Ziskind (1945)	1–6	197	10	5	50	United States
James and Chapman (1975)	?	98	13	6	46	New Zealand
Huston and Locher (1948a, 1948b)	1–15	173	25	10	42	United States
Vestergaard and Aagaard (1991)	5	133	16	7	41	Denmark
Bond and Braceland (1937)	5	204	18	7	38	United States
Bond (1954a, 1954b)	5	946	12	4	37	United States
Newman and Bland (1991)	1–10	3,156	8	3	33	Canada
Martin, Cloniger, Guze, and Clayton (1985a, 1985b)	5–12	250	7	2	33	United States
Anderson (1936)	?	47	6	2	33	United Kingdom
Lee and Murray (1988)	18	88	23	7	30	United Kingdom
Lewis (1936)	?	57	18	5	30	United Kingdom
Weeke (1979, 1986)	1–8	8,096	10	3	30	Denmark
Ziegler and Heersema (1942)	14	84	30	8	28	United States
Fawcett et al. (1990); Fawcett and Scheftner (1993)	8–15	954	14	4	27	United States
Taschev (1973)	?	652	100	26	26	Bulgaria
Kinkelin (1954)	1–72	146	34	9	26	Switzerland
Taschev and Roglev (1973)	1–20	1,846	18	5	26	Bulgaria
Giel, Dijk, and van Weerden-Dijkstra (1978)	2	612	14	4	26	Netherlands

Study						Country
Black, Winokur, and Nasrallah (1987)	2–14	1,593	10	3	26	United States
Avery and Winokur (1976)	3	519	6	2	25	United States
Hastings (1958)	6–12	238	16	4	24	United States
Watts (1956)	1–10	341	7	2	24	United Kingdom
Norton and Whalley (1984)	1–12	784	4	1	24	Scotland
Berglund and Nilsson (1987)	15–28	1,192	40	9	22	Sweden
Perris and d'Elia (1966)	1–15	797	13	3	22	Sweden
Pokorny (1966)	1–14	582	20	4	18	United States
Astrup, Fossum, and Holmboe (1959)	7–19	256	16	3	17	Norway
Brodaty, MacCuspie-Moore, Tickle, and Luscombe (1997)	25	152	53	9	16	United States
Müller-Oerlinghausen et al. (1992)	7	477	9	2	16	Austria, Canada, Denmark, and Germany
Langelüdecke (1941)	1–9	341	79	12	15	Germany
Slater (1938)	1–18	138	43	6	15	Germany
Innes and Millar (1970)	5	706	12	2	15	Scotland
Lundquist (1945)	9–28	319	37	5	14	Sweden
Stenstedt (1952)	1–30	216	19	3	14	Sweden
Pederson, Barry, and Babigian (1972)	4–6	568	16	2	14	United States
Helgason (1964, 1979)	61	496	60	7	12	Iceland
Bratfos and Haug (1968)	1–12	207	16	2	12	Norway
Schulz (1948)	?	1,121	44	5	11	Germany
Kerr, Schapira, and Roth (1969)	4	56	18	2	10	United Kingdom
Tsuang (1978, 1983)	31–40	223	73	7	9	United States
Shobe and Brion (1971)	14–20	111	20	2	9	United States
Oltman and Friedman (1962)	?	187	100	7	7	United States
Petterson (1977)	60–70	69	93	4	5	Sweden
Alström (1942)	1–13	4,437	5	0.2	5	Sweden
Murphy, Monson, Olivier, Sobol, and Leighton (1987)	16	60	40	2	4	Canada
Murphy, Smith, Lindesay, and Slattery (1988)	4	146	34	1	1	United Kingdom
Nyström (1979)	10	94	12	0	0	Sweden
Coppen et al. (1990)	10–11	103	10	0	0	United Kingdom
Petterson (1977)	1–9	123	2	0	0	Sweden

personality disorder. Some studies allowed for multiple diagnoses to be applied to a single patient (comorbidity), while others were limited to a single diagnosis per patient. A second requirement for inclusion was that reports had to specify the number of patients lost to follow-up, the number who died of any cause during follow-up, and the number who died by suicide.

The studies shown in Table 15.3 include inpatient and outpatient samples, first hospital admissions and later hospital admissions, systematic samples of patients in care and "typical cases" chosen by the investigators, and different demographic groups (men and women of different ages). Six of the fifty-seven are population studies of all persons living in a designated region. In these population studies, diagnoses were made by standardized interviews with all persons living in that community. Thus, for those six studies, depressed subjects were not necessarily diagnosed or treated patients.

Some of the groups under study were defined prospectively (for example, by consecutive admissions to a clinical program), and others were defined retrospectively (from available records at a later time). It should be obvious that the quality and reliability of symptom data, diagnostic data, and diagnostic criteria vary greatly among decades and studies. The oldest study in the series was published in 1936 and the most recent in 1997. There is also wide variation in duration of follow-up interval, follow-up success rate, death ascertainment procedures, and cause of death determination. These studies were conducted in fifteen different countries and thus probably reflect national and cultural variations in psychiatric practice.

Figure 15.2 portrays the plot of the fifty-seven studies of suicide mortality among patients with major depressive disorder. The percentages of all deaths that were suicides in this figure range widely and generally show a rate much higher than 15 percent at young ages and early in the course of major depressive disorder, before other deaths have begun to accumulate. As described by Guze and Robins (1970), once 70 percent or more of the patients with major depressive disorder had died, the percentage who died by suicide in the five remaining studies were 5 percent, 7 percent, 9 percent, 15 percent, and 26 percent (Langelüddecke, 1941; Oltman and Friedman, 1962; Taschev, 1973; Petterson, 1977; Tsuang, 1978, 1983). The range of these values is 21 percent, and the central value of this range is about 15 percent.

Is it possible that the lifetime suicide mortality rate has been declining over the last sixty years, explaining why the lifetime suicide rate ranges so broadly over the sixty-year period of reporting? To explore this possibility, the ten mortality studies reported most recently (within the last ten years) are shown as filled circles in Figure 15.2. This labeling makes it obvious that the truly long-term studies (beyond the time when 70 percent or more of patients have died) tend not to include patient samples described by means of structured clinical interviews and modern diagnostic criteria. Only two studies reporting a death rate of 70 percent or more were published within the last twenty years. Tsuang (1978,

Table 15.3. Lifetime Suicide Mortality Risk in Major Affective Disorders: A Reconsideration.

Study	Setting	Diagnoses	Age	Sex-Specific Rates?	Percentage Female	Follow-Up Interval	Number and Percentage of Subjects Dead	Number and Percentage of Subjects Dead by Suicide
Lewis (1936)	Inpatient	Manic-depressive psychosis	15–63 years, X = 30 years	No	?	?	10 (17.5 percent)	3 (5.3 percent)
Anderson (1936)	Inpatient	Depression	41–74 years, X = 52 years	No	100	About 5 years	3 (6.4 percent)	1 (2.1 percent)
Bond and Braceland (1937)	Inpatient, first admission	Manic-depressive psychosis, involutional melancholia	?	No	?	5 years	37 (18.1 percent)	14 (6.9 percent)
Slater (1938)	Inpatient	Manic depression	?	No	?	0–18 years	59 (42.8 percent)	9 (6.5 percent)
Langelüdecke (1941)	Inpatient	Manic depression	?	Yes	70	0–9 years	268 (78.6 percent)	41 (12.0 percent)
Ziegler and Heersema (1942)	Outpatient	Depression	?	No	41	14 years	25 (29.8 percent)	7 (8.3 percent)
Alström (1942)	Inpatient	Manic-depressive psychosis	?	Yes	61	1–13 years	216 (4.9 percent)	10 (0.2 percent)
Lundquist (1945)	Inpatient, first admission	Manic-depressive psychosis	?	Yes	61	9–28 years	119 (37.3 percent)	17 (5.3 percent)
Ziskind, Somerfeld-Ziskind, and Ziskind (1945)	Patients (some ECT)	Affective psychosis	X = 43 years on admission	No	65	6–69 months, X = 40 months	20 (10.2 percent)	10 (5.1 percent)
Huston and Locher (1948a)	Inpatient (some ECT)	Involutional psychosis, melancholic subtype		No				

Table 15.3. Lifetime Suicide Mortality Risk in Major Affective Disorders: A Reconsideration, cont'd.

Study	Setting	Diagnoses	Age	Sex-Specific Rates?	Percentage Female	Follow-Up Interval	Number and Percentage of Subjects Dead	Number and Percentage of Subjects Dead by Suicide
Huston and Locher (1948b)	Inpatient (some ECT)	Manic-depressive psychosis		No				
Schulz (1948)	Inpatient	Manic depression	?	Yes	63	?	492 (43.9 percent)	54 (4.8 percent)
Fremming (1951)	Population	Manic-depressive psychosis	?	No	69	52–56 years	10 (22.2 percent)	5 (11.1 percent)
Stenstedt (1952)	Inpatient	Manic-depressive psychosis	X = 53	Yes	58	1–30 years	42 (19.4 percent)	6 (2.8 percent)
Bond (1954)	Inpatient (some ECT)	Involutional psychotic reaction, manic-depressive reaction	?	No	?	5 years	117 (12.4 percent)	43 (4.5 percent)
Kinkelin (1954)	Inpatient	Simple depression, periodic depression or mania, psychosis with manic and depressive phases, endogenous depression, involutional depression	?	No	50	1–72 years, X = 22 years	50 (34.2 percent)	13 (8.9 percent)
Watts (1956)	Population	Endogenous depression	X = 50 years	No	59	0–10 years	25 (7.3 percent)	6 (1.8 percent)
Hastings (1958)	Inpatient	Manic-depressive psychosis, involutional melancholia, reactive depression	?	No	?	6–12 years	37 (15.5 percent)	9 (3.8 percent)

Study	Setting	Diagnosis	Age		Number	Follow-up period		
Seager (1958)	Inpatient (all ECT)	Manic-depressive psychosis, involutional depression, neurotic depression, puerperal depression	?	No	100	1–3 years	14 (3.9 percent)	8 (2.2 percent)
Astrup, Fossum, and Holmboe (1959)	Inpatient, first admission, ill less than 6 months	Manic-depressive psychosis, reactive psychosis	?	No	?	7–19 years	41 (16.0 percent)	7 (2.7 percent)
Seager (1959)	Inpatient (all ECT)	Manic-depressive psychosis, involutional melancholia, neurotic depression	?	No		6 months postdischarge	2 (1.9 percent)	2 (1.9 percent)
Oltman and Friedman (1962)	Inpatient	Manic-depressive psychosis	?	Yes	55	Variable	187 (100 percent)	13 (7.0 percent)
Perris and d'Elia (1966)	Inpatient	Psychotic depression	?	Yes	49	1–15 years	102 (12.8 percent)	23 (2.9 percent)
Pokorny (1966)	Inpatient	Manic-depressive reaction, depression, depressive reaction, or involutional melancholia with suicide attempt or ideation	?	No	100	1–14 years, X = 4.6 years	116 (19.9 percent)	21 (3.6 percent)
Bratfos and Haug (1968)	Inpatient	Manic-depressive psychosis	X = 53 on admission	No	55	1–12 years, X = 6 years	33 (15.9 percent)	4 (1.9 percent)
Kerr, Schapira, and Roth (1969)	Inpatient	Affective disorder	X = 50 years	Yes	50	4 years	10 (17.9 percent)	1 (1.8 percent)
Innes and Millar (1970)	Inpatient and outpatient	Depression	?	No	68	5 years	81 (11.5 percent)	12 (1.7 percent)

Table 15.3. Lifetime Suicide Mortality Risk in Major Affective Disorders: A Reconsideration, cont'd.

Study	Setting	Diagnoses	Age	Sex-Specific Rates?	Percentage Female	Follow-Up Interval	Number and Percentage of Subjects Dead	Number and Percentage of Subjects Dead by Suicide
Shobe and Brion (1971)	Inpatient (56 percent) and outpatient; 50 percent ECT	Manic-depressive illness; 14 percent bipolar	?	No	74	14–20 years, X = 18 years	22 (19.8 percent)	2 (1.8 percent)
Pederson, Barry, and Babigian (1972)	Inpatient and outpatient	Psychotic depression	Mode = 50–59	Yes	65	4–6 years	93 (16.4 percent)	13 (2.3 percent)
Taschev and Roglev (1973)	Outpatient	Involutional melancholia, periodic melancholia, cyclothymic melancholia, or endogenous depression	?	No	?	1–20 years	332 (18.0 percent)	85 (4.6 percent)
Taschev (1973)	?	Cyclothymic depression, recurrent depression, involutional depression, reactive depression, recurrent mania	?	Yes	54		652 (100 percent)	172 (26.4 percent)
Carlson, Kotin, Davenport, and Adland (1974)	Inpatient	Primary affective disorder, manic state	?	No	?	1–9 years, X = 3.2 years	2 (4.1 percent)	2 (4.1 percent)
Murphy et al. (1974)	Inpatient (more than two-thirds ECT)	Primary affective disorder (16 percent bipolar I)	21–62 years, X = 40 years	No	61	3–6 years, X = 5 years	3 (7.9 percent)	2 (5.3 percent)

Study	Sample	Diagnosis	Age			Follow-up		
James and Chapman (1975)	Inpatient (46 inpatients) and their first-degree relatives (52)	Bipolar affective disorder for subjects, affective disorder for relatives	?	No	?	Variable	13 (13.3 percent)	6 (6.1 percent)
Avery and Winokur (1976)	Inpatient (some ECT)	Manic depression, psychotic depressive reaction, involutional melancholia, depressive neurosis, schizoaffective	X = 51.5 years	No	62	3 years	32 (6.2 percent)	8 (1.5 percent)
Petterson (1977)	Inpatient	Manic-depressive illness	?	Yes	56	60–70 years	64 (92.8 percent)	3 (4.3 percent)
Petterson (1977)	Inpatient	Manic-depressive illness	?	Yes	56	1–9 years	3 (2.4 percent)	0 (0 percent)
Giel, Dijk, and van Weerden-Dijkstra (1978)	Long-term inpatient (more than 2 years)	Affective psychosis	?	No	66	2 years	88 (14.4 percent)	23 (3.8 percent)
Weeke (1979, 1986)	Inpatient, first admission	Manic depression	?	No	65	1–8 years	771 (9.5 percent)	235 (2.9 percent)
Nyström (1979)	Outpatient, all ECT	Depression	?	No	66	10 years	11 (11.7 percent)	0 (0 percent)

Table 15.3. Lifetime Suicide Mortality Risk in Major Affective Disorders: A Reconsideration, cont'd.

Study	Setting	Diagnoses	Age	Sex-Specific Rates?	Percentage Female	Follow-Up Interval	Number and Percentage of Subjects Dead	Number and Percentage of Subjects Dead by Suicide
Helgason (1979)	Population	Manic-depressive psychosis, endogenous depressive syndrome, reactive depressive psychosis, unclassified depressive psychosis, depressive neurosis, affective personality disorder	74–76 years	No	61	61 years	297 (59.9 percent)	36 (7.3 percent)
Tsuang (1978, 1983)	Inpatient	Depression	?	Yes	57	31–40 years	162 (72.6 percent)	15 (6.7 percent)
Norton and Whalley (1984)	Outpatient, taking lithium for more than 2 months	Lithium-treated (unipolar, bipolar, and schizoaffective)	?	No	?	1–12 years	33 (4.2 percent)	8
Martin, Cloninger, Guze, and Clayton (1985a, 1985b)	Outpatient	Affective						
Berglund and Nilsson (1987)	Inpatient	Severe depression or melancholia	X = 40–50 years on admission	Yes	58	15–28 years	478 (40.1 percent)	103 (8.6 percent)
Black, Winokur, and Nasrallah (1987)	Inpatient	Unipolar and bipolar major affective disorder	?	Yes	61	2–14 years	157 (9.9 percent)	41 (2.6 percent)
Murphy et al. (1987)	Population	Depression (DSM-III)	?	No	?	16 years	24 (40.0 percent)	1 (1.7 percent)
Kiloh, Andrews, and Neilson (1988)	Inpatient	Depressive illness	?	No	73	15	42 (31.6 percent)	

Study	Setting	Diagnosis (criteria)	Age		N	Follow-up		
Lehmann et al. (1988)	Inpatient and outpatient	Affective psychosis and depressive neurosis (ICD-8)	X = 53 years	No	77	11 years	20 (21.5 percent)	11 (11.8 percent)
Lee and Murray (1988)	Inpatients	Primary depressive illness (RDC, Kendell)	16–75 years	No	70	18 years	20 (22.7 percent)	6 (6.8 percent) (4 definite)
Murphy, Smith, Lindesay, and Slattery (1988)	Inpatient and outpatient	Primary depression	All over 60 years	No	71	4 years	50 (34.2 percent)	1 (0.7 percent)
Coppen et al. (1990)	Outpatient (lithium clinic)	Mood disorders	X = 60 years	No		10–11 years	10 (9.7 percent)	0 (0 percent)
Newman and Bland (1991)	Inpatient and outpatient (70 percent outpatient)	Manic disorder, bipolar affective disorder, major depressive disorder, and other affective disorder (ICD-9)	?	Yes	62	1–10 years, X = 4.8 years	267 (8.5 percent)	88 (2.8 percent)
Vestergaard and Aagaard (1991)	Inpatient	Mood disorder (Feighner criteria)	X = 43 years	?	No	5 years	22 (16.5 percent)	9 (6.8 percent)
Muller-Oerlinghausen et al. (1992)	Mostly inpatient (all on lithium for more than 6 months; X = 7 years)	Affective disorder (unipolar depression, unipolar mania, bipolar, schizoaffective, and other) (ICD-9 diagnosis)	X = 41 years	No	57	X = 7 years	44 (9.2 percent)	7 (1.5 percent)
Buchholtz-Hansen, Wang, Kragh-Sorenson, and Danish University Antidepressant Group (1993)	Outpatient	Major depression (DSM-III criteria)	X = 50 years	Yes	68	2–10 years, X = 4.6 years	25 (11.4 percent)	16 (7.3 percent)
Fawcett et al. (unpublished)	80 percent inpatient	Major affective disorder	X = 38 years	No	58	8–15 years, X = 11 years	129 (13.5 percent)	35 (3.7 percent)

Figure 15.2. Suicide Mortality Among Patients with a Major Affective Disorder.

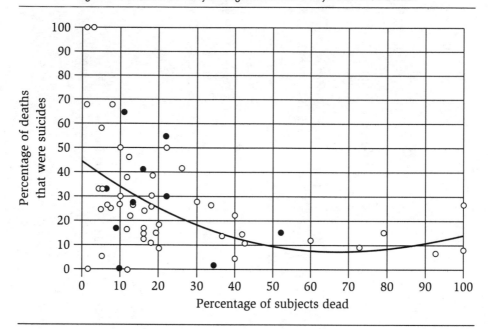

Note: Each circle represents data from one study. Filled circles represent the ten studies that are most recent (they occurred within the last ten years).

1983) found that 9 percent of all patients died by suicide at the point when 73 percent of the total group had died. In a population (community sample) study, Helgason (1979) found that 12 percent of all patients had died by suicide at the point when 60 percent of the total group had died. So although it is possible that lifetime suicide mortality rates have declined in the modern era, there are not sufficient data to draw any firm conclusions.

Of the studies identified in Table 15.2, fourteen report data by gender, so it is possible to consider whether there are any trend differences between males and females. Limiting attention to five studies wherein more than 70 percent of all patients had died, four of these five showed that the percentage of all deaths that were suicides was twice as high for men as for women (25 percent versus 10 percent; 10 percent versus 5 percent; 8 percent versus 3 percent; 12 percent versus 7 percent) (Langelüddecke, 1941; Tsuang, 1978, 1983; Oltman and Friedman, 1962; Petterson, 1977). The fifth study, from Bulgaria, showed that the percentage of all deaths that were suicides was similar for both genders (28 percent versus 25 percent) (Taschev, 1973).

Nine of the studies identified in Table 15.2 report complete data by unipolar as opposed to bipolar lifetime classification, so it is possible to consider whether there are any trend differences between these two patterns of mood disorder.

Keying to the only two of these studies in which more than 70 percent of all patients had died, one (Taschev, 1973) showed that the percentage of all deaths that were suicides was more than three times greater for unipolar than bipolar course (28 percent versus 8 percent). The other (Tsuang, 1978, 1983) showed that the percentage of all deaths that were suicides was similar for both patterns (9 percent versus 11 percent).

Only two studies reported the long-term suicide mortality rate for endogenous versus nonendogenous depressed patients (Kerr, Schapira, and Roth, 1969; Buchholtz-Hansen, Wang, and Kragh-Sørensen, 1993). In both studies, relatively small portions of the total patient groups had died by any cause at follow-up. The suicide mortality rate was higher for endogenous patients in one study and lower for endogenous patients in the other.

IMPLICATIONS FOR THE CLINICIAN

- The studies and data summarized refer (for the most part) to identified, treated patients who were then followed for years or decades. Few of the studies cited provide any data about the mental health treatment status of patients who died by suicide for the weeks or months immediately prior to death. Few provide any data about whether the patients who died by suicide accessed mental health services throughout the follow-up interval. Thus, it remains difficult to draw any new conclusions about long-term suicide mortality among patients with a depressive disorder or to draw conclusions more specific or clinically useful than those originally formulated by Guze and Robins in 1970.

- Until the point when 35 percent to 40 percent of a sample of patients with major depressive disorder have died due to any cause, the percentage of all deaths that were suicides will range from 0 percent to 100 percent, averaging about 20 to 30 percent.

- Although the "central tendency" for suicide mortality appears to be 15 percent when all patients in the sample have died, the methodological and clinical inconsistencies from one study to the next suggest that it would be more precise to acknowledge that lifetime suicide mortality has ranged from 5 percent to 26 percent in the literature.

- The reported lifetime suicide mortality rate for patients with major depressive disorder was twice as high for men as for women, considering studies from fifteen different countries in aggregate.

- There are insufficient data to draw conclusions about differences in lifetime suicide mortality risk between bipolar and unipolar patients or between endogenous and nonendogenous depressed patients.

- Lifetime mortality studies provide insufficient data to draw any conclusions about the effect of any treatment (specifically, pharmacotherapy or ECT) on lifetime risk for suicide in cases of major affective disorder.

- Cannot evaluate effect of treatment.

- The lack of consensual standards for designing and conducting long-term follow-up mortality studies has contributed to our inability to make precise estimates about lifetime risk for suicide and to identify symptoms and features that help identify greater or lesser risk for suicide among patients with major depressive disorder. There is a need for prospective, longitudinal studies that employ real (rather than opportunistic) sampling of patient recruitment strategies, use structured clinical interviews and explicit diagnostic criteria in a reliable and monitored fashion, focus on the few empirically supported risk and protective factors applicable to patients with major depressive disorder, maintain clinical contact with patients at no less than six-month intervals until all subjects have died, and render a cause-of-death verdict for each case by means of case review and predefined operational criteria. Such studies are difficult and costly, but they are necessary if clinicians are ever to be provided with reliable data that would allow them to calculate which severely ill depressed and cycling patients are most likely to die by suicide imminently or over the course of time.

- Only one long-term population-based community sample has been reported that might provide an estimate of the lifetime risk for suicide among untreated persons with major depressive disorders living in the community (12 percent of all deaths that were suicides when 60 percent of the sample had died) (Helgason, 1979). It is impossible to know whether this figure is higher than, lower than, or the same as the corresponding rate for previously treated patients.

- For the U.S. general population, aggregate suicide rates have remained stable since 1945 despite dramatic changes by age over time (for example, elderly rates declined threefold between 1940 and 1990, and youth rates increased threefold between 1956 and 1977).

- Since it appears that post–World War II cohorts in the United States have evidenced higher depression rates and earlier age at first onset of depression, one might reasonably expect that U.S. suicide rates would have increased dramatically after 1945 in the absence of better access to mental health services, antidepressants, and mood stabilizers. Neither clinical nor epidemiological studies can verify this conjecture.

CHAPTER SIXTEEN

Suicide and Schizophrenia

Ming T. Tsuang, M.D., Ph.D., D.Sc.
Jerome A. Fleming, M.S.
John C. Simpson, Ph.D.

Death by suicide has long been of concern to psychiatrists, and therefore the early detection of suicidal individuals is of major importance. To identify the potentially suicidal patient, the clinician must evaluate the patient presenting with psychiatric symptoms within the framework of diagnostic, demographic, and social factors.

EXAMINING RISK

Approximately 90 percent of suicide victims have a psychiatric disturbance (Barraclough et al., 1974). Between 45 and 70 percent of such patients, depending on the study, may carry a diagnosis of mood disorder such as major depression or bipolar illness (Barraclough et al., 1974; Dorpat and Ripley, 1960; Isometsä et al., 1994b). Between 2 and 12 percent of suicide victims have schizophrenia (Black and Winokur, 1990). The purpose of this chapter is to specifically examine the risk of suicide in patients who meet criteria for schizophrenia.

Between 10 and 15 percent of individuals with schizophrenia die from suicide (Tsuang, 1978; Roy, 1986; Amador et al., 1996). In fact, the risk of suicide in

Preparation of this chapter was supported in part by the National Institute of Mental Health Grants R01MH-24189, R01MH-31673, and R37MH-43518.

schizophrenia has not decreased; if anything, it has increased in importance as the result of deinstitutionalization and homelessness among the chronically mentally ill (Caldwell and Gottesman, 1990). Epidemiologic studies have focused on the characteristics that tend to differentiate schizophrenic patients who commit suicide from those who do not (Buda and Tsuang, 1990). Males appear to be at greater risk for suicide than females; they are affected at a younger age, and they tend to be unmarried. Additionally, each exacerbation of the illness often leaves the patient more emotionally handicapped. Most schizophrenic patients are in a depressive state, rather than an intensely psychotic state, when they commit suicide (Drake, Gates, Whitaker, and Cotton, 1985). Furthermore, antipsychotic medications that are used in the treatment of schizophrenia carry with them a substantial risk for side effects, including involuntary movement disorders that at times can incapacitate a patient and thus contribute to the patient's suicidality. Recurring decompensations frequently require repeated hospitalizations. Often patients are left jobless, without prospects for employment, inadequately understood, unaccepted in their family and community, and hopeless about their future. Suicide frequently occurs following hospitalization, although not necessarily after the first or index admission.

In previous studies, schizophrenic patients who committed suicide were found to do so in the first few years of their follow-up (Tsuang, 1978; Tsuang et al., 1980a). Methods chosen by males tended more often to be violent (for example, shooting, jumping, stabbing); women chose less violent means (for example, drug overdoses). There is often a previous attempt for both males and females. According to Shaffer et al. (1974), the number of previous attempts was the most important risk factor associated with suicides in schizophrenia.

Drake, Gates, Whitaker, and Cotton (1985) described most of the schizophrenic patients who committed suicide in their study as having been better educated and often at the beginning of a career when they became ill. Many had jobs, were in school, and functioned reasonably well prior to the onset of the illness. For these patients, awareness of the devastating implications of their illness and a decreased ability to function normally in society may make living intolerable. Often financial, social, and family disintegration accompany their illness. Virkkunen (1976a) found that more schizophrenic suicide victims than schizophrenic controls eventually "gave up." They no longer asked for support or attention and became negative in their attitude toward treatment and indifferent toward staff and personnel. The postdischarge period was especially critical because the structure of the inpatient setting gives way on discharge to joblessness and lack of social supports. For the schizophrenic patient already wary about future prospects, these stresses may tip the balance toward suicide.

Black and Winokur (1990) examined suicide and schizophrenia via a detailed review of the then-current literature. They found a number of risk factors for suicide in schizophrenic patients, including male sex (Cohen et al., 1964; Roy,

1982b; Breier and Astrachan, 1984), age younger than thirty years (Breier and Astrachan, 1984; Roy, 1982b), white race (Breier and Astrachan, 1984; Yarden, 1974), unemployment (Roy, 1982b), a chronic relapsing course (Farberow et al., 1966; Roy, 1982b), prior depression (Cohen et al., 1964; Roy, 1982b), past treatment for depression (Roy, 1982b), depression during the last episode of illness (Roy, 1982b), and a recent discharge (Roy, 1982b). More than half of schizophrenic patients in some samples had made serious suicide attempts (Breier and Astrachan, 1984; Cohen et al., 1964; Warnes, 1968).

Almost 75 to 90 percent of victims are male, a preponderance that has led Miles (1977) to question whether female schizophrenic patients are at any increased risk. Most schizophrenic patients who kill themselves are young; in one study (Black and Winokur, 1988), no suicides occurred among chronic schizophrenic patients after age forty. A possible conclusion from this study is that risk for suicide in schizophrenic illness is age dependent and may be due to changes that occur in the character of schizophrenia over the years. These changes may include a tendency toward less depression and more negative symptoms, such as asociality and amotivation (Pfohl and Winokur, 1983), which may lessen the risk of suicide. Absolute age at time of suicide may be less meaningful than the number of years that have elapsed between onset of the illness and suicide. The majority of suicides occur early in the course of illness, most commonly in the first decade (Lindelius and Kay, 1973). Virkkunen (1974) determined that most suicides occur, on average, after six or seven years of illness. Because women develop schizophrenia later than men (Loranger, 1984), this difference in age of onset is reflected in age at suicide; that is, women kill themselves an average of six years later than men (Black and Winokur, 1988; Virkkunen, 1974).

Schizophrenic patients with a high level of education appear to be at greater risk for suicide (Drake et al., 1984; Farberow et al., 1966; Sletten et al., 1972). This may be due to the "awareness of pathology" that may appear, including feelings of inadequacy and hopelessness, fear of disintegration, and a realization that many of their expectations will never be met (Drake et al., 1984; Warnes, 1968). Unlike most other psychiatric patients who commit suicide, schizophrenic patients apparently fail to communicate their suicidal intentions to the same degree, and the suicide may therefore be unexpected and inexplicable (Allebeck et al., 1987; Breier and Astrachan, 1984). Schizophrenic patients are also reported to use more highly lethal suicide methods (Breier and Astrachan, 1984), although this has been disputed (Black, 1988).

Several studies have suggested that paranoid schizophrenic patients are at a higher risk for suicide than other subgroups (Achté et al., 1966; Levy and Southcombe, 1953; Virkkunen, 1974), and Noreik (1975) observed that hebephrenic patients specifically have a lower rate than paranoid patients. However, Bolin et al. (1968) found no difference in suicide rates between these subtypes. Roy (1982b) found that schizophrenic patients who commit suicide are likely to have a chronic course with many exacerbations and remissions. Risk for suicide is highest early after hospital discharge; as many as 50 percent occur within the first three months (Roy, 1982b). Although intense psychotic behavior has been implicated in many schizophrenic suicides (Black and Winokur, 1990), several well-controlled studies do not support a link between psychosis and suicide (Breier and Astrachan, 1984).

We have previously examined the risk of suicide in schizophrenia as part of our long-term follow-up and family studies of schizophrenia and primary affective disorders (Tsuang, 1978). Two hundred cases of schizophrenia and 325 cases of mood disorder (100 mania and 225 depression) were selected according to specified research criteria from patients admitted to the Department of Psychiatry, University Hospitals at the University of Iowa, from 1935 through 1944. For the analyses, a follow-up period from 1935 to 1974 was selected. This period included the earliest possible year in which an index subject could have committed suicide and allows for a convenient division of the period into four separate decades of follow-up. Using the state of Iowa census data we were able to calculate the expected number of suicides for each sex and each diagnostic group.

Thirty suicides were identified in the course of follow-up work. More than half of these suicides ($n = 17$) were found in the first decade for schizophrenia and mood disorders combined. Twenty-four (80 percent) of the suicides were found in the first two decades of follow-up. In general we found an increased risk of suicide in all psychiatric groups except in female schizophrenics. However, overall for schizophrenia, we found a significant excess for suicide over a forty-year follow-up period. Of all deaths that occurred among schizophrenic patients, suicide accounted for 10.1 percent. The results of the studies reviewed above laid the groundwork for subsequent studies that have examined the role of a range of risk factors for suicide in schizophrenia.

REVIEWING RECENT STUDIES

In this section, we review the results from several well-designed studies that have recently investigated suicide and suicide risk factors in schizophrenia.

High-Risk Factors

Caldwell and Gottesman in 1992 updated a review of the literature in order to determine high-risk factors in schizophrenia and how they relate to the possibility of reducing the risk of suicide in the disorder. They found that among psychiatric patients, schizophrenics are overrepresented among suicides, and that schizophrenics often constitute the majority of inpatient suicides. Concerning the profile of suicide in schizophrenia, they found that the risk for suicide decreases with advancing age, and that the typical schizophrenic suicide is young, unmarried, and has never lived independently. In addition, social adjustment problems are evident at an early age, including chronic social and work impairment. For most suicides, age of onset of schizophrenia is before thirty, the course of illness is lengthy, and there is a long hospitalization. The initial hospitalization is usually longer than a year.

Clinical characteristics common to schizophrenics who commit suicide include depression (either currently or in the past), a sense of hopelessness, suicidal behavior (either currently or in the past), and a history of serious suicide attempts. Other clinical or psychosocial risk factors found in their review of the literature are poor psychosocial functioning, unemployed status, unmarried status, social isolation, deteriorating health, and significant losses. Schizophrenic patients who possess a realistic awareness of the deteriorating effects of their illness and fear progressive mental decline are also at greater risk for suicide. Concerning treatment, schizophrenics with excessive treatment dependence and disillusionment with treatment also show an increased risk.

In summary, Caldwell and Gottesman (1992) found that suicide is the chief cause of premature death among schizophrenics, and that schizophrenia represents a significant risk for suicide. The risk of suicide in schizophrenia is highest in individuals before age forty and declines thereafter. Males and whites are overrepresented in schizophrenia suicides, and symptoms such as hopelessness, suicidal ideation and behavior, and a history of previous suicide attempts present increased risk. Psychosocial factors that point toward a high risk of suicide include inadequate social supports, social isolation, deteriorating health with a high level of premorbid functioning, and significant losses. Early-onset males, patients whose illness course is chronic and who have suffered many exacerbations, patients discharged from a hospital who have high levels of psychopathology and functional impairment, and patients with a realistic awareness of the deteriorating effects of schizophrenia and a fear of further mental decline characterize schizophrenics who are at risk for suicide. The review concludes that a diagnosis of schizophrenia conveys as great a risk, or even a greater risk, of suicide than a diagnosis of mood disorder.

Effects of Age, Gender, and Illness

Heilä et al. (1997) examined the clinical characteristics of suicide victims with schizophrenia in the general population of Finland. Their study is considered the first nationwide population study to investigate all suicides with schizophrenia over a one-year period. This study adds to the previous research on completed suicides among groups of *DSM-III* or *DSM-III-R* schizophrenics (Roy, 1982b; Breier and Astrachan, 1984; Drake et al., 1984; Allebeck et al., 1987; Cheng et al., 1990; Hu et al., 1991; Modestin et al., 1992) in that it examines the effects of age, sex, and illness duration on suicide-related characteristics. The aim of the Heilä et al. (1997) was to analyze the variation of suicide-related characteristics in schizophrenia with age, sex, and illness duration.

This study was part of the National Suicide Prevention Project in Finland (Lönnqvist, 1988). All suicides ($N = 1,397$) occurring in Finland over a twelve-month period (April 1, 1987, to March 31, 1988) were examined. Data collection in this study was extensive: Interviews were conducted with the next-of-kin, the attending health care professional, the suicide's last health or social care contact, and others when necessary. Through a detailed diagnostic assessment of all suicide victims, a total of ninety-two cases (7 percent) were found to have met *DSM-III-R* criteria for schizophrenia. Definition of the key variables included illness duration, age groups, sex, illness course, method of suicide, and principal setting of the treatment.

Of the ninety-two suicide victims with *DSM-III-R* schizophrenia, ninety also met the *DSM-IV* criteria for schizophrenia. In addition, the ninety-two schizophrenia suicides represented 7 percent of all suicides in Finland during the one-year period. The mean age of the suicide victims with schizophrenia was forty years, and of the ninety-two cases sixty-eight (74 percent) were men and twenty-four (26 percent) were women. The mean age at first referral to psychiatric care was 24.4 years and the number of lifetime psychiatric hospital admissions for all suicide victims with schizophrenia averaged 7.9. The victims' clinical characteristics were closely examined and presented the following picture: Most of the suicides (75 percent) were committed during an active phase of illness, and about two-thirds of the women and one-third of the men committed suicide during an acute exacerbation. The most common subtypes of schizophrenia among suicide victims were paranoid and undifferentiated. Only 10 percent of the sample suffered from current suicide-commanding hallucinations. Nearly two-thirds of the schizophrenic suicide victims were positive for a depressive syndrome at the time of death. Alcoholism, either alcohol abuse or alcohol dependence, was found in one-fifth of the schizophrenics who had committed suicide, but only three suicides had a diagnosis of drug abuse. Young and old men suffered more often from depressive syndromes than did middle-aged men, whereas depressive syndromes among women were more common among middle-aged and young women than among older women. At the time of suicide, more than 25 percent of the schizophrenia victims were receiving psychiatric inpatient care and more than 50 percent had psychiatric outpatient treatment contacts. In addition, nearly half the victims committed suicide during the first three months after discharge, and almost 50 percent had their last health care contacts within four days of the suicide. Drug overdose, which is considered nonviolent, was the most common suicide method in these schizophrenics, for both sexes. However, drug overdose as a suicide method was higher in females (58 percent) versus males (29 percent). Violent suicide methods, on the other hand, accounted for 40 percent of the suicide victims with schizophrenia; 46 percent of male suicides were classified as violent compared with 25 percent of female suicides.

The study further examined the age factor. Previous research indicated that suicide victims with schizophrenia tended to be young adults, since suicide in schizophrenia had previously been suggested to be age dependent and uncommon later in life because of characteristic changes in the illness (Black and Winokur, 1990). Heilä et al. (1997), however, found that suicides in schizophrenia had occurred over a large range of age and illness duration. Previous work (Drake et al., 1984) had also shown that young schizophrenics were at the greatest risk for suicide during the nonpsychotic depressed phase. This current study, however, found that over 50 percent of the suicide victims were in the active phase of schizophrenia at the time of suicide regardless of age or illness duration.

In conclusion, Heilä et al. (1997) report that suicides occurred throughout the entire course of schizophrenia and took place most often during an active phase of the illness. They also found that illness duration was not significantly associated with many of the clinical variables studied; however, age, sex, and the interaction between the two did show an association with some clinical characteristics. For example, for women, depressive symptoms were most common for the victims in the middle-aged group, whereas middle age was associated with the lowest rate of depressive symptoms among schizophrenic men. The use of violent methods was greater among the young, whereas drug overdose was more common among middle-aged men and older women. Finally, this study indicates the need for further research into the association between age- and sex-specific risk factors for suicide in schizophrenia.

Other Investigations

Kaplan and Harrow (1996) examined the relationship between negative and positive symptoms and suicidality in schizophrenia versus depression. In this study, seventy schizophrenics and ninety-seven depressives without psychotic symptoms were studied prospectively while in the hospital and at periodic follow-ups. Negative symptoms, positive symptoms, and posthospital functioning were assessed at the two-year follow-up; suicide and suicide attempt were assessed at the 7.5-year follow-up. Analyses of suicide risk showed that psychotic symptoms (that is, hallucinations, delusions) predicted later suicidal activity for schizophrenia patients only; schizophrenics with more psychotic features were at higher risk than those with fewer psychotic symptoms. Negative symptoms (psychomotor retardation, concreteness) predicted later suicidal activity only for the depressive patients. The authors concluded that the adequacy of overall functioning predicts later suicidal activity for both schizophrenics and depressives, and appears to be connected to the effects of psychosis in the schizophrenia group.

Roy and Draper (1995) examined suicide among psychiatric hospital inpatients. They analyzed risk factors for suicide among thirty-seven psychiatric inpatients who committed suicide compared with thirty-seven age- and sex-matched psychiatric inpatient controls. They found that significantly more of the suicide victims had made a previous suicide attempt, suffered from schizophrenia, were involuntary at their last admission, and lived alone. Almost a third of the patients, the majority of whom were schizophrenic, committed suicide after having been in the hospital for more than a year. Although risk factors may vary from one psychiatric hospital to another, these results show that for one inpatient setting, inpatients at risk for suicide typically had previously exhibited suicidal behavior, suffered from schizophrenia, been admitted involuntarily, and lived alone; and that the risk of suicide may remain high among long-stay schizophrenics.

Another interesting, recent study examines suicidal behavior in schizophrenics recruited from various psychiatric hospitals (Amador et al., 1996). With between 20 and 42 percent of patients with schizophrenia attempting suicide (Landmark et al., 1987; Roy et al., 1984; Planansky and Johnston, 1971), there is a very high prevalence of suicidal behavior among individuals with schizophrenia. Specifically, the purpose of this study (Amador et al., 1996) was to examine the relationship between suicidal behavior and awareness of illness in 218 patients with a *DSM-III-R* diagnosis of schizophrenia, based on a hypothesis that greater awareness of illness would increase suicidal behavior in schizophrenia. Data for this study were obtained as part of the *DSM-IV* field trial for schizophrenia and related disorders. The sample of 218 schizophrenics comprised 144 men and seventy-four women. Patients were assessed with an abbreviated version of the Scale to Assess Unawareness of Mental Disorder (Amador et al., 1994) and several scales adapted from the Comprehensive Assessment of Symptoms and History (Andreasen et al., 1992).

Of the 218 schizophrenics studied, 169 (77.5 percent) reported no suicidal behavior, and forty-nine (22.5 percent) reported suicidal behavior. Overall suicidal behavior in schizophrenia was found to be associated with current depressed mood but not with the *DSM-III-R* diagnosis of a major depressive episode. The results also indicated a relationship between suicidal behavior and awareness of delusions in schizophrenia. Specifically, suicidal behavior was significantly less likely to be reported in patients with no awareness of their delusions (18 percent) and those without delusions (17 percent) when compared with patients with moderate (39 percent) or definite (22 percent) awareness of their delusions. In addition, awareness of asociality, blunted affect, and anhedonia were all associated with suicidal behavior. Suicidal and nonsuicidal schizophrenic patients did not differ, however, in the awareness of hallucinations or thought disorder.

In summary, Amador et al. (1996) found that schizophrenic patients with recurrent suicidal thoughts and behavior were generally more aware of their negative symptoms than were nonsuicidal schizophrenic patients. Contrary to expectation, general awareness of having a mental disorder did not predict suicidal behavior. Clinically, these results suggest that awareness of having delusions, flat affect, anhedonia, and asociality may be particularly damaging to one's self-concept and degree of hopefulness about the future. These negative symptoms are commonly mistaken by patients as representing flaws in their character. Amador et al. (1996) suggest that psychological interventions aimed at increasing awareness of illness for treatment purposes should be implemented with caution. Clinicians who wish to evaluate the level of suicidal behavior in schizophrenia patients "should pay close attention to the effects of greater awareness on the patient's degree of demoralization, self-concept, and hopelessness about the future."

In summary, the risk factors for suicide in schizophrenia gleaned from the studies reviewed above are as follows:

- Social or demographic factors
  - Male
  - White
  - Age younger than thirty
  - Unmarried
  - Better educated
  - Unemployed
  - Financial, social, and family disintegration
  - Lack of social supports
  - History of never having lived independently
- Mental state
  - Depressive state
  - Prior depression
  - Depression during last episode of illness
  - Feelings of futility
  - Feelings of inadequacy and hopelessness
  - Awareness of the devastating implications of illness
  - Fear of disintegration
  - Fear that expectations will never be met
  - Fear of progressive mental decline
  - Functional impairment
- Past history
  - Previous suicide attempts
  - Index hospitalization of longer than a year

- Frequent long hospitalizations
- Experience of numerous exacerbations
- Lengthy course of illness
- Chronic relapsing course
- Family history of schizophrenia and suicide
- Current episode
  - Recent discharge from the hospital
  - Failure to communicate suicidal intentions
  - Deteriorating health with a high level of premorbid functioning
  - Significant losses
  - Disillusionment with treatment

In general, no single factor is decisive or even very informative, but the co-occurrence of several risk factors could indicate an increased risk for suicide in this population. For example, Caldwell and Gottesman (1990) note that "among schizophrenia patients, young white males with psychological features of depression and a prior history of suicide attempts are at particularly high risk." Conversely, the absence of a characteristic listed above should not be taken to rule out a risk of suicide. For example, female schizophrenics are at an increased risk of suicide, even though most schizophrenics who commit suicide are male, and therefore "male" is listed as one of the risk factors above.

STUDYING SUICIDE'S GENETIC COMPONENT

Data on suicides from twin studies have shown that concordance rates in monozygotic (MZ) pairs are significantly higher than in dizygotic (DZ) pairs, thus indicating the presence of a genetic component in suicide (Tsuang, 1977; Jule-Nielson and Videbech, 1970). The results of more recent studies have verified these findings (Roy et al., 1991, 1995). Roy et al. (1991) studied 170 twin pairs in which one or both twins had committed suicide. Of these twins, 62 were monozygotic and 114 were dizygotic twins. Seven (11.3 percent) of the monozygotic twin pairs were concordant for suicide compared with two (1.8 percent) of the dizygotic twin pairs. This same trend holds when attempted suicide is examined among twins (Roy et al., 1995). Roy et al. (1995) determined the absence or presence of an attempt at suicide at any time among twenty-six living MZ co-twins and nine living DZ co-twins of twins who had committed suicide. They found that ten of the twenty-six surviving MZ co-twins and none of the nine surviving DZ co-twins had attempted suicide. The data from both studies are consistent with data from previous studies of suicide in twins and suggest that genetic factors may be implicated in suicidal behavior. Evidence for a genetic factor in suicide also comes from findings of the American-Danish adoption studies, which show that suicide in relatives of adoptees who had committed suicide occurred mainly in biological relatives (Kety, 1983; Schulsinger et al., 1979).

Based on these studies and given that the rate of suicide is high in schizophrenia and the risk of schizophrenia in relatives of schizophrenics is high, it is reasonable to hypothesize that relatives of schizophrenics have an increased risk of suicide compared with the general population. We undertook an investigation specifically to look at the risk of suicide in relatives of patients with schizophrenia and mood disorders and to determine whether this risk in relatives increases if the schizophrenic patient also committed suicide (Tsuang, 1983). From 1972 to the end of 1976 we followed up 200 schizophrenics, 100 manics, and 225 depressives who were admitted to a psychiatric hospital between the years 1934 and 1944, as well as their first-degree relatives. We were able to ascertain whether deceased patients and relatives had committed suicide by consulting death certificates, medical records, and by personally interviewing patients and relatives at follow-up.

The risk of suicide among relatives in each diagnostic group were computed by using age-adjusted numbers of subjects exposed to the risk of suicide based on suicide statistics from the general population. We ascertained a total of fifty suicides in relatives of patients.

In general, the risk of suicide in the relatives of patients with schizophrenia and mood disorders combined was nearly eight times greater than the risk in the relatives of controls. In addition, relatives of patients who committed suicide had a risk of suicide almost four times higher than in relatives of patients who did not commit suicide. The suicide risk in the relatives of schizophrenics was similar to the risk in relatives of manics but lower than in the relatives of depressives. This study demonstrated that relatives of patients with schizophrenia are subject to a higher risk of suicide than are relatives of controls. In summary, this study (Tsuang, 1983) supported the presence of a genetic element in suicide suggested by twin studies and adoption studies. The occurrence of a disorder such as schizophrenia additionally increases the genetic risk of suicide in relatives of these patients. Kety (1990) presents the possibility that the genetic factor in suicide is actually an inability to control impulsive behavior, and that mental illness (including schizophrenia) and other stressors trigger the impulsive behavior resulting in a suicide.

We can expect that future studies will continue to explore the genetic dimension of suicide, and that additional studies will be needed to integrate information from genetic research with the considerable information that is already available regarding nongenetic risk factors for suicide. Together, these lines of investigation should inform clinical decision making about issues such as identifying schizophrenic patients at special risk for suicide and planning for possible interventions to help prevent suicide in this patient population.

IMPLICATIONS FOR THE CLINICIAN

In pursuit of these goals, we list some of the salient facts regarding suicide in schizophrenia and suggest some clinical guidelines to help reduce the currently elevated risk of suicide in schizophrenia.

- Suicide is the most serious consequence of psychiatric disorder, and schizophrenia carries a high suicide risk (approximately 10 percent of schizophrenic patients ultimately commit suicide).

- A diagnosis of schizophrenia often conveys a risk of suicide as great or even greater than a diagnosis of a mood disorder.

- Research has identified clinical, historical, and social factors that should alert clinicians to an increased risk of suicide in the schizophrenic patient. No single factor is decisive, but the co-occurrence of several identified risk factors may indicate an increased risk for suicide in this population. The absence of one of these risk factors, however, should not be taken to rule out a risk of suicide, in part because schizophrenia by itself may indicate an elevated suicide risk in many individuals.

- Risk factors for suicide in schizophrenic patients include being male, of age less than thirty years, of white race, and unemployed; and having a high level of education, a chronic relapsing course, prior depression, depression during the last episode of illness, and a recent discharge.

- Unlike most psychiatric patients who commit suicide, schizophrenic patients apparently fail to communicate their suicidal intentions to the same degree; the suicide may be unexpected and inexplicable.

- Schizophrenic patients who commit suicide are likely to have a chronic course with many exacerbations and remissions.

- Schizophrenics who commit suicide seem to have a higher awareness of their pathology, including feelings of inadequacy and hopelessness, fear of disintegration, and a realization that many of their expectations will never be met.

- When faced with an at-risk suicidal schizophrenic patient, the presence of any of the following points should be recognized by the clinician (Appleby, 1992):
    - Sources of staff hostility toward patients
    - Understaffing and poor design of treatment settings
    - Identification of high-risk individuals and stages of illness
    - Changes in location of care

- Isolation
- Depressed mood
- Expressions of intent

- A large percentage of schizophrenia suicides are receiving medical care from a general practitioner, a psychiatrist, or other health care provider at the time of their death (King, 1994).

- Unless effective monitoring and recall systems are used by general practitioners, the growing number of schizophrenic patients discharged to primary care follow-up may be at increased risk for suicide. Good communication between clinicians is essential.

- The use of care plans should enable the social circumstances of vulnerable patients to be monitored so that such potentially stressful situations can be anticipated and increased support can be offered (King, 1994).

- Any social measures that either decrease social disorganization and social isolation or increase social integration and the availability of social supports would be expected to have some effect on suicidal behavior (Adam, 1990).

- The co-occurrence of alcohol or drug abuse in patients with schizophrenia contributes to the suicidal risk.

- Having insight into delusions, flat affect, anhedonia, and asociality may be damaging to patients' self-concept and degree of hopefulness about the future (Amador et al., 1996).

- Clinicians should perform a careful assessment of depression and suicidality in schizophrenia at index admission and during periods of acute psychosis.

- A family history of schizophrenia and suicide increases the risk of suicide in relatives of schizophrenics.

- Because there is high incidence of nonpsychotic depression in schizophrenic patients at the time of suicidal behavior, the addition of antidepressant medication may help to eliminate suicidal ideation in schizophrenics (Drake and Cotton, 1986).

- Clinicians need to be certain that treatment for suicidal patients in their practice includes state-of-the-art psychotherapeutic and psychopharmacologic techniques geared to the treatment of schizophrenia (Blumenthal, 1990).

- Patients with a history of depression and suicidality including suicidal ideation should continue to be monitored for current suicidality even if symptoms improve during a nonpsychotic phase of the illness (Caldwell and Gottesman, 1992).

CHAPTER SEVENTEEN

Substance Abuse and Suicide

Roger D. Weiss, M.D.
Michael R. Hufford, Ph.D.

Substance abuse and dependence are among the most prevalent psychiatric disorders in the United States, and represent two leading causes of death (Kessler et al., 1994; Vaillant, 1995; Rosenberg et al., 1996). One reason for the high mortality rate among individuals with substance use disorders is the elevated rate of suicide associated with these disorders. The frequent use of drugs and alcohol as a vehicle for suicide has been well documented for those with (James et al., 1963; Suokas and Lonnqvist, 1995) or without (Anderson et al., 1995; Borges and Rosovsky, 1996) histories of substance use disorders. The suicide rate among substance abusers is far greater than that among those without psychiatric illness (Murphy and Wetzel, 1990); alcohol use alone increases the risk of suicide by a dramatic margin in comparison with people who are abstinent (Borges and Rosovsky, 1996).

Although individuals with substance use disorder are at greater risk for suicide, determining suicide risk for individuals in this population can be extremely difficult. Studies have found that the differences between substance abusers who contemplate suicide and those who act on their ideation are infrequent and subtle (Adams and Overholser, 1992). To help clinicians make empirically informed decisions regarding the risk of suicide in their substance-abusing patients, we

This study was supported by Grants DA00326 and DA09400 from the National Institute on Drug Abuse and by a grant from the Dr. Ralph and Marian C. Falk Medical Research Trust.

review (1) the prevalence of suicide among substance abusers, (2) the multi-factorial relationship between substance abuse and suicide, (3) the assessment of risk factors for suicide among substance abusers, and (4) the treatment of suicidal substance abusers.

PREVALENCE OF SUICIDE AMONG SUBSTANCE ABUSERS

Determining the prevalence rate of suicide among substance abusers is complicated by a number of issues. Substance abuse can play both a direct and indirect role in suicide. The direct link between suicide and substance abuse includes suicides directly attributable to the deleterious effects of substance abuse, such as an intentional drug overdose. Substance abuse undoubtedly plays numerous indirect roles in suicide as well by increasing the rates of other psychiatric symptoms (for example, depression) and stressful life events (for example, interpersonal losses) that in turn increase the risk of suicide. Some authors have suggested that many sequelae of substance abuse, such as overdoses, propensity for accidents, needle sharing, risky drug-buying practices leading to homicide, and general lack of self-preservation, are all covert or passive suicidal acts (Frances et al., 1987; Marzuk and Mann, 1988).

A number of methodological problems prevent a clear picture from emerging out of the epidemiological data on suicide in substance abusers. Short-term follow-up studies (that is, less than ten years) tend to overestimate the number of suicides, since they are by definition premature deaths. That is, the rate of suicide will become progressively diluted relative to other causes of mortality over time (Berglund, 1984; Murphy and Wetzel, 1990). Moreover, a deterioration of substance abusers' social support network is a frequent consequence of substance use disorders. As a result, studies that rely on psychological autopsies to obtain information regarding the reasons that a substance abuser committed suicide may have considerable difficulty obtaining accurate information.

Despite these methodological problems, numerous studies have attempted to clarify the prevalence of suicide among individuals with substance use disorders. For many years, the prevalence of suicide among substance abusers was reported to be approximately 15 percent (for example, Miles, 1977). However, a careful reanalysis of existing data and a survey of more recent studies led to a very different estimate. Murphy and Wetzel (1990) calculated the annual and lifetime risk of suicide among alcoholics who had sought either outpatient or inpatient treatment. They found that outpatient alcoholics had an annual risk of 0.1 percent (which is ten times the annual rate in the general population) and a lifetime risk of 2.2 percent (which is approximately 60 percent the lifetime risk in the general population) for suicide. Inpatients, who on average have more severe alcohol dependence and increased rates of psychiatric comorbidity, had an annual rate of 0.2 percent and a lifetime risk of 3.4 percent for suicide. These revised data give the clinician little comfort, however, as alcoholics have been reported to contribute to between 25 percent and 43 percent of all suicides (Henriksson et al., 1993; Murphy and Wetzel, 1990). Although completed suicide is more common among men than women, one study of a large population of depressed patients found that controlling for alcohol and drug use negated sex differences in suicide risk (Young et al., 1994). Numerous factors contribute to the increased prevalence rate of suicide among substance abusers compared to the general population. Two of the most important factors include (1) the effects of acute intoxication and (2) comorbid psychopathology such as depression and antisocial personality disorder.

Effects of Acute Intoxication

In addition to the long-term adverse consequences that frequently occur in individuals with substance use disorders, the effects of acute intoxication may also increase the risk of suicidal behavior. For example, acute alcohol or cocaine intoxication can increase aggressiveness, impair judgment, and lead to erosion of restraints against impulsive self-destruction. Alcohol use is strongly related to impulsive suicide attempts (Suokas and Lonnqvist, 1995), and patients treated in an emergency room for attempted suicide show a dose-response relationship between the amount of alcohol consumed and risk for suicide (Borges and Rosovsky, 1996). It is noteworthy that many patients seen in an emergency room for suspected suicide attempts deny that they intended to kill themselves and deny using drugs or alcohol, despite blood tests to the contrary (Suokas and Lonnqvist, 1995).

Acute intoxication is probably a major factor in a number of deaths that could alternatively be considered accidents, passive suicide attempts, or semi-intentional suicidal acts. Suicide has been described by some as an aggressive act against the self (Buie and Maltsberger, 1989), and the use of a drug that increases aggression may provide the momentum to propel ideation into action (Benensohn and Resnik, 1974). For example, one study reported that one-third of fatally injured pedestrians tested positive for alcohol in their blood (Combs-Orme et al., 1983). Interestingly, a substantial percentage of homicide victims also have positive blood alcohol levels (Evans, 1986). Although there are a number of possible reasons for these findings, it is likely that some of this population may engage in high-risk behaviors while intoxicated, thereby increasing the likelihood of a fatal outcome. Sharing needles and engaging in risky sexual practices while intoxicated, both of which increase the likelihood of contracting human immunodeficiency virus (HIV) infection, could also be viewed as an indirect form of self-destruction. For example, responses to the Beck Depression Inventory have been found to be significant predictors of needle sharing among intravenous drug users in an outpatient methadone treatment program (Metzger et al., 1991). Although these behaviors probably represent an active or even passive suicide attempt in only a small minority of cases, it is also probable that a sense of desperation and hopelessness could increase the likelihood or frequency of these high-risk behaviors.

Drug overdoses may also be classified as "accidental" suicidal behavior. For example, when it becomes known in the illicit-drug-using community that someone has died from a heroin overdose, a subgroup of heroin addicts will make great efforts to obtain heroin from the same supply that caused the lethal overdose. As one such individual said, "You figure the stuff is either going to give you an unbelievable high or it's going to put you under. You hope for the high, but if it doesn't work out, it doesn't work out." This type of fatalistic thinking, which is unfortunately quite common among some substance abusers, can obviously increase the mortality rate. Although such a death would not generally be considered a suicide, it represents a form of desperate, high-risk behavior.

The Role of Depression

Psychiatric comorbidity is also strongly associated with attempted and completed suicide among substance abusers. Suominen and colleagues have reported that 82 percent of those who attempt suicide suffer from comorbid mental disorders (Suominen, Henriksson, Suokas, Isometsa, Ostamo, and Lonnqvist, 1996). Depression stands out as something of a sine qua non, since the number of comorbid diagnoses is not associated with an increased risk of suicide unless depression is present (Klerman, 1987). Many studies have shown that the interaction of substance abuse and depression is an especially lethal combination. One consistent finding is that comorbid major depressive disorder is associated with an increased risk of suicidal ideation, suicide attempts, and completed suicide (Black et al., 1986; Berglund, 1984; Cornelius et al., 1995; Hesselbrock et al., 1988; Martin et al., 1985; Salloum et al., 1996; Whitters et al., 1985).

Cornelius and colleagues (1995) found that suicidal ideation was significantly more common in treatment-seeking patients with comorbid major depression and alcohol dependence when compared to patients with either disorder alone. Similarly, Murphy and Wetzel (1990) concluded that suicide in alcoholism is largely dependent on the co-occurrence of a depressive episode, confirming earlier observations that most suicide attempts occur while intoxicated, during periods of worsening depression (Mayfield and Montgomery, 1972).

When evaluating the relationship between substance use disorders, depression, and suicide, one needs to be aware of the patient's current substance use status. Obtaining a clear picture of the role of depression in substance-dependent individuals is greatly enhanced by observing these patients while drug-free (Weiss et al., 1988). Although the most likely outcome of detoxification is a substantial improvement in depressive symptoms (for example, Brown and Schuckit, 1988), clinical depression and increased suicide risk can occasionally emerge during or following detoxification. Although it is unusual to find that so-briety uncovers a lethal depression, it is important to be alert to this possibility.

Data from the National Comorbidity Survey indicate that 24 percent of alco-hol-dependent men in the community and 49 percent of alcohol-dependent women have a lifetime history of depression (Kessler et al., 1997). Comorbid major depressive disorder is present in approximately 10 to 30 percent of treat-ment-seeking cocaine abusers (Gawin and Kleber, 1984; Kidorf et al., 1996; Weiss et al., 1988; Rounsaville et al., 1991). Similar prevalence rates for lifetime history of major depression have been found among studies of treatment-seek-ing patients with opioid dependence (Brooner et al., 1997; Weiss et al., 1992).

The Role of Antisocial Personality Disorder

Antisocial personality disorder is common among substance abusers. Commu-nity data from the Epidemiologic Catchment Area Study indicate that antisocial personality disorder is present in 14.3 percent of individuals with alcohol use disorders, and 17.8 percent of individuals with drug use disorders (Regier et al., 1990). Antisocial behavior and antisocial personality disorder are often charac-terized by impulsiveness and violence that can increase the prevalence of sui-cide (for example, Greenwald et al., 1994). Indeed, antisocial behavior appears to be related to an increased risk for suicidality for many patients with sub-stance use disorders (Black et al., 1986). Among alcohol-dependent patients who have tried to commit suicide, two of three have antisocial personality dis-order (Hesselbrock et al., 1988). The presence of substance abuse problems among patients with antisocial personality often predisposes them to suicide (Murphy and Wetzel, 1990). In fact, when combined with depression, men with antisocial personality are at greater risk for attempting suicide than men with de-pression alone (Lewis et al., 1985).

EVALUATION OF SUICIDE RISK IN SUBSTANCE ABUSERS

Evaluation of suicide risk in substance abusers can be quite difficult. Suicidal behavior can range from impulsive attempts with little or no warning, to esca-lating suicidal ideation over a chronic deteriorating course. Clinicians should be aware of the many ways in which suicide risk can manifest itself among sub-stance abusers. Presentations of suicidal behavior may range from a provoca-tive display of suicidality by an intoxicated patient in an emergency room to a long series of telephone calls from desperate family members of a deteriorating alcoholic or addict. Important areas for careful suicide risk assessment among substance abusers include current precipitants, interpersonal loss, depression, age, communication of suicidal attempt and history of suicide attempts, psy-chiatric history, and lifestyle issues.

Current Precipitants

As is often the case in psychiatric evaluations, asking the question "Why is this occurring now?" may provide important information. In particular, the clinician should ask about interpersonal losses (for example, marital separation) or conflicts, threatened or actual loss of employment, recent physical illness, legal or financial problems, and recent exacerbations of or return to substance abuse. In addition, any change, actual or perceived, in the patient's social support system should also be carefully evaluated, since this may reflect a weakening of the patient's reasons to live.

Interpersonal Loss

It is well known that alcoholics and drug dependent patients experience numerous losses: physical health, vocational functioning, financial status, psychological well-being, and memory are some of the more commonly affected areas. It also appears that experiencing interpersonal loss is an important precipitant of suicidal behavior among substance abusers.

Several studies of alcoholics and drug abusers who commit suicide have shown that interpersonal loss exerts a powerful influence on suicidal behavior (Murphy et al., 1979; Murphy and Robins, 1967; Rich et al., 1988). Studies by Murphy and colleagues have found that as many as one-third of alcoholics who commit suicide had experienced an interpersonal loss within six weeks of killing themselves (Murphy et al., 1979; Murphy and Robins, 1967). Similar results have been found in studies of drug-dependent patients (Rich et al., 1988). The careful assessment of whether a substance-abusing patient has experienced any recent interpersonal losses should therefore be part of a suicide risk assessment.

Depression

A wealth of empirical data indicates that comorbid depression among substance abusers is a significant risk factor for suicide. As a result, patients with substance use disorders should be carefully screened for both depressive symptoms and major depressive disorder. Determining the difference between detoxification-limited depression and independent psychiatric comorbidity remains difficult; evaluation of the presence or absence of depressive symptoms during abstinent periods, family history, and previous treatment response are all components of this differential diagnostic process. Greenfield et al. (1998) have stressed the importance of the distinction between depressive symptoms and major depressive disorder in alcohol-dependent patients; the latter was a poor prognostic sign regarding future drinking behavior in patients hospitalized for alcohol dependence, whereas depressive symptoms themselves during hospitalization had no such prognostic significance.

Age

In middle-to-late adolescence, suicide is a significant cause of death. In 1995, 4789 young people between the ages of fifteen and twenty-four killed themselves, making suicide the third leading cause of death in this age group (Rosenberg et al., 1996). Although precise prevalence rates of suicide in this age group are not known, studies have found that one-third of adolescents who commit suicide have a blood alcohol level greater than 22 mmol/L, or approximately 0.1 percent (Brent et al., 1988). In addition, a psychological autopsy study of completed suicides among adolescents determined that 70 percent of the sample had drug or alcohol problems (Shafii et al., 1985).

Advancing age is also a well-known risk factor for suicide. As many as 80 to 90 percent of alcoholics who commit suicide are males, with suicide frequently occurring as a late phenomenon in the course of alcoholism (Murphy and Wetzel, 1990).

Communication of Suicidal Intent and History of Suicide Attempts

Seventy percent of alcoholics who kill themselves do not have a history of suicide attempts, although 60 percent have made a direct statement regarding their suicidal intent (Murphy et al., 1979). Among adolescents, the communication of suicidal intent is made only to a peer in half of all cases of completed suicides (Brent et al., 1988), thus making professional intervention less likely.

Surprisingly, a history of drug overdoses does not appear to be a useful predictor of suicide potential among patients with opioid dependence (Kosten and Rounsaville, 1988). Use of a particular addictive substance in a previous suicide attempt does, however, appear to be related to the subsequent use of the same substance in a completed suicide. In a prospective study of patients who had attempted suicide, 67 percent of those patients who had consumed alcohol during an initial suicide attempt also used alcohol before subsequently committing suicide, compared to only 13 percent of those patients who had not initially consumed alcohol during a suicide attempt (Suokas and Lönnqvist, 1995). Specific attention should thus be paid to whether the patient has a history of past suicide attempts (Hirschfeld and Davidson, 1988). If so, determining the precipitants and means used in the previous attempt can be important.

Psychiatric History

A careful substance use and psychiatric history can also help in differential diagnosis and determining the potential for suicide. A comprehensive drug and alcohol history should be obtained, preferably in collaboration with the patient's family or friends. A family history of substance use disorder, mood disorder, or suicidal behavior adds further weight to existing risk factors for suicide (Marzuk and Mann, 1988). The clinician should also inquire carefully regarding the availability of means to commit suicide. In particular, access to firearms should be considered in this high-risk population, as availability in and of itself has been correlated with completed suicides (Brent et al., 1988).

Obtaining a thorough assessment of comorbid psychopathology is also useful in a suicide risk assessment. Both axis I and axis II disorders have been found to be more prevalent among substance abusers than in the general population. For example, anxiety disorders, bipolar disorder, major depressive disorder, schizophrenia, and impulse control disorders have all been found to be prevalent among substance abusers (for example, Weiss and Najavits, 1998). Antisocial personality disorder, particularly in men, has been shown to be the most prevalent axis II disorder among substance abusers, with borderline, narcissistic, and histrionic personality disorders also being relatively common (Hesselbrock et al., 1985; Khantzian and Treece, 1985; Weiss et al., 1986). Even among high-risk groups, such as patients with borderline personality disorder, the addition of alcoholism increases the risk for suicide attempts (Nace et al., 1983).

Lifestyle Issues

Questions about the substance abuser's lifestyle and attitudes can help give the clinician insight about suicide risk. Obtaining a history of accidents, overdoses, risky drug-buying practices, needle sharing, unsafe sex, medical complications, and dwindling efforts to preserve significant relationships may provide clues to hopelessness, which may lead to passive or active suicide attempts.

In addition to assessing substance abusers for the presence of the above risk factors, it is important to look for a convergence among risk factors. Suicide is, fortunately, a relatively rare behavior; predicting it with a high degree of certainty is thus likely to remain an unachievable goal (Pokorny, 1983). At the same time, suicide risk assessment is a common clinical activity, requiring considerable skill and a substantial knowledge base. Although no specific cluster of risk factors appears to reliably predict suicide, the clinician should be mindful of meaningful connections among risk factors. For example, when hopelessness following a significant interpersonal loss occurs in the context of a deteriorating social support network, the clinician should be quite concerned.

The following list summarizes some of the areas that are helpful to explore in evaluating suicide risk in patients who are abusing drugs or alcohol.

Evaluation of the Substance Abuser at Risk for Suicide

  Current precipitants—"Why now?"

  Recent interpersonal losses

  Depressive symptoms, with an emphasis on hopelessness

Presence of comorbid axis I or axis II disorders

Past history of suicide attempts

Age

Family history of suicide, mood disorder, or substance use disorder

Comprehensive drug and alcohol history

Availability of means, especially firearms

Poor self-care

CLINICAL MANAGEMENT OF
THE SUICIDAL SUBSTANCE ABUSER

In attempting to lower the risk of suicidal behavior in a chemically dependent patient, the first priority should be to help the patient achieve and maintain sobriety. Completed suicides are far more likely to occur during periods of active use than during recovery (Frances et al., 1987). Furthermore, recovery from alcoholism has been associated with a doubling of the likelihood of recovery from comorbid major depressive disorder (Mueller et al., 1994). The best way to reduce the likelihood of suicide, therefore, as with many other complications associated with substance abuse, is to help patients achieve and maintain abstinence.

Psychosocial interventions with suicidal substance abusers are an integral part of successful clinical management. Given the importance of interpersonal loss and depression in suicide, interventions that help reestablish the substance abuser's social support network may help decrease the risk for suicide. Other aspects of treatment should include connecting the patient to self-help groups in the community, providing education about the nature of addiction and any related comorbid psychiatric conditions, giving attention to vocational issues, and, in some cases, using random urine toxicologic screening.

As our group has noted before (Weiss, Najavits, and Mirin, 1998), the subject of when to administer pharmacotherapy to dually diagnosed patients has long been a subject of controversy. Many clinicians, for instance, are reluctant to use antidepressants to treat depressive symptoms in substance abusers, regardless of the presence of suicidal ideation. There are a number of reasons for this (Weiss and Najavits, 1998). First, clinicians may believe that the depressive symptoms and suicidal ideation will remit as a result of abstinence alone. Second, treaters fear the possibility of a toxic interaction between their prescribed medication and the patient's substance(s) of abuse. Third, many clinicians fear they may be "enabling" their patients by not allowing them to experience the naturalistic negative consequences of their substance abuse, for example, depressed mood. Fourth, clinicians fear that patients may use their prescribed medication to carry out an intentional overdose.

Three recent studies, however, have shown that antidepressant treatment of alcoholics with depression may improve both depressive symptoms and drinking outcomes. McGrath and colleagues (1996) conducted a study of imipramine vs. placebo in sixty-nine actively drinking alcoholic outpatients with current depressive disorder, in which the first episode of depression preceded the alcohol abuse or occurred during long periods of sobriety. Depressive symptoms improved among the imipramine-treated sample, and patients whose mood improved showed a reduction in drinking that was more marked among those treated with imipramine. Cornelius and colleagues (1997) have also found that fluoxetine was effective in reducing depressive symptoms and alcohol consumption among fifty-one patients with comorbid major depressive disorder and alcohol dependence. Mason and colleagues (1996) conducted a double-blind, placebo-controlled trial with desipramine in seventy-one alcohol-dependent patients with secondary major depression; depression was diagnosed after at least one week of abstinence. They found that depressed patients had significantly greater improvement in depressed mood and were abstinent for significantly longer when receiving desipramine, as opposed to placebo. This is a striking finding because clinicians have traditionally been least likely to consider antidepressant treatment for alcoholics whose depression was considered secondary to their drinking. Recent data thus support the potential benefit of antidepressant treatment in patients with coexisting depression and alcoholism.

The studies described above should allay some of the fears that clinicians express about prescribing psychotropic agents for patients with substance use disorders; there were no serious adverse reactions reported, and the fear of enabling (that is, that these patients' drinking patterns would worsen as a result of antidepressant treatment) was not realized. In addition, data from the San Diego suicide study indicate that treating comorbid depression among substance abusers with antidepressants can avert far more suicides than eschewing antidepressant treatment in order to avoid overdoses (Isacsson, Bergman, and Rich, 1994a). Finally, treatment of depression, an illness that is accompanied by substantial morbidity and mortality, including an increased risk of suicide, is an important goal in its own right, even if it is not accompanied by an improvement in the coexisting substance use disorder.

IMPLICATIONS FOR THE CLINICIAN

Having reviewed the empirical literature regarding the multifaceted relationship between substance abuse and suicide, we offer the following implications for the clinician. Such an undertaking is inherently difficult, as the heterogeneity of substance abuse is one of its defining features. However, the following general guidelines should aid the clinician in dealing with this challenging group of patients.

General Points

- Suicidal behavior can be manifested directly (for example, threats to kill oneself) or indirectly (for example, "accidental" overdoses).
- The presence of coexisting major depressive disorder markedly increases the likelihood of suicidal ideation, suicide attempts, and completed suicide.
- Antisocial personality disorder, especially if characterized by impulsiveness and a history of violence, increases suicide risk.

Assessment

- Carefully assess for symptoms of major depressive disorder as well as hopelessness.
- The presence of interpersonal loss in the recent past should be cause for concern.
- Look for meaningful connections among risk factors to help determine suicide risk.

Clinical Management

- The first priority should be to help the patient achieve and maintain sobriety.
- The treatment of coexisting psychiatric conditions can often improve the substance abuse as well, and decrease the risk for suicide.
- Given the importance of interpersonal loss in precipitating suicide among substance abusers, psychosocial interventions should include reconnecting these patients to their social support systems.

CHAPTER EIGHTEEN

Borderline Personality Disorder

Timothy Davis, M.D.
John G. Gunderson, M.D.
Melissa Myers, M.D.

Borderline personality disorder (BPD) is the disorder that is most inextricably intertwined with suicidality in the minds of most clinicians. It is not that these patients commit suicide at a rate that far exceeds that of other psychiatric patients but that this struggle with suicidality is a fundamental part of their illness as well as their treatment. Indeed, with the exception of major depression, BPD is the only diagnosis in *DSM-IV* for which suicidality is a criterion (American Psychiatric Association, 1994).

A comparison of the wording of the criteria suggests a qualitative difference between the suicidality of patients with BPD and those with a depressive disorder. For the diagnosis of a major depressive episode, one may have "recurrent thoughts of death (not just fear of dying), recurrent suicidal ideation without a specific plan, or a suicide attempt or a specific plan for committing suicide." For BPD, one may have recurrent suicidal behavior, gestures or threats, or self-mutilatory behavior. Thus, suicidality in a depressed patient tends to be more intrapsychic, whereas that of a patient with BPD is more typically "in your face" insofar as it is manifested externally in the interpersonal sphere. This is true not only of the more familiar suicidal gestures by borderline patients, but also of completed suicides. A recent study by Runeson, Beskow, and Waern (1996) noted that 44 percent of completed suicides in patients with BPD were witnessed, compared to 17 percent of those in patients with other diagnoses.

This chapter highlights the distinctive features of suicidality in BPD. A review of the epidemiological data, including risk factors for completed suicide, in conjunction with an elucidation of the unique interpersonal dynamics of suicidality in BPD, will provide a framework for the assessment of immediate suicide risk and a foundation for the treatment of both acute and chronic suicidality.

EPIDEMIOLOGY

Suicide attempts are a frequent feature of BPD. Studies have found that 67 to 76 percent of patients with BPD have made at least one suicide attempt in their lives (Gunderson, 1984; Soloff, Lis, Kelly, Cornelius, and Ulrich, 1994b; Stone, Hunt, and Stone, 1987; Zisook, Goff, Sledge, and Schuchter, 1994). Levels of overt suicidal intent vary widely with BPD patients, but in a 1994 study by Soloff, Lis, Kelly, Cornelius, and Ulrich, 64 percent of patients with BPD reported at least one high-intent attempt and 43 percent reported at least one high-medical-lethality suicide attempt. Although suicide threats, gestures, or attempts may in many cases represent efforts to communicate with others or to effect some situational or relational change, it is essential to bear in mind that these still may result in death or may escalate, if dismissed, into more lethal acts. Other behaviors characteristic of or commonly associated with BPD, such as self-mutilation, sexual promiscuity, reckless behavior, and substance abuse, may also represent indirect suicidality.

Despite the high frequency of suicidal behavior in BPD, BPD (as a sole diagnosis) is not overrepresented among psychiatric suicides. Kullgren, Renberg, and Jacobsson (1986) found that the overall proportion of BPD in their study population of completed psychiatric suicides was similar to the proportion of BPD in hospitalized psychiatric patients. The incidence of completed suicide in BPD is about 9 percent in longitudinal studies, a rate comparable to that seen in schizophrenia and 50 percent of mood disorders, in which suicide attempts are much less common (Stone, Hunt, and Stone, 1987; Paris, Brown, and Nowlis, 1987). A lower rate of only 3 percent was found in McGlashan's follow-up (1986) of somewhat older BPD patients who had lengthy psychotherapy treatment at Chestnut Lodge, a private psychiatric hospital in Rockville, Maryland, that specializes in the long-term residential treatment of severely ill patients. Clearly many suicide attempts do not result in death. A number of studies with BPD patients showed that a history of suicide attempts is a significant predictor of completed suicide (Soloff, Lis, Kelly, Cornelius, and Ulrich, 1994a; Kullgren, 1988; Stone, 1993), but given the high baseline rate of suicidal behavior in BPD, it is difficult to discriminate high from low risk based primarily on this factor.

IDENTIFICATION OF RISK FACTORS

Attempts to identify specific risk factors for completed suicide in BPD have been complicated by many factors, including the low general incidence of completed suicide and interstudy variation in patient age, study setting (inpatient versus out-patient), duration and type of treatment, psychiatric comorbidity, and distinction between nonlethal self-destructiveness and suicidal intent. Demographic factors such as older age and male gender, which have been found to be associated with a higher risk of suicide in the general population, have not consistently correlated with suicide risk in studies of borderline patients. Kullgren (1988) found that nei-ther age nor gender differed between a series of fifteen BPD suicides and thirteen BPD inpatients, although Soloff, Lis, Kelly, Cornelius, and Ulrich (1994a) found that BPD patients with high-medical-lethality attempts were older (mean age thirty) than those with low-lethality attempts (mean age twenty-five). The clinical significance of this latter finding is questionable, given that suicide generally oc-curs at a younger age in BPD than in the general population (Stone, Hunt, and Stone, 1987; Kachur, Potter, James, and Powell, 1995; Stone, Stone, and Hurst, 1987). Although Stone, Stone, and Hurst (1987) and Stone (1990) found that 20 percent of male BPD subjects with a history of suicide attempts eventually com-pleted suicide, twice the rate of suicide in female borderline suicide attempts, this finding is confounded by a disproportionate rate among the men of comorbid sociopathy, a factor also associated in this study with completed suicide.

Consistent with data from the general population (Dorpat and Ripley, 1967), most suicides in Stone, Stone, and Hurst's study (1987) were unmarried and unemployed. In addition, several were adopted or came from abusive or inces-tuous families, or both, consistent with Wagner and Linehan's finding (1994) that patients with a history of childhood sexual abuse engaged in more lethal parasuicidal behaviors. Interestingly, Paris, Nowlis, and Brown (1988) found that early separation and loss were less frequent in the backgrounds of those patients who committed suicide. A potentially confounding factor in this study was an inverse correlation between early separation and higher education, the latter of which proved to be an independent risk factor for suicide, perhaps due to shattered expectations.

The severity and extent of BPD symptomatology may correlate with increased suicide risk. Stone (1993) identified this phenomenon among subjects who met all eight *DSM-III* BPD diagnostic items, and Kullgren, Renberg, and Jacobsson (1986) observed that BPD patients who committed suicide were more severely disturbed than those usually reported from clinical settings. However, other studies found that the severity of BPD as measured by the Diagnostic Index for Borderlines (DIB) did not discriminate suicide attempters from nonattempters (Soloff, Lis, Kelly, Cornelius, and Ulrich, 1994a) or suicide completers from con-trols with BPD (Kullgren, 1988).

Attempts to identify specific features of BPD that place a patient at higher risk for suicide have met with mixed results. Psychosis, a risk factor for suicide in the general population, has not been consistently correlated with suicide in BPD. Although some studies (Kullgren, Renberg, and Jacobsson, 1986; Yeomans, Hull, and Clarkin, 1994) have found that psychotic spectrum symptoms in BPD correlated significantly with self-destructiveness and completed suicide, others noted that subjects who committed suicide had lower DIB psychosis scores (Paris, Nowlis, and Brown, 1989) and that schizotypy predicted low suicidal intent (Soloff, Lis, Kelly, Cornelius, and Ulrich, 1994a). Impulsivity has been associated with a higher rate of suicidal behavior in BPD (Soloff, Lis, Kelly, Cornelius, and Ulrich, 1994a), but this has not appeared to translate into increased risk of completed suicide (Stone, Stone, and Hurst, 1987; Paris, Nowlis, and Brown, 1989). Anger has been variously associated with lower or higher suicide risk (Runeson, Beskow, and Waern, 1996; Soloff, Lis, Kelly, Cornelius, and Ulrich, 1994a; Kullgren, Renberg, and Jacobsson, 1986; Kullgren, 1988; Stone, 1993; Stone, Stone, and Hurst, 1987). Unstable interpersonal relationships, reported to correlate with self-destructiveness in one study (Yeomans, Hull, and Clarkin, 1994), did not distinguish between BPD suicides and controls in another (Paris, Nowlis, and Brown, 1989).

Impact of Comorbid Disorders

The impact of comorbid affective disorders on suicidality in BPD remains unclear. Stone, Hunt, and Stone (1987) and Stone, Stone, and Hurst (1987) report that almost 18 percent of BPD males with a concurrent major affective disorder committed suicide. However, he noted high (67 to 75 percent) but comparable rates of major affective disorders in BPD subjects who did and did not complete suicide and found no significant difference in suicide rates between patients with BPD alone versus BPD with concurrent major affective disorder. Paris, Nowlis, and Brown (1989) found no significant differences between fourteen BPD patients who committed suicide and one hundred BPD control subjects with regard to prevalence of affective disorder. Kullgren (1988) and Soloff, Lis, Kelly, Cornelius, and Ulrich (1994a) also found no significant relationship between major affective disorder comorbidity in BPD and attempted lethality or completion. In most studies, there have been high rates of major affective disorder comorbidity in BPD subjects, and it may be that this high baseline correlation weakens the role of major affective comorbidity as a discriminator for serious suicidality. State depression, or depressed mood, has been determined to be associated with high suicide risk (Soloff, Lis, Kelly, Cornelius, and Ulrich, 1994a; Kullgren, 1988) and increased level of self-destructiveness in BPD (Yeomans, Hull, and Clarkin, 1994; Sabo, Gunderson, Najavits, Chauncey, and Disiel, 1995). Kernberg (1993) and Gardner and Cowdry (1985a) argued that the central issue in evaluating suicidal potential in suicidal BPD patients is the discrimination of lower-risk characterologic depression from severe melancholic despair, which is more likely to lead to true suicidal acts.

Substance abuse by BPD patients has been more consistently associated with increased lethality in suicide attempts than is true for BPD patients with no substance abuse (Soloff, Lis, Kelly, Cornelius, and Ulrich, 1994a). Stone (1993) found that BPD patients with alcohol dependence were three times as likely to complete suicide as those with BPD alone. In addition, Links, Heslegrave, Mitton, Van Reekum, and Patrick (1995) observed that BPD patients with co-morbid substance abuse had increased impulsivity, self-mutilatory behavior, and suicidal ideation. The coexistence of BPD, major affective disorder, and alcohol abuse was particularly malignant in Stone's Psychiatric Institute 500 study (1990), with an alarming 38 percent of female patients with this combination of diagnoses committing suicide. Fyer, Frances, Sullivan, Hurt, and Clarkin (1988), in a chart review of hospitalized BPD patients, also found that those with both comorbid affective and substance abuse disorders had a significantly increased risk of serious suicide attempts and a decreased rate of suicidal gestures compared with those with BPD alone.

Interestingly, Stone, Stone, and Hurst (1987) found that the suicide rate among BPD patients with comorbid eating disorders was only a fourth of that of BPD patients in general. Yeomans, Hull, and Clarkin (1994) noted that after BPD patients stopped self-destructive acting out, their level of subjective distress increased. It is possible that nonlethal self-destructive behaviors provide an outlet, however pathological, for discharging distress and thus might reduce a patient's overall risk for more lethal behaviors.

Additional axis II diagnoses or characterologic attributes may also have an impact on suicide risk in BPD. Stone (1989) reported that suicide rates for BPD subjects with narcissistic personality disorder or narcissistic features were double those for BPD alone. He also found (Stone, Stone, and Hurst, 1987) a doubled suicide rate (17 percent) in BPD subjects with comorbid antisocial personality. In contrast, Soloff, Lis, Kelly, Cornelius, and Ulrich (1994a) found that their predominantly male subcohort with BPD, impulsivity, and antisocial personality had made more suicide attempts and reported high-attempt seriousness but overall demonstrated lower lethality than those with BPD alone.

Suicide Risk Levels Following Hospitalization

Similar to other psychiatric disorders, where the suicide rate is highest during the first two years following the index suicide attempt (Dorpat and Ripley, 1967; Pokorny, 1983), the majority of BPD suicides occur within five years of the index hospitalization (Runeson, Beskow, and Waern, 1996; Stone, Stone, and Hurst, 1987; McGlashan, 1986). Sabo, Gunderson, Najavits, Chauncey, and Disiel (1995) noted that suicidal behavior significantly declined during a five-year follow-up of BPD female inpatients, even though suicidal ideation persisted essentially unchanged until year 5, with over 90 percent of subjects reporting suicidal ideation without making suicide attempts throughout the second to fifth study years. This was in contrast to self-harm ideation and behaviors, which did not decline significantly during the follow-up period. A history of multiple hospitalizations has also been associated with a higher rate of completed suicide

(Kullgren, Renberg, and Jacobsson, 1986; Kullgren, 1988). Kullgren (1988) noted that suicide attempts during inpatient treatment were strongly correlated with completed suicides in the hospital, often in the immediate vicinity of staff, or within a month after discharge.

In summary, it is impossible to predict suicide, even in a general psychiatric population, where the baseline level of suicidal behavior is low and a number of clear risk factors have been identified (Pokorny, 1983; Goldstein, Black, Nasrallah, and Winokur, 1991). The difficulty of accurately assessing suicide risk is compounded in BPD, in which nonlethal suicide attempts and self-destructive behavior are common; patient dynamics, motivations, situational factors, and treater responses are varied, complex, and profoundly interrelated; and psychiatric comorbidity is frequent. Studies of suicide in BPD patients have yielded contradictory results regarding the significance of many risk factors, but a few generalizations can be made. Although correlations between completed suicide and individual risk factors are often inconsistent, the coexistence of multiple risk factors for suicide appears to be additive, particularly the combination of BPD, major affective disorder, and substance abuse, or multiple psychosocial stressors such as isolation, unemployment, and history of trauma. It appears that current severe depression, despair, and hopelessness, as contrasted with "characterologic" dysphoria, compound the risk of completed suicide in BPD. More extensive and severe BPD symptomatology may also increase suicide risk, as may concurrent narcissistic or antisocial personality pathology, especially in male borderlines. Hospitalizations and the immediate postdischarge period are emotionally and interpersonally complex times, which represent particularly high-risk periods for BPD suicides. In general, although suicidal ideation tends to persist, the number of suicide attempts and completions tends to decrease markedly over the five years following the index hospitalization in BPD.

ASSESSMENT OF SUICIDE RISK IN BPD

Although the preceding data may be helpful in identifying the relative risk of eventual suicide in an individual patient and even the short-term risk for some patients, it does not address the more frequent and anxiety-producing question in the minds of clinicians working with these patients: What is the risk of this patient's committing suicide right now, if he or she leaves my office?

In considering this question, it is important to distinguish between self-destructive behavior without lethal intent, often termed *parasuicide* or *manipulative suicide attempts,* and a true attempt at suicide. Given that suicidal intent is often ambivalent, this distinction is not always clear-cut. However, in many cases, manipulative suicide attempts can be distinguished on the basis of their having been carried out, usually repetitiously, under circumstances where rescue would be likely and that seemed designed to exact some saving response from a specific other person (Gunderson, Kolb, and Austin, 1981). This distinction is important insofar as the circumstances in which manipulative suicide gestures are likely to occur are quite different from those in which the patient is at significant risk for completed suicide. Gardner and Cowdry (1985a) conceptualized suicidal behaviors in four general categories, each having characteristic affective states, motivations, and outcomes: melancholia, despair, and true suicidal acts; impulsive, nihilistic, or retributive rage; communicative parasuicidal gestures; and self-mutilation or overdose to relieve dysphoria. They suggested that the highest suicide risk is present in the first category, in which BPD with a superimposed major depressive episode may lead to a qualitatively different and more intense despair in which carefully planned, low-rescue-potential, higher-risk suicide attempts are more likely. They caution that although communicative parasuicidal gestures typically involve low actual suicidal intent, unintentional suicides can occur, or the gestures may be rehearsal events of a true suicidal act or attempts to inform the therapist of escalating suicidality.

Many of the general principles for assessing suicidality discussed elsewhere in this book are applicable to the borderline patient. However, there are certain unique characteristics of this patient that should be kept in mind when making this assessment.

Use of the Jacobs Model to Assess Risk

Jacobs (1992) has proposed a tripartite model that takes into account some of these characteristics. The first component identifies the specific psychopathological features of BPD that puts the patient at higher risk for suicide: impulsivity, hopelessness-despair, antisocial features (with dishonesty), interpersonal aloofness, "malignant narcissism," self-mutilating tendencies, and psychosis with bizarre suicide attempts. Jacobs particularly emphasizes the combination of impulsivity and hopelessness as increasing the likelihood of suicide. On the other hand, certain aspects of BPD, such as clinging, dependency, and the use of suicidal behavior to maintain connection, are associated with diminished risk.

The second component of Jacobs's model focuses on evaluation of comorbid Axis I disorders, specifically depressive disorder, substance abuse, eating disorders, and post-traumatic stress disorder. Although the evidence linking any one of these to an increased risk of completed suicide in borderline patients is far from conclusive, in combination with other factors, Jacobs suggests they may increase the risk for an individual patient.

Jacobs terms the third component of his model for assessing suicidal intent "suicide perspective." He divides it into three subcomponents: (1) objectifying suicidal intent and behavior, (2) identifying specific psychological commonalities of suicide, and (3) determining the psychodynamic formulation. Objectifying suicidal intent includes determining the ability to control suicidal thoughts, identifying the deterrents to carrying out the act, distinguishing between active and passive suicidal thoughts, and determining the degree of planning that has occurred. The specific psychological commonalities of suicide in this model draw on the work of Shneidman (1985), who proposed "ten commonalities of suicide," or ten features consistent across all cases of completed suicide. Of these, Jacobs identifies five factors that, in combination, increase the likelihood of completed suicide in borderline patients: intolerable psychological pain, hope-lessness-helplessness, ambivalence, thought constriction, and egression, a reflection of the borderline patient's propensity to action. Jacobs's psychodynamic formulation, which includes assessing the patient's vulnerability to painful affect, the motivational aspects of suicide, the meanings of suicide, and the relationship to death, can help identify the reasons and circumstances under which a borderline patient may be at greater risk for suicide.

Significant Attachments and Suicidal Risk

Gunderson (1984) relates the immediate suicidal risk of borderline patients to their current state of relatedness or attachment with significant others. This method of assessment follows from an appreciation of what some consider to be the central feature of BPD: intolerance of aloneness. Reviewing the earlier work by Modell (1963), Masterson (1972, 1976; Masterson and Rinsley, 1975), and Winnicott (1953), as well as the important refinements by Adler and Buie (1979), Gunderson (1996) posits that the early relationship of the preborderline child to his or her caretakers was sufficiently inconsistent and unstable that a "soothing introject" (that is, an internalized sense of oneself as being cared for) failed to develop, and as a result the borderline patient requires external reassurance. Because borderline patients are unable to evoke this soothing introject, they suffer from an intolerance of aloneness that is relieved only by another person's actual provision of reassuring evidence that they are cared for.

The disruption or anticipated disruption to the relationship with this reassuring other, or primary object, results in a state of aloneness with accompanying anxiety, anger, self-loathing, or panic. The borderline patient, who has difficulty regulating affect, may then attempt to manage this intolerable emotional state by engaging in self-destructive behavior, including suicide gestures and attempts.

The status of the relationship with the primary object determines the borderline patient's affective state and the likelihood and severity of self-destructive acts. In the first level of functioning, when the primary object is present and supportive, the patient may exhibit depressive features but will refrain from serious self-destructive behaviors. In the second level of functioning, when disruption of the relationship is anticipated, the patient will experience anger and may react with manipulative suicide threats and suicidal gestures. In the third level of functioning, in the temporary absence of a sustaining relationship, panic or disassociation is the predominant affect. In desperate attempts to reestablish contact with the self-sustaining relationship, impulsive or psychotically driven self-destructive behaviors of potentially high lethality occur. Sometimes these acts occur under the disinhibiting influence of drugs or alcohol. In a further elaboration of this, Fonagy has suggested that these self-destructive behaviors are directed at a bodily self that the borderline patient disowns and whose death is required to resume being attached to another (1997).

Patients can switch rapidly among these three levels of psychological functioning, often many times within the course of a day or even a single therapy session. The therapeutic response can be guided by the patient's level of functioning. In the first level of functioning, where the risk of suicide is inconsequential, the therapist can proceed as usual. In the second level of functioning, when the therapist is faced with angry, manipulative suicide threats, the therapeutic task is to interpret, confront, and set limits. In the third level of functioning with a panicked, impulsive, and possibly psychotic or dissociative patient, the therapist may need to respond actively and unilaterally to protect the patient until a sustaining relationship can be reestablished.

MANAGEMENT OF SUICIDALITY

The management of suicidality in patients with BPD is commonly an ongoing process that may be punctuated by more discrete episodes of acute suicidal crisis. This contrasts with the management of suicidality in depressed patients, where the episodes of suicidality tend to be more time limited and remit in conjunction with the episode of depression. As such, interventions such as unsolicited provision of support, hospitalization, aggressive pharmacotherapy, or electroconvulsive therapy, which are effective in carrying a depressed patient through a suicidal crisis, may not be effective, and in some cases may be counterproductive, in the long-term management of suicidality in borderline patients. Thus, the clinician must take a more longitudinal perspective in formulating a treatment approach for managing suicidality in BPD. In many ways, the effective management of suicidality with borderline patients is contained in the thoughtful day-to-day attention to roles, boundaries, and relationships that will promote the patient's psychological growth.

Borderline patients frequently express their suicidality in ways that invite concern and encourage active noninterpretative interventions by therapists. This is what is colloquially called "manipulation" or "emotional blackmail." A common example is when a patient misses an appointment after expressing suicidal impulses. It may seem natural for the therapist to telephone to inquire after the patient's well-being. Similarly, it may appear that voicing dismay over a patient's blasé report of driving while intoxicated is the professionally prudent response. However, such indications of concern may lead to the patient's relinquishing the already tenuous self-monitoring and self-preservative functions to the therapist. It may also lead to an escalation of dangerous behaviors in order to test the therapist's willingness to look out for and care for the patient, as in the following case.

Elise reentered therapy with a new psychiatrist after a two-year hiatus, which encompassed her longest period free from self-destructive behavior or hospitalizations since initiating treatment. Within a month of resuming therapy, she reported intensifying suicidal thoughts, escalating self-mutilatory behaviors, the reemergence of anorexia, and the resumption of substance abuse.

Elise began paging her therapist more frequently, reporting that she felt overwhelmed and was unable to implement her previously effective symptom management strategies. The therapist initially responded by engaging actively and empathically in exploring precipitants and suggesting alternative coping strategies. Although effective in defusing the immediate crisis, these interventions led to a rapid increase of suicidal threats, self-mutilation, substance abuse, angry rejections of offers of help, and ultimately a series of involuntary hospitalizations. Attempts to modify this pattern proved fruitless, and a mutual decision to terminate therapy was reached. In a chance encounter several months later, Elise appeared to have regained the lost weight and reported that she was clean and sober and had largely avoided hospitalization.

In fact, borderline patients rarely ask explicitly for the interventions made on their behalf. If it appears that a patient is asking indirectly for something, the appropriate response is to point this out and inquire whether the perception is correct. When it has been clarified that the patient is indeed asking for something specific, there is usually little reason to withhold it. Once the patient's responsibility for requesting the intervention is explicit, the desired sense of magical control is no longer an issue, and the patient will find little reason to continue covert efforts to elicit saving responses.

When a therapist provides a supportive intervention without direct solicitation, the patient's reaction to this intervention should be explored immediately. If such exploration is not undertaken, the provocative signals of impending self-destructive activity will recur, and the danger to the patient will be even greater should one later fail to respond as expected. A fatal incident, like the following, may occur.

Janet periodically rented a motel room and, with a stockpile of pills nearby, called her therapist's home with an urgent message. He responded by engaging in long conversations in which he "talked her down." Even as he told her that she could not count on his always being available, he became more wary of going out evenings without detailed instructions about how he could be reached. One night the patient could not reach him due to a bad telephone connection. She fatally overdosed from what was probably a miscalculated manipulation. The effort to be supportive and available in this case led to a progressive shift of responsibility for the patient's welfare onto the therapist.

Therapists are often aware only that such supportive work gratifies the patient's wishes to be important to the therapist and to exercise control over him or her. Equally important to recognize is the frightening aspects of this invasiveness. As a result of the indistinct boundaries in the background of many of these patients, including sexual and physical abuse, such unrequested therapeutic advances can invoke feelings of terror and self-loathing, leading to an escalation of suicidality.

The counterbalance to this discussion of the risk of supportive interventions is the very real danger of minimizing or ignoring the patient's distress signals. This response will cause the patient to feel neglected or disliked or, at its most extreme, to project cruel punitive or murderous motives onto the clinician. The patient will often proceed by upping the ante with more flagrant and dangerous threats and behaviors. In this setting of conflict, a miscalculation by patient or therapist can easily become fatal. This is particularly likely to become the case when a patient lacks a primary object and is using suicidality as a means of establishing a connection with the therapist, as is illustrated by the case of Louise.

Louise had displayed a pattern of profound regression with a remarkable capacity to elicit overinvolvement from a series of conscientious and committed treaters. Her new therapist was determined not to repeat this pattern and steadfastly confronted and interpreted all intersession contact. A few weeks into therapy, Louise's mother died and her best friend left town on an extended vacation. Louise's suicidality rapidly intensified, and she resumed self-mutilating behaviors, which had been in abeyance for years. Her urgent pleas for emergency sessions were met with the same cool interpretive stance. In a panic, Louise impulsively overdosed, her first such attempt since late adolescence.

Seen narrowly, a therapist's choices can seem to be either "set limits, and don't be manipulated" or "be available, and prevent suicide." The former approach risks the patient's physical welfare, and the latter risks the patient's psychological growth. Kernberg (1975) has described the problem as how to provide sufficient support or structure so that psychotherapy can take place without forgoing the therapist's essential neutrality in the process.

A prudent course from the beginning of therapy is to go along with manipulation, but only if the reason for the intervention is clarified, the meaning of the manipulation is interpreted, and the wisdom of both the patient's behavior and the therapist's responsiveness is explicitly questioned. In addition, early on and repeatedly, the therapist should clarify not only his or her limited ability to prevent suicide, but also his or her legal obligation to intervene if suicide seems imminent and its possible negative effect on therapy. The harmful and potentially irreconcilable effects that the need for any lifesaving activity will have on the therapist's ability to function as a therapist and on the patient's ability to have a useful therapeutic experience need to be emphasized.

The more extreme management approaches of reflexive limit setting or unquestioning support often stem from the therapist's unreasonable view of the borderline patient as either an angry and greedy child or a despairing waif. What is often overlooked is the aspect of the patient that genuinely wishes to use the therapy for constructive change. Treating the patient as a potentially competent, responsible adult is one of the central tenets of the treatment philosophy termed *relationship management* developed by Dawson and MacMillan (1993). They describe the borderline patient's self-concept as a series of dichotomous positions, including good versus bad, strong versus weak, competent versus incompetent, responsible versus irresponsible, and in control versus not in control. This self-concept is context bound in that it shifts from one pole of these dichotomous positions to the other based on the interpersonal context. Thus, in a context in which they are seen as incompetent and not in control, as is the case far too often in their encounters with the mental health profession, borderline patients are likely to act incompetent and not in control. Conversely, if they are treated as competent adults who are in control, they are more likely to act that way.

Another important addition to the management of suicidality in borderline patients is Linehan's dialectical behavior therapy (1993a; Chapter Nine in this book). A key feature of this approach is the delineation of a hierarchy of treatment priorities headed by suicidality. No other issues are addressed until suicidality is no longer in question. This is consistent with the recommendation that psychodynamic therapists advise patients about how suicide-prevention activities endanger their ability to function as agents of growth or change. In addition, in Linehan's model, the reinforcing aspects of self-destructive behavior are minimized by prohibiting contact with the therapist for a set period of time following a self-destructive act. By contrast, contact with the therapist for skills coaching is encouraged prior to acting on self-destructive impulses.

Stone (1993) proposes a kind of primary prevention approach to suicidality that is complementary to the other methods of treatment described here. He focuses attention on several factors that may increase the risk of suicide: aloneness, anger, alcoholism, and antisociality—the so-called Four A's. He encourages patients to feel less alone by strengthening their social skills and work patterns and developing hobbies through individual or group-based occupational and recreational therapy. He suggests that anger can be diminished by therapy focused on developing more harmonious, supportive relationships characterized by realistic expectations and mutuality. Alcoholics Anonymous not only provides an effective treatment for alcoholism, but also may diminish feelings of aloneness and anger through its easily accessible support system. Stone acknowledges that antisociality is seldom directly treatable, but notes that many antisocial men who joined religious organizations that emphasized strict adherence to an acceptable code of behavior made excellent recoveries.

USE OF HOSPITALIZATION

When to hospitalize a chronically suicidal borderline patient is a dilemma that outpatient clinicians commonly face. Part of the dilemma is frequently a wish on the part of the clinician not to gratify the patient's regressive dependent longings or a determination not to be manipulated by the patient. Some have gone so far as to suggest that, if possible, suicidal borderline patients not be hospitalized when they request it, but only when they actively resist it (Goldsmith, Fyer, and Frances, 1990). This approach has several drawbacks, however. First, it deprives the patient of autonomy and undermines the collaborative aspect of the therapeutic relationship. Second, it shames the patient for actively seeking help, resulting in greater self-accusatory preoccupations, with the possible outcome being that the patient seeks relief "outside the system" by engaging in self-destructive behaviors and possibly attempting suicide. Third, it may communicate indirectly to the patient that the clinician alone can and will prevent suicide, quite the opposite of the message that we feel should be conveyed directly to the patient: that the clinician cannot prevent suicide.

Nevertheless, hospitalization is not without risks. Indeed, regression of personality-disordered patients is common on inpatient units. However, it does not follow that all patients with BPD regress in the hospital. Rather than taking a limit-setting approach with borderline patients in regard to hospitalization from the outset, it is preferable to observe whether a pattern of regression develops or whether for any other reason a patient concludes that hospitalizations are not helpful. If so, then clinicians can actively question whether subsequent hospitalizations would be in the patient's best interest.

Clearly hospitalization is neither practical nor indicated at every expression of suicidal ideation. How, then, does a clinician determine when to hospitalize a suicidal borderline patient? When a strong treatment alliance is in place, it is often possible to have a collaborative discussion with the patient, weighing the pros and cons of hospitalization and considering less restrictive and potentially less regressive alternatives, such as a time-limited increase in the frequency of outpatient sessions or the use of day hospital or respite services. However, even with a strong treatment alliance, there are times, particularly following the loss of a primary object, when the patient's thinking becomes too distorted to make true collaboration practical. In these instances, the clinician needs to make a unilateral decision.

The earlier section on assessing risk of suicide provides a starting point for this decision making. Many patients at the third level of functioning (panicked, psychotic, or dissociative in the absence of a primary object) may require hospitalization. This would be the case particularly for patients without a sustaining therapeutic alliance who are actively abusing drugs or alcohol or who have a history of prior suicide attempts, as in the following case example.

Phyllis began an adjunctive treatment with a psychopharmacologist after several years of repeated hospitalizations, often following overdoses of moderate- to high-potential lethality. In the initial sessions, her new psychiatrist emphasized his inability to prevent her suicide, the significant potential for error if he were forced to make unilateral decisions regarding her safety, and his inability to function effectively as her psychiatrist should the pattern of overdoses continue. A collaborative system was developed and functioned effectively until Phyllis's therapist of ten years went on vacation. That week Phyllis presented at her psychiatrist's office with marked psychomotor retardation, flat affect, and a distant, fixed gaze. Her responses to direct questioning were brief and monotonous, and she was unable to engage in a discussion of treatment options. Recognizing that she was most likely in a psychotic or dissociative state, the psychiatrist arranged for Phyllis's hospitalization.

In the session following her discharge, Phyllis thanked her psychiatrist for his intervention. After acknowledging her gratitude, the psychiatrist pointed out the deleterious effects that further unilateral interventions would have on her recovery. The years of treatment that followed were rocky at times, but they were characterized by a progressive decrease in Phyllis's self-destructive behavior without further need for the psychiatrist's unilateral interventions.

Hospitalization may also be indicated for some patients in the second category (angry at a frustrating primary object and engaging in interpersonally directed self-destructive acts). In these cases, hospitalization is used not to actively prevent suicide, but to advance the work of therapy. It may be particularly useful early in treatment to help solidify an alliance (Jacobs, 1992) or later to obtain consultation and work through a "negative therapeutic reaction" (Kernberg, 1984a). Another instance in which it may be necessary is when a more primitive patient engages in a series of escalating parasuicidal acts in order to convey to the therapist the degree of distress he or she is in. When verbal interpretations of this behavior fail to deescalate it, the therapist may be forced to convey behaviorally his or her understanding and caring by hospitalizing the patient. An example of this behavioral dialogue involved a college student named Beth.

Beth entered therapy in a nearly continuous state of perceived suicidal crisis and almost immediately invested her therapist with the role of fantasized rescuer. She ostentatiously displayed evidence of her superficial cutting and frequently ended sessions with threats of elaborate suicide attempts. Beth experienced efforts to help her understand the self-defeating nature of this pattern of relating as rejections. She intensified her self-destructive behaviors and threats and repeatedly insisted that her therapist "pink paper" (involuntarily hospitalize) her. Her therapist refused these requests and indicated to Beth that it was inadvisable for her to judge the depth of his caring by his willingness to comply with a demand that he felt ran counter to her interests.

Beth responded by presenting herself directly to the emergency room following one of her therapy sessions. Admitted to an inpatient unit, she was granted liberal privileges based on her team's assessment of her negligible suicide risk. The following day, Beth ran up to her doctor, displaying fresh superficial cuts on her arms. It was only after her privileges were revoked, thereby behaviorally indicating that her pain was being taken seriously, that the self-destructive behaviors ceased.

Unfortunately, in Beth's case this behavioral dialogue continued to the point that therapy became untenable. In other instances, initial behavioral communication can give way to a useful therapeutic dialogue. In any case, it is crucial to translate behavioral communications explicitly and inform the patient that their continued occurrence will jeopardize the possibility of attaining a psychotherapeutic relationship.

USE OF MEDICATION

The use of medication in the management of patients with borderline personality has become commonplace over the past two decades. Virtually every class of psychotropic medication, including antidepressants, antipsychotics, anticonvulsants, lithium, anxiolytics, and opioid antagonists, has been advocated by one study or another (Soloff, 1993; Davis, Janicak, and Ayd, 1995). The plethora of pharmacological approaches speaks to both the varied and complex array of symptoms presented by borderline patients and the relative ineffectiveness of any one type of medication. Because of the risks that the suicidal borderline patient will misuse or overdose on medication, clinicians must be thoughtful in prescribing them. A few general principles can guide thinking in this area:

1. *Treat comorbid conditions first.* Although many medications have been shown to diminish some symptoms of BPD, there is no evidence that any medication can cause this disorder to remit. By contrast, medications can be highly effective in treating conditions such as major depression or panic disorders. Although there is no direct evidence that such treatment will diminish the risk of completed suicide in borderline patients, the data presented earlier suggesting a higher risk of suicide in borderline patients with comorbid affective disorders provides a compelling rationale for this approach.

2. *Do no harm.* The medication prescribed to alleviate suffering can easily become the means of attempted suicide—manipulative, impulsive, or otherwise. That is not to say that the threat of suicide should dissuade one from providing a potentially helpful treatment, but that the risks of overdose should be considered and discussed with the patient (see principle 5 below) when deciding on the type and amount of medication prescribed. For example, a selective serotonin reuptake inhibitor would be a safer first choice to treat depressive symptoms than a tricyclic antidepressant or a monoamine oxidase inhibitor.

3. *Be realistic.* If medications are prescribed not for a comorbid axis I disorder but for BPD per se, their effect will be limited in ameliorating some of the core features of the disorder. Indeed, intolerance of aloneness, which underlies these patients' suicidal crises, is unlikely to be directly affected by medications to any appreciable degree. Rather, one can hope that when relationships are disrupted, medications might take the edge off the resultant intense affect, delay the impulse to harm oneself, or diminish psychotic or dissociative symptoms. It is important for clinicians not only to acknowledge this but to convey it to patients.

4. *Remember the dynamics.* Medications can have many meanings for the borderline patient, and they are never without significance. On the one hand, medication may be seen as a wonderful gift, an expression of caring and nurturance in an otherwise hostile and unfeeling world. On the other hand, it may be seen as an unwanted, intrusive ploy by a domineering doctor to assert control. Negative feelings about medications can lead to both noncompliance, with resultant worsening of symptoms and increased risk of suicide, and overdose—whether out of anger at the doctor, despair at the ineffectiveness of the treatment, or an attempt to reassert control. Before the patient begins medications, it is important to inquire about his or her feelings toward medication and to reassess them throughout the treatment as one would symptoms and side effects.

5. *Involve the patient.* For the borderline patient, this requires much more than a standard discussion of risks and benefits. Active participation by the patient in decision making must be insisted on. In addition to the benefits to be derived in a general sense from treating the patient as an autonomous, responsible adult, insisting that the patient decide, and not merely consent, to take medication greatly diminishes the gratification to be derived from overdosing on "the doctor's" pills.

FAMILY INTERVENTIONS

Families may inadvertently prompt borderline members to become self-destructive or even to commit suicidal acts. This is due to their usual role as being among the borderline patient's most significant others, a role that ensures major responsibility given the borderline patient's great sensitivity to injury by rejection or separation. Thus, a primary task of mental health professionals is to get the patient's significant family members—parents and spouses most commonly—educated about the issues of particular sensitivity to borderline individuals. Among these issues are separations and hostilities and real or imagined rejections, all likely to be experienced by borderline patients as evidence of being unwanted and evil. This then can precipitate self-destructive responses that serve both to punish oneself and elicit caretaking responses.

When families are informed of their offspring's potential for self-destructive behaviors or their potential to prompt such acts, they often make heroic efforts to prevent this. Here it is an educational task to inform them that unlike their potential to prompt self-destructiveness, they should not believe that they can assume responsibility for preventing such acts. They otherwise may begin an ever-enlarging effort to demonstrate their protectiveness by making it impossible for the borderline family member to hurt himself or herself. Vigilant surveillance may lead to sleepless nights and canceled travel plans. Removing knives or razor blades expands to hiding any sharp objects. Soon the entire family is held hostage by the fear of such acts. This situation is highly gratifying to the borderline patient and harmful to everyone else. The general issue to clarify is that once families begin preventive actions, they are assuming a responsibility that belongs in either the patient's or the professionals' hands. This is not to say that families should ignore dangers like making firearms easily accessible or keeping a well-stocked liquor cabinet when their son or daughter is struggling against relapse.

It is very important that families not ignore evidence of self-destructive behaviors. When they find traces of blood, razor blades placed on the bedstand, or empty liquor bottles, they should identify their fears to the borderline person and not be too quickly reassured by denials. Beyond this, the family members should view such evidences as "cries for help"—communications of a need for caretaking. Thus, the family members should pursue two other lines of communication. First, they should make sure that other family members are aware of the danger and join in addressing the issue. Second, and more important, regardless of whether the patient and even other family members wish to dispel their fears, they should inform and involve professionals. Suicidality cannot safely be assessed, monitored, and prevented within a family. The issue is too complex to assess, and family members are too likely to have personal biases.

COUNTERTRANSFERENCE WITH BPD PATIENTS

Countertransference in work with patients with BPD is often intense, especially in the context of suicidality, where therapist fantasies of being a competent and capable rescuer mix powerfully with feelings of frustration, helplessness, anger, disappointment, devaluation, and hopelessness. Ultimately it can lead to latent or manifest wishes to reject the patient, which may have fatal consequences. Winnicott (1949) wrote frankly of the hateful feelings that difficult patients often evoke in their treaters and argued for the importance of therapists' anticipating and accepting (rather than suppressing) these feelings as essential in managing them therapeutically. With suicidal BPD patients, countertransference is of critical concern because it may lead, if unaddressed, to treaters' behaving in ways that increase the risk of patient suicide.

Countertransference frequently occurs in response to the characteristic defenses of borderline pathology: projection, acting out, splitting, and projective identification. The empathic, earnest efforts of the therapist to establish a mutual working relationship with a borderline patient may unintentionally activate the patient's intense longings for but equally intense terror of closeness. This can lead to intolerable fears and expectations of abandonment, regressive clinging, rageful acting out, and unconscious efforts to externalize inner conflicts in potentially traumatic reenactments. It may play out within the psyche of the therapist, but more typically will manifest in the dynamics of the therapeutic relationship, either in the dyad or as staff splitting in a milieu.

Suicidality can escalate dramatically, as in the case example about Elise, and may be profoundly affected by the countertransferential responses of treaters. Maltsberger and Buie (1974) described the phenomenon of transference-countertransference hate with suicidal patients. They underscored the painful ambivalence about intimacy and trust underlying the suicidal BPD patient's transference hate and frantic efforts to externalize this intolerable hostility onto the therapist using projection and projective identification. These efforts are manifested in various forms of provocative behavior, well targeted toward the therapist's vulnerabilities and designed to elicit confirmatory countertransference hate, which is a mixture of aversion and malice.

These hateful feelings may also be intolerable to the therapist and may be expressed in unconscious and potentially devastating ways toward the patient if the therapist does not acknowledge and address them. The therapist's unconscious countertransference may emerge as therapist self-doubt, giving up on the case, or submitting masochistically to further patient hostility. Inattention to the patient or, conversely, reaction formation and heroic (and regressive) efforts to intervene may also occur. The therapist may reproject the hate back onto the patient, with hostile imposition of repressive controls, denial of real suicidality and insufficient intervention, or premature termination due to "treatment failure." Devaluation of the patient by the therapist may be another nonfeasible manifestation of countertransference hate. Groves (1978) describes the weary aversion, defensive anger, self-doubt, and bland hopelessness that treaters may act out in response to highly dependent, clinging, entitled, help-rejecting, and self-destructive patients. Groves (1978) and Maltsberger and Buie (1974) highlight the danger that unanticipated, unexplored, unacknowledged counter-transference may lead to hostile or abandoning behavior by the therapist. Therapists are usually more concerned about the impact of their hostility. In reality, their unconscious defensive withdrawal from the patient is potentially much more dangerous, confirming the patient's abandonment fears and increasing the risk of suicide.

Countertransference issues with suicidal borderlines are often multiplied in the inpatient or residential treatment setting. Regression is more likely during hospitalization and when several staff are involved, increasing the potential for splitting or for more intense countertransferential responses reinforced by group and staff dynamics. Studies by Kullgren (Kullgren, Renberg, and Jacobsson, 1986; Kullgren, 1988) illustrated the dangers for suicidal BPD patients in these settings. He observed that in-hospital suicide, often in the immediate vicinity of staff, was more characteristic of BPD than of other psychiatric disorders. Staff countertransference reactions leading to repressive and rejecting treatment responses, including mandating patient discharge despite ongoing suicidality and the patient's explicit wishes to remain hospitalized, were very important risk factors for imminent suicide. Significantly, such patients in one study had not been identified as borderline during their hospitalization, and the clinical records did not reveal any awareness of countertransference reactions, highlighting the potentially lethal consequences of failure to recognize and process the dynamics.

Kernberg (1987) also describes the power in the milieu of the patient's projective identification evoking a split in the treatment team and leading to a rejecting reenactment in which there was a "cynical, almost gleeful withdrawal of hospital staff from [the patient] as her treatment gradually fell apart." Gabbard (1989) outlines several strategies for managing countertransference with hospitalized borderlines, beginning with acknowledging its inevitability. He recommends extensively educating staff about the phenomenon and its manifestations, establishing a clinical environment in which staff countertransference feelings are viewed as acceptable and valuable sources of information, and helping staff work toward containment rather than acting out these feelings. He also suggests holding frequent and regular unit staff meetings that include the patient's therapist, and when splitting has occurred, holding meetings with involved staff together with the patient (with a mediating consultant if necessary).

Countertransference is an inevitable part of any therapeutic relationship, and intense positive and negative countertransference responses must be anticipated by therapists who are working with suicidal BPD patients. Countertransference should be suspected when the therapist has reactions to the patient that are unusual in their form or intensity. When they occur, the therapist should work to acknowledge them, contain them, and explore and closely monitor ways they might be affecting the treatment. The therapist must bear in mind that the patient's provocative behaviors are the result of unconscious, dynamic processes and should not take them personally. Particularly in making decisions around treatment parameters, intervention in suicidality, and potential termination, the therapist should carefully weigh emotional and intuitive reactions in the light of specific clinical evidence. Consultation should be considered, using care to do so in a way that does not unduly escalate the patient's abandonment fears. Finally, the therapist should strive to maintain a steady, consistent, empathic, non-reactive, objective stance with the patient, setting limits when appropriate based on clinical evidence. This will maximize the patient's safety and, over time, allow the patient, as Maltsberger and Buie (1974) say, to "acknowledge his transference . . . learn to bear the intensity of his craving and rage, and put them into perspective . . . exchange his impossible narcissistic dreams for real relationships once he finds their fulfillment is not necessary for survival . . . as he internalizes his therapist as a good object, tried and tested through the fire . . . and found trustworthy."

IMPLICATIONS FOR THE CLINICIAN

- Suicidality in borderline patients is extremely common; completed suicides are far less frequent.

- The risk of completed suicide diminishes over time without correlation to suicidal ideation.

- Although it is possible to identify retrospectively risk factors for completed suicide, they have little, if any, predictive power for the individual patient.

- Borderline patients are at greatest risk for serious self-destructive acts when they are panicked due to the absence of a primary object.

- Both a strict limit setting and an unquestioningly supportive approach to suicidality are problematic; active therapeutic interventions can be safely provided, but only if accompanied by clarification, interpretations, and explicit questioning.

- Treating the patient as a responsible adult is likely to result in his or her more responsible behavior.

- Hospitalization is most clearly indicated for patients with a prior history of suicide attempts who are abusing drugs or alcohol in the context of the absence of a primary object and the lack of a strong therapeutic alliance.

- Medications are primarily effective in treating comorbid axis I disorders but may play a modest role in ameliorating some of the symptoms of BPD that contribute to suicide risk.

- Family members should be educated about how to respond to issues of particular sensitivity to borderline individuals, including separation, hostilities, and real or imagined rejections.

- If countertransference reactions, ranging from hatred to rescue fantasies, are unacknowledged and unaddressed, they can lead to treaters' behaving in ways that increase the risk of patient suicide. Consultation, in certain situations, should be considered.

CHAPTER NINETEEN

Trauma and Suicide

James A. Chu, M.D.

Exposure to traumatic events is quite common: the lifetime prevalence of exposure to serious traumatic experiences for persons in the general population in the United States is greater than 50 percent (Kessler, Sonnega, Bromet, Hughes, and Nelson, 1995; Breslau, Davis, Andreski, and Peterson, 1991; Resnick et al., 1993). Such experiences include wartime combat, physical or sexual assault, psychological terror, accidents and natural disasters, and other kinds of exposure to shocking or terrorizing events. Catastrophic events can overwhelm human beings' ability to cope and result in a variety of post-traumatic responses. If the traumatization is severe, prolonged, or occurs early in life, post-traumatic stress disorder (PTSD) and dissociative disorders are likely to develop. One large recent study estimated the lifetime prevalence of PTSD in the general population at 7.8 percent (Kessler, Sonnega, Bromet, Hughes, and Nelson, 1995).

THE LEGACY OF CHRONIC TRAUMATIZATION

The nature and severity of the traumatic events influence the development of psychiatric sequelae. Post-traumatic responses to brief or single overwhelming events in an otherwise intact person tend to be less severe and shorter in dura-

Portions of this chapter are adapted from Chu, 1998.

tion. Persistent and disabling trauma-related responses are seen usually only in those who have been exposed to particularly severe or chronic traumatization. The most severe post-traumatic and dissociative disorders result from certain types of prolonged childhood abuse, chronic combat experiences, and long-term battering relationships. In particular, severe childhood abuse can result in sequelae in the form of a variety of post-traumatic responses and alterations in personality development. Furthermore, since the innate capacity to use dissociative defenses is greatest in childhood (Bernstein and Putnam, 1986; Saunders and Giolas, 1991), traumatized and abused children are at most risk for developing severe dissociative disorders, including dissociative identity disorder. Given the ongoing high prevalence of child maltreatment (more than 1.5 million documented cases per year, according to the U.S. Department of Health and Human Services, 1996), it is not surprising that PTSD and dissociative disorders seen in many acute care settings are most frequently due to severe and persistent childhood traumatization.

Survivors of chronic traumatization are often highly symptomatic. Clinical observations and studies since the 1970s have shown that childhood traumatization can be associated with a wide variety of psychiatric syndromes, including PTSD symptoms (Coons, Cole, Pellow, and Milstein, 1990; Donaldson and Gardner, 1985; Ulman, 1988), dissociative disorders (Bernstein and Putnam, 1986; Ross et al., 1991; Braun, 1990; Chu and Dill, 1990; Kirby, Chu, and Dill, 1993; Saxe et al., 1993), severe personality disorders (Goldman, D'Angelo, DeMaso, and Mezzacappa, 1992; Herman, Perry, and van der Kolk, 1989; Ludolph et al., 1990; Ogata et al., 1990; Westen, Ludolph, Misle, Ruffins, and Block, 1990; Zanarini, Gunderson, and Marino, 1987), substance abuse (Kessler, Sonnega, Bromet, Hughes, and Nelson, 1995; National Victim Center, 1992; Loftus, Polonsky, and Fullilove, 1994) and eating disorders (Welch and Fairburn, 1994; Hall, Tice, Beresford, Wooley, and Hall, 1986), as well as difficulties such as generalized depression and anxiety, emotional lability, impaired self-esteem, social withdrawal, and self-destructive behavior (Bryer, Nelson, Miller, and Krol, 1987; Finkelhor, 1984; Herman, Russell, and Trocki, 1986; Russell, 1986; Shapiro, 1987; Swanson and Biaggo, 1985). Not surprisingly, many traumatized patients with these complex symptoms are suicidal. Many have attempted suicide or made suicidal gestures, and a substantial proportion have chronic suicidal ideation and impulses.

Persons who have been chronically maltreated in childhood often have two fundamental traits—profound mistrust and self-hate—that place them at substantial risk of suicide. Many investigators and clinicians have described the difficulties that impair the relational capacity of chronically traumatized patients (Russell, 1986; Chu, 1992; Briere and Runtz, 1987; Browne and Finkelhor, 1986a; Courtois, 1979; Finkelhor and Browne, 1985; Herman, 1981; Meiselman, 1978). Having been repeatedly victimized, they remain wary—mistrustful of alliances and unable to obtain support and reassurance from others. Janoff-Bulman (1992) has written about the shattered assumptions of trauma survivors. While most people hold basic assumptions about the world as benevolent and meaningful, and about themselves as worthwhile, severely traumatized persons assume that their interpersonal world will mirror their abusive past experiences (p. 86): "The traumatic experience is apt to become fully incorporated into the child's inner world. . . . These children are apt to have negative assumptions in all domains, for core beliefs are less likely to be disentangled at an early age. The trust and optimism, the sense of safety and security, the feeling of relative invulnerability that are afforded the person with positively based assumptions are absent in the psychological world of these children. Instead, their world is largely one of anxiety, threat, and distrust."

Traumatized children remain dependent on their caretakers and hence often are unable to blame their abusers for their maltreatment. Instead, they blame themselves for somehow causing the abuse and for not being good enough. As Shengold (1989) notes:

> If the child must turn to the very parent who inflicts the abuse and who is felt as bad for relief of the distress that the parent has caused, then the child must break with what has been experienced, and out of a desperate need for rescue, must register the parent, *delusionally,* as good. Only the mental image of a good parent who will rescue can help the child deal with the terrifying intensity of fear and rage that is the effect of the tormenting experiences. . . . The absolute need for good mothering makes the child believe in the promise that her parents . . . will be good and rescue her, and to believe that she herself must be bad [pp. 26–28].

Paradoxically, this sense of responsibility for the abuse gives many abused children the illusion of control. They feel as though they somehow caused the abuse, and if they could only be "good," the abuse would stop (Summit, 1983). This belief system evolves into a basic sense of self as defective and unlovable, and leads to persistent self-hate (Gelinas, 1983). It is this self-hate that underlies much of the suicidal behavior of traumatized patients. Particularly following the loss of an important interpersonal connection, they are left alone with their self-hate and unable to access the supportive alliances that might sustain them. They then turn to destruction of the self as the most immediate relief of their intolerable distress. As Maltsberger (1988) notes, "Most commonly, suicide-vulnerable people depend on others to feel real, to feel separate, to keep reasonably calm, and to feel reasonably valuable. The loss or threatened loss of such a sustaining other can lead to an explosion of aloneness, murderous fury, and self-contempt" (p. 51).

SILENT CRIES: PARASUICIDAL BEHAVIOR

Self-destructive acts that are not primarily intended to result in death are commonly called parasuicidal. Such self-harming behavior is extremely common among patients with histories of childhood abuse, and although the behavior may appear bizarre, it has its origins in the assumptions of traumatized patients and the paradox they experience concerning self-care. Learning self-care is an essential step in the treatment of traumatized patients, but most persons who have been victims of early abuse have a very debased sense of self as worthless and defective and have little awareness of the need to care for the self. Traumatized patients often fail to attend to basic care for their physical health. Furthermore, adults who suffered early abuse, particularly those who were physically or sexually abused, have little sense of ownership of their own bodies. Patients often describe a type of detachment concerning their bodies: "I know that somehow this body belongs to me, but it doesn't feel like my body." On looking in the mirror, they sometimes feel as though they are seeing a stranger. Most of the feelings that traumatized patients have about their bodies are pejorative—echoes of what they were told and how they were treated: "bad," "ugly," "fat," "disgusting," "cheap."

Meanings of Self-Harming Behavior

An extremely destructive paradigm in abusive families is that the victimized child's mind and body are available for exploitation. Thus, adult impulses that derive from feelings such as rage or sexual tension are vented on the child. Hence, it is not surprising that when these children become adults, they use themselves, particularly their bodies, in order to relieve tension or act out impulses that often result in self-harm. This tendency to use one's body as a vehicle for tension release is heightened by the relational disturbances that derive from the abusive early environment. When distressed, most humans seek connection with others in order to feel understood and to obtain comfort. This outlet is unavailable to many abuse survivors, since their cries for help have been met with either further abuse or, at best, indifference, and they have learned to avoid human connection.

Self-cutting is common among psychiatric patients, particularly in adolescents (DiClemente, Ponton, and Hartley, 1991), eating disorder patients (Favazza, DeRosario, and Conteiro, 1989), and dissociative disorder patients (Putnam, Guroff, Silberman, Barban, and Post, 1986). Repetitive self-cutting has been associated with histories of childhood sexual abuse (Shapiro, 1987; Himber, 1994; Briere and Runtz, 1988; van der Kolk, Perry, and Herman, 1991; Wise, 1989) and is the most common kind of self-harm seen in adolescents and adults with backgrounds of childhood abuse. (For further discussion of self-mutilation, see Chapter

Eight in this book.) Either superficial or deep cuts to the arms, abdomen, breasts, genitals, legs, throat, or face (in approximate decreasing order of frequency) are repetitively used as tension-reducing mechanisms. There are a variety of similarly destructive behaviors that seem to be variants on this behavior, including burning or abrading the skin; repetitive banging of the hands, arms, head, or feet; swallowing objects such as razor blades, glass, pieces of metal, or caustic substances; inserting objects or foreign bodies into body orifices or actually into the flesh or veins; and washing, douching, or self-administering enemas with caustic substances or painfully hot water. This kind of self-harming behavior is widespread among patients who experience explosive inner tensions and cannot access support from others. In most cases, these self-harmful activities are considered to be parasuicidal and not truly attempts to kill or endanger the self, as in the following example:

> A young woman with the diagnoses of PTSD and borderline personality disorder was admitted to the hospital because she was unable to curb her self-destructive behavior. For many years when she was upset or angry, the patient had swallowed various objects, including fragments of glass and pieces of aluminum soda cans. She generally reported that this behavior was calming to her, and she repeatedly denied suicidal intent. However, the dangerousness of the patient's behavior escalated, and she began swallowing broken-up razor blades, necessitating frequent medical attention, and she appeared to be unable to control this behavior. Despite being under close observation in the hospital, the patient managed to find a pin. Immediately after swallowing the pin, she became quite concerned that she might suffer serious harm and confessed her behavior to the nursing staff. The on-call physician examined the patient and obtained X rays and confirmed that a pin was apparently in her small intestine. He concluded that it was likely that the pin would be pulled through the digestive tract by its head and would most probably pass without serious injury. The patient was not reassured and remained quite tearful and panicky that she would be harmed.

Many self-harming behaviors have the immediate relief of tension as the primary gain. Patients use self-cutting to induce a pleasurable state or at least a kind of numbness, or to end painful dissociated states (Himber, 1994; Grunebaum and Klerman, 1967). Most patients' parasuicidal behavior is stereotyped and consistent over time; that is, most patients seem to choose specific forms of behavior, for example, cutting in specific places with specific kinds of sharp objects. There is often very little pain associated with the cutting. Prior to cutting or other similar behavior, patients often describe experiencing an intolerable sense of inner tension, such as anxiety, dysphoric dissociative states, or anger, which is immediately alleviated after the self-harmful behavior. Patients report that it is often the visualization of blood that results in the feeling of relief from tension (Himber, 1994). Thus, these repetitive self-harming acts are remarkably prompt and effective solutions for self-soothing in patients who have difficulty in obtaining comfort or support from others.

In addition to tension relief, self-cutting and other similar behaviors demonstrate patients' deep-seated sense of defectiveness and self-hate. Some patients report needing to "get the bad blood" out or the impulse to cut out something bad from inside them (Himber, 1994; Grunebaum and Klerman, 1967). Although repetitive self-cutting results in temporary psychological relief, it almost always is associated with shame and secrecy. Patients are generally quite aware that self-cutting is considered abnormal and that others tend to react to this behavior with horror and disgust. Some patients also describe their cutting as compulsive and out of control, leading to increased feelings of shame.

Nonlethal self-cutting or similar behavior has also been described as a nonverbal communication of distress. Kernberg (1968, 1984b) has interpreted some self-harming behavior as attempts to discharge anger at the therapist, and others have emphasized the motivation to manipulate others, gain attention, or deal with threatened loss (Grunebaum and Klerman, 1967). Some traumatized patients do seem to harm themselves for these reasons, particularly in situations of acute distress and explosive anger. When cutting occurs in the context of relational disconnection over feeling abandoned, ungratified, or misunderstood, it may convey messages such as: "This shows you how angry I am!" "*Now* do you take me seriously?" or "See what you made me do?" However, the central intent of self-harmful behavior is not always about attempts to communicate with others. Much self-cutting begins as an inarticulate cry of pain from patients who have no words to describe their distress adequately and feel repeatedly unheard and unseen. Self-cutting often originates as a solitary act that occurs when patients feel intensely alone, absorbed in their distress, and without a conscious intent to communicate or manipulate, and only later sometimes has the role of nonverbal communication.

Therapeutic Responses to Self-Harming Behavior

When a patient reveals self-harming behavior in the context of a therapeutic relationship, it may indeed convey unspoken messages. Revealing self-injury is a mute cry for help, but it often has conflicting messages and is easily misunderstood. There is a nonverbal communication of, "Do you see how much I hurt?" as well as an almost defiant statement of, "Don't you see how different I am from other people, and how I don't need help from anyone else?"

A clinician is in a difficult position in terms of knowing how to respond. A response of only concern or sympathy is gratifying for the patient, who then feels heard, but little is gained in terms of promoting direct or verbal communication. A response that ignores or minimizes the behavior results in the patient's feeling alone and unheard. A response of disgust, frustration, or anger (especially when the behavior is in violation of a therapeutic safety contract) inevitably provokes shame and a confirmation of defectiveness, and it sets into motion the abuse-related scenario of the patient's feeling guilty, as though he or she has been "bad" and deserves punishment. Perhaps the best response in these situations is one that avoids any tone of being shocked or angry, and expresses concern and interest along with a gentle confrontation concerning the dysfunctional aspects of the behavior: "I can see that you have been in a great deal of pain, and I would like to learn more about your cutting and what leads to it. I am sorry that you have not found another way to let me or other people know about your pain, and that you have had to continue to do something that interferes with your ability to grow and heal."

There should also be an assessment concerning the lethality or dangerousness of any parasuicidal behavior. Parasuicidal behavior may not be intended to result in suicide, but particularly dangerous behavior (such as deep cutting or swallowing caustic substances) may inadvertently inflict serious harm that leads to death. Even in the absence of suicidal intent, there may be a risk of death, permanent physical harm, blood loss, and serious infection, which may mandate referral to a physician for ongoing monitoring and treatment. For patients who require frequent medical evaluation for self-harming behaviors, it is almost always helpful to have the regular involvement of a physician, even when the primary clinician is a psychiatrist.

It is important to make the distinction between establishing safety and totally stopping self-harmful behavior. Some patients with childhood histories of neglect and trauma cannot completely extinguish parasuicidal behavior until they develop or restore basic abilities to engage productively with others. However, establishing an alliance about the goal of progressively stopping self-harm is essential. As in the treatment of addictive behaviors, slips and relapses are common, and a sustained commitment to the ultimate goal of abstinence is the most important part of successful treatment. Using an addictions model of treatment, self-harmful behavior should never be regarded moralistically, but as a maladaptive effort at coping that has negative consequences. The patient must supply the primary motivation to control the behavior, although it should be acknowledged that the patient requires considerable support. As noted by Himber:

> Establishing an alliance around safety proceeds hand-in-hand with the development of understanding and communication. Although stopping self-cutting is a final goal of treatment, there are useful intermediate steps. If the patient cannot agree to stop cutting, can she identify and agree to goals which will help her recover? Some patients may disavow the seriousness of their behavior or the shame and fear associated with it, insisting that "it's no big deal," not suicidal, and not worth paying attention to. This can set the stage for a struggle between the patient and the therapist. In such struggles, the patient projects her distress

and anxiety about self-harmful behavior onto the therapist, and then both attacks and devalues the therapist's interventions. As the patient acts less and less concerned about cutting the therapist may become more and more alarmed and the struggle can escalate. It is important to keep the focus on the patient's responsibility for her own safety and to name her attempts to disavow her own distress [1994, pp. 629–630].

Clinicians must be extremely careful not to take on one side of this ambivalence (the "good" side), which allows the patient to feel less conflicted about the self-harmful behavior. Clinicians should provide expert counseling and empathic support but must make it clear that the patient carries the primary responsibility for his or her own behavior and for changing the behavior. The following case illustrates some of the dilemmas and the negotiations concerning the treatment of repetitive parasuicidal behavior.

A thirty-five-year-old mother of two was admitted to the hospital for depression and suicidal ideation. She reported a twenty-year history of repetitive self-cutting, and although she had no major medical problems related to this behavior, both of her forearms were crisscrossed with hundreds of small scars and more recent open and healing wounds. Despite several years of therapy, the patient was making little progress, which she attributed to her own sense of hopelessness and helplessness and to her outpatient therapist: "She just listens and doesn't actually *do* anything." In regard to her self-cutting, she reported that she cut for a variety of reasons, but mostly when she felt intense despair, anger, or aloneness. The cutting numbed these feelings.

Her outpatient therapist was aware of the cutting, and the patient knew that she was uncomfortable about it and wanted it to stop. A number of safety contracts had been established, but she continued to cut somewhat defiantly: "She wants me to stop, but it's my body, and she doesn't understand how much I need it."

The patient's hospital case manager asked about details of the cutting and the circumstances under which it occurred. She underscored both the adaptive role of the cutting and its impact on the patient's life: "I know that cutting has been very helpful to you over the years in coping with intolerable feelings and circumstances. You know that I and your therapist think that you need to find more adaptive ways to express your feelings and move on in your treatment. However, only *you* can decide when and how you are ready to stop cutting. Rather than placing the responsibility on your therapist to make you stop cutting, you should remember that the cutting makes you feel ashamed and out of control at times and has interfered with your treatment."

After considerable discussion, the patient agreed to try to find ways to stop the self-cutting. She used a number of grounding techniques to try to control dysphoric dissociative states and followed through with a plan to try to seek out others when she had the impulse to cut. When she had the irresistible impulse to cut, she instead used a technique of rubbing her forearms with an ice cube, which produced a numbing sensation that reduced the need to hurt herself. Finally, the patient devised a personal and unique solution. Using wooden beads from a craft kit, she painted the name of one of her children on each of two large beads, which she then fashioned into bracelets. Subsequently, when she looked at her arms for a place to cut, she would see the bracelets and recall that she had made a commitment to herself and her family to try to stabilize her life. This proved effective and she was able to stop cutting for the first time in decades.

Two weeks after discharge from the hospital, the outpatient therapist noticed fresh wounds on her arms. The patient shamefully admitted, "Well, I guess I've been forgetting to wear the bracelets." The patient and her therapist were then able to discuss the patient's motivation as being essential in controlling the self-cutting and were able to devise a successful new strategy for addressing this issue in the context of her treatment.

SUICIDE INTERVENTION WITH SEVERELY TRAUMATIZED PATIENTS

The danger of suicide is a complication in the early stages of treating severely traumatized patients. Many patients who have survived extensive early abuse have made suicide gestures or attempts, and nearly all such patients chronically contemplate suicide as a potential relief from their intolerable experiences. The general principles of suicide assessment that are described elsewhere in this book should be respected. In addition, the management of suicide risk in traumatized patients should take into account the following additional principles:

1. Suicidal impulses and behavior must be distinguished from para-suicidal behaviors such as self-cutting or other self-harming behaviors.

2. Clinicians must insist that the threat (or implied threat) of suicide or self-harm not be used as a form of communication or negotiation.

3. Clinicians and patients must agree that the real possibility of suicide constitutes a crisis situation and that any and all interventions may be used in that situation.

4. Although both clinicians and patients together may cooperate in determining the risk of suicide, clinicians may have to act unilaterally to preserve patients' lives and well-being.

These principles are central to managing chronic suicidal threat and are necessary for both patients and clinicians. They must not be compromised, and clear limits must be set concerning any violation of these principles. Interpersonal conflict and struggle are often inherent features of treatment, as the abuse-related dynamics of early experiences are recapitulated in the therapeutic relationship. It is a far safer therapeutic strategy to set clear limits concerning the principles about suicide from the outset and to permit conflict and negotiation to occur in other less lethal areas. Without patients' agreement on these principles, treatment may well be therapeutically untenable, with little hope for a positive outcome, and there is clearly a greater likelihood of stalemate or even death through completed suicide.

The distinction between suicidal and parasuicidal behavior is determined best by direct discussions with patients regarding the motivations and goals of their behavior. Patients are often able to be quite clear about the lack of suicidal intent in certain self-harming activities. However, there are often areas of ambiguity, such as patients who hurt themselves in ways that might or might not be lethal or in behavior that is not intended to be suicidal but might result in serious injury or death, for example, frequent driving while intoxicated. Because of the possible extreme consequences of this kind of ambivalent behavior, clinicians may be placed in the position of acting to safeguard patients' well-being (such as involuntary hospitalization) if there is substantial evidence of imminent danger to self or others

Patients' hints or threats about suicide can be a form of communication, manipulation, or negotiation. Statements such as, "I'm not sure I can keep myself from hurting myself," can be a disguised way of asking, "Do you recognize that I am in pain and feel desperate?" or "What will you do for me if I don't kill myself?" If clinicians sense some underlying message from such statements, they should confront the implied message directly and ask if the patient is trying to communicate the intent to commit suicide or some other message. Once the issue is raised, the burden is on patients to clarify the underlying message in their statements, because unresolved questions concerning suicide are likely to result in hospitalization or other unwelcome outcomes. Such frank and direct discussions about suicide can serve as a deterrent against self-endangering behavior. If patients and clinicians fail to discuss these issues directly, suicidal behavior may actually increase. For example, the patient who says, "I've been thinking about killing myself," as a way of asking, "Do you care about me?" may actually feel impelled to act if the underlying implied question is not clarified and the patient feels disappointed or upset by the therapist's response.

Assessing Ambivalence Concerning Suicide

Many traumatized patients have intense internal conflict about being alive and are ambivalent about suicide. After all, most of those who unambivalently wish to die have already successfully killed themselves. When patients cannot tolerate the pain of their own intense conflicts, clinicians may find themselves assuming one side of the ambivalent feelings—once again, usually the "good" or positive side. Unfortunately, this sometimes allows patients to be unambivalently negative about this complex issue. Clinicians and patients may find themselves in conflict over the issues involving actual survival rather than understanding both sides of the issue as the projections of the patient's intrapsychic conflict, as in the following example:

A thirty-six-year-old married mother of three children began therapy with the goal of wanting to feel "less tortured." She began to describe fragments of memory that suggested extremely severe physical, sexual, and emotional abuse in a chaotic childhood family environment. As therapy continued, she became progressively more aware of the extent of her abuse and overwhelmed by feelings of depression, despair, and loneliness. Her preoccupation with death and suicidal impulses increased. In therapy, the patient reported that she could no longer be responsible for her personal safety and that the therapist had to "hold the hope" for her. This resulted in many discussions in which the patient would argue that her life had become a constant torment and that the therapist should understand and allow her to kill herself. The therapist would then counter with reasons that she should live, including hopes for the future and the value of her life for herself and her family. All such arguments were rejected by the patient as false reassurances, and the therapist became increasingly anxious that she might suicide. Finally, following consultation with a colleague, the therapist said, "I understand that you wish to die and that life is a torment for you. However, you may be oversimplifying the situation. I think you have very mixed feelings about living. Although much of you desperately wishes to die, a small part of you has hope that life might get better. You know that *I* want you to live, but it is much more important for *you* to know that you both want to die and still have some hope to live. I cannot convince you to live, but I can help you sit with the uncomfortable feelings about not knowing what to do." After some discussion, the patient acknowledged the validity of these observations, and the therapy then continued in a more stable manner.

In emergency or crisis situations a clinician may need to assume the responsibility for the patient's safety temporarily, such as invoking involuntary hospitalization when the patient is unable to commit to safety. However, any such stance should be temporary. The treatment itself is untenable unless the patient assumes the burden of working out conflictual feelings about living, with the acknowledgment that the patient has the ultimate responsibility for his or her life.

Some commitment to remain alive should be a prerequisite for therapy. This simple principle is often overlooked by desperately tortured patients and their well-intended therapists. Patients often may be so filled with their own pain that they ignore the fact that they have a fundamental responsibility in any relationship: they must be alive to participate in the relationship, and being alive is a prerequisite for expecting that anyone else will make a commitment to them. Clinicians may be afraid to bring up this issue because of the principle that therapists should not let any of their own feelings contaminate the therapy. However, all relationships, including the therapeutic relationship, depends on the most basic contract: that both parties agree to make a commitment to continue working together. Thus, another effective intervention is often the therapist's interpreting suicide as an abandonment of the relationship: "I understand that you have many reasons to want to die. However, do you recall that you have often asked me to make a commitment to you? I am glad to make a commitment for the foreseeable future, but it is only fair to ask that you do the same: by making some commitment to remaining alive. I have no wish to take away your ultimate control of the decision to live, but I do want you to make a decision for now not to destroy our relationship."

Using Safety Contracts

Agreements that the patient will not commit suicide, so-called safety contracts or no-suicide contracts, present complex issues and are addressed in detail in Chapter Twenty-Six in this book. They are useful for patients who have a rather rigid personal moral code and are able to make a commitment of having to adhere to their promises (for example, "I always keep my word"). They are less effective in patients with significant sociopathic character traits. The most effective safety contracts are made face to face with direct eye contact and with therapists' sensing a sincerity (although often with reluctance on the patient's part) about the agreement. Safety contracts that are sincerely entered into by appropriate patients can be very effective, relieving both clinicians' anxiety and patients' grappling with ambivalence about lethal behavior. Even in the face of trauma-related symptoms, including frequent shifts in affective states and sense of identity, and dissociative amnestic barriers, safety contracts can be maintained by patients who are willing to remain committed to keeping their word.

Virtually all safety contracts also have limitations. For example, it is almost impossible to devise a formal safety contract without loopholes, and patients may adhere to the letter of the agreement while finding ways to violate the substance of the agreement (for example, "I said I wouldn't overdose, but I didn't agree not to drive my car off the road," or "I agreed to be safe until our next appointment, but you rescheduled it"). As a further limitation, safety contracts are usually time limited because few patients can agree to long-term or indefinite contracts not to attempt suicide; to do so compromises their sense of control. Safety contracts must be renewed at agreed-on intervals, and any failure to do so will be seen by the patient as an invitation to engage in self-endangering behavior.

An adolescent girl with a history of severe childhood abuse had made several serious suicide attempts within just a few years. She began working with a therapist, who helped her decrease her self-destructive behavior by making weekly safety contracts on a session-by-session basis. The patient and her therapist took these contracts very seriously, establishing detailed provisions in the contracts about not only the time period of the contracts but various prohibitions against all sorts of self-harming and risk-taking behaviors. Following a session approximately eighteen months into the therapy, the therapist suddenly recalled that she had received an emergency telephone call near the end of the session and had neglected to renew the safety contract. After some thought, she decided that enough trust had developed in the relationship and that a continued safety contract was clearly implied, and she did not act further. The patient, on the other hand, was acutely aware of the failure to renew the safety contract and was convinced that this was a sign that the therapist had finally gotten tired of her and would not mind if she killed herself. She overdosed on all her medication and was subsequently rushed to an emergency room after being found by her roommate.

Although safety contracts are frequently used, the patient's commitment to continue to struggle to stay alive is much more important. As with safety contracts, this commitment to live must be repeatedly discussed and reaffirmed.

Coping with Suicidal Impulses

Coping with both acute and chronic suicidal impulses is a difficult task for traumatized patients, even for those who are committed to remaining alive. Many of the strategies for getting through periods of intense impulses to commit suicide do not differ from those used with other psychiatric difficulties and are discussed elsewhere in this book. Traumatized patients should become particularly adept at self-soothing, distracting themselves from suicidal impulses, and grounding themselves when overwhelmed by intense post-traumatic or dissociative symptomatology. Many patients need to develop a crisis plan for periods when they are particularly overwhelmed. This type of crisis plan consists of a list of interventions that might be useful—for example, calling friends, taking a walk or exercising, reading or watching television, having a warm bath, contacting treating clinicians, calling hot lines, or using emergency services. The success of a crisis plan is dependent on the patient's working on it prior to any major crisis and refining it as they become more adept at coping with their impulses.

Patients who experience post-traumatic and dissociative symptoms must learn strategies that help them maintain contact with current reality, rather than remaining in a state where they reexperience trauma and the feelings of helplessness and despair that bring on suicidal impulses. Most of these strategies fall into the category of grounding techniques (Benham, 1995; Chu, 1998). One of the most basic strategies for effective grounding is to maintain adequate lighting. Patients should be encouraged not to sit in dark or dimly lit environments when they feel anxious and vulnerable to reexperiencing trauma. Seeking "safety" in dark and confined places only facilitates dissociative processes through the lack of visual cues, and actually makes patients more vulnerable to the intrusion of thoughts, feelings, and events associated with past traumatic experiences.

In an interpersonal situation, eye contact is enormously grounding. Many crisis situations have been resolved simply by clinicians' being quietly and firmly directive, asking patients to look at them and to make eye contact. Visual or bodily contact with familiar objects (such as clothing, jewelry, furniture, stuffed animals, or pets) can help remind patients about their current reality. In treatment settings, clinicians can also remind patients that they are in the present (as opposed to being immersed in a past traumatic event) and in a safe place. Using grounding techniques in an office or hospital setting provides the opportunity to learn more about the internal emotional events that precede loss of control. Flashbacks and state switches are experienced as happening abruptly and unpredictably, without any warning. However, careful monitoring of emotional states often shows that dysphoric post-traumatic or dissociative states are often preceded by certain specific kinds of internal emotional states that escape the awareness of most patients. Practicing grounding in a treatment setting offers an opportunity to learn about these internal states and to make interventions before becoming truly overwhelmed.

Managing Crises with Suicidal Patients

Emergency interventions are required in situations where there is risk of actual suicide. Too often, clinicians feel that they are not permitted to use usual and important interventions. Clinicians should never agree to relinquish critical therapeutic options—for example, agreeing never to hospitalize the patient ("I'll just be put into restraints and be retraumatized"), always to discuss all options beforehand ("I'll never be able to trust you again"), or never to contact family members ("I'll never live it down"). It is usually preferable to discuss matters with patients and to respect their wishes, but a possible imminent suicide is an emergency situation that may require extraordinary measures. Such measures may be necessary to save the patient's life, even at the cost of destroying an ongoing therapeutic relationship.

No matter how skilled a clinician may be or how well managed the therapy, there is always the possibility of broken contracts, accidental death when suicide was not intended, and completed suicides. Fortunately, the number of completed suicides is small relative to how common self-harmful behavior and chronic suicidal impulses are in severely traumatized patients. There are situations where there is a serious breach of the substance or spirit of agreements concerning safety. If the patient survives, the clinician needs to consider several options. Is the clinician willing to continue the treatment? A chaotic and anxiety-provoking treatment places considerable burdens on the clinician, and clinicians need to consider whether they are able and willing to continue. Clinicians should be truly candid with themselves about this issue; both the patient's and clinician's well-being depends on it. Too often, clinicians convince themselves that they can continue to treat very anxiety-provoking patients and then subtly act out their frustrations and anger, much to the detriment of the treatment. Consultation is frequently useful in deciding whether to continue to work with an out-of-control suicidal patient. Consultation may be particularly necessary when a decision is made to terminate with a patient to order to help the clinician work through the timing of the termination, address issues of professional responsibility, and avoid abruptly abandoning the patient.

If clinicians are able and willing to continue, they should determine what basic requirements must be met by the patient—for example, agreements concerning safety, impulsive behavior, outside supports, or attitudes—and then ask the patient to meet these requirements as a condition to continuing the therapy. A serious suicide attempt is a major breach of the therapeutic relationship, and it is then incumbent on the patient to demonstrate a willingness to heal the rupture in order for the therapy to continue. When this process is successfully negotiated, patients may find new ways to work in alliance with their clinicians and to make a commitment to continue living.

COUNTERTRANSFERENCE RESPONSES TO SUICIDAL TRAUMA PATIENTS

Countertransference responses in the treatment of traumatized patients are quite complex for therapists. One particular difficulty has been called *vicarious* or *secondary traumatization* (Pearlman and Saakvitne, 1995), in which a therapist's benevolent assumptions about the world are disrupted by exposure to information about the brutality, callousness, sadism, and malevolence that characterize some childhood abuse. Therapists may suffer from shock, disbelief, confusion, and even a pervasive sense of their own vulnerability, and they must then struggle to regain their own sense of safety and stability. Such reactions are common, and clinicians generally use their own interpersonal supports to regain their equilibrium. Fortunately, most clinicians are able to adjust to unpleasant and even horrifying knowledge, integrate such information, and reinstate some healthy perspective and denial in rebuilding a new and workable set of assumptions about the world.

Overidentification

Overidentification with patients, overprotection of patients, and fascination and voyeurism concerning patients and their traumatic histories are also common countertransference difficulties (Chu, 1992; Kluft, 1989; Chu, 1994). However, the most common countertransference problem in working with traumatized patients may be unacknowledged therapist discomfort. The level of involvement necessary with traumatized patients, the recapitulation of abusive interpersonal dynamics, and frequent crises place significant emotional strains on therapists. Many patients are chronically suicidal as they wrestle with intolerable conflicts and unbearable experiences, and they have numerous regressions in which they are unable to take responsibility for themselves or control their actions. In addition, the narcissistic preoccupation of patients, who sometimes seem aware of only their own internal pain, makes them frequently unaware of or indifferent to the impact of their actions on others. The sometimes extraordinary efforts that therapists exert on behalf of their patients over extended periods may not even be acknowledged, leaving therapists feeling that their experience is disregarded or invalidated.

Ongoing risk of suicide or even direct threats of suicide leave therapists with considerable anxiety and confusion. Therapists frequently find it difficult to acknowledge the extent of their own frustration, discomfort, and anger with both the therapeutic process and with patients themselves. Instead, it is usually much more ego syntonic to acknowledge only compassion for the patients' pain and sympathy concerning their past traumatization. Moreover, many patients mold therapists' responses, giving the message not to be upset, frustrated, or angry. Patients fear that the all-important and sustaining interpersonal therapeutic bond would not withstand the therapist's discomfort or anger. Many traumatized patients have experienced anger as out of control and destructive, and they fear any manifestation of therapists' discomfort in the therapy. Therapists often oblige in an unintentional collusion with patients by not acknowledging their dysphoric feelings, even to themselves.

Anger

Manifestations of unacknowledged therapist discomfort, frustration, and anger vary considerably. Few therapists are overtly hostile, but many find themselves becoming avoidant, neglectful, or distant—for example, by failing to follow through with commitments, forgetting appointments, being consistently late to appointments, interrupting sessions to take telephone calls, or scheduling appointments in an erratic or unpredictable manner. Therapists commonly express countertransference discomfort through the use of reaction formation. Rather than acknowledging frustration or angry feelings about patients, they become extremely worried and concerned about patients, redoubling their efforts to protect patients. This type of response is detrimental to the therapy, as therapists avoid bringing up issues that might upset patients and become so overprotective that patients cannot grow and develop psychologically. The overprotective stance is very painful for therapists who feel anxious, enmeshed, and burdened, as in the following example.

A respected therapist worked with a patient who had been profoundly neglected and humiliated throughout childhood by both her parents. The therapist treated the patient for several years, during which there were many crises, usually precipitated by the patient's feeling alone, misunderstood, abandoned, or mal-treated. During these crises, the patient would talk about suicide, take small overdoses of medication, and place herself in dangerous circumstances. In addition, the patient was quite controlling concerning the therapist's responses, often asking, "You're not angry with me, are you?" or "You won't leave me, will you?" with the implied threat of suicide if the therapist responded incorrectly.

The therapist progressively found himself becoming so anxious that he worried constantly about the patient. His sleep was disrupted, and he began to have episodes of stomach pains. He agreed to frequent emergency appointments and even called the patient several additional times a week to make sure she was safe. The therapist finally consulted a trusted colleague, and he found himself highly anxious and tearful as he began to describe his fears about the possibility of the patient's committing suicide. He first denied feeling anger, but after clarifying how he was being controlled and manipulated, he admitted, "I've sometimes wished she would just go away."

After discussing his concerns and acknowledging his anger, the therapist was able to confront the patient gently about the nature of the therapy, reassuring her of his wish to help her but setting reasonable limits concerning her behavior and clarifying his expectations of her active participation in finding ways not to hurt herself. After a period of intense turmoil, the therapy become much more stable and contained. The therapist's overall level of anxiety and sleep returned to normal.

Therapists experience the most painful form of countertransference reactions when they cannot acknowledge their countertransference anger and actually project their own anger and sadism onto their patients. To the therapist, the patient then becomes a seemingly real and substantial threat. The therapist may sometimes develop a mild form of PTSD, complete with unwanted intrusive thoughts, nightmares and disturbed sleep, avoidant and numbing responses, and even startle responses (such as to the ring of the telephone that might be the patient calling). In these situations, the therapist feels acutely threatened by the patient and may dread sessions or other interactions. Furthermore, the therapist feels that he or she cannot abandon (escape from) the patient, and feels helpless to make any kind of positive change in the therapy. This kind of reaction is often a recapitulation of the patient's unresolved early abuse. In response to patients' cues, therapists become involved in enmeshed relationships in which they are highly emotionally invested and from which they feel they cannot exit. They experience dysphoria, anxiety, and despair, and they feel limited in their options. Thus, they have assumed the position of the abused child in a reenactment of the abuse. It is essential for therapists with this type of dilemma to address these issues directly, first in consultation with colleagues and then with patients. The reenactment must be understood and interpreted, with patients and therapists returning to mutually respectful and collaborative stances.

Ongoing professional consultation and education and personal supportive relationships are an essential part of working with traumatized patients who chronically struggle with suicide. Given the episodic crises, the intensity of the therapeutic relationship, the slow pace of treatment, and the real possibility of suicide (even if the therapist exercises maximal skill), there is often little gratification and considerable stress for therapists. Especially when therapists feel the stress of intense and enmeshed therapeutic relationships, they must practice what they preach: interpersonal connection and support are essential parts of human experience and necessary in times of difficulty. After all, traumatized patients are often very astute in observing their therapists, and they look to see how their therapists cope with stress. Therapists' ability to tolerate stress and resolve dilemmas can become a model for how patients can resolve relational impasses.

TRAUMA-RELATED COMORBIDITY AND SUICIDE RISK

Comorbidity of post-traumatic disorders and other *DSM-IV* disorders is extremely common, with a number of studies showing that additional diagnoses can be made in 60 percent or more of patients with trauma-related disorders (Kessler, Sonnega, Bromet, Hughes, and Nelson, 1995; Breslau, Davis, Andreski, and Peterson, 1991; Kulka et al., 1990; Shore, Vollmer, and Tatum, 1989). These findings may make sense in that symptoms of trauma-related disorders are similar to the features of other conditions. Hence, trauma-related disorders have sometimes been described as umbrella disorders, because a wide variety of symptoms may be understood as part of a traumatically based syndrome. For example, the intense dysphoria, emotional constriction, and social withdrawal of PTSD can be similar to symptoms of depressive disorders. The illusions of post-traumatic flashbacks, auditory hallucinations, and thought insertion associated with severe dissociative disorders are easily confused with psychosis (Chu and Dill, 1990; Kluft, 1987). One large national study (Kessler, Sonnega, Bromet, Hughes, and Nelson, 1995) found that traumatic events often preceded the development of other axis I disorders, suggesting that the post-traumatic disorders are often primary umbrella disorders.

The differential diagnosis of post-traumatic disorders from other disorders can be difficult. Brief assessments of patients may fail to distinguish between traumatized patients and those with more biologically oriented mood or psychotic disorders; longitudinal and sophisticated evaluations may be necessary for patients who present with complex symptoms. Nevertheless, such differential diagnosis is critical, for in situations where there is true comorbidity (that is, two or more disorders, and not simply one disorder mimicking another), there may be substantial increased suicide potential. Untreated major depression or psychosis along with trauma-related difficulties may result in patients' experiencing very intense distress and lead them to seek suicide as a relief from their pain. Moreover, although most traumatized patients seem to have some ambivalence about suicide, some severely depressed or psychotic patients are determined to end their lives.

The presentation of true comorbidity of a trauma-related disorder and a mood or psychotic disorder may be misleading. Often the patient will present with pronounced post-traumatic symptoms rather than clear evidence of the other disorder. One hypothesis for this type of clinical presentation is that since PTSD and dissociative disorders are stress-responsive syndromes, the onset of another disorder, such as a mood or psychotic disorder, results in more stress, thus increasing post-traumatic symptoms. In nearly all situations in which there is this type of true comorbidity of axis I disorders, the trauma-related disorder has secondary importance in the hierarchy of treatment. That is, any acute mood disorder or psychosis should be treated prior to embarking on treatment for the post-traumatic or dissociative disorder, as illustrated in the following case example.

A fifty-three-year-old single woman was admitted to a psychiatric hospital with florid PTSD symptoms and strong suicidal impulses. She had continuous intrusive thoughts about well-documented physical and sexual abuse that occurred when she was abandoned as a child and raised in a series of foster homes and institutions. She was particularly fearful after nightfall, having flashbacks of her early abuse and seeing images of menacing figures outside her window. A closer examination of her symptoms suggested that the patient was suffering from a major depression with psychotic features. She showed extreme psychomotor retardation, barely moving from her bed or chair, had sustained a recent twenty-pound weight loss, and spoke of feeling that her "insides" were decaying and wanting to die.

A brief course of electroconvulsive treatment, followed by medication, brought about a substantial change. She recompensated with dramatic improvement in her mood and PTSD symptoms. Although she still reported thinking about her early abuse, the thoughts did not overly disturb her. She was not suicidal and was able to return to her previous level of functioning.

Some axis I disorders may offer ways of coping with the dysphoria of post-traumatic conditions, and there is considerable comorbidity with substance abuse disorders (Kessler, Sonnega, Bromet, Hughes, and Nelson, 1995; National Victim Center, 1992; Loftus, Polonsky, and Fullilove, 1994), eating disorders (Welch and Fairburn, 1994; Hall, Tice, Beresford, Wooley, and Hall, 1986), and somatization disorders (Barsky, Wool, Barnett, and Cleary, 1994; Morrison, 1989; Pribor and Dinwiddie, 1992; Pribor, Yutzy, Dean, and Wetzel, 1993). The psychological numbing of intoxication transiently eases the distress of post-traumatic numbing and intrusion and may mask awareness of disturbing symptoms such as amnesia or state switches. Additionally, intoxication offers an opportunity for persons for release of tension by acting out intense feelings related to traumatic events. Eating and somatization disorders provide arenas in which persons can take the focus away from past distressing events and can structure their lives around preoccupation with bodily concerns.

In situations where these disorders are flagrantly out of control, they may pose substantial risk of injury or death. Risky behaviors while intoxicated can be the cause of accidental death. Severe substance abuse or restricted eating can be a form of slow suicide. Unrelenting somatization, to the extent of patients' undergoing multiple unnecessary medical procedures, can also result in injury, disability, or even death. When substance abuse, eating disorder behaviors, or somatic concerns become patients' primary preoccupation, they should be the primary focus of treatment, rather than futilely attempting to address trauma-related difficulties, as in the following example:

> The patient, an engaging thirty-two-year-old woman, was hospitalized for treatment of her dissociative identity disorder, which was seemingly out of control. Her therapist reported that the patient had escalated her drug use over the past several years, with an alternate personality periodically taking executive control, buying and using drugs, including heroin. The patient's body showed signs of serious self-neglect. She was painfully thin as a result of poor nutrition, her menses were irregular and infrequent, and she was HIV positive but had not yet developed symptoms of AIDS. In the hospital, the patient was seemingly unconcerned about her substance abuse, saying, *"I don't do drugs, an alter does them, and I can't stop her. I don't like to take even aspirin. I need to work on my trauma issues."* The astute inpatient staff recognized the presentation as a primary substance abuse disorder and the patient's lack of concern as a form of denial (albeit with dissociative features). They insisted she address the dangerousness of her behavior and strongly recommended traditional substance abuse treatment rather than a trauma-based treatment program. She was transferred to a dual diagnosis unit and subsequently discharged to a sober house.

PSYCHOPHARMACOLOGY FOR TRAUMA-RELATED DISORDERS

A variety of psychotropic medications have been proposed as effective treatments for trauma-related disorders. Antidepressants have been the agents most investigated in the treatment of PTSD. Studies have shown efficacy of monamine oxidase inhibitors (MAOI) (Kosten, 1992), tricyclic antidepressants (Kosten, 1992; Reist et al., 1989; Davidson et al., 1990; Davidson et al., 1993) and selective serotonin reuptake inhibitors (Nagy, Morgan, Southwick, and Charney, 1993; Klein, 1994; Davidson, Roth, and Newman, 1991; van der Kolk et al., 1994). Studies with PTSD patients also suggest that anticonvulsants (Lipper et al., 1986; Wolf,

Alavi, and Mosnaim, 1988; Fesler, 1991), propranolol (Famularo, Kinscherff, and Fenton, 1988; Kolb, Burris, and Griffiths, 1984), and clonidine (Kolb, Burris, and Griffiths, 1984; Kinzie and Leung, 1989) may be helpful. One open trial suggests that use of clonazepam, a benzodiazepine, is useful for control of post-traumatic symptoms in dissociative identity disorder (Loewenstein, Hornstein, and Farber, 1988). However, the use of medication in dissociative disorders has been less systematically studied than their use in PTSD, and there is a general consensus that psychotherapy rather than medication is the primary therapeutic intervention (Putnam, 1989; Ross, 1989). Despite the evidence from the investigations, the usefulness of medications for the treatment of trauma-related disorders remains unclear. A number of these studies were not controlled, and most investigated specific traumatized populations, such as combat veterans.

Many patients with trauma-related disorders have significant dysphoria, mood lability, disturbed sleep, and hyperarousal that do not readily respond to antidepressant treatment. In practical clinical experience, however, antidepressants frequently are used for PTSD and dissociative disorders even in the absence of a clear comorbid major depression. Although these agents rarely eliminate depressed mood and dysphoria, some increase in energy is seen with the use of activating tricyclic antidepressants such as nortriptyline and desipramine, the MAO inhibitors, or the selective serotonin reuptake inhibitors. Similarly, benzodiazepines often are used for the panic attacks and chronic anxiety commonly seen in trauma-related problems. However, benzodiazepines should be used acutely rather than routinely, reducing the risks of tolerance and habituation, and they may disinhibit destructive impulses and behavioral dyscontrol. Disturbed sleep also is quite common in traumatized patients. Patients are likely to be fearful of going to sleep and often wake up repeatedly with high anxiety or nightmares or both. Benzodiazepines are usually of limited effectiveness because most patients develop tolerance over time. Trazodone, a sedating antidepressant, has been used in doses of 50 mg to 200 mg. Zolpidem (Ambien), the nonbenzodiazepine hypnotic, may also be effective and has a reduced risk of habituation.

Some patients are so overwhelmed by constant flashbacks, intense dysphoria, and intrusive thoughts that they appear to benefit from the use of low-dose neuroleptic medications (Saporta and Case, 1984). Decisions concerning whether antipsychotic medication should be continued on a long-term basis should be carefully reviewed with the patient, considering effects on mental alertness, cognitive abilities, and the risk of tardive dyskinesia. The newer generation of antipsychotic medications may offer some of the advantages of neuroleptics with fewer anticholinergic and Parkinsonian side effects (and perhaps less risk of tardive dyskinesia). Recent clinical experience with risperidone, given as a single bedtime dose of 0.5 mg to 3 mg, has beneficial effects for some patients with post-traumatic conditions; it appears to help with sleep and to reduce chronic anxiety on the following day.

The use of medications in trauma-related disorders is common. In fact, because many medications seem to do some good (although they usually do not eliminate symptoms), the use of multiple medications can easily occur. The benefits of medications are clear in reducing dysphoria and the risk of suicide due to overwhelming symptomatology. However, the benefits must be balanced against the risks of polypharmacy, adverse side effects, addiction and habituation, and suicide. Many of the commonly used psychotropic medications are extremely dangerous in overdose (such as the tricyclic antidepressants), and almost all are potentially lethal in combination. Thus, medications must be used cautiously in trauma patients, who are often both chronically and acutely suicidal. In order for medications to be used safely, psychiatrists and other clinicians must exercise good judgment in prescribing and be aware of how patients are using or misusing them.

IMPLICATIONS FOR THE CLINICIAN

Traumatic disorders in the form of PTSD and dissociative disorders are common in psychiatric patients. Many patients with these disorders, particularly those exposed to ongoing and severe abuse in childhood, have a more chronic clinical course and are likely to have acute and chronic suicidal impulses. Severely traumatized patients frequently have parasuicidal behaviors as well, often with chronic self-harming behaviors that reduce internal tension and that serve as nonverbal communication about their self-hate and intense distress. Clinicians must be astute in distinguishing between suicidal and parasuicidal behaviors through direct and candid discussions with patients and assist them in developing coping mechanisms and finding words for their distress. The treatment of suicidal traumatized patients can be complex and challenging. The basic tenets of traditional treatment are essential for sound treatment, and interventions concerning suicidal impulses are essential in helping these troubled patients through repetitive periods of potential decompensation and danger. The treatment often may be long and difficult, punctuated by periods of crisis and risk. A treatment that combines caring, patience, and commitment with skilled differential diagnosis, assessment of suicide risk, psychotherapy, and psychopharmacology offers the best hope for helping suicidal traumatized patients survive, grow, and thrive.

- Suicidal feelings and impulses are often quite complex, and a part of the treatment of suicidal traumatized patients involves helping them understand their ambivalence about living and bearing the ultimate responsibility for staying alive.
- Safety contracts can be useful for some patients as part of a crisis plan that helps them distract themselves, soothe themselves, and ground themselves.

- A crisis plan is an integral part of dealing with suicidal feelings and impulses and must be well planned, rehearsed, and revised as the treatment proceeds. Clinicians must feel free to act in times of emergency involving suicidal patients and must not be constrained by unwise prior agreements.

- In situations where there is potential for serious self-harm or suicide, clinicians must have the ability to use all appropriate interventions, even if the cost is a disruption of the therapeutic relationship.

- In the aftermath of any serious suicide attempt, all efforts should be made to address the issue of the alliance and the patient's responsibility to work on maintaining a commitment to living. Consultation is often very useful and important, particularly if a clinician is unsure of whether to continue in the treatment after such a major breach of the therapeutic contract.

- Countertransference difficulties, particularly unconscious or unexpressed clinician frustration or anger, are common in treating suicidal traumatized patients. Clinicians must deal with their own feelings directly rather than letting themselves become involved in destructive reactions such as anxiety, self-doubt, acting out, or projection. Consultation and interpersonal supports are often essential to understanding and resolving intense countertransference responses.

- Comorbidity is common in traumatized patients, with many traumatized patients having considerable anxiety and depression as a result of their experiences and symptomatology. Clinicians must be able to identify major comorbid conditions over and above those that are due to the trauma-related disorders. Major mood disorders and psychoses, as well as serious addictive problems, eating disorders, and somatization, must all be addressed as a priority in treatment before actively working on trauma issues.

- Psychopharmacologic interventions may be helpful, although there is not clear evidence of substantial benefit from medications for resolution of the dysphoria and dissociation associated with trauma-related disorders. Various medications, including antidepressants, benzodiazepines, and neuroleptics, may have value in appropriate clinical situations. The newer generation of antipsychotic medications may have promise when used in lower dosages for the autonomic hyperarousal, poor sleep, and chronic anxiety of trauma-related symptoms. The benefits of medication must be balanced against their adverse affects and their potential use as self-destructive agents.

CHAPTER TWENTY

Antisuicidal Effect of Lithium Treatment in Major Mood Disorders

Ross J. Baldessarini, M.D., D.Sc. (hon.)
Leonardo Tondo, M.D.

The melancholic person . . . conceives an intense hatred against his own existence. . . . He usually becomes restless, gloomy, silent and inclined to sigh; he sleeps little and is agitated; he runs away from society . . . and he constantly tries to take his own life, looking all over for deadly tools, imploring people around him to kill him or to help him to achieve death. In a word, everything indicates a more or less suppressed furor against himself and explains the effects of an excessive desperation which is the consequence of a sad passion carried to the extreme degree of intensity.
—Chiarugi, *Della Pazzia, in Genere e in Specie (On Insanity and Its Classification)* [1793] (1987)

There have been major advances in the clinical and epidemiological understanding of suicidal behavior and risk factors in recent decades (Jacobs and Brown, 1989). The ominous association of the depressive phases of major affective disorders with enhanced suicidal risk in persons of all ages—from pediatric to geriatric populations—is now indisputable (Taube and Barrett, 1985; Faedda et al., 1995; Baldessarini et al., 1996c). In bipolar disorders, suicide may account for up to 25 percent of deaths (Goodwin and Jamison, 1990; Tondo et al., 1997, 1998a). These rates may be even greater than in recurrent unipolar major depression (Taube and Barrett, 1985; Roy, 1984, 1989b). Additional excess mortality has been ascribed to highly prevalent comorbid substance abuse as well as cardiovascular and other medical disorders (Angst et al., 1990). All of

This work was supported by NIH Career Investigator Award MH-47370 and grants from the Bruce J. Anderson Foundation and by the Private Donor Neuropharmacology Research Fund at the McLean Laboratories for Psychiatric Research (R.J.B.), as well as by awards from NARSAD, the Theodore and Vada Stanley Foundation, the Harvard Suicide Foundation, and the Italian National Research Council (L.T.). Material summarized in this chapter is based, in part, on research reported in detail elsewhere (Tondo et al., 1997, 1998a).

these causes of premature death may be related to the impact of sustained stress that is inherent in recurrent major mood disorders.

In both unipolar and bipolar forms of depression, and at all ages, appropriate diagnosis and treatment, even now, are attained by only a minority of persons affected with these highly prevalent, often lethal, but eminently treatable major medical disorders (Keller et al., 1986; McCombs et al., 1990; Baldessarini et al., 1996c). Contemporary estimates place lifetime morbid risks for recurrent major depression above 10 percent, and for bipolar disorders, at not less than 1.6 percent (Kessler et al., 1994), and probably over 2 percent if type II bipolar syndromes (depression with hypomania) are included (Tondo et al., 1998b). Annual economic costs of bipolar disorder in the United States were recently estimated to be $45 billion, with at least $8 billion accounted for by direct (treatment) and indirect costs (income losses associated with premature death) ascribed to suicide alone (Wyatt and Henter, 1995). Similar economic costs have been ascribed to major depression (Greenberg et al., 1993b).

Despite the enormous clinical, public health, and economic impact of suicide, remarkably little is known about the specific effects of mood-altering treatments on suicidal behavior that might contribute to its rational prevention or clinical management in persons with major mood disorders (Goodwin and Jamison, 1990; Tondo et al., 1997, 1998b). Available research on suicide prevention through treatment interventions has not yet developed sufficiently to guide either public health policy or clinical practice (Gunell and Frankel, 1994). Although it is plausible to expect that effective treatment and clinical management of depressed or bipolar disorder patients should reduce short-term suicidal risk for individual persons, the proposition that treatment interventions can limit long-term suicide risk is not proved (Gunell and Frankel, 1994). Moreover, specific beneficial effects of otherwise effective antidepressant treatments on suicidal behavior, with the possible exception of electroconvulsive treatment (ECT), have been difficult to demonstrate (Avery and Winokur, 1977; Teicher et al., 1993). It seems particularly ironic that even though bipolar depression is strongly associated with suicide, this syndrome has been systematically excluded from most contemporary studies on antidepressant treatment (Zornberg and Pope, 1993; Baldessarini, 1996). The introduction of safer modern antidepressant medicines has not led to demonstrated reductions in suicide rates in at-risk populations, and their wider use may be associated with a shift toward means of self-destruction more lethal than acute overdoses of antidepressants (Freemantle et al., 1994; Ohberg et al., 1995).

Ethical conflicts arise when fatality is a potential outcome of research, as in the withholding or removal of treatment targeted against clinical conditions, particularly depression or dysphoric manic-depressive states, in which suicide may occur. It follows that controlled prospective studies of the prevention of suicide in depressed or bipolar disorder patients by medical interventions are rare (Goodwin and Jamison, 1990). The problem is further complicated by emerging recognition of high risks of recurrences of mania or depression after discontinuing maintenance treatments with lithium (Baldessarini et al., 1996a, 1996b), antidepressants (Viguera et al., 1997), and other psychotropic agents (Baldessarini et al., 1996a; Viguera et al., 1998).

Despite the many limitations to research on the therapeutics of suicide, some encouraging and enlightening information does exist. This chapter considers previously reported and newly emerging evidence from the research literature that lithium has a strong, and possibly unique, protective effect against suicidal behavior in persons with major affective disorders, and particularly in bipolar forms of manic-depressive illness. In addition, to evaluate relationships between treatment with lithium and suicidal behaviors, a large series of type I and II bipolar manic-depressive patients followed in a collaborating, university-affiliated, mood disorders research clinic were studied for risk of life-threatening acts before, during, and after lithium maintenance treatment.

PREVIOUS STUDIES OF LITHIUM AND SUICIDE

By computerized literature searches and considering references cited in reports so identified, we found twenty-eight studies from the period 1974 to 1997 that included data to permit estimating rates (percentage per year) of suicide attempts or fatalities in persons with major affective illnesses who were treated with lithium. Much of this literature has been reviewed previously (Crundwell, 1994; Tondo et al., 1996, 1997). Of the reports found, thirteen permitted direct comparisons of risks with and without lithium maintenance treatment under matched conditions of diagnosis, follow-up, and assessment; the twenty-two reports that provide data on suicidal rates on lithium are summarized in Table 20.1.

Before summarizing the findings, it is important to emphasize that conclusions derived from this body of data need to be considered cautiously, since many of the reports have substantial limitations (Tondo et al., 1997). These include the following:

1. Many studies follow the original, broad concept of *manic-depressive* illness proposed by Kraepelin (1921) and do not consider unipolar recurrent depressive and bipolar manic-depressive cases, or their subtypes I and II, separately.

2. Suicidal acts are included with a range of severity and potential mortality that is not always specified.

3. Several studies lack direct comparisons of subjects with and without lithium treatment or make comparisons to standardized mortality rates (SMR).

4. Several involve limited numbers of subjects or times at risk in the face of relatively infrequent suicide attempts.

Table 20.1. Summary of Studies of Lithium and Rates (Percentage of Cases per Year) of Suicidal Acts in Major Affective Disorders.

Study	Diagnoses	N	Risk Type	Time (years)	Rates (percentage of cases per year)	
					Lithium	No Lithium
Prien et al. (1974)	BP + UP	327	Deaths	2.0	0.000	0.306
Bech et al. (1976)	MAD	74	Deaths	6.0	0.386	(NA)
Kay and Petterson (1977)	BP	187	Deaths	≤11.0	0.000	0.721
Glen et al. (1979)	BP	784	Deaths	≤9.6	0.186	(NA)
Venkoba-Rao et al. (1988)	MAD	47	Attempts	ca. 8.5	0.000	0.501
Lepkifker et al. (1985)	UP	33	Attempts	8.3	0.000	2.556
Jamison (1986)	MAD	9,000	Deaths	(NA)	0.044	(NA)
Schou and Weeke (1988)	BP + UP	2,640	Deaths	ca. 1.0	0.341	3.137[a]
Nilsson and Axelsson (1990)	MAD	37	Attempts	7.0	0.000	(NA)
Coppen et al. (1991)	MAD	103	Attempts	11.0	0.000	(NA)
Vestargaard and Aagaard (1991)	MAD	133	Deaths	5.0	1.353	(NA)
Modestin and Schwartzenbach (1992a)	MAD	64	Deaths	12.1	0.000	(NA)
Müller-Oerlinghausen et al. (1992)	MAD	68	Attempts + deaths	8.0	1.471	2.022
Rihmer et al. (1993)	BP I & II	36	Attempts	7.2	0.386	5.482
Coppen (1994)	MAD	103	Deaths	16.0	0.066	0.910
Felber and Kyber (1994)	MAD	36	Deaths	7.1	0.404	1.158[b]
Lenz (1994)	MAD	265	Deaths	>0.5	0.194	0.856
Müller-Oerlinghausen (1994)	MAD	394	Deaths	14.2	0.125	(NA)
Ahrens et al. (1995)	MAD	827	Deaths	6.75	0.125	(NA)
Nilsson (1995)	MAD	362	Deaths	14.2	0.184	0.812
Thies-Flechtner et al. (1996)	BP + SA	378	Deaths	2.5	0.000	1.905[c]
Tondo et al. (1997b)	BP I & II	310	Attempts	14.6	0.355	2.752
Summary (22 reports)		16,208	Suicidal acts	ca. 8.22	0.255	1.778
				± 4.53	± 0.403	± 1.444
Apparent risk reduction						6.97 = fold

Note: Many studies include various major affective disorders, lack direct comparisons with persons not treated with lithium, and vary in their inclusion of all suicide attempts or only fatalities. These crude risk estimates suggest an overall lowering of risk of suicidal acts or deaths of about 1.78/0.25 = 7.1-fold (*t* = 3.73) [34 df *p* < 0.001]. All twenty-two of these studies with quantitative data favored lithium, either by providing direct comparisons without lithium treatment or by yielding relatively low risk rates compared to results from studies that included untreated patients; nevertheless, the average rate of suicidal acts of about 0.25 percent per year suggests substantial, but incomplete, protection during treatment with lithium.

BP = bipolar I or II; MAD = major affective disorders; NA = data not reported; SA = schizoaffective disorders; UP = recurrent unipolar major depression.

[a]Risk without lithium is uncorrected for time-at-risk.

[b]When all attempts were included, the difference was 8.74 times as much.

[c]Treated without lithium but with carbamazepine or amitriptyline and antipsychotic agents.

5. Adherence to prescribed treatment is sometimes not verified, such as with assays of circulating concentrations of lithium.

6. Possible confounding effects of the presumed stress of discontinuing treatment usually are not considered.

Despite these methodological limitations, all thirteen studies providing direct numerical comparisons of suicidal rates with and without lithium maintenance treatment consistently found annual rates of suicidal behavior to be substantially lower during maintenance treatment with lithium (Table 20.1). Nine other studies provided information only on the frequency of suicidal behavior during lithium treatment, but their rates (averaging 0.247 percent per year) were far lower than in the thirteen other studies providing rates for subjects not receiving lithium (1.78 percent per year). Although there are risks in combining data across such diagnostically and methodologically heterogeneous studies, the findings are quite consistent. The rate of suicide attempts or deaths with lithium treatment averaged ($\pm$ SD) 0.255 $\pm$ 0.403 percent of subjects per year with lithium treatment in twenty-two studies, compared with 1.78 $\pm$ 1.44 percent per year without lithium treatment in thirteen of the reports (Table 20.1). This sevenfold difference is highly statistically significant ($p < 0.001$). However, the sustained annual risk of 0.255 percent indicates that protection by lithium is not complete.

In addition to the studies summarized in Table 20.1, six other reports also contain information pertinent to the effects of lithium on suicidal behavior in persons with a major mood disorder. Five of these studies support the view that lithium has antisuicidal effects. These reports include an early study by Barraclough (1972), who found approximately 21 percent fewer suicides during follow-up with lithium maintenance among an undefined number of persons at risk, followed for unspecified periods. Similarly, Poole et al. (1978) followed a hundred patients with major affective disorders for unspecified times before and during lithium, and found about a twofold lower rate of suicidal acts with lithium treatment. Weeke (1979) also found suggestive evidence of a lower risk of suicides during lithium maintenance treatment, but did not provide details about diagnoses and duration of follow-up. Hanus and Zalpetálek (1984) found about six times fewer suicidal acts during lithium treatment than without it in ninety-five mixed bipolar and recurrent unipolar disorder patients followed for more than five years. Roy (1984) found a similar effect, with about two times fewer suicidal acts with lithium treatment in twenty-six patients with various major affective disorders, followed for an unspecified time.

Among the twenty-eight studies reviewed, only one failed to find evidence for a protective action of lithium against suicide: Norton and Whalley (1984) reported that suicide rates in nearly 800 patients with major affective disorders were 48.5 times above those expected in the general population; however, they provided no direct comparisons to untreated affectively ill persons. Such direct comparisons may be an important consideration, particularly in evaluating risks for events of infrequent occurrence. For example, even though at least two other studies summarized in Table 20.1 found rates of suicidal behavior above those expected in a general population standardized for age and sex, they both found relatively low rates of suicidal behavior during lithium treatment (Vestergaard and Aagaard, 1991; Ahrens et al., 1995). Without systematic treatment, suicide rates among persons with major affective disorders have been reported to be twenty-nine to seventy-eight times higher than general population rates, and would be even higher if all suicidal acts were included and, presumably, if persons with mood disorders in the general population were excluded (Goodwin and Jamison, 1990). Based on the data summarized in Table 20.1, these rates can be estimated at seven times lower, or, evidently, about 4.1 to 11 percent above rates in the general population, even with lithium maintenance treatment, thus further indicating that protection by lithium is imperfect.

The results just summarized strongly indicate substantial protection against suicide attempts and fatalities with long-term lithium treatment in patients with a variety of severe, recurrent mood disorders. However, this protection appears to be far from complete. This imperfect protection may reflect either limitations of the treatment itself or inconsistent adherence to treatment recommendations. It is not clear whether its evident antisuicidal benefit merely reflects the well-established mood-stabilizing effect of lithium or whether it represents a distinct action on suicidal and perhaps other aggressive behaviors (Wickham and Reed, 1977; Suppes et al., 1993; Baldessarini et al., 1996c; Tondo et al., 1997, 1998a).

Moreover, it should not be assumed that all antimanic and possibly mood-stabilizing agents provide protection against suicidal behavior similar to that found with lithium treatment. For example, in a recent study by Thies-Flechtner and her colleagues (1996) cited in Table 20.1, carbamazepine treatment was associated with suicidal behavior in approximately 2 percent of bipolar or schizoaffective disorder patients who had not been discontinued from lithium (B. Müller-Oerlinghausen, letter to R.J.B., May 1997). A similar rate was also found among patients with recurrent unipolar depression who were maintained with amitriptyline and a neuroleptic. In contrast, there were no suicidal acts among bipolar and schizoaffective disorder patients maintained on lithium in the same study. This unsettling observation requires additional study. Indeed, the effects of various proposed alternatives to lithium maintenance treatment require proof of long-term effectiveness against bipolar depression and suicidal behavior as well as against mania. If the antisuicidal effects of lithium are not shared with other mood-altering agents, this may be due to the cerebral serotonin-enhancing properties of lithium, properties that are not known to be associated with anticonvulsants (Baldessarini, 1996; Baldessarini et al., 1996c; Cappiello et al., 1997).

NEW RESEARCH FINDINGS

We recently carried out an extensive clinical study of life-threatening suicidal acts over time in 310 *DSM-IV* bipolar I (186) and II (124) disorder patients who were evaluated, treated, and followed at the collaborating Lucio Bini mood disorders research clinic in Cagliari, Sardinia. Suicidal events were recorded during observation before and during clinically indicated and medically appropriate treatment. Changes in treatment, and particularly lithium discontinuation, occurred clinically. They were never investigator-initiated for research purposes for obvious ethical reasons pertaining to suicide as a potential outcome. Moreover, the potential morbid risks for early emergence of mania or depression after discontinuing lithium—particularly abruptly or rapidly—had not been well documented until recently (Suppes et al., 1991, 1993; Faedda et al., 1995; Baldessarini et al., 1996a, 1996b). Despite the clinical nature of the data analyzed, the methods employed for clinical assessment and data gathering and recording have been of research quality since the founding of the clinic in the 1970s. Subjects provided informed consent for anonymous use of their clinical records for research.

A Summary of Clinical Data

The 310 bipolar disorder patient-subjects, including 198 (63.9 percent) women and 112 (36.1 percent) men, were at risk over an average of 8.28 ± 8.38 years from the onset of bipolar illness at age averaging ($\pm$ SD) twenty-nine $\pm$ twelve years (range, twelve to sixty-six years) to the start of lithium maintenance treatment. During this period, subjects included for study had been given clinically indicated short-term treatment with antidepressants, antipsychotics, lithium, or other mood-stabilizing agents, but only during acute periods of illness and for not more than three months at a time (a condition of subject selection also required for medicines other than lithium during lithium maintenance). Subjects were followed prospectively thereafter during 6.36 ± 4.98 years of lithium maintenance treatment, and 128 of the subjects also were followed prospectively for an average of 3.70 ± 3.72 years after discontinuing lithium. Discontinuation was medically recommended for clinical indications (typically for adverse effects or pregnancy) or represented a unilateral decision by the patient to stop without medical consultation. Serum lithium concentrations averaged 0.62 ± 0.13 mEq/L, consistent with standard international practice, which is generally conservative and concerned with optimizing compliance (Maj et al., 1986; Coppen, 1994). Suicidal acts were defined as life-threatening and potentially fatal but for timely medical intervention, or as fatal; fatalities prior to lithium treatment could not be included in order to meet the study requirement of evaluating patients before versus during lithium maintenance.

Overall, a total of ninety life-threatening suicidal acts occurred among 58 of the 310 patients; two of those during lithium treatment and six after discontinuing lithium were fatal. In the 8.28 years before regular lithium treatment had been initiated, the rate of life-threatening suicidal acts was 2.34 per one hundred patient-years. The majority of suicide attempts arose early in the illness, and 53 percent of the sixty acts occurring before the start of lithium maintenance treatment arose within the first five years of illness (median latency = 4.79 years from illness onset; see Figure 20.1 and Table 20.2), a period in which 55.5 percent of the 310 subjects-at-risk had not yet entered regular lithium main-

Figure 20.1. Temporal Distribution of Risk for Suicidal Acts.

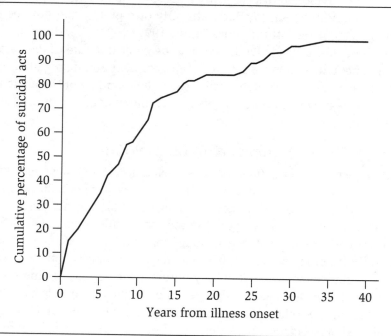

Note: The figure shows the temporal distribution of risk for all ninety reported life-threatening acts among the 310 Sardinian bipolar I and II disorder subjects, at risk for up to forty-three years from the onset of illness. Half of the suicidal acts occurred within the first eight years. The time from illness onset to the start of lithium maintenance treatment in the same population averaged 8.28 ± 8.38 years, thus indicating that much of the suicide risk occurred early and prior to sustained lithium treatment. Suicidal acts often led to sustained treatment. Times to first suicidal acts and latency-to-lithium treatment were closely correlated ($r = 0.93$), with suicidal acts slightly preceding treatment (slope = 0.90). Disparity between suicidal behavior and regular treatment with lithium was particularly marked in the first year of illness, when 22.1 percent of sixty first-lifetime suicidal acts occurred, whereas only 9.6 percent of the patients received lithium maintenance treatment. Nearly three-quarters of initial suicidal acts preceded lithium treatment (Table 20.2). Time-to-lithium maintenance ranked as follows: women > men and bipolar II > I subtype (each factor was independently significant; both $F > 4.0$, $p < 0.05$), thus suggesting relative underrecognition of bipolarity in depressed patients (particularly women), as well as earlier intervention in aggressive or antisocial behavior in manic men.

tenance treatment (Figure 20.1). Suicide attempts also occurred at relatively youthful ages averaging 33.3 ± 12.8 years, although younger onset age was not directly predictive of a shorter latency to a suicide attempt (Table 20.2). Concurrent depression (73 percent) or, less commonly, a mixed-dysphoric mood state (16 percent) was associated with 89 percent of the ninety suicidal acts and all eight fatalities in both type I and II patients; only 11 percent of suicidal acts were associated with mania, and none occurred in a euthymic state.

During lithium maintenance treatment, there were seven suicidal acts (two were fatal) in seven of the 310 subjects over 6.36 years, to yield 0.355 acts per one hundred person-years. This crude risk rate is 6.59-fold lower than that encountered before lithium started (2.34/0.355). The effect of lithium treatment on suicidal risk was further evaluated quantitatively by Kaplan-Meier survival analyses to compare the times-to-first-suicidal-events in the 310 subjects before versus during lithium maintenance (Figure 20.2). This analysis yielded a highly significant difference in suicidal risk-over-time (Wilcoxon $\chi^2 = 22.1$, $p < 0.0001$), with a 4.5-fold difference in the time to 50 percent risk during versus before lithium maintenance treatment (12.5/2.77 months). Additional comparisons of yearly risks of suicidal acts provided by survival analysis (Table 20.3) indicated that by fifteen years of follow-up, the cumulative annual risk rate differed by 8.3-fold (22.9/2.76 percent suicidal). The timing of suicidal acts during lithium treatment indicates that most of the risk was encountered within the first two or three years of treatment, thus suggesting that greater benefits may be found with longer maintenance treatment (Figure 20.2).

After 128 of the patients discontinued lithium, there were twenty-three suicidal acts that included six fatalities, among sixteen patients over an average of

Table 20.2. Timing of Suicidal Acts in Bipolar Disorder Patients Before Lithium Maintenance Treatment.

Years at Risk	Percentage of Acts	Rate (percentage of acts per patient-year)	Age at Acts (years)	Onset Age (year)
0–1	26.7	5.16	27.4 ± 10.8	25.1 ± 9.0
2–5	26.7	1.03	29.8 ± 9.0	27.0 ± 8.6
6–10	23.3	0.90	30.5 ± 7.2	23.9 ± 9.9
11–15	11.7	0.45	36.9 ± 5.5	25.9 ± 7.2
> 15	11.7	0.10	57.1 ± 11.8	27.1 ± 10.8

Note: Distribution of sixty first life-threatening suicide acts prior to starting lithium maintenance treatment in 310 Sardinian bipolar I and II patients, as percentage of suicidal acts within each interval, and the rate of acts per hundred patient-years. More than one-quarter (27 percent) occurred in the first year, 53 percent occurred within five years of illness onset, and average age was ≤ 30 within the first ten years of suicide risk. A majority of acts occurred prior to lithium treatment (74 percent). Time from onset to a suicidal act averaged 7.53 ± 9.17 (median, 4.79) years. Latency to suicidal acts or to treatment was independent of onset age ($r \geq 0.04$, $p > 0.10$).

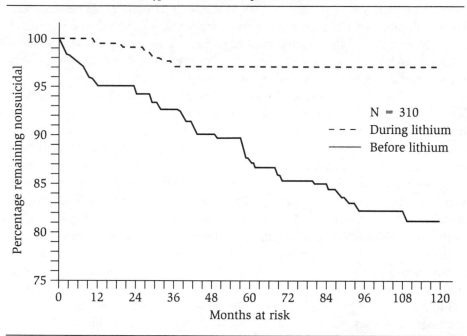

Figure 20.2. Kaplan-Meier Survival Analysis of Time to Suicidal Act
in 310 Type I or II Sardinian Bipolar Disorder Patients.

Note: The figure shows the proportion of persons remaining free of life-threatening suicidal acts up to ten years-at-risk before (lower solid line) and during (upper dotted line) lithium maintenance treatment. Computed suicidal risks ± SE before versus during lithium treatment were 12.5 ± 0.31 percent versus 2.77 ± 0.03 percent up to ten years. Differences in the two survival functions are highly significant (Wilcoxon χ^2 for repeated measures = 22.1, $p < 0.0001$). Comparative computed risks over time are summarized in Table 20.1.

3.70 years of follow-up, to yield crude rates of 4.86 suicidal acts per one hundred person-years of risk (Table 20.4). Moreover, the fatality rate was 1.27 per one hundred patient-years after discontinuing lithium compared to 0.101 during lithium maintenance—an alarming 13.9-fold increase (Table 20.4). After discontinuing lithium, the rate of suicidal acts was 13.7 times (4.86/0.355 per one hundred patient-years) greater than the overall risk during lithium treatment. Moreover, in the first year after discontinuing lithium, the rate of suicidal acts rose especially sharply; it was twenty-two times higher (7.81/0.355) than the time on lithium. Much lower rates were found at later times after discontinuation (3.76), and these compared closely with those found before lithium maintenance had started (2.34). These observations strongly suggest that the first months after discontinuing lithium may carry a particularly high risk of suicidal behavior, including fatalities and multiple attempts, sometimes in persons

**Table 20.3. Suicidal Risk in Bipolar Disorder Patients
Before Versus During Lithium Maintenance Treatment.**

Years at Risk	Percentage Who Are Suicidal (95% CI)		Risk Ratio
	Before Lithium	With Lithium	
1	4.71 (2.30–7.11)	0.65 (0.00–1.54)	7.25
2	5.49 (2.87–8.11)	1.01 (0.00–2.14)	5.44
3	7.26 (4.16–10.4)	2.76 (0.72–4.80)	2.63
4	9.69 (6.02–13.4)	2.76 (0.72–4.80)	3.51
5	11.8 (6.02–13.4)	2.76 (0.72–4.80)	4.28
6	14.2 (7.69–16.0)	2.76 (0.72–4.80)	5.14
8	17.7 (9.54–18.8)	2.76 (0.72–4.80)	6.41
10	18.5 (13.0–24.1)	2.76 (0.72–4.80)	6.70
12	21.5 (15.2–27.8)	2.76 (0.72–4.80)	7.89
15	22.9 (16.1–29.6)	2.76 (0.72–4.80)	8.30

Note: Data are derived from survival functions shown in Figure 20.1 for 310 Sardinian bipolar I and II patients, and represent the cumulative percentage of patients with a life-threatening suicidal act over time, with 95 percent confidence intervals (CI), as well as the ratio of risk rates. The differences are highly significant, even in the first year ($\chi^2 = 22.1$, $p < 0.0001$ for the overall survival functions; Figure 20.1). Note that most of the risk on lithium occurs in the first two to three years, with a rising ratio of protection thereafter, to over eightfold by fifteen years at risk. For the ten periods tabulated here, the average ($\pm$ SD) annual risk was 2.44 ± 0.88 percent before, and 0.481 ± 0.232 percent during lithium maintenance treatment—an overall difference of over fivefold.

Table 20.4. Lithium Treatment and Suicidal Rates in Bipolar Disorder Patients.

Treatment Phase	Suicidal Acts/Patient/Year	Annual Rate (percentage)
All suicidal acts		
Before lithium maintenance	(60 acts/310 cases/8.18 years)	2.34
During lithium treatment	(7 acts/310 cases/6.36 years)	0.355
First year off lithium	(10 acts/128 cases/1.00 year)	7.81
After first year off lithium	(13 acts/128 cases/2.70 years)	3.76
Fatal suicidal acts		
During lithium treatment	(2 deaths/310 cases/6.36 years)	0.101
After discontinuing lithium	(6 deaths/128 cases/3.70 years)	1.27

Note: Data are for 310 Sardinian bipolar I and II disorder patients at risk before and during lithium treatment, of whom 128 were also followed after discontinuing treatment. Risk in the first year of lithium was greater than at later times or before lithium (both $p < 0.01$, based on statistical methods discussed in Tondo et al., 1997b). Fatalities prior to starting lithium were an exclusion criterion so as to evaluate all subjects before and during lithium treatment. The rate of life-threatening suicidal acts per one hundred patient-years was 6.59-fold (2.34/0.355) lower during than before lithium maintenance; in the first year after discontinuing it, the rate rose by 22.0-fold (7.81/0.355), but the subsequent rate was similar to that found before starting lithium treatment (3.76 versus 2.34). The risk of fatalities off lithium increased by 12.6-fold (1.27/0.101).

who were not known to have shown suicidal behavior previously. There was a tendency toward greater risk after abrupt or rapid discontinuation of lithium (one to fourteen days of tapering) versus more gradual discontinuation (more than fourteen days); this trend was not significant, but statistical power was lacking due to the limited number of subjects and relative rarity of suicidal acts, as is discussed elsewhere (Tondo et al., 1997).

Additional analyses, based on multifactorial statistical modeling, reported elsewhere, also attempted to identify factors associated with suicidal events (Tondo et al., 1997a). Preliminary consideration of a large number of descriptive, demographic, diagnostic, family history, and morbidity factors eliminated many potential associations with the presence or absence of suicidal acts at any time. However, three factors were found to be significantly associated with patients who manifested suicidal behavior compared to those who did not. In order of their significance, they were: (1) previous history of a suicidal act, (2) being depressed for a proportion of time above the median, (3) younger age at onset of illness and at the start of each treatment phase.

In summary, this clinical study of relationships of lithium treatment to suicidal acts found that fifty-eight of 310 bipolar I and II disorder patients made ninety suicide attempts (eight were fatal) during a total of over 5,200 patient-years of observation before, during, and after lithium maintenance treatment, with 2.34 life-threatening suicide attempts per one hundred patient-years before lithium maintenance treatment. Important findings include a high risk of suicidal behavior relatively early in bipolar illnesses, with 53 percent of attempts before starting lithium occurring within five years from illness onset, and 74 percent of acts arising prior to the start of lithium treatment. Moreover, most of these patients were younger than age thirty years when they attempted suicide. These findings are consistent with the results of multifactorial modeling, which indicated that suicidal behavior was associated with a relatively early onset of bipolar illness, as we report elsewhere in detail (Tondo et al., 1998a). These observations, taken together, highlight the devastating early emotional impact of bipolar disorder and its high risk of fatal outcome at young ages, as has been noted previously in bipolar disorders as well as in nonbipolar major depression (Johnson and Hunt, 1979; Roy-Byrne et al., 1988; Malone et al., 1995).

It is important to acknowledge the substantial methodological limitations of the work reported, including possibly flawed information gathering, sampling biases, and the obvious ethical constraints to avoid experimental interventions that carry potentially lethal risks. Specific limitations in the present work include

1. Having to reconstruct much of the course of illness from its onset to the start of lithium maintenance from intermittently or retrospectively gathered data

2. Requiring nonlethality of suicidal acts before lithium maintenance was started in order to provide a comparison of subjects with versus without treatment for study

3. Excluding patients with some known risk factors associated with suicidal behavior, including substance abuse

4. Requiring prolonged adherence to essentially lithium monotherapy

5. Having the opportunity to follow only a minority of the patients (41 percent) after discontinuing lithium

The close similarity of suicidal risk before lithium and that based on prospectively gathered data following its discontinuation (particularly at times later than the first year; Table 20.4), however, lends some credence to the methods used and the findings reported. Although the present findings are based on clinically acquired data, the design of a randomized, blind, and prospective study involving life-threatening behavior as a potential outcome would probably not be ethically or clinically feasible given current knowledge of the risks involved (Baldessarini et al., 1996a, 1996b).

In short, the findings summarized here cannot provide a full picture of suicidal behavior in untreated populations of bipolar disorder patients, or deal with the important problem of risk associated with erratic treatment or poor treatment adherence, which, ironically, tends to worsen with emerging affective illness (Baldessarini et al., 1996b, 1996c).

Pertinent Research Findings

The present observations provide new information based on direct comparison of suicidal risk in the bipolar I and II syndromes. Such direct comparison has been rare. We found no significant difference in suicide rates between these diagnostic types. This finding is consistent with other recent observations indicating that type II disorders are not less severe than type I bipolar disorders, despite the absence of mania, nor less life-threatening. Morbidity includes a somewhat higher attack frequency in type II, a similar percentage of total time affectively ill before treatment, similar suicidal risk in both syndromes, and an even more frequent family history of suicidal behavior in type II patients (Baldessarini and Tondo, 1998; Tondo et al., 1998b). Moreover, the present finding that suicidal behavior was closely associated with previous and current bipolar depression is consistent with a high suicidal risk in type II bipolar cases.

Rates of life-threatening suicidal acts as well as levels of affective morbidity were much lower during long-term lithium maintenance treatment than in other periods of observation, with a 6.6-fold lower risk of suicidal acts during treatment than before it was initiated, and up to a 22-fold lower risk than was encountered soon after discontinuing treatment. Survival analysis of time-to-a-suicidal-act also indicated markedly longer periods free of suicidal behavior during lithium treatment, with a 4.5-fold longer time to 50 percent risk on lithium, and an 8.3-fold lower cumulative risk by up to fifteen years of follow-up on lithium (Figure 20.2). In addition, most of the observed risk during lithium treatment occurred during the first three years of treatment, thus suggesting that there may be cumulative benefits of remaining stable on long-term lithium.

Serum concentrations of lithium yielding such protection averaged only 0.6 mEq/L. It is not known whether additional benefits might have been found at higher levels, but the data in Figure 20.1 suggest that it would be difficult to demonstrate additional benefit in view of the extraordinary protection afforded by lithium at these conservative but relatively well-tolerated levels that are less than the 0.75–1.0 mEq/L commonly recommended in the United States (Gelenberg et al., 1989; Baldessarini, 1996). Nevertheless, these levels are highly consistent with contemporary international practice and with evidence that levels of 0.6–0.7 mEq/L provide near-maximal protection against recurrences of bipolar depression and mania and are cost effective with respect to adverse effect risks that seem to be continuously dose-dependent up to toxic and potentially lethal tissue concentrations of lithium (Maj et al., 1986; Coppen, 1994; Baldessarini, 1996; Baldessarini et al., 1996b, 1996c).

Another clinically important finding in our collaborative Sardinian study was that in the first year after discontinuing lithium nonexperimentally for various clinical reasons, the crude rate of suicidal acts (7.81/100 patient-years) was much greater than at any other time, including the years from illness onset to the start of lithium maintenance treatment (4.0-fold) and at times of follow-up without lithium beyond the first year after discontinuing lithium (2.4-fold; Table 20.4). Moreover, the rate of *fatal* suicidal acts was more than eleven times lower during versus after discontinuing lithium (0.101 versus 1.14 deaths per one hundred patient-years at risk).

Previous comparisons of subjects from the same clinic population revealed few and minor differences in demographic or clinical factors in those who did or did not discontinue lithium treatment. In addition, patients included in the present analysis after lithium discontinuation were not maintained on alternative psychotropic medicines or psychotherapy, although they were followed up and received short-term clinical treatment for acute recurrences of affective illness for not more than twelve weeks at a time. These considerations are consistent with a relatively direct clinical impact of the treatment discontinuation itself on the sharply elevated suicidal risk after discontinuing lithium (Baldessarini et al., 1996b).

We suggest, however, that the key intervening variable is early recurrence of bipolar depression and mixed-dysphoric states after discontinuing lithium, which were strongly associated with suicidal behavior. This association may provide a measure of warning and should lead to heightened clinical concern for suicidal risk when such mood states begin to emerge, and to early interventions aimed at protecting such patients and restabilizing their mood. The association with recurrences of depressive or dysphoric illness also offers hope that a slow tapering off of lithium may reduce suicidal risk, since it has been found to sharply reduce rates of early recurrence of bipolar depression as well as mania (Faedda et al., 1995; Baldessarini et al., 1996a, 1996b, 1997). Our preliminary findings are consistent with this expectation, but the data are still too limited to demonstrate a statistically significant association of suicidal risk and the rate of reducing or discontinuing lithium maintenance (Tondo et al., 1998a).

IMPLICATIONS FOR THE CLINICIAN

This chapter considers previously reported and newly emerging evidence that lithium has a strong, and possibly unique, protective effect against suicidal acts in persons with major affective disorders, and particularly in bipolar forms of manic-depressive illness. In twenty-two published studies providing quantitative data pertaining to more than 16,200 patients with major affective illnesses (unipolar recurrent major depression, bipolar manic-depressive disorders, and some with schizoaffective illness), we found a sevenfold lower overall risk of suicidal acts during lithium maintenance treatment (0.25 percent of patients per year) than without it (1.8 percent per year). These findings contrast to the state of knowledge of potential antisuicidal effects of other treatments, in that similar benefits have not been demonstrated during maintenance treatment with mood-altering medicines other than lithium.

Our own new, long-term study of 310 bipolar I and II disorder patients in over 5,200 patient-years of observation found ninety suicide attempts (eight were fatal), again with markedly similar differences between times with versus without lithium maintenance (0.35 percent versus 2.7 percent of patients per year). Suicidal acts were strongly associated with current depression or dysphoria (89 percent) rather than with mania (11 percent of acts), with a history of severe depression and prior attempts, and with relatively early illness onset. Suicidal acts were particularly frequent within five years after onset of bipolar manic-depressive illness prior to lithium maintenance (53 percent; mean age thirty-three years), and the rate in the first year was at least five times greater than at later times. The crude rate of suicidal acts fell by nearly sevenfold during long-term lithium maintenance monotherapy compared with the rate found between illness onset and the start of lithium maintenance. Moreover, survival analysis indicated that cumulative risk of a life-threatening suicidal act over time was reduced highly significantly, by more than eightfold, within fifteen years of follow-up with lithium maintenance therapy. However, after discontinuing lithium, the rate of suicidal behavior was twenty-two times higher within the first year, rising to levels 2.5 times above the average of later risks and above the similar rates found prior to starting lithium treatment. Moreover, fatalities increased by more than 11-fold after discontinuing lithium.

In conclusion, these findings indicate a powerful and long-sustained protective effect of lithium against suicidal behavior. This effect has not been proved to be associated with other mood-altering medical treatment regimens. Our new findings also strongly suggest that there is a sharp, but apparently time-limited, increase in suicidal risk shortly after discontinuing lithium. We suspect that this risk may be even greater after abrupt discontinuation, since this leads to an increased risk of depressive morbidity of bipolar illness, which can be modified by slow tapering off lithium. In general, the lack of experimental therapeutic studies of bipolar depression and the observed close association of suicidality and depression in bipolar disorders emphasizes the need for improved identification and treatment of all forms of major depression, but particularly of bipolar depression. Finally, there was a remarkably long delay (over eight years, and greater in women and patients with bipolar II disorder) between the onset of bipolar illness and regular maintenance treatment, during a period in which at least half of first-lifetime life-threatening suicidal acts occurred. This long latency to protective mood-stabilizing treatment indicates the urgent need for earlier recognition of bipolar disorders (particularly in young persons, and women with unrecognized bipolar II disorders) and much earlier therapeutic interventions.

- Bipolar depression is much more common than had been appreciated formerly—probably more than 2 percent lifetime morbid risk. It carries an unusually high risk of lethality, with suicide accounting for up to 25 percent of deaths among persons with bipolar manic-depressive disorders. In addition, bipolar disorders are associated with some of the highest rates of substance abuse comorbidity of any psychiatric disorder. Premature mortality rates in bipolar disorder patients are also several times higher due to substance abuse and presumably stress-related comorbid medical illnesses, all of which may also contribute to suicidal risk.

- Bipolar depression has largely been systematically excluded from research on modern therapeutics for major depressive disorders. Reasons include concerns about liability in persons who have a high risk of impulsive and self-injurious behaviors due to switching from depressive to manic or psychotic phases of the disorder when they are not protected with lithium or alternative mood-stabilizing agents.

- Bipolar depression and dysphoric mixed manic-depressive states accounted for nearly 90 percent of ninety suicidal acts among 310 bipolar disorder patients under observation for up to 18.8 years (1.8 percent per year) under various conditions of treatment and follow-up. Age at the time of sixty suicidal acts prior to lithium maintenance treatment was young (mean age thirty-three); 53 percent of initial life-threatening acts occurred within five years after illness onset, and 74 percent of these occurred prior to the start of regular lithium treatment. Moreover, more than half of first-lifetime potentially fatal suicidal acts occurred before the start of regular lithium treatment (delayed, on average, by more than eight years from illness onset).

- Systematic studies of reduction of suicidal risk with mood-altering agents have been rare and face severe ethical constraints. Evidence that antidepressants have led to specific reductions of long-term suicidal risk in depression or bipolar disorders is absent, and the introduction of safer antidepressants probably has not reduced suicide rates appreciably owing to the use of other, more lethal means of self-destruction.

- Our meta-analysis of published and new data comparing suicidal risk rates in treated and untreated bipolar disorder patients indicated strong support for an antisuicidal effect of lithium, with a sevenfold overall reduction of rates of suicidal behavior. At least one recent study has found that carbamazepine provided much less antisuicidal protection in bipolar disorders.

- New data based on the long-term observation of bipolar I and II disorder patients in a collaborating Sardinian mood disorders clinic further supported a strong antisuicidal effect of lithium. However, stopping lithium was followed by a sharp rise in recurrences of manic-depressive affective morbidity, which, in turn, was associated with a marked rise in rates of suicidal acts (twenty-two times higher in the first year) and fatalities (eleven times higher).

- These findings strongly support the need for more assertive and specific attention to the clinical diagnosis and safe management of persons with bipolar depression, and for further studies of all mood-altering agents for their effect on suicidal behavior. The evidence reviewed here indicates that lithium maintenance therapy virtually stands alone as a medical treatment with substantial evidence of a selective and long-sustained antisuicide effect. The findings also support the need for much earlier diagnosis and intervention into these frequently fatal disorders, particularly to minimize the impact of the high rates of suicidal acts that occur early in the course of the illness.

CHAPTER TWENTY-ONE

Treatment of the Suicidal Patient with Psychotropic Drugs and ECT

Carl Salzman, M.D.

S uicide almost always occurs in the context of serious mental illness (Clark and Fawcett, 1992b). It is self-evident, therefore, that treatment of a mental illness should also prevent the occurrence of suicide. Yet literature that specifically demonstrates the prevention of suicide by successful treatment is surprisingly sparse. This chapter reviews the literature on the pharmacological treatment of the suicidal patient and addresses the following questions:

1. What is the evidence for the prevention of suicide by pharmacological treatment? Is there specific evidence for the prevention of suicide in patients with a diagnosis of major depression, bipolar illness, schizophrenia, anxiety disorders, or personality disorder?

2. If there is evidence for the efficacy of psychotropic drugs in preventing suicide, are there differences among the drugs that are used to treat each category of illness regarding their suicide-preventing qualities? Is electroconvulsive treatment (ECT) effective in preventing suicide, and, if so, how does it compare in efficacy with chemical antidepressants?

3. Are there neurobiologic mechanisms that underlie suicidal thought and behavior, independent of diagnosis, that suggest a specific psychotropic drug treatment?

4. Do some psychotropic drugs make suicidal ideation or behavior worse?

5. Is it true that depressed patients are at greater risk of suicide as their symptoms begin to resolve with successful psychotropic drug treatment?

PREVENTING SUICIDES BY TREATING DEPRESSION

The relation between suicide and depression is well known (Fawcett et al., 1987). Patients with major depression have at least a 15 percent lifetime risk of suicide (Guze and Robins, 1970, and Chapter Fifteen in this book); depression is present in 40 to 85 percent of all completed suicides (Isacsson et al., 1994a; Cheng, 1995). The presence of severe hopelessness, suicidal ideation, history of previous suicide attempts (Fawcett, Scheftner, Fogg, and Clark, 1990; Fawcett, Clark, and Busch, 1993), and severe anxiety (Fawcett, 1992) are strong correlates of potential suicide, both early and late, in a depressed patient. As a general proposition, the link between depression and suicidal thought or behavior is convincing.

Does Antidepressant Treatment Prevent Suicide?

Although it is plausible to assume that reduction of depressive symptoms will secondarily prevent suicide, there are relatively few controlled studies regarding the efficacy of antidepressant treatments in preventing suicide. There is controversy regarding the available evidence for antidepressant efficacy. One interpretation of the data strongly indicates that antidepressant medication is more effective than placebo in reducing suicidal ideation, although it is not as clear that medication reduces suicide attempts (Malone, 1997). Another opinion holds that the value of antidepressants in preventing suicide has not yet been established (Montgomery et al., 1992).

No trials of tricyclic antidepressants have been undertaken that specifically demonstrate their ability to prevent suicide. For example, Avery and Winokur (1978) found no significant difference in suicide attempts between those who received antidepressant medication and those who did not receive treatment. Black, Winokur, Mohandoss, Woolson, and Nasrallah (1989) also reported no significant difference in the risk of suicide between patients who were acutely treated with adequate antidepressants and those who did not receive antidepressant treatment, but these studies may not be representative of clinical patients, since suicidal patients are usually excluded from clinical trials (Malone, 1997).

It is also possible that patients in these tricyclic antidepressant studies did not receive sufficient doses or medication for a time to produce an adequate therapeutic effect. Studies clearly indicate that depressed patients frequently take inadequate therapeutic doses (for review, see Keller, 1994). In one study of affectively ill patients who were suicidal, only two of eleven were receiving lithium carbonate at the time of treatment and, overall, fewer than 20 percent were receiving adequate tricyclic antidepressant or lithium carbonate medication (Roy, 1982a; Roy and Chir, 1994).

Data regarding the effect of selective serotonin reuptake inhibitor (SSRI) antidepressants in preventing suicide are slightly more positive but still equivocal. These studies (for review see Malone, 1997) suggest that there may be a more rapid reduction in suicidal ideation with SSRI antidepressants as compared with nonserotonergic antidepressants, which is apparent at about two weeks. By four to six weeks of treatment, however, there are no longer any differences between SSRIs and other classes of antidepressants, thus suggesting that the serotonergic antidepressants may be more useful in reducing suicidal behavior only during the early phases of treatment. A study by Sacchetti et al. (1991) further suggested that serotonergic antidepressants were more effective in patients who had a history of suicidal behavior compared with patients without a history of suicidal behavior. Other studies, however, concluded that the SSRI antidepressants were "equivocal" in preventing suicide (Montgomery and Montgomery, 1982, 1984; Schifano and De Leo, 1991; Freemantle et al., 1994).

The efficacy with which ECT prevents suicide is considerably more robust. Avery and Winoker (1977, 1978) compared suicide attempts in previously depressed patients six months after treatment either with ECT or with antidepressants. There was zero percent suicide in the ECT group compared to 10 percent among patients who had received antidepressants. Although these older studies are frequently cited as support for the efficacy of ECT in suicidally depressed patients, the preponderance of evidence comes from extensive clinical experience. A National Institute of Mental Health (NIMH) Consensus conference (Rose et al., 1985) as well as standard references (e.g., Goodwin and Jamison, 1990) consistently mention ECT as the most efficacious treatment for the suicidal patient.

Since placebo-controlled trials of antidepressant treatment in the suicidal depressed patient are unethical, only retrospective reviews of treated versus untreated (or inadequately treated) patients can be used to assess the overall efficacy of treatment in preventing suicide. Three studies clearly indicate that the incidence of suicide in depressed patients is greater in those who are *not* taking antidepressants than for those who are adequately medicated. Isacsson et al. (1994a) found that less than half of the patients who committed suicide in San Diego were prescribed antidepressants and commented that "more suicides might be averted by decisively treating depressed patients with antidepressants than by not treating them to avoid antidepressant overdoses." Isacsson et al. (1992, 1994b) also published similar data from a population of people committing suicide in Sweden, finding that of patients who committed suicide only 15 percent had received antidepressant treatment during the previous three months. Marzuk et al. (1995) reported virtually identical data from a population of suicide patients in New York City. Eighty-four percent of these patients were not taking an antidepressant (or neuroleptic) medication. These authors agree that "the potential of these drugs [antidepressants] to prevent suicide has not yet been realized" (Isacsson et al., 1996; Marzuk et al., 1996). Nevertheless, in the majority of patients, treatment results in substantial improvement or total remission of suicidal ideation and impulses (ACNP, 1993).

Differences Among Antidepressants and the Neurobiology of Suicide

In 1976 Åsberg first observed that the serotonin metabolite 5-hydroxy-indole acetic acid (5-HIAA) was reduced in the spinal fluid of patients who made violent suicide attempts (Åsberg et al., 1976). This seminal observation, confirmed many times and discussed in detail in Chapter Six, has led to the so-called serotonergic hypothesis of suicidal behavior. As articulated in Chapter Six, this hypothesis proposes that serotonin functions as a modulator of aggression and impulsive behavior. Reduced or dysfunctional serotonin neurotransmission may therefore result in increased impulsive and aggressive behavior. Violent (and usually impulsive) suicide is seen as one category of such impulsive and aggressive behavior. A large body of evidence has been marshaled to support this hypothesis (Malone and Mann, 1993) and suggests that drugs that facilitate serotonin neurotransmission may be especially useful for the treatment of the suicidally depressed patient.

Given the data that suggest a relative therapeutic superiority for antidepressants that affect serotonin neurotransmission, it is reasonable to ask whether serotonergic antidepressants are more effective than others in preventing suicide. Unfortunately, there are no data to suggest that any class of antidepressant is more or less effective in the treatment of the suicidally depressed patient, assuming that all drugs are prescribed in adequate doses. Adequate doses of all classes of antidepressants are more highly correlated with suicide prevention than differences among drugs.

For some suicidal patients, however, combining the therapeutic effect of drugs may help prevent suicide. For example, there is a clear need for neuroleptic augmentation of antidepressant medication for treatment of the delusionally depressed patient (Spiker et al., 1981; Roose et al., 1983). Recent evidence also suggests that rapid reduction of anxiety in a hospitalized depressed patient may also prevent suicide (Fawcett et al., 1993). High anxiety may predispose a depressed inpatient to suicide even when suicidal intent is denied, a finding that points to the importance of decreasing anxiety rapidly while instituting adequate antidepressant therapy (Busch et al., 1993). Bipolar depressed patients should receive mood-stabilizing medication in conjunction with antidepressant treatment to prevent the development of mania. See Chapter Twenty for further discussion of this point, particularly as it relates to lithium.

Do Antidepressants Cause Suicide?

There are three categories of concern regarding whether antidepressant treatment increases rather than prevents suicide: the increased risk of suicide during early recovery from depression, suicide by antidepressant overdose, and the possibility that antidepressants increase suicidal behavior.

Increased Risk of Suicidal Behavior During Early Recovery

It is a clinical aphorism that risk of suicide increases as patients start to symptomatically improve. Surprisingly, there are no data to support this observation despite its common acceptance. Clinical observations, however, suggest that the mood of some depressed patients may improve for one to three days preceding a suicide (Clark and Fawcett, 1992b). Several hypotheses have been proposed to explain improved mood just preceding suicide. Ostow (1962) commented that "enhanced physical energy propels murderous rage towards the introjected object," that is, increased physical energy during the early recovery period may predispose the still depressed subject to self-destructive behavior. Although psychoanalytically plausible, it should be noted that this hypothesis of self-directed anger has not been supported by research observations (Goldney et al., 1997). Detre and Jarecki (1991) noted that since depressive symptoms may remit in the reverse order of their appearance, a phenomenon they called "temporal and symptomatic rollback," suicidal thoughts in depressed patients may persist as vegetative symptoms begin to improve. Many authors (for example, Himmelhoch, 1987) have similarly suggested that antidepressants, by alleviating psychomotor retardation before the affective despair or hopelessness resolves, may provide the depressed patient with the energy to commit suicide. However, since many (if not most) patients do not experience an increase in suicidality as they start to improve, the actual risk of suicide during early recovery cannot be calculated. Although clinicians should remain alert to the possibility of suicide as a patient starts to recover, this time-honored belief may be wrong as often (or more often) than it is correct.

Fatality from Antidepressant Overdose

The potentially fatal toxicity of tricyclic antidepressant overdose also links antidepressant treatment with suicidal behavior. The risk of suicidal behavior by overdose does not appear to differ among antidepressants; however, tricyclic antidepressants are associated with a higher rate of death from overdose (Kapur et al., 1992). Furthermore, previously cited studies (Marzuk et al., 1995; Isaccson et al., 1992, 1994a, 1994b) indicate that patients who attempted or committed suicide tended *not* to be taking antidepressants. Lack of data limit conclusions about nontricyclic (and non-MAOI) overdose fatalities.

Do SSRI Antidepressants Cause Suicide or Increase Suicide Potential?

The possibility that antidepressants might increase or cause suicidal behavior was first raised by Teicher et al. (1990) with regard to fluoxetine. Subsequent reviews of fluoxetine and the emergence of suicidality (Mann and Kapur, 1991; Tollefson et al., 1994; Beaseley et al., 1992; Fava and Rosenbaum, 1992; Wirshing et al., 1992) have failed to confirm this observation. There are also no data from studies of newer antidepressants such as venlafaxine, nefazodone, bupropion, and mirtazapine, that suggest an increase in suicidality. Overall, Mann and Kapur (1991) concluded that these antidepressants were not associated with an increase in suicidal ideation or behavior except in a very small number of unusual patients. Molcho and Stanley (1992) have even suggested that SSRI antidepressants are the antidepressants of choice for treatment of depressed patients who are at risk for suicide because of reduced risk of fatal overdose. Isacsson et al. (1996), Freemantle et al. (1994), and Jick et al. (1995), however, failed to find that pharmacological toxicity was a significant factor in suicide when all methods for suicide were considered; that is, low-toxic antidepressants did not carry lower risks than tricyclics. Rather, underprescribing or therapeutic failure correlated with suicide.

The initial observations of Teicher have not been replicated in a controlled study, and it is now hypothesized that rare emergence of increased suicidality with SSRIs is either idiosyncratic or the result of increased agitation or akathisia (Drake and Erlich, 1985; Lipinski et al., 1989; Hamilton and Opler, 1992; Rothschild and Locke, 1991, Wirshing et al., 1992).

Newer antidepressants have also been implicated in increasing suicidal behavior. For example, maprotiline was associated with five successfully completed suicides out of fourteen attempts, compared with only one in a placebo group (Montgomery, 1990). On the basis of this proportional difference, it was concluded that maprotiline may provoke suicide attempts and that its mechanism of suicide provocation differs from the mechanism of its antidepressant effect (Montgomery, et al., 1992).

TREATING SUICIDALITY IN OTHER DISORDERS

Depression is not the only presenting problem when treating suicidality, patients displaying bipolar disorders, anxiety disorders, schizophrenia, and personality disorders are also at risk.

Bipolar Disorder

Bipolar depressed patients are at a particular risk for suicide in the depressive phase of their illness, although there is no significant difference in rates between bipolar I and bipolar II depressed patients (Chapters Fourteen and Twenty). The treatment of the depressed phase of bipolar illness is not different from the treatment of the unipolar depressed patient except that a mood stabilizer such as lithium or an anticonvulsant is usually employed to prevent a switch into mania. A large body of data (Tondo et al., 1996; Tondo, Jamison, and Baldessarini, 1997) confirm that the risk of suicidal behavior in patients with bipolar disorder is sharply reduced during lithium maintenance treatment. There are no data to suggest that other mood stabilizers such as the anticonvulsants or neuroleptics are more or less effective than lithium in preventing suicide in bipolar depressed patients. However, new data (Chapter Twenty) emphasize the lethal risk of bipolar illness, especially in young adults, and the necessity for ongoing maintenance treatment. Discontinuation of mood stabilization in a bipolar patient is very likely to lead to relapse (Baldessarini et al., 1996b), and regardless of subtype of illness, the risk of suicide increases markedly when lithium is discontinued (2.2 versus 0.39).

Anxiety Disorders

It has been established that panic disorder carries with it a significant risk of suicide (Weissman, Klerman, and Markowitz, 1989). However, a reanalysis of this data concluded that this association occurs only in the presence of comorbid conditions (Hornig and McNally, 1995). Fawcett et al. (1993) have demonstrated that the presence of anxiety in a suicidally depressed patient increases the risk of suicidal behavior. It is reasonable to assume, therefore, that reduction of anxiety may reduce the risk of suicide in a depressed patient, and effective antipanic treatment may reduce the risk of suicide associated with this disorder.

There are no data to suggest that a specific class of medication is more or less likely to prevent suicidal ideation or behavior in patients with anxiety or anxiety spectrum disorders. Anxiety and panic disorder are commonly treated with benzodiazepine anxiolytics (as well as other drugs), and successful treatment presumably decreases suicidal risk. However, it has also been suggested that benzodiazepines induce behavioral disinhibition that results in suicide attempts. One study of a small number of patients noted an increased suicidality with alprazolam in patients with a personality disorder (Gardner and Cowdry, 1985b). Other studies, however, concluded that there is no evidence to suggest that therapeutic benzodiazepine treatment of anxiety or panic disorder is associated with an increased risk of suicidality (Smith and Salzman, 1991; Jonas and Hearron, 1996). Overall, the successful treatment of panic, anxiety, and other anxiety-related syndromes appears to be associated with a decreased risk of suicidal behavior.

Schizophrenia

Suicide occurs in 9 to 13 percent of patients with schizophrenia over the course of a lifetime, and the mortality from suicide in schizophrenia is twenty times higher than among nonschizophrenic people (Harkavy-Friedman and Nelson, 1997). The suicide rate is 0.4 to 1.1 percent per year, and if a patient with schizophrenia has made one suicide attempt, there is a 35 to 40 percent chance of a second attempt. On the basis of these statistics, it is plausible to assume that adequate treatment of schizophrenic symptoms, although not curing the illness, may nevertheless diminish the risk for suicidality. This assumption is supported by the observation that the suicide rate decreases dramatically to 0.009 to 0.18 percent per year with adequate neuroleptic treatment. Furthermore, when clozapine is discontinued, the suicide rate increases (Meltzer and Okayli, 1995). These observations emphasize the necessity for ongoing adequate neuroleptic treatment of schizophrenia. See Chapter Sixteen for further discussion of suicide and schizophrenia.

Personality Disorders

As is reviewed in Chapter Eighteen, borderline personality disorder is associated with suicidal ideation and self-destructive (sometimes suicidal) behavior. Suicide may be a higher risk for the patient who is suffering from major depression and also has this form of personality disorder (Corbitt et al., 1996). Patients with borderline personality disorder may actually experience an increase in suicidal behavior during treatment with antidepressants (Gardner and Cowdry, 1985b; Soloff et al., 1986a, 1987). Two of the six hospitalized patients who experienced increased suicidality during fluoxetine treatment carried a diagnosis of major depression and borderline personality disorder, and two others may also have had characteristics of borderline personality disorder (dissociation, multiple personality) in conjunction with major depression (Teicher et al., 1990). In contrast, mildly symptomatic research volunteer subjects with borderline personality disorder without comorbid major depression did not report an increase in suicidal ideation or behavior during treatment with fluoxetine (Salzman et al., 1995). Regardless of whether antidepressant treatment actually increases the risk of suicidality in a patient with borderline personality disorder, the role for antidepressant treatment needs to be clarified with further studies.

Neuroleptics have been shown to decrease suicidal tendencies in patients with personality disorder. Cowdry and Gardner (1988) found a significant reduction in suicidal tendencies in patients with personality disorders treated with trifluoperazine compared with placebo. Soloff et al. (1986b) reported similar effects with haloperidol.

Psychotropic medications may be useful for other aspects of this personality disorder, but there may be a greater role for psychotherapy rather than specific pharmacotherapy for suicidal ideation and behavior (Goldblatt and Schatzberg, 1992; Malone, 1997).

FORMULATING TREATMENT GUIDELINES

The following treatment guidelines can be formulated based on the above review. It must be emphasized, however, that thoughtful treatment of an individual patient takes precedence over treatment recommendations or algorithms suggested by this or any other publication. Regardless of which specific treatment or medication is chosen, the following basic principles emerge:

1. All studies of the treatment of a potentially suicidal patient emphasize the importance of adequate doses of medication or adequate use of ECT in order to intervene against suicide. However, most suicides occur in the context of no treatment or undertreatment.

2. An empathic therapeutic relationship within which prescribing strategies can be formulated and treatment carried out is essential. Psychotropic drug treatment is not a cure for suicidality but is part of a comprehensive treatment program.

3. Psychiatric illness tends to be chronic and recurring. All evidence supports the importance of adequate maintenance therapy after initial symptoms have resolved or have moderated. Risk of suicide clearly increases when maintenance treatments are discontinued.

4. There is no evidence that antidepressants or other psychotropic medications trigger emergent suicidal ideation in a reliable and predictable manner. It is clear that most patients receive substantial benefit from treatment with psychotropic drugs.

5. It is good clinical practice to closely monitor suicidal patients receiving treatment with psychotropic drugs. Some depressed patients who are responding to treatment may occasionally have brief relapses lasting one or two days in which their symptoms may recur.

IMPLICATIONS FOR THE CLINICIAN

- There are no data to support the recommendation of any specific antidepressant class or individual antidepressant drug for the treatment of the depressed suicidal patient. Although studies suggest a role for dysfunctional serotonin neurotransmission in the suicidal patient, there are no data to suggest that serotonergic antidepressants are more therapeutic for the suicidally depressed patient or are more likely to prevent suicide.

- Regardless of which antidepressant medication is selected, the dose must be maintained at therapeutic levels. All antidepressant drugs appear to be equally effective in reducing suicide ideation and behavior when given in full therapeutic doses.

- An advantage of the tricyclic class of antidepressants is the ability to monitor blood levels within the therapeutic range.

- A disadvantage of tricyclic antidepressants (and MAOIs) is the potential for lethal overdose. However, although nontricyclics and non-MAOIs may be safer in overdose, potential toxicity is usually less critical to treatment response than adequate dose. If a tricyclic or MAOI is selected, it is prudent to prescribe small quantities of therapeutic doses to reduce the risk of an overdose fatality.

- There is no evidence that SSRI or other antidepressants increase suicidal ideation or behavior for the average patient with major depressive disorder. Although it is possible that an occasional patient who also suffers from comorbid borderline personality disorder may experience a transient increase in suicidal ideation, a causal relationship has not been proven. SSRI antidepressants may produce akathisia in some individuals; it is unclear whether akathisia increases the risk of suicidal ideation and behavior.

- Bipolar patients who are depressed should receive a mood-stabilizing medication in conjunction with antidepressant treatments. The risk of suicide increases dramatically, as does relapse, when mood stabilizing medication is discontinued. As yet no evidence supports the superiority of any specific mood-stabilizing medication in preventing suicide.

- ECT is as effective as antidepressant medications in preventing suicide in a depressed patient, and may be more effective and more rapidly acting than chemical antidepressants for some patients, especially those with delusions. Although a precise number of ECT treatments cannot be recommended, adequate treatments are necessary to reduce suicidal ideation and prevent relapse.

- Delusionally depressed patients who do not receive ECT should be treated with a combination of neuroleptics and antidepressants.

- Anxiety may increase the risk of suicide in depressed patients, especially those who are hospitalized. When anxiety is significant, depressed patients should receive anxiolytic treatment in conjunction with antidepressant treatment.

The following conclusions bear specifically on the treatment of panic disorder, schizophrenia, and personality disorder.

- Panic disorder in the presence of comorbidity carries a significant risk of suicide; all adequate treatments will reduce this risk. The use of therapeutic doses of benzodiazepines to treat panic disorder (or severe anxiety) does not increase the risk of suicide.

- Schizophrenia also increases the risk of suicide. Thoughtful treatment should be directed at improving quality of life as well as reducing symptoms of schizophrenia. Adequate neuroleptic doses must be used for treatment, but doses must be carefully balanced against antipsychotic medication side effects to avoid noncompliance.

- Individuals with borderline personality disorder often experience suicidal ideation or display suicidal behavior. No specific pharmacological treatments (or ECT) have been demonstrated to reliably reduce these symptoms. Empathic, effective psychotherapy may be useful.

CHAPTER TWENTY-TWO

The Inpatient Management
of Suicidality

Gary Jacobson, M.D.

Suicidality is the single most common precipitant for psychiatric inpatient admission, and it has been for the past decade (Friedman, 1989). Various surveys report that between 60 and 75 percent of child, adolescent, and adult patients and 40 to 55 percent of geriatric patients are admitted to inpatient units in the United States with concerns of self-harm. Suicidality is even more common in readmission within thirty days after discharge, approaching 80 percent of the precipitating reasons for admission (personal communication from national mental health managed care company, December 1997).

Since resolution of suicidal ideation, intent, and behavior usually triggers rapid discharge from inpatient status, the concentration of patients remaining on inpatient units with various levels of suicidality has become pronounced. Nonetheless, there are a few published studies of suicide on the inpatient unit itself. Older studies suggest that between 5 and 6 percent of all suicides in the United States and Great Britain were occurring in psychiatric hospitals (Robins et al., 1959b; Crammer, 1984). For patients who did commit suicide while hospitalized, the largest group (43 percent) were hospitalized for less than one week, suggesting the particular need for vigilance at a point when the patient is not yet well known. Long hospitalizations, however, did not prevent hospital suicides, some of which occurred after six months of inpatient care (Busch, Clark, Fawcett, and Kravitz, 1993).

A study of patients who killed themselves on the unit or had made an attempt on the unit serious enough to have caused anoxic encephalopathy showed correlations with the diagnosis of schizophrenia, a history of prior attempts of potentially high lethality, the history of living alone or living in a household without younger children, and finally with involuntarily hospitalization (Roy and Draper, 1995). Recent studies have shown a shift toward a greater percentage of suicides occurring within two months of discharge (Morgan and Stanton, 1997). These findings reemphasize the importance of aftercare planning and treatment.

ORIENTATION OF THE INPATIENT CLINICIAN

Much of inpatient psychiatry has taken the form of an extended emergency service where critical evaluations need to be made and remade, diagnoses and treatments undertaken without delay, and a coordinated set of clinical interventions called into play, sometimes with incomplete knowledge of the patient. The inpatient clinician treating suicidal patients is faced with and should be aware of two sets of contradictory forces: the suicidal patient's own ambivalence in choosing life or death and outside pressures for thoroughness on the one hand and brevity on the other.

Few other interventions in medicine are as satisfying as directly saving a life. Yet when it comes to saving a life by hospitalizing an acutely suicidal patient, the doctor is often met by an uncooperative and at times ungrateful person. "Why shouldn't I have the right to kill myself if I want to?" asked a seventeen-year-old hospitalized after a major overdose. "You are not the boss of me. I am old enough to do what I want, including ending my life if that is what I want to do."

More subtle is the patient who appears to permit the resolution of the immediate suicidal crisis but then wishes to terminate treatment abruptly. A study contrasting patients who completed treatment with those who withdrew within the first two days showed that those who withdrew prematurely presented avoidant, negativistic, and passive-aggressive personality traits and that abrupt unilateral withdrawal by the patient shortly after a suicidal crisis represented a generally maladaptive and high-risk style of coping (Rudd, Joiner, and Rajav, 1995). The patient's judgment or that of the family regarding the patient's suicidality risk is certainly a factor to be considered but cannot be relied on as definitive by the clinician, who has the duty to make a broader, more comprehensive, expert judgment independent of the patient's opinion.

The structure of contemporary medical insurance can increase the pressure to take risks for the sake of economics. Economic pressure is an unavoidable part of society's need to conserve resources, but such pressure cannot be yielded to as the determining factor for discharge decisions in the individual case. Because suicide is a low-frequency occurrence and many experts have held that it is not predictable in the individual case (Roy and Draper, 1995; Pokorny, 1983,

1993), insurance review pressure is sometimes brought to bear on a clinician to discharge an individual patient as being "not suicidal" without the clinician's having adequate tools of rebuttal. The clinician must bear in mind that it is he or she who is primarily responsible for the patient's safety and treatment. If there is a difference of opinion regarding the safe discharge of a suicidal patient, it may be the clinician's duty to appeal the insurance reviewer's opinion that the patient does not meet standards for inpatient care. A second opinion of a peer can be requested to assist in this appeal.

Although suicide may not be individually predictable in the usual sense of the word, the expectation of the family and the legal community is that the clinician and the hospital not take risks that *foreseeably* might result in suicide. Contradictions inherent in the terms *predictability* and *foreseeability* are fortunately made somewhat easier by the way the term *foreseeability* is used forensically. The courts have held the clinician liable for "foreseeable" suicide when that suicide was deemed to be part of the negligent failure to exercise appropriate "duty of care," that is, when the clinician had failed to assess risk properly or, once risk had been assessed, had failed to take proper protective action (Simon, 1992b; Appelbaum and Gutheil, 1991; Bongar, Maris, and Berman, 1993). If the clinician appropriately assesses risk; reevaluates that risk at selected points along the treatment; communicates with the nursing staff, the patient's family, and others who have relevant knowledge of the patient; documents the risks and benefits of various treatment plans; assesses the patient's suicidal risk prior to discharge; and makes reasonable disposition arrangements for the patient, and following this the patient commits suicide, then the great likelihood is that the death, unfortunate and difficult as it is for the patient's family and the clinician, will not be deemed to have been "foreseeable." If, however, the clinician omits one of these steps and the omission of that step can be shown to be causally related to the patient's death, the clinician may very well be held professionally liable. The perspective of this chapter is that in the inpatient treatment of suicidal patients, optimum patient care and optimum risk management have an identical goal: the use of knowledge, skill, and organization to save lives by reducing, to the extent possible, "foreseeable" suicide.

COMPREHENSIVE ASSESSMENT OF SUICIDALITY

Since the issuance of draft guidelines in 1993 for the assessment of suicidality by the Suicide Risk Advisory Committee of the Harvard Medical Institutions (see Appendix), the identification of suicidality has included clinical factors, historical factors, and factors related to the patient's capacity to interact with others, particularly with caregivers. A number of inpatient systems have adopted a uniform approach to both assessment and documentation of suicidality. In these systems, suicidality is assessed on admission and on discharge for most, if not all, inpatients (Henschen, 1997).

The rationale for a uniform approach is threefold. First, to the extent that a uniform approach is comprehensive, there is an increased chance that the right clinical questions will be asked and relevant information obtained. For example when a research team using a uniform questionnaire reviewed fifty patients with attempted suicide to a university inpatient service that did not have a standardized assessment instrument, almost a quarter of the clinicians (24 percent) failed to document the presence of a prior suicide attempt, one of the risk factors to consider in assessing suicidality (Malone et al., 1995a).

A second rationale for comprehensive and uniform documentation is its assistance in reducing the malpractice risk to the clinician and the hospital. A recent review by a major malpractice insurance company of the medical records of suicide patients revealed that more than 50 percent had inadequate or absent documentation for defense (Ellis and Schaefer, 1995).

Finally, compiling statistical data and research is made easier by the uniformity of documentation. If an inpatient service uses a standardized assessment form, however, there should be a clear understanding that the form does not substitute for clinical judgment and whatever uniform approach is used, adequate opportunity should be left for the clinician to make additional comments or observations.

The approach to a comprehensive assessment in this chapter examines suicidal ideation, history of self-destructiveness, diagnoses or symptoms associated with a higher incidence of suicides, a review of stressful life circumstances, and an assessment of the patient's mental competence and capacity for therapeutic alliance.

Suicidal Ideation

Grouped under suicidal ideation are three components: (1) *thoughts* about suicide, which can be either specific or vague and either active, in which the patient is the agent of the suicide, or passive, in which the patient accepts or even wishes for circumstances in which he or she might be killed; (2) *intent,* in which the patient has the conscious intent to act on his or her suicidal ideation; and (3) *plan,* in which the patient has formulated a plan to engage in suicidal behavior. If a plan exists, the feasibility and potential for high lethality of that plan are also assessed. Feasibility questions often examine access to the means of suicide, and in this context, it is important to ask about access to firearms. Finally, since a small but important number of suicides are accompanied by homicide (Lester, 1989; Cohen, Llorente, and Eisdorfer, 1998), investigation of ideation involving wishes to harm others should be investigated as well. (See Chapter Ten in this book for further discussion of this topic.)

The absence of suicidal ideation at the time of the examination does not preclude the clinical judgment that the patient is suicidal and requires hospitalization. A common precipitant for evaluation for hospital care is a suicide attempt itself. Following that attempt, the patient may be temporarily relieved and have no suicidal ideation at the time of the examination but nonetheless be at risk for return to suicidality. The clinician must review the other factors involved in the assessment to make a judgment as to whether the absence of suicidal ideation following an attempt will most likely be sustained or whether the patient is in near-term danger of relapse.

The elements of suicidal ideation that involve identification with a family member or friend who has committed suicide, a longing to join a loved one who has died, or containing delusional material may be especially worrisome and should be monitored as part of the treatment plan. Certain patients, especially those with a diagnosis of borderline personality or chronic depression, live with frequent thoughts about suicide that can last for years or even decades. If chronic suicidal ideation is stable, that ideation may not alone be a reason for hospitalization or a reason to delay discharge. However, the assessment of chronic suicidal ideation should concentrate on similarities or differences of the present suicidal ideation and its clinical circumstances with those that have existed in the past.

History of Suicide Attempts

The history of suicide attempts, the frequency and total number of such attempts, and the potential lethality of those attempts are all important risk factors in anticipating future suicides (Rich, Young, and Fowler, 1986c). There is little useful distinction between the term *suicide attempt* and the term *suicide gesture*. The latter generally implies that the patient engaged in a suicide-appearing action intended to impress others or to relieve internal states of tension temporarily but did not "really" wish to die. Since patients are generally not pharmacologists or otherwise expert in predicting the precise effects of their suicidal actions, so-called gestures may turn out to be fatal. A useful distinction can be made by appreciating the intent of the behavior.

So-called aborted suicide attempts, in which the patient begins but does not complete a suicide act and therefore avoids injury, do carry a high degree of suicide intent and are highly associated with actual attempts (Barber, Marzuk, Leon, and Portera, 1998). The term *self-mutilation* implies the absence of suicide intent. Clinically, however, patients who mutilate themselves, usually by cutting or burning, may also have a history of suicide attempts (see Chapter Eight in this book).

The behavior and communications of the patient during and following a suicide attempt are instructive (Shneidman, 1993). These help focus the therapeutic intervention both as to the patient's psychological development and to the patient's family and social relationships. Messages in a "suicide note" such as feelings of worthlessness and mention of specific people being "better off" with the patient dead provide reference for the clinician's intervention. The following note from a college student written prior to a near-lethal suicide attempt is illustrative.

> Dear Mom and Dad:
>   I love you so much. Please know that I will be better off this way. I love you. I'm sorry,
>
> Sam
> P.S. Everything life gave me my whole life, I didn't want. All I want is you guys. Bye.

The poignancy of the note, as well as the fact that the patient made no attempt to reach anyone prior to initiating his suicidal behavior, left no doubt as to the seriousness of his intent.

Finally, a history of two types of suicide attempts have special relevance for inpatient clinicians: attempts made while in an intensive treatment setting and a "surprise" suicide attempt that occurred directly following an evaluation of nonsuicidality. In both of these special circumstances, the clinician should document how the current treatment plan takes these elements into account to avoid their repetition if possible.

Diagnostic Status

A number of diagnoses have been established in the literature as being associated with a significantly higher incidence of suicide. These correlations are not fixed but are being refined over time with new observations. The diagnostic areas commonly associated with higher suicide rates are major depression, manic-depressive disorder, alcohol or substance abuse and dependency, borderline personality disorder, schizophrenia, and certain types of panic or anxiety disorder (Mościcki, 1995a).

Major Depressive Disorder. Major depressive disorder is the most common diagnostic correlate of suicidality, with a suicide rate of more than ten times that of the general population. A correlation has also been shown between suicide and the duration and severity of depression, and depression has been implicated as a comorbid diagnosis in the suicide rates of a number of other diagnostic states, especially alcoholism and schizophrenia (Jones et al., 1994). Major depression that reaches the level of severity to warrant consideration of inpatient care is itself an indication for a comprehensive suicide evaluation, even in the absence of suicidal ideation. Independent of the duration and severity of the depression, the highest period of risk for suicide is generally within the first three months of any specific major depressive episode and within five years of the lifetime onset of depression (Malone, Haas, Sweeney, and Mann, 1995).

Bipolar Disorder. In a large study of nine thousand individuals with manic-depressive illness, suicide accounted for almost 19 percent of the deaths in this population. A close look showed that a subgroup of manic patients, sometimes called mixed state, with concurrent depressive symptoms in mania, are particularly at risk (Swann, 1995). (See Chapters Fourteen and Twenty for a fuller discussion of this high-risk population.)

Substance Abuse. The most common comorbid factor in both completed and attempted suicides is alcohol or substance abuse and dependency. This factor is associated with higher levels of suicidal ideation and increased lethality of attempts (Nielson, Stenager, and Brahe, 1993). Chemically dependent adolescents are particularly at risk. In a study of three hundred chemically dependent adolescents, ages fifteen to nineteen, a high proportion—between one-third and three-fourths of various subpopulations—reported prolonged thoughts of death and prolonged desires to be dead, along with a significant number of attempts (between 28 percent and 68 percent), with females more than males. Moreover, alcohol levels showing intoxication have been found in almost half of actual adolescent suicides (Deykin and Buka, 1994).

When suicide attempts occur in patients with alcohol dependence, the lethality of those attempts may have little to do with the actual intent (Nielson, Stenager, and Brahe, 1993). Alcohol intoxication not only affects judgment about what is and is not lethal but also intensifies the lethality of barbiturates, benzodiazepines, and a number of other medications that the alcohol-dependent patient might abuse. While the intent of intoxification might be to obtund life rather than to end it, the alcoholic patient is significantly at risk for miscalculation.

Borderline Personality Disorder. A problem for inpatient clinicians is that borderline patients may use suicidality as a prominent manipulative tactic, including a ploy to gain admission to the hospital. Furthermore, hospitalization, and particularly prolonged hospitalization, may be regressive and not in the patient's longer-term best interest. Complicating the picture is the high proportion of borderline patients who make suicide attempts that are nonlethal, make many such attempts, and mutilate themselves. A number of studies have placed the lifetime incidence of suicide attempts in borderline personality disorder patients at about 70 percent, with a recent review showing an average between three and four significant attempts per patient (Soloff et al., 1994a). The clinician may be misled by these "false positives" into viewing suicidality in the borderline patient as a pathological but not particularly lethal state. In fact, the death rate by suicide of borderline personality disorder is not insignificant (Stone, 1993a). (See Chapter Eighteen.)

A highly serious intent to commit suicide in borderline patients as judged by the lethality of the attempt is associated with both the number of lifetime attempts and the persistence of a subjective dysphoria, which may or may not meet formal diagnostic criteria for major depressive disorder (Soloff et al., 1994a). Suicidal behavior in the borderline patient should not be taken merely as background morbidity; rather, each episode should be examined on its own for the risks and benefits of inpatient care and for the presence of a comorbid axis I disorder.

Schizophrenia. Various reports have shown that between 9 and 13 percent of deaths in schizophrenic patients are as a result of suicide. Although the precipitants of suicide in schizophrenic patients may be diverse and include social maladaptation, poor self-esteem, and delusional processes, it is probable that the most important correlates of suicide in schizophrenic patients are depressive symptoms and depressive symptoms combined with alcohol abuse (Jones et al., 1994). In a study of schizophrenic admissions, 50 percent of patients had auditory hallucinations, and half of those experienced command hallucinations, many of them violent (Zisook, Byrd, Kuck, and Jeste, 1995). The few patients in this series who did commit suicide had command hallucinations to do so. However, neither this nor other studies reached a level of statistical correlation between command hallucinations to suicide and actual death. Despite the insufficiency of statistical certainty, management of risk is clearly in favor of treating a patient with the acute onset of command hallucinations to suicide as a person in imminent danger. If a patient with persistent but chronic "voices telling me to kill myself" is judged not to be in danger, documentation of nonacuity and a supporting opinion by a second clinician may be prudent.

Anxiety and Panic Disorders. Fawcett (1995) and others have suggested that severe subjective anxiety at the time of discharge is correlated with an increased rate of suicide attempts. Others have shown that in patients with panic attacks associated with depression, substance abuse, or personality disorders, there appears to be an increased incidence of suicide attempts, although panic attack alone is not clearly associated with increased suicidality (Mannuzza, 1992; Johnson, Weissman, and Klerman, 1990; King, Schmaling, Cowley, and Dunner, 1995; Henriksson et al., 1996). Combined with other factors, severe anxiety and panic disorders should be considered as part of a comprehensive suicide evaluation.

Life Circumstances

Social, interpersonal, or medical circumstances that produce physical or psychic pain, helplessness, or intolerable shame or guilt should be investigated for increased suicidality (Barber, Marzuk, Leon, and Portera, 1998; Rich, Fowler, Fogarty, and Young, 1988a). The threatened loss of a close person, which is perceived by the patient to be a rejection, may precipitate a suicidal act in order to manipulate or avert the threat. After a loss such as separation or divorce has taken place, a suicide attempt may be intended as an act of revenge. The radical loss of financial status may precipitate suicide as a protection against anticipated humiliation. Suicide may be seen by the patient as a way of restoring honor following a defeat in which humiliation has already occurred. Adverse legal judgments may not only feel humiliating but may also produce intolerable physical threats, such as assault or rape.

Older adults commit suicide at far greater rates than others. The suicide rate in the general population is between 11 and 12 per 100,000, but for those over age sixty-five, it is 17 per 100,000 and for those over age eighty, 22 per 100,000. However, depression, the most common diagnosis correlated with suicide, may be no more frequent in the older adult than in younger adults once we remove the effects of medical illness and disability (Roberts et al., 1997). A recent study of medically hospitalized elders followed for a little under one year showed a prevalence of major depression from 10 to 21 percent and an additional similar prevalence of partially expressed depression (Koening et al., 1997). When it does occur, depression in the elderly appears to be dramatically more lethal than depression in younger age groups. The ratio of attempted suicide to completed suicide is approximately two hundred to three hundred attempts to one death in younger patients and approximately four attempts to one death in the elderly (Bharucha and Satlin, 1997). Often there is no warning, and the first attempt is lethal.

Responses to changed circumstances are highly individual. Some people may survive a holocaust with loss of family and country without becoming suicidal, while others will become suicidal when floods or hurricanes have altered familiar surroundings (Krug et al., 1998). Assessing the impact of changed circumstances on a specific patient includes understanding the patient's cultural context, family supports, and range of coping mechanisms. It is helpful to know if there is a sustaining relationship with a therapist who will continue with the treatment after discharge and to assess whether the patient, with help, can process threats and losses in a manner enabling the sustenance of hope.

Competence and Alliance

When the clinician relies on the patient's communication of his or her internal status, including suicidal ideation or intent, two clinical factors are implied. The first assumption is that the patient has the mental competence to understand the nature of the questions and the importance of the communications being asked for. The second assumption is a measure of alliance, that is, whether the patient is willing to communicate critical thoughts and feelings to the clinician (Gutheil, 1993).

Without both competence and alliance, it is more difficult to assess safety and therefore to adjust the suicidal patient's inpatient privileges accurately. Common practices such as the no-harm or no-suicide contract between patient and clinical staff, in which the patient agrees to maintain his or her own safety as a condition for clinical privileges, are relatively meaningless with insufficient mental competence or therapeutic alliance. A number of authors (Miller, Jacobs, and Gutheil, 1998; Jacobs, 1995) have advised against relying on the no-suicide contract, particularly as a stand-alone index of a patient's safety (see Chapter Twenty-Six in this book). Although this type of contract is in common use in inpatient services, its chief utility may be in the negative, that is, in intensifying staff attention to those who refuse such an agreement. Refusal is often an indication that the patient is delusional, confused, or provocative; any one of these conditions requires specific attention.

Indications of alliance, such as the patient's outreach to nursing staff at times of increased distress and the patient's candor with the therapist, can be assessed early in inpatient treatment and at intervals throughout the inpatient stay. Questions such as the following may assist in assessing the initial potential for alliance: If the patient has made a suicide attempt, is he or she relieved or sorry that it failed? Does the patient accept the need for treatment? Is the patient able to request staff assistance if, in his or her own opinion, safety is in jeopardy? Finally, the patient's history of alliance in prior similar crises may be helpful if it is available.

Special Considerations with Child and Adolescent Patients

In the United States and Europe, suicide ranks among the five leading causes of deaths in adolescents (Diekstra and Guldinat, 1993). As with adults, there is a correlation between the severity of suicidality and the symptoms and diagnosis of depression (Brent et al., 1986; Brent, 1995). Because the assessment of children and adolescents involves the patient's family whenever possible, special issues arise. Often a child or adolescent patient will tell his or her parents of suicidal ideas and plans and withhold this information from a new therapist even on direct questioning. Conversely, an adequate relationship with a therapist may elicit valid suicidal ideation from a child that is withheld from parents. Even when suicidality is known by a patient and the family and communicated to the therapist, there is often poor agreement between parent and child on the severity of that suicidality. Because of the seriousness of potential risk, the clinician has little choice but to explore the more severe rating.

Children and younger adolescents may not clearly understand that death is final and irreversible (Orbach, Rosenheim, and Hary, 1987). A three-year-old girl was brought to the clinic by her mother who feared that her daughter was psychotic, suicidal, or both. The child appeared to have developed a new obsession about ladders and on several occasions expressed to her mother the wish to die.

She was able to tell her therapist her determination to go to heaven, where she believed her recently deceased grandfather resided. She saw ladders, particularly tall construction ladders, as the most obvious route to her destination.

Somewhere between the ages of seven and thirteen, children do appear to understand the immutability of death. Older adolescents are reasonably accurate about predicting which methods of suicide would be fatal. Adolescent fantasies of death by suicide tend to be explicit and include major overdoses, laceration, and hanging. Latency-age children, on the other hand, often can give no specific fantasies how suicide could occur and they have incomplete notions of fatality, such as, "I could choke myself with my hands." When young children make suicide attempts that appear sublethal, such as attempting to drown themselves in the bathtub, overdosing on a small number of pills, or inflicting minor stab wounds, the intent to die may be just as serious as a child who runs in front of a truck or attempts hanging.

The assessment of suicidality for children and adolescents uses many of the same factors as that for adults, but with added emphasis on the immediate family situation. The degree of depression, presence of a conduct disorder, substance abuse, a history of previous attempts, the presence of a suicidal relative, the loss of a family member, and low family support are all factors commonly reviewed by child and adolescent clinicians concerned with suicide (Morano, Cisler, Lemerond, 1993; Pfeffer, 1997; Gould et al., 1996).

A large sampling of children between the ages of five and eighteen years showed that the onset by age fourteen of a psychiatric disorder significantly increased the risk for suicidal ideation by age fifteen and suicide attempts by age eighteen (Reinherz et al., 1995). Adolescent patients who have made suicide attempts compared with those who were never suicidal showed correlation with social impairment and borderline personality. This study showed little correlation with a general history of aggression or with assaultive behavior toward others (Brent et al., 1993a). Physical and sexual abuse were found to be significantly associated with suicide attempts in both children and adolescents (Shaunesey, Cohen, Plummer, and Berman, 1993). One study reviewed 120 consecutive suicides of patients under the age of twenty for correlation with homosexuality. No evidence could be found that death by suicide in gay teenagers was a consequence of stigmatization (Shaffer et al., 1995). The presence of a learning disorder or newly discovered physical disability in an adolescent should be explored for suicidal potential because of the impact of these conditions on the formation of self-image of the adolescent, and attention deficit hyperactivity disorder associated with pronounced mood fluctuations should be explored for adolescent mania (Sachs, 1997).

One of the special concerns surrounding adolescent suicide, in both the inpatient unit and the community, is the potential for the contagion of suicidal behavior with or without an explicit suicide pact. A number of studies in the

United States and elsewhere have shown clustering among adolescent age groups of suicide attempts that could not be explained by seasonality (Gould, Petrie, Kleinman, and Wallenstein, 1994). A major attempt or actual death on the inpatient unit of an adolescent by suicide generally alerts the entire adolescent service in an attempt to inhibit other attempts. Suicides of hospitalized adolescents (or indeed hospital patients of any age) can have a profound impact on the hospital staff manifested by symptoms of grief and PTSD that require sensitive administrative handling (Cooper, 1955).

TREATMENT ENVIRONMENT

In order to reduce the opportunities for hospitalized patients who are still determined to end their lives, a combination of design features and operational procedures are first-line prevention measures. Safety regulations vary from locality to locality. Prevention measures are generally targeted at limiting the patient's access to means of hanging or other asphyxiation, cutting, poisoning, or burning. Common safety design features found on the inpatient unit are protuberances such as shower rods, shower heads, and ceiling water sprinklers designed to break off at low test weights, provision of mirrors and windows of nonbreakable material, provision of interior safety screens in front of external breakable windows, and the shortening of electrical cords to their minimal necessary length. But no unit can be "suicide proof" due to the determination of some patients.

The ability to observe the intently suicidal patient at all times and at all places is particularly important. Determined patients have successfully committed suicide in an otherwise safe treatment environment by hanging on sheets draped over a door and attached to the doorknob on the other side of the door. Other patients have used articles of clothing or electrical cords. Most inpatient units provide for the capacity to observe a patient anywhere in his or her room, often by means of a window in the patient door combined with strategically placed convex or other mirrors allowing corners of the room to be seen or at times by means of a closed circuit television camera. In certain jurisdictions where these arrangements conflict with patient privacy rights, hospitals may post members of the nursing staff in the room in a one-to-one observation of the patient or move the patient to an open sleeping arrangement within sight of a nursing staff member.

Furniture has been taken apart and used as a weapon against the patient himself or herself or staff members. Furniture is used that can stand abuse or can be removed from the room. Beds that have the capacity to accept restraints are common. Finally, doors to the unit itself must be lockable, or there should be a personnel system in place to guard against unauthorized departure from the unit. A significant proportion of suicide deaths of hospitalized patients have occurred off the psychiatric unit itself, either on the hospital grounds or in the community following unauthorized departure (Morgan and Priest, 1991). Design features such as locked doors that restrict egress and transparent materials used for internal observation (such as wire-reinforced glass or transparent plastic) should be reviewed for conformity with local fire ordinances.

Administrative Procedures

Architectural safety features, although important, are static; they are no substitute for the preventive and monitoring procedures generally carried out by the nursing staff. Preventative action on admission includes a search of the patient for dangerous items and, where a high degree of lethality is anticipated, the removal of items of the patient's clothing such as belts and shoelaces that could be used for hanging attempts. Matches, lighters, and sharp items are secured out of patient reach.

The problem of smuggling drugs onto the unit by visitors, particularly on adolescent units, has been significant. As a means of limiting this problem, some units request identification of all visitors and in certain instances supervise all visitors

From time to time, police are called to the unit to assist with a dangerous patient. Alternatively, police may request access to a unit to interview a patient suspected of having committed a crime. In these cases, police are generally asked to leave firearms outside the unit.

Finally, the training of nonclinical hospital staff such as food, cleaning, and maintenance services personnel is an important part of unit safety. Many patients have bolted from an otherwise locked unit when doors have been left open by an inattentive nonclinical service provider. Toxic cleaning chemicals should be guarded and plastic bags not used in patient area waste baskets.

Level-of-Care Decisions

Suicide precautions are physician or other clinician written orders that specify a series of actions and a level of surveillance by the nursing staff on the inpatient unit. There is no single assessment format or rating that automatically dictates the prescription for a specific suicide precaution level, and these prescriptions remain a broadly based clinical judgment. Beck, Kovacs, and Weissman have emphasized a strong association between suicidal behavior and the level of hopelessness (1975) and have incorporated this observation in a scale for suicide ideation (1979).

The findings obtained from a comprehensive suicide risk assessment, the clinical interview, and patient observation form a basis for documenting the clinician's reasoning in prescribing for the patient's safety. Although there are no published correlations between assessment factors and prescribed levels of suicide precaution, trends have begun to emerge. If patients present at risk for suicide and are unable or unwilling to form an alliance with the hospital staff, they are frequently placed on a level of precaution beyond the base level of surveillance provided by the unit to all admissions. If, in addition to lack of alliance with the hospital staff, the patient has demonstrated potential lethality in prior attempts and is severely symptomatic with a mood disorder or psychosis, he or she is often placed on one of the more secure levels of suicide precaution.

Precautions can involve constant observation or intermittent observation, usually every fifteen minutes or more frequently. At the higher levels of suicide risk, intermittent observation, even every five minutes, may be inadequate because the patient may have the capacity to hurt himself or herself within that time interval and because unit duties may inadvertently extend the time between intended observations.

The following are examples of defined levels of care:

Level 1: Close One-to-One Observation. At the highest level of suicide precaution, a staff member is assigned to be with the patient at all times, and a flow sheet is maintained for documenting the patient's symptoms and behaviors. Some precaution protocols specify that the staff member be within arm's length or other close proximity to the patient so as to be able to intervene rapidly in destructive behavior. The patient is supervised even during bathroom breaks and toileting. Belts, cords, and laces are removed from the patient's clothing. No sharp objects, such as razors, are permitted, even under supervision. A room search is undertaken to ascertain that there are no secreted or dangerous objects, and all visits are supervised.

Level 2: Close Observation, Group. This level of precaution is similar to the first, although the patient is observed as part of a small group of patients, generally not more than four. Often the difference between placing a patient on Level 1 or Level 2 is the degree of the patient's overt hostility or behavioral dyscontrol. Patients who have hurt themselves or threatened themselves or others even while a staff member was present are usually not suitable for group observation without significant improvement.

Level 3: Intermittent Observation. The patient is checked on regular intervals, usually every fifteen minutes or less. They are often permitted to use sharp objects such as a safety razor with direct supervision. Bathroom time is not under direct supervision, although checks for the patient's whereabouts and safety continue by means of establishing voice contact even if the patient is toileting. Unsupervised visiting may be allowed. Patients who are placed on intermittent observation status generally have not made previous recent suicide attempts in a hospital setting and have sufficient capacity to communicate verbally with the hospital staff and accurately convey inner states.

Alertness to the possibility of inpatient suicide, even when the admission suicide assessment does not result in suicide precautions, is important in prevention. A retrospective analysis of suicides occurring during hospitalization showed that between 17 and 26 percent of inpatient suicides had not been recognized as having suicidal ideation, and up to half of those who died on the unit or shortly after discharge were thought to be nonsuicidal at the time of admission (Morgan and Priest, 1991; Dennehey et al., 1996; Morgan, 1979). Therefore, even without a formal order for suicide precaution, new admissions to an inpatient unit are often initially restricted to the unit and are monitored at regular intervals.

For patients who are placed on various levels of suicide precautions, it is useful to have contingency plans for crises, such as the evaluation of the unit in case of a fire, and also for more routine situations, such as changes of nursing shift and periods of nursing shortage.

In some ways, it is easier to impose than to reduce suicide precautions. Before reducing suicide precautions, the clinician's own observations should be compared with the observations of others, including the nursing staff. The clinician order to reduce or eliminate suicide precautions should be accompanied by a progress note in the medical record reviewing the examination of the patient, stipulating the clinical basis for the decision and the risks and benefits of it. As part of risk management, this examination and progress note is so important that many inpatient units prohibit the nursing staff from carrying out a clinician order to reduce suicidal precautions unless this progress note is written (personal communication, Westwood Lodge Hospital, Westwood, Massachusetts, 1990). Finally, it is important for the nursing staff to have the capacity to initiate or increase suicide precautions in an emergency when the clinician who usually writes such orders is unavailable. The reasons for these emergency precautions also should be clearly documented in the medical chart.

CLINICAL STRATEGIES

There are generally three goals of inpatient treatment: (1) the preservation of life and safety, (2) the reduction or elimination of suicidal intent and ideation together with the treatment of underlying disorders, and (3) the improvement of an array of intrapsychic capacities, interpersonal factors, and psychosocial circumstances, sufficient to permit the patient to cope following discharge with a diminished risk of the return of suicidality. These goals are not separate from one another, but often one or another goal is prominent during different phases of the patient's hospital treatment. The goal is for all to be achieved before discharge.

The restrictions of suicide precautions and, in the case of otherwise uncontrollable danger, the restrictions of seclusion and restraint (Gutheil, 1978) preserve the patient's safety by preventing suicidal behavior. The majority of suicidal patients seem comforted by the structure, support, and limit setting of the inpatient unit. Most patients on the higher levels of suicide precaution may struggle against or test their limits but generally engage staff in a process that addresses issues of trust, self-restraint, and alliance building. Thus, the negotiation between patient and staff to reduce a clinical restriction is an opportunity to engage the patient in an ongoing assessment, to make progress in the restoration of affective and cognitive capacities, and to reverse hopelessness and helplessness (Beck, 1989).

The continuous process of assessment and alliance building is also a forum for discussion of reality testing, social judgment, anger and disappointment, diminished self-esteem, and anxiety, all frequently occurring problems in suicidal inpatients. As the restrictions of suicide precautions along with negotiations surrounding them recede, these topics remain and become the focus of group and individual therapy. Consistency in the therapeutic milieu, which includes frequent clinical visits with the same therapist, and group and activity therapies permit the patient to develop an acceptance of clinical support in reappraising his or her previous maladaptive assumptions and coping mechanisms.

Cognitive therapy, as either a primary or an auxiliary treatment, is particularly adapted to the reduction of hopelessness as a recurrent negative automatic thought. With the exception of patients whose thought processes are significantly disrupted, it has been used successfully in a wide array of clinical situations (Wright, Thace, Beck, and Ludgate, 1993).

A number of cognitive therapy techniques can also be specifically directed at self-esteem issues, often central in suicidality. Techniques that assist the patient in recognizing distortions in his or her self-evaluation and have been used in successful intervention include inquiring about or keeping a daily journal of positive thoughts and events, a self-inventory of positive traits, and instructions on the recognition of absolutist and negative thinking (McKay and Fanning, 1987; Beck, Rush, Shaw, and Emery, 1979).

Patients whose depressed mood is alleviated but still see themselves as worthless, as deserving punishment for their deeds, or as legitimately responsible for intolerable events raise concerns about their vulnerability to the return of suicidal behavior. When the patient's self-condemnation is in fact tied to his or her negligence in an event such as serious injury to a third party, the empathic acceptance of the reality of the situation by the therapist, support by fellow patients in group therapy, explicit apologies by the patient, and meetings with clergy are often critical factors in reducing the potential return of suicidality.

The reduction of symptoms associated with affective and thought disorder syndromes is clearly a first-order strategy. Electroconvulsive therapy may be necessary to intervene more rapidly than antidepressants, particularly when intense suicidal behavior persists on the inpatient unit. Almost all of the neuroleptic and newer antipsychotic medications have been used with success in the acute clinical management of schizophrenia and bipolar disorder with suicidality. A number of prominent psychopharmacologists have preferred the newer antipsychotics over the phenothiazines or haloperidol because of the lessened risk of tardive dyskinesia and the apparent superior therapeutic effect on the deficit syndrome in schizophrenia, chiefly anergy, avolition, and anhedonia (personal communication with D. J. Borrelli, 1998; Liberman, 1996).

Indeed, olanzapine, risperidone, quetiapine, and clozapine have all demonstrated a broad spectrum of efficacy for treating both the positive and the negative symptoms for schizophrenia (Perry, 1995; Tollefson et al., 1997; Blin, Azorinn, and Bouhours, 1996). In the longer term, clozapine has been shown to have a positive effect on the suicide risk in schizophrenic patients as compared to patients treated with older neuroleptics. This decrease in suicidality with clozapine treatment patients was associated with improvement in depression and hopelessness (Meltzer, 1995). However, when agitated, hallucinating, and delusional suicidal patients do not respond rapidly or fully with the newer antipsychotic medications, substituting the phenothiazines or haloperidol or, alternatively, adding these medications to the newer antipsychotics have been effective in selected cases, including with patients with command hallucinations (personal communication with C. Adler, May 1998).

A number of studies have demonstrated the usefulness of Lorazepam, either alone or as an adjunct with haloperidol, in psychotic agitation and as an adjunct with lithium during a manic episode (Bataglia et al., 1997; Foster, Kessel, Berman, and Simpson, 1997; Lenox, Newhous, Creelman, and Whitaker, 1992). Lorazepam alone may be preferable to neuroleptics when alcohol has been used as part of a suicide attempt because of concerns about lowering the seizure threshold with alcohol withdrawal.

Suicidal ideation, intent, and behavior may all recede as the acute symptoms diminish. In some patients, especially those with pronounced affective disorder, it is clear that suicidality comes and goes with acute symptomatology; the key to longer-term treatment of the suicidality is prevention, to the extent possible, of the return of those symptoms. In other patients, however, where symptom improvement was not accompanied by resolution of the relevant psychosocial stressors, patients may remain actively suicidal. In a study of patients who committed suicide in the hospital or shortly after discharge, approximately half had shown significant clinical improvement prior to their deaths (Morgan and Priest, 1991).

Among the most common psychosocial stressors are those that involve family members. The clinician must judge whether certain family meetings would be constructive for the patient or whether the patient needs protection from that engagement, at least for the time being. A significant number of inpatients with suicidality have experienced sexual abuse (Beck, James, and van der Kolk, 1987;

Jacobsen and Richardson, 1987). Overt confrontation of sexual abuse in a family meeting needs careful preparation and follow-up if it is to occur within a brief hospital stay. When suicidal behavior is related to family conflict, resolution of that conflict in family meetings may be critical to the ability of the patient to return home.

Since marital disputes are a common precipitant for suicide attempts, couple assessment and the beginnings of couple treatment occur frequently during hospitalization. Unlike most outpatient couple therapy, one member of the marital dyad is clearly labeled "the patient." Therefore, the therapist should take special care so that the nonhospitalized spouse is not regarded as a superior marital partner, to the detriment of the patient's self-esteem (Jacobson, 1983).

The spouse of a suicidal hospitalized patient may also take the occasion of the hospitalization to finalize plans for separation or divorce. This circumstance quickly becomes apparent when the outside spouse refuses to come to couple therapy meetings with the patient or else announces the decision directly. Although the announcement intensifies the crisis for the patient, it also serves to clarify the situation. Clinician assistance can then be directed toward organizing the skills and outside arrangements that the patient will need to cope with the divorce and begin to plan for life alternatives.

Suicidal patients who are admitted with acute affective or psychotic symptoms generally respond to treatment by following a course of diminishing symptoms. Some patients, such as those with borderline personality, may not show significant changes in suicidal ideation despite improvements in mood, relationships, and psychosocial stressors. Some, such as patients with post-traumatic stress disorder, may present sharp fluctuations in suicidality as they experience flashbacks, associations with traumatic memories, hyperarousal, hypervigilance, sleep deprivation, depressed mood, irritability, and at times explosive states (Southwick, Bremnor, Krystal, and Charney, 1994; Kramer et al., 1994; Smith, 1996).

A wide variety of medications have been used directed at the range of symptoms, among them tricyclic antidepressants, the MAOIs and more recently, both the SSRIs and anticonvulsants. Although there is little evidence for the effectiveness of benzodiazepines alone, they are occasionally used as adjunctive treatment. Beta blockers have been used to address autonomic hyperactivity and clonidine to address flashbacks. The use of low-dose neuroleptics or the newer antipsychotic medications on an as-needed (prn) basis may be calming to post-traumatic stress or borderline patients who experience an episodic drive to hurt or kill themselves. In addition to the relief from the extreme tension of self-destructive urges, prn dosing can provide a sense of control for the patient who is otherwise experiencing little mastery of mind or body (personal communication with C. Adler, May 1998). Since the use of these medications is often empirical and without support of large published studies, careful monitoring of developments in the literature and explanations to the patient are in order.

The current inpatient treatment bias for PTSD patients is in favor of brief hospitalizations to protect against regression. Traumatic events are opened for examination enough to understand their content and form a reasonable hypothesis on their etiology. In addition to medication, patients are taught behavioral methods of terminating flashbacks and containing anxiety.

Finally, there is a danger that suicidality will be treated as a mere symptom to be added to a checklist and to be reduced and in that sense treated as similar to other symptoms such as hallucinations, depression, or anxiety. Suicidality is a symptom, but it is frequently a signal that meaning and purpose in the patient's life are not being sustained. As Victor Frankl (1977) and others have found, meaning can be restored or discovered through human encounters and by attitudes taken even in the face of unavoidable suffering.

DISCHARGE PROCEDURES

Several reviews have seen a disturbing number of suicides shortly following hospitalization, frequently within the first twenty-four to forty-eight hours (Morgan and Stanton, 1997). In general, patients who are on suicidal precautions are not discharged except to be transferred to another hospital. While a small minority of patients have successfully persuaded the courts to obtain release despite medical opinion of suicidality, the majority of patients who were discharged and committed suicide shortly after are commonly seen as not suicidal or, at minimum, not suicidal with the support of their aftercare treatment program. All patients admitted with a concern about suicidality should have a specific assessment for suicidality on or proximate to the day of discharge. Assessment can be similar to the admission assessment already described, or, because the medical record will have contained significant information on the patient's progress in the reduction of suicidality, an abbreviated note is acceptable.

Before discharge, the patient should be informed about those elements that might increase his or her risk of the return of suicidality, such as self-discontinuation of medication and noncompliance with the treatment plan following hospitalization. At some point during the patient's treatment, it is helpful to explain to the patient explicitly that the clinician needs to rely on the patient's truthfulness in reporting inner states of the presence or absence of suicidal feelings and to garner from the patient an agreement to communicate these inner states truthfully. Often this is done in the course of clinical interviews at the beginning of the patient's hospital stay, but if not, this communication should be considered at the end of the hospital stay and documented in the patient's chart. The patient needs explicit information on how to access emergency services after discharge, the date of appointment or the mechanism for gaining an appointment with a specific posthospital treatment arrangement, laboratory tests and medical or surgical follow-up that may be needed following discharge, and an ample discussion of the effects and side effects of postdischarge medications. Finally, it is useful to record the assent of the patient to the specific elements of the discharge plan and postdischarge care arrangements. Similar information, with permission, can be conveyed to members of the patient's family; if the patient is a minor or under guardianship, it is often mandatory to supply this information. Communication with the postdischarge treatment provider usually takes place verbally prior to discharge, and in addition, excerpts of the patient's medical chart and written transfer forms are routinely forwarded to the aftercare treaters.

Problems arise when the information provided is not sufficiently specific or is untimely. Since the immediate postdischarge period is of special concern for the suicidal patient, timely transmission of details, such as the hospital's assessment of the patient's suicidality or destructiveness to others, the hospital's recommendations for postdischarge treatment plans, and information on the hospital's recommendation for discharge medications, laboratory, and medical follow-up, as well as actual medications given or prescriptions written, should be transmitted, and a record should be made in the patient's medical chart of the transmission of that information.

Considerations for Requesting a Second Opinion

In many instances, the clinician is uncertain about the patient's suicide risk following discharge, and yet it appears to be in the best interest of the patient's getting on with his or her life to discharge the patient to a less than twenty-four-hour supervised setting. An explanation of the clinician's reasoning about both the risks and the benefits of the discharge should be placed in the medical record, and, to the extent possible, efforts of plans to mitigate the risk should be documented. Mitigating the risk will often involve information to the patient and family to maintain vigilance for certain prodromal symptoms such as hypomania in a bipolar patient, the return of depression or alcohol abuse, or the return of painful circumstances. Informing the patient and family about such early warning systems and providing explicit information on accessing urgent care are common means of mitigating risk.

Requests from a peer for a second opinion on the discharge or aftercare plan is useful when a risk is assumed but mitigation of that risk is difficult. Conditions just prior to discharge that might trigger a second opinion include the persistence of suicidal ideation with a feasible plan, a recent history of having had the ideation to harm others, a recent history of suicide attempt with residual symptoms of depression, severe anxiety or psychosis, a history of suicide attempt in a patient who is refusing assistance following discharge, and a history of previous "surprise" suicide attempts.

Many patients are admitted with a history of suicidality but following inpatient treatment appear to become less anxious, less depressed, have a greater alliance with the staff, are handling privileges well, have plans for the future, and accept a well-thought-out proposal for a support system following discharge. When such patients then make a serious suicidal attempt shortly following discharge, the staff is usually surprised, as well as disconcerted, because the suicide attempt occurred despite their vigilance. Clinicians are left with the sense that they were either misled by the patient or that they themselves failed to take into account factors that they could not identify. A second opinion for patients with a history of a serious surprise suicide attempt should be considered prior to the patient's being given any hospital privileges in which he or she is unattended and also prior to discharge. The clinician's progress notes, as well as the second opinion consultant's note, should address the patient's history of suicide attempts in the face of appearing to be "nonsuicidal," the patient's perspectives on that fact, and the clinician's perspectives on why the present clinical condition and circumstances as well as the postdischarge treatment plan are different from those that occurred previously.

Among the most difficult conundrums are patients who have made a serious suicide attempt and state in a predischarge evaluation that they are not suicidal "now" but let it be known that they have a clear and persistent wish to end their life at some undetermined future point. Under these circumstances, a second opinion consult serves not only as a review of the patient's readiness for discharge but also as a diagnostic and treatment review. A number of second opinions have changed the course of treatment and in certain instances have uncovered explicit suicide plans on the part of the patient who was unwilling to reveal them to the attending clinician.

So-called psychological autopsies of suicidal deaths have indicated that approximately 90 percent of these deaths exhibited prodromal indicia of the suicide in the form of verbal and behavioral clues (Shneidman, 1994). Of the 10 percent whose lethal outcome was hidden, some may have intentionally and skillfully masked their intent, some may have been the victims of impulsivity or sudden changes in stress, and some are victims of factors that are simply unpredictable. When suicide does occur following discharge, a careful predischarge suicide assessment and a second opinion, when warranted, will give some comfort to the inpatient clinician in knowing that he or she made a full and conscious effort to preserve the patient's life.

Review of the Discharge Plan

A study of over fifteen hundred suicide attempters showed the suicide mortality to be approximately 6 percent within the first five years after the attempt, with the risk of death by suicide particularly high during the first year. Mortality among men was nearly twice that of women. Both older and younger men who had made suicide attempts were at higher risk of death than women, and older women were at substantially higher risk of death than younger women (Nordström, Samuelsson, and Åsberg, 1995a). These data and others showing a shift in deaths among suicidal patients from the inpatient setting to the postdischarge period (Morgan and Stanton, 1997) suggest that failure to comply with referral to outpatient aftercare and inadequate outpatient aftercare is a significant problem

In the case of individuals who have repeatedly failed to keep outpatient appointments following hospitalization for suicidality, inpatient clinicians should look to altering the aftercare plan so as to avoid repeating the past. Useful variations have included several forms of outreach to the patient. In a study of attempted-suicide patients with a history of failing to comply with referrals for outpatient care, compliance significantly improved after visits in their homes by community nurses (Van Heeringen et al., 1995). In a large study of follow-up intervention with depressed elderly patients, telephone contact at home reduced the suicide rate in this population by sevenfold over a four-year period (De Leo et al., 1995).

Although means for suicide are ubiquitous, the discharge plan should be reviewed for selective prescribing in suicidal patients who habitually overdose on their prescription medications (Rynn, Graf, and Palovcek, 1997). Nationwide, between 9 and 25 percent of self-poisoning deaths have involved antidepressant medication (Litovitz et al., 1996).

IMPLICATIONS FOR THE CLINICIAN

- As inpatient clinicians are called on to see and treat increased numbers of suicidal patients over shorter durations, the broad range of issues to which the clinician must attend becomes compressed into a smaller time frame.

- Standardizing the assessment, suicide precautions, and discharge procedures helps the clinician attend to the multiple elements involved in an organized and comprehensive fashion. The tendency toward standardization, however, also raises the risk for clinicians who do not follow the hospital's procedures, should harm befall their patients.

- Purposeful variation from standardized hospital expectations can be handled by documenting the clinical reasons for these variations and, if necessary, obtaining consultation. Inadvertent omissions are more troublesome.

- The assistance of the inpatient unit's quality assurance program in monitoring clinician compliance with standardized expectations is of particular risk management importance, as is updating these expectations by bringing to bear new clinical research and taking into account changes in clinical practice.

- For patients admitted with suicidality, a predischarge assessment of suicidality should be made and recorded. In constructing the discharge plan, an attempt should be made to anticipate the risks inherent in relapse after discharge. When these risks are prominent and difficult to mitigate, a peer second opinion consultation on the patient's readiness for discharge and postdischarge plans is useful.

- As aftercare assumes a larger role in preserving the gains of the suicidal patient, explicit communication, including the transfer of written records to the aftercare source, is an important part of treatment.

- Informing the patient, and to the extent indicated the family, of the availability of emergency resources, the importance of vigilance for the return of symptoms that may signal relapse, and the risks of not following through on medication or aftercare plans may help in the postdischarge period.

- The clinician's empathic attention to the painful and disruptive experiences of the suicidal patient and the clinician's attempt to understand the patient's potential to find and sustain meaning in his or her life moves the treatment beyond a collection of symptoms abated to that of a human life enhanced.

CHAPTER TWENTY-THREE

ECT and Suicide

Eran D. Metzger, M.D.

The safety and efficacy of electroconvulsive therapy (ECT) in the treatment of mood disorders is well established (Avery and Winokur, 1977). Since the first administration of ECT in the United States in 1940, advances in pretreatment screening, the introduction of general anesthesia, and modifications in how the ECT stimulus is administered have all served to decrease iatrogenic morbidity and mortality. The mortality rate for ECT has come to equal that for general anesthesia given for other short procedures, on the order of two deaths per 100,000 treatments (Abrams, 1992; Kramer, 1985; Fink, 1979). Interestingly, despite this treatment's success, rates of utilization in this country vary significantly from state to state (Hermann et al., 1995). Furthermore, research into areas such as mechanism, predictors of response, technique, and maintenance of symptom remission has not kept pace with similar research in the pharmacotherapies. A recent editorial in the *American Journal of Psychiatry* (Salzman, 1998) states:

> It appears that ECT has failed to attract current scientific curiosity. Despite a journal devoted exclusively to convulsive therapy, and a society of dedicated researchers and clinicians, there has not been the same systematic accretion of clinical research into ECT's mechanisms and efficacy as there has been for antidepressants. . . . What is to be done? We lack comparisons of ECT's efficacy with adequately dosed trials of new antidepressants for all categories of depression, especially for our sickest patients. We need carefully collected data on the therapeutic impact of ECT for the suicidally depressed patient, both acutely and after treatment.

This chapter surveys the data currently available on ECT's effect on suicidal behavior. In addition, the chapter reviews patient selection, risk of suicide during ECT, biological considerations, and areas for further research.

HISTORY OF ECT

A brief history of this unique treatment, currently the lone medical procedure in psychiatry widely used, will help elucidate the role of ECT in the treatment of the suicidal patient. Although the use of induced convulsions to treat mental illness dates back over two centuries, credit for the first application is attributed to the Italian psychiatrists Cerletti and Bini, who treated their first patient in 1938 (Cerletti and Bini, 1938). Although crude by today's standards, ECT was much safer and more effective than other contemporary treatments and thus gained rapid acceptance. Unfortunately, the success of ECT came to threaten its own existence. Over the next two decades, its clinical application outpaced research, leading to public charges of overuse and, in some jurisdictions, legal barriers to psychiatrists' employment of this modality. The response to both public skepticism and professional concern stimulated two important American Psychiatric Association Task Force reports (1978, 1990) and a National Institute of Health Consensus Conference (1985). These reports addressed important issues such as patient selection, informed consent, medical screening, technique, and duration of treatments. Salzman's introductory quote notwithstanding, current research in both anesthesia and stimulus delivery has made ECT a much safer and better tolerated treatment than even ten years ago. The absence of absolute medical contraindications to ECT has made possible its use in patients who have suffered severe illness or injury after suicide attempts. Although ECT may present fewer risks for some medically ill patients than a trial of antidepressant medication, patients are rarely referred for ECT prior to psychopharmacologic failure (APA, 1990; Prudic et al., 1996).

Unipolar and bipolar major depressive episodes and mania respond most predictably to ECT, with success rates as high as 80 to 90 percent. This success rate is even more impressive given the difficulty in identifying predictors of response (see below) and given that ECT is often reserved for patients who have depression refractory to medications. Use of ECT for treatment of schizophrenia has dropped off in the face of newer neuroleptic medications and an absence of data to support sustained improvement. A growing case literature supports the use of ECT in catatonia (Fink, 1992), and gratifying improvement of varying duration may be seen in the signs and symptoms of Parkinson's disease (Fink, 1988).

Abrams has reviewed the current research on which depressed patients are most responsive to ECT (1992). Although one might assume that endogenous depressions would be most responsive to ECT, the presence of endogenous or *DSM-III* melancholic features has not consistently predicted a better outcome (Coryell and Zimmerman, 1984; Zimmerman et al., 1986). The discrepancies in these data serve as a reminder of the problems inherent to the endogenous or reactive question. Similarly, Hamilton Rating Scale for Depression scores based on selecting items specific for melancholic depression are also not predictive of improved response to ECT (Hamilton, 1960; Prudic et al., 1989; Abrams and Vedak, 1991). Clinical variables consistently correlated with good outcome in the Abrams review include increased age, shorter duration of illness, and female gender. There is a surprising lack of data to support any association between the presence of suicidal ideation or suicide attempt and outcome from ECT (Carney et al., 1965; Hamilton and White, 1960; Hobson, 1953; Mendels, 1965; Roberts, 1959).

SUICIDAL IDEATION AND THE USE OF ECT

Despite the lack of association between suicidal ideation and ECT response, the presence of suicidal ideation in a patient may trigger a consultation for ECT. Without the risk of suicide present in such a patient, alternate modes of therapy would most likely be considered. The risk of suicide in a patient understandably impels the clinician to employ a treatment modality that is expeditious and that has a high success rate. Even among those knowledgeable about ECT's safety and tolerability, it may be thought of as a means of last resort; particularly violent or otherwise disturbing suicide attempts (for example, in-hospital attempts) may prompt some to consider such "heroic measures." The suicidal patient may request ECT himself or herself to alleviate suicidal feelings. In an alternative scenario in which the suicidal patient is refusing all treatment, a clinician may request ECT as the only "antidepressant" that can be administered involuntarily. As a symptom of mood disorder, suicidal ideation must be considered among other signs and symptoms when determining the appropriateness of ECT for a given patient. In a discussion of the topic, Frankel's (1984) assessment remains valid: "What needs to be stated . . . is that for many instances of suicidal behavior ECT is not the appropriate treatment, and in many cases of major affective illness requiring ECT there is no clear evidence of suicidal ideation or behavior. . . . We cannot assume that the higher the potential for suicide in any patient, the greater the need for ECT."

ECT practitioners are commonly asked to consult on a patient with character disorder and suicidal ideation. Chronic suicidal ideation in such a patient may prompt a clinician to request ECT in reaction to a sense of futility. Though a blanket response to such a request along the lines of, "ECT is not indicated in the treatment of character disorder," may not be, strictly speaking, inaccurate, it relegates to others the challenge and responsibility of ruling out in this patient a comorbid major depression. Ample evidence supports the increased vulnerability to major depression of patients with character disorder. (See Chapter Eighteen.) In addition, one study of patients with major depression treated with ECT found no difference in response between those with and without a comorbid character disorder (Zimmerman et al., 1986). In sum, although suicidal ideation in a patient with character disorder may prompt a request for ECT for the "wrong reasons," the presence of a comorbid major depression needs to be ruled out before deciding whether or not to proceed with ECT.

A patient with major depression and a comorbid character disorder who embarks on a course of ECT should be informed as to which of her symptoms are expected to respond to this treatment. To date, ECT's efficacy in the treatment of symptoms of character disorder, obsessive compulsive disorder, addictive disorders, and post-traumatic stress disorder, has not been demonstrated. Thus, in the case of a patient with comorbid character disorder, ECT might successfully treat the major depression, although the patient's parasuicidal behavior still persists.

ECT and Suicide Prevention

The relative infrequency of suicide even in depressed patients presents one obstacle to studying the effectiveness of ECT in preventing suicide. Retrospective studies may also be influenced by ECT referral patterns, whereby ECT is reserved for more seriously depressed and suicidal patients. Nevertheless, results of studies employing several methodologies suggest a role for ECT in reducing the rate of suicide in patients with depression (see review in Tanney, 1986). Epidemiologic studies comparing suicide rates in a particular geographical area over time generally support a reduction of suicide rates when ECT was available compared to when tricyclic medications were favored (Krieger, 1966; Jaasskelainen and Viukari, 1976; Lönnqvist et al., 1974).

In an initial study of mortality rates between groups of depressed patients receiving different treatment modalities at three-year follow-up, Avery and Winokur were unable to detect an effect of ECT on the rate of suicide (1976). In the 519 patients studied, only eight suicides occurred, distributed across four treatment groups. In a follow-up study of the same patients, suicide and suicide attempts were analyzed at six and twelve months after hospital discharge (Avery and Winokur, 1978). After six months, suicide attempt rates were significantly higher in patients who took antidepressant medication than in patients who received ECT. After one year, four successful suicides had occurred. Though none were in the ECT group, this difference did not achieve statistical significance. Methodological problems in this study include the absence of a definition of what constitutes a suicide attempt and the designation of 150 mg of imipramine (or equivalent) as adequate pharmacotherapy.

Indirect evidence for the efficacy of ECT in depression is provided by a recent Finnish study that reviewed 1,397 completed suicides over a twelve-month period to determine how many of these persons had received ECT within three months of death (Isometsä et al., 1996a). Only two such cases were identified. Both patients had relapsed, one after receiving what appeared to have been suboptimal treatment.

While the above studies are encouraging, definitive evidence of the efficacy of ECT in preventing suicide is lacking. In particular, studies are needed to compare ECT against the new antidepressants currently dominating clinical practice for effectiveness in reducing suicidal behavior in depression. Until such data are available, one must presume that a treatment as highly effective as ECT against depression is similarly effective against one of depression's cardinal symptoms.

Suicide During ECT

Since the development of imipramine almost half a century ago, no antidepressant medication synthesized since has improved on its efficacy. Rather, the advantages of the newer medications lie in their improved side-effect profiles and particularly in their relative safety if used in overdoses.

Suicide attempts during a course of ECT are extremely rare. One explanation for this observation is that until recently the majority of patients who received ECT were inpatients in a supervised setting, who would thus have had less opportunity to attempt suicide. However, isolated case reports do exist. A psychopharmacology graduate student requested ECT for major depression with psychotic features. At her first ECT session, conducted as an inpatient, she experienced prolonged paralysis after administration of a routine dose of succinylcholine for the procedure. A subsequent toxicology screen suggested, later confirmed by the patient, the ingestion of an organophosphate insecticide twenty days prior to the treatment in a suicide attempt (Jaksa and Palahniuk, 1994). A twenty-one-year-old patient with a history of two suicide attempts was unresponsive for two hours after her fifth inpatient ECT session. A toxicology screen revealing benzodiazepine led to her subsequent admission to having taken an overdose of temazepam, which she had been collecting in her room (Surgenor et al., 1996). These two case reports highlight the prudence of performing a thorough medical workup, including toxicology screen, of a patient whose ECT session departs from the usual course.

Several factors have led to an increase in the use of outpatient ECT. It is not uncommon for ECT practitioners to perform the majority of treatments on outpatients. Managed care organizations are less likely to reimburse hospitalization for the duration of a course of ECT if the patient does not exhibit acute suicidal ideation or psychosis. Outpatient maintenance ECT has gained increasing acceptance as a means to prevent relapse of depression. These developments would suggest that the ECT psychiatrist devote increased attention to screening patients for the presence of suicide risk factors before treatments.

Although there is much debate on this subject, the early phases of antidepressant treatment, in some patients, have been temporally associated with an increase in suicide risk. If improvements in energy and psychomotor retardation precede improvement in mood and suicidal ideation, the result may be that the patient now has the wherewithal to act upon suicidal feelings against which anergia might have previously served as a protective factor. Because patients receiving ECT generally respond more quickly than those on medication, one might predict that this period of increased vulnerability to suicide would be similarly shortened. One study of thirty-seven patients receiving ECT found that mean suicidal ideation scores actually improved *earlier* than energy items (Rich et al., 1986b). However, the study's authors caution against a revision of clinical wisdom in this area based on these data. Until more studies indicate otherwise, it is reasonable to approach the initial response to ECT with the same level of concern about the potential for increased risk for suicide as one does for the patient in the initial stages of antidepressant treatment.

Although transient mild amnesia is not uncommon in ECT, frank delirium lasting beyond the immediate post-ictal period is decidedly rare. If prolonged delirium secondary to ECT does occur, it often does so toward the end of a course, when suicide risk has decreased. Nevertheless, delirium always deserves respect as a risk factor for suicide, and the ECT patient who becomes delirious deserves increased vigilance (Goldberg, 1987).

ECT AND THE BIOLOGY OF SUICIDE

The mechanism of therapeutic action of ECT remains a mystery. Preclinical studies abound but reviewers have found their data to be of questionable relevance to actual human conditions (Abrams, 1992). Human studies suffer from small sample sizes and serious methodological problems. Nevertheless, studies of the effect of ECT on serotonin activity are intriguing because of their relevance to biological findings in suicide. (See Chapter Six for an explication of the association between serotonin levels and suicide.) Several lines of research suggest that ECT has serotonergic effects. Preclinical studies have shown that electroconvulsive shock (ECS), in contrast to antidepressant medications, decreases the density of central serotonin 5-HT_2 receptors (Sackeim et al., 1995). ECS has also been shown to increase postsynaptic receptor sensitivity to serotonin, while leaving gamma-amminobutyric acid and norepinephrine receptor sensitivity unchanged (de Montigny, 1984). In humans, studies of urinary and cerebral spinal fluid metabolite 5-hydroxy-indole-acetic acid (CSF 5-HIAA) after ECT have yielded inconsistent results. A small study found that ECT increased CSF 5-HIAA while leaving concentrations of the norepinephrine metabolite 3-methoxy-4-hydroxyphenyl-glycol unchanged (Rudorfer et al., 1991).

Fenfluramine hydrochloride stimulates presynaptic release of serotonin and has been used as a probe to assess serotonin activity in a number of psychiatric conditions. Fenfluramine-stimulated prolactin release serves as an indirect measure of serotonin activity and has been shown to be blunted in depressed patients (Coccaro et al., 1989). In a study of eighteen patients with major depression, serum prolactin levels showed a twofold increase after a series of ECT (Shapira et al., 1992). Using an alternative paradigm of acute tryptophan depletion, a recent study found no reemergence of depressive symptoms in five successfully treated patients (Cassidy et al., 1997). Study size limits the conclusions that can be drawn from these data. Nevertheless, the results are interesting in that they again contrast with findings from analogous studies using antidepressant medications, in which tryptophan challenge did produce reemergence of depressive symptoms (Delgado et al., 1990).

AREAS FOR FUTURE RESEARCH

As discussed at the beginning of this chapter, it is somewhat of a paradox that a therapy so successful in treating depression and, in turn, suicidal behavior has been an area of relative neglect by researchers. Although a significant decrease in the use of ECT in the 1960s and 1970s might have exonerated psychiatry for a comparable paucity of research, that excuse is no longer viable. In each of the areas presented in this chapter, opportunities exist for further study. The availability of refined diagnostic criteria and structured diagnostic interviews now makes possible multicenter epidemiological and cohort studies on the effects of ECT on suicidal behavior. For such data to be meaningful, increased attention must be given to distinguishing between suicide attempts and parasuicidal acts.

In an era of briefer hospitalizations and use of alternatives to hospitalization, screening methods must be devised for identifying which patients can and cannot safely receive ECT in an outpatient setting. Systems must be developed for safely treating depressed outpatients with ECT and for monitoring suicide risk over the course of treatments. Relapse rates of 20 to 50 percent are observed even when antidepressant medications are used after a course of ECT. Rigorously controlled protocols for maintenance ECT are needed that include suicide and suicidal ideation among the variables studied.

ECT is clinically unrivaled among the somatic therapies for mood disorder in its ability to help otherwise refractory patients and bring about rapid improvement of symptoms. Studies are needed to follow-up on the preliminary findings of the unique neuroendocrine changes associated with ECT, particu-

larly in the area of serotonin function. Such studies have the potential to further the understandings of the biology of suicide and suicidal ideation.

IMPLICATIONS FOR THE CLINICIAN

The review of ECT and suicide elicits the following implications for the clinician.

- ECT is a safe and highly effective treatment for major depression and
  mania, with response rates as high as 80 to 90 percent in these disorders. Modifications in anesthesia, medical monitoring, and stimulus
  delivery have increased the safety and comfort of the procedure.

- Accompanying the improvement that occurs in these mood disorders
  with ECT is the significant improvement in suicidal behavior. The duration of this improvement and how to maintain these benefits are topics
  deserving further study.

- The presence of suicidal behavior in a patient does not predict outcome
  from ECT. Not all suicidal patients are good candidates for ECT, and not
  all good candidates for ECT are suicidal.

- In major depression, response to ECT is more rapid than response to
  antidepressant medication, thus shortening the period of vulnerability
  to suicidal behavior. A rare side effect of ECT is delirium beyond the
  immediate post-ictal phase, which may transiently increase the risk of
  suicide.

- There is no evidence for a direct action of ECT on suicidal behavior.
  Research suggests a state of decreased serotonin availability associated
  with violent suicide. Preliminary studies suggest ECT may affect serotonin function differently from antidepressant medication. Further studies are needed to elucidate the association between serotonin, suicide,
  and ECT.

- Current changes in ECT practice patterns, with more patients being
  treated on an outpatient basis, necessitate the development of protocols
  for assessing suicidal risk over the course of treatments.

PART THREE

SPECIAL ISSUES

CHAPTER TWENTY-FOUR

Suicide in Children and Adolescents

Stuart Goldman, M.D.
William R. Beardslee, M.D.

S uicide in childhood and adolescence is a serious and rapidly growing public health problem. At present it is the third most common cause of death in adolescents and the fifth most common cause of death in school-aged children (Centers for Disease Control, 1992). Suicide attempts among children and adolescents are even more common. In 1997 it was estimated that upward of 9 percent of adolescents and 1 percent of school-aged children attempted to harm themselves; even more contemplated self-harm. As researchers in the 1980s began to identify disorders of childhood psychopathology, they also initiated more rigorous studies of all aspects of suicidal behaviors, including epidemiology, comorbidity, and familial studies. Although much progress has been made in identifying factors that are statistically associated with increased suicide risk, such as comorbid depression, substance abuse, and the presence of handguns in homes (Brent et al., 1988), differentiating and treating cases on an individual clinical basis has been and remains quite challenging. Clinicians, when treating a child and family, may feel stymied in their efforts to proceed with treatment. Researchers have not been able (Kosky, Silburn, and Zubrick, 1990) to differentiate reliably among suicide ideators, attempters, and completers, making the clinical task of assessing and treating at-risk children all the more difficult. Because of the difficulty of differentiating among these groups, concerns expressed by parents, teachers, and children about suicide in their children, students, or friends must always be taken seriously and fully evaluated.

What has emerged from these systematic studies is that suicidal children are "not a distinct diagnostic group" (Shaffer and Fisher, 1981). It has become increasingly clear that the act of suicide is a result of a complex set of behaviors and that many of the factors leading to suicidal behavior are difficult to assess, particularly since they most often can only be studied retrospectively. The act of suicide represents a final, desperate attempt by a child at some type of resolution to what he or she perceives to be otherwise unsolvable troubles. The reasons a child sees suicide as the only solution are highly individualized and may defy initial attempts at understanding. The decision to attempt suicide is usually, but not always, made in the context of underlying serious psychopathology (which may or may not have been previously identified). Another factor that makes understanding suicidal behaviors all the more difficult is that certain cognitive aspects of the suicidal ideation may exist only transiently (Asarnow, Carlson, and Gutherie, 1987), and the child may not remember them at all, thus making them impossible to assess later. Evaluating both the common and the unique aspects of each case becomes the primary task of the clinician and the clinical researcher.

In this chapter, we review the epidemiology and risk factors for childhood and adolescent suicidal behaviors. We will integrate this information into a clinical model that can be used for assessing, understanding, and treating the individual suicidal child and end with some recommendations for future areas of investigation.

EPIDEMIOLOGY

The rates of suicide have risen dramatically over the past four decades. In 1950 the rate for adolescents was 2.7 per 100,000. This doubled by 1960 and has plateaued at over four times the 1950 rate during the past ten years at approximately 13 per 100,000. (See Table 24.1.) Suicide accounts for 13 percent of all adolescent deaths and ranks third overall as a cause of death in adolescents, after accidents and homicide. In children ages five to fourteen, it is the fifth leading cause of death, ranking behind accidents, malignancies, homicide, and

Table 24.1. Rates of Suicide per 100,000.

Year	Ages 5–14	Ages 15–24
1950		2.7
1960		5.2
1979	0.4	12.4
1992	0.9	13.0
1994	0.9	13.8

congenital abnormalities (Kochanek and Hudson, 1994). Although suicide is far rarer in this age group than in older adolescents, the fairly recent doubling of this rate reflects a growing phenomenon of increasing concern.

Although the reasons for the dramatic rise in the rates of suicide among youths of all ages are unclear, it is clear that it is not simply a change in the rates of reporting (Brent, Perper, and Allman, 1987). Speculation about the increase has been attributed to the increase in the rates of alcohol abuse and depression (Brent, Perper, and Allman, 1987), the increased availability of firearms (Boyd and Mościcki, 1986), and changes in the American family, including increased rates of divorce, greater mobility, and decreased religious practice (McAnarney, 1979). Today's societal pressures for children to act "grown up" in ways that both appeal to and overwhelm adolescents may also be a contributing factor. These pressures bombard children from every direction: from peers, media, and inadvertently from parents who need their children to adapt to a two-parent-working or single-parent family structure. These pressures, when coupled with the breakdown of consistent and predictable support systems such as families and friends, create life choices and options that many adolescents can neither avoid nor comfortably choose and may lead to a profound sense of desperation and helplessness.

Age

Suicide attempts or completions are very rare prior to puberty, although suicidal ideation is not. The suicide rate for children and adolescents increases with age throughout adolescence. In preadolescent children, the lower rates are attributed to more immature cognitive and psychosocial development, lower rates of comorbidity, and decreased access to lethal methods or agents. More specifically, from a developmental perspective, the preadolescent's ability to plan and execute a completed suicide is lower (Shaffer and Fisher, 1981). Hopelessness and helplessness, two risk factors for suicide, are also experienced differently by younger children than by adolescents. The preadolescent's sense of time (living in the present and not envisioning the future) diminishes the angst of being hopeless forever, which an adolescent more keenly feels. For the younger child, being helpless is also more familiar and hence less distressing. Dependency is a normal state of childhood, whereas adolescents are often fighting for independence. A child's dependency also means that he or she is more connected to and supervised by parents and teachers, who generally provide attachment, support, and monitoring. Younger children also have lower rates of depression and substance abuse, both of which are associated with increased risk of suicide. Finally, younger children have less access to the most lethal methods of self-destruction, particularly handguns.

Many of the factors believed to be protective in earlier childhood become risk factors for suicide as children grow older. Their cognitive capacity is more fully developed, which allows them to envision a hopeless future and contemplate their own helplessness in relation to their current situation and future possibilities. In addition, adolescents are more able to consider an array of "solutions" to their problems, which may include taking their life. The capacity to plan and execute their own demise is also greater. The increased rates of high-risk comorbid diagnosis (depression and substance abuse) statistically increase the suicide risk, as does their access to guns and alcohol, both risk factors for completed suicide.

From the psychosocial vantage point, adolescents experience increased pressure to develop autonomy and mastery as they grow older. Teenagers move away from depending on parents and teachers, thus reducing contact and supervision, and possibly increasing isolation. There may be frequent and drastic changes in peer relationships, adding to their distress and alienation. Finally, the pressures to cope with their changing bodies, develop intimate relationships, and define a career can be overwhelming. All of these stresses occur under extreme pressure to "do it all on their own," yet adolescents' identities, coping mechanisms, and senses of self are still too underdeveloped and unstable to weather the storm these challenges present. The adolescents' inevitable failures only add to their feelings of hopelessness and worthlessness, further disheartening vulnerable adolescents and hurling them into a downward spiral of hopelessness and helplessness.

The psychological pressures on families, increased by the breakdown of family structure and a rise in poverty, also come to bear on the rise in suicide rates. These pressures can splinter family resources, decreasing the amount of support and supervision that a child has at home and increasing the child's feelings of hopelessness and helplessness.

Gender

There are dramatic differences between males and females in suicide ideation, attempts, and completions. Suicidal ideation and attempts are far more common in girls, and completions are far more common in boys, as is also true for adults. Joffe, Offord, and Boyle (1988) found suicidal ideation in over four times as many girls as boys (14.5 percent versus 3.3 percent) and suicide attempts in over three times as many girls as boys (7.1 percent versus 2.4 percent). This is in contrast to completed suicides, in which boys outnumbered girls nearly five to one.

Explanations for the differences in rates of ideation, attempts, and completions between girls and boys fall into two broad areas. First, girls have a higher incidence of depression than do boys, by a factor of two to one. This depression, coupled with a greater inclination toward internalizing emotions (coping with feelings through reflection and personal responsibility rather than action), may partially explain the increased rates of ideation and nonfatal attempts. In other words, girls may contemplate suicide more often, but their tendencies toward thought versus action help to contain the number of fatal attempts. Girls may also be at lower risk secondary to protective factors, such as their focus on attachments and relationships, which both offer support and create a reluctance to severing these ties through suicide. Second, the increased completion rate in males tends to be attributed to their more outwardly aggressive and disruptive behaviors (Offord, Boyle, and Szartmari, 1987), coupled with their increased alcohol abuse. Boys tend to choose far more lethal methods than girls, with the majority of boys using firearms as opposed to pills, the more common method among girls. This combination of impulsive aggressiveness, intoxication, and firearms is highly lethal (Brent, Perper, and Allman, 1987). Other protective or risk factors probably exist but are yet to be identified.

Sexual Orientation

Anecdotal and uncontrolled studies (Remafedi, Farrow, and Deisher, 1993) have suggested that the rates of suicide attempts and completion are much higher in gay and lesbian populations than would be expected. To date, this observation has not been observed in careful studies. Many gay and lesbian adolescents report a great deal of stress and loneliness, much of it revolving around either "coming out" or having to keep their secret. There are also many situations in which prejudicial treatments or attitudes may make the life of a gay or lesbian adolescent far more challenging than that of his or her heterosexual peers. The resultant combination of stress and isolation that many gay and lesbian adolescents face is believed to be general, as opposed to specific, risk factors for suicidal behaviors that have relevance when there is associated depression, substance abuse, or personality disorder.

Ethnicity and Race

It is well known that the rates of suicide vary a great deal from culture to culture and group to group. The rates of suicide in black adolescents are lower than they are for white adolescents (Centers for Disease Control, 1998). Native American males have higher rates than all other adolescent groups. The increased rate in Native Americans is highest in tribes in which traditional values have been most eroded (Berlin, 1987). It is this erosion of traditional values and family structures that may account for the varying regional rates for suicide among black adolescent males. The highest rates are in the Northeast and Midwest, where family structure is the most eroded. In these regions, the rate of suicide in black males approaches that of white males.

A CLINICAL UNDERSTANDING OF SUICIDE

Children and adolescents who have suicidal ideation, have attempted suicide, or have completed suicide are not a homogeneous group, which makes a broad understanding of the phenomenon quite difficult. Suicidal thoughts or acts have intense individual meanings and purposes that can be understood only in the context of an individual's life. Suicide may be a way of attempting to regain control for someone who feels truly out of control and unable to handle the situation more reasonably and rationally. It may be retaliatory—an action purposely made against those around the child who are perceived to have done the child wrong. It may be a desperate attempt at reunion or a result of unbearable pain. In all cases, suicide is the final symptom of an individual's disturbed life. Suicide in itself is not the disease. Most clinicians appreciate that the pathway to a suicide attempt or completion involves a complex set of factors. Specific factors alone cannot explain the act. When one takes a set of factors in concert and applies them to a specific case, the suicidal behaviors can often be understood. Once this understanding exists, interventions for treatment and prevention can be built upon it.

The factors that lead to suicide can be divided broadly into vulnerability to suicide, internal or external stress, inability to consider alternatives or problem-solve, and access to methods of suicide. By assessing each of these factors in detail, the clinician can evaluate and understand the suicidal ideation and thereby develop a clinical intervention plan that may lead to preventative interventions.

Vulnerability

Vulnerability to suicide has been written about extensively (Pfeffer, 1986; Group for the Advancement of Psychiatry, 1996) and encompasses biological, developmental, familial, and cultural factors. At the most basic level, Tsuang (1983) has shown a genetic link for suicide in adult twins, as well as increased rates of suicide in the relatives of suicide completers.

On a more diagnostic level, depression, substance abuse, and conduct disorders have all been shown to increase the risk of suicide and are well known to have familial links. In one study (Shaffer, Gould, and Fisher, 1996), 90 percent of adolescent suicide attempters had an axis I *DSM-III* diagnosis, with rates of major depression up to 80 percent and conduct disorder approaching 50 percent. Other reports have linked serious acts to bipolar disorder, anorexia and bulimia nervosa, and substance abuse (Shaffer, Gould, and Fisher, 1996). Certain axis II type disorders, including borderline and antisocial personality disorders in adults and conduct disorder in those under age eighteen (Shaffer, Gould, and Fisher, 1996), have also been shown to be linked to increased rates of suicide. Conventional clinical wisdom holds that clinical comorbidity is likely to be synergistic as a risk factor for almost any adverse outcome.

Studies of biological vulnerability (Kruesi, Rapoport, and Hamburger, 1990) have shown that, as in adults, there is a biochemical factor in children and adolescents. The levels of 5-HIAA, a serotonin breakdown product, are lower in the cerebrospinal fluid of children and adolescents with aggressive and impulsive behaviors. This tendency toward violence has been linked to suicide by Plutchik and van Praag (1990), who found that 10 to 20 percent of all suicidal people have a history of significant violence and 30 percent of all violent people have a history of suicidal behaviors. Whether this finding ultimately will turn out to be related causally or just be associated is unclear. To date, the demonstration of a primary biochemical abnormality in suicidal youths has not appeared in the literature. (See Chapter Six for more details.)

On another biochemical front, Brent (1986) has shown that adolescent epilepsy is associated with increased suicidal risk. Whether this reflects general or specific brain pathology, medical stress, some combination of these factors, or currently unidentified factors is unclear.

Finally, additional evidence for the role of biological vulnerability is found in the tenfold increase in the rates of both attempts (1 percent to 9 percent) and completions (1 per 100,000 to 1 per 10,000) as one moves from childhood to adolescence. Although there are many other factors that may contribute to this increase, it parallels the increases in the rates of many of the psychiatric disorders, possibly suggesting an unfolding biological process that accounts for the dramatic increases in psychopathology and suicide in adolescence.

Developmental Factors. We have described what is believed to be some of the biological factors and now review the posited developmental factors that are believed to be contributory (although any separation of biological and developmental factors is really artificial; at the most critical levels they are inextricably linked).

The first major developmental factor stems from the primary tasks of adolescence: separation and identity formation. Developing a core sense of self that is loved and valued by oneself and others, as well as competent to enter the world, is the major work of adolescence. Complex theories of the self have been elaborated by Kohut, Bowlby, and Stern, among others; the overarching concept of an individual's sense of self is the internal representation of perceived experience with others and the response of others to oneself. An individual's self-perception is a direct reflection of his or her feelings about how he or she has been treated by others. We know that in the most extreme cases of real or perceived mistreatment, such as intrafamilial abuse, the rates of suicidal behaviors are much higher (Shaunesey, Cohen, Plummer, and Berman, 1993). The severity of the suicidal act in adolescents correlates to the severity of the abuse by others (Hibbard, Brack, and Rauch, 1988). The increased suicide rate among abused children is certainly consistent with this hypothesis regarding sense of self, but in a broader way may also be a result of the loss of basic family functions.

Even in adolescents whose core sense of self is basically intact, there may be periods of challenge or change that are quite daunting. Realistic appraisal of one's self and one's capabilities is one of the cornerstones of identity formation. Most adolescents incur trials and tribulations while testing out their skills in interpersonal relationships and in the school or workplace. Developmentally, these skills have attained a certain priority and can no longer be ignored. Fantasies of the future can offer temporary relief but are more difficult to rely on or believe in as a child develops. As they reach their teens, their real-world experiences of school, peers, intimacy, and families are prominent. Many adolescents doubt their abilities to cope with these experiences, possibly leading to a cycle of self-doubt. To counter or cope with feelings of self-doubt, the adolescent may set unrealistic goals or demands and then attempt to test or prove these goals, which often leads to failure and subsequent frustration, resulting in more self-doubt. This pattern can lead to a downward spiral of shame or guilt, or both, over one's perceived incompetence. This shame and guilt can be overwhelming and lead to true despair.

All of this occurs as the adolescent moves away from the support, structure, and supervision that most families and schools offer. The vulnerable adolescent is more likely to be isolated and therefore unidentified and unaided at a time when asking for help is counter to his or her developmental needs. This conundrum can make for marked desperation that appears to emerge from nowhere, and leaves the adolescent with no place to turn to for help. Open communication and early identification tend to counter this desperation. Many adolescents need an adult to normalize the ups and downs of adolescence and development, help them to be less self-critical, and emphasize the appropriate environmental supports. This support can be crucial to the prevention of suicidal behaviors.

Adding to this set of developmental challenges are cognitive changes that are also believed to make adolescents more vulnerable to suicide. The capacity for normal operations, or abstract thinking, described by Piaget, means that adolescents have the potential for propositional thought. That is, they can ponder about abstract or possible scenarios and cognate in a way that makes situations that were impossible to imagine earlier far more real. Thinking about suicide thus takes on new dimensions as an act that could actually be done if life is truly intolerable. It is believed that as many as 15 to 40 percent (Kosky, Silburn, and Zubrick, 1990) of a nonclinical sample of adolescents think about suicide in a given year. Of course, there is great range to "thinking" about suicide, from the mere ideation to the attempt to the actual completion. It may be the prevalence of suicidal thoughts, however, that contributes to the phenomenon of cluster suicides seen in some communities. Finally, the adolescent's greater cognitive capacities mean that his or her ability to plan and carry out suicidal thoughts is much greater than in the past, placing the adolescent at higher risk for completion (Borst, Noam, and Bartok, 1991).

Family Vulnerability. All children and adolescents exist actively and intensely in a family matrix. Although this is generally an asset, any factor that compromises or impairs the functioning of the family matrix—certain identified patterns of family dysfunctionality such as excessive rigidity, blurring of boundaries, or a failure to communicate (Brent et al., 1988)—puts the child or adolescent at greater risk. Increased family-based vulnerability is also associated with major family psychiatric disorders (especially depression), a family history of suicide, family relocations, separations, and divorce. In families where there is major distress or dysfunctioning, the child may feel unsupported, unwanted, or even expendable (Sabbath, 1969). For example, children of divorcing parents may be propelled into using self-destructive behaviors to cope with their feelings of isolation or abandonment. From a family systems perspective, a child's suicidal behaviors would generally be seen as both embedded in and a response to the family's distress or dysfunction. Understanding the behavior and addressing the problem should then occur within the family context.

All families, even those that are not dysfunctional, are subject to periods of stress. Family illness, poverty, and divorce, among other stressors, can disrupt most families. All families undergo stress during periods of transition such as births, entrance of children to school, adolescence, and children's leaving home. Most families handle these transitions in stride, but some become dysfunctional and are unable to perform the necessary tasks of a family unit. During the children's adolescence, when parents may relive or reexperience their own unresolved issues, these transitional stress points can become all the more difficult to negotiate. Parents may become stuck reworking their own past and unable to respond to their child's needs, thus rendering themselves unavailable to respond appropriately to their troubled adolescent and resulting in greater risk for the child. This can lead to the same feelings of lack of support and unwantedness that are seen in families with major dysfunction or distress.

Cultural and Social Factors. Certain cultural and social factors that are transmitted to and through the family and child can increase the risk of suicidal behaviors (Jilek-Aall, 1988). Cultures that are undergoing major periods of change with shifts in the familial and social structure norms are reported to have higher rates of suicide. This has been posited to account for the increased rates of suicide in Micronesia and in Native Americans, both of which have experienced dramatic shifts in their cultures fairly recently (Jilek-Aall, 1988). It is noteworthy that Native American tribes with the more preserved traditional structures are at the least risk (Berlin, 1987). It has also been proposed that some of the shifts in American social structure, including increased rates of divorce, greater mobility, and decreased family cohesiveness (McAnarney, 1979), have contributed to the marked increase in suicide in the post–World War II era. Other studies (Gould, Shaffer, Fisher, and Garfinkel, 1998) have shown that divorce alone is not responsible.

On a broader level, it has been noted that even in countries that have experienced comparable rates of change in the social structures over the past decades, there are still differences in rates of suicide. Cross-cultural studies (Jilek-Aall, 1988) have concluded that countries such as the United States, Japan, and Sweden, which have been characterized as highly competitive and goal-directed societies, have appreciably higher rates of suicide than countries such as Norway, which has been characterized as having a less competitive, less goal-directed set of social values.

Stress

Stress is a significant factor in any model of understanding suicidal behavior. Stress is defined as anything that makes the activities and tasks of life more difficult to accomplish; it can be external or internal in origin, and encompasses biological and developmental factors. Clearly the majority of suicidal children are at some increased premorbid risk, but it is their inability to cope with their stress that may shift the balance toward self-destructiveness. The common state of extreme hopelessness and helplessness that often precedes the suicidal act is precipitated by a perceived, identifiable stressor. The individual's perception of the stressor plays a key role in the development of suicidal behavior; indeed, some of the precipitants may be considered minor by more objective standards.

Developmentally, younger children handle stress in two characteristic manners: either they take some immediate action (hopefully countering) or they seek out the aid of a caring adult. Since their capacities to tolerate and discuss their feelings or to generate alternate strategies are limited by their developmental stage, their dependence on others to help them cope with stress is generally accepted and welcomed. From this perspective, it naturally follows that the stressor most often associated with suicidal behaviors in school-aged children is perceived or actual abandonment or object loss.

Adolescents generally have a greater capacity than younger children to tolerate ambivalent or negative feelings and develop alternative problem-solving options, which also look toward the future. However, adolescents who are in the hopeless and helpless presuicidal state lose their capacity to problem-solve. They too, like younger children, turn to others during times of stress. The acute stressor for most adolescent suicide attempts or completions is also the loss of or abandonment by a significant other. Marttunen, Aro, and Lönnqvist (1993) have estimated that interpersonal loss or major conflict with a parent or a boyfriend or girlfriend is present in up to 70 percent of cases of suicide attempts or completions.

As adolescents' cognitive skills develop during adolescence, so does their appreciation of the long-term ramifications of certain behaviors. This understanding, coupled with a growing sense of personal responsibility, makes adolescents more susceptible to the distress associated with school, legal, or social problems. They now can anticipate the impact of their behaviors over time, so it is understandable that issues perceived as a possible cause of future stress or problems are commonly identified precipitants of self-destructive acts in the adolescent population.

Problem-Solving Abilities

Many children and adolescents face major life stressors. Although underlying risk factors are not uncommon, only a minority of adolescents confronted with these stressors attempt to harm themselves (less than 10 percent) and complete suicide (less than 0.015 percent). What specifically differentiates those who attempt or complete suicide from the vast majority of young people has not been clearly identifiable in epidemiologic or other factor studies, but certain patterns have emerged.

Since self-destructive behaviors could readily be described as a fundamental breakdown in problem solving by less drastic means, researchers have looked at suicide attempters and completers to see if any patterns emerge in the cognitive processes (thinking patterns) of these groups. Suicide attempters and completers are characterized by cognitive inflexibility, cognitive distortions (Patsiokas, Clum, and Luscumb, 1979), and poor coping strategies. Orbach, Rosenheim, and Hary (1987) have shown that suicidal school-aged children are unable to produce alternative problem-solving strategies, resulting in diminished flexibility in meeting life's challenges. Decreased problem solving and poor social skills have also been associated with suicidal behavior in adolescents. Carlson and Cantwell (1982) noted that poor school performance is a risk factor, but low IQ is not. This suggests that it is the level of functioning rather than the underlying capacity that connotes risk.

The relevance of exposure to models of suicidal behavior is a controversial factor, with conflicting reports about cluster suicides and the role of the media. Although the impact of the media may be unclear, it is clear from Coleman (1987) and others that in certain situations, suicide can spread within a group as though it were contagious, resulting in what has been described by many authors as clustering. Although the exact mechanism of this spreading is uncertain, identification with the victim, modeling, and notoriety are among the factors considered to play a role in cluster suicides. In any case, it appears that once the taboo of suicide is breached, it becomes a far more accessible and acceptable possibility to vulnerable members of the group or community.

Within families, the risk of suicidal behaviors increases with a positive history of family suicidal behaviors, mediated by a combination of genetic, environmental, and modeling mechanisms. Finally, the risk for future suicide attempts increases twentyfold with an individual's history of a prior attempt (Shaffer, 1988). The contribution of cognitive modeling, priming the pump, or other associated factors is unclear.

There are two common factors, however, that are found almost universally among suicidal youth: the cognitive states of profound hopelessness and helplessness (Spirito, Williams, Stark, and Hart, 1988) and Beck's triad of negative perspectives about oneself, the world, and the future. Some authors (Gladstone and Kaslow, 1995) have focused on a negative attribution model, which reflects an individual's overall approach to life, to account for the noted observations.

Access to Lethal Means

The final factor in understanding suicidal behaviors is access to methods of suicide. Vulnerability, stress, and problem-solving limitations are all important, but without access to the means, a serious self-destructive act is less likely. Access to serious methods of self-harm, particularly firearms and motor vehicles, increases the risk of suicide. Without ready access to these methods, many self-destructive impulses can be contained.

Access to certain methods of self-destruction changes with age. Older children and adolescents have readier access than younger children to more lethal methods, such as guns, cars, and drugs. This may help to explain the increase in the rates of completed suicide with age. Many authors (Brent, Perper, and Allman, 1987) have shown that access to the most lethal method, guns, significantly increases the risk of suicide. Access to alcohol and other drugs, risk factors for suicide, also increases with age. Alcohol, a depressant, impairs judgment, is associated with emotional lability, and may be disinhibiting. This leads to impaired problem solving and produces subsequent difficulties. Several authors have shown (Brent, Perper, and Allman, 1987) that the combination of alcohol (with its detrimental effects on judgment and behavior) and firearms (which are irreversible) is highly lethal.

The role of access to methods is often underappreciated and may be one that is often readily addressable through preventative efforts at curbing substance abuse and the availability of firearms. Psychological autopsies do not differentiate attempters from completers except for the presence of alcohol and guns. This indicates that the differentiating factor between attempters and completers may be access to a lethal method rather than a cognitive, developmental, or psychological factor.

THE ETIOLOGIC MODEL

The etiologic model that evolves from these contributing factors is complex and multidimensional. Although statistical models that help identify certain high-risk populations and indicate preventative interventions have come out of some studies, the majority of the individuals in the identified high-risk groups neither seriously contemplate nor act on suicidal thoughts. We therefore have to move

SUICIDE IN CHILDREN AND ADOLESCENTS **429**

beyond who is at high risk for suicide. Since there are many patients who would not be identified as high risk by this group approach, we must attempt to understand the individual meaning of the act or the ideation to provide a clinically useful model of intervention for most patients.

Although the meaning of suicidal behavior is always highly individualized, certain broad patterns do reoccur among attempters and completers. Central to suicidal behavior or ideation in almost all children and adolescents is a profound sense of loss of control of one's life, which leads to pervasive feelings of helplessness and hopelessness. The child or adolescent therefore perceives suicide as the "only" available solution to the problem. Most often he or she is experiencing depressive symptoms but can also be enraged. The most common motivation described for the act is the intense wish for relief or escape from an unbearably painful situation. This desire often is secondary to the loss of an important relationship, which the patient feels is irreplaceable. It may also be in response to abusive treatment from another or a result of the patient's own relentless self-reproach. Regardless, the individual is impelled to escape, and suicide appears to be the only route (Pfeffer, 1986). This may be true for both the chronically troubled child and the impulsive child who feels transiently overwhelmed after a series of setbacks.

The second common pattern of personal meaning is using suicide as revenge against another person. The patient believes that the act of suicide will cause the offending or neglecting party to be "sorry" for what he or she has done. Often associated with this is a desire for attention or to be noticed, even in a negative way. Commonly when attention is the driving force, the attempt is of lower lethality, since gestures or attempts may have the same desired effect (Pfeffer, 1986).

Reunion with a dead loved one is the third category of personal meaning associated with suicidal behaviors. The behavior is often used to counter a sense of loss or aloneness. The desire to be reunited with an idealized object may be coupled with the desire to escape the pain of a loss, offering a powerful motivation for some children and adolescents (Pfeffer, 1986).

Finally, the child's behavior might be motivated by meaning that is best understood in a family context (Sabbath, 1969). The meaning may range from the child's seeing himself or herself as the family's scapegoat ("they'll be better off without me"), to distracting the family from other family issues (such as stopping a divorce), or to acting out a real wish on the parent's part to be rid of the child (a parent's lamenting how different his or her life would be without the child), among others.

Since multiple factors and motivations are involved in the etiology of suicide attempts and completed suicide, it is important to recognize that those who are at the highest risk are individuals with the most risk factors occurring concurrently. Those children and adolescents who are acutely experiencing family crises, personal losses, erosion of self-esteem, and setbacks in interpersonal relationships, in combination with social isolation and access to lethal means, are likely to be in the highest risk category.

ASSESSMENT AND INTERVENTION

The identification and subsequent assessment of children who might be at risk follow from the description of contributing factors. The dilemma is to select from the large number of children who will be identified as having some risk those who need early intervention. Clearly the prevention of suicide attempts is the optimal intervention strategy. This is both because of the inherent value of primary prevention and because differentiating attempters from completers is so difficult. Children who meet several of the identified risk factors in Table 24.2 and are reported to have thoughts about suicide or have attempted to harm themselves should be considered to be at the highest risk and carefully evaluated. However, any child who expresses significant suicidal thoughts or has harmed himself or herself in some way needs to be taken seriously and evaluated promptly.

The process of assessing suicidal youths in any context is a complex and challenging task, especially when the child is school aged (Jacobsen, Rabinowitz, and Popper, 1994). This is true whether the assessment occurs as part of a general assessment, as in the evaluation of a depressed child, or in a focused evaluation as might occur in an emergency room setting. The most accurate picture is obtained by interviewing the child and his or her parents, as well as by gathering information from as many other sources (such as school, siblings, and peers) as possible. This comprehensive evaluation must be immediate if the child is at serious risk and as near to the event as possible if the child is at lower risk. Quite often the child or adolescent, along with his or her family, will minimize the events over time as they realize the severity of what has transpired and want to deny the meaning of the act. This makes an accurate assessment increasingly difficult as possible distortions of the scenario develop as the history is recounted serially.

The first task of the clinician is to assess the severity of the situation in order to determine the activity level that the suicidal child needs. This means assessing the risks as well as resources of the patient and his or her family. It is useful to determine the likelihood of a reoccurrence of the overwhelming feelings, events, or actions that led to the current problem. The patient's level of safety and the need for active protection are based on the assessment and the balancing of these factors. The personal meaning of the act or ideation must also be assessed and understood from the patient's perspective. It is critical to understand the reason from the patient's vantage point, both to establish and maximize a responsive

Table 24.2. At-Risk Vulnerability to Suicide.

Psychiatric disorders or dysfunction
    Depression, especially major depression; bipolar disorder
    Substance abuse
    Conduct disorder, intermittent explosive disorder
    Psychosis
    Borderline personality disorder
    Anorexia, bulimia nervosa
    Suicidal threats or attempts in the past
    Undiagnosed but marked impulsivity

Family history
    Depression, substance abuse, psychosis
    Antisocial or borderline personality disorder
    Medical illness, epilepsy
    History of suicide attempts and suicide
    Domestic violence, abuse

Stress
    Interpersonal loss of conflict
    Divorce or separation
    Legal trouble
    Academic failure or dysfunction
    Isolation

Alternatives and problem solving
    Limited options
    Social isolation
    Impulsivity
    History of suicidal behaviors
    Helplessness and hopelessness

Access
    Presence of firearms

treatment plan. Next, the clinician must assess whether the act was a solitary behavior or occurred in the context of another set of underlying difficulties, which themselves may need to be treated.

The assessment of the patient's relative balance of risks and resources can be sorted into four categories: underlying risk factors, lethality of the attempt, individual resources, and family resources. Evaluating the positive and negative aspects of each category provides a relative measure of the risk and conveys either a high- or low-risk situation, as reflected in Table 24.3. Subsequent intervention and treatment must then be based on the risk level of the situation.

The clinician who is reviewing the details of the situation and its precipitants as reported by the child and his or her family has two principal tasks: (1) assessing the degree of risk and the need for protection, always erring on the side of caution, and (2) assessing the reasons for the situation, such as the precipitating events, and identifying the underlying factors. Since the history is from multiple informants, resolving conflicts among different accounts can be quite challenging and requires time and patience. It is vital that even if there are differing views, if any informant indicates a high risk, regardless of lack of substantiation from others, the concern needs to be thoroughly evaluated. Definitive clinical decisions can be made when the assessment of factors points to either the very high or very low risk or resource, making the assessment more complex and the clinical decisions less clear. Again with conflicting reports or with mixed components of risks and resources, it is usually safer to opt for the conservative, protective approach. The example that follows illustrates risk assessments.

Sally was a fourteen-year-old girl who presented in the early fall because of suicidal ideation. She lived with a single, working mother and was a freshman in high school. Through middle school, she had been a better-than-average student, as a result of her very hard work and help she had received from her neighbor and a tutor. Over the summer, she experienced her first boyfriend, but he had broken up with her just as school began. She used some alcohol over the summer months, but denied using any since school started. Her mother and Sally both reported that she had been increasingly isolated since the previous spring, when her maternal grandmother had died. The summertime had been better, but she had dramatically worsened since returning to school.

At interview she was an attractive but somewhat unkempt girl, appearing her age. She was quite tearful, complained of dense anhedonia, and had both sleep and appetite disturbances and poor concentration. She said she felt that she could not handle high school and could not do the work. She was profoundly ashamed of being "stupid" and was sure that she had let everyone down. She said that she was unsafe and had vague plans about an overdose. When questioned further, she said that she had gone to her mother's medicine cabinet to look for something the night before, rummaging through and then stopping. She said she would rather die than go back to school and that she could see no ways of making the situation better. Her mother said that she was concerned, but

Table 24.3. Risks and Resources.

	High Risk	Low Risk
Risk/Vulnerability		
Psychopathology	Depression, conduct disorder, substance abuse, character diagnosis, prior suicide attempts	Minimal
Family factors	Significant family psychopathology (as above), history of abuse or violence, history of prior attempts, family dysfunction or divorce	Mild or absent
Current stress	Interpersonal loss or conflict, legal or school difficulties, divorce, separation, abuse, recent exposure to suicide	Low
Individual resources		
Coping skills	Poor, especially impulsiveness, prior attempts, impaired judgment, hopelessness or helplessness, low communication skills	Good (opposite of high-risk coping skills)
Social network	Poor, isolated, alienated, fragmented	Intact
Family resources	Limited, dysfunctional, disorganized, lack of empathy, inability to respond, tendency to minimize	Supportive, empathetic, realistic
Attempt		
Nature	Planned, solitary attempt; accidental discovery; intoxicated	Unplanned, disclosed attempt; planned discovery
Intent to die	High	Low
Method	High lethality; guns, violence, major overdose	Low lethality: minor overdose, superficial wounds
Meaning of death	Ego syntonic, low ambivalence, no regrets, resentment of discovery, continued wish	High ambivalence, no choice at time, high regrets, appreciation of discovery
Precipitant	Impasse or dilemma remains	Impasse is resolved

added, "I have no time for this nonsense, I don't know why she feels this way [so stupid]. She has always been an A/B student." At this point, Sally got up and paced the floor. She cried as she said, "I just don't know what I'm going to do. It really scares me."

Family history was not significant for depression, substance abuse, or past suicidal behaviors. Sally was hospitalized that day.

Although Sally had made no direct attempts at hurting herself, she did have a plausible plan and had partially sought the means to carrying it out. This plan, coupled with her major depression, acute stressors, social isolation, lack of family resources, and helpless and hopeless state, put her at quite high risk. With this level of risk and her profound worry that she "did not know what she was going to do," it was clinically impossible to predict what she would do under the current circumstances. Additionally, there were no readily identifiable factors that could be addressed to alter her risk. The clinician weighing these factors was justifiably concerned and placed Sally in a protective environment.

Sally was hospitalized for the next three weeks while her situation was being assessed and stabilized. Her suicidality worsened for a period of time, and there were episodes of considerable agitation. It was discovered on psychological testing that she had a significant learning disability and low average overall cognitive skills. Her sense that she was unable to handle the work was not just depressed, negative thoughts; it was an accurate reflection of her situation. When she was told that testing showed that she was right when she complained of the difficulty of the work, she was in part relieved and in part distressed at being "dumb." She was started on a selective serotonin reuptake inhibitor (SSRI) with a modest initial response and discharged to home with a gradual transition to school, with every-other-day outpatient therapy.

Within days Sally presented to the emergency room with an acute overdose of seven Aleve. She stated that she just felt that she could not do the work and she never would be able to, so she impulsively "took the pills." This time she did not want to die. She told her mother within thirty minutes what she had done and with some cognitive reframing could imagine a plan to address her schoolwork. Her mother agreed that she could take the next week off to help support the treatment plan. We made an appointment to meet again the next day, and Sally went home with an agreement to call if she should feel self-destructive at all.

At first glance, the second scenario may appear more serious since there was an actual overdose. However, the risk and resource balance was quite different. The patient's depression, although still present, was beginning to respond to the SSRI. Sally was appreciably less hopeless, and her ability to collaborate in her treatment plan was evident. She reported feeling understood when complaining of her fears of failure (less isolation and alienation) and was amenable to a cognitively based intervention. The suicidal act was impulsive, of minimal lethality, and rapidly reversed. Also, she could agree to participate actively in a safety plan. Finally, her mother was able to collaborate in a supportive intervention strategy, which was not previously the case. All of these factors had shifted the risk-to-resource ratio in a positive direction, allowing Sally to return home. In sum, the act was minimal, the patient could collaborate therapeutically (including a safety contract), and she now felt understood, as opposed to alienated, as the alliance with her mother was established.

Treatment

There are no controlled treatment studies of suicidal children and adolescents to guide clinical interventions, although there have been follow-up reports that have appeared in the literature (Pfeffer, Peskin, and Siefker, 1992). The clinician therefore must rely on his or her individual assessment of the situation to guide the intervention. Nevertheless, there are certain guidelines that should be followed.

The first clinical question, after careful assessment, focuses on the weighing of the risk and resource factors to determine the level of care and protection needed. Children with a ratio of high risk to low resources are usually placed in a protective environment. Traditionally, this has been on a psychiatric ward, but other structured, supervised settings may also be appropriate. Children with more favorable risk-to-resource ratios may be discharged to home but need close follow-up over the next days and weeks as the situation unfolds. Patients whose risk-to-resource ratio is unclear should be placed in a protective environment until their safety is clearly established.

Clinical safety becomes the core of the first phase of intervention for both inpatients and outpatients. For inpatients, the decision has already been made that they are unable, either alone or with their family's help, to maintain their own safety. On inpatient units, maximizing the patient's safety is the staff's responsibility. In the most severe situations, patients may require continuous eyesight observation at arm's length. The level of protective restriction is slowly eased as the patient demonstrates symptomatic improvement and becomes capable of participating in his or her own safety planning and control. Over time, the levels of observation are decreased and the levels of privileges are increased, often with reliance on safety or no-suicide contracts. The primary goals of this first phase of treatment are to keep the child safe, complete the assessment, mobilize the appropriate resources, begin treating any underlying disorders, and develop and implement a longitudinal treatment plan. When a child and his or her family are able to collaborate on a reasonable safety and treatment plan, the child is usually ready for discharge.

In many phases of both inpatient and outpatient care, especially early on, the no-suicide or safety contract is one of the major elements of treatment. Some authors (Rotheram, 1987) have described contracts as the key component of the outpatient plan. The contract typically specifies that the patient will not harm himself or herself or will call the therapist or some other specified key person if he or she is feeling unable to maintain his or her own safety. The inability to negotiate a no-suicide contract is reason for grave clinical concern and often leads to ongoing protective (inpatient) treatments. Although these contracts have utility and can be quite reassuring to patients, families, and clinicians, the technique is subject to several major reservations. (See Chapter Twenty-Six.)

The first reservation is whether the patient and family are able to adhere to the contract. Suicide attempters are often impulsive people with cognitive distortions and coexistent psychopathology. They feel overwhelmed and, despite their sincere and best intentions, are often unable to honor any contract. If the underlying precipitating circumstances or factors have not changed, the likelihood of compliance is even smaller. After the central precipitants have been identified, the clinician should then evaluate with the patient, "What is different about the situation now?" If there is no clear answer, it becomes difficult to justify why the situation will not reoccur. This makes uncertain many aspects of the patient's care, especially safety. It should lead to a major reassessment and refocusing of the clinician plan directed at addressing the precipitating events, and not a continued emphasis on the contract.

The family has a critical role. Their capacity to be supportive of the safety plan is crucial. This requires adjustments to their work and family schedules and responding interpersonally to their son or daughter. In this regard, the family must be assessed of its ability to contract to keep the child safe and provide the necessary resources to return the child to the appropriate caretaking facility should difficulties develop. Since distress and dysfunction within the family are often part of the precipitating stresses to the suicidal act, the immediate correction and improvement of the family difficulties, including an appropriate response, may be impossible.

The second reservation about contracts arises from the reliance on the therapeutic relationship, among other factors, to help curb or control self-destructive behaviors. Many suicidal patients have acute or chronic problems with maintaining relationships; therefore, the establishment of a positive relationship becomes quite problematic. These vulnerable patients have usually struggled to establish meaningful relationships, so it is unrealistic to expect them to do so with a relative stranger. When the patient is being evaluated in an acute setting, such as an emergency room, the appearance of a positive relationship can be deceptive and should not be relied on. This is in contradistinction to established therapeutic relationships with proven direction and magnitude. In cases of established relationships, the counterbalancing vector of the therapeutic relationship may allow the connection to provide a basis for maintaining a contract. However, as a note of caution, in one of the few follow-up studies of suicidal children, Pfeffer, Peskin, and Siefker (1992) found that more than half of the repeat attempters were in treatment at the time of the attempt. One can presume that a significant portion of these cases had an active no-suicide contract at the time of their attempt, highlighting the concern about the value of these contracts.

Despite these reservations or limitations, the no-suicide contract has some real clinical value in certain contexts. This value can be optimized by including these components:

- Explicitly negotiating the contract and making sure that the parameters are clear. This is often done in writing and needs to be regularly checked and updated.

- Including significant others in the negotiation and enlisting their help in carrying out the plan. This provides additional resources and reconnects families. Negotiations should be discussed in an open forum since secret negotiations can lead to splitting of the family alliances.

- Denying access to any lethal means of self-harm (such as guns and pills). By collaborating with both patients and their families to deny access, the clinician can assess basic elements of his or her alliance with the family. For example, a refusal to restrict access to guns, perhaps by storing them at the local police station, may imply a low level of concern for the child's safety.

- Ensuring twenty-four-hour availability of the primary clinician or backup. Situations rapidly evolve, and the team needs to be ready to intervene. Twenty-four-hour availability is also seen by patients and families as both a reflection of the seriousness of the situation and of the clinician's concern for their well-being. No-suicide contracts, like all other forms of treatment, must be grounded in the appropriate clinical alliance.

After the acute phase has been resolved, the longer-term, more definitive treatment of the suicidal child or adolescent can be undertaken. The treatment should contain these key elements:

- Understanding and addressing the dilemma that gave rise to the attempt. This requires time as the clinician tries to view the situation from the child's perspective and then correct it.

- Treating the underlying psychopathology. This includes a rigorous diagnostic assessment of the child and may encompass a prolonged data-gathering phase from multiple sources, including psychological testing. A more detailed assessment of the family is also indicated.

- Individual and family therapy, including psychoeducational components, to treat the underlying factors or disorder. The psychoeducational component allows families to understand the pre-event elements, teaches them how to identify risk, and helps them to feel empowered for the future. This is particularly helpful since almost every family is terrified that the suicidal behavior will reoccur.

- Improving problem solving and social functioning through means including cognitive behavioral work with the child and family. Involving or reinvolving the child with social groups (school, church, sports, scouts) helps him or her feel connected and less alienated.

Understanding the personal meaning of an attempt is at the core of all interventions as one designs a plan to counter the suicidal urge and occurs in parallel with treating the underlying psychopathology with medications; interpersonal, family, and psychoeducational work; and social system interventions as indicated. This is illustrated in the integrated care of the following case.

Joanna was a nine-year-old who presented with an acute overdose of ten to fifteen Tylenol. She lived with her aunt in the family home. Her parents were not in the picture. She was doing fairly well in school and had friends and no prior psychiatric history. She did report symptoms consistent with a major depression and lived in a rather overwhelmed household. She was sent home from the emergency room with a no-suicide contract, a plan to see her the following day, and an agreement with her aunt to take the next two days (Thursday and Friday) off from work so that she could be with Joanna.

In the second interview, after she had drawn a picture of heaven, she spoke at length of her desire for a reunion with her deceased grandmother. She had a detailed idea of what her grandmother's life must be like there and had a burning desire to join her. It became very clear that her grandmother had been the glue that had held Joanna together and that the void she had left behind was unfilled.

Joanna was started on an SSRI and met with the clinician to review her longings. The clinician then worked with her aunt to improve the overall life of this girl by making a number of environmental changes: moving Joanna out of her deceased grandmother's bedroom (which she had moved into to have her own room), starting an after-school program at the local neighborhood club, and "prescribing" fifteen minutes a day of mutually enjoyable activity between Joanna and her aunt. Her aunt and the clinician also met to review what the aunt knew about depression and suicide, and she was presented with a brief psychoeducational piece to bolster her knowledge base and help her feel more empowered.

Joanna and the clinician spoke at length about her relationship with her grandmother: how she knew that her grandmother would never give up on her and how that increased her resolve about not giving up on herself by wanting to leave this earth. They made lists of all the things that her grandmother would be proud of her for and wrote private messages about the things she wanted to talk with her grandmother about and would borrow her grandmother's wisdom to solve the problems she faced at home, with her peers, and in school. Her suicidality rapidly stabilized. She continued to improve gradually over the next several months with a marked lessening of her depressive symptoms and a full return to good functioning. The meetings tapered, but she continued the SSRI. She reported at follow-up that she often would say to herself, "Now what would Grams say about this?" and would then follow her grandmother's advice.

Clearly this intervention borrows and builds on the four treatment points outlined above and was not confined to a single therapeutic model. It assessed the strengths and weaknesses in all spheres of this child's life and then developed the intervention to meet the specifics of the case. In this particular instance, the family and child were fully cooperative, helping to ensure a positive outcome. On an individual basis, Joanna was able to grieve the loss of her grandmother and progress in the mourning process. She was enabled to integrate the lost object (her grandmother) through constructive approaches to problem solving by using the therapy and therapist. Her depression was treated pharmacologically with a positive response. Her aunt was aided by the behavioral recommendations and developed a more sophisticated understanding of her niece's difficulties. There was a real synergy of the approaches. Unfortunately, this is not always the case, even if one follows a carefully thought out treatment plan, as is illustrated by the following case.

> Mike was a fifteen-year-old who presented after ingesting twenty-five of his Zoloft pills. He had been in treatment for depression and substance abuse at the time of his overdose. He was acutely hospitalized for medical and psychiatric stabilization. His parents were unable to attend family meetings, and his father tended to minimize the attempt. "He was only trying to get attention," he often repeated. Despite clinical recognition of the importance of engaging the family, and many attempts to do so, the family treatment never got off the ground.
>
> The treatment alliance with Mike was equally shaky. The apparent precipitant for the overdose was the breakup with a girlfriend. Mike refused to talk about it at all. His first passes off the unit were disastrous, with marijuana and alcohol abuse. He convinced his parents to sign him out against medical advice four days after the incident. Since he was not suicidal, he was allowed to leave. The family refused outpatient follow-up.

Mike's clinical precariousness coupled with the family's inability to support the needed treatment led to the request for state protective services on the grounds of medical neglect, but the case was screened out. Mike and his family were lost to follow-up.

The case conference had centered on the inability to form an alliance with either the parents or the teenager. Many hypotheses were offered to account for this difficulty, including an inability to tolerate affect by both the parents and Mike, parental guilt regarding Mike's desperate state, and the parents' expressed wish for Mike to "just get out of our lives." Primary features in the therapeutic alliance will sabotage, derail, or at least delay almost all treatment plans.

In the treatment realm, certain patterns or themes occur as one works with children and the families of children who attempt or complete suicide. For most families, the idea that their child would be so desperate, pained, and over-whelmed that he or she feels that suicide is the only way out is their worst night-mare come true. Many families become despairing, with a profound sense of helplessness and failure. Other families become enraged at the child for what they see as the child's victimizing them. All families, in our opinion, need non-judgmental, clinical support, something that can be quite challenging since these same families also engender marked negative countertransference. Families need education about suicide and the underlying disorders that their children have. They need to review their family's functioning without being unduly self-critical. Finally, they need to feel less helpless and more empowered to resume success-ful parenting so that they will not be terrified that the self-destructive acts will reoccur or will feel more competent to deal with them if they do. This includes helping the family to recognize warning signs of depression and substance abuse, and to develop a plan of action once something has been noted.

Intervention After Suicide

For those rare families in which suicide has occurred, the need for intervention is critical. The unspeakable has happened. Programs to support all family mem-bers are absolutely essential. Parents and surviving children need an opportu-nity to review the situation and attempt to grapple with the aftermath and their emotions, including remorse, misunderstanding, and survivor guilt. Families often need the opportunity to tell their story again and again. There is a real pos-sibility of further negative sequelae in the survivors, including depression (25 percent), post-traumatic stress disorder (40 percent), suicidal ideation (31 per-cent), or acting out, divorce, or future suicide attempts (Pfeffer, Martins, and Mann, 1997). The risk increases if survivors are untreated. Preventive interven-tions such as those described by Beardslee et al. (1996) for families with de-pression can be adapted for use with this at-risk population of suicide survivors. Interventions can include psychoeducational meetings, opportunities for the fam-ily unit to review the events and illness and identification, monitoring, and early treatment for family members at risk.

Just as it is necessary to intervene with families in which a suicide has oc-curred, so too is it necessary to intervene in schools that have experienced a suicide. The other students, as well as the teachers, will need help and support in dealing with the confusion and pain that inevitably occur in the aftermath of a suicide. Rapid consultation and support may help diminish the contagion ef-fect that has been noted in some communities following a suicide.

PREVENTION

The identification of children and adolescents who are at risk for suicidal be-haviors has been challenging, in large part due to their heterogeneity. These children share a final common pathway but not a common disease. Despite this phenomenon, there are preventative principles that are recommended to address suicidal behaviors in children and adolescents:

- All care providers, parents, and educators should be educated about childhood suicide, with an emphasis on the role of underlying risk factors, such as major loss, abuse, depression, substance abuse, and recent suicides within a community.

- The urgent need to evaluate all children who express self-destructiveness in order to facilitate early treatment should be stressed. Families and schools can educate all children about some of the warning signs of suicide, including hopelessness and helplessness, social isolation, and substance abuse, and advise children to seek adult help if they are concerned for themselves or one of their peers.

- Children who are at the highest risk for suicide can be identified through this educational process, allowing for intervention at an earlier stage.

- Broad social programs may be implemented to address the core of the known risk factors. Programs should focus on the early treatment of depression, prevention of physical and sexual abuse, prevention and treatment for substance abuse, and decreasing the availability of firearms. One of the most important avenues to pursue in this regards the prevention of depression. Recent studies by Clarke, Hawkins, Murphy, and Sheeber (1995) have indicated that treatment of children with depressive symptoms who do not yet meet the criteria for depression may prevent episodes of depression. Other research by Beardslee et al. (1997) has shown that improving family understanding in the situation of severe parental depression can diminish risk factors for depression in their children and may even improve their children's functioning.

In sum, education, identification, and early intervention are the keys to preventing child and adolescent suicidal behavior.

IMPLICATIONS FOR THE CLINICIAN

- Although suicide, particularly in school-aged children, is quite rare, suicidal ideation and suicide attempts are not. Models based on vulnerability, resources, and stress have general utility and are statistically helpful, but assessing and differentiating patients requires a highly individualized approach.

- We believe that the refinement of techniques and tools that can be specifically applied to individual patients and the development of clinical algorithms specific for suicidal children and adolescents will bring interventions to the next level. With increased understanding and ability to identify those individuals at the greatest risk for self-harm, more effective prevention strategies will ensue. It is through primary prevention that we will stem the rising tide of suicide.

- Suicide rates have rapidly risen over the past four decades, quadrupling to 0.9 per 100,000 in children and 13.8 per 100,000 in adolescents. Suicidal ideation or attempts are far more common, with estimates for ideation in the 10 to 15 percent range and attempts around 5 percent. Differentiating ideators and attempters from completers has been very challenging, but addressing those risk factors that are identifiable is the key to prevention.

- Multifactoral etiologic models acknowledge the clinical reality: suicidal behaviors are a final symptom, not a specific illness. There will be no Rosetta Stone for suicide, but one should tailor the intervention to address each identifiable factor.

- Intervention is based on assessing the individual's risk-to-resource balance, coupled with an understanding of the meaning of the act. Personal meaning defines both the act and the treatment. One must understand "why" to understand "why not."

- The therapeutic alliance with the child and his or her family is critical. Asking the family to remove lethal weapons from the home can often be the litmus test for family alliance.

- When in doubt, be conservative. Safety and protection come first.

CHAPTER TWENTY-FIVE

Suicide in the Elderly

David C. Steffens, M.D.
Dan G. Blazer, M.D., Ph.D.

Our thoughts about suicide in late life are different from our thoughts about suicide in younger people. The image of a seventy-eight-year-old man with severe and chronic medical problems, recently widowed, quietly ending his life by taking an overdose differs sharply from our image of a twenty-four-year-old married woman with two young children found in her car with a self-inflicted gunshot wound to the head. Yet each individual has terminated his or her life, having made the decision that death is the only solution to the problems that life has presented. In this chapter we assume that most suicides in the elderly, like most suicides in younger people, are preventable tragedies. After providing a historical context, we review the epidemiology of suicide in the elderly, its risk factors and consequences. Then we discuss the clinical management of suicide in the elderly, including assessment, prevention, crisis intervention, and working with family and loved ones when a suicide occurs. We conclude with a discussion of societal and ethical implications of suicide in the elderly, with a brief overview of physician-assisted suicide.

HISTORICAL PERSPECTIVE

Accounts of suicide in late life date back thousands of years. Seneca, the personal teacher of the Emperor Nero, eloquently and clearly described suicidal thinking:

> For this reason, but for this alone, life is not an evil—that no one is obliged to live. If life pleases you, live. If not, you have a right to return whence you came.

443

I will not relinquish old age if it leaves my better part intact. But if it begins to shake my mind, if it destroys its facilities one by one, if it leaves me not life but breath, I will depart from the putrid or tottering edifice. I will not escape by death from disease so long as it may be healed, and leaves my mind unimpaired. I will not raise my hand against myself on account of pain, for so to die is to be conquered. But if I know that I must suffer without hope of relief, I will depart, not through fear of the pain itself, but because it prevents all for which I would live [Lecky, 1869].

Seneca's own suicide, however, was anything but a rational decision. Having fallen out of favor with Nero late in his life and confronted with the choice of taking his own life or having it taken by someone else, Seneca chose the former. Herein lies the dilemma facing clinicians and, indeed, society, as we confront the specter of suicide in late life. Is suicide among the elderly a rational solution to a set of problems, or is it a psychiatric disorder, or even a response to a disorder? Suicide in older people is, in most cases according to the authors of this chapter, an irrational response to severe psychological pain that results from diagnosable psychiatric disorders.

Yet factors other than mental illness are associated with suicide and, perhaps, lower the threshold for committing suicide. For Albert Camus, whether one should commit suicide was the only serious philosophical problem. He struggled with thoughts of suicide through much of his life, and though he did not actively commit suicide, many believed the automobile accident that led to his death was, in fact, an indirect suicide. The philosophical question about suicide raised by Camus, described in his work, *The Myth of Sisyphus* (1964), may become a reality that many older persons confront. For example, the elderly are more likely to experience severe physical illnesses that inevitably lead to death. Therefore, physician-assisted suicide to relieve pain and suffering or the specter of death has involved the elderly more than other age groups. In addition, many older people fear becoming burdens to themselves, friends, and society. The weight of chronic, debilitating illnesses, such as Alzheimer's disease, which burden families, leads some elders to justify suicide. Older persons also recognize that they have "lived longer than they will live," have accomplished most of what they wished to accomplish, and therefore see little future compared to the past memories, whether the past was pleasant or unpleasant. Seneca's reflections, therefore, are as applicable today as they were two thousand years ago.

SCOPE OF SUICIDE IN THE ELDERLY

The concept of suicide in the elderly spans many other behavioral and cognitive constructs. In this section we examine acute versus chronic suicide, direct versus indirect suicide, suicidal ideation, suicide attempts versus completed suicides, and physician-assisted suicide and euthanasia.

Acute Versus Chronic Suicide

Suicide usually implies an acute, decisive action that leads to death, such as shooting oneself, hanging oneself, overdosing on medications, crashing one's automobile in a single car accident, or asphyxiation with carbon monoxide. These methods of suicide are usually identifiable, recorded on death certificates, and used to compile statistics regarding suicide. In late life, however, even these methods may be attributed to natural or accidental causes of death, thus leading to an underestimate of the frequency of suicide in the elderly. For example, the older person involved in a single car accident, such as crashing into a tree, would rarely be assumed to have committed suicide. Rather, we tend to make the assumption that some acute medical event occurred prior to the accident. Older persons found dead in their homes may not be subjected to a thorough postmortem examination to rule out possible self-inflicted causes of death, in part because they are "expected" to die from conditions such as cardiac disease. Medical examiners are reticent to embarrass older persons and their families if no evidence of participation by another person in the death can be found.

Far more difficult for the clinician working with older adults is chronic suicide. By far the most common form of chronic suicide is failure to eat, therefore leading to slow but definite starvation. Other forms of chronic suicide include sustained drug and alcohol abuse, refusal to use life-sustaining medications (such as insulin), and self-neglect. Such behavior has also been termed "silent suicide" (Simon, 1989), and it has important clinical, legal, and societal implications. Karl Menninger, in *Man Against Himself* (1938), explored in detail the potential to chronic suicide in society and suggested that such behavior is perhaps more applicable to older persons than persons of other ages. Such forms of slow and frequently not obvious suicide represent real challenges to clinicians and families. First, the behavior must be recognized by all parties caring for the older person, and there are strong barriers to such recognition. It is unacceptable for most people to even consider that someone would be willing to slowly and methodically starve themselves to death. And once we have reached that conclusion about a loved one or patient, we must fight the tendency to become an accomplice to the process. Notions that "if his will to die is that strong, there is little we can and should do about it," or "she's so old and her health is so poor, maybe death is the best thing" may prevent us from confronting the patient and undertaking a thorough psychiatric assessment.

Direct Versus Indirect Suicide

Indirect suicide is closely associated with chronic suicide, but some differences do emerge. Direct actions to take one's life, such as self-inflicted gunshot wounds and overdoses of medication, are the most noticeable attempts of suicide. Nevertheless, a number of indirect approaches to suicide are prevalent in our society. Some older persons submit themselves to dangerous, even reckless situations. For example, an older man may wander into the woods of his farm during the middle of winter with inadequate clothing, submitting his safety to the elements. Others refuse adequate medical care for a potentially fatal condition that could be treated. Such behavior is exemplified by an older woman who suffers from a significant and severe cardiac arrhythmia that can be controlled by medications, yet she refuses to take the medications, therefore increasing the likelihood that she will die from the arrhythmia.

Passive Death Wishes

Chronic suicide and indirect suicide should also be distinguished from passive death wishes, or the presence of thoughts that one would rather be dead but no intent, either directly or indirectly, to end one's life. Such thinking is common in the elderly and may or may not be associated with psychiatric or medical illness. Often experiencing guilt over being a burden to loved ones or to society, older individuals with passive death wishes may feel that they themselves as well as those around them would be better off if they were dead. Statements such as "it wouldn't be the end of the world if I didn't wake up tomorrow" typify passive death wishes. As religion and spirituality often play a prominent role in the lives of the elderly, passive death wishes may be expressed in prayers for life and its misery to come to an end. It is not uncommon for depressed elders to report "I have asked God to take me." It is unclear how frequently passive death wishes may lead to active suicidal behavior in the elderly, or even if there is a connection between the two. For example, older patients with chronic depression may carry thoughts of death with them on a daily basis, but never seriously entertain ideas of taking steps to end their life.

Suicide Attempts Versus Completed Suicides

Suicide attempts range widely, and some clinicians may attempt to categorize these attempts. From a clinical perspective, these categorizations are of little value, for they are generally based on the concept that some "attempts" are more serious than others. In reality, all suicide attempts are serious, even if the intent of the gesture is not to die but perhaps to call for help. For example, persons who knew Marilyn Monroe believed she did not actually wish to end her life when she died of an overdose of medications. Rather, she was attempting to gain attention and help. Regardless of the actual motivation, suicide attempts range from taking a few pills that are highly unlikely to lead to death to a self-inflicted gunshot wound from which a person miraculously survives. Reports of attempted suicide are less frequent in late life (less than 1 percent report an attempt at some time in their lives) compared to younger ages, where the lifetime frequency of attempted suicide is between 1 and 2 percent (Blazer et al., 1986).

As noted above, completed suicides are not always easy to identify. Even so, there is little doubt that completed suicides are more frequent in late life than at other stages of the life cycle, but this is almost entirely due to an increased frequency of suicide deaths among older white males ("Suicide among older persons," 1996). It is equally clear that one of the best predictors of completed suicide is history of previous attempts. This well-documented finding is particularly true in the elderly.

Euthanasia and Physician-Assisted Suicide

Euthanasia and suicide with the assistance of someone else have taken place since antiquity. These approaches of taking one's life run counter to a culture that views suicide as a sign of mental illness and have received considerable attention in the press in recent years. Euthanasia has been a topic of many conversations recently, stimulated in large part by the foundation of the Hemlock Society, and is closely connected with physician-assisted suicide. Physician-assisted suicide has made headline news during the 1990s since Dr. Jack Kevorkian assisted Mrs. Janet Adkins to end her life while parked in a van later found in a Michigan suburb. She was attached to a so-called "suicide machine" provided by Dr. Kevorkian. Mrs. Adkins had been diagnosed as suffering from probable Alzheimer's disease (in its early stages) and made the decision to end her life rather than undergo the slow decline in her cognitive abilities. (The ethical and legal aspects of physician-assisted suicide are discussed at the end of this chapter.) See also Chapter Thirty.

EPIDEMIOLOGY OF SUICIDE IN THE ELDERLY

Older people have consistently shown higher rates of suicide compared to other age groups. The overall suicide rate in persons sixty-five years and older had been dropping from the early 1940s until the 1980s (Meehan et al., 1991). During the period from 1980 to 1992, the number of suicides in this older age group increased 36 percent, from 4537 to 6160 (Kachur et al., 1995; "Suicide among older persons," 1996). In 1992, persons sixty-five years and older accounted for 13 percent of the population but almost 20 percent of suicides. Between 1980 and 1992, suicide rates actually decreased for persons aged sixty-five to seventy-four but increased substantially in older persons: 11 percent for those age seventy-five to seventy-nine years, 35 percent for eighty to eighty-four-year-olds, and 15 percent for those eighty-five and older.

Suicide frequency varies significantly by gender and race or ethnicity among older adults. Prevalence (per 100,000) in 1986 was 45.6 for white males, 16.2 for black males, 7.5 for white females, and 2.4 for black females. Even so, the rates for black males are increasing at a much faster pace than for white males (Meehan et al., 1991). In 1992, among those eighty-five and older, the suicide frequency was 67.6 for white men, 6.3 for white women, 17.1 for black men, and 3.0 for black women (Kachur et al., 1995).

The methods used for committing suicide also vary by age and gender. Two-thirds of suicides among the elderly are committed by use of firearms (compared to 57 percent among persons under the age of 65). In 1986, 75 percent of male victims over the age of sixty-five died of gunshot wounds compared to 61 percent of male victims under the age of sixty-five (M. S. Kaplan et al., 1994). During the same year, only 31 percent of female suicides over sixty-five died of gunshot wounds compared to 41 percent under the age of sixty-five. Yet the trend is for women to use firearms in completing suicide at an increasing rate, with firearms accounting for 38 percent of all suicides among women 65 and older in 1992 (Adamek and Kaplan, 1996). In the last decade, the use of firearms surpassed the use of drugs and poisons as the most common method of committing suicide among older women. White men consistently are at greatest risk for using a firearm to commit suicide. Of the 14,887 cases of suicide in this group from 1989 to 1991, 77 percent were committed with firearms (Kaplan et al., 1996). Specific predictors of firearm-associated suicide among elderly white men were age sixty-five to eighty-four, living in a nonmetropolitan area, not completing high school, and being married, divorced, or widowed (not single). Although married older men have lower suicide frequencies than single older men, the proportion of suicides involving guns was higher in the married men. Less commonly used methods of completed suicide in elderly men include (in order of decreasing frequency) strangulation, poisoning, and cutting (Kachur et al., 1995).

Recent data from the Centers for Disease Control demonstrate geographic differences for suicide within the United States among all age groups ("Regional Variations," 1997). Regional crude suicide frequencies were highest for persons residing in the West (14.1 per 100,000 population), followed by the South (13.1), Midwest (11.4), and Northeast (9.3). Whether similar geographic differences in suicide frequencies exist for the elderly remains unclear.

Suicide Rates in Other Countries Compared with U.S. Rates

Though the frequency of suicide has increased among older persons in the United States, the prevalence is not as high as that among other industrialized societies (Pritchard, 1996a). For example, the suicide prevalence among men seventy-five and older in Austria between 1974 and 1992 increased 125 percent from 873 to 1095 per million. Sweden, West Germany, France, Denmark, Switzerland, Portugal, Belgium, and Japan reported higher prevalence among elders than found in the United States. However, between 1974 and 1992, the frequency of male suicide in the United States increased at a faster pace than that for the remainder of the industrialized world.

There are interesting and notable cultural differences in suicide rates. For example, in the People's Republic of China, although younger women have a higher suicide rate than younger men (male-to-female ratio of 0.77), in the age group of fifty-five years and older, the male suicide prevalence is higher (Pritchard, 1996b). Living in rural areas of China greatly increases the risk of suicide. In Japan, suicide by drowning is a common method of suicide in the elderly, with a higher frequency of intentional drowning among women (Rockett and Smith, 1993). In the multiethnic city of Singapore, the annual suicide rate per 100,000 was 52.0; however, it was highest among ethnic Chinese (59.3), followed by Indians (33.9), and lowest among Malays (3.0). The Malay population consists largely of devout Muslims, so religious prohibitions may play a significant role in the rarity of suicide (Ko and Kua, 1995).

Cohort Analyses

Birth cohort appears to be a strong predictor of suicide frequency. Persons born between 1900 and 1920 have experienced lower suicide rates at every age than persons born prior to 1900 and persons born after 1920 (Blazer et al., 1986). This, in part, explains the decline in the frequency of suicide among older persons from 1950 to 1980 and the subsequent upswing in prevalence since 1980. Why do some birth cohorts suffer from higher frequencies of suicide than others? Suicide frequency may be related to the relative size of birth cohorts compared with other cohorts within the population (Holinger et al., 1988). For example, successively younger birth cohorts are facing a more competitive job market, increased social stress, delayed marriage (and therefore delayed establishment of close relationships), fewer children, and smaller social networks. More prevalent divorce, secularization, and perhaps a subsequent feeling of alienation may also explain the increased suicide frequency in younger birth cohorts. There is also evidence that cohort size may have differential effects on different age groups, with large cohort size raising the suicide frequency for the young and middle-aged, but reducing it for the elderly (Pampel, 1996). These are theories only and can scarcely be tested by using national suicide data. Even so, tracing suicide frequency by age through the twentieth century is most useful to understand the relative well-being of older persons compared to the remainder of society through time.

Gender Difference in Suicide

Gender is one of the most important correlates of suicide in older persons, as in other age groups, for older women do not experience an increase in prevalence with age as do older white men (Canetto, 1992). One possibility for explaining these gender differences in suicide mortality is that women exhibit differences in coping that protect them from suicide compared to men. In contrast to men (at least through most of the twentieth century), women tend to experience several role shifts during adulthood. In addition to a period of mothering, women have traditionally moved in and out of the work force depending on their age. Men, in contrast, have tended to follow a relatively stable course. The change from work to retirement for men, therefore, may be more difficult and men may not have developed the coping skills necessary for such changes, a lack that in turn increases their likelihood of suicide. Women are more likely to maintain close relationships outside the marriage relationship than are men, and this may also explain part of the difference. An older man, recently widowed, may find that much of his prior social contact depended on relationships that his wife had maintained, and any reluctance to preserve such relationships may isolate him from potential sources of support. Finally, men are more likely to use violent means of suicide, such as gunshot wounds, which tend to be fatal more often than taking pills, although, as noted above, the prevalence of suicide by means of firearms is increasing among older women.

Suicidal Ideation

Suicidal ideation is relatively common throughout the life cycle. In a large survey of older adults in the community (Blazer et al., 1986), 6.1 percent expressed thoughts about death within two weeks before the time of the interview and 4.4 percent expressed a desire to die at some point in their life; 1.2 percent expressed this desire within the two weeks before the interview; 3.5 percent reported that they had contemplated suicide at some point in their lives. In the entire sample (persons eighteen and above), 7.5 percent reported having thoughts of suicide sometime during their life. In a study of older primary care patients, the estimated prevalence of suicidal ideation was 0.7 to 1.2 percent (Callahan, et al., 1996). Among eighty-five-year-olds in a community in Sweden, 4.0 percent of those without mental illness reported thinking that life was not worth living in the last month, 4.0 percent wished for death, 0.9 percent thought about taking their own life, but none had seriously considered suicide (Skoog et al., 1996). Among those with mental disorders, these figures were 29.2 percent, 27.5 percent, 9.2 percent, and 1.7 percent.

Suicide Attempts

Although the prevalence of suicide in the elderly is high, the prevalence of attempted (unsuccessful) suicide is low (Sendbuehler and Goldstein, 1977). There is very little literature on the epidemiology of suicide attempts, and it tends to focus on specific populations at risk. For example, in a population of 126 elderly depressed inpatients followed for one year, 8.7 percent made a suicide attempt. Compared with nonattempters, attempters were of higher socioeconomic status, had more of a history of past suicide attempts, and were more likely not to have had a remission of their index depressive episode (Zweig and Hinrichsen, 1993).

RISK FACTORS FOR SUICIDE IN LATE LIFE

As described above, increased age is a risk for suicide throughout life, irrespective of birth cohort effects (Kachur et al., 1995). This increased risk does not plateau at age of sixty-five; rather, persons eighty-five plus years of age have the highest prevalence of suicide in our society. The association of age and suicide is explained exclusively by the association of age and suicide among males in the United States, in that the frequency of suicide among females (both white and nonwhite) changes relatively little across mid and late life. Males are much more likely to commit suicide than females, and whites have a higher suicide frequency than nonwhites, though among older persons, the prevalence among black males is increasing at a faster pace than for white males. Suicide frequencies are also higher among persons single, separated or divorced, or widowed compared to persons who are married at all ages. This is especially true for males. Suicide frequency usually increases during troublesome economic times and decreases during times of prosperity. Frequencies also exhibit age-specific temporal cycles (McLeary, Chew, Hellsten, and Flynn-Bransford, 1991). For example, day-of-the-week effects (whereby Monday has the highest suicide rate and Saturday has the lowest) are found almost exclusively in middle-aged suicide. On the other hand, older persons are more likely to commit suicide during the summer months, whereas teenagers are more likely to commit suicide during the winter months. Recently, a large five-year retrospective study demonstrated a significant positive association between suicide in persons older than sixty-five and hours of sunshine and higher relative humidity (Salib, 1997). It is unclear how such meteorological factors influence suicidal behavior in the elderly, but it probably occurs through an interaction with biological and social variables.

Psychiatric Disorders

Psychiatric disorders are the most important risk factors for suicide in the elderly, especially depression and alcohol abuse or dependence (Blazer, 1991). In fact, suicide among the elderly without a diagnosable mental disorder seems to be rare (Henriksson et al., 1995). In one study, 80 percent of persons who had attempted suicide and were later admitted to an adult psychiatric inpatient unit, had experienced a major depression of late onset, especially a psychotic depression (Lyness et al., 1992). Among completed suicide victims aged seventy-five to ninety-two, 71.4 percent had a mood disorder; in a group aged fifty-five to seventy-four, 63.9 percent had a mood disorder (Conwell et al., 1996). In depressed elderly patients, those with three or more prior depressive episodes were more likely to report suicidal ideation than those with two or fewer prior episodes (Steffens et al., 1996). Alcohol abuse is also a known risk factor of suicide (Blumenthal, 1988), though the impact of alcohol abuse on suicide prevalence in older persons is not conclusive (Mäkelä, 1996) and may be confounded by comorbid depressive disorders (Conwell et al., 1996; see also Chapter Seventeen in this book). Finally, older patients with anxiety neurosis have been shown to be at higher risk of suicide (Allgulander and Lavori, 1993).

Physical Illness and Functional Disability

Chronic physical illness as a risk factor for suicide has received significant attention in the press during recent years. The prospect of living many years with chronic pain or disability and subsequently becoming dependent upon the health care system or family members is especially difficult for older persons who have traditionally accepted an independent lifestyle and cling to our society's valuation of self-sufficiency. Some have suggested that physical illness may contribute to suicide in over one-third of older persons. In one study, 94 percent of older suicides had physical problems at the time of death, 59 percent had an active axis III disorder, and 57 percent had seen a health professional in the thirty days prior to death (Carney et al., 1994). The illnesses most frequently cited are diseases of the central nervous systems (especially Alzheimer's disease), malignancies, cardiopulmonary conditions, and urogenital diseases in men. Those with mixed Alzheimer and vascular dementia may be at a particularly high risk for suicidal ideation (Rao et al., 1997).

Previous Suicide Attempts

A previous history of a suicide attempt is well known to contribute to the risk for future suicide attempts (Blazer, 1991). Each attempt increases the risk of a successful suicide in the future. In some ways, having made a suicide attempt breaks through a psychological barrier to suicide and therefore decreases the threshold for future suicide attempts. Clinicians must be especially vigilant in working with older persons who have made suicide attempts, given that, in general, older persons do not attempt suicide as frequently as younger persons but do complete suicides with a higher frequency.

Psychological Factors

The association of hopelessness with suicide is intuitive, and in recent years, the relationship between hopelessness and suicide attempts in older persons has been demonstrated (Rifai et al., 1994). Persons who are experiencing recurrent major depression and are treated with standard psychotherapy and pharmacotherapy are of a higher risk for a suicide attempt if they exhibit a higher degree of hopelessness. In addition, loss of pleasure or interest, significant cycling of mood, which can lead to severe experiences of depression following periods of well-being, can also contribute to an increased risk for suicide. As noted above, coping styles also may increase the risk for suicide. For example, older persons who tend to act out their conflicts and psychological pain as opposed to expressing them to a confidant, are at greater risk for suicide (Blazer and Koenig, 1996).

Social Factors

Investigators have examined the occurrence of stressful life events prior to suicide. In the elderly, generally the most frequently cited life event was a severe medical illness, especially in men (Heikkinen et al., 1995a). Another stressor associated with suicidal ideation in the elderly is bereavement (Szanto et al., 1997). Widowed or divorced older men have a significantly increased risk of suicide (Tsuang et al., 1992). However, apart from marital status, very few other social factors have been consistently associated with suicide in the elderly. Contrary to expectation, one group found no excess of social isolation among older suicides compared to younger, although among the elderly, more suicide victims lived alone (Heikkinen et al., 1995b). Death and illness in the family were frequent recent life events but occurred with similar frequency between younger and older victims (Heikkinen et al., 1995a). Financial trouble does not appear to be as important a risk factor for the elderly as it is in younger populations (Heikkinen et al., 1995a). There was no difference in stressful life events between older men and women (Heikkinen and Lönnqvist, 1995).

Biological Susceptibility

In recent years, two areas of psychobiological research have been related to suicide: the hypothalamic-pituitary-adrenal (HPA) axis and the serotonin system (Conwell et al., 1995). For example, HPA dysfunction has been associated with significant changes in cognitive function, such as confusion, which may contribute to the propensity to suicide. Decreased levels of 5-hydroxy-indole-acetic acid (5-HIAA, a metabolite of serotonin) have been found in a number of studies of persons who have either died of violent suicide or have shown an increased propensity to attempt suicide, including one study in the elderly (Jones et al., 1990). There is no evidence that the serotonin system is changed in normal aging. See Chapter Six for further discussion.

EVALUATION OF THE POTENTIALLY SUICIDAL OLDER ADULT

The evaluation of the potentially suicidal older adult can be divided into the evaluation of the direct and indirect risk of suicide. Neither of these approaches to an evaluation is highly predictive of suicide, primarily because suicide is such a rare event. Therefore suicidal risk is, by its very nature, subject to overestimation. Even so, given the tragedy of suicide, this overestimation may be helpful.

Early intervention to prevent suicide based on the assessment of the potential for suicide could save the lives of many older persons. Unfortunately, we will never know the degree to which our efforts are successful, primarily because of the rarity of the event. Moreover, due to ethical constraints, it would be impossible to perform a "controlled study" of interventive prevention in a high-risk group of suicidal patients compared to a controlled group in order to determine the effectiveness of that intervention. For further reading on assessment and management of suicide in the elderly, we refer the reader to *Now I Lay Me Down: Suicide in the Elderly* (Lester and Tallmer, 1994).

Direct Assessment

The clinician undertakes the direct assessment of suicide in the interview with the potentially suicidal older adult (Osgood, 1992). A four-item screen for identification of suicidal ideation among general medical patients has been developed (Cooper-Patrick et al., 1994). Many clinicians feel uncomfortable asking older adults directly about their intentions to harm themselves. A fourfold, layered approach to assessment is useful in obtaining the necessary data without disrupting the therapeutic relationship with the potentially suicidal elder. The first inquiry should be, "Have you ever felt life is not worth living?" As noted above, this question is answered affirmatively in a significant minority of older persons. Among depressed older persons the frequency of a positive response is much greater. Yet many older persons who wish they were dead would never act upon that wish. The reasons vary from moral or religious prohibitions to fears of the pain of killing oneself.

The second inquiry, if the first is positive, is "Have you ever thought of hurting or harming yourself?" Though this question does not specifically inquire about "suicide," the elder will almost always interpret the question accurately and will usually provide an honest response in return. If the elder states that he or she has not considered inflicting personal harm, the inquiry can cease and the older person may be considered, at least from the perspective of direct assessment, at low risk for suicide.

If the answer to the second question is positive, however, the clinician should inquire, "Have you considered specific methods for harming yourself?" Many elders who have thought of harming themselves have only thought so in general terms. Others, however, have considered specific means by which they might harm themselves, such as shooting themselves, taking medications, or refusing necessary medical therapies. If an individual has considered a specific method for inflicting personal harm and that method is readily available to him—for example, an older person states that he will shoot himself and in fact possesses a gun—a critical threshold has been crossed and a risk of suicide is much higher.

Finally, the clinician should inquire, "Have you ever made a suicide attempt?" The importance of suicide attempts as part of the overall risk-factor profile of the potentially suicidal older adult has been emphasized above. Yet "attempts" vary in severity. Some persons will simply walk to the medicine cabinet to determine whether he or she has sufficient medications for an attempt. Others, however, have actually taken guns from their bureaus within the bedroom, loaded their guns, and placed the gun to their heads, only to decide, at the last moment, not to pull the trigger. Still others have actually made attempts, either by taking medications or by wounding themselves in an attempt at suicide.

In summary, the direct assessment of the potential for suicide ranges from suicidal ideation in its broadest terms to serious attempts to end one's life. The more severe the attempt, or the more specific the ideation, the greater the risk for suicide.

Indirect Assessment and Risk Factors

Given the rarity of completed suicides and the difficulty of establishing a clear relationship between direct assessment of suicidal risk and suicide over short periods (for example, a few days), clinicians treating persons at risk for suicide would do well to emulate physicians in their approach to reducing the risk for myocardial infarction. Direct assessment of risk should be coupled with known indirect risk factors, as described above: older age, male gender, white race or ethnicity, physical illness, psychological factors such as hopelessness, previous suicide attempts, and psychiatric disorders such depression and alcohol abuse. Clinicians can then develop a risk factor profile. This profile is analogous to that for cardiovascular disease, which includes obesity, hypertension, cholesterol and lipid levels, lack of exercise, and demographics such as age, gender, race or ethnicity, and lifestyle. The clinician can then assess the interaction of various risk factors to determine risk for suicide in a particular patient (Johnston and Walker, 1996).

Even though suicide and myocardial infarction might at first glance exhibit little in common, there are similarities in the approach to preventing these two tragic events. First, both are isolated, severe events that decrease life expectancy among persons at greater risk. Studies abound that demonstrate that, among the depressed, life expectancy is decreased in large part by suicide just as studies abound demonstrating that persons with a high risk for myocardial infarction have a shortened life expectancy. A second similarity is that death is usually not the outcome of the event. Most persons experiencing a myocardial infarction do not die, as is the case with most persons who make a suicide attempt. Those persons, however, are known to be at especially high risk for future fatal events regardless of the presence or absence of other risk factors. Therefore, preventive efforts are especially directed toward persons who have experienced a nonfatal event. Third, risk for both suicide and myocardial infarction derive from a combination of risk factors rather than any single factor. Therefore, an aggressive, generic approach to prevention is more appropriate than an isolated, specific approach. The clinician must call on every resource to decrease the risk of suicide as much as possible.

CLINICAL MANAGEMENT OF THE SUICIDAL OLDER PERSON: INTERVENTION AS PREVENTION

The management of the older person at risk for suicide consists of intervention strategies directed at preventing future suicide attempts. In other words, intervention is preventive. The intervention can be conveniently divided into two phases, crisis intervention and treatment of underlying problems. These strategies are not always successful, however, and clinicians must also be prepared to assist family and health care workers when an older adult commits suicide.

Crisis Intervention

Crisis intervention consists of three phases. First and perhaps foremost is protection of the person at significant suicidal risk. These persons may come to the attention of the clinician through making a suicide attempt that was unsuccessful or through an expressed desire to end their lives, conveyed perhaps to a family member or the clinician. Adequate assessment of suicidality in older adults also requires a working knowledge of high-risk groups, such as whites, males, and recently widowed, depressed, or alcoholic patients (Osgood, 1992). When a clinician deems the risk for suicide at crisis level, extraordinary measures are indicated, including involuntary hospitalization. If the older person refuses voluntary hospitalization, around-the-clock vigils by family members and twenty-four-hour-a-day availability by the clinician may substitute for involuntary hospitalization. The crisis of suicide generally is brief, as immediate suicide intentions rarely last more than a few days. Therefore, protecting the older adult through the period of crisis is paramount. If hospitalization is not elected, the clinician must be sensitive to the pressure being placed on the family and offer considerable support to them as they struggle with the wrenching challenges of caring for a suicidal individual.

A second phase in crisis intervention is the suicide contract. If an older adult expresses the intent to commit suicide, the clinician often can obtain a promise from the older person that he or she will not make a suicide attempt without contacting the clinician and speaking to the clinician about her or his specific intent. For a suicide contract to be effective, an alliance must be established, the potentially suicidal elder must be cognitively intact, and the clinician must be available either by telephone or by immediate visit to a clinic facility. Older persons in the late twentieth century in the United States are generally faithful to their word, and therefore the suicide contract, if it can be negotiated, is an effective means for deterring suicide through the period of crisis (see Chapter Twenty-Six). Why would an older person intent upon harming himself submit to a contract with the clinician? The intent to kill one's self is, by its very nature, ambivalent, for the desire to live is clearly present if the elder is still alive. The clinician therefore takes advantage of this ambivalence through the crisis period.

In the midst of the crisis of suicide, the clinician can involve the family. First, if the older person is not hospitalized and the responsibility includes family involvement for vigilance during the period of increased risk for suicide, the family can be instructed as to what to do to assist in minimizing risk of suicide. For example, family members can be told to remove any potentially harmful instruments, such as guns and knives, from availability to the older person, and also should be instructed to take responsibility for medications. Frequent checks by the clinician with the elder, family members, or friends who stay with the elder during the period of crisis can assist the family.

Engaging whole families in preventing suicides during the crisis period will probably become more important in the future, given the decreased resources for hospitalizing older persons. Families must be cautioned, however, that even their best efforts may prove ineffective and this is no different than what could be expected in a hospital setting. Older persons, even in the best of medical facilities, have managed to commit suicide. In other words, families must not be given the "responsibility" (or it should not even be suggested that families can take the responsibility) to prevent an older person from harming herself or himself. If families cannot manage to garner the necessary support, or if they show significant ambivalence regarding the management of an older adult during a suicidal crises, then that older person must be hospitalized.

Treatment of the Underlying Problem

The crisis of suicide is short term. In contrast, the problems leading to the crisis generally build up over a considerable period and are complex and multifactorial. Once the crisis has abated, the clinician should aggressively address the problems that may have contributed to the crisis, whether by treating a major depressive disorder, treating alcohol abuse or dependence, or assisting the older person to adjust to a recent loss. Some problems can be addressed more easily than others; for example, a chronic and progressive illness such as cancer or Alzheimer's disease cannot be reversed. In these situations, the clinician can only work with the older person and family (if available) to help the elder adjust to the problem presented. Though in some cases even the clinician may deem a suicide "rational," given the alternatives available to the elder, the clinician has a responsibility from the outset to assume that suicidal thoughts and behavior are abnormal and reflective of underlying psychopathology and therefore call for the best medical and psychiatric intervention available for the patient. Because older men are at greatly increased risk for suicide, some have suggested that suicide prevention strategies should target at-risk elderly males to bolster internal cognitive deterrents to suicide (Range and Stringer, 1996).

Other Prevention Strategies

Because suicide in the elderly is now recognized as a growing public health concern (Conwell, 1994), a number of programs have been developed to target this problem. One strategy is based on the traditional telephone crisis intervention model. Patients with geriatric depression can call in, or alternatively may be called by staff, for ongoing contact, assessment, and reminders to take prescribed medication (McIntosh, 1995). Such use of telephone contact has been shown to decrease the expected frequency of suicide among an elderly population (De Leo et al., 1995). Future models of prevention may include in-home visits to patients in crisis by volunteers and staff familiar to the patient (McIntosh, 1995).

Perhaps the most effective way of preventing suicide is through primary prevention. Educating both health care providers and the general public about risk factors for suicide in the elderly may help affect the conditions that can lead to suicide, such as worsening depression, alcoholism, and presence of a firearm in the household. Community-based programs can provide information and teach skills needed to recognize and respond to depression and suicidal behavior in the elderly. Such comprehensive public health measures have been implemented in several U.S. cities (Pratt et al., 1991; McIntosh, 1995). The National Institute of Mental Health will be supporting several initiatives targeting prevention of suicide in the elderly in the coming years.

If a Suicide Occurs

Arnold Toynbee, in his book *Man's Concern with Death* (1969), said, "There are always two parties to a death; the person who dies and the survivors who are bereaved . . . and in the proportionment of suffering, the survivor takes the brunt." If an older person commits suicide, the clinicians who treated that elder should assist the family. Families often feel guilty and tend to project that guilt onto the health care profession, despite the best efforts of the profession to instruct the family of its limitations. Lawyers often suggest that if a suicide occurs, clinicians should have little if any contact with family. However, it is the responsibility of the clinician to provide family members with an opportunity to vent their anger and frustration. The clinician may also vent his frustration (without suggesting that he had made a mistake) in preventing a suicide. (Chapter Thirty-One discusses these issues further.)

Both families and physicians must recognize that suicide, in the last analysis, cannot always be prevented. Even the best efforts of clinicians and family members, or the most compulsive procedures, directed toward preventing suicide are not always effective. Families express many concerns, not the least of which is embarrassment, over the fact that a valued family member has committed, according to some, an unpardonable sin. Family members feel guilt that they did not provide an environment that could rescue the elder from a sense of profound hopelessness and helplessness. Family members need to talk, and that talk must cover the spectrum of suicide, from the specific details of the actual event to the ethical and religious issues surrounding suicide. Each of these needs felt by family members are also felt by clinicians who have worked closely with older persons who commit suicide. Yet despite the variety of feelings and even frank psychiatric symptoms experienced acutely in survivors of elderly suicide, these survivors do not appear to experience any greater psychopathology at two-month follow-up than individuals who lost a loved one due to natural causes (Farberow et al., 1987).

Both the professionals who worked with the elder and the family members must work through their grief. Initially, they may share this work but ultimately the grief work must be individual. Any clinician who has treated an older person who has committed suicide cannot easily dismiss the outcome of that treatment. Clinicians should never become comfortable with an unnatural death, and this is especially true when that death is voluntary. Suicide therefore challenges the existential core of those left behind. The host of emotions experienced by a person bereaved from a suicide is beautifully described by Fine (1997) in her book *No Time to Say Goodbye: Surviving the Suicide of a Loved One.*

ETHICAL AND LEGAL ISSUES

The phenomena of suicide spans many fields of inquiry, not just the psychiatric or the medical. As noted above, many physicians and other health care professionals, clergy, and scholars support the free choice of an older person to experience "death with dignity." In Greek society, the Stoics and Epicureans viewed suicide as not only acceptable but especially relevant for escaping the problems of pain and old age. In recent years, the Hemlock Society, which accepts suicide as an acceptable solution to certain human conditions such as painful illness, has grown in membership dramatically. Even so, the recognition that suicide, more often than not, is an irrational act and the strong beliefs by some that suicide is unacceptable under any circumstances render societal discussions of elderly suicides especially relevant. We now discuss three issues related to the ethical and legal parameters of suicide.

Societal Intervention

As noted above, firearms are a favored means of committing suicide by many older adults, especially males. Given that suicide is often irrational and impulsive, limiting availability of the instruments to commit suicide is one means for its reduction. Just as arguments have been made that violent crimes can be decreased by gun control, equally cogent arguments have been made that suicide can be reduced by gun controls as well. A parallel example suggesting that suicide prevalence can be lowered, at least for a time, by removing an instrument of suicide has been demonstrated in England. During the early 1960s, a toxic form of cooking gas was replaced by a nontoxic form. A favorite means of suicide in England at that time was placing one's head in an oven and turning on the gas. At approximately the time nontoxic cooking gas replaced toxic gas, the frequency of suicide dropped dramatically, especially among elderly white males.

Rational Suicide on the Grounds of Old Age

Despite the optimistic approach to aging among many gerontologists in concept, the fact of an old age relatively free of illness for the vast majority of elders is not a reality and not expected to be a reality in the future (Moody, 1991). Though people are living longer and have achieved greater economic security during this century, we find more elders who are nonetheless subsequently relegated to a discouraging dependence, frequently during years lived in a nursing home. This fact has lead many to suggest that suicide is a rational alternative to frailty in late life. These advocates of rational suicide are not simply advocating the voluntary withdrawal of life supports when a medical condition is hopeless or cognitive functioning is severely impaired. They have revived an interest in legally facilitating older people to make a choice regarding life supports under certain circumstances in the future, as evidenced by a new law that requires hospitals to present older persons admitted an opportunity to provide "advance directives" regarding life supports.

The debate regarding rational suicide transcends the science of gerontology and the practice of the mental health professionals (Carpenter, 1993). If the issue were to remain as simply an ethical debate in society, the subject could be relegated to the ethicists and the theologians. With a rise of physician-assisted suicide, which has an impact upon the laws of our society and the practice of medicine, "rational suicide" becomes an issue of central importance to all who work with older adults.

Physician-Assisted Suicide

Physician-assisted suicide has received much attention throughout the lay press in recent years, predominantly through the activities of the Michigan physician Jack Kevorkian. As noted above, Kevorkian constructed a device for intravenously administering a lethal chemical that permits an apparent painless death at the choice of an individual who seeks the assistance of the physician. Sometimes Dr. Kevorkian has been present when the lethal chemical was administered and sometimes he has been absent. He has been arrested on several occasions but has not been incarcerated for an extended period.

Kevorkian has confronted society with the necessity of making legal decisions regarding physician-assisted suicide. Society, in turn, has shown its ambivalence toward physician-assisted suicide through its circuitous legal approaches. In 1996, the State of Oregon established a law permitting physician-assisted suicide, the first such law in this country. That law has withstood court challenges and has recently been confirmed in another statewide referendum. Surveys of both physicians and nonphysicians reveal a relative acceptance of physician-assisted suicide, more than half of persons surveyed in most cases. In contrast, among the elderly, many have less lenient attitudes toward assisted suicide; those demographic groups at highest risk for suicide are most in favor of legalization (Seidlitz et al., 1995). When physicians are specifically asked about their willingness to assist a person in committing suicide, however, the likelihood of a positive response drops significantly. It is unknown at this point whether physicians hesitate because physician-assisted suicide in most states is illegal or "questionably illegal," or because the physicians' own ethical and moral values preclude it.

Society has been forced to confront physician-assisted suicide as a phenomenon and make decisions accordingly. A more detailed discussion of this complicated issue is presented in Chapter Thirty.

IMPLICATIONS FOR THE CLINICIAN

- Older people have the highest prevalence of suicide.
- Risk factors for suicide in the elderly include male gender, white race, presence of depression, severe and chronic medical conditions, early dementia or alcoholism, a past history of suicide attempt, recent loss, and availability of a firearm. Knowledge of these risk factors will help clinicians identify patients with a high potential for suicide.
- A stepwise approach to detection of suicide risk includes inquiring about vague suicidal thoughts, wishes to die, past attempts, and development of a suicide plan.

- When faced with a patient at risk for suicide, clinicians must be prepared to engage both the patient and the family in a discussion of suicide risk and prevention: Intervention *is* prevention.

- As the medical community and society as a whole grapple with the issue of physician-assisted suicide, clinicians must examine their own views on this subject, as well as their potential age bias with respect to suicide in the elderly, avoiding the trap of thinking, "It's understandable that he would want to die under the circumstances."

- Having a clear understanding of both the patient's clinical risk and one's own attitudes about suicide may help avert what might be termed, with hindsight, a "preventable tragedy."

CHAPTER TWENTY-SIX

Suicide-Prevention Contracts

Advantages, Disadvantages, and an Alternative Approach

Michael Craig Miller, M.D.

When cases of completed suicide are reviewed postmortem, it is not un-common to find that a responsible clinician or hospital staff member has made a "contract" with the patient to avoid self-destructive behavior or to promise to call the clinician if the impulse to commit suicide returns. This finding raises the question of the effectiveness of this commonly employed treatment device. The purpose of this chapter is to define the suicide-prevention contract, review its history, outline indications and contraindications, understand the influence of collateral topics, and discuss an alternative approach for managing the risk of suicide.

From recent surveys, we know that such contracts, alternatively named no-suicide contracts or contracts for safety, are commonly used as a risk management technique with suicidal patients. However, there has been very little formal training about the technique, and its use derives more from an oral tradition than a didactic one. It is rare to find formal lectures on no-suicide contracts in psychiatry residency or psychology training programs. The literature in peer review journals is scant, especially compared to the extent of its use.

THE SUICIDE-PREVENTION CONTRACT: A DEFINITION

The suicide-prevention contract is a common risk management technique used by clinicians to obtain a patient's commitment to not act on suicidal or self-destructive urges, and to inform clinicians of the status of those urges. It is usually employed in the context of acute suicidal thoughts, impulses, or behaviors but may be used at any time in the treatment of a patient when the risk of suicide is considered.

By the end of this chapter, the following conclusions regarding such contracts will be presented. Suicide-prevention contracts are

- Infrequently studied but widely used
- Overvalued as a risk management device
- Sometimes therapeutic when utilized as part of a comprehensive treatment plan
- Limited by the unpredictability of suicide and by the multiple and varied antecedents to completed suicides
- Instigated in part by the psychological reactions of clinicians to suicidal patients, including their fear of litigation
- Used in a clinical setting without enough regard to the important meaning of the word in the legal context
- Frequently charted in short phrases like *contract for safety* without appropriate ancillary documentation
- Advised to be supplemented or replaced by an approach based on the basic tenets of informed consent

The literature on suicide-prevention contracts is quite small. Ewalt, in the first (1967) edition of Freedman and Kaplan's *Comprehensive Textbook of Psychiatry,* captures the essence of the negotiation with a patient threatening suicide. He laces his discussion with direct, clinical, commonsense advice about how to respond to individuals in crisis. Ewalt outlines several emotional states and interpersonal circumstances through which crises confront clinicians. In his discussion of suicide, Ewalt focuses on interpersonal rather than symptomatic elements, emphasizing "finding out what is going on—preferably from the patient," and describing the kinds of communication that may be embedded in suicidal statements and actions. The suicide threat is characterized as "a signal or indication that the person is asking for assistance" or (following Shneidman and Farberow, 1957) as a "cry for help." Ewalt advises that suicidal patients should be encouraged to talk about their feelings, and cautions that the patient should not "be asked to promise not to commit suicide," but rather "put it off until we talk about it. . . . After the physician knows he is being taken seriously, he can point out that the opportunity for suicide always exists and that it is desirable to discuss the situation before this step, from which there is no return, is taken. In most instances an individual can be persuaded to come to the physician's office or emergency room or can be persuaded to allow the physician to send someone around to escort him to the hospital" (p. 1183).

The suicide-prevention contract was first formally recommended in the psychiatric literature when it appeared in a 1973 paper by Drye, Goulding, and Goulding. This paper was written without reference to the statistical data about suicide prediction that has been gathered over the last four decades. It made claims for the technique that were not supported by data, but did identify the need to inquire directly about suicidal thoughts and to actively assess risk. The paper presents a technique that depends upon a precise definition of suicide risk so as to prevent suicide in an individual patient. Drye, Goulding, and Goulding (1973) outlined their technique quite specifically, including the language of the contract, the kinds of responses to look for in the patient, and the kinds of conclusions that the clinician can draw from those responses. As proof of its usefulness, they provided case examples. The authors did not provide specific data or analysis to support the technique's effectiveness. They did state that in over five years of using the technique, with over 600 patients, they had no fatalities. We will see below why this analysis of the technique's efficacy is flawed.

Drye, Goulding, and Goulding (1973) did, however, make the useful, logical point that there are advantages to sharing "the evaluation task with the patient. Since he is the one who is making the decision to kill himself . . ., he has the best data—not only on how intense his urge is, but on how strong his controls are" (p. 171). They also rightly emphasized the advantage of helping the patient to be the author of his own treatment plan (presaging the modern-day informed-consent approach), since authorship may lead to a greater sense of patient responsibility for the treatment. They also pointed out the limitations of such planning with patients whose competence is impaired. These points figure in the informed consent process described in the final sections of this chapter.

In the late 1970s and early 1980s, a handful of articles appeared in the nonpsychiatric literature. The suicide-prevention contract was described in textbook and review articles (Cox, 1979; Goulding and Goulding, 1979; Hipple and Cimpolic, 1979; Twiname, 1981; O'Farrell, Goodenough, and Cutter, 1981; Horoshak, 1982; Getz, Allen, and Myers, 1983; Assey, 1985; Neville and Barnes, 1985), but there were few papers on the subject in mainstream psychiatric or psychological publications. The most recent articles that appear in the mainstream literature survey attitudes toward the technique and tend to outline its limitations critically (Simon, 1991; Mahrer and Bongar, 1993; Davidson, Wagner, and Range, 1995; Green and Grindel, 1996).

Suicide-prevention contracts probably originated as a specialized form of the *therapeutic contract*. The theory behind the therapeutic contract, however, does not apply to no-suicide contracts. The therapeutic contract emphasizes shared responsibility between the clinician and patient and defines respective contributions, obligations, and roles in the treatment relationship (Hollender and Ford, 1990; Etchegoyen, 1991). Collaborative decisions about treatment aims and plans are made between individuals who are both competent and rational. The "contract" is constantly updated as the relationship and treatment evolve. The principles of the therapeutic contract have been absorbed into clinical practice and govern treatment relationships in all areas of medicine (Gutheil and Havens, 1979; Gutheil, 1982).

The threat of suicide makes a true therapeutic contract impossible. The central feature of that contract, the element of patient choice, may be restricted or removed. When suicide risk is judged to be high, the clinician may need to abandon the collaborative aspect of the relationship and make a plan that the patient dislikes. The patient is no longer permitted to choose, since the clinician feels obliged to act to protect the patient from harm, for instance, by seeking an involuntary hospitalization. In such a case, the patient's consent is not ignored, but is supplanted by more urgent clinical needs.

SUICIDE: IS IT PREDICTABLE?

An important prerequisite to understanding treatment planning with suicidal patients is the limitation on our ability to predict suicidal behavior in individuals. The difficulty in understanding the limitations of our predictive ability—and our wish to do better—contributes to the tendency to utilize devices such as suicide-prevention contracts.

The standard approach to evaluating suicide risk is to enumerate demographic and clinical data, typically called *risk factors*. Suicide risk factors have relevance for identifying populations at risk but do not specify which *individuals* are most likely to commit suicide. The most commonly known suicide risk factors are the demographic risk factors, which identify subpopulations (according to age, sex, marital status, race, or ethnicity) with the highest suicide rates. In evaluating risk, we include the patient's diagnosis, support system, and recent life context as part of the data base to establish the likelihood that a given individual will commit suicide. These factors, and the important ways to use them, are reviewed in detail elsewhere in this book. (See Chapters One and Nine.)

These risk factors are considered part of the suicide assessment but need to be placed in the context of the limitations of our ability to predict individual future behavior based on statistical factors. This limitation was demonstrated by Pokorny in a classic 1983 paper, in which he followed 4800 Veterans Administration Hospital patients prospectively over a five-year period. Pokorny selected known risk factors previously correlated with extremely high suicide rates. Prospective analyses of the predictive value of these risk factors revealed that they were of extremely limited practical use because of the enormous number of false positives: 90 to 99 percent of the patients that fell into the highest risk categories did not go on to commit suicide in the course of one year. Furthermore, more than 75 percent of patients who actually committed suicide were not detected when the risk factors were applied as a screening test. That is, there were a significant number of false negatives as well. Pokorny emphasized that when events occur rarely (like suicide, which occurs at a low base rate), false positives and false negatives confound efforts to predict that event. (The low base rate thus undermines the proof of efficacy offered by Drye, Goulding, and Goulding, 1973, that 600 patients making no-suicide contracts had no fatalities.) Also, Jacobs highlights in Chapter One that even among a high-risk group, such as those with affective disorders, 99 percent do not suicide in any given year.

Another limitation of basing a screen for suicide on demographic or descriptive risk factors alone is that they do not encompass the patient's current clinical state. State-dependent factors change over time. They include aspects such as affective states (for example, hopelessness or anxiety), thought disorders, psychotic symptoms, or physiological changes due to intoxication or physical illness. These variables often change rapidly and alter the level of suicide risk; they are impossible to assess by strict objective measures and in many cases are unknowable.

In summary, clinicians must be cognizant of the inability to predict suicide in the individual case. However, this should not deter the clinician from making a clinical judgment of risk based on clinical data, in spite of the inability to assign risk precisely.

FACTORS INFLUENCING CONTRACT USE

Several factors influence clinicians' use of the suicide-prevention contract, including fear of lawsuits, interpersonal factors, and unconscious emotional responses.

Fear of Lawsuits

Medicolegal concerns clearly influence clinicians confronting difficult clinical situations. The fear of lawsuits derives from the unrealistic expectations (on the part of clinician, patient, and family) related to the fallacy of suicide prediction. If we are held to that impossible standard, our clinical responses are likely to be adversely affected. The fear of being sued is understandable. Gutheil, Bursztajn, and Brodsky (1984) have described (see Chapter Thirty-One) the mechanisms operating in families who have lost a loved one to suicide. Families will often transfer and transform their guilt about the death of their family member and place blame onto the clinician or the hospital treating the patient. Families may have an automatic tendency to hold clinicians to a strict liability standard; that is, if the patient committed suicide, it must have been predictable, and the clinician must be liable. Clinicians anticipating such a response from families may unrealistically rely upon suicide-prevention contracts as a magical source of protection against being sued.

Interpersonal and Unconscious Factors

Interpersonal and unconscious factors serve as another influence. Maltsberger and Buie (1974) described the particularly complex but understandable emotional responses to suicidal patients. The fear of lawsuit intensifies the emotional reactions engendered in clinicians by patients who are acutely suicidal. Their classic paper outlined the problem of countertransference hate in the work with suicidal patients. Complicated responses (anger, frustration, despair, hopelessness) can lead to aversive reactions to suicidal patients, resulting in any of the following feelings or actions: reaction formation leading to unrealistic attempts at rescue; abandonment of the patient as a result of becoming bored, narcissistically injured, or convinced that the patient is "untreatable"; self-criticism on the clinician's part, that is, feeling worthless, a problem particularly difficult for clinicians in training. This conceptualization explains numerous pitfalls in the treatment of suicidal patients. Pertinent to the issue of suicide-prevention contracts, any of these responses may contribute to making a contract that is responsive to the clinicians' reactions rather than the patient's needs.

Maltsberger and Buie (1974) described the complicated mechanism behind these reactions. Some suicidal patients have a tendency to disavow their own hateful feelings and to elicit hate in the therapist or psychiatrist. Patient behavior that elicits hateful feelings is often complemented by attempts on the patient's part to positively engage the clinician in order to sustain a relationship. Furthermore, the doctor's duty to the patient and the prohibition against abandoning a patient serves as a sustaining force in the treatment relationship. Thus, in many ongoing therapeutic relationships, a doctor and patient may have extended periods in which the patient sees the doctor as bad, hurtful, or hateful, yet the patient makes no effort to leave the doctor in favor of another. Unless the patient's complicated motivations are understood, the clinician may be led to measures that are countertherapeutic. In this context, the suicide-prevention contract may represent an enactment of the therapist's unconscious desire to retaliate against the patient's projection of hate.

Clinician Attitudes

In recent years, there have been a series of surveys of clinician attitudes toward suicide-prevention contracts. Davidson, Wagner, and Range (1995) analyzed forty-six questionnaires completed by licensed psychologists. The respondents believed that contracts were useful for moderately suicidal adult and adolescent patients but less helpful for slightly or severely suicidal ones. Overall, this group did not believe that contracts reduce liability for treatment outcome. Green and Grindel (1996) surveyed the head nurses of psychiatric inpatient units about their management of suicidal patients. They found that more than 80 percent of the units used suicide-prevention contracts and thought that such contracts were useful.

In a survey of Harvard Medical School psychiatry faculty in January 1994, attendees of a conference were surveyed about the extent of their formal education in the use of suicide-prevention contracts (Miller, Jacobs, and Gutheil, 1998). Formal training was defined as a lecture or lectures on the history and the use of contracts, their indications and contraindications, or risks and benefits. Whereas virtually all psychiatrists and psychologists observed contracts in use at some point during their careers and approximately three-quarters worked in places where they were regularly used, 60 to 70 percent said they had never received formal training on the use of contracts.

These data highlight the disparity between the widespread use of contracts and the relative absence of formal training. The use of contracts appears to be based on impressionistic rather than objective data.

SUICIDE-PREVENTION CONTRACTS: INDICATIONS

Since suicide occurs so rarely, it is extremely difficult to prove or disprove the usefulness of any technique for managing suicide risk. And because the majority of patients, even suicidal patients, do not commit suicide, a clinician is likely to believe that suicide-prevention contracts work. Although there is no statistical proof of risk reduction, there may be some advantages or indications for using this technique as long as other important clinical and risk management principles are observed. Suicide-prevention contracts are best utilized under the following circumstances:

- As one of the components of a comprehensive evaluation and treatment plan
- In the context of an established and currently positive treatment relationship
- In conjunction with a formal assessment of suicide risk
- In recognition that risk will never be zero and that agreement to a contract does not abolish risk
- With evidence that clinical data were weighed and that clinical judgment was used
- With documentation that avoids shorthand (such as "patient contracted for safety") and includes documentation such as suicide assessment, the basis for the clinical judgment, and the plan for managing suicide risk

The nature of such planning and documentation will be addressed later in the chapter.

Assessing the Nature of the Therapeutic Alliance

The suicide-prevention contract may test the adequacy of the therapeutic alliance. Patient refusal to accede to a contract may be an indication that the alliance is shaky and can be taken seriously as an indicator of suicide risk. In some patients, the refusal may indicate contrariness or anger rather than suicide risk, but that judgment should be made only after an evaluation of other factors, including history, nature of interpersonal relationships, symptoms, and current environmental factors.

If a patient does agree to a contract, the meaning may still be uncertain. Although it may indicate that the alliance is intact, the agreement could be motivated by compliance or deception. Judgment about the nature of the alliance is always informed by many other factors, of which the acceptance or refusal of a contract is only one factor.

Identifying Explicit Treatment Goals

The strain on the clinician and the patient when there is a crisis may be diminished by any tool that makes the treatment goals explicit. A contract can serve the aim of outlining the goals of the treatment and may formally establish the connection between the clinician and the patient. It may also, if done in the context of a positive relationship, demonstrate the clinician's concern. Many systems of care have moved in the last decade toward documents that provide an explicit outline of the treatment for the patient. Written materials that outline the nature of the treatment, its goals, and the expectation of the patient will have a beneficial educational effect and may reduce strain.

Supporting Adaptive Defenses

The suicidal patient with a personality disorder, and some patients with affective or psychotic disorders, may benefit greatly from a technique that supports their coping mechanisms or adaptive defenses. The patient with obsessional defenses may find it useful to have the plan written down and may be relieved to know what to do. The narcissistic patient may benefit from personally designing how the plan or contract is constructed. A depressed patient's experience of dysphoria as interminable may be alleviated by a plan that focuses on shortening the time horizon. A psychotic patient may find a "concrete" piece of paper a useful "reality" check.

The patient's defenses are best supported by explicitly identifying the goals of the suicide-prevention contract to provide an understanding with the patient about his dangerous behavior. For instance, is the patient being enlisted to refrain specifically from self-mutilation or self-harm? Is he being asked to contact the clinician if he has suicidal thoughts or if feelings emerge that may precipitate suicidal behavior? Since there are many types of agreements and a wide range of interpretations possible, it may be helpful to define a specific plan with the patient.

PITFALLS OF THE SUICIDE-PREVENTION CONTRACT

The most difficult problem with the suicide-prevention contract is the possibility that practitioners will consider it the beginning and end of suicide risk management. Some patients may be comfortable with the idea of making a contract or a commitment in order to bind their own anxiety about suicide. However, especially with new patients, promises of safety must be viewed in the overall context of the clinical situation. For example, a clinician on call for emergencies asks a suicidal patient to contract for safety, or a newly admitted hospital patient is asked by staff nurses to adhere to the same promise. The problem in both of these instances is that the patient has no investment in the relationship, so the promise or the contract means little. We may assess the patient's intentions and should accept any commitment that is offered (to encourage the patient's efforts at self-control), but we should avoid relying solely on such promises.

The clinician is cautioned to remember that patients who agree to a contract continue to be at risk. They are not necessarily at *more* risk than the demographics and the clinical situation would suggest, but they are probably not at less risk either. Treatment decisions about the management of suicide risk are solely dependent upon clinical judgment, after the collection of historical data and conduct of a mental status examination and discussion with the patient. See the final sections of this chapter for specific recommendations.

The Contract's Hidden Messages

If one confines the largest portion of an interaction with a suicidal patient to obtaining a contract for safety, other important aspects of the communication may be negatively affected. The process of obtaining a contract may paradoxically discourage or impede the patient's conveying painful affects or suicidal thoughts to the people trying to help them. One aim in the treatment of suicidal patients is to encourage frank and open discussion of suicidal or self-destructive thoughts. If a patient feels that a discussion of these thoughts represents a violation of the contract, they may be less inclined to share them.

A focus on "contracting" also may lead the patient to believe that the clinician (or clinical staff of an inpatient unit) is more interested in pro forma administrative maneuvers than in the patient's distress or the treatment. Especially if the contract becomes a prerequisite to the patient's getting other desired or needed attentions, it may encourage a less sincere compliance with the aims of the contract. For example, a patient may view a signature as a necessary step to obtaining an increase in privileges on an inpatient unit or to influencing an outpatient therapist's decision to treat him or become closer. The perception of a power differential between clinician and patient may lead to the patient's feeling coerced, a position that is contrary to the underpinnings of the therapeutic contract as discussed above.

A decrease in communication may lead to the patient's feeling more isolated. The isolation can intensify despair and increase suicide risk. The patient may also resort to increasingly unconscious or indirect modes of communication, using behavior more than conversation to let the clinician know what is felt—for example, by suicide attempts or regression. The most troubling form of communication in these instances is so-called "manipulative" behavior. This behavior may be the patient's way of informing the clinician about his state of mind, but the behavior may result in the patient's obtaining the opposite of what is desired or needed, that is, causing clinicians to have aversive or angry reactions and respond with increased therapeutic distancing.

The description here is quite stereotyped and extreme. Many patients, especially those with personality disorders, have a tendency to communicate through action rather than words despite the excellent efforts of capable clinicians. For the purposes of this review, the stereotype helps outline the pitfall and contraindication clearly so it can be avoided.

Contract: The Legal Term

From the point of view of risk management, clinicians may consider avoiding the word *contract* in their clinical negotiations, since the word has specific meanings in a court of law that are rarely intended by the clinician. The suicide-prevention contract is not a legal contract. In its most elementary legal sense, a contract implies an exchange of goods. The suicide-prevention contract demands that the patient give a promise to stay safe. The clinician does not offer anything in exchange that is not already due the patient. In other words, since the clinician already has the duty to provide care to the patient that meets acceptable standards, the patient has nothing additional to gain by agreeing to any contract.

Furthermore, the "contract for safety" may carry the added burden of appearing to attempt to free the clinician from blame for any bad outcome in the treatment. The bad outcome of suicide is a rare but inevitable occurrence in the careers of practitioners, whether or not they specialize in treating high-risk patients. The clinician should avoid practices that focus on liability prevention rather than appropriate clinical intervention. Should an occurrence of suicide lead to a lawsuit, and should that case find its way to a courtroom, the outcome of the legal case and judgments about the clinician's care are improved if it can be demonstrated that a comprehensive assessment and treatment was provided to the patient rather than a reliance on the suicide-prevention contract.

AN ALTERNATIVE APPROACH: INFORMED CONSENT

The proposition of the suicide-prevention contract and the values of the therapeutic contract can both be appropriately subsumed under the doctrine of informed consent. Informed consent provides a useful and realistic framework for the management of suicide risk, as it allows the clinician to achieve therapeutic aims and to manage risk. As with the suicide-prevention contract, the informed consent procedure itself is not the intervention that reduces risk. Risk is reduced by treating underlying pathology, providing support and containment (or encouraging progress when appropriate), and modifying risk factors when possible.

At important decision points in the treatment of the suicidal patient, the clinician can review the variety of treatment options with the patient and clarify the risks and benefits of each option. The various treatment options can be completely explained so as to encourage full and voluntary participation of the patient in the mutually agreed upon treatment goals. Included in that discussion can be a frank acknowledgment of the risk of death from suicide. Suicide is not the only risk. Risks of overly restrictive plans must also be discussed. For example, there is a risk of regression and dependence that accompanies plans that require the patient to give up more autonomy. Furthermore, entering a hospital or curtailing activities may expose patients to real-life morbidity, such as interruptions of family life or threats of job loss.

Case Example One
Ms. A was a twenty-one-year-old student at a local college, brought to the emergency room by her roommate after taking a handful of aspirin and diphenhydramine. She came home late after an evening out with her boyfriend. She says they had a fight and she just wanted to go to sleep "to forget it all." She had no previous psychiatric history, but said her parents brought her to see a psychologist when she was a junior in high school for "behavior problems." She looked a little disheveled but talked with the evaluating psychiatrist easily and did not appear depressed. She appreciated the doctor's concern but wanted to return to her dorm as soon as possible because she had an early class the next day.

Although it is impossible to make a prediction about her future behavior, Ms. A's suicide attempt puts her in a higher-risk group than the general population. The clinician should stay alert to her minimization of the attempt, the impulsive nature of the action, and her apparent lack of awareness that she needs further evaluation and treatment. However, the attempt was of low lethality and the patient did not fall into a high-risk demographic group. Her mental status examination was also negative for symptoms of depression and she had no immediate plan to hurt herself again. She also said she was looking forward to getting back on track quickly, although the suspicious clinician would want to stay alert to the possibility that the patient was saying what she needed to say in order to get out of the hospital.

Most clinicians would not have recommended hospitalization in this case. However, one should avoid merely asking the patient whether she can "contract for safety." First of all, this novice to the mental health system would not have understood the meaning of the phrase. Furthermore, she might have acceded to such a request merely to be discharged from the hospital. Instead, the clinician can clearly tell the patient about the risk she would bear upon leaving the hospital, that is, her impulsive suicide attempt was not to be dismissed and she could, at some point, find herself under the sway of similar emotions and a desire to act self-destructively again. She may not feel distress imminently, but she needed to understand the possibility. There was minimal lethality, which did not warrant hospitalizing her against her will, but she needed to be aware that an impulsive self-destructive act could lead to her death. Ultimately the risk to her would be less if she kept a follow-up appointment for an outpatient psychiatric evaluation, at which time longer-term treatment options would be discussed. Rather than asking her "to contract," the emergency psychiatrist would write down the instructions for follow-up with instructions about whom to call if self-destructive impulses returned. The psychiatrist would then assess whether the patient understood the risks and recommendations before discharging her and would document this interaction.

In the previous vignette, the discussion about the risk of death and the recommendations for follow-up are meaningful only if the patient understands the explanations and the plans. The value of the discussion of risks and benefits of treatment options and the patient's choosing among those options depends upon the patient's competence to understand the treatment options and capacity to weigh information in order to make a decision among those options. Without these abilities, it is impossible to depend upon the patient's understanding and consent. With these abilities, a patient is entitled to make an "unwise" choice. (See also Chapter Thirty-One.) With a competent patient, the informed consent procedure allows the clinician to focus clearly on real options, move away from magical solutions, and openly discuss the risks attending various approaches.

Case Example Two

Mr. B, a fifty-four-year-old man with dysthymia, came for his regularly scheduled appointment with his psychologist, who had been treating him in weekly psychotherapy over the previous six months. During the prior several weeks, the man had been feeling worse and they had begun to discuss the need for a psychopharmacology referral, previously refused by the patient. He looked gaunt and forlorn. He had been waking up at 3:30 A.M., unable to get back to sleep. He was kept awake by fears that his wife was having an affair with another man and worried that his boss was about to fire him. He had no appetite and thought maybe he had lost about five pounds. He had also given up reading novels, one of the few activities that consistently gave him pleasure.

The therapist asked whether his thoughts were turning to death or suicide. The patient denied it. The therapist again raised the issue of a psychopharmacology referral and the patient said he had given it thought and had decided not to pursue it. "Those drugs are not going to help me. Nothing will."

Mr. B's level of depression had increased, with deepening discomfort and anhedonia, some anxiety and agitation, and classic neurovegetative symptoms. There was no evidence that his marriage or his job was insecure, so the worries about his wife and boss may have been delusional. Furthermore, his turning down a psychopharmacology referral, although consistent with his prior preference, now seemed linked to pessimism about the overall benefits of any treatment, a possible mood-congruent distortion.

This patient, as an older, male patient with a severe depression, was in a significant demographic risk group. An evaluator should be suspicious of his denial of suicidal plans. Also, the clinician should question Mr. B's competence to weigh the risks and benefits of treatment options appropriately. A contract or commitment for safety from this man would be difficult to trust. He may be sincere, but the clinical information suggests interventions aimed specifically at enhancing the patient's safety. With uncertainty about the patient's reality testing, it would be difficult to accept his assurances about any plan without following him closely or getting corroboration from someone in the family who knows him well.

This case reveals another important point regarding the management of suicide risk, that is, the aggressive treatment of depression is as important as any assurance about the patient's safety in the short term. If the clinician's judgment in this case is that there is significant risk of suicide, a change in intervention (such as hospitalization, an appointment the next day, calling the spouse, and so forth) is called for, based in this case on the combination of the severity of the patient's symptoms and the inability of the patient to give reliably informed consent to a treatment plan.

How do we assess a patient's competence to give informed consent? Because competence is a legal concept, it is reasonable to start with a definition. According to the *American Heritage College Dictionary* (1997), *competence* means "being adequately or well qualified; a specific range of skill, knowledge, or ability; being legally qualified to perform an act." Generally, an individual must be able to comprehend the nature of the particular issue in question and to understand its quality and its consequences. Only a court can declare an individual legally incompetent. Physicians and other clinicians must think instead in terms of capacities rather than competencies (see below).

Evaluating Competence to Give Informed Consent

- Give the patient adequate instruction regarding
  - Diagnosis
  - Treatment proposed
  - Purpose of treatment
  - Likelihood of success
  - Side effects and risks of treatment
  - Alternatives proposed, including no treatment
- Assess understanding of this instruction
- Assess ability to think and use the data rationally
- Assess the emotional impact of the illness and treatment proposed
- Consider evaluating the patient at several different times to establish competence over time
- Consider using alternative evaluators

Physicians are most likely to question a patient's capacity to give informed consent when the patient refuses what the doctor believes is reasonable treatment (Roth, Meisel, and Lidz, 1977). When evaluating suicide risk, the competence assessment may be usefully integrated into the evaluation, for clinical rather than legal reasons. Since the patient's ability to collaborate in the treatment is central to managing suicide risk, the assessment of the patient's ability to work competently with the clinician toward developing a reasonably safe treatment plan is arguably a key feature of that work. Although the issue of a formal guardianship proceeding may arise, the clinical issue is to assess the patient's capacity to collaborate, understand the needs brought on by his illness, and weigh the information relevant to treatment decisions.

Certain psychiatric illnesses are more likely to compromise the patient's capacity to give informed consent. Dementia, delirium, stroke, and many other neurological illnesses can impair cognition and competence to understand relevant data. Psychotic symptoms such as those found in schizophrenia or mood disorders may distort the patient's understanding of isolated elements of a treatment decision, and require careful exploration on the part of the clinician to discover the distortion of thought. A diagnosis of cognitive impairment or psychotic illness does not in itself mean that the person's ability to give informed consent is impaired. The illness must lead to a specific deficit, which can be defined by the clinician.

A patient with a personality disorder presents particular problems with regard to competence assessment. Patients with personality disorder often make decisions that will seem unreasonable to the clinician (and they will often make such decisions when they are suicidal). Although the individual may have some element of psychosis or cognitive impairment, frequently neither problem exists. Patients with personality disorder are often simply the victim of their own bad judgment, under the sway of impressively painful and conflicting emotions. Competent individuals are entitled to make bad judgments, so long as they are capable of understanding the issues involved. One is also entitled to refuse to weigh all the issues, ignore advice, or shut off any discussion.

In the evaluation of a patient at risk for suicide, the evaluator may assess the patient's understanding of the specific treatment situation, understanding of the pertinent facts, and ability to think rationally. The clinician is advised to determine that adequate information has been provided to the patient regarding the illness, the current state of the illness, and the various options available for treatment. Moving to an educational mode can be helpful because of the content and process of explaining rational options may diffuse the affect in charged situations, and thus reassure a troubled patient. At the same time, educating the patient may also take great patience. Once satisfied that the patient's situation has been explained sufficiently, one may ask him to repeat back his understanding of it. In this way, one will determine the patient's grasp of the facts: the purpose of treatment and the likelihood of its success, the side effects and risks of the treatment, the alternatives proposed including that of no treatment. One can pay close attention to errors in logic that may indicate subtle or blatant psychotic thought process or cognitive deficit.

Case Example Three

Ms. C was a twenty-eight-year-old woman with a history of three prior suicide attempts admitted to the inpatient unit on Monday, July 1, following a visit from her mother. She reported to her therapist intense thoughts about suicide, with a plan to take an overdose of barbiturates, which she could obtain from a friend. She also had a regular tendency to cut her wrists and ankles, not with death as the aim, but for the management of anxiety. A small package of straight razor blades was found and removed from her backpack when she was searched on admission.

On Tuesday and Wednesday, Ms. C said she felt much better and was gradually advanced from fifteen-minute, to thirty-minute, and finally to hourly checks on the unit. She never required constant observation. She told staff that her suicidal thoughts had completely abated and she also had not had a desire to cut herself for the first forty-eight hours of her hospitalization. Outwardly she appeared comfortable, and there was no evidence that she had cut herself.

On Thursday, July 4, rounds were being conducted by Dr. Q, the psychiatrist on call for the Independence Day holiday. She had just met Ms. C, who told her that she had renewed thoughts of cutting herself late the previous evening. She did tell the nursing staff of these thoughts and was now feeling well, without thoughts of cutting or suicide. She requested the privilege to join the group of patients accompanied by the staff for periodic brief walks off the ward during the day.

Ms. C was at low to moderate chronic risk for suicide. She had multiple suicide attempts and was chronically affectively unstable. She had a diagnosis of borderline personality disorder, which carries an increased lifetime risk for suicide. She had access to a means for lethal overdose. Thus, by risk factors, she was in a risk group that was higher than the general population. She had been doing very well, but had a worrisome episode the night before. She sought out a nurse to get support, but the episode underscored the rapid changes possible in Ms. C's clinical state. When queried, she was unable to describe the reasons for feeling worse the night before, and talked only in general terms about an empty feeling coming over her without knowing why.

As an on-call physician, the psychiatrist was further handicapped because she was entirely new to the case and had not even the two-day relationship that the ward attending had with the patient. The attending physician's sign-out instructions and progress notes from the day before instructed the covering psychiatrist to "assess for group passes tomorrow."

The most conservative approach to this patient would be to maintain the current level of observation for the patient, or (on the basis of the previous night's events) to increase the level of observation. The advantage of maintaining the status quo (that is, the decrease in suicide risk) must, however, be weighed against the possibility that the patient will become alienated from the treatment team and develop more regressive behavior in response to the continued confinement and her anger about it. The advantage of accepting the patient's request for an advancement of her privileges in this setting is that it supports her desire to take more responsibility for herself and may lead her to progress more rapidly out of the hospital. Both plans involve some risk.

This case demonstrates a typical dilemma in the treatment of patients with borderline personality disorder. In the judgment of the psychiatrist after interviewing the patient, reviewing the record, and discussing the patient with nursing staff, Ms. C was competent and therefore free to weigh the risks and benefits and decide among the alternative plans. Furthermore, given the rare occurrence of suicide, it was quite unlikely, even given the increased risk, that the patient would commit suicide. The psychiatrist explained the risks and benefits of each choice, emphasizing that by making the stepwise advance to group privileges, the patient had to be ready to bear the small increase in risk that she might lose control of her impulses, but that the risk was acceptable in light of the potential gains. Dr. Q also arranged for the patient and nursing staff to review the need to communicate openly about her feelings, particularly with regard to suicide or self-harm, throughout the day.

RECOMMENDATIONS FOR MANAGING SUICIDAL RISK

Although some clinicians may still choose to use the suicide-prevention contract, many may find that the exercise of avoiding the contract leads to more robust, direct, and grounded management of suicidal risk.

The first step in the management of suicide risk is to encourage communication about suicidal thoughts and impulses and to document the patient's statements about suicide. Some practitioners may want to shape or limit the patient's statements for fear that the discussion itself can lead to regression. The patient's expressions of distress can be met with sympathy by the clinician who responds directly with suggestions about how to work collaboratively with the patient to avert a bad outcome by developing strategies to manage it. Eliciting the distressing thoughts and accompanying self-destructive plans is the first step toward managing the risk of suicide.

This discussion may form the beginnings of an alliance with new patients or may help solidify a relationship with a well-known patient. In either case, the clinician should make a judgment about the nature of the relationship, erring on the side of caution. The inpatient, emergency, or covering clinician or the initial evaluator should make the assumption that there is no working (or usable) relationship and caution should be exercised. In longer, ongoing treatment relationships, the clinician may judge that the relationship is intact, but should always consider the possibility that there is a rift or negative phase. It is helpful to address the nature of the relationship in treatment notes.

The patient's competence to understand her problems, the proposed treatments and ability to carry out the treatment should be addressed, at least implicitly, in the evaluation. If the patient is competent, the various treatment alternatives should be discussed in detail, with the relative risks and benefits of those alternatives. All discussions with the patient should be geared toward dispelling "magic." All patients will be helped by a short course in the uncertainty of medical decision making, stressing that all decisions bear some risk, especially decisions involving the treatment of a potential suicide. This discussion, if carried out supportively, may appeal to the patient's "healthiest self," to whatever intact adaptive defenses or coping mechanisms may be available to assist the patient in the attempt to make progress.

With this approach, the clinician is sharing the waxing and waning risk of suicide with the patient and the patient bears responsibility for communicating with the clinician about his or her clinical state. The clinician may explain to the patient that the patient may not always be able to bear that responsibility.

In the treatment of suicidal patients, at some point in the treatment that risk must be borne in order to make progress.

Documentation of this procedure may seem daunting. It may make sense, especially with patients who will be treated over time, for the practitioner to write one longer note that describes the character of the discussion with the patient about suicide risk. The clinician may then reference this note when there is a repeat of the discussion, or may describe changes or modifications as the patient either regresses or improves. This approach revives the central intentions of the therapeutic contract and emphasizes the collaboration between clinician and patient.

All risk managers recommend writing more frequent and longer notes, but practical time constraints make it impossible to follow that recommendation. The practitioner is urged to develop his or her own creative way of capturing the discussion concisely, avoiding hackneyed phrases (like "contracted for safety") that have lost clinical meaning. One cannot write voluminous entries after every patient encounter. At some point, though, it is useful to outline

- Risks discussed
- Treatment options weighed
- Treatment choices selected and for what reason
- Evidence that indicates the patient understood the discussion and was capable of making a free choice based on his or her understanding of the options

An important key in the management of risk is the sharing of the clinical burden with the patient. The preceding list, at the very least, demonstrates the partnership that the clinician and the patient have entered to treat the illness. (See below.)

Informed Consent and the Management of Suicide Risk
- Avoid pitfalls of pro forma interventions
- Depend upon informed consent to create a realistic framework for the appraisal of treatment options
- Educate the patient about the uncertainty inherent in medical treatments
- Underscore the mutual responsibility of sharing the burden of managing the waxing and waning of suicidal ideas
- Review the risks and benefits of each treatment option, including the option of no treatment
- Discuss directly the risk of death from suicide

- Explain all treatments to obtain patient participation that is knowledgeable and voluntary
- Consider risks other than suicide and discuss those with the patient (for example, dependence, regression, increase in morbidity)
- Assess the patient's competence or capacity to give informed consent
- Accept that competent individuals are entitled to make bad choices
- Consult with a peer if warranted
- Provide concise, but not stereotyped, documentation of assessment and treatment planning, emphasizing collaboration (or its absence)

IMPLICATIONS FOR THE CLINICIAN

- The suicide-prevention contract is overvalued as a clinical or risk management technique.
- The discussion of a contract is one possible test of the therapeutic alliance and may provide some structure, but it does not in itself reduce the risk of suicide.
- A limited focus on the contract may direct the clinician's attention away from other important matters. Like suicide risk factors, acceding to a contract has no predictive value for the individual patient who is at some risk for suicide.
- The clinician should avoid shortcuts, both in the suicide assessment and in the documentation of the assessment.
- As an alternative to using suicide-prevention contracts, the clinician can assess the patient's competence to participate in treatment planning and then conduct such treatment in the context of the well-established principles of informed consent.
- Conscious and unconscious determinants of the clinician's response, particularly anything that would lead to aversive reactions, should be acknowledged.
- The clinician should actively defend against the fear of lawsuits, which can lead to unwanted, unproductive, and even illogical thinking and defensive medical practice.
- The clinician may supportively share the uncertainty and responsibility of assessment and treatment with competent patients. This cooperation, although at first anxiety-provoking, may lead to a more realistic approach to treatment and may encourage the patient to develop a capacity to bear painful feelings and avoid self-destructive action.

CHAPTER TWENTY-SEVEN

Guidelines for Conducting a Suicide Review

Steve Stelovich, M.D.

Completed suicide is a brutal fact of life that almost all mental health practitioners must confront in one way or another. Nonetheless, medicine's overwhelming preoccupation has been with matters of etiology and prevention. In a recent bibliography of over seventeen hundred scientific articles devoted to the subject of suicide, fewer than ten focused on methods for managing such deaths. This lack of guidelines or recommendations for practice in the area leaves the health care provider in a lonely and difficult situation at best.

The problem is compounded by the fact that evolving systems of health care delivery scrutinize provider performance as never before. And in view of the fact that increasing numbers of patients are being treated in outpatient as opposed to inpatient settings, those few supports that hospitals can and have furnished in such situations become less and less relevant to the current practice of psychiatry.

In my experience of conducting nearly one hundred suicide reviews over some twenty years, I have found that participating providers repeatedly raise similar questions:

- Can something be learned from the case that might help prevent future suicides, attempts at suicide, or harm to others suffering from similar conditions?

- Was the care delivered of high quality, and might a different outcome have been reasonably expected were the care to have been modified— or, more bluntly, "Did I do the right thing?"

- Was the cause of death associated with social or delivery system issues that interfered with treatment, and how might these be addressed?
- What is or was the emotional impact of the suicide on those who were providing care?
- Are there risk management issues that would be in the best interest of all to learn about?

Concern focuses on the patient, the illness, the providers, and the social and health care surround. Without a means for regularly reviewing cases of completed suicide, most of the questions raised are difficult to answer at best. Not infrequently, clinicians are left unsure of themselves and vulnerable from a risk management point of view.

Harvard Pilgrim Health Care (HPHC) is a health maintenance organization with approximately 1.25 million members across most of the New England states. It is composed of staff, group, and Independent Practice Association components and does not carve out its mental health programs. As such, it should expect to encounter approximately 125 suicides per year if one assumes that the general rate of suicide is 1 in 10,000. Having at least indirect, and often direct, involvement with the care delivered to its members, HPHC and other large programs of organized health care delivery face problems over and above those confronting individual providers. Aside from public health issues raised by the simple magnitude of the numbers, large health care organizations must ask whether their own systems in any way contribute to completed suicides, whether the providers they retain are impaired in their functioning, and whether steps can be taken to provide support and education to their providers that might reduce the future rate of such deaths.

In the context of these concerns, ad hoc reviews of completed suicides began to be conducted at HPHC on both outpatient and inpatient suicides some twenty years ago. Initially, the reviewing process was loosely based on procedures in place among several of Harvard University's teaching hospitals. However, as HPHC grew to include a network of more and more providers, most of whom had little inpatient experience, cognizance had to be taken of two facts: (1) most outpatient practitioners never formally reviewed findings after the fact of suicide, and (2) structures configured to suit inpatient needs had to be modified to serve outpatient settings. At HPHC, the development of such structures led to the establishment of a formal corporate suicide review committee as part of its risk management activities.

This chapter discusses in detail the policy and procedures supporting the activity of HPHC's suicide committee as a representation of distilled experience in practice gained over twenty years in conducting regular suicide reviews in outpatient as well as inpatient settings. This material will be most easy to use by providers practicing in clinics, groups, or other organized settings. Individual providers, however, should be able to use the various elements, making appropriate modifications where needed; some of these will be specifically suggested in the course of the following discussion.

PURPOSE AND GOALS

A carefully formulated suicide review policy can support providers by providing uniform guidelines for reviewing cases of completed suicide that also can be easily generalized to cover serious attempts at suicide as well as other events associated with adverse outcomes. In addition, standardized practices configured to provide maximal clinician protection using peer review processes allow for the free exchange of information, which is vital for improving practice patterns in the future.

In the course of developing its standards for suicide review, HPHC has repeatedly encountered and ultimately settled on ten goals for such reviews:

1. To learn about and make recommendations regarding issues in the delivery of care that might specifically prevent suicides, attempts at suicide, and harm to others

2. To evaluate and make recommendations regarding the quality of clinical treatment being rendered to patients in danger of harming themselves or others

3. To evaluate and make recommendations regarding internal systems issues that have an impact on treatment being rendered to patients in danger of harming themselves or others

4. To learn of and make recommendations about the emotional impact on staff involved with a patient's suicide or harm to others

5. To provide support, through the review process, to staff involved with a patient's suicide or harm to others

6. To refer to appropriate risk management review cases in which there is reason to believe that a provider's actions may call into question his or her fitness to provide clinical services

7. To assess and make recommendations regarding the documentation of care in situations associated with suicide, attempts at suicide, and harm to others

8. To explore risk management issues in the situations outlined above

9. To evaluate the need for and make recommendations with respect to the establishment of studies concerning suicide or danger to others within the population

10. To develop educational programs as appropriate

AUTHORITY AND PROTECTION

In an age of ubiquitous litigation, many clinicians, if not all, are hesitant to discuss completed suicides in an open fashion. At the same time, it is only through open discussion of such cases that information can be gained that will stand both providers and patients in a better stead so they can move forward.

At HPHC, suicide reviews are carefully conducted under the rules regarding peer review activities as outlined by the Board of Registration in Medicine for the Commonwealth of Massachusetts. Providers undertaking such reviews are strongly encouraged to explore the protections available to them through their local boards of medicine and professional societies. Individual providers wishing to conduct formal reviews, if they are not clearly protected under the laws of their respective states, might consider approaching their local medical society or psychiatric association, which might be willing to extend formal protection for such undertakings. Once such protection is made available, its limits and requirements need to be carefully explained to all participants in such reviews, both to encourage an open exchange of information and prevent inappropriate access to the review material once it has been completed.

At HPHC, the corporate Patient Care and Assessment Committee (PCAC), a peer review committee established according to the rules and regulations of the Massachusetts Board of Registration in Medicine, has established a formal subcommittee, the Corporate Risk Management Committee (CRMC), for peer review protection. This committee in turn established the Suicide Review Committee, which convenes local ad hoc subcommittees for the completion of specific case reviews. Local findings are regularly reviewed by the Corporate Suicide Review Committee, and these are reported to the CRMC and then to the PCAC.

RESPONSIBILITIES AND ACTIVITIES

Local reviews are scheduled within two to six weeks of learning of a suicide or other adverse event to be examined. The chair of the Corporate Suicide Review Committee appoints a reviewer to chair the review. The chair, in turn, determines the membership for each ad hoc review committee. The local committee should include those providers directly involved in the care of the patient prior to death. The membership generally includes, but is not limited to:

- The chair and reviewer
- The psychiatrist and other mental health professionals (both inpatient and outpatient) involved in the care of the deceased
- The primary care provider

- Relevant medical and surgical specialists
- Relevant clinical supervisors or care coordinators

The chair of the Corporate Suicide Review Committee, or his or her designee, distributes the following information:

- A notification form to the local committee's leader outlining his or her responsibilities and confidentiality guidelines (see Exhibit 27.1 for sample memo)
- An explanatory memo to each review participant (see Exhibit 27.2 for sample memo)
- Notification to the Corporate Risk Management Committee regarding the appointment of a local ad hoc suicide review committee

The chair of the local review group assembles copies of all pertinent records and documents and labels them, "Confidential, Peer Review Material, Not to Be Duplicated." Additionally, all backup data, printouts, copies of records, and other materials brought to the suicide review meeting are designated, "information and records necessary to comply with risk management and quality assurance programs established by the Board of Registration in Medicine and necessary to the work product of the Patient Care Assessment Committee." Providers working in other states and in other circumstances should acquaint themselves with the protections provided by law through their own boards of registration in medicine and modify their procedures accordingly. In Massachusetts, all such records are kept securely locked and following the reviews are destroyed, with the exception of the final reports.

Approximately one and one-half hours are devoted to the review itself. The local committee, under the direction of the chair, is expected to assess the matters salient to the suicide and produce a report that includes the following material:

- A case abstract.
- A brief description of the suicide itself.
- A review of the course of treatment.
- Specific consideration, with particular attention to the adequacy of medical record documentation, is given to (1) the appropriate identification and assessment of risk, (2) evidence of ongoing assessment at critical points in the case, (3) evidence of appropriate protective and preventative measures being ordered and used, (4) utilization of appropriate monitoring and observation procedures, (5) evidence of appropriate interclinician communication, (6) assessment of the patient's ability to participate in the prescribed treatment, and (7) rationale for the treatment plan as prescribed.

Exhibit 27.1. Memo to Appoint a Chair for a Local Suicide Review Committee.

To: (Name)
From: (Chair of HPHC's Corporate Suicide Review Committee)
Date: _____ Confidential, Peer Review Material, Not to Be Duplicated
Re: Appointment of Suicide Review Committee

You are hereby appointed to chair a local Suicide Review Committee, a medical peer review committee, which shall function as an ad-hoc subcommittee of the HPHC Corporate Suicide Review Committee and the HPHC Corporate Risk Management Committee (CRMC). The purpose of your committee is to review the facts surrounding the recent suicide of (patient's name). Should you believe the scope of this charge needs to be broadened or changed, approval must be proposed and sought and permission granted in writing from the CRMC through the Corporate Suicide Review Committee. In addition to yourself, the subcommittee's membership will consist of (list of participants).

CRMC subcommittees generally consider relevant clinical facts and make recommendations as to possible improvements based upon their findings, as well as identify and analyze patient risks as they occur in our clinical settings. To achieve these goals, they are expected to evaluate the quality of health care rendered by our staff and network providers, determine whether clinical activities were performed in compliance with applicable standards of care, and to alert the CRMC through the Corporate Suicide Committee as to the need for possible evaluation if there is evidence that health care providers may be found to be impaired or allegedly impaired by reasons of alcohol, drugs, physical disability, mental instability, or otherwise.

Your notes should remain in a secure place. Any written comments or document you create or copy must be labeled, "Confidential, Peer Review Material, Not to Be Duplicated." Minutes or other documents should not be distributed to anyone outside of your subcommittee or the Corporate Suicide Review Committee. Periodic reports must be forwarded to me. Any person with whom you find it necessary to speak during the course of your work must be advised of the confidential nature of your activities and that this assignment is a peer review process. In addition, discussion between or among subcommittee members or between subcommittee members and other HPHC staff or members must be regarded as confidential discussions.

Work products of your subcommittee should be objective. They should not contain patient identifying information but, when necessary, codes should be used instead of names and the Chair shall maintain the identifying list when needed. "Back up" data, printouts, records, or data brought to the meeting for review should be designated by you as "information and records necessary to comply with risk management and quality assurance programs established by the Board of Registration in Medicine and necessary to the work product of the Patient Care Assessment Committee." This material should be destroyed when no longer needed.

Exhibit 27.1. Memo to Appoint a Chair for a Local Suicide Review Committee, cont'd.

You should be aware that Massachusetts General Law (Chapter 231, Section 85K) provides that "no . . . duly appointed member of a committee of a medical staff or a . . . health maintenance organization . . . shall be liable in suit for damages as a result of this act, omissions, or proceedings, undertaken or performed within the scope of his duties as such subcommittee members, provided that he acts in good faith and in the reasonable belief that based on all the facts, the action or inaction of his part was warranted."

Subcommittee members shall confine their discussions to the group's meetings. Any discussion outside formal subcommittee meetings may be subject to discovery. Further discussions and reporting of your subcommittee's findings should be limited to the Corporate Suicide Committee.

Exhibit 27.2. Explanatory Memo to Review Team Members.

This memo is sent as a general explanatory cover note to each member of an ad hoc local suicide committee in order to orient them to the process. The member also receives a formal note of appointment and a copy of HPHC's policy

To: (Appointed members of a Local Suicide Review Team)
From: (Chair, Corporate Suicide Review Committee)
Date: _____ Confidential, Peer Review Material, Not to Be Duplicated
Re: Suicide Review Activities at HPHC

Each of you may be aware that most known suicides are reviewed on a case-by-case basis at HPHC as a peer review/quality assurance activity with the primary aim of improving care to our members in the future. These reviews are carried out under the authority of HPHC's Patient Care and Assessment Committee (PCAC) and are completed by local suicide review committees which are constituted for that purpose and are afforded peer review protection.

As you may have never taken part in such a review, I have included a copy of the HPHC policy covering these activities in order to better acquaint you with the aims, procedures, and medical/legal guidelines which need to be followed in order to guarantee confidentiality for the process. In addition, a formal memorandum is included establishing the specific local suicide review committee being convened to review the current case which outlines the procedures which must be followed in order to guarantee us peer review protection.

If there are questions that you have about the procedure, please feel free to contact (name).

Following the review, all copies of materials relevant to the undertaking of the individual reviews are destroyed when no longer needed.

In the preparation of the final summary report, the chair of the local committee removes patient identifying data. When such information is necessary to follow through on recommendations or further evaluation, codes should be used in place of names.

Although free and open discussions are usually allowable in formal peer review proceedings, all conversations and written reference to related events that are not part of the formal proceedings themselves are readily discoverable in a court of law.

As might be anticipated, the emotional stress attending completed suicide often contributes to the paucity or superabundance of material that can potentially emerge in a suicide review. It has been my experience that communication with individual participants under the provisions of peer review guidelines prior to the meeting itself to prepare the participant and to help determine the nature of the material that might emerge is of enormous help in contributing to the efficient use of time.

LESSONS LEARNED

After some twenty years of experience in conducting inpatient and outpatient suicide reviews, I can report unequivocally that information immediately germane to the improvement of patient care can be expected in each instance when such reviews are undertaken. At HPHC, the well-known association among depressive states, alcohol abuse, and suicide was brought starkly to the light when the majority of a series of cases reviewed revealed that alcohol abuse was playing an active role at the time of death; an educational reminder article was planned for inclusion in the physician practice newsletter. Two outpatient providers, particularly troubled regarding their perception regarding care rendered to a patient prior to suicide, were posed to submit complaints against one another to the board of medicine; following a difficult but very productive review, the providers recognized major contributing factors to the death of which neither of them had been aware. Their plans subsequent to the review included consideration of the possibility of collaborating on a clinical paper elaborating on the role of such problems when participating with multiple providers in the delivery of care of seriously disturbed individuals. The all-too-common experience of encountering outpatient records of less than ideal composition among network providers has led HPHC to review and expand its requirements for outpatient record keeping in an attempt to ensure quality care and adequately protect its participant providers.

Aside from individual experiences, from a corporate standpoint, the regular reviewing of completed suicides has been felt to be a valuable instrument in the process of continually improving patient care.

IMPLICATIONS FOR THE CLINICIAN

- Many inpatient and alternative-to-hospitalization facilities seldom conduct reviews on completed suicides, and regular guidelines are not readily available for those that do.

- With rare exceptions, outpatient clinicians do not conduct such reviews.

- Regular and uniform suicide reviews can provide a ready instrument for improving patient care, a mechanism for identifying risk management vulnerability and developing remedial recommendations, and a means for supporting clinicians in handling the distress associated with the suicide of one of their patients.

- Suicide reviews should be convened under strict guidelines prescribed for peer review proceedings as outlined by local statutes or regulations in order to guarantee maximum protection for the privacy needed to conduct such activities.

- The rules and guarantees afforded to participants should be clearly explained to participating clinicians prior to meeting in order to guarantee the most efficient use of time.

- Information immediately germane to the improvement of patient care can be expected to emerge in each instance when such reviews are undertaken.

Relevant Readings

Bengesser G. Postvention for bereaved family members: Some therapeutic possibilities. *Crisis* 1985;9:45–48.

Chance S. Surviving suicide: A journey to resolution. *Bull Menninger Clin* 1988;52:30–39.

Cotton P. Dealing with suicide on a psychiatric inpatient unit. *Hosp Comm Psychiatry* 1983;34:55–59.

Hodgkinson P. Responding to inpatient suicide. *Br J Med Psychol* 1987;60:387–392.

Jacobs DG, Klein-Benheim M. The psychological autopsy: A useful tool for determining proximate causation in suicide cases. *Bull Am Acad Psychiatry Law* 1995;23:1–18.

Litman R. When patients commit suicide. *Am J Psychother* 1965;19:570–576.

Neill K. The psychological autopsy: A technique for investigating a hospital suicide. *Hosp Comm Psychiatry* 1974;25:33–36.

Stelovich S. Framework for handling adverse events. *Forum, Risk Management Foundation of the Harvard Medical Institutions* Apr 1997;8–9.

CHAPTER TWENTY-EIGHT

Medical Settings and Suicide

Martin J. Kelly, M.D.
Michael J. Mufson, M.D.
Malcolm P. Rogers, M.D.

Whe considering the issue of suicide in medical settings it is useful to separate concepts related to patients and their problems from those of settings and systems. Clearly patients interact with systems, but the issues may be better understood by separating them. This chapter is therefore organized into two sections, the first addressing patients and the second discussing the medical settings and systems.

PATIENT ASSESSMENT

Of the hundreds of thousands of people who attempt suicide in the United States each year (see Chapter Two), almost all will go through the emergency rooms of general hospitals. There they will be evaluated by the medical staff for the medical effects of the attempt and most often by a psychiatrist or other mental health personnel for the psychiatric issues. Since suicidal behaviors are common to medical settings, all caretakers in acute medical settings should have some familiarity with the problem and approaches to evaluating it. Experienced emergency room staff eventually develop clinical acumen about suicidal patients and probably have a reasonable sense about who remains at considerable risk after an attempt. These clinical skills are refined with each encounter, thus adding to the sophistication in dealing with future patients. Though there may be some situations in which the emergency room staff feels confident to make dispositions without psychiatric consultation, this should be a rare circumstance. An example might include a small overdose of nonprescription medications by a girl in early adolescence who had been drinking and was recently rejected by a boyfriend, and who has an intact, stable, and concerned family and available psychological counseling. Another example would be an individual with a long pattern of suicidal gestures (low-risk acts with manipulative intent) in a respected treatment program, which, when consulted, supports return to the ongoing program.

Such decisions should be rarely made and only by experienced medical staff. In most settings suicidal patients are evaluated by a mental health professional, ordinarily a psychiatrist. Expedience or cost considerations may lead to less experienced and less well-trained individuals making the crucial decisions about suicidal risk and psychiatric disposition. Because this decision is of great consequence both to the individual (and to the allocation of resources), whenever possible it should be made by a psychiatrist with expertise in assessing acutely suicidal patients and patients who survive life-threatening, self-inflicted acts. Some settings will not have on-site psychiatric coverage in the emergency room and may use affiliated psychiatric facilities.

The overwhelming number of suicide attempts in the United States are by overdose of prescription medications. These overdoses range from a handful of pills from a parent's medicine cabinet to a serious ingestion by a medical professional who knew of the likely lethality and who would have succeeded but for some accident of discovery. Some suicidal acts, for example, self-inflicted gunshots, are inherently so potentially lethal as to leave no doubt about intent. Other acts, such as slashing with razors or knives, require a more comprehensive and more subtle evaluation of the circumstances and motivation of the individual.

The most common confounding variable in the assessment of suicide risk is intoxication either with drugs or alcohol. The disinhibiting effect of intoxication may reveal an underlying serious wish to die or it can allow an individual to engage in help-seeking behavior otherwise unacceptable for expression. The disinhibition of intoxication challenges the clinical acumen and biases of even experienced clinicians; for example, a patient is at low risk without alcohol, but at high risk if intoxicated.

Some types of suicidal behavior, particularly hanging, also are challenges. This type of suicide attempt can reflect a very serious wish to die or an attempt to draw attention to oneself. Unlike overdoses, slashing, and shootings, whereby the underlying intent is often reflected in the seriousness of the act, hanging is inherently harder to assess. Sometimes there is a phenomenon of contagion; for example, adolescents from neighborhoods where others have committed suicide by hanging (or overdose). These evaluations require particular caution, even if the indicia of depression and active wish to die are not present.

Though there is ongoing debate about the utility of the term suicide *gesture* as opposed to suicide *attempt,* the clinician making decisions has to consider the seriousness or lethality of the act. The concept of *gesture* concerns the intentionality component of the act. The concept implies that a person does not have a desire to die but rather is expressing a psychological state in which she or he consciously or unconsciously wishes to change. The affects prompting the act include helplessness, the need to involve others, and some degree of despair. The individual hopes the act will mobilize help and does not reflect a conscious intent to end life. In most instances, the intent is not to seek psychiatric hospitalization.

In contrast, in common clinical parlance a suicide *attempt* refers to an act that is inherently very serious and the intent is to end life. Merely sending a message to others or stimulating environmental rearrangements is not the conscious or the major wish. The psychodynamic considerations and unconscious wishes in such acts are addressed elsewhere in this volume (Chapter Four).

The clinical dilemma of distinguishing a *gesture* from the range of other suicidal behaviors has received extensive attention (Jacobs and Brown, 1989; Maris et al., 1992). Often this includes the assessment of the lethality of the act and the likelihood of discovery (Weisman and Worden, 1972). This information is usually known in the emergency room. But there are many factors that may surround suicide attempts that are unknown and unknowable in the emergency room or in a typical acute medical setting. The most common is the true mental state of the patient just before and at the time of the act.

Evaluating Suicide Attempts

In assessing a suicide attempt, ideally one would like to know the patient's premorbid psychological history, the circumstances leading up to the act, and, if possible, the meaning of the act in psychological terms. Remember that most patients are limited in their capacity to express other than in general ways how they are feeling just a short time before. Therefore, especially when assessing suicide in the emergency room, one tries to seek out information from available sources. Suicide notes can be helpful but are surprisingly infrequent.

Those who discovered the patient often have important observations. Any comments of the patient close in time to the event are particularly valuable in gauging seriousness. Observers may also be able to describe the circumstances, physical and otherwise, of the attempt and provide information about whether the suicide attempt was a reflection of a conflict with another person or represented a more global sense of despair. Similarly detailed information about the means and implements are often critical. The type of medication, where and when obtained, whether it belonged to someone else, what the attempter understood of its actual harmfulness, the number of pills in the bottle, and whether they were all consumed, and so forth, are all logical inquiries.

If the attempt was by cutting or slashing, the specific details of the weapon including not only its type but also how the person obtained it, who owned it, and how long had it been available can be important. Also of some importance is the issue of how the person was found. Was the act relatively open or public such that discovery was likely, or was it secretive and discovered only by chance? What was the patient's appearance? What was he or she wearing? Did the clothes have any particular meaning? Were there sexualized or erotic components? Was there evidence of intoxication? Were there unusual objects in the area?

Those with this information may only stay for a brief time in the emergency department after they have brought in the patient. Prompt interview of these informants while the patient is receiving acute medical treatment is extremely worthwhile though occasionally overlooked. Secretarial and support staff can be trained to collect some of this information or at a minimum get information on how to contact these individuals afterward. Those who can provide valuable information include not only family and friends, but also emergency medical technicians, ambulance attendants, firefighters, police, and others.

The behavior of the patient while undergoing acute medical care in the emergency room is also useful data. What is the patient's attitude about the suicide attempt? Is the patient relieved, or does he regret being alive? Is he withdrawn, sullen, apparently depressed, or are is he cooperative with medical care? What is her mental status? Is there evidence of major mental illness such as psychosis? Is there evidence of major depression? Does the patient have paranoid delusions? Does she appear intoxicated (drugs or alcohol)?

It is often surprising how limited the patient's insight and capacity to communicate is in the acute period following the suicide attempt; any nonverbal sources of information are therefore useful. If a patient is admitted following an overdose, is there indication on physical examination that he has previously tried to hang or slash himself? Critically, what is the evolution of the patient's emotional state while she is in the emergency room, a period that often spans several hours. If a problem in a relationship or a threatened breakup triggered the attempt, has there been some further communication or reconciliation either in person or by phone? If someone was admitted in an intoxicated state, the intoxication may well have cleared by the time a decision about disposition needs to be made. But while intoxicated and disinhibited, the patient may be more candid about his level of despair. However, it may have triggered an impulsive act that, though very dangerous, was out of keeping with the patient's usual behavior and hence represents a less ominous act.

The issues in the direct evaluation of the patient and of the mental status is addressed elsewhere in this volume, especially Chapters One and Twelve.

Addressing Safety Issues in
the Emergency Room

The need to keep the patient safe after a suicide attempt is obvious. However, the emergency room at any moment may go into full response mode with the arrival of trauma victims or patients in crisis, a status that demands the attention of most of the emergency room staff. It is wise for hospitals to have policies that take into account these occasionally hectic circumstances and the distractions that might allow someone who remains suicidal to make another attempt or to escape from the emergency room. The design of most modern emergency rooms is such that patients are often in clear view of many staff and there are other staff members very close by. Visual surveillance from a nursing station or the use of restraints is necessary if a staff person cannot be with the patient all the time. If surveillance cannot be done by emergency room staff, family members and friends can be utilized. This also often comforts the patient and can be of assistance in the workup because the interaction between the patient and others in their lives sheds some light on the context, circumstances, and meaning of the act. It may also provide data regarding the safety and reasonableness of discharge to home.

Concern about safety is a consideration if the pattern of trauma is inconsistent with the history as given. Skepticism by an emergency room staff member has uncovered situations in which a husband has injected a near lethal dose of insulin into his diabetic wife, nearly causing death and resulting in irreversible brain damage. In another case an individual driving home from a hospital childbirth class called the police, claiming that he and his wife had been shot and wounded in a robbery attempt a short distance from the hospital. It eventually emerged that he had fatally shot his wife and deliberately inflicted a nonfatal wound to his own abdomen. Ironically, a couple of months later, he killed himself by jumping from a bridge as authorities were preparing to arrest him. In several instances the hospital staff has suspected staged suicide attempts to avoid arrest and incarceration.

It is optimum if the psychiatrist can be involved throughout the care in the emergency department. The evolution of the patient's mental status, observed over a period of several hours, is probably the most important factor in deciding whether the patient will be sent to a psychiatric hospital or some other disposition. Too often the psychiatric evaluation is seen as something that happens at the end of the medical workup rather than in parallel. It is suboptimum for the patient to be seen only after there is medical clearance for discharge. Practicalities may force this from time to time, but observing the patient at several points throughout medical treatment often can lead to more enlightened and therapeutic decisions.

Assessing the Need for Hospitalization

A twenty-five-year-old man took an overdose of Tylenol impulsively after his girlfriend broke off the relationship. He found himself alone on the holiday, began drinking and using cocaine, which he had not done for months. In the aftermath of his intoxication and cocaine high, he became more depressed and took the overdose. He had no idea whether it would be harmful, but knew that his friend took them to "get a better night's sleep." On evaluation, the patient revealed that he wasn't relieved after he took the overdose. In fact he was frightened, but quickly felt too sick and immobilized to act and slipped into a profound sleep. Upon waking the next day, in the apartment he was sharing with a friend (who was there while he was sleeping), he felt sick and realized what he had done. He immediately called his therapist, whom he had been seeing once a week and with whom he had a very positive alliance. She told him to get to an ER immediately. He drove to a hospital fifteen to twenty minutes away and sought help. Only after he was seen did he learn of the potentially serious risk the medicine (acetaminophen) might have on his liver. He was admitted, treated, and monitored carefully. While in the hospital he was in touch with his former girlfriend, who came to visit. They agreed to work on their relationship, with the help of couples therapy. To the consultant psychiatrists he sometimes seemed angry and labile. He emphasized how "stupid" he now felt the attempt had been and spoke with amazement about how close he had come to death and about a sense of renewed meaning, purpose, and opportunity in his life that came after the overdose. He also spoke about the importance of his job as a foreman in a small furniture factory, which he had held for the past year. He was expected to be at work in a few days, and felt that his presence there was important to the stability of the company. He was also in touch with his therapist and agreed with the possible addition of psychopharmacologic treatment to his ongoing psychotherapy. The psychiatric resident was going to hospitalize the patient and thought it was "brave" of the attending psychiatrist to let him return home. "I wouldn't risk losing my license for that."

Many psychiatrists may lean toward self-protection and distance themselves in recommending hospitalization after some suicide attempts. They may worry about malpractice litigation or criticism from their peers and supervisors, and are not inclined to accept additional risk. They may also at times feel uncomfortable and angry because of the hostility of the patient.

If medical hospitalization is warranted after a suicide attempt, the seriousness of the attempt needs to be established. In some instances the psychiatric management of the patient is primarily to assure safety awaiting the transfer to a psychiatric hospital. But in a number of cases, developments during the course of the medical hospitalization make the psychiatric hospitalization unnecessary. The suicidal act itself may have "changed" the patient and discharged the psychological and emotional tension, thus rendering them less suicidal. It often brings about changes in the interpersonal environment and relationships so that outpatient therapy may be more appropriate despite the seriousness of the attempt. In fact a psychiatric hospitalization can be experienced by the patient as punitive.

Antidepressant medication, when initiated following a suicide attempt in the general hospital setting, is often credited with improvement in the patient's mental status or lessened suicidal ideation when this is due to interpersonal and acute intrapsychic changes. The stability of the patient's living arrangement, therapeutic connection, work life, and social supports are all part of the consideration regarding the decision to hospitalize or not. It is also important to remember that hospitalization, though it might seem to increase safety in the short run, may not promote a therapeutic alliance but in fact might interfere with one. It is also important to be realistic about the stigma of psychiatric hospitalization, which sometimes becomes a kind of scarlet letter that will always remain with the patient. The voluntariness of a hospitalization certainly has major implications for its therapeutic prospects. Because of the profound effects of loss of freedom, involuntary hospitalization should never be sought in a reflexive fashion.

Survivors of the most serious suicide attempts—for example, following gun shot wounds to the head, jump survivors, or patients who have set themselves on fire—will probably have prolonged medical treatment. Remarkably, they are unlikely to require psychiatric hospitalization at the end of acute medical treatment. More commonly they are discharged to a rehabilitation facility or to their homes with supportive services. Their lives are fundamentally changed by the physical damage of the suicidal act, and with surprising frequency often they are no longer suicidal, thus rendering psychiatric hospitalization unnecessary and possibly counterproductive. Further, most psychiatric hospitals are resistant to having patients with medical needs such as frequent dressing changes, intravenous therapy, and so forth, and they are not ordinarily equipped to provide this care. Some specialized "Med-Psych" units can accommodate these needs but they are unavailable in most areas. These units are often more skilled at meeting the medical needs of patients after a suicide attempt than addressing in depth the psychological ones.

The role of the psychiatrist in the medical inpatient management of patients following a suicide attempt is multifaceted. The primary responsibility is for safety and psychiatric treatment and arranging the appropriate and most therapeutic disposition. Within these roles are many others, including educating the nursing and medical staff about suicidal patients. Most medical units will have only sporadic (and usually infrequent contact) with suicidal patients, and this must be taken into consideration in the treatment plan. Typically, more than one visit each day to the patient or floor is helpful, especially early in the admission. Changes in nursing procedures in most institutions have resulted in the designation of a primary nurse for each patient. This nurse coordinates the nursing care and formulates a treatment plan for the patient on the unit. Beyond the informal practical educational role of the psychiatrist, there is often a need to consider the staff's attitudes about the patient. These can significantly influence how the patient is perceived and treated, and often have implications for safety.

For most medical staffs, a suicide attempt is an emotionally evocative event. Among the emotions stirred up by such an event can be anger and extreme disapproval. Identification with the patient and excessive "sympathy" can also come into play. It is impossible to identify and manage the affects of all who will have contact with the patient. However, the psychiatrist can work with the nursing staff to establish clear and unambiguous elements in the treatment plan that limit the risk that these personal attitudes and biases pose.

Since the predominant mode of suicide attempt is by overdose, delirium is a frequent consequence. Because it is the most serious risk factor for successful suicide in a medical hospital (Reich and Kelly, 1976), the delirious patient must be carefully observed. Beyond watchfulness, the vigorous treatment of the delirium, if possible, is primary suicide prevention. In emergency rooms and intensive care units, where observation is readily available, a delirious patient is relatively safe, but in a single room without observation on a typical floor, such a patient is at risk.

In some circumstances the medical and psychiatric condition of the patient after a suicide attempt are both serious and both require vigorous treatment. If a suicidal patient is resistant to medical care, refusing hydration and nutrition because of depression, emergency treatment can be instituted after the appropriate medicolegal review. Emergency treatment can include electroconvulsive therapy or acute medical intervention. There are a wide range of conditions that might require this, including profound depression, psychosis, catatonia, postpartum depression, and other serious psychiatric syndromes.

Later in this chapter, we address psychiatric management techniques in the general hospital medical setting. In the emergency room and inpatient setting, however, thresholds for physical as opposed to interpersonal management techniques are lower than in psychiatric facilities. Medical personnel and nursing staff are acculturated to respond to crisis manifested by acute, concrete signals and operate on the presumption that patients will actively seek them out if in extremis. The suicidal patient does not participate in this implicit contract.

SUICIDE PRECAUTIONS IN THE GENERAL HOSPITAL

Psychiatric hospitals and general hospitals differ in the implementation of suicide precautions. In psychiatric institutions there are clear gradations of suicidal watchfulness, with a range from constant observation through five-minute checks and fifteen-minute checks, as well as room or ward restrictions. In medical institutions all patients are acutely ill and often precariously so. The staff is therefore generally alert and vigilant for untoward medical events signaled by monitors, alarms, or patient calls of distress and need for assistance. The patient who is suicidal in the hospital is atypical in this culture.

This atypicality is also reflected in the somewhat bimodal arrangement of suicide-risk management of these settings. The suicidal patient in the medical hospital has, as a practical matter, *all or nothing* suicide watch. They are either restrained or under constant observation (usually by so-called "sitters"), or they are regarded as a typical and presumptively compliant patient. A patient who is no longer suicidal will be regarded as typical of the medical patients on the ward and expected to signal distress if in need. Patients who continue to be suicidal are unlikely to bring attention to themselves. Rather, they are likely to take advantage of any lessened staff attention, for example, a medical crisis of another patient, as an opportunity for additional suicidal behavior.

In psychiatric institutions, interpersonal relationships and interpersonal management of emotional crisis and suicidality are key. In that setting, *no-suicide contracts* (NSC) operate on this principle of an interpersonal connection between the patient and the staff member. (See Chapter Twenty-Six for further discussion.) In the medical setting, there are so many more people involved in the care than is typical of psychiatric units that interpersonal management as a practical matter is risky. Nevertheless, the nursing and medical staff have many important opportunities to observe the patient's behavior and mental status, as well as the interaction with family and friends. Such observations should be encouraged and recorded in the hospital chart. They can be critical in the disposition.

Special Risks for Medical Patients: Traumatic Information and Loss

Medical facilities are replete with stories of patients receiving sudden traumatic information. Some patients may learn through genetic testing that they will eventually develop an illness such as Huntington's chorea. Patients may learn from test results (Weil and Hawker, 1997) that they have cancer and a limited time to live. They may become aware suddenly of life-changing and disfiguring injuries. A new diagnosis of HIV can be unexpected and precipitate acute depression. Family members and friends may suddenly learn of the death of a loved one. Emotional reactions to such events are intense and require a period of integration. During that process some individuals are at acute risk. Medically ill elderly patients may be at particular risk. One study of suicides in the elderly concluded that 50 percent were despondent over illness (Younger et al., 1990).

Reich and Kelly (1976) described the nature of suicide attempts in the general hospital. The attempts were impulsive acts without warning and without factors typically thought to be associated with suicide risk. The "impulsive" suicide was associated with stress leading to psychic tension, anger, agitation, and sudden mood changes. The stress was commonly acute and related to loss of emotional support both due to family conflicts or disruptions in relationships with medical personnel. This study emphasized that loss of impulse control was a vulnerability related to conditions including personality disorders, affective disorder, psychotic states, and delirium.

Other Issues in the General Hospital Pertaining to Suicide

In the face of certain medical problems, some patients engage in high-risk behavior. Some may drive recklessly. Some may deliberately expose themselves to HIV. Some patients with peripheral vascular disease may continue smoking out of a sense of hopelessness. A patient with cirrhosis may go on an alcohol binge. Psychiatric consultation may be sought to help interpret the meaning of such behavior and assess whether psychosocial intervention would be helpful. Some acute trauma may be ambiguous in terms of suicidality. Psychiatric consultation is sensibly requested for unusual accidents, such as falls from buildings, gunshot wounds, electrocution, single occupant motor vehicle accidents, burns, and so forth. Another consideration is that medical therapies may sometimes give patients ready means for suicide, like the dialysis patients who bleed to death as a result of disconnecting the arteriovenous shunt (Kasi-Visweswaran et al., 1982) or the diabetic who takes an overdose of insulin. Psychiatric consultation to medical staff around complex psychosocial issues involved in noncompliance is quite useful in these cases, as the following example displays.

> A twenty-two-year-old female diabetic was admitted to the hospital for noncompliance resulting in severe diabetic ketoacidosis with confusion. There had been a history of increasingly severe noncompliance, and the current episode was in the context of problems with a boyfriend and school difficulties. Prior to admission the patient was working, living with a roommate, and attempting to function more autonomously. On interview she acknowledged how close to death she had come and that it was related to her noncompliance. At times she felt she would be better off dead. She did not voice acute suicidal ideation and agreed to outpatient treatment. The patient's managed care plan did not feel it could mobilize acute outpatient treatment and transferred the patient against her will to a psychiatric facility for the weekend. The patient expressed the feeling she was being punished for her noncompliance. She was reevaluated in the psychiatric hospital, judged to be no longer in need of hospitalization, and allowed to leave after a weekend admission.

Noncompliance, if it leads to life-threatening complications, may raise serious questions about suicidal intent. However, in the absence of suicidal intent, in-depth psychiatric evaluation is warranted because noncompliance most often reflects complicated interactions between the patient and the health care providers as well as the patient's difficulties in adapting to emotional demands.

In this case, the hospital consulting psychiatrist had mobilized appropriate family support and felt that the patient could return home safely, to be seen as a psychiatric outpatient after the weekend. The psychiatrist for her managed care organization insisted the patient be hospitalized against her will, and she was. Following the weekend psychiatric hospitalization, having experienced the hospitalization as punitive and disruptive, she signed herself out and had no further alliance with the psychiatric or medical team.

Suicide Among Special Medical Populations

There is an increase in depression in patients with medical illness. The prevalence rate of depression is 10 to 15 percent in the general medical population as compared with 5 percent in the general population (Nesse et al., 1996). In patients with selected chronic illnesses, prevalence rates range between 25 and 50 percent (Nesse and Finlayson, 1996). Pancreatic cancer and lung cancer are well-known examples and the incidence of depression is also increased in AIDS, chronic pain syndromes, chronic renal failure, acute burn injuries, cancer, lupus, rheumatoid arthritis, multiple sclerosis, and central nervous system disorders. It is notable that depressed patients are high utilizers of medical care (Henk, Katzelnick, Kobak, Greist, and Jefferson, 1996) and that over two-thirds of people who commit suicide had consulted their general practitioner in the previous month, and 40 percent had done so in the previous week (Hirschfeld and Russell, 1997).

Higher suicide rates have been noted in patients with acute spinal cord injuries, epilepsy, and in other neurologic disorders, such as Huntington's chorea, migraine, amyotrophic lateral sclerosis, brain tumors, cranial trauma (Stenager and Stenager, 1992), cancer (Allebeck, 1989), chronic renal failure (Degoulet et al., 1982), and AIDS (Marzuk et al., 1988). Harris (1994) did a comprehensive search of the literature and identified the specific medical disorders that have an increased risk of suicide (see Table 28.1). Pregnancy and the puerperium, interestingly, are associated with decreased risk. However, the evidence was inconclusive for amputation, heart valve replacement and surgery, Crohn's disease, ulcerative colitis, hormone replacement therapy, alcoholic liver disease, neurofibromatosis, systemic sclerosis, and Parkinson's disease.

It should be noted that these data describe medical illnesses in which suicide rates have been described and documented. The list is not necessarily exhaustive, and the reader should also note that the rates are often higher because of comorbid psychiatric or substance abuse problems (see Table 28.2).

HIV or AIDS. The data for suicide following HIV or AIDS diagnoses may be better documented because of the generally better statistics kept on patients with these diagnoses. The higher suicide rates, nearly a sevenfold increase, probably results from a combination of the effect of HIV on the brain, the increased likelihood of substance abuse as a comorbid problem, the perception

Table 28.1. Medical Conditions with Increased Suicidal Risk.

Illness	Increased Risk
HIV or AIDS	6.6x
Huntington's disease	2.9
Malignant neoplasms	
All sites	1.8
Head and neck	11.4
Multiple sclerosis	2.4
Peptic ulcer	2.1
Chronic renal failure	
Dialysis	14.5
Transplantation	3.8
Spinal cord injuries	3.8
Systemic lupus erythematosus	4.3

Table 28.2. Neuropsychiatric and Psychiatric Conditions Associated with Increased Suicidal Risk.

Neuropsychiatric syndromes	Alcohol withdrawal
	Substance abuse
	Delirium
	Brain injury
Major psychiatric disorders	Depressive disorder
	Acute psychosis
	Personality disorder
	Panic disorder
	Schizophrenia

of a grim prognosis (though that has changed dramatically with new treatments), and the stigmatizing aspects of the illness. In fact, the early recognition of higher suicide rates has led to careful management of the circumstances under which patients receive bad news regarding the outcome of HIV testing. With improved treatments and prognoses, perhaps the suicide rate will drop.

Huntington's Disease. There has been much concern about the impact of genetic testing and counseling for Huntington's disease. Data from some reports suggest that patients may also be at risk simply from the symptoms even before a formal diagnosis is made (Di Maio et al., 1993). Huntington's disease causes progressive dementia, neurologic deterioration, and personality changes. Reviews of the risk of suicide in Huntington's disease cases have been inconclusive. Early studies suggested increased risk of suicide, but more recent studies raise doubts (Farrer, 1986; Schoenfield et al., 1984; Stenager and Stenager, 1992). Risk factors may include growing up in a family with an affected member, living with an awareness of the risk of contracting the disease, and having neuropsychiatric sequela including depression, irritability, and psychosis with delusions and hallucinations (Jensen et al., 1993). These symptoms may be related to dysfunction in the orbitofrontal cortex, thus making the patient more prone to impulsivity and emotional instability.

Malignant Neoplasms. Cancer patients appear to be at a higher risk for suicide, particularly during the first two years after diagnosis (Allebeck, Bolund, and Ringback, 1989; Storm et al., 1992). Risk is greater among patients with disseminated as opposed to localized cancers (Storm et al., 1992). Lung and upper airway cancers were associated with greater rates of suicide in both genders, and rates were greater in gastrointestinal cancers for men. Cancers of the head and neck have an elevenfold increase in rates of suicide, whereas cancer generally has a relatively modest, twofold increase. The reason for the much higher rates among head and neck cancer patients is unclear but may relate to the association with alcohol and tobacco use, facial disfigurement, and the loss of voice.

> After receiving the diagnosis of metastatic intestinal cancer, a sixty-eight-year-old man feared becoming a burden to his wife and voiced feelings of depression and hopelessness in the medical clinic. One week later he returned to the parking lot of the hospital and shot himself in the abdomen. He survived the shooting, and when interviewed stated that he did not want to become a burden to his wife and wanted to make it easy for everyone by killing himself on hospital grounds. Over a period of several days he stated he no longer felt suicidal and was glad he had survived the attempt. He was easily managed on the hospital ward and accepted supportive therapy. He voiced no further suicidal ideation and said he felt shame for what he had done and hoped his wife would forgive him. He was eventually discharged home and followed in the psychiatry clinic in the hospital at which he received medical treatment.

This man had multiple risk factors for suicide, including advanced age, new diagnosis of cancer, and depression with hopelessness. He also voiced the feelings of hopelessness to his primary care doctor shortly before the attempt, although without voicing active suicidal ideation or plans. In this population, prediction of suicide is particularly hard even with psychiatric consultation. This patient's return to the hospital grounds can be interpreted as an expression of ambivalence in terms of his desire to die or be saved. The acute psychological disturbance cleared after the suicide attempt, and the patient was then able to involve himself and his wife in psychiatric outpatient treatment that addressed his fears and feelings about the future.

Multiple Sclerosis and Degenerative Neurologic States. Suicide risk appears to be greater earlier in the course of these diseases, especially in younger, less disabled males. The predisposition to psychiatric disorder and organic mental syndromes may also play a role in the increase in suicidality.

> A sixty-eight-year-old man was admitted to the neurology service for treatment of a degenerative neurologic condition that caused weakness and inability to use his hands in any functional capacity. This man was a very successful graphic designer who felt his whole identity and pleasure in life derived from his ability to do this work. He was widowed and had still been active at work prior to his illness. Over an eighteen-month period he became increasingly disabled and began to openly state that if there was no cure for him he would rather die and, in fact, had plans to kill himself. There was no evidence of major depressive illness, and this man spoke openly and rationally about dying. In an attempt to address this suicidal ideation he volunteered to transfer to a psychiatric ward. He was discharged after two weeks of treatment, which included antidepressants. Six months later he successfully committed suicide at home.

Certain patients with devastating medical conditions that cause severe disability openly express their intent to commit suicide. These suicides often reflect the patient's loss of will to live, especially if the loss of self-esteem is severe and the patient is aging and has little social support. Even when psychiatric treatment is in place, such individuals may ultimately commit suicide, and preventing the suicide is impossible. In such cases it is very helpful for the primary care physician to have the support of psychiatric consultation to review treatment early on in the case, assess fully all treatment alternatives, and ensure that the patient's talk of suicidality does not alienate the primary care givers.

Because the most common means of suicide attempt and a frequent means of suicide is by prescription medication, patients' doctors often feel quite upset if they have provided the means of suicide. Psychiatrists in medical settings help the practitioners in that setting deal with these events and their personal emotional responses to them.

Peptic Ulcer. The most likely reason for the higher suicide rate among peptic ulcer patients is the frequent occurrence of psychiatric disorder, substance abuse, or alcoholism in ulcer patients.

Epilepsy. Although there are few reliable studies examining the correlation between epilepsy and suicide risk, the largest follow up study showed a fivefold increase in suicide in this population. Other studies suggest that increased suicide attempts in epileptics are associated with character disorder, psychotic disorders, and a history of prior suicide attempts.

Chronic Renal Failure: Dialysis and Transplantation. Since hemodialysis and peritoneal dialysis became widely available for patients with chronic renal failure, there have been some reports of higher than expected suicide rates and issues regarding the appropriate assessment of patients' requests for stopping therapy, which, of course results in death. This has been referred to by some as "veiled" suicide, and by others as "rational" suicide. Whether decisions to terminate treatment are viewed or recorded as suicide is unclear. Chronic renal disease is complicated by uremic encephalopathy, hypertensive encephalopathy, hemodialysis disequilibrium syndrome, and dialysis dementia, all of which can present with confusional states. Uremic neuropathy can cause chronic pain syndromes and periodic leg movement disorders that disrupt sleep.

From a practical point of view, decisions to terminate treatment require careful assessment of capacity to refuse treatment and the role of any psychiatric illness interfering with that capacity. Further, the degree of openness of the patient, not only with the medical staff but with their own families, is an important dimension to consider.

Spinal Cord Injuries. Patients with spinal cord injuries (SCI) carry a higher risk of suicide. This relates both to the impact of a sudden devastating injury on an individual's self-concept and self-esteem and to the high association of major psychiatric disorders in the SCI population, including alcohol and drug abuse, psychosis, and depression. Each of these disorders can lead to suicide attempts that inadvertently can cause SCI. Risk management necessitates distinguishing between the two groups. The patients who are actively adjusting to the injury do better with psychotherapy; the group with major psychiatric disorders need alcohol and drug treatment or treatment with psychopharmacologic means in addition to supportive therapy.

The acute and chronic effects of head injury must also be attended to in this group of patients. This includes postconcussive syndromes and post-traumatic brain injury. These patients are vulnerable to episodes of delirium and impulsivity. The following vignettes illustrate suicidality in various SCI patients.

Case One: A Substance-Abusing SCI Patient
Mr. A was a thirty-seven-year-old man with a long history of polysubstance abuse. He was dependent on alcohol and Valium (diazepam). After he became intoxicated and abusive at home, his wife locked him out of the house. He told her he was going to kill himself if she did not let him back into the house to get to his alcohol and drugs. When his wife refused, he attempted to get in by climbing on the roof and breaking in a window. During this attempt, he fell off the roof, and as a result became paraplegic. In the hospital, treatment consisted

of detoxification from the alcohol and minor tranquilizers. Because the patient reported ongoing suicidal ideation, a sitter was arranged. When the intoxication cleared, the patient was found to be neither severely depressed nor suicidal. He was managed on a spinal cord unit for his injury. In the hospital he began attending AA and was eventually discharged home with outpatient psychotherapy and family therapy.

Case Two: SCI in the Psychotic Patient

A twenty-year-old man attempted suicide by hanging himself in the woods near his home. The tree branch broke and he fell, suffering a SCI with paraplegia. On admission he was found to be in the midst of an acute paranoid psychosis. Despite significant paranoid ideation and disorganized thinking, he voiced no further suicidal ideation and denied any desire to die. He could not talk in any meaningful way about the attempted hanging. He was treated with antipsychotic medication and supportive psychotherapy. He was initially under the supervision of a sitter, a precaution that was discontinued after one week. The patient had an uneventful course for three months until one week before planned discharge. Without any warning, while on pass, the patient attempted to wheel himself into a river near the hospital but was discovered by passers-by. He was taken back to the hospital, where he discussed that he was afraid to leave the hospital and return home. There had been no worsening of his psychosis. Further supportive therapy was provided on the medical ward, which facilitated his eventual transfer home. The patient had no further suicidal attempts in follow-up for ten years.

Clinical experience also suggests that some patients with sudden disabling illnesses may be more at risk after the acute medical hospitalization, either in a rehabilitation setting (Missel, 1978) or upon discharge home.

Case Three: Adjustment to SCI with Chronic Pain Syndrome and Depression

A fifty-five-year-old man suffered an SCI while at work on a construction site. He was admitted to the hospital and after stabilization became depressed. He also developed a chronic pain syndrome and began voicing a wish to die. He did not describe any plans to harm himself and did not feel he would act on his feelings, yet he felt angry and out of control. He had a prior history of a major depressive episode and a family history of suicide in a sibling and parent. This patient agreed to begin antidepressants but refused individual psychotherapy. With his wife and family he engaged in family therapy to address issues of discharge before the actual discharge. Suicidal ideation diminished with improvement in the depression and ongoing family therapy, which addressed issues around self-esteem and his need to be in control. The chronic pain syndrome continued to pose a significant problem and at times led to recurrent suicidal ideation.

These cases illustrate the spectrum of clinical dilemmas seen in patients with SCI. The first case illustrates the relationship between substance abuse and risk of SCI. The suicidal threat was followed by a severe but accidental injury while intoxicated. When the intoxication cleared, the treatment focus was on the SCI and the traditional treatment of alcohol or drug abuse. As often occurs, the acute suicidal ideation resolved when the patient was no longer intoxicated.

Case Two illustrates the occurrence of SCI in patients with psychotic disorders. Psychosis poses a high risk for suicide, even when the patient is under treatment with appropriate antipsychotic medication. Skilled inpatient SCI units can manage these complex patients with psychiatric consultation based on the patient's needs.

Case Three illustrates how multiple risk factors may emerge in the SCI patient. In this case, adjustments to loss, major depression, chronic pain, and family history all combine to increase risk for suicide. The mobilization of acute psychiatric treatment becomes a necessity in managing this type of patient.

Systemic Lupus Erythematosus. The roughly fourfold increased risk of suicide among these patients probably results from the disease's effects on the central nervous system, which can include acute psychosis, cognitive impairment, and depression. Associated organ failure—for example, in chronic renal failure—and the possibility of steroid-induced psychosis may also add to the higher than expected rate.

Chronic Pain Syndrome. Chronic pain is underappreciated as a psychophysiologic state that can cause enormous psychological stress leading to suicide in a vulnerable patient. The primary care physician should be attentive to this specialized group of patients and inquire about suicidal ideation. The threshold for psychiatric consultation should be low. Inpatient treatment on a specialized pain unit may be necessary.

Given the nature of chronic pain, decisions around psychiatric hospitalization can be quite difficult. The patient seeks the "cure" of the pain syndrome and is very prone to frustration and anger as treatment moves forward without improvement. There is a much higher than expected incidence of major depressive disorder in patients with chronic pain. The following vignette displays a patient's unresolved grief and depression as related to a chronic pain syndrome.

A thirty-nine-year-old woman was seen in the pain clinic for a chronic pain syndrome. She had suffered a nonunion of a fracture of her clavicle in a bicycle accident, necessitating bone grafting surgery from her pelvis. Following the procedure she developed an ilioinguinal neuropathy. Shortly before the injury her husband suffered a heart attack and died while they were on a hiking excursion. She had been in therapy for depression and was maintained on antidepressants. She was an honors college graduate and was fully employed. As the pain syndrome continued, she began to voice suicidal ideation. The neuropathy proved refractory to pharmacologic trials, and as each trial failed her suicidal ideation intensified. Her therapist requested psychiatric consultation from a multidisciplinary pain clinic. In the midst of the evaluation, the patient was visited by her parents. This relationship had been a chronically conflicted one. While the parents were visiting, the patient went into the garage and committed suicide by carbon monoxide poisoning.

Individuals with a chronic pain syndrome refractory to treatment are vulnerable to demoralization and the emergence of depressive syndromes. This alone can lead to suicidal ideation, necessitating psychiatric consultation. In certain patients a host of risk factors emerge that increases the risk even more. In this woman, an unresolved grief reaction, chronic family discord, and a chronic pain syndrome form the backdrop for a completed suicide despite aggressive treatment attempts.

Rational Suicide

No discussion of higher suicide rates in the medically ill would be complete without some mention of the concept of rational suicide. There are circumstances under which patients choose to die, either actively or by discontinuing treatment. This is uncommon, however, considering the number of people with terminal illness. The following vignette concerns a family who wants to stop a patient's cancer treatment and considers the option of suicide.

A thirty-eight-year-old computer programmer was diagnosed as having a glioblastoma multiforme, a malignant brain tumor with a grim prognosis. He underwent surgery, followed by radiation, and then chemotherapy. He lost his appetite during the chemotherapy and experienced marked fatigue. He was unable to work, and his stamina diminished. His marriage revolved around mutual work and a shared passion for gourmet cooking. There were no children. Both the patient and his wife felt that life as they had known it was over. The patient himself had little tolerance for any further medical intervention. He wanted to "hurry up and get it over with." He and his wife had discussed suicide but dismissed it as an option because the life insurance policy would be nullified by suicide.

This case is exceptional. Both the patient and his wife were starkly realistic about the future. They had permitted themselves to be hopeful for some time, but now wanted no medical intervention, no false hope, or anything that would merely prolong a life without value to them. They had already grieved the loss of their life together.

There certainly was an element of depression in his response, but also a rational wish for death. His fatigue, loss of interest, and loss of pleasure in available activities were evident. His internist prescribed fluoxetine, which was rejected after a few days because of nausea. He was also seen in psychiatric consultation. A stimulant, methylphenidate, was prescribed, which had a brief dramatic effect on his energy level and desire to do things. However, he found the stimulating effect to be too intense and stopped taking it after two to three days rather than titrating the dosage downward. The event confirmed their decision to avoid any further medical intervention.

The most important gift friends and family can give to those who are dying is simply to be with them. The last few months of life can be particularly meaningful. Fear of abandonment, fear of loss of control, and intense suffering are generally the greatest worries of those who are dying.

Assisted suicide is a highly public and controversial issue. Many disagree with the methods of the most highly publicized practitioner, Dr. Kevorkian, but few doubt the need for renewed attention to this complicated issue. Other physicians, such as Timothy Quill and colleagues, have approached and written about this issue in a balanced and thoughtful fashion (Quill, 1993; Quill and Brody, 1995; Quill et al., 1992).

The level of public support for change in this area became evident with the 1994 Death with Dignity Act, passed by a majority of voters in the State of Oregon. This act would allow certain terminally ill patients with less than six months to live to commit suicide with the assistance of their attending physicians. It requires that the patient be competent and not mentally ill. The law is currently being challenged in the courts, based on the inadequacy of the process of excluding incompetency and mental illness.

There are differences of opinion about the prevalence of so-called "rational suicide." Most studies that have actually investigated the issue have found that the desire for death in the terminally ill is closely associated with clinical depression in most cases. Chochinov and his group (1995) studied 200 terminally ill patients, assessing both the prevalence of clinical depression and their wish for an early death. Only 8 percent acknowledged a serious and pervasive desire to die, although 44 percent of patients had experienced occasional wishes for an earlier death. For those with a desire to die the prevalence of depression was 59 percent compared with 8 percent among those not wishing to die. Other studies support the need for careful evaluation of depression. During a two week follow-up period, Brown and colleagues (1986) studied the final days of forty-four terminally ill patients. They found that the majority (77 percent) had never wished for death to come early. Of the remaining ten patients, three had been suicidal and seven had wished for an early death. All ten of these patients were found to be suffering from clinical depression.

When one looks carefully for psychiatric diagnosis among people who have committed suicide, one finds compelling evidence for the presence of significant mental illness (see Chapter One). One group of investigators (Lesage et al., 1994) found that in young men completing suicide, the combination of borderline personality disorder, affective disorder, and untreated alcoholism was particularly lethal. Well-known risk factors include male gender, increasing age, living alone, recent loss, early parental loss, and family history of suicide.

There is thus compelling evidence that depression can be driving the seemingly rational wish to die, and therefore should be carefully evaluated in every terminally ill patient. Nevertheless, most physicians also agree that the decision of a terminally ill patient to shorten the period of suffering before death can be rational (see Chapter Thirty).

When care of dying patients is as thoughtful and attentive as our most aggressive therapies, patients do not commonly seek assisted suicides (Sachs et al., 1995). One should strive to create an approach that allows death to be a natural, expected milestone of human existence, rather than simply an unwanted outcome of disease (McCue, 1995).

Psychiatric Illnesses and Suicide

Other chapters in this volume focus on the relationship between various psychiatric disorders and suicide. We do not cover the same ground here, except to note these disorders (see Table 28.2) and to comment on those with special connections to medical facilities. Conditions such as panic disorder and intoxication, which can greatly enhance suicidality, are commonly seen in the ER. Organic mental syndromes, for obvious reasons, are also very commonly seen both in the ER and in the medical and surgical inpatient setting. Delirium poses a very high risk of suicidality but is time-limited.

Delirium After Coronary Bypass Surgery

A fifty-eight-year-old factory foreman with no prior psychiatric history underwent a coronary artery bypass graft. He was noted to be intermittently confused postoperatively before he was discharged home on day four. The fact that he spoke limited English may have led his doctors to underestimate his confusion. After discharge, his family became aware that he was frightened, apparently in response to continued auditory and visual hallucinations at home. On day six he was brought to the hospital's ER, where he underwent a medical and psychiatric evaluation. A computed tomography head scan and EKG were both normal, as were blood gases and a battery of blood tests. The psychiatrist felt that he was still delirious, though it was resolving, and would benefit from being admitted. The medical team felt that there was insufficient medical justification for rehospitalization. The patient and family declined psychiatric hospitalization, which would have required transfer to another facility, and opted to return home. The patient was given a prescription for haloperidol, 2 mg at night. The family was instructed to observe the patient closely. The family continued to watch him closely throughout the next day, during which he appeared calmer. That night, however, while in the same bed with his sleeping wife, he saw and heard demons threatening him. He got out of bed and jumped out the window, landing twenty-two feet below. He was found by his family the next morning and brought to the hospital, where he was found to have a fractured pelvis and was readmitted.

Complicated Grief with Major Depression

A sixty-five-year-old man had left his home, planning to drive to his vacation home, where he had hunting guns. Along the way he stopped in the ER, complaining of chest pain and depression. He had no evidence of cardiac disease but told the ER doctor that in the past few days he had feared he would shoot himself or his grandchild. A psychiatry consultation was called. On evaluation the man expressed the feeling of being "brokenhearted" due to the sudden death of his wife six months earlier. He became frightened over the thought that he was going to harm himself or his grandchild. Fearing he would hurt the child, he had left his home to drive to his vacation home. His evaluation revealed unresolved grief and symptoms of a major depression with hopelessness, melancholia, anhedonia, a ten-pound weight loss, and insomnia. He feared he would harm himself if he went to his home in Maine. Consent was obtained to talk with his daughter, who agreed to confiscate his weapons. A psychiatric hospitalization was arranged and accepted by the patient.

This case illustrates the need for the ER doctor (or outpatient doctor) to listen closely to the patient's physical complaint, which may contain a communication beyond the manifest complaint. This man's complaint of chest pain was a somatic derivative of the depression and possibly a symbolic expression of a "broken heart." A full history revealed a major depressive disorder and unresolved grief reaction. This depression contained morbid rumination with suicidal ideation and homicidal ideation. In addition to psychiatric hospitalization, this clinical treatment plan necessitated informing the family about the risk of having firearms available to a man with depression and suicidal or homicidal ideation. The patient consented to having the family informed of the team's concerns about the weapons and the recommendation that they be confiscated. If the patient had refused consent in this regard, forensic consultation around duty to inform and warn would have been indicated.

Personality Disorder with Multiple Suicide Attempts: Evaluation in the ER Setting

A twenty-one-year-old college student was directed by her therapist to the ER after she called and told the therapist that she had taken an overdose of Zoloft (sertraline). Her psychopharmacologist was on the hospital staff. The patient carried the diagnosis of personality disorder and depression. She took the overdose impulsively after becoming angry at her therapist and upset over stress at school. She had a history of several prior overdoses, only one of which necessitated psychiatric hospitalization. The patient arrived at the ER and was given Ipecac. Psychiatric consultation revealed a sullen but engageable young woman who apologized for her behavior and said she would understand if everyone was angry with her and wanted to hospitalize her. She denied acute suicidal ideation and talked about the impulsive overdose. After the initial psychiatric evaluation, the patient was left to medical attention and subsequently eloped from the ER. She called the ER from her therapist's office and returned after attending her regularly scheduled appointment with her therapist. She had taken a taxi both ways in her hospital robe and street jacket! In consultation with her therapist, she was discharged home to see her therapist again the next day. The anxiety generated by this patient's behavior in ER staff was addressed with the staff as part of the consultation.

Patients with personality disorder, chronic depression, and emotional instability often present with a history of recurrent suicide attempts. The provocative behavior invites a response to punish the patient or to treat the patient as a helpless child. The patient's initial phone call provoked a rapid response from the therapist, which was appropriate. In the ER, however, with the patient's elopement and return, the staff had to choose between a possibly unnecessary psychiatric hospitalization (though experienced by the patient as punitive and as infantilizing) or returning her to her therapist in an attempt to increase autonomy.

In this situation the clinical decision was made in the context of ongoing treatment and the availability of that treatment after discharge. Documentation was made that this patient will remain a chronic suicide risk but was not an acute risk.

Consultation to the ER staff focused on the anger the patient stimulated with her behavior and the desire of the staff to respond to the anger by moving the patient to a psychiatric hospital. The patient kept her appointment with the therapist, and at follow-up two years later had not made another suicide attempt.

MEDICAL SYSTEMS AND MEDICAL CARETAKERS

The medical setting differs from psychiatric facilities in a number of essential aspects. In addition, there have been dramatic changes in the health care delivery system in the past twenty years. The length of stay in medical hospitals has halved from approximately ten days to five or under. The level of morbidity on discharge has markedly increased, and many patients are discharged from the hospital in much sicker and more infirm states. Much more complicated care is now rendered at home or in a variety of extended care facilities such as rehabilitation hospitals, skilled nursing facilities, and nursing homes. Patients who in the past were not discharged until they were relatively self-sufficient and able to care for themselves, now leave the hospital still in need of a variety of sophisticated medical procedures, such as home intravenous therapy and other treatments. This change is relevant because earlier studies in general hospitals showed clusters of suicidal behavior at the end of the hospital stays. With shorter hospital stays and earlier discharges, the risk of suicide may shift to these outpatient settings and even to the patient's home. In the earlier studies, suicide gestures at the end of hospitalization often were aimed at delaying discharge (Reich and Kelly, 1976). Subtle or intermittent confusional states of delirium may also be missed before discharge, and this also shifts the risk to outpatient and other settings (see earlier case vignette earlier under "Rational Suicide").

The dramatic changes in health care are paralleled by an explosion in hospital construction and changes in architecture. Hospitals with opening windows, balconies, open stairwells, and access to roofs and porches have been replaced by safer, more restricted, and environmentally controlled buildings with less inherent possibilities for suicide risk. Other changes such as centrally located nursing stations with the capacity to view most patient rooms and glass walls and partitions in intensive care units contribute to safer and more controlled surroundings.

Some changes, however, have probably raised the risk. Tertiary care institutions, often large urban institutions, are growing while smaller more personal community hospitals are losing beds and closing. These larger institutions, though rendering technologically superior care, may be less able to respond to emotional and psychological needs. The demands for greater productivity from smaller staffs and increasing reliance on technology regrettably makes it unlikely that doctors, nurses, and others will be found as often at the bedside listening and talking to patients. The older models of "the doctor" and the "head nurse" have given way to multidisciplinary teams organized by specialty and organ system. It is often difficult to know who has primary responsibility for the psychosocial aspects of care. The implications for the care of the suicidal patient are obvious.

The doctor-patient relationship of the past now more resembles a loose contract with a medical team composed of doctors, nurses, psychiatrists, social workers, physician assistants, and many others, all of whom will have contact, usually brief, with a patient in the course of any given day. For the acutely ill patient and his family, this situation is bewildering, as they struggle to discover who is in charge. Because the contacts with the patient are so brief and so focused around narrow medical issues, the possibility of a true relationship and treatment alliance is less common than it was previously. Though this is true for all patients, it is a more serious issue for patients following a suicide attempt and for those at risk for suicide.

Psychiatrists are also affected. They are pressured more for medical and neurologic recommendations and decisions about medications than for providing psychiatric and emotional care for the patient. They are too often most valued for a ready psychiatric disposition at the moment of medical discharge. The psychiatrist must be aware of these pressures and avoid being marginalized merely to the role of neuropsychiatrist, psychopharmacologist, or discharge planner. The patient and the family are most likely to find the primary nurse and the psychiatrist to be the key people on the treatment team and often the most accessible.

Suicide Watch and Sitters

Following a serious suicide attempt, the person who has the most contact with the patient would probably become "the sitter." This is likely to be a person without any formal medical or nursing training whose function is literally to sit in the patient's room and call for help if anything unusual takes place. These individuals are often not actual employees of the hospital but are provided by temporary agencies for this sitting activity on an eight-hour shift basis. There are often serious cultural and language limitations, and sitters cannot be used for other tasks should the patient no longer be suicidal or ready to be discharged. When the sitters are discontinued, the patient is regarded as requiring only ordinary or routine care. The most serious implication for the use of sitters with a suicidal patient is that it is functionally an all-or-nothing situation—the patient either receives constant observation or nothing more than regular medical monitoring and care (see earlier discussion). This makes the psychiatric assessment of present suicidality all the more critical, and often results in continuing sitters for longer than is necessary.

Approaches that are inappropriate in psychiatric settings in the management of acutely suicidal patients are not uncommon in medical hospitals. This includes using family members or friends to sit with the patient for extended periods, including entire shifts on occasion. Such an approach may be influenced by staffing and other factors not directly related to the patient, but it can be more beneficial than the physical presence of a sitter with whom the patient cannot communicate or finds frightening. Constant observation is certainly preferable to the use of physical restraints, which can cause distress and agitation. Family members or others with the patient work collaboratively with the nursing and psychiatrist staff. Input from those who have known the patient prior to the suicide attempt often will be very useful in the assessment of current suicidal risk and in making the most informed discharged planning.

Contracts of Safety

Chapter Twenty-Six provides a sophisticated discussion of no-suicide contracts, or contracts for safety. Acuity of medical problems and level of illness place practical limitations on a hospitalized patient's capacity to effectuate a suicidal plan and will also probably limit the patient's capacity to make relationships. Because medical hospitalizations are so brief and so many people have brief contact with the patient, it is unlikely that relationships of sufficient depth will form to make contracts for safety particularly meaningful. Although suicide prevention through no-suicide contracts is problematic in medical hospitals, asking patients about their current suicidal feelings is useful.

The management of suicide risk in the medical hospital is primarily based on the active treatment of medical problems such as delirium, focused psychiatric treatment including ECT, and, if needed, physical restraints for patient safety. The psychiatrist in the medical setting needs to be particularly informed about medications and drug interactions to be helpful in the medical management of patients. The psychiatrist here also has an important educational role, including setting up a structured care plan and stressing the risk of delirium in suicide.

In recent years in psychiatry there has been a medicalization of depression and an enthusiasm for antidepressant medications. This has fed a bias toward biological causes of depression and less emphasis on the interpersonal components of depression and suicide. Medical colleagues are easily persuaded by this view and bias, because they have seen a similar explosion of biological treatments in the medical field. This can be a problem, for example, if the medical or nursing staff assumes that antidepressant medications can diminish or substantially remove suicide risk within a few days.

There is an allied issue about antidepressants for the depressed patient who is not suicidal. As a practical matter, it is almost impossible to assess the benefit of antidepressant medications in the span of a medical hospitalization. The patient's mood and outlook often vary with the state of the underlying medical problem. The hospital-based psychiatrist should be reluctant to change the antidepressant regimen of the patient in current psychiatric treatment. Any changes in antidepressant regimens should be done in respectful consultation with the psychiatrist who will be following the patient after discharge. Even suicide attempts should not invite gratuitous changing of antidepressant medication without such consultation.

Outpatient Medical Care and Suicide Prevention

The following vignette illustrates inappropriate voluntary hospitalization as a result of systems problem in a hospital setting.

A thirty-seven-year-old separated woman with severe systemic lupus erythematosus (SLE) began to experience auditory hallucinations. Her medical illness began acutely approximately two years earlier when she developed shortness of breath, high fever, and delirium, requiring a prolonged ICU admission with ventilator support. She required resuscitation several times. She also required pacemaker implantation and was unconscious for close to thirty days. Following her acute care, she was transferred to a rehabilitation hospital, where she "learned to walk and talk again." The auditory hallucinations started after she returned home. Initially there were single words and phrases and then whole paragraphs, which seemed very real and outside her head. The voices became increasingly critical, intrusive, and frightening. Initially, she did not complain about these voices, but mentioned it to a cardiologist during a routine follow-up visit for her pacemaker. The cardiologist sent her to the hospital's ER for psychiatric evaluation. There the on-call psychiatric resident felt that she was acutely in danger, presumably from self-injurious behavior, and arranged for an involuntary hospitalization. She remained in the psychiatric hospital for three days, where she was treated with antipsychotic medications, and left as soon as she was allowed. The auditory hallucinations continued, but she avoided all contact with psychiatrists for about one and a half years before accepting another referral.

Although auditory hallucinations could suggest an acute and unstable psychosis, the decision to involuntarily hospitalize this patient was premature and probably unwise. The worst consequence was the creation of distrust and avoidance of contact with psychiatrists, which lasted for some time. Involuntary hospitalizations should never be pursued without a compelling, well-grounded, and intuitive sense that a patient is in a life-threatening situation. It should never be an automatic, self-protective response to a circumstance suggesting that the patient might be suicidal. One suspects that this patient would not have been hospitalized had she been dealing with a clinician who knew her or a psychiatrist with experience with organic mental syndromes who could put her symptoms in better perspective. As it happened, this patient's transfer to the ER created an ersatz emergency which reflexively fed an inappropriate and counterproductive psychiatric hospitalization.

Cultural and System Changes

There are some who believe that increased integration of psychiatric practice into outpatient medical settings and a drift away from mental health clinics and psychiatric hospitals are inevitable. All health care institutions are undergoing profound changes in culture and organization. An increasing percentage of care is being "managed." It is inevitable that psychiatric practices will change. Certainly there have been changes in the culture of medical settings. Not long ago it was common to hear the term *family doctor* or individuals pursuing training in *family practice.* These terms have all but dropped from the medical lexicon to be replaced by *primary care* and *primary care providers* and *PCPs.* These terms describe widely disparate practices. They can represent physicians who know their patients well and have followed them for a number of years, or they can mean a "doc in a box" and refer to physicians whose function is primarily to triage all but the simplest problems. Regrettably, these terms might signify a commissioned medical broker as a substitute for an actual provider of medical services. The patient's primary care physician today may not be in the network of the new insurer chosen by the patient's employer next year. The pressure for efficiency can be an incentive to restrict and ration care, and to justify poor care. A common expectation of the proponents of these new arrangements is that the primary care physician will take on greater portions of the psychiatric and other medical specialty care and will be selective and parsimonious in referring to specialists of all types.

Terms like *covered lives, clients,* and *subscribers* have replaced the term *patient* in the business-speak of these organizations. And *risk* or *at risk* refers to *consuming* medical resources rather than *patient risk, medical risk,* or *suicidal risk.* Even with the increasing time pressures, it is doubtful that a shortcut will be found to spending unhurried, quiet moments with the patient, listening for depression and potential suicidal risk. Suicidal patients who are ambivalent debate in their own minds about seeking help. If they are hurried or perceive the physician to be inconvenienced by getting into this complicated area, they will opt for silence. As noted, up to two-thirds of patients who commit suicide have had contact with medical caretakers within weeks of the act (Matthews et al., 1994; Hirschfeld and Russell, 1997). This indicates, unfortunately, that the suicidality or its seriousness was not picked up and effectively addressed.

> A fifty-year-old woman presented to the ER with major depressive disorder, suicidal ideation, and the question of new neuropsychiatric deficits (decreased memory, inattention). A preliminary neurologic evaluation was unrevealing, and the psychiatrist recommended psychiatric hospitalization. The managed care company refused approval for psychiatric transfer, claiming the patient warranted a medical admission to neurology. The medical house staff refused admission, emphasizing that the neuropsychiatric evaluation could be performed on an outpatient basis. The psychiatric consultant refused to send the patient home and had to go through several layers of appeal to gain psychiatric hospitalization. She sought supervisory consultation and was advised not to discharge the patient until approval for psychiatric admission was obtained or until the managed care group assumed responsibility for the patient in their emergency triage setting. It took more than eight hours of phone calls and appeals to resolve the dilemma around hospitalization.

Courts have ruled that the physician who complies with third party payors in decisions made about patients, without protest and when his medical judgment dictates otherwise, is the one ultimately responsible for the outcome of the decision. Although from a forensic standpoint this responsibility is shared with the third party, the individual clinician must never make a decision regarding the management of a suicidal patient to comply with pressures exerted by managed care. Any disagreement with a third party payor must be appealed, and the medical judgment of the responsible clinician should never be relegated to the third party. Although this can cause "systems" conflict, the clinician's ultimate responsibility is to the patient (see Chapter Thirty-One).

The evaluation and management of suicidal patients is invariably time-intensive and unavoidably requires the attention of a trained professional. A trained professional is, of course, more expensive than physician extenders of whatever sort, or questionnaires filled out in a waiting area. But evaluation and management by a trained professional is more likely to identify individuals at risk, and therefore to add to acute cost or expense. Medical business organizations can regard suicidal liability as merely a cost of doing business. This is very different from the traditional medical culture and its values (McArthur and Moore, 1997).

In the changing medical world psychiatrists will more and more be called on to educate colleagues in primary care and specialties about identifying suicidal patients. But even if more professionals are involved, suicide evaluations take time—each minute takes sixty seconds and each hour sixty minutes.

IMPLICATIONS FOR THE CLINICIAN

In review, the foregoing discussion has the following implications for the clinician:

- Decisions about disposition of patients after suicide attempts should be made only after psychiatric consultation because of the serious implications of releasing patients still at risk as well as the stigmatization of involuntary hospitalization.

- Intoxication is a confounding circumstance and an opportunity. Patients might reveal serious feelings of despair that might be denied when the patient is sober.

- Make every effort to collect information from all sources—police, ambulance, attendants, friends, family, security personnel, those who discovered the attempt—and also inquire about physical evidence at the scene.

- Many patients are limited acutely in what they can say about their state of mind and circumstances at the time of the act, and suicide notes, though helpful, are rare.

- Some data is for all intents unknowable in the emergency room, and the evolution of the mental status over time is often the most reliable indication of suicide risk.

- Suicide watch in the hospital is, as a practical matter, all-or-nothing; the patient is either under constant observation by a "sitter" or just another patient on the floor.

- Improvements in depressed affect in a typical medical stay (days) are probably not due to antidepressant medication but to psychological and interpersonal factors.

- Despite the seriousness and poor prognosis of many medical conditions, suicide is relatively rare. However, certain illnesses have relatively high suicide rates, including chronic renal failure, head and neck cancers, HIV or AIDS, lupus, SCI, Huntington's disease, and others (see Table 28.1).

- Though medical progress and changes have made the hospital setting physically safer, they have probably lessened the opportunity for meaningful treatment relationships. This has implications for the understanding of the patient's inner emotional state as well as for reliance on contracts for safety, or no-suicide contracts, in medical facilities.

- The culture and forms of medical care are changing to prize efficiency and mitigate against ongoing primary medical relationships and the concept of family doctor, thus reducing the likelihood that medical caretakers will have the inclination or the time to explore a patient's feelings of depression and suicide.

CHAPTER TWENTY-NINE

Suicide Assessment in the Primary Care Setting

Michael Craig Miller, M.D.
Randall Howard Paulsen, M.D.

There is strong evidence that many depressed and suicidal patients seek care first from their primary care physicians (Regier, Goldberg, and Taube, 1978), a tendency reinforced by the managed health care gatekeeper model. Perhaps half of all depressed patients receive their treatment from an internist or family practitioner (Regier et al., 1988b). Access to collaboration with psychiatric colleagues is a key element for primary care providers to be able to care for these patients. In the primary care setting, one may think of psychiatrists as collaborative primary care providers rather than specialists (Paulsen, 1996).

Primary care physicians are aware of the burden of psychopathology in their practices and request active involvement from mental health clinicians. They also know that psychiatric symptoms are important from a risk management perspective, that is, these physicians may be held accountable for patients who attempt or commit suicide. In suicide-related claims for a large insurance underwriter for general hospitals and physicians in the Boston area, 42 percent of the physicians named as defendants were nonpsychiatric, and 30 percent of those cases involved patients being cared for in nonpsychiatric settings. Thus, all physicians will find it helpful to be familiar with clues that might suggest the presence of suicidal thoughts, know how to respond, and know when to refer for psychiatric evaluation.

The purpose of this chapter is to heighten physician awareness of general principles of suicide risk assessment, help them identify patients who might be at increased risk for suicide, and provide guidance about the evaluation and treatment of primary care patients in whom suicide risk is suspected. We will refer also to areas of collaboration at the interface of primary care and psychiatry, which may be an indispensable part of reducing the risk of suicide among populations at risk.

A FOUNDATION FOR UNDERSTANDING

The modern study of suicide began with the work of French sociologist Emile Durkheim. In his 1897 treatise, *Le Suicide,* Durkheim (1951) attributed suicide to the failed relationship of the individual to society. The suicidal person either feels he must sacrifice himself for society ("altruistic" suicide), has poor social supports ("egoistic" suicide), or feels cut off from society ("anomic" suicide). Shrinking resources in medicine force the physician to consider the needs of patients in the context of the community they live in, giving Durkheim's model a new relevance. A primary care physician's knowledge of the patient's social context or support system is an important source of information.

Today's views of the psychological lives of depressed, suicidal patients commence with Freud (1917), who understood melancholia or depression as hostility aimed at the self, hostility that derives from ambivalent feelings about loved ones. Some depressed individuals may have not developed the psychological tools to be able to tolerate the vicissitudes (or take the good with the bad) in important relationships.

Another basic concept relating to suicide risk is the problem of self-esteem. In the absence of a healthy self-concept, an individual may be extraordinarily vulnerable. Interpersonal relationships may be shallower, leading to deficits in actual or perceived social support. Clinicians interested in existential theory note that any individual may have trouble finding meaning in life, a situation that can lead to suicidal thoughts (Yalom, 1980).

A history of chaotic, traumatic, or neglectful family relationships may lead to the development of personality disorders, in which a patient may be plagued by persistent feelings of emptiness and isolation or with difficulties managing anger. These patients may be particularly ill equipped to deal with ordinary frustration and may easily fall into suicidal despair (Gunderson, 1985).

Even a person with normative psychological reserves may be overwhelmed by a catastrophic stress (Greenspan and Samuel, 1989). In the primary care setting, suicide risk is often abruptly increased when a dreadful diagnosis is communicated to a patient or when a terrible illness fails to respond to treatment (Fawcett, 1972). The shock can overwhelm a patient's coping capacity. Experienced primary care physicians often arrange for a family member to be present when they deliver such news and then ask for a follow-up call from the patient and family within twenty-four hours. These actions can be taken whether or not a psychiatric referral is sought.

In today's multicultural medical care setting, it is important to take cultural tradition into account. For example, suicide for a Japanese patient who has experienced a great humiliation does not run counter to the cultural expectations in the same way that it would in American or European traditions.

Recent biomedical developments demonstrate that the biology of depression is not to be underestimated, even when life stresses or medical setbacks would seem to explain a patient's despondency. A major metabolite of serotonin, 5-hydroxyindoleacetic acid (5-HIAA), has been found in lower concentrations in the cerebrospinal fluid of patients who commit suicide (Stanley and Stanley, 1990). Studies in twin populations and homogeneous ethnic groups have shown genetic links to suicidal behavior (Lester, 1996; Roy, Rylander, and Sarchiapone, 1997b). Although there are no clinical laboratory tests available to detect the presence of a mood disorder or determine suicide risk, the weight of genetic evidence does show that suicide, like affective disorder and alcoholism, runs in families. It is therefore useful to ask about family history of suicide where there is depression or suicidal thoughts.

Suicide Risk Factors in the Primary Care Setting

Family, social, and psychiatric histories are useful to identify higher-risk patients. Three important identifiers likely to emerge in a medical evaluation are a history of previous suicide attempts by the patient, the presence of a diagnosis of depression or substance abuse, and a history of suicide in a first-degree relative (Hirschfeld and Russell, 1997). Primary care physicians may be in a good position to learn about major losses (a spouse, a job, or physical functioning) in the lives of their patients. At particularly high risk are older male patients, since men commit suicide four times as often as women and suicide risk increases with age.

Screening tests for suicide are neither sensitive nor specific. Use of risk factors to identify high-risk patients always yields numerous false positives, and those criteria used to define lower risk always yield some false negatives. Thus, the application of risk factors is of limited use. However, for general populations, an increase in sensitivity in all physicians to the issue of suicide will lead to good, direct questions about intent, plan, supports, and the need for psychiatric follow-up and assessment.

Suicide intent is state dependent; that is, it is not constant over time in an individual. Suicide intent varies widely with the level of stress, fluctuations in any underlying psychiatric disorder, and internal psychological factors. Once a patient has experienced a suicidal state, there is a greater likelihood of repeated episodes (Hirschfeld et al., 1983). The primary care provider can label suicide as an active problem for discussion. Keeping the concern about suicide an active part of the ambulatory problem list can eventually result in successful referral, evaluation, and treatment and to meaningful changes in the patient's experience of hopelessness about life circumstances.

There is no reason that the inherent limitations on predicting suicide should lead to nihilism. Turning the treatment focus to the possible causes of suicidal behavior in the context of a stable primary care alliance may reduce the number of suicides over a large population of patients. Patients and families can help their doctors monitor the level of risk and the need for treatment over time. Primary care physicians who do not hesitate to ask direct questions about suicide do the best screening. By identifying illnesses that give rise to suicide and using the primary care relationship to keep suicide on the active problem list, we move closer to the public health goal of reducing the overall number of suicides.

The Suicide Population

One excellent reason for primary care physicians to be concerned about suicide is that 75 percent of suicides have had contact with a physician within six months prior to their death, and 50 percent of suicides have never had psychiatric contact (Blumenthal, 1988). More than three-quarters of individuals seek medical care rather than psychiatric care during their first emotional crisis (Schulberg and Burns, 1988). A third of all primary care patients may be depressed, and of all patients being treated for depression, half of them are treated in the medical setting (Katon and Schulberg, 1992).

In 1996, there were approximately 30,862 suicides in the United States, making it the ninth leading cause of death overall, accounting for 1.3 percent of all deaths, just behind HIV infection, which ranks eighth (Anderson, Kochanek, and Murphy, 1997). The national suicide rate has remained fairly constant over the past half-century, but there have been changes within demographic groups. The western and southern states have higher rates of suicide; there is some evidence that the suicide rate is correlated with the access to firearms (Lester and Murrell, 1980), which makes clinical sense since death by firearms is the leading cause of suicide in every region and a major public health issue.

Men commit suicide more commonly than women do, by a four-to-one ratio, despite the fact that women attempt suicide more frequently than men do, by a two-to-one ratio. The highest suicide rates are for people over age sixty-five, but suicide is the third leading cause of death for people ages fifteen to twenty-four after injuries and homicide, with an even more lopsided male-to-female ratio of six to one. The lifetime risk of suicide is increased for patients with mood disorders, schizophrenia, or alcoholism. Whites commit suicide more than blacks, but the rate is increasing dramatically among young black men (Holinger, Offer, and Ostrov, 1987). The rate of suicide among the Native American population is high (Dinges and Duong-Tran, 1994).

Violent methods of committing suicide are obviously more frequently lethal, with firearm deaths accounting for more than half of all suicides (55 to 60 percent). Hanging is the second most common way of committing suicide (14 percent). Ingestions and cutting are frequent methods for attempting suicide, but account for less than 15 percent of suicide deaths (Monk, 1987). Men are more likely to commit suicide by firearms, women by ingestion (Mościcki, 1995a).

Individuals who are divorced or separated, living alone, unemployed, or recently bereaved are also at higher risk. Interpersonal conflict or discord, chaos or abuse at home, or anything else that diminishes emotional support or causes humiliation can also precipitate suicidal action (Mościcki, 1995a).

Suicide Attempts

The risk of suicide for patients who make suicide attempts, or who hurt or mutilate without suicidal intent, may be underestimated. There is a tendency to dismiss self-destructive behavior as attention-getting "gestures." The use of the word *gesture* minimizes the significance of the action, since people who exhibit such behavior are at higher risk for suicide than the general population. They commit suicide at a rate of 1 percent per year (Goldstein, Black, Nasrallah, and Winokur, 1991); 10 to 20 percent eventually end their life by suicide (Hillard, 1995). Of those who die by suicide, 20 to 40 percent have made prior attempts (Cullberg, Wasserman, and Stefansson, 1988).

In contrast to those who complete suicides (men, older, using premeditated lethal methods), people making suicide attempts are more likely younger, are more frequently women, and are more impulsive. Mood disorders, alcoholism, and schizophrenia predominate in the group of patients who commit suicide, whereas suicide attempts are made more frequently by patients with personality or situational disorders, and those who are chemically dependent. (See Chapters Fifteen, Sixteen, and Seventeen.)

Self-mutilation is distinguished from suicide by the absence of the overt intention to die. Self-destructive acts, cutting being the most common (Bach-y-Rita, 1974), are often a form of self-punishment. Paradoxically, hurting oneself when one feels self-critical can be experienced as soothing. Much of this behavior is carried out in private, completely apart from the goal of getting attention. The psychological aims are internal and highly individual. These patients often carry diagnoses of borderline personality disorder, post-traumatic stress disorder, or dissociative disorder. (See Chapters Eight and Eighteen.)

In the wake of a suicide attempt, one evaluates the lethality of the attempt and the patient's intentions. Lethality refers to the choice of method and the circumstances of the attempt. A high degree of planning (such as going out of the way to arrange not to be discovered and rescued) indicates higher lethality. The patient's suicidal intent may be quite different from what the lethality indicates. The patient may have miscalculated the seriousness of the method, or his or her reality testing may be impaired.

A patient's intentions can be assessed in the reaction after the attempt. Is remorse or surprise expressed, or does the patient wish the attempt had succeeded?

CLINICAL EVALUATION OF
SUICIDE RISK BY PRIMARY CARE PHYSICIANS

The psychiatric interview and assessment for primary care physicians contain the following elements:

- Screening for symptoms of depression, anxiety, psychosis, and signs of substance abuse

- Asking about suicidal thoughts, plans, or behaviors

- Investigating the presence of medical conditions associated with suicide

- Searching for physiological or cognitive changes that may increase the risk of suicide

- Asking about any previous history of suicide attempts

Close collaboration with psychiatrists, psychologists, and psychiatric social workers can complement primary care physicians' skills in assessing risk, developing a psychiatric differential diagnosis, determining the dynamic meanings or motivation for suicide, assessing the patient's coping mechanisms, evaluating the social support system, and developing a comprehensive treatment plan for the suicidal patient.

Psychiatric Diagnosis

Increased risk of suicide is attached to almost every psychiatric disorder. In approximately four-fifths of all suicides, the victim has had a major depression, alcoholism, or a combination of the two (Fawcett et al., 1990). A minority of individuals with those disorders seek treatment.

Mood disorders carry a lifetime suicide risk of 15 percent and account for more than 60 percent of suicide deaths (van Praag and Plutchik, 1988). These disorders, particularly depression in all its forms, are highly prevalent: 10 percent of men and 25 percent of women will be depressed at some point in life. Table 29.1 sets out diagnostic criteria of major depression and dysthymia, a milder form of depression.

Risk is greatest when psychotic symptoms accompany a mood disorder (Black, Winokur, and Nasrallah, 1988), although the absence of psychosis does not imply safety. Anhedonia (a persistent lack of pleasure), anxiety, and hopelessness are associated with higher suicide risk (Silberman and Sullivan, 1984). The relationship to anxiety is particularly interesting since anxiety disorders themselves carry an increased risk of suicide. There is a great deal of comorbidity between alcoholism and affective disorder, and patients who are

Table 29.1. Diagnostic Criteria of Major Depression and Dysthymia.

Major Depressive Episode	
Criteria	Symptoms
By *DSM-IV* criteria, a patient must have at least five of these symptoms for two weeks; patient must have depressed mood or anhedonia.	Depressed mood
	Anhedonia (diminished interest or pleasure)
	Significant weight loss or gain
	Insomnia or hypersomnia
These symptoms must cause distress or impairment in functioning.	Psychomotor agitation or retardation
	Fatigue or low energy
	Feeling worthless or guilty
	Indecisiveness or poor concentration
	Thoughts of death or suicide

Dysthymia	
Patients with dysthymia have a chronically depressed mood during most days over a two-year period. By *DSM-IV* criteria, a patient must have at least two of the symptoms while depressed.	Poor appetite or overeating
	Insomnia or hypersomnia
	Low energy or fatigue
	Low self-esteem
	Poor concentration or indecisiveness
	Hopelessness
Usually symptoms are less severe than in a major depressive episode.	

actively drinking will be at some increased risk (Murphy, Wetzel, Robins, and McEvoy, 1992).

The pervasiveness of alcoholism in our society and the disinhibiting effects and impairment of judgment that are a feature of alcohol intoxication lead to its association with a disproportionate number of suicides. Although lifetime risk of suicide is 3 percent, alcohol is involved in up to half of all suicides. There is a particularly strong connection between alcohol and adolescent suicide (Murphy, Wetzel, Robins, and McEvoy, 1992). There is also significant comorbidity with both mood disorders and personality disorders in all age groups (Motto, 1980). Primary care training, and family practice as well, has successfully increased providers' use of screening tools. Use of simple, time-efficient questions has markedly increased detection of symptomatic drinking behavior (Murphy and Wetzel, 1990). Alcohol use is sometimes conceptualized as "self-treatment" for an anxiety or mood disorder. Suicide risk for alcoholics is greatest during periods of active drinking, during the second or third decade of illness, or if there is a recent or anticipated loss.

Patients with alcoholism and chemical dependency are easy to overlook in the medical setting. Not only is drug use often occult, but physicians may have experienced the sociopathic side of these patients (forging prescriptions or obtaining multiple prescriptions from different providers, for example). These negative experiences can naturally cause resentment in a well-meaning primary care provider, reducing the likelihood of exploring secondary depressive symptoms or suicidal thoughts.

The following questions provide an efficient screening tool for primary care providers:

- Have you felt you ought to *cut* down on your drinking or drug use?

- Have people *annoyed* you by criticizing your drinking or drug use?

- Have you felt bad or *guilty* about your drinking or drug use?

- Have you ever had a drink or used drugs first thing in the morning *(eye-opener)* to steady your nerves or get rid of a hangover or to get the day started?

These are called the CAGEAID questions, referring to the mnemonic CAGE Adapted to Include Drugs. (See Chapter Seventeen for more information on alcohol and substance abuse.)

Primary care physicians are often involved in the medical care of patients with chronic psychotic disorders. Schizophrenia is a diagnosis that is difficult to make, and its modern treatment is not generally the province of primary care providers. The affiliated mental health system should take the responsibility to educate medical colleagues about key disorders, with frequent updates on new medications, possible drug interactions, the role of stress, and the meaning of symptomatic exacerbations in the course of this illness. This collaborative channel of communication is indispensable to primary care providers if they are to play a useful part in the detection of increased suicidal risk in a psychotic patient.

The lifetime risk of suicide in this diagnosis is quite high—about 10 to 15 percent. One-third to one-half make suicide attempts (Cohen, Test, and Brown, 1990). Command hallucinations—voices that instruct the patient to commit suicide and also sometimes appear in mood disorders—should always be taken seriously when present, but are not clearly implicated in suicides. The following questions are useful for inquiring about the presence of psychotic symptoms:

- Have you ever had trouble with your thoughts?

- Have your thoughts ever been so confused that you lost track of your ideas?

- Are your thoughts ever frightening or disturbing?

- Do you ever feel as if you lose control of your thoughts?
- Have you ever felt that people were watching or following you? Have you ever felt people wanted to hurt you?
- Have your eyes or ears ever played tricks on you? Have you ever heard a voice when nobody else was with you or seen things that were not actually there?

The depression and demoralization of this chronic, deteriorating illness may lead to suicide (Drake, Gates, Cotton, and Whitaker, 1984). Learning of the diagnosis is a significant blow to self-esteem. Those most at risk are patients in early phases of the illness who had good prior functioning and recognize their own deterioration. For example, young, unemployed males who were functioning at a high level prior to the onset of illness are particularly at risk (Drake, Gates, Cotton, and Whitaker, 1984).

Akathisia, an uncomfortable adverse effect of antipsychotic medications, has also been implicated in suicide deaths. It can be easily mistaken for psychotic agitation by observers. If the clinician increases the dosage of antipsychotic medication and agitation gets worse instead of better, the diagnosis of akathisia should be considered. The patient may find it an unbearable symptom, similar to the intolerable nature of certain anxiety states. In its worst presentations, patients are unable to sit still, and they worry that they will never shake the feeling, which when combined with an attitude of demoralization can lead to suicidal action. Akathisia provides another example of the importance of adequate communication between psychiatric provider and primary care physician.

The important connection between anxiety or panic states and suicide has come to light only in this decade (Beck, Steer, Sanderson, and Skeie, 1991). The lifetime risk of suicide may be quite similar to mood disorders (Coryell, Noyes, and Clancy, 1982) when there is comorbidity (see Chapters One and Twenty-One). Severe anxiety and agitation may be more unbearable and demoralizing than depression and may be a significant state-of-mind factor and a direct cause for suicide.

Personality disorders, particularly borderline, narcissistic, histrionic, and dependent types, have a lifetime suicide risk of 7 percent (Gardner and Cowdry, 1985b). Traits that predispose to suicide are hostility, impulsiveness, aggression, social isolation, low self-esteem, helplessness, and negativity. Many of these patients have a pattern of poor adaptation and vulnerability to stress. They also may alienate important supports, such as family members and medical personnel. Mood disorders and chemical dependency are also commonly comorbid. Constitutional factors (genetic factors that affect the individual's emotional reactions to environmental strains) may have affected the individual's development. These patients are particularly at risk when they are under the sway of disinhibiting substances and at those times are especially prone to self-destructive behavior (Joffe and Regan, 1989).

Patients with personality disorders can have stormy interpersonal relationships, with ambivalent attachments to most of the people in their lives. They also have few tools to deal with the expectable difficulties of life, either at work or in intimate relationships. What tools they do have they have difficulty applying flexibly. Therefore, they tend to be emotionally more isolated than average. The treatment of these patients is made more difficult by a tendency of some to push caregivers away at the same time that they seek help, a characteristic sometimes named "help rejecting." They may come from unusually chaotic or traumatic backgrounds, leading many clinicians to emphasize the diagnosis of post-traumatic stress disorder (PTSD) rather than personality disorder. Psychiatrists are still struggling to define the limits of the diagnosis, but suspicion of trauma or abuse should lead the clinician to seek a family assessment voluntarily or involuntarily when mandated by law. It is often sensitive primary care physicians who detect domestic violence for the first time.

For many patients with personality disorders, suicide attempts may become a way of life, and it may become easy to dismiss their suicidal behavior as gestures or manipulations. They may express their anger or frustration through a variety of self-destructive acts. This group of patients may use self-mutilation as a way to control or modulate painful emotions. Some do in fact go on to suicide.

Medical Populations

Geriatric patients are a particularly important group because they have frequent complex comorbid medical problems. As the demographic data suggest, suicide rates increase with age, and older men are particularly prone to suicide. Those men who have used action rather than language to cope with emotional stress may be more at risk later in life if their activity is curtailed and if they are unable to discuss depression or suicidal feelings openly. A form of mood disorder called masked depression (Johnston and Walker, 1996) consists of prominent vegetative or somatic symptoms of depression in the absence of any awareness of depressed mood. Here the primary care provider, with or without a consulting or collaborating psychiatrist, may initiate an empirical trial of an antidepressant after a thorough search for possible medical causes of loss of energy and appetite. Such patients can respond well to antidepressant treatment, with a broadening range of affect and a retrospective subjective improvement in mood.

Higher suicide rates are generally associated with diagnoses of cancer (Allebeck, Bolund, and Ringback, 1989; Allebeck and Bolund, 1991), AIDS and HIV infection (McKegney and Ma, 1992; Marzuk et al., 1988; Perry, Jacobsberg, and Fishman, 1990), peptic ulcer disease (Katon and Sullivan, 1990), renal failure, epilepsy (Carrieri et al., 1993), Huntington's chorea, multiple sclerosis, and spinal cord injuries. Patients with delirium must also be watched carefully, especially if they are also overtly depressed (Reich and Kelly, 1976). The statistical correlations between these populations and suicide should not lull the clinician, however, into believing that depression is a normal consequence of chronic, severe medical illness. In fact, these depressions can and often do respond to psychiatric treatment. For a more in-depth discussion of medical settings and suicide, see Chapter Twenty-Eight.

ELEMENTS OF SUICIDE ASSESSMENT IN PRIMARY CARE

Knowledge about suicide is of little use to primary care physicians without a practical way of putting that knowledge to use in the clinical setting. A greater familiarity with the epidemiology of suicide and the association of suicide with demographic and diagnostic groups will increase the likelihood that a physician will detect patients at risk. On an operational and pragmatic level, providers will be more inclined to ask about clinical problems when they know that consulting help is available. Since internists expect to be interrupted by telephone calls and pagers, they are most comfortable with psychiatrists who make rapid contact. This type of access functionally improves the effectiveness of psychiatric consultation, referral, and crisis management (Paulsen, 1996).

Since patients at risk often are ambivalent about discussing depression or suicide, the first challenge is to create opportunities for them to talk about these subjects. The physician can create an opening by asking about depressive symptoms. He or she might notice sadness or sullenness, low energy, paucity of speech, or the psychomotor retardation of depression. Questions about the patient's appetite, weight, sleep, sexual activity, and capacity for pleasure can routinely become part of the review of systems. These items are summarized in Table 29.2. The screening effort can be integrated naturally into practice by keeping materials about depression in waiting rooms or other patient areas— for example, hospital cafeterias or admitting areas. There are many succinct, well-designed, and informative pamphlets available from organizations such as the American Psychiatric Association, the U.S. Public Health Service, and the Alliance for the Mentally Ill.

Table 29.2. Identifying the Depressed Patient.

Observations	Symptoms
Sadness or sullenness	Decreased appetite
Low energy	Change in weight
Paucity of speech	Sleep disorder
Psychomotor retardation of depression	Decreased sexual activity
	Decreased capacity for pleasure

A routine review of potential risk factors for suicide can be included when depression or suicidal thoughts are suspected (see Table 29.3). The clinician can make note of current or past substance abuse; ask about a family history of suicide or mood disorder or other psychiatric illness; and inquire about the patient's social supports, current employment or marital status, or recent losses. Many physicians use general health questionnaires as part of a medical evaluation; such questionnaires should contain sections on psychiatric symptoms, marital and employment status, or the occurrence of stressful events.

These suggestions can be applied according to the provider's judgment about a patient's needs at a given time. Primary care physicians are faced with many competing clinical and administrative pressures that make it impossible for psychiatric review items to be addressed at every visit. Especially when other acute medical problems are present, the psychiatric issues will fall toward the periphery. In some settings, where the primary care group has decided to include psychiatrists as part of the practice, ongoing relationships allow "curbside" consults and a heightened awareness of psychiatric issues. This organizational or structural solution can help keep psychiatric problems in the mainstream (Paulsen, 1996).

Some primary care physicians take advantage of a medical hospitalization as a time to introduce a psychiatric evaluation, especially in hospitals where psychiatric consultation services are available. Since families converge on the hospital during visits, a social worker may more easily evaluate the support network.

Table 29.3. Risk Factors for Suicide.

Under Age Thirty	Over Age Thirty
Family history of suicide	Family history of suicide
Males more than females	Males more than females
History of previous attempts	History of previous attempts
Native American	Native American
Psychiatric diagnosis: mood disorders and substance abuse	Psychiatric diagnosis: mood disorders, schizophrenia, alcoholism
White more than black	Single, especially separated, widowed or divorced
Miniepidemic in community	
History of delinquent or semi-delinquent behavior, even without current depression	Lack of social supports
	Concurrent medical illness(es)
	Unemployment
Presence of firearms (when other factors are present)	Decline in socioeconomic status
	Psychological turmoil

Source: GL Klerman, Clinical epidemiology of suicide, *The Journal of Clinical Psychiatry.* 48[12, Suppl]:33–38, 1987. Copyright 1987, Physicians Postgraduate Press. Reprinted by permission.

Although most pharmacological interventions are quite safe, it can be even easier to start a psychotropic medication in the hospital, especially if there is concern about adverse reactions or drug-drug interactions.

Asking About Suicide

Even for the physician sensitive to suicide risk, it is a significant hurdle to learn how to ask direct questions about suicide. Many clinicians have an automatic tendency to be reassuring and optimistic. Although it is always the physician's job to offer hope and succor, a cheerful appeal may give the patient the message to keep troubling thoughts quiet. The patient may then go away feeling alienated and may be less likely to get help. Instead of trying to "cheer up" the patient, the physician can offer reassurance and hope based on the idea that effective treatment is available for depression and other psychiatric illnesses and then offer to initiate that help.

Depressed and suicidal patients can present varied and subtle challenges to the practitioner. It may be simplest to invite the patient to talk in general terms about the sources of his or her distress with follow-up review of systems questions about depression. At the very least, expressing this interest can reassure the patient that raising the issues with their doctor was the right thing to do. If a patient cannot cooperate with the primary care physician's exploration or evaluation, it is a good indication for urgent referral to a colleague or an emergency service. The primary care provider needs to know that in most jurisdictions, any physician is entitled to initiate an emergency order for psychiatric evaluation if he or she perceives a high degree of perceived risk in the patient,

The following questions provide a suggested script to use when suicidal thoughts may be present:

- How depressed (or sad) do you get? Ever so depressed that you think that life is not worth living?
- Do you think of acting on the feelings by hurting yourself or taking your own life?
- What kinds of ideas do you have about suicide?
- When do you feel most like hurting yourself?
- Do you have a plan?
- When would you be tempted to implement such a plan?
- Do you have the means to implement the plan?
- How do you actually react in situations that trigger thoughts of suicide?
- What might you do to stop yourself, or are you not interested in stopping yourself?
- Are you frightened by the temptation to take your own life?
- What do you think of suicide as a solution to your troubles?

Evaluating a Suicide Plan

When asking about depressive symptoms or suicidal feelings or plans, it is simplest to follow the well-worn path that any doctor follows when elucidating a chief complaint or a positive item on the review of symptoms. For example, we ask a patient who has chest pain to describe the feeling: when did it start, how often does it occur, how long does it last, and how bad is it? The same kinds of questions apply to suicide: what is the content of the patient's thoughts, when did they start, how often do they occur, and how long do they last? Additional specific questions focus on whether the patient plans to act or is plagued more by a passive wish for death, such as, "I sometimes wish I wouldn't wake up in the morning." Does the patient ruminate about death or feel unable to control suicidal impulses? Is there a particular motivation for committing suicide or avoiding suicide?

The primary care physician may feel more comfortable deferring the evaluation of a suicide plan to a psychiatrist or other mental health professional. However, if a patient admits to planning suicide, it may help to collect some information about that plan. A key item to determine is the method under consideration by the patient. Lethal methods of suicide such as shooting and hanging are quite worrisome and make the need for referral urgent, especially if the means are immediately available to the patient. If there are firearms in the home, they can be removed to another location by a family member; the police are often willing to hold guns if there is no other safe and inaccessible place to put them.

The extent of the patient's planning is also significant. Is the patient's plan feasible? Is the patient capable of isolating himself or herself so as not to be rescued? Is the patient putting his or her affairs in order, for example, by making a will or giving away possessions? There may be both overt and covert goals intended by the suicide plan. One important distinction is between the wish to die and the wish to hurt oneself. The symbolic aims of suicide are important but may be left for a mental health clinician to explore. Any overt suicidal behavior should not be minimized and should ultimately be the subject of a psychiatric evaluation.

An important special case is the patient who is in a terminal stage of a medical illness. Patients are entitled to make judgments about treatment and their own survival based on the current quality of life, the nature of relationships with loved ones, and the desire to retain their dignity. A physician may occasionally interpret as suicidal the refusal to participate in lifesaving or extended burdensome treatments.

It is often very difficult to distinguish a patient's wish for relief from suffering due to the illness or the treatment from a more active suicidal wish. The primary care relationship is indispensable in such cases. The modern primary care provider actively advocates for health care proxies and carries out the difficult but necessary discussions with patients about their wishes regarding care at the end of life. The relationship with the patient and family members is a genuine source of support. When a patient chooses to cease treatment, the primary care physician will have historical information that will help distinguish between a suicidal idea related to depression and a consistent, natural, and recognizable expression of the patient's values and character.

ROLE OF PRIMARY CARE IN TREATMENT

We do not expect primary care physicians to conduct treatment as psychiatrists do. They can and do intervene by providing realistic encouragement and support, addressing related medical conditions, and initiating treatment with an antidepressant.

Treatment of the Underlying Medical Condition

For patients who have the potential to commit suicide, certain early interventions may increase the possibility of diverting a lethal outcome. Such interventions overlap with good standard medical care, with the primary care physician attending carefully to the evaluation and treatment of possible medical causes of depression. In addition to medical illnesses, a variety of medications and substances are also commonly implicated in depression (see Table 29.4). It is often not enough to treat the underlying or related medical condition. The patient may improve somewhat, exposing a comorbid primary mood disorder requiring psychiatric evaluation, possible medication, and therapy.

In the primary care setting, Barrett, Barrett, Oxman, and Gerber (1988) and others have found that many treatment-responsive forms of depression do not meet *DSM-IV* criteria for depression, but fall into the "not otherwise specified" category of depression. Combined with full-fledged major depression, these two groups make a significant population of treatable depression. Frequently a course of treatment is begun on empiric grounds even when the patient does not meet the complete criteria for depression.

Psychiatric diagnoses may be included in an initial differential diagnosis, rather than making them "diagnoses of exclusion." Thus, if a patient is depressed or suicidal, basic psychiatric treatment can be initiated earlier in the course of the illness (rather than waiting to rule out all medical causes of the symptoms). This approach is also very important in panic disorder, where psychotherapy and early treatment with medication can prevent agoraphobic and dysfunctional medical utilization behaviors (for example, frequent urgent care visits or unnecessary invasive cardiac procedures).

A patient at risk for suicide should be referred but not dismissed. The relationship with the primary care physician has enormous value to the patient, and the connection can be sustaining. Furthermore, suicidal patients may be un-

Table 29.4. Medications and Substances Implicated in Depression.

Medical Causes	Medications and Substances
Cerebral neoplasm	ACTH/glucocorticoids
Cerebrovascular disease	Alcohol
Coronary artery disease	Alpha-methyldopa
Degenerative disorders	Anabolic steroids
Fahr's disease	Antipsychotics
Huntington's disease	Baclofen
Parkinson's disease	Benzodiazepines
Wilson's disease	Cimetidine
Endrocrine disorders	Clonidine
Addison's disease	Cycloserine
Cushing's disease	Digitalis
Diabetes mellitus	Disulfiram
Hyperthyroidism	Ethambutol
Hypothyroidism	Guanethidine
Pituitary disorders	L-dopa
Epilepsy	Metoclopramide
HIV	Nonsteroidal anti-inflammatory agents
Multiple sclerosis	Oral contraceptives
Systemic lupus erythematosus	Propranolol
	Ranitidine
	Reserpine
	Sulfonamides
	Thiazide diuretics

usually vulnerable and experience slights when they are certainly not intended. Thus, it is helpful for the physician to clarify the limits of her or his expertise, but emphasize that the problem is not entirely out of her or his province. By making follow-up appointments, the physician can demonstrate interest in the patient's psychiatric treatment and follow any medical conditions that may affect psychiatric symptoms or come up as a consequence of psychopharmacological treatment. In those settings where medical and psychiatric care are integrated, the patient will feel additionally reassured that he or she is not being referred to a "stranger." It also reinforces the idea that the psychiatric treatment is one of inclusion, not exclusion.

When an urgent evaluation is necessary, there may be a role for psychiatric hospitalization or some other intensive treatment setting, such as partial or day hospital, respite care, or emergency room evaluation. In general, physicians should consider hospitalization in the following situations:

- The patient's life appears to be in immediate danger.
- The patient has little or no viable family or community support.
- The patient exhibits extremely impulsive behavior or poor judgment.
- The patient has had a sudden change in mental status or decline in functioning.
- A comorbid medical or neurological problem makes the diagnostic problem particularly complex and impossible to evaluate in the out-patient setting.

Pharmacological Interventions

It is generally safe to offer treatment with an antidepressant if there is a suspicion that the patient meets criteria for a diagnosis of depression or dysthymia (see Table 29.1). The introduction of serotonin-specific reuptake inhibitors (SSRI) to the pharmacopoeia has made antidepressants easier to administer because they have more tolerable side effects and because dosing schemes are simpler. If the patient has target symptoms of depression, one might begin treating with sertraline 25 mg or fluoxetine 10 mg in the morning with food. These dosages are low, but the typical side effects of nausea, diarrhea, headache, or sleeplessness are often better tolerated or completely avoided if the dosage is increased slowly. After several days to a week on the initial dosage, it is generally safe to begin increasing the dosage incrementally, to 50 to 100 mg per day of sertraline or 20 to 40 mg per day of fluoxetine. Most patients who are going to respond will respond within two to four weeks on a therapeutic dosage. Sleeplessness, one of the most common side effects of these drugs, can often be safely managed with a small (25 to 50 mg) dosage of the sedating antidepressant trazodone in the evening.

There is a dispute whether the SSRIs are as effective as the older tricyclic antidepressants (TCA) in the treatment of some depressions. Assuming the patient does not have a conduction disturbance that can be exacerbated by TCAs, it is often quite safe to proceed with nortriptyline, initially with a dose of 10 to 25 mg at bedtime, titrating to a daily dosage of 50 to 100 mg as tolerated. The most common side effects of tricyclics are sedation and a variety of anticholinergic effects, including dry mouth, blurred vision, constipation, and urinary retention. If the patient tolerates the first few days of the initial dosage, it is safe to move the dosage up into the average therapeutic range. However, one may have to move more slowly if the side effects are marked or the patient is elderly. Serum levels can help determine the proper dosage. The common SSRI and TCA medications are summarized with starting and average dosages in Table 29.5.

A key concern in prescribing TCAs is the risk of overdose. These agents have a relatively low therapeutic index. They too frequently can cause fatal arrhythmias when taken even in a small overdose, making them more dangerous for patients whose intent to die is low but impulsively take a few extra pills, mis-

Table 29.5. Common Medications for Depression, with Dosages.

Agent (Trade Name)	Class	Starting Dosage	Average Dosage Range (Maximum)
Sertraline (Zoloft)	SSRI	25–50 mg	50–100 mg (200 mg)
Fluoxetine (Prozac)	SSRI	10–20 mg	20–40 mg (80 mg)
Paroxetine (Paxil)	SSRI	10–20 mg	20–30 mg (50 mg)
Nortriptyline (Pamelor/generics)	TCA	10–25 mg	75–100 mg (150 mg)
Amitriptyline (Elavil/generics)	TCA	25 mg	150–200 mg (300 mg)
Desipramine (Norpramin/generics)	TCA	25 mg	150–200 mg (300 mg)
Imipramine (Tofranil/generics)	TCA	25 mg	150–200 mg (300 mg)
Bupropion (Wellbutrin)	Other	75 mg	150–300 mg (450 mg)
Venlafaxine (Effexor)	Other	25–50 mg	150–300 mg (450 mg)
Nefazodone (Serzone)	Other	100–200 mg	300–600 mg (600 mg)
Mirtazapine (Remeron)	Other	15 mg	15–45 mg (45 mg)

calculating the risk of this action. The risk of arrhythmia should be clearly explained to the patient. Most psychiatrists argue that patients truly intending suicide can find other means, so TCAs should not be withheld if they are the drug of choice. However, it is safer at the beginning of treatment to dispense only a week's supply. This approach also reinforces weekly contact and follow-up. Once the patient is feeling better, it is safer to dispense more convenient quantities, as long as the risks of overdose have been outlined.

Since anxiety is a significant risk factor in some individuals, it is useful to consider the use of benzodiazepines in judicious dosages. Lorazepam (Ativan) 0.5 to 1.0 mg two to four times per day or clonazepam (Klonopin) 0.25 to 0.5 mg two to three times per day are safe dosages to start. We recommend avoiding shorter-acting benzodiazepines, like alprazolam (Xanax), because they may increase the potential for dependence and the risk for developing rebound anxiety. Although the potential for dependence or abuse in susceptible individuals is always of concern, it seems wise to err in the direction of a short course of benzodiazepines in an anxious or distraught patient who is considered at risk for suicide.

Some primary care physicians are less comfortable prescribing antipsychotic medications. Although these medications may be an important part of initiating treatment with a suicidal patient, the suspicion of psychosis may then prompt a rapid referral for management of psychotic symptoms.

When to Refer to a Psychiatrist

It is impossible to give specific recommendations about when to refer to a psychiatrist, because the level of comfort with psychiatric symptoms is so variable among primary care physicians. In systems where psychiatric and mental health services are more or less integrated into the system of primary care, primary care doctors tend to feel more comfortable taking on more of the psychiatric treatment and may have a higher threshold for referral. Much can be done in these systems through quick telephone consultations or a five-minute discussion in the corridor between offices.

An important rule in the use of a consultant is to refer when in any doubt about the diagnosis, the level of suicide risk, or the course of treatment. Some physicians who are comfortable treating depression in the absence of suicidal thoughts will want to refer to a psychiatrist if there is any mention of suicide in the evaluation.

The other advantage of referral has less to do with a physician's area of medical knowledge and more to do with the advantage of increasing the resources available to the patient. Treatment by a psychiatrist or other mental health professional allows more time for supportive psychotherapy. Social workers and resource personnel can focus on the issues of family support and other supportive structures.

Primary care physicians need no justification for referral to a psychiatrist beyond their own judgment. Certain clinical factors, parallel to suicide risk factors, may trigger a referral, including the severity of depressive, anxiety, or psychotic symptoms; the absence of family or social support; a family history of suicide; past history of a suicide attempt; the age and sex of the patient (older men); or a recent significant loss. See Table 29.6 for reasons to refer to a psychiatrist.

IMPLICATIONS FOR THE CLINICIAN

- Suicidal thoughts are a significant source of distress for patients of primary care physicians, and suicide is a significant source of risk for that population.
- Psychiatric liaison is an indispensable part of educating primary care physicians in the recognition and management of this problem. How-

Table 29.6. Reasons to Refer to a Psychiatrist.

Severe depressive or anxiety symptoms
Presence of significant suicidality
Any psychosis
Poor family or social support
Family history of suicide
Past history of suicide attempts
Patient's age and sex (older men)
Recent significant loss

ever, economic pressures give doctors little time for collaboration and also decrease the time available for seeking the warning signs of suicide.

- It is very helpful to have a network of consultants available to answer questions on the run and to accept referrals for evaluating complex problems. Such a network can include psychiatrists, psychologists, social workers, and psychiatric nurses who are comfortable working with the medical population. Psychiatrists are obviously best equipped to manage the psychopharmacological issues, but the other disciplines have much to offer regarding evaluation, psychotherapy, or family treatment.

- Comprehensive diagnostic evaluation is important, but with the costs of medical evaluation and treatment under close scrutiny, a number of factors may restrict the definition of comprehensiveness. The clinician should strive for balance between medical and psychiatric evaluation and try to give equal attention to biological and psychosocial evaluation and treatment. This balance can never be perfectly achieved, but keeping balance in mind can be a helpful guiding principle in the work with suicidal patients.

- One cannot determine with any certainty the acuity of an individual patient's suicide risk. We cannot rule out or rule in suicide risk on prognostic grounds alone. Once suicidal thinking has been observed and discussed, it is important to make it an active problem until significant change or treatment occurs. Patients are rarely, if ever, put off by a primary care physician's concern about their safety. Unfortunate outcomes can occur when a risk of suicide has been prematurely dropped from active consideration.

- The guidelines set forth in this chapter should not be used as rigid rules. Rather, they are a helpful source of information to guide primary care physicians in their work with a puzzling and humbling population of patients.

CHAPTER THIRTY

Suicide, Assisted Suicide, and Euthanasia

Herbert Hendin, M.D.

Euthanasia is a word coined from the Greek language (*eu* for "good or noble" and *thanatos* for "death") in the seventeenth century by Francis Bacon to refer to an easy, painless, happy death. In modern times it has come to mean the active causation of a patient's death by a physician, usually through the injection of a lethal dose of medication. In physician-assisted suicide, the patient self-administers the lethal dose, which has been prescribed by a physician who knows the patient intends to use it to end his or her life.

HISTORICAL BACKGROUND

Throughout history, individual philosophers from Plato and Seneca to Montaigne and Hume justified self-induced death for those who were severely sick and suffering. The idea that physicians should assist in the suicide, however, was not seriously proposed until the discovery in the last century of analgesics and anesthetics that could relieve suffering in dying patients as well as easily and painlessly end life (Emanuel, 1994).

Interest in medical euthanasia also coincided with the birth a century ago of the modern hospital as an institution that could provide curative medical and surgical treatment. As medical science learned to control acute infectious disease, and as life expectancy began its gradual increase from a norm of forty in 1850 to almost double that figure today, degenerative and late-onset diseases, of which cancer was the epitome, made the discussion of end-of-life care more urgent and the role of the physician more important. By the beginning of this century the principle of the *double effect* was introduced into medicine; that is, in the interests of relieving suffering it was appropriate to give treatments that risked death. The first articles advocating euthanasia in the context of modern medicine appeared in the United States and England in the 1870s. The first proposal for the legalization of euthanasia was made and defeated in Ohio in 1905. Following a similar defeat in Iowa, no further proposals were made in the United States for three decades.

Interest in euthanasia revived in the United States and was even stronger in England in the 1930s. Euthanasia societies were formed in both countries, and accounts of suffering patients who desired euthanasia began to appear, as well as accounts by physicians who had performed it surreptitiously. In 1936 the British House of Lords rejected by a vote of thirty-five to fourteen a bill to legalize euthanasia. In 1937 the Nebraska legislature also defeated such a proposal (Pappas, 1996).

The postwar revulsion to the use of euthanasia by German doctors to end the lives of mentally ill children and adults considered incurable, and subsequently to eliminate Jews, gypsies, and others designated as inimical to the so-called racial and genetic potential of the German people, discredited the movement. Modern medical technology that permits us to maintain a pointless semblance of life and creates fear of painful and undignified deaths was blamed for the revival of interest in euthanasia in the 1970s and 1980s, now centered on compassion for suffering patients. The Netherlands became the first country to give legal sanction to physician-assisted suicide and euthanasia. In 1994, Oregon became the only state to pass a law permitting physician-assisted suicide. In November 1997, that law was reaffirmed by Oregon voters.

ILLNESS, SUICIDE, AND ASSISTED SUICIDE

People assume that seriously or terminally ill people who wish to end their lives are different from those who are suicidal for other reasons. Yet clinicians who treat such patients know otherwise. Terror, depression, and a wish to die are the first reactions of many people who learn that they have a serious or deadly illness. Such patients are not significantly different from people who meet other crises with the desire to end the crisis by ending their lives (Hendin and Klerman, 1993).

Physical illness is a motivation for suicide; this was known long before today's movement to legalize assisted suicides of patients who are seriously or terminally ill. Medical illness plays an important role in 25 percent of suicides, and this percentage rises with age: from 50 percent in suicides who are over 50 years old to over 70 percent in suicides older than 60 (Mackenzie and Popkin, 1990). Medical conditions shown to be associated with high suicide rates include cancer, AIDS, peptic ulcer (although alcoholism is a confounding variable here), Huntington's chorea, head injury, and renal disease. (See Chapter Twenty-Eight for further discussion.)

Most suicide attempts reflect a person's ambivalence about dying, and patients requesting assisted suicide show an equal ambivalence. When interviewed two weeks after a request for assisted suicide, two-thirds of these patients show a significant decrease in the strength of the desire to die (Emanuel et al., 1996). Patients may voice suicidal thoughts in response to transient depression or severe pain, but these patients usually find relief with treatment of their depression or with pain medication, and are grateful to be alive. Strikingly, the overwhelming majority of people who are terminally ill fight for life to the end: Only 2 to 4 percent of suicides occur in the context of terminal illness.

Link Between Suicide and Depression

Mental illness raises the suicide risk even more than physical illness. Nearly 95 percent of all people who kill themselves have a psychiatric illness diagnosable in the months before suicide (Robins et al., 1959b; Dorpat and Ripley, 1960; Barraclough et al., 1974). The majority suffer from depression that can be treated. This is particularly true of those over fifty who are more prone than younger victims to take their lives during an acute depressive episode.

Like other suicidal individuals, patients who desire an early death during a serious or terminal illness are usually suffering from a treatable depressive condition. Although pain and other factors, such as a lack of family support, contribute to their wish for death, depression is the most important factor, and researchers have found it to be the only factor that significantly correlates with the wish for death (Chochinov et al., 1995).

Depression, often precipitated by discovering one has a serious illness, exaggerates the suicidal patient's tendency to see problems in absolute, black-and-white terms, overlooking solutions and alternative possibilities. Suicidal patients are especially prone to setting such absolute conditions on life: "I won't live . . . without my husband," "if I lose my looks, power, prestige, or health," or "if I am going to die soon." These patients are afflicted by the need to make demands on life that cannot be fulfilled. Determining the time, place, and circumstances of their death is the most dramatic expression of their need for control.

Studies of suicide clarify the nonrational elements of the wish to die in reaction to serious illness. Suicidal patients may have the unconscious wish to be put to death by their doctor. Psychiatrists treating suicidal patients may assume the patient sees them as a savior, when actually they are cast in the role of executioner (Asch, 1980; Rich, Young, and Fowler, 1986c), with the patient sometimes fantasizing closeness or union with the doctor through death. Patients can feel that getting rid of a perceived bad part of themselves is necessary for such a union, and they may see death as a deserved punishment in this process (Hendin, 1995).

Similar dynamics can be seen in patients requesting assisted suicide and euthanasia. Often the illness is seen as part of the bad self that must be eliminated by death before the desired union can take place. Fantasies of achieving closeness through death are often shared by patient and doctor.

Patients who attempt suicide and those who request assisted suicide often test the affection and care of others, confiding feelings like, "I don't want to be a burden to my family," or "My family would be better off without me." Such expressions usually reflect depressed feelings of worthlessness or guilt or may be a plea for reassurance. Not surprisingly, they are also classic indicators of suicidal depression in people who are in good physical health. Whether physically healthy or terminally ill, these individuals need assurance that they are still wanted; they also need treatment for their depression. Unfortunately, depression is commonly underdiagnosed and inadequately treated. Although most people who kill themselves are under medical care at the time of death, their physicians often fail to recognize the symptoms of their depressive illness, or fail to provide adequate treatment (Murphy, 1975).

The fact that a patient finds relief in the prospect of death is not a sign that the decision is appropriate. Patients who are depressed and suicidal may appear calm and less depressed after deciding to end their lives, whether by themselves or with the help of a doctor. It is coping with the uncertainties of life and death that agitate and depress them.

Fear of Death

The uncertainties surrounding death also play a role in patient requests for assisted suicide. Tim, for example, was a professional in his early thirties when he developed acute myelocytic leukemia. He was told that medical treatment would give him a 25 percent chance of survival and that without it he would die in a few months.

His immediate reaction was a desperate, angry preoccupation with suicide and a request for support in carrying it out. He was worried about becoming dependent and feared both the symptoms of his disease and the side effects of treatment.

Tim's anxieties about the painful circumstances that would surround his death were not irrational, but all his fears about dying amplified them. Once Tim could talk about the possibility or likelihood of his dying, and what separation from his family and the destruction of his body meant to him, his desperation subsided. He accepted medical treatment and used the remaining months of his life to become closer to his wife and parents.

At first he would not talk to his wife about his illness because of his resentment that she was going on with her life whereas he would likely not be going on with his. A session with the two of them cleared the air and made it possible for them to talk openly with each other. Two days before he died, Tim talked about what he would have missed without the opportunity for a loving parting (Hendin, 1998).

Like Tim, the majority of those who request assisted suicide or euthanasia are motivated primarily by dread of what will happen to them rather than by current pain or suffering—they fear pain, dependency on others, loss of dignity, the side effects of medical treatment, and, of course, death itself (see Table 30.1). Patients do not know what to expect and cannot foresee how their conditions will unfold as they decline toward death. Facing this uncertainty, they fill the vacuum with their fantasies and fears. When these fears are dealt with by a car-

Table 30.1. Physician-Assisted Suicide and Euthanasia.

Reasons given for requesting
- Pain and suffering
- Loss of dignity
- Dependence on others
- Losing control of one's life
- Side effects of treatment
- Impoverishing treatment costs
- Burden to family

Psychological factors
- Presence of depression
- Fear of death
- Desire to test the affection of others
- Fear of abandonment
- Desire to seize control by determining the time and place of death
- Desire to be purified by destroying a bad part of the self
- Desire to receive a deserved punishment
- Desire to reunite with others who died
- Desire to unite with the physician

Social factors
- Presence or absence of family support
- Availability of a competent doctor
- Ability to afford treatment
- Earlier experiences with relatives and friends who died

ing and knowledgeable physician, the request for an expedited death usually disappears.

It is difficult to understand the relation of suicide to assisted suicide or to understand what assisted suicide and euthanasia mean in actuality without studying the Netherlands, where both have been practiced with legal sanction for two decades.

EUTHANASIA IN THE NETHERLANDS

What happens in the Netherlands to patients, like Tim, who become suicidal when confronted with serious or terminal illness? Early in my work in the Netherlands I was shown *Appointment with Death,* a film by the Dutch Voluntary Euthanasia Society that was intended to promote euthanasia. In the film, a forty-one-year-old artist was diagnosed as HIV positive. He had no physical symptoms but had seen others suffer with them and wanted his physician's assistance in dying.

The doctor compassionately explained to him that he might live for some years symptom-free. Despite this, over time the patient repeated his request for euthanasia. Although the doctor thought his patient was acting unwisely and prematurely, he did not know how to deal with his patient's terror. He rationalized that respect for the patient's autonomy required that he grant the patient's request.

Consultation in the case was pro forma; a colleague of the doctor saw the patient briefly to confirm his wishes. Although the primary doctor kept establishing that the patient was persistent in his request and competent to make the decision, thus formally meeting those criteria, the doctor did not address the terror underlying the patient's request.

This patient had clearly been depressed and overwhelmed by the news of his situation. Had his physician been able to deal with more than formal criteria regarding a request to die—more likely to be pursued in a culture not so accepting of assisted suicide and euthanasia—this man would probably not have been assisted in suicide (Hendin, 1996).

In the decade between 1983 and 1992, by making assisted suicide and euthanasia easily available, the Dutch reduced the suicide rate of those over fifty in the population by one-third (see Figure 30.1). This occurred in the age group containing the highest numbers of euthanasia cases (86 percent of the men and 78 percent of the women) and the greatest number of suicides (Hendin, 1995a). This was the period of growing Dutch acceptance of euthanasia. The remarkable drop in the older age group appears to be due to older suicidal patients' asking to receive euthanasia. The likelihood that patients would end their own lives if euthanasia was not available to them was one of the justifications given by Dutch doctors for providing such help.

Figure 30.1. Suicide Rates in the Netherlands, 1983–1992.

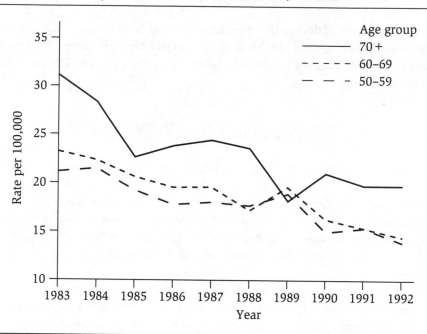

Of course, euthanasia advocates can maintain that making suicide "unnecessary" for those over fifty who are physically ill is a benefit of legalization rather than a sign of abuse. Justification for such an attitude depends, of course, on whether one believes that there are alternatives to assisted suicide or euthanasia for dealing with the problems of older people who become ill.

Among an older population, physical illness of all types is common, and many who have trouble coping with physical illness became suicidal. In a culture accepting of euthanasia, their distress is accepted as a legitimate reason for dying. It may be more than ironic to describe euthanasia as the Dutch cure for suicide.

Problems of Regulation

Ignoring patients' fears and depression is not the only problem that has arisen in the Dutch system. During the past two decades, the Netherlands has moved from considering assisted suicide to giving legal sanction to both physician-assisted suicide and euthanasia, from euthanasia for terminally ill patients to euthanasia for those who are chronically ill, from euthanasia for physical illness to euthanasia for psychological distress, and from voluntary euthanasia to nonvoluntary and involuntary euthanasia.

According to the Royal Dutch Medical Association (1995), it did not seem reasonable medically, legally, or morally to sanction only assisted suicide, thereby denying more active medical help in the form of euthanasia to those who could not effect their own deaths. Nor could the Dutch deny assisted suicide or euthanasia to the chronically ill who have longer to suffer than the terminally ill, nor to those who have psychological pain not associated with physical disease. To do so would be a form of discrimination. Involuntary euthanasia is not legally sanctioned by the Dutch but it is increasingly excused as necessary to end suffering in patients not competent to choose for themselves.

Even more troublesome than the extension of euthanasia to more patients is the inability to regulate the process within the following established guidelines: the patient must make a well-considered voluntary request; the patient must be experiencing intolerable suffering that cannot be relieved; there must be consultation with a second physician; and all cases of physician-assisted suicide and euthanasia must be reported.

These guidelines have been modified and violated, and have failed to protect patients. Concern over charges of abuse led the Dutch government to sanction 1990 and 1995 studies of assisted suicide and euthanasia (Van der Maas, Van Delden, and Pijnenborg, 1992; Van der Maas et al., 1996). The studies won the support of the Royal Dutch Medical Association with the promise that physicians would be immune from prosecution for anything they revealed.

Many of the violations are evident from these two studies. For example, more than 50 percent of physicians reported that they felt free to suggest euthanasia to patients. Neither the physicians nor the study's investigators seem to acknowledge how much the voluntariness of the process is compromised by such a suggestion. Frightened and suffering patients, however, are inclined to listen to suggestions made to them by doctors, even when the doctor is implying that their life is not worth living.

Underreporting is a serious problem. Despite a simplified reporting procedure and statute that protects them from prosecution if they follow established guidelines, 60 percent of Dutch cases are still not reported, a fact that by itself makes regulation impossible.

Of equal concern is the substance of what is not being reported. The 1995 study's interviews with physicians revealed that in only 11 percent of the unreported cases was there consultation with another physician. Moreover, almost 20 percent of the physicians' most recent unreported cases involved the ending of a life without the patient's consent (Van der Wal et al., 1996). Official regulations are being ignored, and physicians are getting around this by not reporting those cases.

Death Without Consent

The most alarming concern to arise from the Dutch studies has been the documentation of cases in which patients who have not given their consent have their lives ended by physicians. The studies revealed that in about one thousand deaths each year, physicians admitted they actively caused death without the explicit consent of the patient. In addition, about a quarter of physicians stated that they had "terminated the lives of patients without an explicit request" from the patient to do so, and a third more of the physicians could conceive of doing so. The use of the word "explicit" is somewhat inaccurate, since in 48 percent of these cases there was no request of any kind, and in the others there were mainly references to patients' earlier statements of not wanting to suffer (Hendin, Rutenfrans, and Zylicz, 1997).

The 1990 study revealed, and the 1995 study confirms, that cases classified as "termination of the patient without explicit request" were a fraction of the nonvoluntary and involuntary euthanasia cases. International attention had centered on the 1,350 cases (1 percent of all Dutch deaths) in 1990 in which physicians gave pain medication with the explicit intention of ending the patient's life.

The investigators minimized the number of patients put to death who had not requested it by not including these 1,350 patients in that category. By 1995, there had been an increase in the number of deaths in which physician's gave pain medication with the explicit intention of ending the patient's life from 1,350 cases to about 1,900 (1.4 percent of all Dutch deaths).

As reported by the physicians in the 1995 study, in more than 80 percent of these cases (1,537 deaths) no request for death was made by the patient. Since researchers around the world have treated these deaths as cases of nonvoluntary euthanasia (a term used when a patient is not competent to make a decision) and involuntary euthanasia (if the patient is competent), they see this as a striking increase in the number of cases terminated without request and a refutation of the Dutch investigators' claim that there has been perhaps a slight decrease in the number of such cases.

The Dutch investigators try to minimize the significance of the number of deaths without consent by explaining that the patients were incompetent. But in the 1995 study, 21 percent of the cases classified as "patients whose lives were ended without explicit request," were competent; in the 1990 study 37 percent of these cases were competent. When asked the reasons for not discussing the decisions with their competent patients, physicians usually said that they had previously had some discussion of the subject with the patient. Yet it seems incomprehensible that a physician would end the life of a competent patient on the basis of a previous discussion without checking how the patient currently felt.

An illustration given of why it was at times necessary for physicians to end the lives of competent patients without their consent was the case of a nun whose physician ended her life a few days before she would have died. The physician felt that although the patient was in excruciating pain, her religious convictions did not permit her to ask for death. In another documented case, a Dutch patient with disseminated breast cancer who had said she did not want euthanasia had her life ended because in the physician's words, "It could have taken another week before she died. I just needed this bed."

If one totals all the deaths from euthanasia, assisted suicide, ending the life of a patient without consent, and giving opioids with the explicit intention of ending life, the total number of deaths caused by active intervention by physicians has increased from 4,813 (3.7 percent) of all deaths in 1990 to 6,368 (4.7 percent of all deaths) in 1995. This is an increase of 27 percent in cases in which physicians actively intervened to cause death. Although minimizing the increase, the Dutch investigators concede that generational and cultural changes in attitudes may be responsible for it.

Interactive Decisions

Since the government-sanctioned Dutch studies are primarily numerical and categorical, they do not examine the interaction among physicians, patients, and families that determines the decision for euthanasia. We need to look elsewhere for a fuller picture.

Other studies conducted in the Netherlands have indicated how voluntariness is compromised, alternatives are not presented, and the criterion of unrelievable suffering is bypassed. A few examples help to illustrate how this occurs:

> A wife who no longer wished to care for her sick, elderly husband gave him a choice between euthanasia and admission to a home for the chronically ill. The man, afraid of being left to the mercy of strangers in an unfamiliar place, chose to have his life ended; the doctor, although aware of the coercion, ended the man's life. In a study of euthanasia done in Dutch hospitals, doctors and nurses reported that more requests for euthanasia came from families than from patients themselves. The investigator concluded that the families, the doctors, and the nurses were involved in pressuring patients to request euthanasia (Hilhorst, 1983).

> A physically healthy, fifty-year-old woman who had lost her son recently to cancer, subsequently refused all psychiatric treatment and said she would accept help only in dying. She was assisted in suicide by a psychiatrist within four months of her son's death. The psychiatrist had told the woman that he could not make such a decision until he knew her better, implying that if after time he considered her decision appropriate he would assist her. The woman saw him for a number of sessions over a two-month period, eventually telling him she would leave if he did not help her, at which point he did. During the course of our interviews the psychiatrist told me that his patient suffered from incurable grief. Her refusal of treatment was considered by the physician and the Dutch courts to make her suffering unrelievable. The woman had told the psychiatrist that if he did not help her she would kill herself without him. He seemed, on the one hand, to be succumbing to emotional blackmail and, on the other, to be ignoring the fact that even without treatment, experience has shown that time alone was likely to have affected her wish to die.

Another Dutch physician, who was filmed ending the life of a patient recently diagnosed with amyotrophic lateral sclerosis, says of the patient, "I can give him the finest wheelchair there is, but in the end it is only a stopgap. He is going to die and he knows it." That death may be years away but a physician with this attitude may not be able to present alternatives to this patient. The patient in this case was clearly ambivalent about proceeding and wanted to put off the date for his death. This ambivalence was ignored by the doctor, who was supporting the desire of the patient's wife to move forward quickly. The doctor never saw the patient alone, permitted the wife to answer all questions for him about whether he wanted to die, and presented an exaggerated picture of the death that awaited him without euthanasia (Hendin, 1995a).

It would seem evident that there has been an erosion of medical standards in the care of terminally ill patients in the Netherlands when, as the government-sanctioned studies document, 60 percent of Dutch cases of assisted suicide and euthanasia are not reported, more than 50 percent of Dutch doctors feel free to suggest euthanasia to their patients, and 25 percent admit to ending patients' lives without their consent.

Given legal sanction, euthanasia, intended originally for the exceptional case, has become an accepted way of dealing with serious or terminal illness in the Netherlands. In the process, palliative care has become one of the casualties whereas hospice care has lagged behind that of other countries. For the Dutch, accepting the option of euthanasia seems to be costing them the opportunity to take advantage of the developments in palliative care of the past decade.

Parallels in the United States

What parallels do we already see or are we likely to see between the Dutch experience and our own? Our legal system and our medical and ethical values would make it difficult for us to make a distinction between assisted suicide and euthanasia. Patients wanting to die make no such distinction, and since many of them cannot swallow medication they have only one choice.

Nor, if we legalize assisted suicide or euthanasia, would we find it easy to exclude people who are suffering but are not terminally ill. Terminal illness is not, in any case, a definable medical category. It is even less so when the illness may be terminal because patients exercise their right to refuse treatment.

The leading medical advocates of assisted suicide in the United States have authored model proposals that make clear that legalization of assisted suicide for so-called terminally ill patients is but a first step. For example, in the *New England Journal of Medicine*, Timothy Quill, one of the most prominent advocates of assisted suicide, and five coauthors call for the legalization of euthanasia as well as assisted suicide for "competent patients suffering not only from terminal illness" but also for those with "incurable, debilitating disease who voluntarily request to end their lives" (Miller et al., 1994). "Incurable debilitating disease" would include conditions like diabetes and arthritis.

Proponents of legalization have maintained that since both assisted suicide and euthanasia are already taking place in this country, legalization would make it possible to regulate their practice. In 1998, Diane Meier and six colleagues published the results of a survey of physicians indicating that 3.3 percent have prescribed lethal medications at least once and that 4.7 percent have given lethal injections at least once (Meier et al., 1998). Perhaps most disturbing about the study was that in 79 percent of cases, physicians who gave lethal injections to patients had received no direct request from the patient to do so.

Meier has said elsewhere that if physicians are willing to do this with the law as it now stands, the likelihood that such practices would increase with legalization and the fact that they cannot be regulated have led her to stop favoring legalization of assisted suicide and euthanasia (Hendin, 1998; Meier et al., 1998). The Dutch experience would tend to support her conclusion.

In both the United States and the Netherlands, ignorance of how to relieve suffering is probably the most frequent reason doctors comply with or encourage patients' requests for assisted suicide and euthanasia, although they rationalize what they do as respecting patient autonomy. At a small, international workshop that addressed problems in the care of the terminally ill, two American cases were presented in which terminally ill patients requested assisted suicide.

In one case a man was confined to a wheelchair with advanced symptoms of AIDS that included cystic lung infection, severe pain due to inflammation of the nerves in his limbs, and marked weight loss. By the appropriate use of steroids, antidepressants, and psychological sensitivity in dealing with his fears of abandonment, he was able to gain weight, be free of his pain and his wheelchair, and live an additional ten months, for which he was grateful (Gomez, 1996).

In another case a woman with great pain due to lung cancer that invaded her chest wall wished for assisted suicide. A nerve block relieved her pain, and she was happy to be able to leave the hospital and live her remaining months at home (Foley, 1996).

I presented these cases to several euthanasia advocates in the Netherlands and in this country. They at first agreed that the patient with AIDS had a right to have euthanasia performed, but were not so sure after they heard the actual outcome. In the second case, aware that a nerve block could provide relief, most would not perform euthanasia.

In other words, doctors felt free to ignore patient autonomy when they knew how to help the patient. "Patient autonomy" was in essence a rationale for assisted suicide when doctors felt helpless and did not know what else to do. This seems an argument for educating physicians, not for legalizing assisted suicide (Hendin, 1996).

Studies have shown that the more physicians know about palliative care, the less they favor legalization; the less they know, the more they favor it (Portenoy et al., 1997). Caring for people at the end of life takes considerable skill and requires a great deal emotionally of a physician; the Dutch experience suggests that legal sanction for the easier option of assisted suicide and euthanasia makes it harder to engage physicians in the process.

Nor is this so surprising. According to the American Medical Association's report on medical education, only a handful of medical schools in the United States require a course in the care of dying patients. Only a quarter of residency programs do so. Only 17 percent of more than a thousand accredited residency programs surveyed offer a hospice rotation, and only half of those programs require it. In a survey conducted by the American Board of Internal Medicine, only 32 percent of 1,400 residents surveyed felt they had received adequate training in talking to patients who request assistance in dying or a hastened death.

The case of the physically healthy woman who was assisted in suicide while grieving the recent loss of her son aroused such concern outside of the Netherlands that we are not likely to soon see pressure in the United States for assisted suicide or euthanasia for distress unaccompanied by physical illness. As should be clear by now, however, psychological distress is most often at the basis of the request for assisted suicide even when the patient has a physical illness. If legalization occurs, the combination of the two is as likely to be accepted as justification for assisted suicide here as it is in the Netherlands.

Some areas where there is not a parallel are also sources of concern. The United States is alone among the industrialized democracies in not guaranteeing medical care to large numbers of its population. Without such care, euthanasia could become essentially a forced choice for large numbers of the poor, the disabled, minority groups, and older people; many of them would be vulnerable to pressure for assisted suicide and euthanasia by family, physicians, hospitals, and nursing homes, or by the unnecessary suffering they are experiencing because they cannot obtain proper palliative care.

Some awareness of this may be responsible for the fact that in contrast to younger groups that support euthanasia (56 percent of those in the eighteen to thirty-four age group favor it), it is supported by only 37 percent of those over sixty-five, the presumed beneficiaries of the practice. And whereas a slight majority of whites favor the practice, African Americans oppose it by more than two to one (Tarrance Group, 1994).

A more equitable medical system, however, has not protected the Dutch. Ultimately, by virtue of their helplessness and dependence, all seriously or terminally ill people are vulnerable.

THE PSYCHIATRIST'S ROLE
WHEN EUTHANASIA IS REQUESTED

Although the evaluation by a psychiatrist of a patient who is requesting euthanasia or assisted suicide cannot provide a simple solution to the situation, it can make a difference in the patient's choice of whether to choose life or death. (See Table 30.2.)

Diagnosing Underlying Psychiatric Disorders

A thorough psychiatric evaluation can help detect the presence of treatable disorders that may be affecting the individual's current desire to die. Once the underlying disorder is treated, the desire for death may diminish or disappear altogether.

The request for death ordinarily comes from patients who are desperate, whether or not they are medically ill. Supporting or denying such a request to die is an inadequate response. A comprehensive psychiatric assessment must include inquiring into the source of the patient's desperation and undertaking to relieve it. That inquiry must include a history of the patient's experiences with the deaths of those close to him or her, a history of past crises in the patient's life and how they were dealt with, and of course a past history of depression as well as any suicide attempts.

Why is such an exploration done so seldom by physicians responding to a patient's request for assistance in suicide? Partly because physicians are not trained to undertake an extensive psychiatric evaluation or to deal with patients' anxieties about dying. They may be inexperienced or uncomfortable in referring patients for psychiatric evaluation. Pieter Admiraal, a prominent Dutch practitioner of euthanasia, says that underlying anxiety about "spiritual and physical decay" is far more important than pain as the reason for requesting euthanasia (Hendin, 1998). He will nevertheless not refer such patients to a

---

Table 30.2. Physician-Assisted Suicide and Euthanasia: The Role of the Psychiatrist.

Diagnose underlying psychiatric disorders, such as depression

Understand and relieve the desperation that underlies the request for assisted suicide

Understand the ambivalence that is present in most requests for assisted suicide

Help the physician deal with his or her feelings of helplessness in the face of death

Help the patient and the caregivers come to terms with and address the patient's unfinished business

Recognize the interactive nature of the decision to request assisted suicide or euthanasia and facilitate communication between families and physicians involved in the decision

Do not act merely as a gatekeeper to decide issues of competence

Insist that all patients requesting assisted suicide be referred for psychiatric evaluation

---

psychiatrist, considering it insulting to do so. Psychiatrists, however, are trained to explore and relieve the hidden anxieties of patients, whether or not those patients are mentally ill.

The physician's own fears and anxieties may also determine how he or she interacts with a terminally ill patient and whether an evaluation of the patient's psychiatric state and underlying emotions is undertaken. Lewis Thomas, one of the deans of modern American medicine, wrote insightfully about the sense of failure and helplessness that physicians may experience in the face of death (Thomas, 1984). Such feelings may explain why doctors, including psychiatrists, have such difficulty discussing terminal illness with patients. A majority of doctors avoid such discussion, whereas most patients would prefer frank talk.

These feelings may also explain both the doctors' tendency to use excessive measures to maintain life and their need to make life a physician's decision. Physicians who unwisely prolong the dying process and those who practice euthanasia may have more in common than they realize.

By deciding when patients die, by making death a medical decision, the physician preserves the illusion of mastery over the disease and the accompanying feelings of helplessness. The physician, not the illness, is responsible for the death. Assisting suicide and euthanasia become ways of dealing with the frustration of being unable to cure the disease.

Psychiatrists, too, may be paralyzed in the face of death and a dying patient's request to die. Their normal processes of inquiry sometimes seem suspended, leading to no real exploration of the nature of the patient's desperation. Unable to prevent death, the psychiatrist seems to forget all else and to simply regard the patient as a condemned person whose last wish should be granted.

Psychiatrists are trained to recognize depression, but only a relative few have experience in dealing with depression in seriously or terminally ill patients. Psychiatrists should be able to recognize ambivalence, including the ambivalence that is usually present in patients who insist they want to die. They are also knowledgeable about counterphobic behavior, although they have more trouble recognizing and dealing with it when terrified patients embrace death.

Because of the underlying anxieties that may accompany an individual's desire for death, as well as the comorbidity between depression and physical illnesses, a patient's request and desire for death should be evaluated psychiatrically beyond the surface of the patient's stated reasons. In addition, a psychiatrist may be able to help a physician who is treating a terminally ill patient come to grip with his or her own anxieties and fears about the patient's death.

Helping Patients Resolve Unfinished Business

The last days of most dying patients can be given meaning if those treating them know how to engage them, and here the psychiatrist can be helpful to the patient and those directly responsible for the patient's care. Tim, the patient with acute myelocytic leukemia, needed to communicate with his wife, communication that was not possible till he voiced his envy and resentment over her going on with her life while he was probably not going to be doing so; his situation finds parallels in the lives of most dying patients.

In a twist on conventional wisdom, the English palliative care specialist Robert Twycross has written, "Where there is hope there is life," referring not to hope of a cure, but hope of doing something that gives meaning to life as long as it lasts (Twycross, 1995). Virtually everyone who is dying has unfinished business, even if only the need to share their life and their death with friends, family, a doctor, or a hospice worker. Without such purpose terminally ill patients who are not in great physical distress may be tortured by the feeling that they are only waiting to die and may want to die at once. A psychiatrist may be able to help a dying patient and his or her caregivers come to terms with and address the patient's unfinished business and create a sense of purpose and closure that can be comforting for the patient and all those involved.

Facilitating Communication Between Families and Physicians

Psychiatrists are more experienced than most physicians in recognizing the interactive nature of crucial decisions. This is particularly important in evaluating requests for assisted suicide and euthanasia, which are usually the result of an interaction in which the needs and character of family, friends, and doctor play as big and often bigger role than those of the patient. A Swedish study has shown that when chronically ill patients attempt suicide, their families, overburdened by caring for them, often do not want them resuscitated. When social intervention relieves the burden on the family, the patients want to live, and their families want them to live (Wasserman, 1989). By facilitating communication between families and patients the psychiatrist can clarify and often relieve the burdens and anxieties that lead family members to influence patients to request assisted suicide or euthanasia.

Although psychiatrists are experienced in dealing with patients who are being pressured or coerced by families, the problem is more difficult for the psychiatrist when the patient's physician becomes caught up in the pressuring process. Here the psychiatrist must be careful not to suspend his powers of observation and simply defer to medical colleagues.

Understanding Physicians' Emotional Issues

Physicians who perform euthanasia are often troubled by it even years afterward. Some speak of a need for absolution. If euthanasia was a legitimate medical procedure, most doctors would not feel so disturbed by performing it. Although withdrawal of futile treatment that is only prolonging the dying process may be difficult for physicians, it produces no such reaction afterward.

The average doctor's discomfort with ending a patient's life is not so surprising. Even when justified by the exigencies of war, most soldiers pay a price for participating in killing. Just as a minority of soldiers deal with the horror of war by embracing the power that being able to end someone's life confers, a minority of doctors embrace assisted suicide and euthanasia with fervor. That a small number of doctors do a great number of the cases is one of the unexamined aspects of the Dutch euthanasia story; one admits to close to a hundred, another is proud to have done many times that number. Several described the bonding with the patients they put to death as one of the closest and most meaningful experience of their lives. For some, continued participation in and advocacy of euthanasia appear to be a way of denying the guilt they feel over their initial involvement. One psychiatric advocate has even argued that the doctor being troubled afterward is a sign that the euthanasia is appropriate (Klagsbrun, 1997). Another seems to maintain that providing absolution to medical colleagues is a legitimate function for psychiatrists in such cases (Block, 1995).

Assessing Competence

In considerations of legalizing assisted suicide, psychiatrists are generally assigned the role of assessing whether patients are competent to make the request. Such an assessment is supposed to include an evaluation to determine the presence of depression and to distinguish it from the sadness that may accompany illness. Even patients with severe depression may pass tests of legal competence to make medical decisions. In the Netherlands, and in statutes proposed in several of our states, depression per se is not accepted as indicating incompetence.

If assisted suicide were legal nationally, as it now is in Oregon, Tim probably would have gone to a doctor whom he knew was likely to support his request. Because he was mentally competent, he would have qualified for assisted suicide and would surely have found a doctor who would have agreed to his request.

Because the Oregon law, and similar laws being considered in other states, does not require an independently referred doctor for a second opinion, Tim would likely have been referred by a physician supportive of assisted suicide to a colleague who was equally supportive; the evaluation would have been pro forma. He could have been put to death in an unrecognized state of terror, unable to give himself the chance of getting well or of dying in the dignified way he did. It was the fact that I was not the arbiter of his fate but rather a sympathetic but engaged listener that permitted Tim to talk freely with me.

The Dutch physician who assisted in the suicide of his HIV-positive patient who had no symptoms thought his patient was acting prematurely. Unable to deal with the patient's terror, he fell back on reliance on guidelines such as competence and respect for the patient's autonomy. A knowledgeable psychiatrist could play an important therapeutic role in such a case. If the psychiatrist is reduced to the role of gatekeeper, the patient tends to simply say or do what is necessary to persuade the psychiatrist to go along with the request to die.

Psychiatrists in the Netherlands played a relatively passive role in the growing normalization of suicide and euthanasia, even though this has meant that patients who are basically suicidal, whether physically ill or not, are being assisted in death. American psychiatrists should learn from that experience to be more involved, educating the public that legalization will become a license to exploit the fears of the ill and depressed. They should insist that all patients requesting assisted suicide—not just those who are obviously disturbed—should be referred for psychiatric consultation.

CONCLUSION

Although inadequate psychiatric and medical training of physicians is a major obstacle to our providing adequate palliative care to patients who are seriously or terminally ill, problems in our health care delivery system compound the problem. State laws written before the advent of modern palliative care and designed to prevent drug abuse will have to be revised because they often make it impossible for hospitals to stock adequate amounts of analgesic medication.

Insurance companies and managed care companies will need to be obliged to make palliative care an integral part of their policies. In particular, we will need to insist that treatment of depression in terminally ill patients be covered. At present, there are financial disincentives to providing such care. Although palliative care is cheaper than unwise medical care that only prolongs the process of dying and that characterized our medical system in the past, assisted suicide is the cheapest solution of all.

When I began studying assisted suicide and euthanasia, the apprehensions I had about it were rooted in experience with people who became suicidal in response to serious illness. I feared they would become willing victims if assisted suicide and euthanasia were given legal sanction. What I learned in the Netherlands indicated that such fears were justified.

I had assumed, however, that euthanasia in the Netherlands, where there is comprehensive health insurance for everyone, was surely set in a framework of providing better care for patients who were terminally ill than we were providing in this country. I learned that not only was that not true but that the development of palliative care was being stunted in the Netherlands by the Dutch acceptance of euthanasia as an alternative. Euthanasia, which had been proposed as an unfortunate but necessary solution in refractory cases, had become an easy way of dealing with anxiety, depression, and pain in seriously or terminally ill patients. What I have seen subsequently in the Netherlands and in this country has persuaded me that legalization should be prevented because it would markedly worsen the care we provide to terminally ill patients.

What was as surprising to me as this discovery was my realization that, contrary to the expectations of its proponents, legal sanction for assisted suicide and euthanasia increases the power and control of doctors, not patients. This happens because the doctor can suggest euthanasia (which has a powerful impact on patients' decisions), ignore patient ambivalence, fail to present suitable alternatives, and even end the lives of patients who have not requested it.

No group of suicidal patients has been more ignored than those who become suicidal in response to serious or terminal illness. No suicide-prevention measure holds more immediate promise of success than providing the psychological and medical care that makes suicide not seem the only option for these patients.

Knowledge of how to minister to the need of terminally ill people is, I believe, one of medicine's finest achievements in the past two decades, but dissemination of that knowledge has only begun. Our challenge is to bring that knowledge and that care to all patients who are terminally ill. If we succeed, the issue of assisted suicide and euthanasia will become irrelevant.

IMPLICATIONS FOR THE CLINICIAN

- Medical illness plays an important role in 25 percent of suicides, and this percentage rises with age: from 50 percent in suicides who are over fifty years old to over 70 percent in suicides older than sixty.

- Most suicide attempts reflect a person's ambivalence about dying; patients requesting assisted suicide show an equal ambivalence. When interviewed two weeks after a request for assisted suicide, two-thirds of these patients show a significant decrease in the strength of the desire to die.

- Like other suicidal individuals, patients who desire an early death during a serious or terminal illness are usually suffering from a treatable depressive condition. Although pain and other factors, such as a lack of family support, contribute to their wish for death, depression is the most important factor, and researchers have found it to be the only factor that significantly correlates with the wish for death.

- Suicidal patients are especially prone to setting absolute conditions on life, such as: "I won't live . . . without my husband," "if I lose my looks, power, prestige, or health," or "if I am going to die soon." These patients are afflicted by the need to make demands on life that cannot be fulfilled. Determining the time, place, and circumstances of their death is the most dramatic expression of their need for control.

- Patients who attempt suicide and those who request assisted suicide often test the affection and care of others. Expression such as, "I don't want to be a burden to my family," or "My family would be better off without me," usually reflect depressed feelings of worthlessness or guilt or may be a plea for reassurance. Not surprisingly, they are also classic indicators of suicidal depression in people who are in good physical health. Whether physically healthy or terminally ill, these individuals need assurance that they are still wanted; they also need treatment for their depression.

- The fact that a patient finds relief in the prospect of death is not a sign that the decision is appropriate. Patients who are depressed and suicidal may appear calm and less depressed after deciding to end their lives, whether by themselves or with the help of a doctor. It is coping with the uncertainties of life and death that agitate and depress them.

- In the decade between 1983 and 1992 by making assisted suicide and euthanasia easily available, the Dutch have significantly reduced—by a third—the suicide rate of those over fifty in the population, the age group containing the highest numbers of euthanasia cases. This appears to be due to the fact that older suicidal patients are now asking to receive euthanasia. The likelihood that patients would end their own lives if euthanasia was unavailable to them was one of the justifications given by Dutch doctors for providing such help.

- Ignoring patients' fears and depression is not the only problem that has arisen in the Dutch system. During the past two decades, the Netherlands has moved from considering assisted suicide to giving legal sanction to both physician-assisted suicide and euthanasia, from euthanasia for terminally ill patients to euthanasia for those who are chronically ill, from euthanasia for physical illness to euthanasia for psychological distress, and from voluntary euthanasia to nonvoluntary and involuntary euthanasia.

- Psychiatrists are more experienced than most physicians in recognizing the interactive nature of crucial decisions. This is particularly important in evaluating requests for assisted suicide and euthanasia, which are usually the result of an interaction in which the needs and character of family, friends, and doctor play as big and often bigger role than those of the patient. A Swedish study has shown that when chronically ill patients attempt suicide, their families, overburdened by caring for them, often do not want them resuscitated. When social intervention relieves the burden on the family, the patients wanted to live and their families wanted them to live as well.

- The request for death ordinarily comes from patients who are desperate, whether or not they are medically ill. Supporting or denying such a request to die is an inadequate response. A comprehensive psychiatric assessment must include inquiring into the source of the patient's desperation and undertaking to relieve it. That inquiry must include a history of the patient's experiences with the deaths of those close to him or her, a history of past crises in the patient's life and how they were dealt with, and of course a past history of depression as well as any suicide attempts.

CHAPTER THIRTY-ONE

Liability Issues and Liability Prevention in Suicide

Thomas G. Gutheil, M.D.

For the average clinician, few events are as devastating as the death of a patient through suicide. That experience may be rendered even more distressing by one possible aftermath of such a death: a malpractice suit against the psychiatrist or other health care provider for failure to prevent that death.

Clinicians who are the target of such litigation describe the emotional reactions to being sued as resonating malignantly with the promptings of their own consciences and neurotic guilt, even in cases where the treater is objectively blameless and has rendered proper treatment (Carter, 1971; Maltsberger, 1992). Other legal developments, such as the National Practitioner Data Bank described in this chapter, complicate the human response to suit. Finally, suicide remains the most common cause of litigation against all mental health professionals (personal communication with P. B. Martin, January 13, 1998). For all these and other reasons, a book discussing suicide may appropriately contain an examination of the dynamics of suicide litigation and recommendations directed to avoiding this outcome.

This chapter places the issue of liability for suicide in a contemporary social context, reviews some aspects of the theory of malpractice law and its relevant

---

An earlier version of this chapter was given as a presentation in a Harvard Medical School Continuing Education Symposium on suicide in September 1997.

application, discusses the standard of care in relation to suicide liability, and addresses the practical principles of risk management to aid in decreasing the risk of liability in the event of a patient's suicide.

THE SOCIAL CONTEXT

Much of the social context of our modern world is captured in cartoons, and the matter of prevention of liability for suicide is no exception. For example, one cartoon shows a dinosaur lecturing to a large audience of other dinosaurs and saying, "The picture's pretty bleak, gentlemen. The world's climates are changing. The mammals are taking over and we all have a brain about the size of a walnut." We might imagine that the modern version of this vision might read instead that the economic climates are changing, managed care is taking over, and when it comes to deciding what exactly it is that the law wants from us, we do indeed have brains about the size of a walnut.

Managed care, among other impacts, has tended to shorten the length of stay for inpatients in psychiatric hospitals. This trend has had several effects: it has altered conceptions of what a standard length of hospitalization should be for certain clinical conditions; required that thorough intake evaluations occur in a shorter period of time; decreased the amount of time within which a patient may form alliances with staff and within which patients and staff can come to know and understand each other; and decreased the time available for staff to observe the effects, if any, of the various treatment approaches used for the patient (Ostergard, 1997).

Yet another contextual factor is the social attitude that might be styled contemporary narcissistic entitlement or, as our Canadian friends refer to it, the "American disease." This attitude is fostered by widely distributed advertisements, in print, radio, and television media, of the following general stripe, usually printed in end-of-the-world-size type: "INJURED? You may have a case! Call the XYZ law firm for a free first consultation." Thus, every injury is associated in the public mind with litigation rather than grief, mature acceptance, and the resolve to be more careful next time.

Further complication of these factors is provided by sheer numbers; some estimate that there are more attorneys in the state of California alone than in any other country in the world (except, of course, our own).

The attitudes of physicians are also a part of the social context of liability. Another modern cartoon shows a physician proffering a bottle of medication to a patient and saying, "Take thirty-two of these and sue me in the morning." This image perfectly captures a kind of feeling of hopeless resignation that many clinicians have about the daunting prospect of being sued. An educational objective for this chapter is to decrease the feeling of hopelessness by identifying proven principles of risk management that rest, as all such approaches should rest, on a foundation of sound clinical practice (Appelbaum and Gutheil, 1991).

THE INSURANCE CONTEXT

The data on liability payments for suicide cases are rendered complex because of terminology. The clinical event of suicide may be described for insurance or claim purposes as misdiagnosis (even though suicidality is not a diagnosis), inadequate treatment (in the sense of suicide prevention), or wrongful death (wrongful because it is claimed to have resulted from negligence) (personal communication with P. B. Martin, January 13, 1998). How suicide is designated may be dependent on how the plaintiff's attorney chooses to word the claim.

Recent data (personal communication with P. B. Martin, January 13, 1998) from the Risk Management Foundation, the malpractice insurer for the Harvard hospital system, reveals that in the first twenty years of the foundation's existence (1976–1996), there were 237 suicide-related actions, with 202 involving psychiatry and with 35 involving other caretakers, such as internists. Completed suicides and attempts numbered 51 (35 of those psychiatric, of which 19 were inpatient and 16 outpatient). These outcomes generated 42 claims or suits, 37 of which were closed in the time period. Of this final pool of psychiatric malpractice claims closed as of 1996, 21 involved no payment and 16 were closed with some payment, most through settlement. The most common methods employed by psychiatric patients were jumping and hanging. With occasional exceptions, these data can be regarded as typical for the average insurer covering malpractice claims in relation to suicide.

The establishment of the National Practitioner Data Bank is the most recent change in the landscape of malpractice litigation. Since not only successful suits against a doctor but also settlements, even minor ones, must be reported to the bank, and since credentialing agencies are obligated to check with the bank before hiring physicians, even a perfectly rational decision to settle a nuisance case for a trivial amount may well result in the physician's having to explain the result to all subsequent employers. Since only a "win" by the physician is *not* reported, physicians may be tempted to fight every case. This is not necessarily a bad strategy, but it does remove the significant benefit of settlement in putting a case behind you and going on with your life. Loss of this benefit is most relevant because of the emotional devastation that accrues from even a baseless suit (Carter, 1971; Maltsberger, 1992).

Note also that more dismissals or dropping of cases may occur simply because the doctor will not settle, and the plaintiff's lawyer does not want to take the economic risk of trial. That is, from the plaintiffs' viewpoint, the case may make sense economically only if they can look toward a speedy settlement. If no one will settle because of the data bank, then the plaintiff's attorney, who is, after all, fronting the money to develop the case, now has to accept a hugely increased economic risk, a risk further increased because of the high proportion of defense verdicts in suicide cases.

In sum, the National Practitioner Data Bank has altered the playing field for malpractice litigation, but the actual effects are still developing.

THE LEGAL CONTEXT

A brief foray into legal theory may provide an additional context in which to consider suicide liability. Malpractice is considered in the law to be a tort (that is, a civil wrong) of the negligent type (that is, a claimed "sin of omission," or failure to do something) rather than an intentional tort, or "sin of commission," as it were.

Malpractice occurs when the plaintiff, or the patient who has turned on a physician, proves all four of the elements of malpractice by a preponderance of the evidence (that is, that they are more likely than not to be true).

First, the plaintiff must prove that there existed from the physician who administered the diagnosis, treatment, or service to this patient a duty to deliver reasonable care. This duty can be established (and most often is established) by the fact of the physician's actual evaluation and treatment of the patient or, under some circumstances, even by a mere offer to treat that person.

Then it must be established that the physician was derelict in this duty; he or she was neglectful or negligent in carrying out the duty to deliver reasonable care. In this context, the notion of the standard of care becomes relevant; this term represents the yardstick against which the quality of care is measured. Although the terminology may vary among jurisdictions, a typical wording might go something like this: "The defendant failed to exercise the care and skill of the average prudent practitioner in that profession and under similar circumstances." Variations might phrase it as "average reasonable practitioner," "practitioner in that specialty," "practitioner taking into account the relevant literature," and so on. Many jurisdictions use what is called a "national standard," whereby practitioners are presumed to practice at the same general level from coast to coast. Other jurisdictions use a locality rule, whereby the doctor accused of malpractice is compared only to practitioners from the same locality. Clinicians should be familiar with their local standard.

How is the lay jury to know the standard of care for professional practice? Explaining this standard to the jury is the task of the expert witness on the case; the expert must usually demonstrate knowledge of the standard, then explain it and relate it to the facts of the case at hand.

Third, since the tort system exists as a mechanism for the compensation of victims, the plaintiff must prove that damages occurred. In suicide cases, the damages are those that flow from the death itself as it affects the survivors, family, and heirs. These damages may constitute straightforward financial losses, such as lost income that would have been earned from the deceased, or subtler emotional injuries such as grief, suffering, and "loss of consortium," a legal term for loss of those benefits of the relationship itself, such as companionship, comfort, and, with partners, sexual relations.

The final burden on the plaintiff in a malpractice case is to prove that the damages were caused by the alleged negligence, that is, that there existed a linkage of direct causation between negligence and damages. This element implies that a doctor may have been negligent in some way in treating a patient. If this negligence is not causally linked to the damage, malpractice has not occurred.

A handy mnemonic for remembering these elements is that malpractice consists of dereliction of a duty directly causing damages: the four D's of malpractice (Appelbaum and Gutheil, 1991). Although all elements must be present to constitute malpractice, a case might focus on one or a combination of these elements as the core of the dispute.

THE ROLE OF "BAD FEELINGS" IN SUICIDE LITIGATION

In the real world, malpractice litigation results from the malignant synergy of a bad outcome for any reason and what might be termed "bad feelings" (Gutheil, 1992). In the context here, the "bad outcome" is suicide. Here we gain further insight into why suicide is the most common claim against all mental health disciplines: doctors, nurses, psychologists, and social workers. Everyone understands that a suicide is one of the worst outcomes for survivors (the usual litigants in such cases) and an outcome that leaves some of the worst, and most conflicted, feelings in its wake (Gutheil, Bursztajn, Brodsky, and Alexander, 1991).

In this context, the term *bad feelings* refers to all the predictable affects stirred up by the suicide of someone close to us. Although descriptions of the experience of survivors have been addressed elsewhere (Alexander, 1998), this section reviews those feelings as they represent stimuli to malpractice litigation.

Guilt

A primary dysphoric affect triggered by suicide is guilt in the survivors. This can be distinguished from classic survivor guilt about being alive while others in the same situation (such as war or prison camp) have died. Survivors of suicide are often racked by a particular self-recrimination of the type: "We should have done something, noticed something, done more, prevented this somehow."

This form of guilt is highly intensified if the survivors have treated the deceased badly or feel that they have done so. A paradigmatic situation, actually played out in many famous suicide cases, might take this form: wife leaves depressed husband; husband commits suicide; wife sues husband's doctor for malpractice in failing to prevent the suicide.

The wife's actual responsibility for the suicide in this example is a matter of metaphysics beyond the scope of this chapter; however, the wife's *feeling* of responsibility and consequent guilt are fully understandable to anyone. In this and comparable scenarios, we might readily grasp the temptation of the survivor to fix the blame elsewhere; hence, the suit against the husband's treating doctor might be viewed as the wife's displacement of guilt through the tort system. The search for displacement in this manner may be undertaken even in less blatant sequences of events; the best and most devoted of spouses and partners may yet feel they "should have done more."

Let us pause in the discussion of the "bad feelings" to identify immediately the risk management implication that flows from the above formulation. If, by some intervention, a physician can alleviate the guilt of the survivors, not only is he or she helping them through a crisis and decreasing their psychiatric morbidity from their loss; he or she is also practicing sound risk management.

Family guilt can take the most complex forms. In a famous local case, a young outpatient hanged himself from a beam in the basement of the family home. At a later point it was revealed that, tied on the same beam next to the fatal rope, there was an old, broken rope, gray with dust. Apparently there had been a previous suicide attempt that had failed because the rope broke. And that old rope had been dangling there in the basement for years during much family traffic; no one had taken notice of the silent message.

Rage

A related "bad feeling" is rage, an affect commonly transformed from guilt or diverted from the deceased to the doctor. In addition to its obvious connection to the wish to blame someone for the suicide, rage may be fomented by the clinician's arrogance, insensitivity, and inaccessibility, the last especially when the family is in crisis. In one case, the emotional wellspring of the suit appeared to be the fact that the doctor was perceived as never returning telephone calls. In another case, a patient had committed suicide, and the psychiatrist sent the widow a very thoughtful condolence card—in the same envelope as the final bill. This was likely to have been the trigger of the litigation.

Grief

The fact that grief is a natural healing process designed by nature to deal with loss does not make it pleasant to endure, and the wish to avoid grief by, say, activity is also a natural one. Litigation after a loss from suicide provides just such a vehicle of activity into which survivors may plunge to postpone or avoid working through the loss; litigation may well keep one busy for the next seven years or so, permitting focus on the lawyer, the next affidavit, and the next deposition. From a risk management viewpoint, helping survivors deal maturely with their grief is thus doubly helpful.

Note also that litigation interferes with the grief process in several ways. For example, the adversarial process clouds normal ambivalence toward the deceased and removes the loss from the realm of workable affect into an arena where others control the process. Public exposure of affect in legal proceedings may disrupt private grieving and emotional growth. Finally, the stress of litigation and its subsequent letdown, even after a plaintiff's verdict, may predispose to eventual depression in survivors.

Surprise

In general medicine, the toxic effect of surprise is well known; for example, patients fully informed about recovery room conditions are said to need less postoperative analgesia. My own experience in psychiatry suggests that patients can tolerate significant amounts of dysphoria if they are prepared for it; when surprised, patients note that their tolerance decreases, and paranoia and other alliance threats supervene.

In the context of this chapter, families who were aware that their relative was profoundly depressed may yet not feel prepared, because of a variety of mental mechanisms, for a suicide. Surprise may lead (and often does lead) in sequence to feelings of betrayal, helplessness, anger, distrust, blaming, and, ultimately, litigation.

Once again, preparation of the family has a dual effect. The diminution of surprise both readies the family for the possible trauma of the tragedy and decreases the impulse to seek targets for blame. Here again, as always, risk management rests on a clinical foundation.

The approach to preparing the family involves alerting the family to the fact that suicidal intent is one of the effects or morbidities of depression and recruiting the family to assist in the observation of the patient for significant behaviors, such as giving away possessions, revising a will, and so on.

The issue of weapons, especially firearms in the home, deserves separate mention. Both families and clinicians may be tempted into denial of the risks associated with guns in the household of a person with suicidal leanings. Inquiry about the presence of firearms and subsequent arrangement for their removal to a place of safety (friends, relatives, local police) are important elements of negotiation with the family. The recommendation to remove firearms should be followed up to ensure it has been followed through; cases exist where families have merely hidden the guns or changed their location, only to have the weapons found and used.

Betrayal of Trust

Betrayal of trust is the "bad feeling" that is most often a product of the most misguided form of risk management: defensive practice. Defensive practice not only fails to prevent litigation; it may actually foster it (Gutheil, Bursztajn, and Brodsky, 1984). Defensive practice places the physician and patient in adversarial positions, losing the therapeutic alliance. This posture anticipates the adversarial context of the courtroom and may predispose survivors of suicide to adopt the mentality of that arena. The patient or family may feel that trust in an ally has been betrayed.

Even more important, patients themselves who feel "defended against," rather than allied with, may feel cut off from the therapist as a source of emotional support, a critical element in suicide prevention. Patients (or family) may even feel that the physician is not genuinely treating them; instead, he or she is defending against future lawyers. Consequently, this is not a real relationship, not worth staying alive for, a result that increases suicide risk.

Psychological Abandonment

In a liability context, there is a cause of action called "abandonment," when a patient is left abruptly without resources. The subject here is slightly different: psychological abandonment occurs when bereft survivors of a suicide feel that they have been left emotionally alone with the terrible outcome. At that point, for a variety of obvious reasons, mental health professionals may retreat: the nurses do not meet the family's eyes, and the doctor does not return telephone calls. Even more destructively, families who are desperate to find out or understand what happened may be referred to the hospital's attorney, a move that is highly ill advised since it may well communicate to the distressed family a tone of a cover-up of wrongdoing or an evasion. Bereft families want to talk to the doctor on the case. Indeed, there are cases where families go to an attorney for the simple reason that no one in the health care system will talk to them or give them a straight answer. Clinicians uncertain about how to approach this sensitive situation should consult with knowledgeable peers or the risk managers from their institution or insurance carrier.

THE MALPRACTICE CASE IN SUICIDE

Despite the extensive variability of patients who commit suicide, the suicide suit itself reveals a rigid formalism that would put a Japanese Noh drama to shame (Perr, 1965; Gutheil, 1984, 1987). As long as the situational status of the suicide is given—regardless of the patient's age, sex, diagnosis, demographics, condition, or state of intoxication—an expert can promptly identify the crucial factor in the case and supply a rough outline of the plaintiff's and defense's legal strategy. If the patient is an outpatient, the critical question will turn on whether the patient should have been hospitalized or committed; for an inpatient, the case will focus on observation (for example, frequency of checks) or environment (for example, breakaway shower rods); for an escapee, escape precautions; for a recent dischargee, the indications for discharge and the aftercare plan; and for a patient on pass, the prepass assessment.

To digress for a moment regarding inpatients, a surprisingly large number of physicians do not know precisely what is meant by "suicide precautions" in their local hospital. Is it constant observation, or checks every five, ten, fifteen, or thirty minutes? Physicians should spell it out exactly as they intend it.

Suicidologists estimate that there are twenty-three suicide attempts for every completed suicide (Goodwin and Runck, 1992). This number of "false positives" demonstrates the challenges for clinicians of identifying true suicidal intent; hence, families are suing clinicians for a rare occurrence. Even when the suicide attempt is not "successful," tort law permits patients themselves to sue their own doctors for injuries sustained in their own suicide attempt.

Models of the Psychiatric Patient

To understand how suicide is portrayed in malpractice litigation, consider some models of the psychiatric patient. The "model" in this context may represent either the plaintiff's attorney's intended image of the patient who has committed suicide, or the jury's perceived image, or both. Such images, which may actually be nearly subliminal in nature, may yet be highly influential in jury decision making (Gutheil, 1992).

The usual private practice model pictures the patient as an autonomous adult seeking a consultation for study of his or her life. A common plaintiff's model of the patient, in contrast, is a functionally comatose person, fully dependent on the physician for all needs, including life support. The patient's suicide, then, is a failure of the physician's life support.

Another model is the patient as "product." When a company makes a defective product, the company is responsible or liable for injuries that may result. If the patient is portrayed as a product of the hospital or of the treatment process itself, then the jury might view the patient who committed suicide as a defective product and thus find the "company" (that is, the treaters) liable for that "defect." Note how this model casts the treaters as warrantors of the patient's safety.

Another common model, similar to the life support model, is the patient as child. In an actual case, the opposing expert described a fully competent, nonpsychotic adult outpatient as "a helpless child in the hands of his caretakers." Here the suicide is portrayed as the result of a negligent failure of the treater's "parenting."

A related pair of models might be called the "victim-agent" dilemma. If the patient is the victim of suicidal tendencies, then perhaps the doctor should have protected the patient better; if the patient is the agent of suicidal action, then the suicide is something the patient is doing to himself or herself, and the doctor "feels" less culpable to the jury.

The Problem of Strict Liability

Under the theory certain of strict liability, activities (usually particularly hazardous activities such as dynamite manufacture) are not governed by the theory of ordinary negligence, which holds that everyone has the duty to exercise reasonable care. Instead, the activities are governed by strict liability, whereby, regardless of negligence, the actor must pay "anyway." Thus, if dynamite blows up prematurely, the effort to find out who was last smoking in the dynamite shack is not useful because he or she is spread out all over the landscape; instead, the manufacturer must pay the damages and pass the cost on to the consumer, where part of the price of the dynamite goes to buy the manufacturer a liability insurance policy (Gutheil, 1992).

Note well that this analysis has absolutely nothing to do with those issues of professional negligence relevant to malpractice in suicide. However, legitimate legal reasoning aside, it would clearly be in the plaintiff's interest for the jury to adopt a "pay anyway" attitude toward the case: a patient has died; a family has suffered a loss; and, as advertisements everywhere proclaim, "Someone should pay."

Because such strict liability reasoning lies outside the notions of standards of care and good clinical practice, it is difficult to defeat in court. A jury whose attitude is, "Just pay the family the money," will not be influenced by the quality of care delivered; hence, there is no valid defense to this position. There is, however, a possible approach.

A New Competence

The approach in question evolved from the medicolegal research of the Program in Psychiatry and the Law at the Massachusetts Mental Health Center and Harvard Medical School (Gutheil, Bursztajn, and Brodsky, 1986). The study was aimed at clarifying negotiations between the suicidal patient and the treater. For example, before sending a patient out of the hospital for a pass or for discharge, or when deciding whether to hospitalize an outpatient, the clinician usually asks the patient directly about the presence of suicidal intent. The patient may reply candidly, may conceal secret suicidal intent to prevent interference, or may simply not be in touch with those feelings in the interview yet may be vulnerable to their recurrence later. Clearly, questions about the patient's honesty or authenticity in denying suicidal intent are quite important to clinical decision making.

To approach this problem systematically, a new competence was defined, discussed in detail elsewhere (Gutheil, Bursztajn, and Brodsky, 1986). This was the patient's competence (or capacity or ability) to weigh the risks and benefits of sharing with or withholding from treaters information about suicidal ideation or intent. This formulation in terms of the patient's weighing risks and benefits intentionally parallels informed consent.

A number of capacities are invoked by this model: the patient's awareness of internal states and the ability to introspect, the patient's cognitive clarity, the state of the patient's familiarity with his or her own history, and the like. Conversely, a patient's psychosis, dissociation, or organic impairment may diminish or eliminate this capacity.

The value of this approach is its separation from purely subjective assessments of credibility—"I believed the patient" or "I thought the patient was lying to me"—which are influenced by countertransference and other forces in the treater; and its provision of a model for assessment of the patient that can be reliably performed and clearly documented.

The strength of this model is based on the fact that in all jurisdictions, a competent patient may refuse even lifesaving medical or surgical treatment. By obvious analogy, a competent patient could knowingly refuse lifesaving psychiatric treatment by not revealing suicidal intent. Focusing on competence aids in distinguishing patients who cannot report their own suicidality (because of being too sick or impaired) from those who decide not to report it. For the former population, the clinician has a responsibility to allow for the deficit and act more conservatively and protectively (for example, by increasing the monitoring or hospitalizing the patient at a lower threshold); for the latter, the clinician is not at fault for the suicide of a patient who could have revealed suicidal intent but chose not to. This approach also frees the clinician from the impossible task of reading the patient's mind. This model has been successfully employed in several states, suggesting that juries can grasp this concept.

An Example from Clinical Practice

Consider the example of a highly functional yet impulsively suicidal borderline patient who is admitted to a hospital for overt concern about suicidality. Her past contains both serious and less serious suicide attempts; she has never been psychotic. The patient responds to treatment and is now considered for a first pass. Thus, the issue of suicidality is on the table from the point of admission, and since this is the first pass, there has been no previous pass to serve as an empirical test of the patient's safety. The clinician's approach should generally use the following systematic inquiry:

1. Does the patient understand that clinicians, not being mind readers, must be informed directly by the patient as to his or her intent? Does

the patient realize that the clinician cannot help unless the patient levels with him or her?

2. Does the patient understand the risks and expected benefits of the pass itself: its goal, purpose, and value in the treatment plan?

3. Does the patient know what to do if suicidal feelings rise up again, if the pass goes sour, if the impulse to hurt himself or herself grows stronger, if panic sets in? Does the patient know the usual fail-safe mechanisms (calling the ward; cutting short the pass; having someone, even an ambulance, drive him or her back)? Does the patient know whom to call on nights and weekends?

These issues constitute the material of the patient's demonstrated competence to weigh the risks and benefits of giving information to or withholding it from treaters (Gutheil, 1992). This inquiry should then be documented in concise form, such as, "Patient knows what to do if pass becomes stressful, how to deal with possible increase in suicidality, risks and benefits of pass, responses to emergency."

This approach and its documentation take advantage of the clinician's actual presence in the room with the patient; no one else has access to this information, and the clinician has determined by a specific test rather than by guessing that the patient demonstrates the critical competence. Also, a patient who is not able to respond appropriately to the inquiry is probably not ready to go on the pass at that time; here, again, the risk management idea rests on a clinical foundation, as it must do to be valid.

Patients easily flooded by affect or those with concreteness of thought may be given a card with the clinic's or hospital's telephone number and a written list of problem situations and what to do when they are encountered; a copy of this guide may be placed in the chart as documentation.

Should the patient indeed commit suicide on the pass without warning the treaters, a sound defense to the accusation of negligence is the care shown in the assessment and the fact (as a jury can grasp) that this patient demonstrated before going out that he or she could have reached out. The patient knew, by actual test, what to do but apparently elected not to do it, and that is not the clinician's fault. This analysis has significant power in the courtroom.

ACUTE VERSUS CHRONIC SUICIDALITY

I have elsewhere noted (Gutheil, 1985) that acute suicidality is a problem in the metabolism of despair; chronic suicidality is a problem in the metabolism of responsibility. This epigram captures the point that we frequently encounter acutely suicidal patients in practice whose management, if not simple, is at least straightforward. Those less common patients who are chronically suicidal are an especially problematic group. For these patients, suicidality is a way of life—paradox intended. Although some of this group use suicidality as a learned manipulative force to control others, including treaters, in their environment (Sifneos, 1966; Basescu, 1965), others are more existentially suicidal; they cling to the idea of suicide as an ever-present escape hatch from an often intolerable living situation (Farber, 1962); hence, they are never not suicidal. Their posture is, "If the world disappoints me one more time, I will pull the ace from my sleeve: I will play my trump card and commit suicide. Thus, I am in control at all times."

I have suggested that these latter patients "hold the world by the throat," but it is their own throats. The clinician's posture must often be, "I cannot keep you alive single-handedly, but I can help you learn to take care of your own life and learn to take responsibility for your feelings and the task of bearing them." In practice, this approach will inevitably involve the clinician's and the patient's assuming together some calculated risks, such as electively not hospitalizing the patient on some occasions (in part because of the lack of any end point and in part to aid the development of the patient's capacity to bear feelings) (Olin, 1976; Schwartz, 1979). Scholars have suggested that the above approach is related to the work of Linehan (1993a; see Chapters One and Nine in this book) with chronically suicidal borderline patients.

Pitfalls of the Suicide Contract

In contemporary practice, the term *suicide contract* (also called the *antisuicide contract* and *contracting for safety*) is commonly bandied about in relation to the treatment of suicidal patients (Miller, Jacobs, and Gutheil, 1998; Jacobs, 1993; Chapter Twenty-Six in this book). A progress note, in cryptic entirety, may say: "Patient contracted," as though some puzzling diminution in patient size were taking place.

This regrettable term is used in several different ways, a point further impeding its utility. To heighten the confusion, lawyers always assume that clinicians mean by contract the same highly specific term of art they use in the law.

Clinically, one meaning of this kind of contract is the patient's moral commitment or "pledge" to notify caretakers of new or increased suicidal intent; in a more primitive and plaintive version, the treater asks for a promise that the patient will not act on suicidal intent. The most glaring flaws in this approach are that (1) the patient may not be competent to make such an agreement; (2) the treater may not have become important enough to the patient at that point to make a promise meaningful; (3) the request may be seen as aimed at the treater's distress, not the patient's (of course, this may be quite accurate); (4) the achievement of a contract may inappropriately replace or distract from careful clinical assessment of the patient's state; and (5) treaters may be lulled into a false and dangerous sense that the patient has somehow been "suicide-proofed" by this pledge.

A second sense of this contract is as mastery of time. Depressed patients feeling that they face an eternity of dysphoria may feel better and more in control if asked if they can hold off on suicidal action for one day at a time or, in desperate straits, even for an hour at a time. The message is, "You needn't agree to try staying alive for years to come, a prospect that seems to overwhelm you; let us focus instead on your trying to hold on for just one day for now."

Rather than using a contract, Jacobs (1993) has suggested that the treater focus on an "alliance for safety," where patient and treater agree to devote themselves to the task of treatment in a collaborative manner. The message is, "We will work together. You will tell me how you are feeling and will observe and monitor yourself; and I will help your monitoring and coordinate the treatment."

Dates with Death: A Special Problem

Time-contingent or situation-contingent suicidality poses special difficulties for the clinician (Gutheil and Schetky, 1998). Here the patient states something like the following: "If I don't feel better in a month, I'll commit suicide," "If I'm not married by the time I'm thirty, I'll commit suicide," or "If I get one more rejection, I'll commit suicide." For the clinician, the disconcerting dilemma posed by such statements is that they represent declared suicidal intent, usually an emergency condition, but are unusually placed in some definite or indefinite future, clearly altering the typical imminence of the emergency.

Recommendations for this paradoxical situation are addressed elsewhere (Gutheil and Schetky, 1998) but may be summarized thus:

1. Explore the statement as a communication of a feeling state, particularly of felt helplessness and a desire for control.

2. Avoid power struggles by pacing the therapy carefully, teaching cognitive skills of affect management, and refraining from asserting that you can single-handedly prevent suicide.

3. Assess the patient's competence to collaborate in treatment planning (Gutheil, Bursztajn, and Brodsky, 1986) and maintain a low threshold for hospitalization voluntarily or petitioning for commitment, especially as the "target date" nears.

TRADITIONAL RISK MANAGEMENT APPROACHES

Nothing reviewed in this chapter is intended in any way to replace the more familiar approaches to risk management commonly used and described in detail elsewhere (Appelbaum and Gutheil, 1991; Gutheil, 1992; Gutheil, Bursztajn, and Brodsky, 1984); these include careful documentation (especially as to the patient's capacity to participate in treatment planning); consultation, where a second opinion, even obtained anonymously so that confidentiality is not breached, brings the physician into touch with the standard of care; and sharing uncertainty (Gutheil, Bursztajn, and Brodsky, 1984), where the physician allies with patients' wishes for certainty and magical guarantees but gently disabuses them of the reality of those wishes, by commenting, for example, "I sure wish I could keep you alive all by myself or guarantee that this treatment would be sure to work on your depression."

OUTREACH AFTER SUICIDE

Outreach to the survivors of suicide—including interventions in the form of attending a funeral or wake, inviting the family to meet to discuss the suicide, or, at the very least, sending a condolence letter—is an important clinical response to the bereaved, which physicians have performed since time immemorial. Outreach is aimed at decreasing the psychiatric morbidity of survivors of suicide as well as assisting the clinician to process his or her own grief and permitting final termination. In addition to these humane goals, outreach may serve a risk management function insofar as it aids the family in dealing with the "bad feelings" that occur in the wake of a suicide and aids in the preservation of an alliance with the doctor (Appelbaum and Gutheil, 1991; Gutheil, 1992). Yet a caveat is in order.

Clinicians having experienced a patient's suicide are usually torn between two extremes: feeling completely responsible for the suicide and disclaiming any responsibility for it (Carter, 1971; Maltsberger, 1992). Neither extreme should be enacted with the family, as this is not helpful. Similarly, any regrets the clinician feels should be shared with supervisors or peers, not the family.

I recommend that the treaters, rather than either wallowing in self-excoriation or asserting self-exoneration, find something both true and admiring or positive to say or write to the family about the deceased—for example, "I really admired your husband's stamina in the face of so much adversity," "I was impressed by the strength of your daughter's religious faith and what a source of comfort it was for her," "I will really miss your grandfather's dry wit, even when things looked bleak." Finding something to admire places the treater in an alliance with the family, who are often groping for some positive, eulogizing thing to say about the deceased.

Younger clinicians often express fear of encountering the family—fearing being attacked or abused—because of their own neurotic guilt and fear of the family's anger. Experience reveals that families usually see the doctor's appearance at the funeral as a positive expression of respect and welcome the participation in the mourning process.

COMMONLY ASKED QUESTIONS

In risk management conferences around the country, some questions come up so frequently that I include them here as a miscellany for the sake of completeness.

How do you foster responsibility when dealing with chronic suicidality?

The critical point is to understand that not all suicidality is alike. Everyone may have fleeting suicidal ideation, but this differs profoundly from the acutely lethal, despairing individuals who are hopeless and at the end of their rope, and those in what might be called an existential suicidal position, who essentially are always suicidal because they never learned about pleasure, relationships, and living. For them, suicidality is not a spike in the pattern of their mood; it is a steady state over time. Its management is different from that of acute suicidality, just as the management of acute pneumonia is different from that of diabetes. As with diabetes, the patient has to learn to master the condition in an ongoing, sometimes lifelong manner.

For the clinician, a useful posture is, "I sure hope you don't kill yourself, but I know I can't stop you." (This part of the response avoids threatening the patient with removal of the "trump card.") "What I can offer is a chance to take your situation seriously, which means no alcohol, attending AA, and coming to your appointments Tuesdays at 2:00 so that we can work on managing your affect better."

What should one do if faced with an outstanding bill for the patient who committed suicide? Is forgiving the bill an admission of guilt? Is asking for payment a provocation to sue?

The critical point to understand is that you do not know what to do. Those who do know are called risk managers, and they work for insurance companies. Unlike physicians, they have been specifically trained to make this kind of decision. Take no action without consulting them.

I was told after a suicide a couple of years ago that I had to get the consent of the administrator of the estate and get a court order before I could release information to family members.

This advice was legally correct; you do need such consent or permission of an executor to reveal what the patient disclosed to you in confidence. However, you do *not* need such permission to talk about your own feelings toward the patient, or to offer support, comfort, and therapeutic work to the family. Even with the above consents, the doctor should use some discretion and tact in revealing the patient's material to family.

But the families want more. They want the details of what happened. They are ruminating; they are obsessing.

In a way, the question has answered itself. If the family is not satisfied with your statements about the situation in general or your feelings, you can tell them that you need certain releases and then you will do your best to clarify more of the details of the case. Remember always that the release—and this is true for the release of information about the living as well as the dead—overcomes only the legal barrier to discussion. It does not overcome the ethical and the sensitivity barriers to discussion.

Yes, but those legal barriers do take a little while for the administrator of the estate to get the paperwork done.

But nothing stops you from meeting every week with the family to see how they are doing, to have them continue to work on their grief with you, to talk to them about your experience. Confidentiality is not a barrier to support, to empathy, to exploring the family's experiences—their fantasies, their feelings, their wishes, their guilt, their sadness, and so on. Of course, you should document these meetings or, if the family refuses to meet with you, document your referral of them to alternative agencies to deal with their needs.

Could you comment on the effects on the standard of practice of mental health providers as a result of all this litigation for negligence?

The most direct and obvious answer is that a misapplied fear of litigation has led to the ironically self-destructive approach called defensive medicine. Defensive medicine oppositionalizes, alienates, and adversarializes the relationship of the clinician and patient, just where, ironically, the collaborative alliance with the patient (and family) is the soundest form of risk management.

There are two pieces of good news emerging from this chaos: practitioners have become more sensitive to the use of documentation and consultation. Over the years I have been working in this area, I have been impressed with the way the records have improved.

I recommend keeping records for something like ten years. At the end of the ten years, I reduce the record to a one-page summary of the case and keep that forever.

Can you say something about the termination summary after a suicide?

It is probably useful to write one. It will aid your own internal termination, and you are making a record while events are fresh in your mind—a record of use to you, your insurer, and your institution for a number of purposes, including peer review.

Keep in mind the possibility that this might end up in public; hence, it should reflect well on you as a doctor, a person, and a clinician, rather than being either a self-flagellation or a self-exoneration. Keep it clinical and neutral.

IMPLICATIONS FOR THE CLINICIAN

Already bereaved by a patient's suicide, clinicians may find their suffering increased by becoming the recipient of a malpractice suit after the suicide. While it is still a truism that anyone can sue anyone for anything, the clinically based risk management principles outlined here will help decrease the likelihood of litigation in the first place and the likelihood of the plaintiff's prevailing if suit is filed. To sum up:

- The core of liability prevention is care of the patient in alliance-based, nondefensive ways.

- The critical elements of clinically based risk management are attention to documentation, consultation, sharing uncertainty, and patient competence.

- Outreach to survivors serves both humanitarian and risk management goals.

- "Suicide contracts" should not replace careful clinical assessment or work within the therapeutic alliance.

- Anticipating bad feelings that might follow the outcome of suicide will aid in both working with the patient and the family and decreasing litigation risk.

APPENDIX

Guidelines for Identification, Assessment, and Treatment Planning for Suicidality

Risk Management Foundation of the Harvard Medical Institutions

IDENTIFICATION AND ASSESSMENT

Purposes

To provide a model for the assessment of suicidality in all clinical settings.

To provide information to be incorporated into institution-specific protocols.

These guidelines are not to be construed or to serve as a standard of care. Standards of medical care are determined on the basis of all clinical data available for an individual case and are subject to change as scientific knowledge and technology advance and patterns evolve. This model should be considered only as a guideline. Adherence to it will not ensure a successful outcome in every case. It should not be construed as including all proper methods aimed at the same results. The ultimate judgment of suicidality regarding a particular patient must be made by the clinician in light of the clinical data presented by the patient and other available information (adapted from Practice guidelines for major depressive disorder in adults. *Am J Psychiatry* 1993; 150[supp14]).

When to Use These Guidelines

Assessment and documentation of suicidality are integral components of any psychiatric evaluation and become primary concerns in that evaluation at the following times:

1. During initial interview or on admission to a facility or program
2. With the occurrence of any suicidal/self-destructive behavior or ideation
3. On the occasion of any noteworthy clinical change (e.g., significant new symptoms, mental status changes, stressors)
4. For inpatients who have been assessed to be suicidal, the following situations may prompt any additional assessment:
   a. On progression to a less restrictive level of precautions or privileges (including therapeutic passes).
   b. At time of discharge from hospital.

Data for Assessing Suicidality/General

The assessment of a potentially suicidal patient begins with a comprehensive psychiatric evaluation. At subsequent evaluations, the breadth of questioning will vary depending on circumstances. Such inquiry often includes relevant complaint(s) and history, a limited mental status examination, and relevant physical and laboratory examinations that do not unnecessarily duplicate previous assessments.

Psychiatric Evaluation Psychiatric Diagnosis

The clinician performs a diagnostic assessment to identify whether the patient suffers from a psychiatric illness associated with higher suicide risk, especially mood disorders, schizophrenia, substance abuse, anxiety disorders, borderline personality disorder, and other personality disorders and traits, or patients with comorbid illness. See "Disorders Correlated with Suicidal Behavior" section for details on suicide risk with specific diagnostic considerations.

Other Conditions Which Can Increase Suicide Risk

1. Physical illness, particularly associated with chronic pain
2. Delirium associated with organic illness
3. Other personality disorders/traits
4. Psychopathology in family and social milieu, including life stress and crisis
5. Family history of psychiatric illness and particularly of suicide
6. The presence of firearms in the home (particularly for adolescents)

The assessment of suicidality is an active process during which clinicians evaluate:

1. Suicidal intent and lethality
2. Dynamic meanings and motivation for suicide
3. Presence of a suicidal plan
4. Presence of overt suicidal/self-destructive behavior
5. The patient's physiological, cognitive, and affective states
6. The patient's coping potential
7. The patient's epidemiologic risk factors

Many of these observations are made during the general psychiatric evaluation and mental status examination. However, a number of suicide specific questions may be included in this process.

The Detection of Suicidality—Suicide-Specific Questions

1. Is the patient able/competent to participate in treatment?
2. Is the patient able to develop a therapeutic alliance?
3. Are suicidal thoughts/feelings present?
4. What form does the patient's wish for suicide take?
5. What does suicide mean to the patient?
6. Has the patient lost or anticipates losing an essential sustaining relationship?
7. Has the patient lost or anticipates losing his/her main reason for living?
8. How far has the suicide planning process proceeded?
9. Have suicidal behaviors occurred in the past?
10. Has the patient engaged in self-mutilating behaviors?
11. Does the patient's mental state increase the potential for suicide?
12. Are depression and/or despair present?
13. Does the patient's physiologic state increase the potential for suicide? (e.g., physical illness, intoxication, pain, delirium, organic impairment)
14. Is the patient vulnerable to painful affects such as aloneness, self-contempt, murderous rage, shame, or panic?
15. Are there recent stresses in the patient's life?
16. What are the patient's capacities for self-regulation?
17. Is the patient able/competent to participate in treatment?
18. Loss of coping mechanism?
19. An expanded version with more detailed questions is included in the section called "Detection of Suicidality: Expanded Outline and Questions."
20. Are epidemiologic risk factors present?

See "Suicide Risk Factors" section for a list of these risk factors. These factors do not predict suicide. Rather, they are part of a suicide assessment because of their demonstrated statistical correlation with suicide.

TREATMENT PLANNING

Once an assessment of the patient's suicide risk has been made, an individual treatment plan must be designed. Treatment planning is a dynamic process, shaped by and communicated between the patient and involved caregivers in light of changing information or behaviors. Sometimes it may be possible and clinically indicated to include significant others in treatment planning. Because suicidality can be an acute (state) or chronic (trait) condition, treatment planning may need to consider both short and long term goals. Treatment planning takes into account the patient's potential for suicide, capacity to form a treatment alliance, and range of available treatment alternatives from outpatient follow-up to hospitalization with constant observation.

Collect Data Before Treatment Planning

Success is more likely when the treatment plan rests on a firm foundation of data and assessment.

Identify a Range of Treatment Alternatives

1. Weigh the risks and benefits of each alternative, including the alternative "no treatment."
2. There is no unique correct plan. Select a plan based upon assessment and judgment.

Involve the Patient and Family in the Treatment Planning Process to the Degree Possible

1. When a patient lacks the capacity to participate in treatment planning, the clinician must make judgments about the most appropriate treatment plan.
2. Information from the patient's significant others may be of use in the planning process.

Incorporate Existing Treatment Modalities Into the Plan

1. Involve a current treating clinician and/or appropriate significant others in planning and follow-up.
2. Continue or reassess ongoing pharmacotherapy, with involvement of prescribing physician.

Be Aware that Contracts Will
Not Guarantee the Patient's Safety

1. Patient's ability to understand and participate in treatment should be assessed.
2. Treatment focus should be on alliance with the patient.
3. Contracts can play a role if utilized as part of a comprehensive evaluation and treatment plan.
4. However, contracts can give staff a false sense of security and interfere with a thorough suicide assessment.

Choose Appropriate Levels of
Observation, Supervision, and Privileges

1. The inpatient unit is especially effective in the treatment of acute rather than chronic suicidality. It offers safety, support, and hope (although no unit is suicide proof). Inpatient treatment planning is determined on an individual basis to meet the patient's need for maximal safety in the least restrictive environment. Although precautions and privileges have restrictive elements, they are applied in the context of a treatment plan that aims to enable a patient to tolerate suicidal feelings.
2. Inpatient treatment of suicidal patients relies upon a progression through a hierarchy of observation levels, supervision levels, privileges, and therapeutic passes.
3. With clinical improvement, suicidality may still persist. Although the ultimate goal is toward a less restrictive environment, the clinical decision must be based on an assessment that the suicide risk has been reduced.

The Levels of Observation, Supervision, and Privileges
Parallel the Patient's Potential for Suicidal Behavior

1. Examples of observation levels are:
   a. Continuous observation (1:1 or remaining in sight of staff members)
   b. Restricting the patient to an area where he or she can be seen at all times by staff
   c. Restricting the patient to public areas; not allowing him or her to be alone in room
   d. Checks at intervals of 5, 15, or 30 minutes
   e. Periodic checks at intervals greater than every 30 minutes
2. Examples of when staff supervision is necessary include during the patient's use of:
   a. Sharps (nail cutters, razors, scissors)
   b. Cigarettes and matches

    c. Poisons (cleaning supplies)

    d. Bathroom

    e. Kitchen

    f. Occupational therapy

3. Examples of privilege levels are:

    a. Restricted to unit

    b. Accompanied off-unit by staff (specify 1:1 versus group, number and gender of staff person, legal status of patient when relevant)

    c. Accompanied off-unit by non-staff (reliable family member or friend)

    d. Unaccompanied off-unit

Document the Treatment Planning Process and the Plan

1. Document the range of options considered and why one was chosen over others.

2. Document communication with the patient. With suicidal inpatients, documentation of suicidality occurs, at (but not limited to) the following treatment stages:

    a. Admission

    b. First unaccompanied pass

    c. Discharge (Especially at discharge, the issue of chronic suicide risk must be considered. The chronic risk can be assessed according to the same model, though a longer view is taken of the risks and benefits of various treatment options.)

3. Document discharge planning to include:

    a. Living arrangements, work, communication with significant others

    b. Follow-up appointments or contact with outpatient provider

    c. Medications (include prescriptions)

    d. Current suicide assessment

In Planning Treatment for a Chronically Suicidal Patient, Some of the Following Considerations May Apply:

1. Safety may wax and wane.

2. Despair over treatment failure may increase suicide potential.

3. The treatment team may decide to tolerate short term risk to foster long-term growth.

    a. Such a decision should include informed consent.

    b. Documentation should make clear the choices and rationale.

4. Assess the risk of continued hospitalization.

DISORDERS CORRELATED WITH SUICIDAL BEHAVIOR

The following five DSM IV disorders are correlated with suicide and suicidal behavior:[1]

Mood Disorders (15 percent lifetime risk of suicide)

1. The absence of psychosis does not imply safety.
2. A misleading reduction of anxious or depressed affect can occur in some patients who have resolved their ambivalence by deciding to commit suicide. A patient who has made the decision to die may appear at peace and not show signs of an inner struggle. Concern is warranted especially when the patient appears emotionally removed, shows constricted affect, or is known to have given away belongings.
3. The likelihood of suicide within 1 year is increased when the patient exhibits:
   a. Panic attacks
   b. Psychic anxiety
   c. Anhedonia
   d. Alcohol abuse
4. The likelihood of suicide during the ensuing 1–5 years is increased when the patient exhibits:
   a. Increased hopelessness
   b. Suicidal ideation
   c. History of suicide attempts

Panic Disorder (7–15 percent lifetime risk of suicide)[2]

1. Suicide rate may be similar to that of mood disorders
2. Greater likelihood is correlated with more severe illness or comorbidity
3. Suicide does not necessarily occur during a panic attack
4. Demoralization or significant loss increase the likelihood of suicide
5. Agitation may increase the likelihood of translating impulses into action

---

[1]More than 90 percent of completed suicides carry a diagnosis of alcoholism, depression, schizophrenia, or some combination of these.

[2]Recent studies have demonstrated that an association of panic disorder with attempted and completed suicide appears to be indirect, and that panic disorder is not an independent risk factor (Beck at al., 1991; Henriksson et al., 1996; Johnson et al., 1990). See Chapter Two for further information.

Schizophrenia (10 percent lifetime risk of suicide)

1. Suicide is relatively uncommon during psychotic episodes
2. The relationship between command hallucinations and actual suicide is not clearly causal
3. Suicidal ideation occurs in 60–80 percent of patients
4. Suicide attempts occur in 30–55 percent of patients
5. Suicide potential is increased by:
   a. Good premorbid functioning
   b. Early phase of illness
   c. Hopelessness or depression
   d. Recognition of deterioration, e.g., during a post-psychotic depressed phase

Alcoholism (3 percent lifetime risk of suicide)

1. Abusers of alcohol/drugs comprise 15–25 percent of suicides
2. Alcohol is associated with nearly 50 percent of all suicides
3. Increased suicide potential in an alcoholic patient correlates with:
   a. Active substance abuse
   b. Adolescence
   c. Second or third decades of illness
   d. Comorbid psychiatric illness
   e. Recent or anticipated interpersonal loss
4. Substance abuse can represent self treatment to blunt the anxiety or mood disturbance associated with a masked, comorbid psychiatric disorder

Borderline Personality Disorder (7 percent lifetime risk of suicide)

1. Much higher risk associated with comorbidity, especially with mood disorder and substance abuse
2. Psychopathology associated with increased risk:
   a. Impulsivity, hopelessness/despair
   b. Antisocial features (with dishonesty)
   c. Interpersonal aloofness ("malignant narcissism")
   d. Self-mutilating tendencies
   e. Psychosis with bizarre suicide attempts
3. Psychopathology associated with diminished risk:
   a. Infantile personality (with hysterical features)
   b. Masochistic personality

DETECTION OF SUICIDALITY: EXPANDED OUTLINE AND QUESTIONS

Suicidal Intent and Lethality

1. Are suicidal thoughts/feelings present?
   a. What are they?
   b. Are they active/volitional or passive/non-volitional?
   c. When did they begin?
   d. How frequent are they?
   e. How persistent are they?
   f. Are they obsessive?
   g. Can the patient control them?
   h. What motivates the patient to die or to continue living?
2. Dynamic meanings and motivation for suicide
3. What form does the patient's wish for suicide take?
   Is there a wish to die, to hurt someone else, to escape, to punish self?
4. What does suicide mean to the patient?
   a. Is there a wish for rebirth or reunion?
   b. Is there an identification with a significant other?
   c. What is the person's view of death and relationship to it?
   d. Does death have a positive meaning for the patient?
5. Has the patient lost an essential sustaining relationship?
6. Has the patient lost his/her main reason for living? (These losses can be threatened.)

Presence of a Suicidal Plan

1. How far has the suicide planning process proceeded?
2. Specific method, place, time?
   a. Available means?
   b. Planned sequence of events?
   c. Intended goal? (e.g., death, self-injury, or another outcome)
3. Feasibility of plan?
   Access to weapons (Document any conversation about access to guns or other lethal weapons. Consider the possibility of misinformation.)
4. Lethality of planned actions?
   a. Objectively assess danger to life.
   b. Objectively question patient's conception of lethality.
   c. Avoid terms such as gesture or manipulation, because they imply a motive that may be absent or irrelevant to lethality.

d. Bizarre methods have less predictable results and may therefore carry greater risk.

e. Pay attention to violent, irreversible methods such as shooting or jumping.

5. Likelihood of rescue?

Patients who contemplate a plan likely to end in discovery may be more ambivalent and/or attached to people than others who plan their suicidal behavior to occur in an isolated setting.

6. What preparation has the patient made (e.g., obtaining pills, suicide note, making financial arrangements)?

7. Has the patient rehearsed for suicide (e.g., rigging a noose, putting gun to head, driving near a bridge)?

History of Overt Suicidal/Self-Destructive Behavior

1. Have suicidal behaviors occurred in the past?

2. It is useful to explore the circumstances of any past suicide attempts. If the patient can describe the past event, this may provide the best window into the current state of mind. Absence of previous suicidality, however, does not eliminate the risk of current or future attempts.

3. Statistical relationships of suicide attempts to suicide completion are:

a. Attempters are at increased risk for suicide over the general population by 7–10 percent.

b. 18–38 percent of those who died by suicide have made a prior attempt.

c. 90 percent of attempters do not go on to complete suicide.

d. 1 percent of past attempters kill themselves each year.

4. Has the patient engaged in self-mutilating behaviors?

a. Wrist-cutting or other self-mutilation suggests consideration of the diagnoses of PTSD or dissociative disorders among others. When a history of trauma or abuse is present, it may be valuable to assess the presence of a mood disorder.

b. Although self-mutilation is frequently an act of self soothing rather than an attempt to die, patients who self-mutilate do sometimes commit suicide.

c. In assessing risk of further self-mutilation, one useful question is, "How do you calm yourself down?"

The Patient's Physiological, Cognitive, and Affective States

1. Does the patient's mental state increase the potential for suicide?

a. Does the patient have the capacity to act?

(1) Suicide requires both the ability to organize and the energy to implement a plan.

(2) Suicide potential may be heightened when there is greater energy (as in early recovery from depression) or lowered inhibition (as during intoxication or rage).

    b. Is the patient hopeless?

      (1) Hopelessness is a key psychological factor in suicidal intent and behavior.

      (2) It is often accompanied by pervasive negative expectations.

2. Are depression and/or despair present?

    Depression is a mood state or syndromal disorder associated with vegetative symptoms. Despair is a cognitive state that features a sense of futility about alternatives, no personal sense of a future role, and a lack of human connections that might offer support.

    a. Is a diagnosable psychiatric disorder present that is correlated with suicidality or poor treatment compliance?

3. Does the patient's physiologic state increase the potential for suicide? (illness, intoxication, pain)

    a. Are intoxicants present?

      (1) Acute intoxication or withdrawal can lead to an acute increase in suicide risk

        a. State dependent: decreased inhibition, poor judgment, denial

        b. Importance of precipitants such as interpersonal loss

      (2) Thorough evaluation difficult when patient is intoxicated

        a. Provide safe place until sober

        b. Reassess suicide risk when sober

      (3) Chronic abuse or dependence leads to a chronic risk

        a. Trait dependent self-destruction and decreased self-care

        b. Suicide risk can be elevated when a relapse occurs

4. Is the patient vulnerable to painful affects such as aloneness, self-contempt, murderous rage, shame or panic?

The Patient's Coping Potential

1. Are there recent stressors in the patient's life?

    a. Is the patient facing a real or imagined loss, disappointment, humiliation or failure?

    b. Has there been a disruption in the patient's support system (including treatment)?

2. What are the patient's capacities for self-regulation?

    a. Does the patient have a history of impulsive behavior?

    b. Does the patient need, and can he or she use external sustaining resources to regulate self-esteem?

3. Is the patient able to participate in treatment?

    a. Does the patient verbalize a willingness to comply with treatment plan?

    b. Does the patient possess the capacity for making an alliance?

SUICIDE RISK FACTORS

The following risk factors provide explicit criteria for identifying the presence of factors correlated with a greater likelihood of suicide risk. They can be used as a screen, to heighten risk awareness. With any individual patient, they assume greater or lesser importance. The list of factors most relevant to adults over age 30 differs from that for individuals younger than 30 (adapted from Klerman, 1987).

Under 30 (Adolescents and Young Adults)

1. Family history of suicide
2. Males > females
3. History of previous attempts
4. Native American
5. Psychiatric diagnosis: mood disorders and substance abuse
6. White > black
7. Mini-epidemic in community
8. History of delinquent or semi-delinquent behavior even without depression in current mental state
9. Presence of firearms (when other factors are present)

Over 30

1. Family history of suicide
2. Males > females
3. History of previous attempts
4. Native American
5. Psychiatric diagnosis: mood disorder, schizophrenia, alcoholism
6. Single: especially separated, widowed, or divorced
7. Lack of social supports
8. Concurrent medical illness(es)
9. Unemployment
10. Decline in socioeconomic status
11. Psychological turmoil

DEVELOPED BY THE SUICIDE RISK ADVISORY COMMITTEE OF THE RISK MANAGEMENT FOUNDATION OF THE HARVARD MEDICAL INSTITUTIONS

Committee Members

Douglas Jacobs, M.D., Chairman
Thomas G. Gutheil, M.D.
James Harburger, M.D.
Martin J. Kelly, M.D.
John T. Maltsberger, M.D.
Michael Craig Miller, M.D.
Ron Schouten, M.D.
Lloyd I. Sederer, M.D.

Consultants

Margaret Brewer, R.N., M.B.A.
James M. Ellison, M.D., M.P.H.

Risk Management Foundation Staff

Eileen M. Ryan, R.N., M.S., M.P.H., Co-chairperson
Priscilla S. Dasse, R.N., M.P.H.
Carol McL. Shapiro, R. N.

Reviewers

William Adams, M.D.
Andrew Brotman, M.D.
Randolph Catlin, M.D.

REFERENCES

Abrams R. *Electroconvulsive therapy,* 2d ed. New York: Oxford University Press 1992.

Abrams R, Vedak C. Prediction of ECT response in melancholia. *Convulsive Ther* 1991;7:81–84.

Achté K, Stenbäck A, Teräinen H. On suicides committed during treatment in psychiatric hospitals. *Acta Psychiatr Scand* 1966;42:272–284.

Adam KS. Environmental, psychosocial and psychoanalytic aspects of suicidal behavior. In SJ Blumenthal, DJ Kupfer (eds), *Suicide over the life cycle: Risk factors, assessment, and treatment of suicidal patients.* Washington DC: American Psychiatric Press 1990:39–96.

Adamek ME, Kaplan MS. The growing use of firearms by suicidal older women, 1979–1992: A research note. *Suicide Life-Threat Behav* 1996;26:71–78.

Adams DM, Overholser JC. Suicidal behavior and history of substance abuse. *Am J Drug Alcohol Abuse* 1992;18:343–354.

Adelson L. Pedicide revisited: The slaughter continues. *Am J Forensic Med Pathol* 1991;12:16–26.

Adler D. Schizophrenia and the life cycle. *Community Ment Health J* 1995;31:249–262.

Adler G, Buie DH Jr. Aloneness and borderline psychopathology: The possible relevance of child development issues. *Int J Psychoanal* 1979;60:83–96.

Ågren H. Symptom patterns in unipolar and bipolar depression correlating with monoamine metabolites in the cerebrospinal fluid: II. Suicide. *Psychiatry Res* 1980;3:225–236.

Ågren H. Depressive symptom patterns and urinary MHPG excretion. *Psychiatry Res* 1982;6:185–196.

Ågren H, Niklasson F. Suicidal potential in depression: Focus on CSF monoamine and purine metabolites. *Psychopharmacol Bull* 1986;22:656–660.

Ahrens B, Müller-Oerlinghausen B, Schou M, et al. Excess cardiovascular and suicide mortality of affective disorders may be reduced by lithium prophylaxis. *J Affective Disord* 1995;33:67–75.

Akiskal HS, Chen SE, Davis GC, et al. Borderline: An adjective in search of a noun. *J Clin Psychiatry* 1985;46:41–48.

Alexander V. *In the wake of suicide: Stories of the people left behind.* San Francisco: Jossey-Bass 1998.

Allebeck P. Schizophrenia: A life-shortening disease. *Schizophr Bull* 1989;15:81–88.

Allebeck P, Bolund C. Suicides and suicide attempts in cancer patients. *Psychol Med* 1991;21:979–984.

Allebeck P, Bolund C, Ringback G. Increased suicide rate in cancer patients: A cohort study based on the Swedish Cancer-Environment Register. *J Clin Epidemiol* 1989;42:611–616.

Allebeck P, Varla A, Kristjansson E, et al. Risk factors for suicide among patients with schizophrenia. *Acta Psychiatr Scand* 1987;76:414–419.

Allen NH. Homicide followed by suicide: Los Angeles, 1970–1979. *Suicide Life-Threat Behav* 1983;13:155–165.

Allgulander C, Lavori PW. Causes of death among 936 elderly patients with "pure" anxiety neurosis in Stockholm County, Sweden, and in patients with depressive neurosis or both diagnoses. *Comp Psychiatry* 1993;34:299–302.

Alström CH. Mortality in mental hospitals with especial regard to tuberculosis. *Acta Psychiatr Neurol Scand* 1942;24(suppl):1–422.

Alvarez, A. *The savage god.* New York: Random House 1970.

Amador XF, Flaum M, Andreasen NC, et al. Awareness of illness in schizophrenia and schizoaffective and mood disorders. *Arch Gen Psychiatry* 1994;51:826–836.

Amador XF, Friedman JH, Kasapis C, et al. Suicidal behavior in schizophrenia and its relationship to awareness of illness. *Am J Psychiatry* 1996;153:1185–1188.

American College of Neuropsychopharmacology. Consensus statement, March 2, 1992. *Neuropsychopharmacology* 1993;8:177–183.

American Heritage College Dictionary, 3d ed. Boston: Houghton Mifflin 1997.

American Psychiatric Association. *Diagnostic and statistical manual of mental disorders,* 3d ed. Washington DC: American Psychiatric Association 1980.

American Psychiatric Association. *Diagnostic and statistical manual of mental disorders,* 4th ed. Washington DC: American Psychiatric Association 1994.

American Psychiatric Association, Task Force on Electroconvulsive Therapy. *Report no. 14.* Washington DC: American Psychiatric Association 1978.

American Psychiatric Association, Task Force on Electroconvulsive Therapy. *The practice of electroconvulsive therapy: Recommendations for treatment, training, and privileging.* Washington DC: American Psychiatric Association 1990.

Anderson BA, Howard MO, Walker RD, Suchinsky RT. Characteristics of substance-abusing veterans attempting suicide: A national study. *Psychol Rep* 1995;77:1231–1242.

Anderson EW. Prognosis of depressions of late life. *J Ment Sci* 1936;82:559–588.

Anderson IM, Ware CJ, Da Roza-Davis JM, Cowen PJ. Decreased 5-HT-mediated prolactin release in major depression. *Br J Psychiatry* 1992;160:372–378.

Anderson RN, Kochanek KD, Murphy SL. Report of final mortality statistics, 1995. *Monthly vital statistics report,* vol 45, no 11, suppl 2. Hyattsville MD: National Center for Health Statistics 1997.

Andersson A, Eriksson A, Marcusson JO. Unaltered number of brain serotonin uptake sites in suicide victims, *J Psychopharmacol* 1992;6:509–513.

Andreasen NC, Flaum M, Arndt S. The Comprehensive Assessment of Symptoms and History (CASH): An instrument for assessing diagnosis and psychopathology. *Arch Gen Psychiatry* 1992;49:615–623.

Andrews JA, Lewinsohn PM. Suicidal attempts among older adolescents: Prevalence and co-occurrence with psychiatric disorders. *J Am Acad Child Adol Psychiatry* 1992;31:655–662.

Andrus JK, Fleming DW, Heumann MA, et al. Surveillance of attempted suicide among adolescents in Oregon, 1988. *Am J Public Health* 1991;81:1067–1069.

Angst J, Stassen HH, Gross G, et al. Suicide in affective and schizoaffective disorders. In A Marneros, MT Tsuang (eds), *Affective and schizoaffective disorders.* Berlin: Springer-Verlag 1990:168–185.

Appelbaum PS. *Tarasoff* and the clinician: Problems in fulfilling the duty to protect. *Am J Psychiatry* 1985;142:425–429.

Appelbaum PS, Gutheil TG. *Clinical handbook of psychiatry and the law,* 2d ed. Baltimore: Williams & Wilkins 1991.

Appleby L. Suicide in psychiatric patients. Risk and prevention. *Br J Psychiatry* 1992;161:749–758.

Appleby L, Amos T, Doyle U, et al. General practitioners and young suicides: A preventive role for primary care. *Br J Psychiatry* 1996;168:330.

Arango V, Ernsberger P, Marzuk PM, et al. Autoradiographic demonstration of increased serotonin 5-HT$_2$ and ß-adrenergic receptor binding sites in the brain of suicide victims. *Arch Gen Psychiatry* 1990;47:1038–1047.

Arango V, Ernsberger P, Sved AF, Mann JJ. Quantitative autoradiography of a$_1$- and a$_2$-adrenergic receptors in the cerebral cortex of controls and suicide victims. *Brain Res* 1993;630:271–282.

Arango V, Mann JJ. Relevance of serotonergic postmortem studies to suicidal behavior. *Int Rev Psychiatry* 1992;4:131–140.

Arango V, Underwood MD, Gubbi AV, Mann JJ. Localized alterations in pre- and post-synaptic serotonin binding sites in the ventrolateral prefrontal cortex of suicide victims. *Brain Res* 1995;688:121–133.

Arango V, Underwood MD, Mann JJ. Fewer pigmented locus ceruleus neurons in suicide victims: Preliminary results. *Biol Psychiatry* 1996;39:112–120.

Arató M, Tekes K, Palkovits M, et al. Serotonergic split brain and suicide. *Psychiatry Res* 1987;21:355–356.

Arató M, Tekes K, Tóthfalusi L, et al. Reversed hemispheric asymmetry of imipramine binding in suicide victims. *Biol Psychiatry* 1991;29:699–702.

Arora RC, Meltzer HY. Serotonergic measures in the brains of suicide victims: 5-HT$_2$ binding sites in the frontal cortex of suicide victims and control subjects. *Am J Psychiatry* 1989a; 160:730–736.

Arora RC, Meltzer HY. ^{3}H-imipramine binding in the frontal cortex of suicides. *Psychiatry Res* 1989b;30:125–135.

Arora RC, Meltzer HY. Laterality and ^{3}H-imipramine binding: Studies in the frontal cortex of normal controls and suicide victims. *Biol Psychiatry* 1991;29:1016–1022.

Arranz B, Blennow K, Eriksson A, et al. Serotonergic, noradrenergic, and dopaminergic measures in suicide brains. *Biol Psychiatry* 1997;41:1000–1009.

Arranz B, Eriksson A, Mellerup E, et al. Brain 5-HT$_{1A,}$ 5-HT$_{1D,}$ and 5-HT$_2$ receptors in suicide victims. *Biol Psychiatry* 1994;35:457–463.

Asarnow UR, Carlson GA, Gutherie D. Coping strategies, self-perceptions, hopelessness and perceived family environments in depressed and suicidal children. *J Contemp Clin Psychol* 1987;55:361–366.

Åsberg M, Schalling D, Träskman-Bendz L, Wägner A. Psychobiology of suicide, impulsivity and related phenomena. In HY Meltzer (ed), *Psychopharmacology: The third generation of progress.* New York: Raven Press 1987.

Åsberg M, Thorén P, Träskman L, et al. "Serotonin depression": A biochemical subgroup within the affective disorders? *Science* 1976;191:478–480.

Åsberg M, Träskman L, Thorén P. 5-HIAA in the cerebrospinal fluid: A biochemical suicide predictor? *Arch Gen Psychiatry* 1976;33:1193–1197.

Asch SS. Suicide and the hidden executioner. *Int J Psychoanal* 1980;7:51–60.

Asnis GM, Eisenberg J, van Praag HM, et al. The neuroendocrine response to fenfluramine in depressives and normal controls. *Biol Psychiatry* 1988;24:117–120.

Assey JL. The suicide prevention contract. *Perspect Psychiatr Care* 1985;23:99–103.

Astrup C, Fossum A, Holmboe R. A follow-up study of 270 patients with acute affective psychosis. *Acta Psychiatr Neurol Scand* 1959;135(suppl):1–65.

Avery D, Winokur G. Mortality in depressed patients treated with electroconvulsive therapy and antidepressants. *Arch Gen Psychiatry* 1976;33:1029–1037.

Avery D, Winokur G. The efficacy of electroconvulsive therapy and antidepressants in depression. *Biol Psychiatry* 1977;12:507–523.

Avery D, Winoker G. Suicide, attempted suicide, and relapse rates in depression: Occurrence after ECT and antidepressant therapy. *Arch Gen Psychiatry* 1978;35:749–753.

Bach-y-Rita G. Habitual violence and self-mutilation. *Am J Psychiatry* 1974;131: 1018–1020.

Baker J. Monitoring of suicidal behavior among patients in the VA health care system. *Psychiatr Ann* 1984;14:272–275.

Baldessarini RJ. Drugs and the treatment of psychiatric disorders: Antimanic and antidepressant agents. In JG Hardman, LE Limbird, PB Molinoff, et al (eds), *Goodman and Gilman's pharmacological basis of therapeutics,* 9th ed. New York: McGraw-Hill 1996:431–459.

Baldessarini RJ. Critical issues in assessment and treatment. Presentation to the Harvard Medical School–Continuing Medical Education, Boston, Sept 1997.

Baldessarini RJ, Suppes T, Tondo L. Lithium withdrawal in bipolar disorder: Implications for clinical practice and experimental therapeutics research. *Am J Therapeutics* 1996a;3:492–496.

Baldessarini RJ, Tondo L. Effects of lithium treatment in bipolar disorders and post-treatment-discontinuation recurrence risk. *Clin Drug Investig* 1998;15:337–351.

Baldessarini RJ, Tondo L, Faedda GL, et al. Effects of the rate of discontinuing lithium maintenance treatment in bipolar disorders. *J Clin Psychiatry* 1996b; 57:441–448.

Baldessarini RJ, Tondo L, Floris G, Rudas N. Reduced morbidity after gradually discontinuing lithium in bipolar I and II disorders: A replication study. *Am J Psychiatry* 1997;154:548–550.

Baldessarini RJ, Tondo L, Suppes T, et al. Pharmacological treatment of bipolar disorder throughout the life-cycle. In KI Shulman, M Tohen, S Kutcher (eds), *Bipolar disorder through the life-cycle.* New York: Wiley 1996c:299–338.

Ball TS, Sebback L, Jones R. An accelerometer-activated device to control assaultive and self-destructive behaviors in retardants. *J Behav Ther Exp Psychiatry* 1975;6:223–228.

Ballard CG. Benign intracranial hypertension and repeated self-mutilation. *Br J Psychiatry* 1989;155:570–571.

Banki CM, Arató M. Amine metabolites and neuroendocrine responses related to depression and suicide. *J Affective Disord* 1983;5:223–232.

Barber ME, Marzuk PM, Leon AC, Portera L. Aborted suicide attempts: A new classification of suicidal behavior. *Am J Psychiatry* 1998;155:385–389.

Barley WD, Buie SE, Peterson EW, et al. The development of an inpatient cognitive-behavioral treatment program for borderline personality disorder. *J Pers Disord* 1993;7:232–240.

Barraclough BM. Suicide in the elderly. *Br J Psychiatry* 1971;120(suppl 6):87–97.

Barraclough BM. Suicide prevention, recurrent affective disorder and lithium. *Br J Psychiatry* 1972;121:391–392.

Barraclough BM. *Suicide: Clinical and epidemiological studies.* London: Croom Helm 1987.

Barraclough BM, Bunch J, Nelson B, Sainsbury P. A hundred cases of suicide: Clinical aspects. *Br J Psychiatry* 1974;125:355–373.

Barrett JE, Barrett JA, Oxman TE, Gerber PD. The prevalence of psychiatric disorders in a primary care practice. *Arch Gen Psychiatry* 1988;45:1100–1106.

Barsky AJ, Wool C, Barnett MC, Cleary PD. Histories of childhood trauma in adult hypochondriacal patients. *Am J Psychiatry* 1994;151:397–401.

Basescu S. The threat of suicide in psychotherapy. *Am J Psychother* 1965;19:99–105.

Bataglia J, Moss S, Rush J, et al. Haloperidol, lorazepam, or both for psychotic agitation? *Am J Emerg Med* 1997;15:335–340.

Beardslee WR et al. Response of families to two preventative intervention strategies: Long-term differences and attitude change. *J Am Acad Child Adolesc Psychiatry* 1996;35:774–782.

Beardslee WR, Wright EBJ, Salt P, et al. Examination of children's responses to two preventative child strategies over time. *J Am Acad Child Adolesc Psychiatry* 1997;36:196–204.

Beasley CM, Potvin J Jr, Masica DN, et al. Fluoxetine: No association with suicidality in obsessive-compulsive disorder. *J Affective Disord* 1992;24:1–10.

Beautrais AL, Joyce PR, Mulder RT, et al. Prevalence and comorbidity of mental disorders in persons making serious suicide attempts: A case-control study. *Am J Psychiatry* 1996;153:1009–1014.

Bech P, Vendsborg PB, Rafaelsen O. Lithium maintenance treatment of manic-melancholic patients: Its role in the daily routine. *Acta Psychiatr Scand* 1976; 53:70–81.

Beck AT. Predictor of eventual suicide in psychiatric inpatients by clinical rating of hopelessness. *J Consult Clin Psychol* 1989;57:309–310.

Beck AT, Brown G, Berchik RJ, et al. Relationship between hopelessness and ultimate suicide: A replication with psychiatric outpatients. *Am J Psychiatry* 1990;147: 190–195.

Beck AT, James C, van der Kolk BA. Reports of childhood incest and current behavior of chronically hospitalized psychotic women. *Am J Psychiatry* 1987;144:1474–1476.

Beck AT, Kovacs M, Weissman A. Hopelessness and suicidal behavior: An overview. *JAMA* 1975;234:1146–1149.

Beck AT, Kovacs M, Weissman A. Assessment of suicidal intention: The scale for suicide ideation. *J Consult Clin Psychol* 1979;47:343–352.

Beck AT, Rush AJ, Shaw BF, Emery G. *Cognitive therapy of depression.* New York: Guilford Press 1979.

Beck AT, Steer RA, Kovacs M, et al. Hopelessness and eventual suicide: A 10-year prospective study of patients hospitalized with suicidal ideation. *Am J Psychiatry* 1985;142:559–563.

Beck AT, Steer RA, Sanderson WC, Skeie TM. Panic disorder and suicidal ideation and behavior: Discrepant findings in psychiatric outpatients. *Am J Psychiatry* 1991;148:1195–1199.

Beck AT, Weissman A, Lester D, Trexler L. Classification of suicidal behaviors: II. Dimensions of suicidal intent. *Arch Gen Psychiatry* 1976;33:835–837.

Beck RW, Morris J, Lester D. Suicide notes and risk of future suicide. *JAMA* 1974;288: 495–496.

Benensohn HS, Resnik HLP. A jigger of alcohol, a dash of depression, and bitters: A suicidal mix. *Ann NY Acad Sci* 1974;233:40–46.

Benham E. Coping strategies: A psychoeducational approach to posttraumatic symptomatology. *Am J Psychosoc Nurs* 1995;33:30–35.

Berglund M. Suicide in alcoholism. *Arch Gen Psychiatry* 1984;41:888–891.

Berglund M, Nilsson K. Mortality in severe depression: A prospective study including 103 suicides. *Acta Psychiatr Scand* 1987;76:372–380.

Berlin IN. Suicide among American Indian adolescents: An overview. *Suicide Life-Threat Behav* 1987;17:218–232.

Berman A. Dyadic death: Murder-suicide. *Suicide Life-Threat Behav* 1979;9:15–23.

Bernstein EM, Putnam FW. Development, reliability, and validity of a dissociation scale. *J Nerv Ment Dis* 1986;174:727–734.

Beskow J. Suicide and mental disorder in Swedish men. *Acta Psychiatr Scand* 1979; 277(suppl):1–138.

Beskow J, Gottfries CG, Roos BE, Winblad B. Determination of monoamine and monoamine metabolites in the human brain: Post mortem studies in a group of suicides and in a control group. *Acta Psychiatr Scand* 1976;53:7–20.

Beskow J, Runeson BS, Asgard U. Psychological autopsies: Methods and ethics. *Suicide Life-Threat Behav* 1990;20:307–323.

Bharucha AJ, Satlin A. Late life suicide: A review. *Harvard Rev Psychiatry* 1997;5: 55–65.

Biegon A, Israeli M. Regionally selective increases in b-adrenergic receptor density in the brains of suicide victims. *Brain Res* 1988;442:199–203.

Black DW. Mortality in schizophrenia: The Iowa record linkage study. *Psychosomatics* 1988;29:55–60.

Black DW, Warrack G, Winokur G. The Iowa record linkage study: I. Suicides and accidental deaths among psychiatric patients. *Arch Gen Psychiatry* 1985;42:71–74.

Black DW, Winokur G. Age, mortality, and chronic schizophrenia. *Schizophr Res* 1988;1:267–272.

Black DW, Winokur G. Suicide and psychiatric diagnosis. In SJ Blumenthal, DJ Kupfer (eds), *Suicide over the life cycle: Risk factors, assessment, and treatment of suicidal patients.* Washington DC: American Psychiatric Press 1990:135–153.

Black DW, Winokur G, Mohandoss E, et al. Does treatment influence mortality in depressives? A follow-up of 1,076 patients with major affective disorders. *Ann Clin Psychiatry* 1989;1:165–173.

Black DW, Winokur G, Nasrallah A. Suicide in subtypes of major affective disorder: A comparison with general population suicide mortality. *Arch Gen Psychiatry* 1987;44:878–880.

Black DW, Winokur G, Nasrallah A. Effect of psychosis on suicide risk in 1,593 patients with unipolar and bipolar affective disorders. *Am J Psychiatry* 1988; 145:849–852.

Black DW, Yates W, Petty F, et al. Suicidal behavior in alcoholic males. *Comp Psychiatry* 1986;27:227–233.

Black HC, Nolan JR, Connolly MJ. *Black's law dictionary,* 5th ed. St Paul MN: West 1979.

Blacker KH, Wong N. Four cases of autocastration. *Arch Gen Psychiatry* 1963;8:169–176.

Blackwell B. Treatment adherence. *Br J Psychiatry* 1976;129:513–531.

Blair-West GW, Mellsop GW, Eyeson-Annan ML. Down-rating lifetime suicide risk in major depression. *Acta Psychiatr Scand* 1997;5:259–263.

Blazer DG. Suicide risk factors in the elderly: An epidemiological study. *J Geriatr Psychiatry* 1991;24:175.

Blazer DG, Bachar JR, Manton JG. Suicide in late life: Review and commentary. *J Am Geriatr Soc* 1986;34:519.

Blazer DG, Kessler RC, McGonagle KA, Swartz MS. The prevalence and distribution of major depression in a national community sample: The National Comorbidity Study. *Am J Psychiatry* 1994;151:979–986.

Blazer DG, Koenig HG. Suicide. In JE Birren (ed), *Encyclopedia of gerontology: Age, aging, and the aged.* Orlando FL: Academic Press 1996.

Blin O, Azorinn JM, Bouhours P. Antipsychotic and anxiolitic properties of respiridone, haloperidol and methotrimeprazine in schizophrenia patients. *J Clin Psychopharmacol* 1996;16:38–44.

Block S. Patient requests for euthanasia and assisted suicide in terminal illness: The role of the psychiatrist. *Psychosomatics* 1995;36:445–457.

Blumenthal SJ. Suicide: A guide to risk factors, assessment, and treatment of suicidal patients. *Med Clin North Am* 1988;72:937–971.

Blumenthal SJ. An overview and synopsis of risk factors, assessment, and treatment of suicidal patients over the life cycle. In SJ Blumenthal, DJ Kupfer (eds), *Suicide over the life cycle: Risk factors, assessment, and treatment of suicidal patients.* Washington DC: American Psychiatric Press 1990:685–733.

Bolin RK, Wright RE, Wilkinson MN, et al. Survey of suicide among patients on home leave from a mental hospital. *Psychiatr Q* 1968;42:81–89.

Bond ED. Results of treatment in psychoses with a control series: II. Involutional psychotic reaction. *Am J Psychiatry* 1954a;110:881–883.

Bond ED. Results of treatment in psychoses with a control series: III. Manic-depressive reactions. *Am J Psychiatry* 1954b;110:883–885.

Bond ED, Braceland FJ. Prognosis in mental disease: The use of one-page abstracts. *Am J Psychiatry* 1937;94:263–274.

Bongar B, Maris RW, Berman AL, et al. Inpatient standards of care and the suicidal patient: I. General clinical formulations and legal considerations. *Suicide Life-Threat Behav* 1993;23:245–256.

Borges G, Rosovsky H. Suicide attempts and alcohol consumption in an emergency room sample. *J Stud Alcohol* 1996;57:543–548.

Borkovec TD, Inz J. The nature of worry in generalized anxiety disorder: A predominance of thought activity. *Behav Res Ther* 1990;28:153–158.

Borst SR, Noam GG, Bartok JA. Adolescent suicidality: A clinical developmental approach. *J Am Acad Child Adolesc Psychiatry* 1991;30:796–803.

Bourne HR, Bunney WE Jr, Colburn RW, et al. Noradrenaline, 5-hydroxytryptamine, and 5-hydroxyindoleacetic acid in hindbrains of suicidal patients. *Lancet* 1968; 2:805–808.

Boyd JH. The increasing rate of suicide by firearms. *N Engl J Med* 1983;308:872–874.

Boyd JH, Moscicki EK. Firearms and youth suicide. *Am J Public Health* 1986;76: 1240–1242.

Bratfos O, Haug JO. The course of manic-depressive psychosis: A follow-up investigation of 215 patients. *Acta Psychiatr Scand* 1968;44:89–112.

Braun BG. Dissociative disorders as sequelae to incest. In RP Kluft (ed), *Incest-related syndromes of adult psychopathology.* Washington DC: American Psychiatric Press 1990:227–246.

Breed W. Occupational mobility and suicide among white males. *Am Sociol Rev* 1963;28:179–188.

Breier A, Astrachan BM. Characterization of schizophrenic patients who commit suicide. *Am J Psychiatry* 1984;141:206–209.

Brent DA. Overrepresentation of epileptics in a consecutive series of suicide attempters seen at a children's hospital, 1978–1983. *J Am Acad Child Adolesc Psychiatry* 1986;25:242–246.

Brent DA. Correlates of medical lethality of suicide attempts in children and adolescents. *J Am Acad Child Adolesc Psychiatry* 1987;26:87–89.

Brent DA. Risk factors for adolescent suicide and suicidal behavior. *Suicide Life-Threat Behav* 1995;25:52–63.

Brent DA, Bridge J, Johnson BA, Connolly J. Suicidal behavior runs in families. *Arch Gen Psychiatry* 1996;53:1145–1152.

Brent DA, Johnson BA, Bartle S, et al. Personality disorder, tendency to impulsive violence, and suicidal behavior in adolescents. *J Am Acad Child Adolesc Psychiatry* 1993a;32:69–75.

Brent DA, Kalas R, Edelbrock C, et al. Psychopathology and its relationship to suicidal ideation in childhood and adolescence. *J Am Acad Child Adolesc Psychiatry* 1986; 25:666–673.

Brent DA, Kerr MM, Goldstein CE, et al. An outbreak of suicide and suicidal behavior in a high school. *J Am Acad Child Adolesc Psychiatry* 1989;28:918–924.

Brent DA, Kolko DJ. Suicidality in affectively disordered adolescent inpatients. *J Am Acad Child Adolesc Psychiatry* 1990;29:587–593.

Brent DA, Perper JA. Research in adolescent suicide: Implications for training, service delivery, and public policy. *Suicide Life-Threat Behav* 1995;25:222–230.

Brent DA, Perper JA, Allman CJ. Alcohol, firearms, and suicide among youth. *JAMA* 1987;257:3369–3372.

Brent DA, Perper JA, Allman CJ, et al. The presence and accessibility of firearms in the homes of adolescent suicides: A case-control study. *JAMA* 1991;266:2989–2995.

Brent DA, Perper JA, Goldstein CE, et al. Risk factors for adolescent suicide: A comparison of adolescent suicide victims with suicidal inpatients. *Arch Gen Psychiatry* 1988;45:581–588.

Brent DA, Perper JA, Moritz GM, et al. Stressful life events, psychopathology, and adolescent suicide: A case-control study. *Suicide Life-Threat Beh* 1993b;23:179–187.

Brent DA, Perper JA, Moritz GM, et al. The validity of diagnoses obtained through the psychological autopsy procedure in adolescent suicide victims: Use of family history. *Acta Psychiatr Scand* 1993c;87:118–122.

Breslau N, Davis GC, Andreski P, Peterson E. Traumatic events and posttraumatic stress disorder in an urban population of young adults. *Arch Gen Psychiatry* 1991;48:216–222.

Briere J, Runtz M. Post sexual abuse trauma: Data and implications for clinical practice. *J Interpers Viol* 1987;2:367–379.

Briere J, Runtz M. Symptomatology associated with childhood sexual victimization in a non-clinical adult sample. *Child Abuse Negl* 1988;12:331–341.

Briere J, Zaidi LY. Sexual abuse histories and sequelae in female psychiatric emergency room patients. *Am J Psychiatry* 1989;146:1602–1606.

Brodsky BS, Malone KM, Ellis SP, et al. Characteristics of borderline personality disorder associated with suicidal behavior. *Am J Psychiatry* 1997;154:1715–1719.

Bronisch T. The typology of personality disorders, diagnostic problems and their relevance for suicide behavior. *Crisis* 1996;17:55–58.

Brooner RK, King VL, Kidorf M, et al. Psychiatric and substance use comorbidity among treatment-seeking opioid abusers. *Arch Gen Psychiatry* 1997;54:71–80.

Brown GL, Ebert MH, Goyer PF, et al. Aggression, suicide and serotonin: Relationships to CSF amine metabolites. *Am J Psychiatry* 1982;139:741–746.

Brown GL, Goodwin FK. Cerebrospinal fluid correlates of suicide attempts and aggression. *Ann NY Acad Sci* 1986;487:175–188.

Brown GL, Goodwin FK, Ballenger JC, et al. Aggression in humans correlates with cerebrospinal fluid amine metabolites. *Psychiatry Res* 1979;1:131–139.

Brown JH, Henteleff P, Barakat S, Rowe CJ. Is it normal for terminally ill patients to desire death? *Am J Psychiatry* 1986;143:208–211.

Brown SA, Schuckit MA. Changes in depression among abstinent alcoholics. *J Stud Alcohol* 1988;49:412–417.

Browne A. Assault and homicide in the home: When battered women kill. In MJ Saks, L Saxe (eds), *Advances in social psychology,* vol. 3. Hillsdale NJ: Erlbaum 1987.

Browne A, Finkelhor D. Impact of child sexual abuse: A review of the research. *Psychology Bulletin* 1986a; 99:66–77.

Browne A, Finkelhor D. Initial and long-term effects: A review of the research. In D Finkelhor (ed), *A sourcebook on child sexual abuse.* Thousand Oaks CA: Sage 1986b:143–179.

Browne WJ, Palmer AJ. A preliminary study of schizophrenic women who murdered their children. *Hosp Community Psychiatry* 1975;26:71–75.

Bryer JB, Nelson BA, Miller JB, Krol PA. Childhood sexual and physical abuse as factors in adult psychiatric illness. *Am J Psychiatry* 1987;144:1426–1430.

Buchholtz-Hansen PE, Wang AG, Kragh-Sørensen P. The Danish University Antidepressant Group: Mortality in major affective disorder: Relationship to subtype of depression. *Acta Psychiatr Scand* 1993;87:329–335.

Buda M, Tsuang MT. The epidemiology of suicide: Implications for clinical practice. In SJ Blumenthal, DJ Kupfer (eds), *Suicide over the life cycle: Risk factors, assessment, and treatment of suicidal patients.* Washington DC: American Psychiatric Press 1990:17–37.

Buie DH Jr. Empathy: Its nature and limitations. *J Am Psychoanal Assoc* 1981;299:281–307.

Buie DH Jr, Maltsberger JT. The psychological vulnerability to suicide. In DG Jacobs, HN Brown (eds.), *Suicide: Understanding and responding.* Madison CT: International Universities Press 1989:59–71.

Busch KA, Clark DC, Fawcett JA, Kravitz H. Clinical features of inpatient suicide. *Psychiatr Ann* 1993;23:256–262.

Buteau J, Lesage AD, Kiely MC. Homicide followed by suicide: A Quebec case series, 1988–1990. *Can J Psychiatry* 1993;38:552–556.

Caldwell CB, Gottesman II. Schizophrenics kill themselves too: A review of risk factors for suicide. *Schizophr Bull* 1990;16:571–589.

Caldwell CB, Gottesman II. Schizophrenia—a high-risk factor for suicide: Clues to risk reduction. *Suicide Life-Threat Behav* 1992;22:479–493.

Callado LF, Meana JJ, Grijalba B, et al. Selective increase of a_{2A}-adrenoceptor agonist binding sites in brains of depressed suicide victims. *J Neurochem* 1998;70:1114–1123.

Callahan CM, Hendrie HC, Nienaber NA, Tierney WM. Suicidal ideation among older primary care patients. *J Am Geriatr Soc* 1996;44:1205–1209.

Callahan J. Documentation of client dangerousness in a managed care environment. *Health Soc Work* 1996;21:202–207.

Camus A. *"The myth of Sisyphus" and other essays* (trans J O'Brien). New York: Knopf 1964.

Canetto SS. Gender and suicide in the elderly. *Suicide Life-Threat Behav* 1992;22:80–97.

Cappiello A, Sernyak MJ, Malison RT, et al. Effects of acute tryptophan depletion in lithium-remitted manic patients: A pilot study. *Biol Psychiatry* 1997;42:1076–1978.

Card JJ. Lethality of suicidal methods and suicide risk: Two distinct concepts. *Omega* 1974;5:37–45.

Carlson GA, Cantwell DP. Suicidal behavior and depression in children and adolescents. *J Am Acad Child Adolesc Psychiatry* 1982;21:361–368.

Carlson GA, Kotin J, Davenport YB, Adland M. Follow-up of 53 bipolar manic-depressive patients. *Br J Psychiatry* 1974;124:134–139.

Carney MWP, Roth M, Garside RF. The diagnosis of depressive syndromes and the prediction of ECT response. *Br J Psychiatr* 1965;111:659–674.

Carney SS, Rich DL, Burke PA, Fowler RC. Suicide over 60: The San Diego study. *J Am Geriatr Soc* 1994;42:174–180.

Carpenter BD. A review and new look at ethical suicide in advanced age. *Gerontologist* 1993;33:359–365.

Carrieri PB, Provitera V, Iacovitti B, et al. Mood disorders in epilepsy. *Acta Neurol (Napoli)* 1993;15:62–67.

Carter RE: Some effects of client suicide on the therapist. *Psychotherapy* 1971;8:287–289.

Cassidy F, Murry E, Weiner WD, Carroll BJ. Lack of relapse with tryptophan depletion following successful treatment with ECT. *Am J Psychiatry* 1997;154:1151–1152.

Cavan R. *Suicide.* Chicago: University of Chicago Press 1928.

Centers for Disease Control. *Youth suicide prevention programs: A resource guide.* Atlanta: Centers for Disease Control 1992.

Centers for Disease Control. Suicide among black youths: United States, 1980–1995. *MMWR* 1998;47(10).

Cerletti U, Bini L. Un nuovo metodo di shock-terapie "l'eletro-shock." *Boll Acad Med Roma* 1938;64:136–138.

Cheetham SC, Crompton MR, Czuclek C, et al. Serotonin concentrations and turnover in brains of depressed suicides. *Brain Res* 1989;502:332–340.

Cheetham SC, Crompton MR, Katona CLE, Horton RW. Brain 5-HT$_1$ binding sites in depressed suicides. *Psychopharmacology (Berlin)* 1990;102:544–548.

Cheng ATA. Mental illness and suicide. *Arch Gen Psychiatry* 1995;52:594–603.

Cheng KK, Leung CM, Lo WH, Lam TH. Risk factors of suicide among schizophrenics. *Acta Psychiatr Scand* 1990;81:220–224.

Chiarugi V. Della pazzia, in genere e in specie (On insanity and its classification) (trans G Mora). Canton MA: Watson 1987:109–187. (Originally published 1793)

Chochinov HM, Wilson KG, Enns M, et al. Desire for death in the terminally ill. *Am J Psychiatry* 1995;152:1185–1191.

Choron J. *Suicide.* New York: Scribner 1972.

Christensen GA, Popkin MK, Mackenzie TB, Realmuto GM. Lithium treatment for chronic hair pulling. *J Clin Psychiatry* 1991;52:116–120.

Christie R, Bay C, Kaufman IA. Lesch-Nyhan disease. *Dev Med Child Neurol* 1982;24: 293–296.

Chu JA. The therapeutic roller coaster: Dilemmas in the treatment of childhood abuse survivors. *J Psychother Pract Res* 1992;1:351–370.

Chu JA. The rational treatment of multiple personality disorder. *Psychotherapy* 1994; 31:94–100.

Chu JA. Controlling posttraumatic and dissociative symptoms. In *Rebuilding shattered lives: The responsible treatment of complex posttraumatic and dissociative disorders.* New York: Wiley 1998:108–117.

Chu JA, Dill DL. Dissociative symptoms in relation to childhood physical and sexual abuse. *Am J Psychiatry* 1990;147:887–892.

Clark DC. Narcissistic crises of aging and suicidal despair. *Suicide Life-Threat Behav* 1993;23:21–26.

Clark DC, Fawcett JA. An empirically based model of suicide risk assessment for patients with affective disorders. In DG Jacobs (ed), *Suicide and clinical practice.* Washington DC: American Psychiatric Press 1992a:55–73.

Clark DC, Fawcett JA. Review of empirical risk factors for evaluation of the suicidal patient. In B Bongar (ed), *Suicide: Guidelines for assessment, management, and treatment.* New York: Oxford University Press 1992b:16–48.

Clark DC, Horton-Deutsch SL. Assessment *in absentia*: The value of the psychological autopsy method for studying antecedents of suicide and predicting future suicides. In RW Maris, AL Berman, JT Maltsberger, RY Yufit (eds), *Assessment and prediction of suicide.* New York: Guilford Press 1992:144–182.

Clarke GN, Hawkins W, Murphy M, Sheeber LB. Targeted prevention of unipolar depressive disorder in an at-risk sample of high school adolescents: A randomized trial of group cognitive intervention. *J Am Acad Child Adolesc Psychiatry* 1995; 34:312–321.

Clarkin JF, Widiger TA, Frances A, et al. Prototypic typology and the borderline personality disorder. *J Abnorm Psychol* 1983;92:263–275.

Clayton PJ et al. Follow-up and family study of anxious depression. *Am J Psychiatry* 1991;148:1512–1517.

Coccaro EF, Kavoussi RJ, Hauger R. PRL responses to d-fenfluramine and D,L-fenfluramine in man. American College of Neuropsychopharmacology 32nd Annual Meeting, Maui, Hawaii, 1993(abstract):160.

Coccaro EF, Siever LJ, Klar HM, et al. Serotonergic studies in patients with affective and personality disorders. *Arch Gen Psychiatry* 1989;46:587–599.

Cochran E, Robins E, Grote S. Regional serotonin levels in brain: A comparison of depressive suicides and alcoholic suicides with controls. *Biol Psychiatry* 1976;11:283–294.

Cochran SD. Strategies for preventing lithium noncompliance in bipolar affective illness. Doctoral dissertation, University of California, Los Angeles, 1982.

Cochran SD. Preventing noncompliance in the outpatient treatment of bipolar affective disorders. *J Consult Clin Psychol* 1984;52:873–878.

Cohen D, Llorente M, Eisdorfer C. Homicide-suicide in older persons. *Am J Psychiatry* 1998;155:390–396.

Cohen LJ, Test MA, Brown RL. Suicide and schizophrenia: Data from a prospective community treatment study. *Am J Psychiatry* 1990;147:602–607; erratum: *Am J Psychiatry* 1990;147:1110.

Cohen S, Leonard CV, Barberow NL, et al. Tranquilizers and suicide in the schizophrenic patient. *Arch Gen Psychiatry* 1964;11:312–321.

Coid J. The epidemiology of abnormal homicide and murder followed by suicide. *Psychol Med* 1983;13:855–860.

Coleman L. *Suicide clusters.* Boston: Faber & Faber 1987.

Colletta ND. At risk for depression: A study of young mothers. *J Genet Psychol* 1983; 142:301–310.

Combs-Orme T, Taylor JR, Scott EB, Holmes SJ. Violent deaths among alcoholics: A descriptive study. *J Stud Alcohol* 1983;44:938–949.

Committee on Prevention of Mental Disorders, Division of Biobehavioral Science and Mental Disorders, Institute of Medicine. New directions and definitions. In PJ Maracek, RJ Haggerty (eds), *Reducing risks for mental disorders: Frontiers for preventive intervention research.* Washington DC: National Academy Press 1994:19–32.

Compas BE, Slavin LA, Wagner BM, Vannatta K. Relationship of life events and social support with psychological dysfunction among adolescents. *J Youth Adolesc* 1986; 15:205–221.

Conwell Y. Suicide in elderly patients. In LS Schneider, CF Reynolds, BD Lebowitz, AJ Friedhoff (eds), *Diagnosis and treatment of depression in late life.* Washington DC: American Psychiatric Press 1994:397–418.

Conwell Y, Brent DA. Suicide and aging: I. Patterns of psychiatric diagnosis. *Int Psychogeriatr* 1995;7:149–164.

Conwell Y, Duberstein PR, Cox C, et al. Relationships of age and axis I diagnoses in victims of completed suicide: A psychological autopsy study. *Am J Psychiatry* 1996;153:1001–1008.

Conwell Y, Raby WN, Caine ED. Suicide and aging: II. The psychobiological interface. *Int Psychogeriatr* 1995;7:165–181.

Coons PM, Cole C, Pellow T, Milstein V. Symptoms of posttraumatic stress and dissociation in women victims of abuse. In RP Kluft (ed), *Incest-related syndromes of adult psychopathology*. Washington DC: American Psychiatric Press 1990:205–225.

Cooper C. Patient suicide and assault. *J Psychosoc Nurs Ment Health Serv* 1955;33(6): 26–29.

Cooper JM. Mental disease situations in certain cultures: A new field for research. *J Abnorm Soc Psychol* 1934;29:10–17.

Cooper M, Eaves D. Suicide following homicide in the family. *Viol Victims* 1996;11: 99–112.

Cooper-Patrick L, Crum RM, Ford DE. Identifying suicidal ideation in general medical patients. *JAMA* 1994;272:1757–1762.

Copeland AR. Dyadic death—revisited. *J Forensic Sci Soc* 1985;25:181–188.

Coppen A. Depression as a lethal disease: Prevention strategies. *J Clin Psychiatry* 1994;55(suppl 4):37–45.

Coppen A, Standish-Barry H, Bailey J, et al. Long-term lithium and mortality. *Lancet* 1990;335(8701):1347.

Coppen A, Standish-Barry H, Bailey J, et al. Does lithium reduce mortality of recurrent mood disorders? *J Affective Disord* 1991;23:1–7.

Corbitt EM, Malone KM, Haas GL, et al. Suicidal behavior in patients with major depression and comorbid personality disorders. *J Affective Disord* 1996;39:61–72.

Cornelius JR, Salloum IM, Ehler JG, et al. Fluoxetine in depressed alcoholics. *Arch Gen Psychiatry* 1997;54:700–705.

Cornelius JR, Salloum IM, Mezzich J, et al. Disproportionate suicidality in patients with comorbid major depression and alcoholism. *Am J Psychiatry* 1995;152:358–364.

Corrigan PW, Yudofsky SC, Silver JM. Pharmacological and behavioral treatments for aggressive psychiatric patients. *Hosp Community Psychiatry* 1993;44:125–133.

Corte HE, Wolff MM, Locke BJ. Comparison for procedures for eliminating self-injurious behavior of retarded adolescents. *J Appl Behav Anal* 1971;4:201–207.

Coryell W, Noyes R Jr, Clancy J. Excess mortality in panic disorder: A comparison with primary unipolar depression. *Arch Gen Psychiatry* 1982;39:701–703.

Coryell W, Noyes R Jr, House JD. Mortality among outpatients with anxiety disorders. *Am J Psychiatry* 1986;143:508–510.

Coryell W, Zimmerman M. Outcome following ECT for primary unipolar depression: A test of newly proposed response predictors. *Am J Psychiatry* 1984;141:862–867.

Courtois CA. The incest experience and its aftermath. *Victimology* 1979;4:337–347.

Cowburn RF, Marcusson JO, Eriksson A, et al. Adenylyl cyclase activity and G-protein subunit levels in postmortem frontal cortex of suicide victims. *Brain Res* 1994;633: 297–304.

Cowdry RW, Gardner DL. Pharmacotherapy of borderline personality disorder: Alprazolam, carbamazepine, trifluoperazine, and tranylcypromine. *Arch Gen Psychiatry* 1988;45:111–119.

Cowdry RW, Pickar D, Davies R. Symptoms and EEG findings in the borderline syndrome. *Int J Psychiatr Med* 1985;15:201–211.

Cowen PJ, McCance SL, Gelder MG, Grahame-Smith DG. Effect of amitriptyline on endocrine responses to intravenous L-tryptophan. *Psychiatry Res* 1990;31:201–208.

Cowen PJ, Power AC, Ware CJ, Anderson IM. 5-HT$_{1A}$ receptor sensitivity in major depression: A neuroendocrine study with buspirone. *Br J Psychiatry* 1994;164:372–379.

Cox JG. Rehabilitation and the suicidal client. *J Appl Rehab Counseling* 1979;10:20–22.

Coyle J. "Neurobiology of suicide." Speech presented at Sucide: Critical Issues in Assessment and Treatment conference. Sept. 12–13, 1997, Boston.

Crabtree LH. A psychotherapeutic encounter with a self-mutilating patient. *Psychiatry* 1967;30:91–100.

Crammer JL. Special characteristics of suicide in hospital inpatients. *Br J Psychiatry* 1984;145:460–476.

Crook T, Raskin A, Davis D. Factors associated with attempted suicide among hospitalized depressed patients. *Psychol Med* 1975;5:381–388.

Cross JA, Cheetham SC, Crompton MR, et al. Brain GABA$_B$ binding sites in depressed suicide victims. *Psychiatry Res* 1988;26:119–129.

Crow TJ, Cross AJ, Cooper SJ, et al. Neurotransmitter receptors and monoamine metabolites in the brains of patients with Alzheimer-type dementia and depression, and suicides. *Neuropharmacology* 1984;23:1561–1569.

Crowder JE, Gross CA, Heiser JF. Self-mutilation of the eye. *J Clin Psychiatry* 1979;24:420–423.

Crumley FE. Adolescent suicide attempts. *JAMA* 1979;241:2404–2407.

Crumley FE. Substance abuse and adolescent suicidal behavior. *JAMA* 1990;263:3051–3056.

Crundwell JK. Lithium and its potential benefit in reducing increased mortality rates due to suicide. *Lithium* 1994;5:193–204.

Cullberg J, Wasserman D, Stefansson CG. Who commits suicide after a suicide attempt? An 8-to 10-year follow-up in a suburban catchment area. *Acta Psychiatr Scand* 1988;77:598–603.

Currens S, Fritsch T, Jones D, et al. Homicide followed by suicide: Kentucky, 1985–1990. *MMWR* 1991;40:652–653, 659.

Dahlström A, Fuxe K. Evidence for the existence of monoamine-containing neurons in the central nervous system: I. Demonstration of monoamines in the cell bodies of brain stem neurons. *Acta Physiol Scand* 1964;62(232):1–55.

Daly M, Wilson M. *Homicide.* Hawthorne NY: Aldine de Gruyter 1988.

Davidson JRT, Kudler HS, Saunders WB, et al. Predicting response to amitriptyline in posttraumatic stress disorder. *Am J Psychiatry* 1993;150:1024–1029.

Davidson JRT, Kudler HS, Smith R, et al. Treatment of posttraumatic stress disorder with amitriptyline and placebo. *Arch Gen Psychiatry* 1990;47:259–266.

Davidson JRT, Roth S, Newman E. Fluoxitine in posttraumatic stress disorder. *J Traum Stress* 1991;4:418–423.

Davidson LE, Rosenberg ML, Mercy JA, et al. An epidemiologic study of risk factors in two teenage suicide clusters. *JAMA* 1989;262:2687–2692.

Davidson MW, Wagner WG, Range LM. Clinicians' attitudes toward no-suicide agreements. *Suicide Life-Threat Behav* 1995;25:410–414.

Davis J, Janicak P, Ayd F. Psychopharmacotherapy of the personality-disordered patient. *Psychiatr Ann* 1995;25:614–620.

Dawson D, MacMillan H. *Relationship management of the borderline patient: From understanding to treatment.* New York: Brunner/Mazel 1993.

Deakin JF, Pennell L, Upadhyaya AJ, Lofthouse R. A neuroendocrine study of 5-HT function in depression: Evidence for biological mechanisms of endogenous and psychosocial causation. *Psychopharmacology (Berlin)* 1990;101:85–92.

De Berniernes L. Legends of the fall. In I Frazier, R Atwan (eds), *The best American essays 1997*. New York: Houghton Mifflin 1997:37–46.

Degoulet P et al. Mortality risk factors in patients treated by chronic hemodialysis: Report of the Diaphane Collaborative Study. *Nephron* 1982;31:103–110.

De Leo D, Carollo G, Dello Buono ML. Lower suicide rates associated with a tele-help/tele-check service for the elderly at home. *Am J Psychiatry* 1995;152:632–634.

Delgado P, Charney D, Price L, et al. Serotonergic function and the mechanism of antidepressant action. *Arch Gen Psychiatry* 1990;47:411–418.

de Montigny C. Electroconvulsive shock treatments enhance responsiveness of forebrain neurons to serotonin. *J Pharmacol Exp Ther* 1984;228:230–234.

Dennehey JA, Appleby L, Thomas CS, et al. Case control study of suicides by discharged psychiatric patients. *Br Med J* 1996;312:1580.

De Paermentier F, Cheetham SC, Crompton MR, et al. Brain b-adrenoceptor binding sites in antidepressant-free depressed suicide victims. *Brain Res* 1990;525:71–77.

Detre TP, Jarecki HG. *Modern psychiatric treatment.* Philadelphia: Lipincott 1991.

de Wilde E, Kienhorst ICWM, Diekstra RFW, et al. The relationship between adolescent suicidal behavior and life events in childhood and adolescence. *Am J Psychiatry* 1991;149:45–51.

Deykin EY, Buka SL. Suicidal ideation and attempts among chemically dependent adolescents. *Am J Public Health* 1994;84:634–639.

Di Clemente RJ, Ponton LE, Hartley D. Prevalence and correlates of cutting behavior: Risk for HIV transmission. *J Am Acad Child Adolesc Psychiatry* 1991;30:735–739.

Diekstra RFW, Guldinat W. The epidemiology of suicidal behavior: A review of three continents. *World Health Stat Q* 1993;46:52–68.

Dietz PE. Mass, serial, and sensational homicides. *Bull NY Acad Med* 1986;62:477–491.

Dillon KA, Gross-Isseroff R, Israeli M, Biegon A. Autoradiographic analysis of serotonin 5-HT$_{1A}$ receptor binding in the human brain postmortem: Effects of age and alcohol. *Brain Res* 1991;554:56–64.

Di Maio L, Squitieri F, Napolitano G, et al. Suicide risk in Huntington's disease. *J Med Genet* 1993;30:293–295.

Dinges NG, Duong-Tran Q. Suicide ideation and suicide attempt among American Indian and Alaska Native boarding school adolescents. *Am Indian Alaska Native Ment Health Res Monogr Ser* 1994;4:167–182; discussion 182–188.

Donaldson MA, Gardner R. Diagnosis and treatment of traumatic stress among women after childhood incest. In C Figley (ed), *Trauma and its wake.* New York: Brunner/Mazel 1985:356–377.

d'Orbán PT. Women who kill their children. *Br J Psychiatry* 1979;134:560–571.

Dorpat TL. Suicide in murderers. *Psychiatry Digest* 1966;27(6):51–55.

Dorpat TL, Boswell JW. An evaluation of suicidal intent in suicide attempts. *Compr Psychiatry* 1963;4:117–125.

Dorpat TL, Ripley HS. A study of suicide in the Seattle area. *Compr Psychiatry* 1960;1:349–359.

Dorpat TL, Ripley HS. The relationship between attempted suicide and committed suicide. *Compr Psychiatry* 1967;8:74–79.

Dorwart RA, Chartock L. Suicide: A public health perspective. In DG Jacobs, HN Brown (eds), *Suicide: Understanding and responding.* Madison CT: International Universities Press 1989.

Dorwart RA, Epstein S. *Privatization of mental health care: A fragile balance.* Westport CT: Auburn House/Greenwood 1993.

Dorwart RA et al. A national survey of psychiatrists' professional activities. *Am J Psychiatry* 1992;149:1499–1505.

Douglas JD. *The social meanings of suicide.* Princeton NJ: Princeton University Press 1967.

Drake RE, Cotton PG. Depression, hopelessness and suicide in chronic schizophrenia. *Br J Psychiatry* 1986;148:554–559.

Drake RE, Ehrlich J. Suicide attempts associated with akathisia. *Am J Psychiatry* 1985;142:499–501.

Drake RE, Gates C, Cotton PG, Whitaker A. Suicide among schizophrenics: Who is at risk? *J Nerv Ment Dis* 1984;172:613–617.

Drake RE, Gates C, Whitaker A, Cotton PG. Suicide among schizophrenics: A review. *Compr Psychiatry* 1985;26:90–100.

Draper BM. Suicidal behavior in the elderly. *Int J Geriatr Psychiatry* 1994;9:655–661.

Draper BM. Prevention of suicide in old age. *Med J Aust* 1995;162:533–534.

Drye RC, Goulding RL, Goulding ME. No-suicide decisions: Patient monitoring of suicidal risk. *Am J Psychiatry* 1973;130:171–174.

Dublin LI. *Suicide: A sociological and statistical study.* New York: Ronald Press 1963.

Dubovsky SL. "Experimental" self-mutilation. *Am J Psychiatry* 1978;135:1240–1241.

Dunner DL, Gershon ES, Goodwin FK. Heritable factors in the severity of affective illness. *Biol Psychiatry* 1976;11:31–42.

Durkheim E. *Suicide: A study in sociology* (ed G Simpson; trans JA Spaulding, G Simpson). New York: Free Press 1951. (Originally published 1897)

Dvoskin JA, Steadman HJ. Using intensive case management to reduce violence by mentally ill persons in the community. *Hosp Community Psychiatry* 1994;45:679–684.

Easteal P. Homicide-suicides between adult sexual intimates: An Australian study. *Suicide Life–Threat Behav* 1994;24:140–151.

Edleson JL, Syers M. The effects of group treatment for men who batter: An 18-month follow-up study. *Res Soc Work Prac* 1991;1:227–243.

Edman G, Åsberg M, Levander S, Schalling D. Skin conductance habituation and cerebrospinal fluid 5-hydroxyindoleacetic acid in suicidal patients. *Arch Gen Psychiatry* 1986;43:586–592.

Egan J. The thin red line. *New York Times Magazine*, July 27, 1997:21–48.

Egan MP. Contracting for safety: A concept analysis. *Crisis* 1997;18:17–23.

Egeland JA, Sussex JN. Suicide and family loading for affective disorders. *JAMA* 1985;254:915–918.

Ellis BR, Schaefer M. *Medical Professional Mutual Insurance Company,* Nov 1995.

Emanuel EJ. The history of euthanasia in the United States and Britain. *Ann Intern Med* 1994;121:793–802.

Emanuel EJ, Fairclough DL, Daniels ER, et al. Euthanasia and physician-assisted suicide: Attitudes and experiences of oncology patients, oncologists, and the public. *Lancet* 1996;347(1908):1805–1810.

Endicott J, Nee J, Andreasen NC, et al. Bipolar II: Combine or keep separate. *J Affective Disord* 1985;8:17–28.

Endicott J, Spitzer RL. A diagnostic interview: The schedule for affective disorders and schizophrenia. *Arch Gen Psychiatry* 1978;35:837–844.

Englesman ER, Polito G, Perley J. Traumatic amputation of the penis. *J Urol* 1974;112: 774–778.

Ernst FA. Self-recording and counterconditioning of a self-mutilative compulsion. *Behav Ther* 1973;4:144–146.

Etchegoyen RH. *The fundamentals of psychoanalytic technique.* New York: Karnac Books 1991.

Etzerdorfer E, Sonneck G, Nagel-Keuss S. Newspaper reports and suicide. *N Engl J Med* 1992;327:502–503.

Evans CM. Alcohol and violence: Problems relating to methodology, statistics and causation. In PF Brian (ed), *Alcohol and aggression.* London: Croom Helm 1986:138–160.

Ewalt JR. Other psychiatric emergencies. In AM Freedman, HI Kaplan (eds), *Comprehensive textbook of psychiatry.* Baltimore: Williams & Wilkins, 1967:1179–1187.

Faedda GL, Baldessarini RJ, Suppes T, et al. Pediatric-onset bipolar disorder: A neglected clinical and public health problem. *Sex Marital Ther* 1995;3:171–195.

Fairbairn WD. *Psychoanalytic studies of the personality.* London: Tavistock 1952. (Published in the United States as *An object-relations theory of the personality.* New York: Basic Books 1952.)

Famularo R, Kinscherff R, Fenton T. Propranolol treatment for childhood posttraumatic stress disorder. *Am J Dis Child* 1988;142:1244–1247.

Farber LH. Despair and the life of suicide. *Rev Existential Psychol Psychiatry* 1962;2: 125–139.

Farberow NL (ed). *The many faces of suicide: Indirect self-destructive behavior.* New York: McGraw-Hill 1980.

Farberow NL, Gallagher DE, Gilewski MJ, et al. An examination of the early impact of bereavement on psychological distress in survivors of suicide. *Gerontologist* 1987;27:592–598.

Farberow NL, Shneidman ES, Neuringer C. Case history and hospitalization factors in suicides of neuropsychiatric hospital patients. *J Nerv Ment Dis* 1966;142:32–44.

Farmer R. The differences between those who repeat and those who do not. In R Farmer, S Hirsch (eds), *The suicide syndrome.* London: Croom Helm 1980.

Farrer L. Suicide and attempted suicide in Huntington's disease: Implications for preclinical testing of persons at risk. *Am J Med Genet* 1986;24:305–311.

Fava M, Rosenbaum JF. Suicidality and fluoxetine: Is there a relationship? *J Clin Psychiatry* 1992;53:103.

Favazza A. Why patients mutilate themselves. *Hosp Community Psychiatry* 1989;40: 137–145.

Favazza A. *Bodies under siege: Self-mutilation and body modification in culture and psychiatry,* 2d ed. Baltimore: Johns Hopkins University Press 1996.

Favazza A, Conterio K. Female habitual self-mutilators. *Acta Psychiatr Scand* 1989;79: 283–289.

Favazza A, De Rosario L, Conteiro K. Self-mutilation and eating disorders. *Suicide Life-Threat Behav* 1989;19:352–361.

Favazza A, Rosenthal R. Varieties of pathological self-mutilation. *Behav Neurol* 1990;3: 77–85.

Favazza A, Rosenthal R. Diagnostic issues in self-mutilation. *Hosp Community Psychiatry* 1993;44:134–140.

Favazza A, Simeon D. Self-mutilation. In E Hollander, D Stein (eds), *Impulsivity and aggression.* New York: Wiley 1995.

Fawcett JA. Suicidal depression and physical illness. *JAMA* 1972;219:1303–1306.

Fawcett JA. Predictors of early suicide identification and appropriate intervention. *J Clin Psychiatry* 1988;49(suppl 10):7–8.

Fawcett JA. Suicide risk factors in depressive disorders and in panic disorder. *J Clin Psychiatry* 1992;53:9–13.

Fawcett JA. Assessing and treating the patient at risk for suicide. *Psychiatr Ann* 1995; 23:244–255.

Fawcett JA. The detection and consequences of anxiety in clinical depression. *J Clin Psychiatry* 1997;58(suppl 8):35–40.

Fawcett JA, Busch KA, Jacobs D, et al. Suicide: A four-pathway clinical-biochemical model. *Ann NY Acad Sci* 1997;836:288–301.

Fawcett JA, Clark DC, Busch KA. Assessing and treating the patient at risk for suicide. *Psychiatr Ann* 1993;23:244–255.

Fawcett JA, Clark DC, Scheftner WA. The assessment and management of the suicidal patient. *Psychiatr Med* 1991;9:299–311.

Fawcett JA, Kravitz HM. Anxiety syndromes and their relationship to depressive illness. *J Clin Psychiatr* 1983;44:8–11.

Fawcett JA, Scheftner WA. Personal communication. 1993.

Fawcett JA, Scheftner WA, Clark DC, et al. Clinical predictors of suicide in patients with major affective disorders: A controlled prospective study. *Am J Psychiatry* 1987;144:35–40.

Fawcett JA, Scheftner WA, Fogg LF, et al. Time-related predictors of suicide in major affective disorder. *Am J Psychiatry* 1990;147:1189–1194.

Felber W, Kyber A. Suizide und Parasuizide während und ausserhalb einer Lithium prophylaxe. In B Müller-Oerlinghausen, A Berghöfer (eds), *Ziele und Ergebnisse der Medikamentosen Prophylaxe Affektiver Psychosen.* Stuttgart: Thieme 1994:53–59.

Fenn HH, Robinson D, Luby V, et al. Trends in pharmacotherapy of schizoaffective and bipolar affective disorders: A 5-year naturalistic study. *Am J Psychiatry* 1996;153: 711–713.

Fenton WS, McGlashan TH. Natural history of schizophrenia subtypes: I. Longitudinal course of paranoid, hebephrenic, and undifferentiated schizophrenia. *Arch Gen Psychiatry* 1991a;48:969–977.

Fenton WS, McGlashan TH. Natural history of schizophrenia subtypes: II. Positive and negative symptoms and long-term course. *Arch Gen Psychiatry* 1991b;48:978–986.

Fenton WS, McGlashan TH, Victor BJ, Blyler CR. Symptoms, subtype, and suicidality in patients with schizophrenia spectrum disorders. *Am J Psychiatry* 1997;154: 199–204.

Fesler FA. Valproate in combat-related posttraumatic stress disorder. *J Clin Psychiatry* 1991;52:361–364.

Fichter M, Quadflieg N, Rief W. Course of multi-impulsive bulimia. *Psychol Med* 1994; 24:592–604.

Fine C. *No time to say goodbye: Surviving the suicide of a loved one.* New York: Doubleday 1997.

Fink M. *Convulsive therapy: Theory and practice.* New York: Raven Press 1979.

Fink M. ECT for Parkinson's disease? *Convulsive Ther* 1988;4:189–191.

Fink M. Catatonia and DSM-IV. *Convulsive Ther* 1992;8:159–162.

Fink WL, Roth LH. Altruistic murder-suicide: A case report and clinical implications. *Hosp Community Psychiatry* 1979;30:558–559.

Finkelhor D. *Child sexual abuse: New theory and research.* New York: Free Press 1984.

Finkelhor D, Browne A. The traumatic impact of child sexual abuse: A conceptualization. *Am J Orthopsychiatry* 1985;55:530–541.

Fishbain DA, Goldberg M, Rosomoff RS, Rosomoff HL. Homicide-suicide and chronic pain. *Clin J Pain* 1989;5:275–277.

Fishbain DA, Rao VJ, Aldrich TE. Female homicide-suicide perpetrators: A controlled study. *J Forensic Sci* 1985;30:1148–1156.

Foley HA. *Community mental health legislation: The formative process.* Lexington MA: Heath 1975.

Foley K. Case presentation at the Bellagio Workshop on Care of the Terminally Ill, Aug 1996.

Fonagy P. Attachment and borderline personality disorder: A theory and some evidence. Stanton Lecture, McLean Hospital, Belmont MA, Oct 24, 1997.

Foster S, Kessel J, Berman ME, Simpson GM. Efficacy of lorazepam and haloperidol for rapid tranquilization in a psychiatric emergency room setting. *Int Clin Psychopharmacol* 1997;12:175–179.

Fowler RC, Rich CL, Young D. San Diego suicide study: Substance abuse in young cases. *Arch Gen Psychiatry* 1986;43:962–965.

Frances A. Introduction to the section on self-mutilation. *J Pers Dis* 1987;1:316.

Frances A, Fyer M, Clarkin JF. Personality and suicide. *Ann NY Acad Sci* 1986;487:281–293.

Frances RJ, Franklin J, Flavin DK. Suicide and alcoholism. *Am J Drug Alcohol Abuse* 1987;13:327–341.

Frank E, Prien RF, Kupfer DJ, Alberts L. Implications of noncompliance on research in affective disorders. *Psychopharmacol Bull* 1985;21:1,37–42.

Frankel FH. The use of electroconvulsive therapy in suicidal patients. *Am J Psychother* 1984;38:384–391.

Frankl V. *Man's search for ultimate meaning.* New York: Plenum 1977.

Franklin RK. Deliberate self-harm: Self-injurious behavior within a correctional mental health population. *Crim Justice* 1988;15:210–218.

Frazier SH. Murder—single and multiple. *Res Public Assoc Res Nerv Ment Dis* 1974;52:304–312.

Freedman DS, Byers T, Barrett DR, et al. Plasma lipid levels and psychologic characteristics in men. *Am J Epidemiol* 1995;141:507–517.

Freedman R, Foote SL, Bloom FE. Histochemical characterization of a neocortical projection of the nucleus locus ceruleus in the squirrel monkey. *J Comp Neurol* 1975;164:209–232.

Freemantle N, House A, Song F, et al. Prescribing selective serotonin reuptake inhibitors as strategy for prevention of suicide. *Br Med J* 1994;309:249–253.

Fremming KH. *The expectation of mental infirmity in a sample of the Danish population.* London: Cassell 1951.

Freud S. Mourning and melancholia. In *The standard edition of complete psychological works* (trans, ed J Strachey), vol. 14. London: Hogarth Press 1957:238–260. (Originally published 1917)

Freud S. Inhibitions, symptoms, and anxiety. In *The standard edition of complete psychological works* (trans, ed J Strachey), vol. 20. London: Hogarth Press 1959:77–175. (Originally published 1926)

Freud S. The ego and the id. In *The standard edition of complete psychological works* (trans, ed J Strachey), vol. 19. London: Hogarth Press 1961:3–66. (Originally published 1923)

Freud S. An outline of psychoanalysis. In *The standard edition of complete psychological works* (trans, ed J Strachey), vol. 23. London: Hogarth Press 1964:141–207. (Originally published 1940)

Friedlander K. On the "longing to die." *Int J Psychoanal* 1940;21:416–426.

Friedman P (ed). *On suicide, with particular reference to suicide among young students.* Madison CT: International Universities Press 1967.

Friedman RC, Aronoff MS, Clarkin JF, et al. History of suicidal behavior in depressed borderline inpatients. *Am J Psychiatry* 1983;140:1023–1026.

Friedman RC, Clarkin JF, Corn R, et al. DSM-III and affective pathology in hospitalized adolescents. *J Nerv Ment Dis* 1982;170:511–521.

Friedman RS. Hospital treatment of the suicidal patient. In DG Jacobs, HP Brown (eds), *Suicide: Understanding and responding*: Madison CT: International Universities Press 1989:379–402.

Frierson RL. Suicides by the old and very old. *Arch Intern Med* 1991;151:141–144.

Fuller RW, Snoddy HD, Robertson DW. Mechanisms of effects of d-fenfluramine on brain serotonin metabolism in rats: Uptake inhibition versus release. *Pharmacol Biochem Behav* 1988;30:715–721.

Fyer M, Frances A, Sullivan T, et al. Suicide attempts in patients with borderline personality disorder. *Am J Psychiatry* 1988;145:737–739.

Gabbard G. Splitting in hospital treatment. *Am J Psychiatry* 1989;146:444–451.

Gabilondo AM, Meana JJ, García-Sevilla JA. Increased density of mu-opioid receptors in the postmortem brain of suicide victims. *Brain Res* 1995;682:245–250.

Gardner DL, Cowdry RW. Alprazolam-induced dyscontrol in borderline personality disorder. *Am J Psychaitry* 1985a;142:98–100.

Gardner DL, Cowdry RW. Suicidal and parasuicidal behavior in borderline personality disorder. *Psychiatr Clin North Am* 1985b;8:389–403.

Garrison CZ, McKeown RE, Valois RF, et al. Aggression, substance use, and suicidal behaviors in high school students. *Am J Public Health* 1993;83:179–184.

Gaw AC, Bernstein RL. Classification of amok in DSM-IV. *Hosp Community Psychiatry* 1992;43:789–793.

Gawin FH, Kleber HD. Cocaine abuse treatment: Open pilot trial with desipramine and lithium carbonate. *Arch Gen Psychiatry* 1984;41:903–909.

Gelenberg AJ, Kane JM, Keller MB, et al. Comparison of standard and low serum levels of lithium for maintenance treatment of bipolar disorder. *N Engl J Med* 1989;321:1489–1493.

Gelinas DJ. The persisting negative effects of incest. *Psychiatry* 1983;46:312–332.

Getz WL, Allen DB, Myers RK. *Brief counseling with suicidal persons.* Lexington KY: Lexington Books 1983.

Giel R, Dijk S, van Weerden-Dijkstra JR. Mortality in the long-stay population of all Dutch mental hospitals. *Acta Psychiatr Scand* 1978;57:361–368.

Gladstone TR, Kaslow NJ. Depression and attributions in children and adolescents: A meta-analytic review. *J Abnorm Child Psychol* 1995;23:597–606.

Glass RM. AIDS and suicide. *JAMA* 1988;259:1369–1370.

Glen AIM, Dodd M, Hulme EB, Kreitman N. Mortality on lithium. *Neuropsychobiology* 1979;5:167–173.

Glick ID, Clarkin JF, Spencer JH, et al. A controlled evaluation of inpatient family intervention: Preliminary results of the six-month follow-up. *Arch Gen Psychiatry* 1985;42:882–886.

Glueck CJ et al. Hypocholesterolemia and affective disorders. *Am J Med Sci* 1994;308:218–225.

Goldacre M, Seagrott V, Hawton K. Suicide after discharge from psychiatric in-patient care. *Lancet* 1993;342(8866):283–286.

Goldberg RJ. The assessment of suicide risk in the general hospital. *Gen Hosp Psychiatry* 1987;9:446–452.

Goldblatt M, Schatzberg A. Medication and the suicidal patient. In DG Jacobs (ed), *Suicide and clinical practice.* Washington DC: American Psychiatric Press 1992:23–42.

Golden RN, Ekstrom D, Brown, TM, et al. Neuroendocrine effects of intravenous clomipramine in depressed patients and healthy subjects. *Am J Psychiatry* 1992;149:1168–1175.

Goldenberg E, Sata LS. Religious delusions and self-mutilation. *Curr Concepts Psychiatry* 1978;Sept./Oct.:2–5.

Goldman SJ, D'Angelo EJ, De Maso DR, Mezzacappa E. Physical and sexual abuse among children with borderline personality disorder. *Am J Psychiatry* 1992;149:1723–1726.

Goldney RD. Homicide and suicide by aircraft. *Forensic Sci Int* 1983;21:161–163.

Goldney RD, Winefield A, Saebel J, et al. Anger, suicidal ideation, and attempted suicide: A prospective study. *Comp Psychiatry* 1997;38:264–268.

Goldsmith SJ, Fyer M, Frances A. Personality and suicide. In SJ Blumenthal, DJ Kupfer (eds), *Suicide over the life cycle: Risk factors, assessment, and treatment of suicidal patients.* Washington DC: American Psychiatric Press 1990:155–176.

Goldstein RB, Black DW, Nasrallah A, Winokur G. The prediction of suicide: Sensitivity, specificity, and predictive value of a multivariate model applied to suicide among 1,906 patients with affective disorders. *Arch Gen Psychiatry* 1991;48:418–422.

Gomez C. Case presentation at the Bellagio Workshop on the Care of the Terminally Ill, Aug 1996.

González AM, Pascual J, Meana JJ, et al. Autoradiographic demonstration of increased a_2-adrenoceptor agonist binding sites in the hippocampus and frontal cortex of depressed suicide victims. *J Neurochem* 1994;63:256–265.

Goodhart S, Savitsky N. Self-mutilation in chronic encephalitis. *Am J Sci* 1933;185:674–684.

Goodstein J. Cognitive characteristics of suicide attempters. *Diss Abstr Int* 1982;43:1613.

Goodwin FK, Jamison KR. *Manic-depressive illness.* New York: Oxford University Press 1990.

Goodwin FK, Runck BL. Suicide intervention: Integration of psychosocial, clinical, and biomedical traditions. In DG Jacobs (ed), *Suicide and clinical practice.* Washington DC: American Psychiatric Press 1992:1–22.

Gordon R. An operational classification of disease prevention. In JA Steinberg, MM Silverman (eds), *Preventing mental disorders.* Rockville MD: U.S. Department of Health and Human Services 1987:20–26.

Gould MS, Fischer P, Parides M, et al. Psychosocial risk factors of child and adolescent completed suicide. *Arch Gen Psych* 1996;53:1155–1162.

Gould MS, Petrie K, Kleinman MH, Wallenstein S. Clustering of attempted suicide. *Int J Epidemiol* 1994;23:1185–1189.

Gould MS, Shaffer DA. The impact of suicide in television movies. *N Eng J Med* 1986; 315:690–694.

Gould MS, Shaffer DA, Fisher P, Garfinkel R. Separation/divorce and child and adolescent completed suicide. *J Am Acad Child Adolesc Psychiatry* 1998;37:155–162.

Gould MS, Wallenstein S, Kleinman MH. Time-space clustering of teenage suicide. *Am J Epidemiol* 1990a;131:71–78.

Gould MS, Wallenstein S, Kleinman MH, et al. Suicide clusters: An examination of age-specific effects. *Am J Public Health* 1990b;80:211–212.

Goulding ME, Goulding RL. *Changing lives through redecision therapy.* New York: Brunner/Mazel 1979.

Graff H, Mallin R. The syndrome of the wrist cutter. *Am J Psychiatry* 1967;124:74–79.

Grahame K. *The wind in the willows.* New York: Scribner 1991. (Originally published 1933)

Green JS, Grindel CG. Supervision of suicidal patients in adult inpatient psychiatric units in general hospitals. *Psychiatr Services* 1996;47:859–863.

Greenberg PE, Stiglin LE, Finkelstein SN, Berndt ER. Depression: A neglected major illness. *J Clin Psychiatry* 1993a;54:419–424.

Greenberg PE, Stiglin LE, Finkelstein SN, Berndt ER. The economic burden of depression in 1990. *J Clin Psychiatry* 1993b;54:405–418.

Greenfield SF, Weiss RD, Muenz LR, et al. The effects of depression on return to drinking: A prospective study. *Arch Gen Psychiatry* 1998;55:259–265.

Greenspan GC, Samuel SE. Self-cutting after rape. *Am J Psychiatry* 1989;146:789–790.

Greenwald DJ, Reznikoff M, Plutchik R. Suicide risk and violence risk in alcoholics: Predictors of aggressive risk. *J Nerv Ment Dis* 1994;182:3–8.

Griffin JC, Williams DE, Stark MT. Self-injurious behavior. *Appl Res Ment Retard* 1985;7:105–116.

Griffin N, Webb M, Parker R. A case of self-inflicted eye injuries. *J Nerv Ment Dis* 1982;170:53–56.

Gross-Isseroff R, Dillon KA, Fieldust SJ, Biegon A. Autoradiographic analysis of a_1-noradrenergic receptors in the human brain post mortem. *Arch Gen Psychiatry* 1990;47:1049–1053.

Gross-Isseroff R, Israeli M, Biegon A. Autoradiographic analysis of tritiated imipramine binding in the human brain post mortem: Effects of suicide. *Arch Gen Psychiatry* 1989;46:237–241.

Gross-Isseroff R, Salama D, Israeli M, Biegon A. Autoradiographic analysis of [^{3}H-]ketanserin binding in the human brain post mortem: Effect of suicide. *Brain Res* 1990;507:208–215.

Group for the Advancement of Psychiatry Report. *Beyond symptom suppression: Long-term views of schizophrenia.* Washington DC: Group for the Advancement of Psychiatry 1992.

Group for the Advancement of Psychiatry. *Adolescent suicide.* Washington DC: American Psychiatric Press 1996.

Groves J. Taking care of the hateful patient. *N Engl J Med* 1978;298:883–887.

Grunebaum H, Klerman GL. Wrist slashing. *Am J Psychiatry* 1967;124:524–534.

Gunderson JG. *Borderline personality disorder.* Washington DC: American Psychiatric Press 1984.

Gunderson JG. The interface between borderline personality disorder and affective disorder. *Am J Psychiatry* 1985;142:277–288.

Gunderson JG. Personality disorders. In AM Nicholi Jr (ed), *The new Harvard guide to psychiatry.* Cambridge MA: Belknap Press 1988.

Gunderson JG. The borderline patient's intolerance of aloneness: Insecure attachments and therapist availability. *Am J Psychiatry* 1996;153:752–758.

Gunderson JG, Kolb JE, Austin V. The diagnostic interview for borderline patients. *Am J Psychiatry* 1981;138:896–903.

Gunderson JG, Zanarini MC. Current overview of the borderline diagnosis. *J Clin Psychiatry* 1987;48(suppl):5–11.

Gunnell D, Frankel S. Prevention of suicide: Aspirations and evidence. *Br Med J* 1994;308:1227–1233.

Gutheil TG. Observations on the theoretical basis for seclusion of the psychiatric inpatient. *Am J Psychiatry* 1978;135:325–338.

Gutheil TG. On the therapy in clinical administration: II. The administrative contract, alliance, ultimatum and goal. *Psychiatr Q* 1982;54:11–17.

Gutheil TG. Malpractice liability in suicide. *Leg Aspects Psychiatr Prac* 1984;1:1–4.

Gutheil TG. Medicolegal pitfalls in the treatment of borderline patients. *Am J Psychiatry* 1985;142:9–14.

Gutheil TG. Clinical and legal ramifications of suicide. In DM Szemborski (ed), *Risk factors in psychiatric management.* Elizabeth NJ: Healthways Communications 1987.

Gutheil TG. Suicide and suit: Liability after self-destruction. In DG Jacobs (ed), *Suicide and clinical practice.* Washington DC: American Psychiatric Press 1992.

Gutheil TG. Competence assessment in suicide evaluation. *Forum* 1993;14(6):9–10.

Gutheil TG, Bursztajn H, Brodsky A. Malpractice prevention through the sharing of uncertainty: Informed consent and the therapeutic alliance. *N Engl J Med* 1984;311:49–51.

Gutheil TG, Bursztajn H, Brodsky A. The multidimensional assessment of dangerousness: Competence assessment in patient care and liability prevention. *Bull Am Acad Psychiatry Law* 1986;14:123–129.

Gutheil TG, Bursztajn H, Brodsky A, Alexander T. *Decision making in psychiatry and law.* Baltimore: Williams & Wilkins 1991.

Gutheil TG, Havens LL. The therapeutic alliance: Contemporary meanings and confusions. *Int Rev Psychoanal* 1979;6:467–481.

Gutheil TG, Schetky D. A date with death: Time-based and contingent suicidal intent and its management. *Am J Psychiatry* 1998.

Guze SB, Robins E. Suicide and primary affective disorders. *Br J Psychiatry* 1970;117:437–438.

Haberlandt W. Der Suizid als genetisches Problem (Zwillings-und Familienanalyse). *Anthropol Anz* 1965;29:65–89.

Haberlandt W. Aportacion a la genética del suicidio. *Folia Clin Int* 1967;17:319–322.

Hagnell O, Lanke J, Rorsman B. Suicide rates in the Lundby study: Mental illness as a risk factor for suicide. *Neuropsychobiology* 1981;7:248–253.

Hagnell O, Rorsman B. Suicide in the Lundby study: A comparative investigation of clinical aspects. *Neuropsychobiology* 1979;5:61–73.

Hall RCW, Tice L, Beresford TP, et al. Sexual abuse in patients with anorexia and bulimia. *Psychosomatics* 1986;30:73–79.

Hall SM, Havassy BE, Wasserman DA. Commitment to abstinence and acute stress in relapse to alcohol, opiates, and nicotine. *J Consult Clin Psychol* 1990;58:175–181.

Hamilton M. A rating scale for depression. *J Neurol Neurosurg Psychiatry* 1960;23:56–62.

Hamilton M, White JM. Factors related to the outcome of depression treated with ECT. *J Ment Sci* 1960;106:1031–1041.

Hamilton MS, Opler LA. Akathisia, suicidality, and fluoxetine. *J Clin Psychiatry* 1992;53:401–406.

Hansen JP, Bjarnason O. Homicide in Iceland, 1946–1970. *Forensic Sci* 1974;4:107–117.

Hanus K, Zalpetálek M. Suicidal activity of patients with affective disorders in the course of lithium prophylaxis. *Cesk Psychiatr* 1984;80:97–100.

Hanzlick R, Koponen M. Murder-suicide in Fulton County, Georgia, 1988–1991. *Am J Forensic Med Pathol* 1994;15:168–173.

Harder T. The psychopathology of infanticide. *Acta Psychiatr Scand* 1967;43:196–246.

Harkavy-Friedman J, Nelson E. Management of the suicidal patient with schizophrenia. *Psychiatr Clin North Am* 1997;20:625–641.

Harrer VG, Urban HJ. Zur Selbstblendung and Selbstverstummelung. *Wien Med Wochenschr* 1950;100:37–40.

Harris EC, Barraclough BM. Suicide as an outcome for medical disorders. *Medicine* 1994;73:281–296.

Harris EC, Barraclough BM. Suicide as an outcome for mental disorders: A meta-analysis. *Br J Psychiatry* 1997;170:205–228.

Harry J. Sexual identity issues. In U.S. Department of Health and Human Services; Alcohol, Drug Abuse, and Mental Health Administration, *Report of the Secretary's Task Force on Youth Suicide, vol 2: Risk factors for youth suicide.* DHHS Publication No. (ADM)89–1624. Washington DC: U.S. Government Printing Office 1989: 2-131-2-142.

Harvard Medical Institutions, Risk Advisory Committee (DG Jacobs, chair). Draft suicide assessment guidelines. *Forum* 1993;14(6):14–19.

Hastings DW. Follow-up results in psychiatric illness. *Am J Psychiatry* 1958;114:1057–1066.

Haught K, Grossman D, Connell F. Parents' attitudes toward firearm injury prevention counseling in urban pediatric clinics. *Pediatrics* 1995;96:649–653.

Hawthorne N. *The scarlet letter.* London: Ward Lock 1850.

Hawton K. Self-cutting. In K Hawton, P Cowen (eds), *Dilemmas and difficulties in the management of psychiatric patients.* Oxford: Oxford University Press 1990.

Hayes LM. National study of jail suicides: Seven years later. *Psychiatr Q* 1989;60(1):7–29.

Hayes LM. Suicidal or manipulative: Does it really matter? *Crisis* 1993;14:154–156.

Hayes LM. Controversial issues in jail suicide prevention. *Crisis* 1995;16:107–110.

Hazell P, King R. Arguments for and against teaching suicide prevention in schools. *Aust NZ J Psychiatry* 1996;30:633–642.

Heikkinen ME, Isometsä ET, Aro HM, et al. Age-related variation in recent life events preceding suicide. *J Nerv Ment Dis* 1995a;183:325–331.

Heikkinen ME, Isometsä ET, Marttunen MJ, et al. Social factors in suicide. *Br J Psychiatry* 1995b;167:747–753.

Heikkinen ME, Lönnqvist JK. Recent life events in elderly suicide: A nationwide study in Finland. *Int Psychogeriatr* 1995;7:287–300.

Heilä H, Isometsä ET, Henriksson MM, et al. Suicide and schizophrenia: A nationwide psychological autopsy study on age- and sex-specific clinical characteristics of 92 suicide victims with schizophrenia. *Am J Psychiatry* 1997;154:1235–1242.

Helgason T. Epidemiology of mental disorders in Iceland. *Acta Psychiatr Scand* 1964; 173(suppl):1–258.

Helgason T. Epidemiological investigations concerning affective disorders. In M Schou, E Strömgren (eds), *Origin, prevention, and treatment of affective disorders.* Orlando FL: Academic Press 1979.

Hellman ID, Morrison TL, Abramowitz SI. The stresses of psychotherapeutic work: A replication and extension. *J Clin Psychiatry* 1986;42:197–205.

Hemphill RE. A case of genital self-mutilation. *Br J Med Psychol* 1951;24:291–295.

Hendin H. Fall from power: Suicide of an executive. *Suicide Life-Threat Behav* 1994; 24:293–301.

Hendin H. Assisted suicide, euthanasia, and suicide prevention: The implications of the Dutch experience. *Suicide Life-Threat Behav* 1995a;25:193–204.

Hendin H. Selling death and dignity. *Hastings Center Rep* 1995b;25:19–23.

Hendin H. *Suicide in America.* New York: Norton 1995c.

Hendin H. The slippery slope: The Dutch example. *Duquesne Law Rev* 1996a;35: 427–442.

Hendin H. Suicide and the request for assisted suicide: Meaning and motivation. *Duquesne Law Rev* 1996b;35:285–310.

Hendin H. *Seduced by death: Doctors, patients, and assisted suicide.* New York: Norton 1998.

Hendin H, Klerman GL. Physician-assisted suicide: The dangers of legalization. *Am J Psychiatry* 1993;150:143–145.

Hendin H, Rutenfrans C, Zylicz Z. Physician-assisted suicide and euthanasia in the Netherlands: Lessons from the Dutch. *JAMA* 1997;277:1720–1722.

Heninger GR, Charney DS, Sternberg DE. Serotonergic function in depression: Prolactin response to intravenous tryptophan in depressed patients and healthy subjects. *Arch Gen Psychiatry* 1984;41:398–402.

Henk HJ, Katzelnick DJ, Kobak KA, et al. Medical costs attributed to depression among patients with a history of high medical expenses in a health maintenance organization. *Arch Gen Psychiatry* 1996;53:899–904.

Henriksson MM, Aro HM, Marttunen MJ, et al. Mental disorders and comorbidity in suicide. *Am J Psychiatry* 1993;150:935–940.

Henriksson MM, Isometsä ET, Kuoppasalmi KI, et al. Panic disorder in completed suicide. *J Clin Psychiatry* 1996;57:275–281.

Henriksson MM, Marttunen MJ, Isometsä ET, et al. Mental disorders in elderly suicide. *Int Psychogeriatr* 1995;7:275–286.

Henry A, Short J. *Suicide and homicide: Some economic, sociological, and psychological aspects of aggression.* New York: Free Press 1954.

Henschen GM. Risk reduction guidelines problem memorandum, Charter Behavioral Health Systems, Sept 1997.

Herman JL. *Father-daughter incest.* Cambridge MA: Harvard University Press 1981.

Herman JL. *Trauma and recovery.* New York: Basic Books 1992.

Herman JL, Perry JC, van der Kolk BA. Childhood trauma in borderline personality disorder. *Am J Psychiatry* 1989;146:490–495.

Herman JL, Russell D, Trocki K. Long-term effects of incestuous abuse in childhood. *Am J Psychiatry* 1986;143:1293–1296.

Hermann RC, Dorwart RA, Hoover CW, Brody J. Variation in ECT use in the United States. *Am J Psychiatry* 1995;152:869–875.

Hesselbrock MN, Hesselbrock V, Syzmanski K, Weidenman M. Suicide attempts and alcoholism. *J Stud Alcohol* 1988;49:436–442.

Hesselbrock MN, Meyer RE, Keener JJ. Psychopathology in hospitalized alcoholics. *Arch Gen Psychiatry* 1985;42:1050–1055.

Hibbard RA, Brack CJ, Rauch S. Abuse, feelings and health behaviors in a student population. *Am J Dis Child* 1988;142:326–330.

Hilhorst HW. *Euthanasie in het ziekenhuis.* Lochem NL: Tijdstroom 1983.

Hillard JR. Predicting suicide. *Psychiatr Services* 1995;46:223–225.

Himber J. Blood rituals: Self-cutting in female psychiatric patients. *Psychotherapy* 1994;31:620–631.

Himmelhoch JM. Lest treatment abet suicide. *J Clin Psychiatry* 1987;48(suppl 12):44–54.

Hipple JL, Cimpolic P. *The counselor and suicidal crisis.* Springfield IL: Thomas 1979.

Hirose S. Depression and homicide. *Acta Psychiatr Scand* 1979;59:211–217.

Hirschfeld RMA. Algorithm for the evaluation and treatment of suicidal patients. *Primary Psychiatry* 1996;Feb.:26–29.

Hirschfeld RMA, Davidson L. Clinical risk factors for suicide. *Psychiatr Ann* 1988;18: 628–635.

Hirschfeld RMA, Klerman GL, Clayton PJ, et al. Assessing personality: Effects of the depressive state on trait measurement. *Am J Psychiatry* 1983;140:695–699.

Hirschfeld RMA, Russell JM. Assessment and treatment of suicidal patients. *N Engl J Med* 1997;337:910–915.

Hlady WG, Middaugh JP. Suicides in Alaska: Firearms and alcohol. *Am J Public Health* 1988;78:179–180.

Hobson RF. Prognostic factors in electroconvulsive therapy. *J Neurol Neurosurg Psychiatry* 1953;16:275–281.

Holinger PC, Offer D, Ostrov E. Suicide and homicide in the United States: An epidemiologic study of violent death, population changes, and the potential for prediction. *Am J Psychiatry* 1987;144:215–219.

Holinger PC, Offer D, Zola MA. A prediction model of suicide among youth. *J Nerv Ment Dis* 1988;176:275–279.

Hollender MH, Ford CV. *Dynamic psychotherapy: An introductory approach.* Washington DC: American Psychiatric Press 1990.

Hornig CD, McNally RJ. Panic disorder and suicide attempt: A reanalysis of data from the Epidemiologic Cachment Area Study. *Br J Psychiatry* 1995;167:76–79.

Horoshak I. How to handle high-risk patients. In N Miller (ed), *Suicide intervention by nurses.* New York: Springer 1982:63–68.

Hrdina PD, Demeter E, Vu TB, et al. 5-HT uptake sites and 5-HT$_2$ receptors in the brain of antidepressant-free suicide victims/depressives: Increase in 5-HT$_2$ sites in cortex and amygdala. *Brain Res* 1993;614:37–44.

Hu WH, Sun CM, Lee CT, et al. A clinical study of schizophrenic suicides: 42 cases in Taiwan. *Schizophr Res* 1991;5:43–50.

Hughes DH. Suicide and violence assessment in psychiatry. *Gen Hosp Psychiatry* 1996; 18:416–421.

Huston PE, Locher LM. Involutional psychosis: Course when untreated and when treated with electric shock. *Arch Neurol Psychiatry* 1948a;59:385–394.

Huston PE, Locher LM. Manic-depressive psychosis: Course when treated and untreated with electric shock. *Arch Neurol Psychiatry* 1948b;60:37–48.

Ikeda M, Mackay KB, Dewar D, McCulloch J. Differential alterations in adenosine A$_1$ and kappa$_1$ opioid receptors in the striatum in Alzheimer's disease. *Brain Res* 1993;616:211–217.

Ikeda Y, Noda H, Sugita S. Olivocerebellar and cerebelloolivary connections of the oculomotor region of the fastigial nucleus in the macaque monkey. *J Comp Neurol* 1989;284:463–488.

Indian Health Service. *Regional differences in Indian health, 1996.* Rockville MD: U.S. Department of Health and Human Services, Indian Health Service, Office of Planning, Evaluation, and Legislation, Division of Program Statistics 1996a.

Indian Health Service: *Trends in Indian health, 1996.* Rockville MD: U.S. Department of Health and Human Services, Indian Health Service, Office of Planning, Evaluation, and Legislation, Division of Program Statistics 1996b.

Innes G, Millar WM. Mortality among psychiatric patients. *Scott Med J* 1970;15:143–148.

Inskip HM, Harris EC, Barraclough BM. Lifetime risk of suicide for affective disorder, alcoholism and schizophrenia. *Br J Psychiatry* 1998;172:35–37.

Institute of Medicine, Committee on Prevention for Mental Disorders, Division of Biobehavioral Science and Mental Disorders. New directions and definitions. In PJ Maracek, RH Haggerty (eds), *Reducing risks for mental disorders: Frontiers for preventive intervention research.* Washington DC: National Academy Press 1994:19–32.

Isacsson G, Bergman U, Rich CL. Antidepressants, depression, and suicide: An analysis of the San Diego study. *J Affective Disord* 1994a;32:277–286.

Isacsson G, Boëthius G, Bergman U. Low level of antidepressant prescription for people who later commit suicide: 15 years of experience from a population-based drug database in Sweden. *Acta Psychiatr Scand* 1992;85:444–448.

Isacsson G, Holmgren P, Wasserman D, et al. Use of antidepressants among people committing suicide in Sweden. *Br Med J* 1994b;308:506–509.

Isacsson G, Rich CL, Bergman U. Antidepressants and suicide prevention (letter). *Am J Psychiatry* 1996;153:1659.

Isometsä ET, Henriksson MM, Aro HM, Lönnqvist JK. Suicide in bipolar disorder in Finland. *Am J Psychiatry* 1994a;151:1020–1024.

Isometsä ET, Henriksson MM, Aro HM, et al. Suicide in major depression. *Am J Psychiatry* 1994b;151:530–536.

Isometsä ET, Henriksson MM, Heikkinen ME, Lönnqvist JK. Completed suicide and recent electroconvulsive therapy in Finland. *Convulsive Ther* 1996a;12:152–155.

Isometsä ET, Henriksson MM, Heikkinen ME, et al. Suicide among subjects with personality disorders. *Am J Psychiatry* 1996b;153:667–673.

Isometsä ET, Henriksson MM, Lönnqvist JK. Completed suicide and recent lithium treatment. *J Affective Disord* 1992;26:101–104.

Jaasskelainen J, Viukari NMA. Do tricyclic antidepressants work? *Lancet* 1976;1:424.

Jacobs DG. Evaluating and treating suicidal behavior in the borderline patient. In DG Jacobs (ed), *Suicide and clinical practice.* Washington DC: American Psychiatric Press 1992:116–123.

Jacobs DG. The no-suicide contract. *Forum* 1993;14(6):9.

Jacobs DG. Suicide: What's new and what you need to know. Presentation, Medicolegal Pitfalls for the Practicing Psychiatrist, Massachusetts Psychiatric Society, Boston, Mar 18, 1995.

Jacobs DG, Brown HN (eds), *Suicide: Understanding and responding.* Madison CT: International Universities Press 1989.

Jacobs DR, Muldoon MF, Rastam L. Invited commentary: Low blood cholesterol, nonillness mortality, and other nonatherosclerotic disease mortality: A search for causes and confounders. *Am J Epidemiol* 1995;141:518–522.

Jacobsen A, Richardson B. Assault experiences of 100 psychiatric inpatients: Evidence for the need of positive inquiry. *Am J Psychiatry* 1987;144:908–913.

Jacobsen LK, Rabinowitz I, Popper MS. Interviewing prepubertal children about suicidal ideation and behavior. *J Am Acad Child Adolesc Psychiatry* 1994;33:439–452.

Jacobson G. The couple. In L Sederer (ed), *Inpatient psychiatry: Diagnosis and treatment.* Baltimore: Williams & Wilkins 1983:281–288.

Jaksa RJ, Palahniuk RJ. Attempted organophosphate suicide: A unique cause of prolonged paralysis during electroconvulsive therapy. *Anesth Analg* 1994;80:832–833.

Jameison GR. Suicide and mental disease: A clinical analysis of one hundred cases. *Arch Neurol Psychiatry* 1936;36:1–12.

Jameison GR, Wall JH. Some psychiatric aspects of suicide. *Psychiatr Q* 1933;7:211–229.

James IP, Scott-Orr DN, Curnow DH. Blood alcohol levels following attempted suicide. *Q J Stud Alcohol* 1963;24:14–22.

James NM, Chapman CJ. A genetic study of bipolar affective disorder. *Br J Psychiatry* 1975;126:449–456.

Jamison KR. Suicide and bipolar disorders. *Ann NY Acad Sci* 1986;487:301–315.

Jamison KR. *An unquiet mind: A memoir of moods and madness.* New York: Knopf 1995.

Jamison KR, Akiskal HS. Medication compliance in patients with bipolar disorders. *Psychiatr Clin North Am* 1983;6:175–192.

Jamison KR, Gerner RH, Goodwin FK. Patient and physician attitudes toward lithium: Relationship to compliance. *Arch Gen Psychiatry* 1979;36:866–869.

Janoff-Bulman R. *Shattered assumptions: Towards a new psychology of trauma.* New York: Free Press 1992.

Jensen P, Sorensen S, Fenger K, Bulwig T. A study of psychiatric morbidity in patients with Huntington's disease, their relatives and controls. *Br J Psychiatry* 1993;163: 790–797.

Jensen VW, Petty TA. The fantasy of being rescued in suicide. *Psychoanal Q* 1958;27: 327–339.

Jick SS, Dean AD, Jick H. Antidepressants and suicide. *Br Med J* 1995;310:215–218.

Jilek-Aall L. Suicidal behavior among youth: A cross-cultural comparison. *Transcult Psychiatr Res Rev* 1988;25:86–105.

Joffe RT, Offord D, Boyle MH. Ontario Child Health Study: Suicidal behavior in youths 12–16 years. *Am J Psychiatry* 1988;145:1420–1423.

Joffe RT, Regan JJ. Personality and suicidal behavior in depressed patients. *Compr Psychiatry* 1989;30:157–160.

Johnson EH, Britt B. *Self-mutilation in prison.* Carbondale: Southern Illinois University Center for the Study of Crime, Delinquency, and Corrections 1967.

Johnson GF, Hunt G. Suicidal behavior in bipolar manic-depressive patients and their families. *Compr Psychiatry* 1979;20:159–164.

Johnson J, Weissman MM, Klerman GL. Panic disorder, comorbidity, and suicide attempts. *Arch Gen Psychiatry* 1990;47:805–808.

Johnston M, Walker M. Suicide in the elderly: Recognizing the signs. *Gen Hosp Psychiatry* 1996;18:257–260.

Jonas JM, Hearron AE Jr. Alprazolam and suicidal ideation: A meta-analysis of controlled trials in the treatment of depression. *J Clin Psychopharmacol* 1996;16: 208–211.

Jones BE, Moore RY. Ascending projections of the locus ceruleus in the rat II autoradiographic study. *Brain Res* 1977;127:23–53.

Jones JS, Stanley B, Mann JJ, et al. CSF 5-HIAA and HVA concentrations in elderly depressed patients who attempted suicide. *Am J Psychiatry* 1990;147:1225–1227.

Jones JS, Stein DJ, Stanley B, et al. Negative and depressive symptoms in suicidal schizophrenia. *Acta Psychiatr Scand* 1994;89:81–87.

Joyce JN, Shane A, Lexow N, et al. Serotonin uptake sites and serotonin receptors are altered in the limbic system of schizophrenics. *Neuropsychopharmacology* 1993;8:315–336.

Jule-Nielson N, Videbech T. A twin study of suicide. *Acta Genet Med Gemellol* 1970; 19:307–310.

Kachur SP, Potter LB, James SP, Powell KE. *Suicide in the United States, 1980–1992.* Violence Surveillance Summary Series No. 125. Atlanta: Centers for Disease Control and Prevention, National Center for Injury Prevention and Control 1995.

Kalafat J, Elias M. An evaluation of a school-based suicide awareness intervention. *Suicide Life-Threat Behav* 1994;24:224–233.

Kalafat J, Elias M, Gara J. The relationship of bystander intervention variables to adolescents' responses to suicidal peers. *J Primary Prevention* 1993;13:231–244.

Kallman F, Anastasio M. Twin studies on the psychopathology of suicide. *J Nerv Ment Dis* 1947;105:40–55.

Kaplan KJ, Harrow M. Positive and negative symptoms as risk factors for later suicidal activity in schizophrenics versus depressives. *Suicide Life-Threat Behav* 1996;26:105–121.

Kaplan JR et al. Demonstration of an association among dietary cholesterol, central serotonergic activity, and social behavior in monkeys. *Psychosom Med* 1994;56:479–484.

Kaplan JR, Muldoon MF, Manuck SB, et al. Assessing the observed relationship between low cholesterol and violence-related mortality. In DM Stoff, JJ Mann (eds), *The neurobiology of suicide: From the bench to the clinic.* New York: New York Academy of Sciences 1997:57–80.

Kaplan MS, Adamek ME, Gelling O. Sociodemographic predictors of firearm suicide among older white males. *Gerontologist* 1996;36:530–533.

Kaplan MS, Adamek ME, Johnson S. Trends in firearm suicide among older American males, 1979–1988. *Gerontologist* 1994;34:59–65.

Kapur S, Mann JJ. Role of the dopaminergic system in depression. *Biol Psychiatry* 1992;32:1–17.

Kapur S, Mieczkowski T, Mann JJ. Antidepressant medications and the relative risk of suicide attempt and suicide. *JAMA* 1992;268:3441–3445.

Karasu TB. Psychoanalysis and psychoanalytic psychotherapy. In HI Kaplan, BJ Sadock (eds), *Comprehensive textbook of psychiatry,* 5th ed. Baltimore: Williams & Wilkins 1989:1442–1461.

Kasi-Visweswaran R, Khan AS, Narayan G, et al. Suicide by disconnection of arteriovenous shunts: Report of 3 cases. *J Assoc Physicians India* 1982;30:179–181.

Kasper S, Vieira A, Schmidt R, Richter P. Multiple hormone responses to stimulation with *dl*-fenfluramine in patients with major depression before and after antidepressive treatment. *Pharmacopsychiatry* 1990;23:76–84.

Katon W, Schulberg HC. Epidemiology of depression in primary care. *Gen Hosp Psychiatry* 1992;14:237–247.

Katon W, Sullivan MD. Depression and chronic medical illness. *J Clin Psychiatry* 1990;51(suppl):3–11; discussion 12–14.

Kay DWK, Petterson U. Manic-depressive illness. *Acta Psychiatr Scand* 1977;269(suppl):55–60.

Keith-Spiegel P, Spiegel DE. Affective states of patients immediately preceding suicide. *J Psychiatr Res* 1967;5:89–93.

Keller MB. Chronicity, relapse, recurrence, and psychosocial morbidity in severe depression and the role of maintenance treatment. In L Grunhaus, JF Greden (eds), *Severe depressive disorders.* Washington DC: American Psychiatric Press 1994:139.

Keller MB, Klerman GL, Lavori PW, et al. Treatment received by depressed patients. *JAMA* 1982;248:1848–1855.

Keller MB, Lavori PW, Klerman GL, et al. Low levels and lack of predictors of somatotherapy and psychotherapy received by depressed patients. *Arch Gen Psychiatry* 1986;43:458–466.

Kellerman AL, Reay DT. Protection or peril? An analysis of firearm-related deaths in the home. *N Eng J Med* 1986;314:1557–1560.

Kellerman AL, Rivara FP, Somes G, et al. Suicide in the home in relation to gun ownership. *N Engl J Med* 1992;327:467–472.

Kerkhof AJFM, Bernasco W. Suicidal behavior in jails and prisons in the Netherlands: Incidence, characteristics, and prevention. *Suicide Life-Threat Behav* 1990;20: 123–137.

Kernberg OF. Structural derivatives of object relationships. *Int J Psychoanal* 1966;47: 236–253.

Kernberg OF. The treatment of patients with borderline personality organization. *Int J Psychoanal* 1968;49:600–619.

Kernberg OF. *Borderline conditions and pathological narcissism.* Northvale NJ: Aronson 1975.

Kernberg OF. Clinical management of suicidal potential in borderline patients. In *Severe personality disorders: Psychotherapeutic strategies.* New Haven CT: Yale University Press 1984a:254–263.

Kernberg OF. *Severe personality disorders: Psychotherapeutic strategies.* New Haven CT: Yale University Press 1984b.

Kernberg OF. Projective identification, countertransference, and hospital treatment. *Psychiatr Clin North Am* 1987;10:257–272.

Kernberg OF. *Aggression in personality disorders and perversions.* New Haven CT: Yale University Press 1992.

Kernberg OF. Suicidal behavior in borderline patients diagnosis and psychotherapeutic considerations. *Am J Psychother* 1993;47:245–254.

Kerr TA, Schapira K, Roth M. The relationship between premature death and affective disorders. *Br J Psychiatry* 1969;115:1277–1282.

Kessler RC, Crum RM, Warner LA, et al. Lifetime and co-occurrence of DSM-III-R alcohol abuse and dependence with other psychiatric disorders in the national comorbidity survey. *Arch Gen Psychiatry* 1997;54:313–321.

Kessler RC, McGonigle KA, Zhao S, et al. Lifetime and 12–month prevalence of DSM-III-R psychiatric disorders in the United States: Results from the national comorbidity study. *Arch Gen Psychiatry* 1994;51:8–19.

Kessler RC, Sonnega A, Bromet E, et al. Posttraumatic stress disorder in the National Comorbidity Study. *Arch Gen Psychiatry* 1995;52:1048–1060.

Kety SS. Observations on genetic and environmental influences in the etiology of mental disorder from studies on adoptees and their relatives. In SS Kety, LP Rowland, RL Sidman, SW Matthysse (eds), *Genetics of neurological and psychiatric disorders.* New York: Raven Press 1983.

Kety SS. Genetic factors in suicide: Family, twin and adoption studies. In SJ Blumenthal, DJ Kupfer (eds), *Suicide over the life cycle: Risk factors, assessment, and treatment of suicidal patients.* Washington DC: American Psychiatric Press 1990:127–133.

Khantzian EJ, Treece C. DSM-III psychiatric diagnosis of narcotic addicts. *Arch Gen Psychiatry* 1985;42:1067–1071.

Khuri R, Akiskal HS. Suicide prevention: The necessity of treating contributory psychiatric disorders. *J Clin North Am* 1983;6:193–207.

Kidorf M, Brooner RK, King LV, Chutuape MA. Concurrent validity of cocaine and sedative dependence diagnoses in opioid-dependent outpatients. *Drug Alcohol Depend* 1996;42:117–123.

Kienhorst CWM, de Wilde EJ, van den Bout J, et al. Self-reported suicidal behavior in Dutch secondary education students. *Suicide Life-Threat Behav* 1990;20:101–112.

Kiloh LG, Andrews G, Neilson M. The long-term outcome of depressive illness. *Br J Psychiatry* 1988;153:752–757.

Kind P, Sorensen J. The costs of depression. *Intl Clin Psychopharmacol* 1993;7:191–195.

King E. Suicide in the mentally ill: An epidemiological sample and implications for clinicians. *Br J Psychiatry* 1994;165:658–663.

King MK, Schmaling KB, Cowley DS, Dunner DL. Suicide attempt history in depressed patients with and without a history of panic attacks. *Compr Psychiatry* 1995;36:25–30.

Kinkelin M. Verlauf und Prognose des manisch-depressiven Irreseins. *Schweiz Arch Neurol Neurochir Psychiatr* 1954;73:100–146.

Kinzie JD, Leung P. Clonidine in Cambodian patients with posttraumatic stress disorder. *J Nerv Ment Dis* 1989;177:546–550.

Kirby JS, Chu JA, Dill DL. Severity, frequency, and age of onset of physical and sexual abuse as factors in the development of dissociative symptoms. *Comp Psychiatry* 1993;34:258–263.

Kirmayer LJ, Robbins JM, Dworkind M, et al. Somatization and the recognition of depression in anxiety in primary care. *Am J Psychiatry* 1993;150:734–741.

Kjellman BF, Ljunggren JG, Beck-Friis J, Wetterberg L. Effect of TRH on TSH and prolactin levels in affective disorders. *Psychiatry Res* 1983;14:353–363.

Kjelsberg-Eikeseth PH, Dahl AA. Suicide in borderline patients: Predictive factors. *Acta Psychiatr Scand* 1991;84:283–287.

Klagsbrun S. Case in favor of physician-assisted suicide. Presented at the American Academy of Forensic Sciences annual meeting, Feb 21, 1997, New York.

Klein M. On the development of mental functioning. *Int J Psychoanal* 1958;39:84–90.

Klein NA. Sertraline efficacy in depressed combat veterans with posttraumatic stress disorder. *Am J Psychiatry* 1994;151:621.

Klerman GL. Clinical epidemiology of suicide. *J Clin Psychiatry* 1987;48(suppl 12):33–38.

Klerman GL, Weissman MM. Increasing rates of depression. *JAMA* 1989;261:2229–2235.

Klimek V, Stockmeier C, Overholser J, et al. Reduced levels of norepinephrine transporters in the locus ceruleus in major depression. *J Neurosci* 1997;17:8451–8458.

Kluft RP. First-rank symptoms as a diagnostic clue to multiple personality disorder. *Am J Psychiatry* 1987;144:293–298.

Kluft RP. The rehabilitation of therapists overwhelmed by their work with multiple personality disorder patients. *Dissociation* 1989;2:244–250.

Ko SM, Kua EH. Ethnicity and elderly suicide in Singapore. *Int Psychogeriatr* 1995;7:309–317.

Kochanek KD, Hudson BL. Advance report of final mortality statistics, 1992. *Monthly Vital Statistics Report* 1994;43(suppl 6).

Koening H et al. Depression in medically ill hospitalized older adults: Prevalence, characteristics, and course of symptoms according to six diagnostic schemes. *Am J Psychiatry* 1997;154:1376–1383.

Kohut H. *The analysis of the self.* Madison CT: International Universities Press 1971.

Kolb LC, Burris B, Griffiths S. Propranolol and clonidine in the treatment of chronic posttraumatic stress of war. In BA van der Kolk (ed), *Posttraumatic stress disorder: Psychological and biological sequelae.* Washington DC: American Psychiatric Press, 1984:97–107.

Koo JYM. *Current concepts: Psychodermatology.* Kalamazoo MI: Upjohn Company 1989.

Korpi ER, Kleinman J, Goodman SI, et al. Serotonin and 5-hydroxyindoleacetic acid in brains of suicide victims: Comparison in chronic schizophrenic patients with suicide as cause of death. *Arch Gen Psychiatry* 1986;43:594–600.

Kosky R, Silburn S, Zubrick SR. Are children and adolescents who have suicidal thoughts different from those who attempt suicide? *J Nerv Ment Dis* 1990;178:38–43.

Koss MP, Goodman LA, Brown A, et al. *No safe haven: Male violence against women at home, at work, and in the community.* Washington DC: American Psychological Association 1994.

Kosten TR. Alexithymia as a predictor of treatment response in PTSD. *J Traumatic Stress* 1992;5:563–573.

Kosten TR, Rounsaville BJ. Suicidality among opioid addicts: 2.5 year follow-up. *Am J Drug Alcohol Abuse* 1988;14:357–369.

Kotin J, Post RM, Goodwin FK. Drug treatment of depressed patients referred for hospitalization. *Am J Psychiatry* 1973;130:1139–1141.

Koyama T, Lowy MT, Meltzer HY. 5-hydroxytryptophan-induced cortisol response and CSF 5-HIAA in depressed patients. *Am J Psychiatry* 1987;144:334–337.

Kraemer HC, Kazdin AE, Offord DR, et al. Coming to terms with the terms of risk. *Arch Gen Psychiatr* 1997;54:337–343.

Kraepelin E. *Manic-depressive insanity and paranoia* (trans RM Barclay; ed GM Robertson). Edinburgh: Livingston 1921.

Kramer BA. Use of ECT in California, 1977–1983. *Am J Psychiatry* 1985;142:1190–1192.

Kramer TL, Lindy JD, Green BL, et al. The comorbidity of posttraumatic stress disorder and suicidality in Vietnam veterans. *Suicide Life-Threat Behav* 1994;24:58–67.

Krieger G. Suicides, drugs, and the open hospital. *Hosp Community Psychiatry* 1966; 17:196–199.

Kruesi MJP, Rapoport JL, Hamburger S. CSF monoamine metabolites, aggression, and impulsivity in disruptive behavior disorders in children and adolescents. *Arch Gen Psychiatry* 1990;47:419–426.

Krug EG, Kresnow J, Peddicord JP, et al. Suicide after natural disasters. *N Engl J Med* 1998;338:373–378.

Krystal H. Affect regulation and narcissism. In EF Ronningstam (ed), *Disorders of narcissism*. Washington DC: American Psychiatric Press 1998:299–325.

Kulka RA, Schlenger WE, Fairbank JA, et al. *Trauma and the Vietnam War generation*. New York: Brunner/Mazel 1990.

Kullgren G. Factors associated with completed suicide in borderline personality disorder. *J Nerv Ment Dis* 1988;176:40–44.

Kullgren G, Renberg E, Jacobsson L. An empirical study of borderline personality disorder and psychiatric suicides. *J Nerv Ment Dis* 1986;174:328–331.

Kushner AW. Two case of auto-castration due to religious delusions. *Br J Med Psychol* 1967;40:293–298.

Landmark J, Cernovsky ZZ, Mersky H. Correlates of suicide attempts and ideation in schizophrenia. *Br J Psychiatry* 1987;151:18–20.

Landwirth J. Sensory radicular neuropathy and retinitis pigmentosa. *Pediatrics* 1964; 34:519–524.

Langelüddecke A. Über Lebensartung und Rückfallhäufigkeit bei Manisch-Depressiven. *Z Psych Hygiene* 1941;14:1–14.

Laruelle M, Abi-Dargham A, Casanova MF, et al. Selective abnormalities of prefrontal serotonergic receptors in schizophrenia: A postmortem study. *Arch Gen Psychiatry* 1993;50:810–818.

Last JM. *A dictionary of epidemiology.* New York: Oxford University Press 1983.

Laufer M. The body image, the function of masturbation, and adolescence. *Psychoanal Study Child* 1968;23:114–137.

Laufer M (ed). *The suicidal adolescent.* Madison CT: International Universities Press 1995.

Laufer M, Laufer ME. *Adolescence and developmental breakdown.* New Haven CT: Yale University Press 1984.

Lawrence KM, De Paermentier F, Cheetham SC, et al. Brain 5-HT uptake sites, labelled with paroxetine, in antidepressant-free depressed suicides. *Brain Res* 1990a;526: 17–22.

Lawrence KM, De Paermentier F, Cheetham SC, et al. Symmetrical hemispheric distribution of ³H-paroxetine binding sites in postmortem human brain from controls and suicides. *Biol Psychiatr* 1990b;28:544–546.

Lecky WEH. *History of European morals from Augustus to Charlemagne.* New York: Appleton 1869:219–220.

Lee AS, Murray RM. The long-term outcome of Maudsley depressives. *Br J Psychiatry* 1988;153:741–750.

Lehmann HE, Fenton FR, Deutsch M, et al. An 11-year follow-up study of 110 depressed patients. *Acta Psychiatr Scand* 1988;78:57–65.

Lennon S. Genital self-mutilation in acute mania. *Med J Aust* 1963;50:79–81.

Lenox RH, Newhous PA, Creelman WL, Whitaker TM. Adjunctive treatment of manic agitation with lorazepam vs haloperidol: A double-blind study. *J Clin Psychiatry* 1992;53:47–52.

Lenz G. Increased mortality after drop-out from lithium clinic. *Neuropsychopharmacology* 1994;10:682S.

Lenzi A, Lazzerini F, Placidi GF, et al. Predictors of compliance with lithium and carbamazepine regimens in the long-term treatment of recurrent mood and related psychotic disorders. *Pharmacopsychiatry* 1989;22:34–37.

Lepkifker E, Horesh N, Floru S. Long-term lithium prophylaxis in recurrent unipolar depression. *Acta Psychiatr Belg* 1985;85:434–443.

Lesage AD, Boyer R, Grunberg F, et al. Suicide and mental disorders: A case-control study of young men. *Am J Psychiatry* 1994;151:1063–1068.

Lesch KP. The ipsapirone/5-HT$_{1A}$ receptor challenge in anxiety disorders and depression. *Excerpta Med Int Congress Series 968* 1991;2:905–908.

Lester D. Suicide as an aggressive act: A replication with a control for neuroticism. *J Gen Psychol* 1968;79:83–86.

Lester D. Murder followed by suicide in those who murder police officers. *Psychol Rep* 1987;60:1130.

Lester D. National suicide and homicide rates: Correlates vs predictors. *Soc Sci Med* 1989;29:1249–1252.

Lester D. *Understanding and preventing suicide: New perspectives.* Springfield IL: Thomas 1990.

Lester D. State initiatives in addressing youth suicide: Evidence for their effectiveness. *Soc Psychiatry Psychiatr Epidemiol* 1992;27:75–77.

Lester D. Genetics, twin studies, and suicide. *Suicide Life-Threat Behav* 1996;16:274–285.

Lester D. The effectiveness of suicide prevention centers: A review. *Suicide Life-Threat Behav* 1997;27:304–310.

Lester D, Beck AT. What the suicide's choice of method signifies. *Omega* 1980–1981; 11:271–277.

Lester D, Murrell ME. The influence of gun control laws on suicidal behavior. *Am J Psychiatry* 1980;137:121–122.

Lester D, Tallmer M. *Now I lay me down: Suicide in the elderly.* Philadelphia: Charles Press 1994.

Levenson M. Cognitive and perceptual factors in suicidal individuals. *Diss Abstr Int* 1973;33:5521.

Levenson M, Neuringer C. Problem-solving behavior in suicidal adolescents. *J Consult Clin Psychol* 1971;37:433–436.

Leviton J, Riley M. Seven deadly days. *Time* July 7, 1989:31–61.

Levitt P, Moore RY. Noradrenaline neuron innervation of the neocortex in the rat. *Brain Res* 1978;139:219–231.

Levy S, Southcombe RH. Suicide in a state hospital for the mentally ill. *J Nerv Ment Dis* 1953;117:504–514.

Lew EO. Homicidal hanging in dyadic death. *Am J Forensic Med Path* 1988;9:283–286.

Lewin BD. *The psychoanalysis of elation.* New York: Norton 1950.

Lewinsohn PM, Rohde P, Seeley JR. Adolescent suicidal ideation and attempts: Prevalence, risk factors, and clinical implications. *Clin Psychol Sci Prac* 1996;3:25–46.

Lewis A. Manic-depressive psychosis. *J Ment Sci* 1936;82:488–558.

Lewis CE, Rice J, Andreasen NC, et al. Alcoholism in antisocial and nonantisocial men with unipolar depression. *J Affective Disord* 1985;9:253–263.

Liberman JA. Atypical antipsychotic drugs as a first-line treatment of schizophrenia. *J Clin Psychiatry* 1996;57(suppl):68–71.

Lichtenberg P, Shapira B, Gillon D, et al. Hormone responses to fenfluramine and placebo challenge in endogenous depression. *Psychiatry Res* 1992;43:137–146.

Lidberg L, Tuck JR, Åsberg M, et al. Homicide, suicide, and CSF 5-HIAA. *Acta Psychiatr Scand* 1985;71:230–236.

Lidberg L, Winborg IM, Åsberg M. Low cerebrospinal fluid levels of 5-hydroxyindoleacetic acid and murder-suicide. *Nord J Psychiatry* 1992;46:419–420.

Lifton RJ. Suicide: The quest for a future. In DG Jacobs, HN Brown (eds), *Suicide: Understanding and responding.* Madison CT: International Universities Press 1989:459–469.

Lin N, Simeone RS, Ensel WM, Kuo W. Social support, stressful life events, and illness: A model and an empirical test. *J Health Soc Behav* 1979;20:108–119.

Lindelius R, Kay DWK. Some changes in the pattern of mortality in schizophrenia in Sweden. *Acta Psychiatr Scand* 1973;49:315–323.

Lindqvist P. Criminal homicide in northern Sweden, 1970–1981: Alcohol intoxication, alcohol abuse, and mental disease. *Int J Law Psychiatry* 1986;8:19–37.

Lindqvist P, Gustafsson L. Homicide followed by the offender's suicide in northern Sweden. *Nord J Psychiatry* 1995;49:17–24.

Linehan MM. A social-behavioral analysis of suicide and parasuicide: Implications for clinical assessment and treatment. In H Glaezer, JF Clarkin (eds), *Depression: Behavioral and directive intervention strategies.* New York: Garland 1981;229–294.

Linehan MM. *Cognitive-behavioral treatment of borderline personality disorder.* New York: Guilford Press 1993a.

Linehan MM. *Skills training manual for treating borderline personality disorder.* New York: Guilford Press 1993b.

Linehan MM, Armstrong HE, Suarez A, et al. Cognitive-behavioral treatment of chronically parasuicidal borderline patients. *Arch Gen Psychiatry* 1991;48:1060–1064.

Linehan MM, Camper P, Chiles JA, et al. Interpersonal problem solving and parasuicide. *Cogn Ther Res* 1987;11:1–12.

Linehan MM, Heard HL, Armstrong HE. Naturalistic follow-up of a behavioral treatment for chronically suicidal borderline patients. *Arch Gen Psychiatry* 1993;50:971–974.

Links P, Heslegrave R, Mitton J, et al. Borderline personality disorder and substance abuse: Consequences of comorbidity. *Can J Psychiatry* 1995;40:9–14.

Linnoila M, Virkkunen M, Scheinin M, et al. Low cerebrospinal fluid 5-hydroxyindoleacetic acid concentration differentiates impulsive from nonimpulsive violent behavior. *Life Sci* 1983;33:2609–2614.

Lipinski JF, Gopinath M, Zimmerman P, et al. Fluoxetine-induced akathisia: Clinical and theoretical implications. *J Clin Psychiatry* 1989;50:339–342.

Lipper S, Davidson JRT, Grady TA, et al. Preliminary study of carbamazepine in posttraumatic stress disorder. *Psychosomatics* 1986;27:849–854.

Litman R. Psychodynamics of indirect self-destructive behavior. In NL Farberow (ed), *The many faces of suicide: Indirect self-destructive behavior.* New York: McGraw-Hill 1980.

Litovitz TL, Feldberg L, White S, et al. Annual report of the American Association of Poison Control Centers. *Am J Emerg Med* 1996;14:487–537.

Little KY, Clark TB, Ranc J, Duncan GE. b-Adrenergic receptor binding in frontal cortex from suicide victims. *Biol Psychiatry* 1993;34:596–605.

Little KY, McLauglin DP, Ranc J, et al. Serotonin transporter binding sites and mRNA levels in depressed persons committing suicide. *Biol Psychiatry* 1997;41:1156–1164.

Lloyd KG, Farley IJ, Deck JHN, Hornykiewicz O. Serotonin and 5-hydroxyindoleacetic acid in discrete areas of the brainstem of suicide victims and control patients. *Adv Biochem Psychopharmacol* 1974;11:387–397.

Loewenstein RJ, Hornstein N, Farber B. Open trial of clonazepam in the treatment of posttraumatic stress symptoms in multiple personality disorder. *Dissociation* 1988;1:3–12.

Loftus EF, Polonsky S, Fullilove MT. Memories of childhood sexual abuse. *Psychol Women Q* 1994;18:64–84.

Lönnqvist JK. National Suicide Prevention Project in Finland: A research phase of the project. *Psychiatria Fennica* 1988;19:125–132.

Lönnqvist JK, Niskanen P, Rinta-Manty R, et al. Suicides in psychiatric hospitals in different therapeutic eras: A review of literature and own studies. *Psychatria Fennica* 1974;5:265–273.

Lopez JF, Chalmers DT, Little KY, Watson SJ. Regulation of serotonin$_{1A}$, glucocorticoid, and mineralocorticoid receptor in rat and human hippocampus: Implications for the neurobiology of depression. *Biol Psychiatry* 1998;43:547–573.

Lopez-Ibor JJ Jr, Lana F, Saiz-Ruiz J. Impulsive suicidal behavior and serotonin. *Actas Luso-Esp Neurol Psiquiatr* 1990;18:316–325.

Lopez-Ibor JJ Jr, Saiz-Ruiz J, Iglesias LM. The fenfluramine challenge test in the affective spectrum: A possible marker of endogeneity and severity. *Pharmacopsychiatry* 1988;21:9–14.

Loranger AW. Sex difference in age at onset of schizophrenia. *Arch Gen Psychiatry* 1984;41:157–161.

Lowry FH, Kilivakis TL. Autocastration by a male transsexual. *Can Psychiatr Assoc J* 1971;16:399–405.

Lowther S, De Paermentier F, Crompton MR, et al. Brain 5-HT$_2$ receptors in suicide victims: Violence of death, depression, and effects of antidepressant treatment. *Brain Res* 1994;642:281–289.

Lowther S, Katona CLE, Crompton MR, Horton RW. 5HT$_{1D}$ and 5-HT$_{1E/1F}$ binding sites in depressed suicides: Increased 5-HT$_{1D}$ binding in globus pallidus but not cortex. *Molec Psychiatry* 1997;2:314–321.

Lucero WJ, Fireman J, Spoering K. Comparison of three procedures in reducing self-injurious behavior. *Am J Ment Deficiency* 1976;180:548–554.

Ludolph PS, Westen D, Misle B, et al. The borderline diagnosis in adolescents: Symptoms and developmental history. *Am J Psychiatry* 1990;147:470–476.

Lundquist G. Prognosis and course in manic-depressive psychoses: A follow-up study of 319 first admissions. *Acta Psychiatr Neurol* 1945;35(suppl):1–96.

Lyness JM, Conwell Y, Nelson JC. Suicide attempts in elderly psychiatric inpatients. *J Am Geriatr Soc* 1992;40:320.

Mackenzie TB, Popkin MK. Medical illness and suicide. In SJ Blumenthal, DJ Kupfer (eds), *Suicide over the life cycle.* Washington DC: American Psychiatric Press 1990:205–232.

MacKinnon D, Farberow NL. An assessment of the utility of suicide prediction. *Suicide Life-Threat Behav* 1975;6:86–91.

MacKinnon DF, Jamison KR, De Paulo JR. Genetics of manic depressive illness. *Ann Rev Neurosci* 1977;20:355–373.

Maddison D, Mackey KH. Suicide: The clinical problem. *Br J Psychiatry* 1966;112:693–703.

Maes M, Jacobs MP, Suy E, et al. Cortisol, ACTH, prolactin and beta-endorphin responses to fenfluramine administration in major-depressed patients. *Neuropsychobiology* 1989;21:192–196.

Magie D. What is being predicted? The definition of suicide. In RW Maris, AL Berman, JT Maltsberger, RI Yufit (eds), *Assessment and prediction of suicide.* New York: Guilford Press 1992:105–129.

Mahrer J, Bongar B. Assessment and management of suicide risk and the use of the no-suicide contract. In L Van de Creek, S Knapp, TL Jackson (eds), *Innovations in clinical practice,* vol. 12. Sarasota FL: Professional Resource Press 1993:277–293.

Maj M, Starace F, Nolfe G, Kemali D. Minimum plasma lithium levels required for effective prophylaxis in DSM-III bipolar disorder: A prospective study. *Pharmacopsychiatry* 1986;19:420–423.

Mäkelä P. Alcohol consumption and suicide mortality by age among Finnish men, 1950–1991. *Addiction* 1996;91:101–112.

Malmquist CP. Psychiatric aspects of familicide. *Bull Am Acad Psychiatry Law* 1981;8:298–304.

Malone KM. Pharmacotherapy of affectively ill suicidal patients. *Psychiatr Clin North Am* 1997;20:613–625.

Malone KM, Chanto K, Corbitt EM, et al. Clinical assessment versus research methods in the assessment of suicidal behavior. *Am J Psychiatry* 1995a;152:1601–1607.

Malone KM, Corbitt EM, Li S, Mann JJ. Prolactin response to fenfluramine and suicide attempt lethality in major depression. *Br J Psychiatry* 1996;168:324–329.

Malone KM, Haas GL, Sweeney JA, Mann JJ. Major depression and the risk of attempted suicide. *J Affective Disord* 1995b;34:173–185.

Malone KM, Mann JJ. Serotonin and major depression. In JJ Mann, DJ Kupfer (eds), *Biology of depressive disorders, Part A: A systems perspective.* New York: Plenum Press 1993:29–49.

Maltsberger JT. *Suicide risk: The formulation of clinical judgment.* New York: New York University Press 1986.

Maltsberger JT. Suicide danger: Clinical estimation and decision. *Suicide Life-Threat Behav* 1988;18:47–54.

Maltsberger JT. The implications of patient suicide for the surviving psychotherapist. In DG Jacobs (ed), *Suicide and clinical practice.* Washington DC: American Psychiatric Press 1992.

Maltsberger JT. Confusions of the body, the self, and others in suicidal states. In A Leenaars (ed), *Suicidology: Essays in honor of Edwin S. Shneidman.* Northvale NJ: Aronson 1993:148–171.

Maltsberger JT. Ecstatic suicide. *Arch Suicide Res* 1997;3:283–301.

Maltsberger JT. Pathological narcissism and self-regulatory processes in suicidal states. In EF Ronningstam (ed), *Disorders of narcissism.* Washington DC: American Psychiatric Press 1998:327–344.

Maltsberger JT, Buie DH Jr. Countertransference hate in the treatment of suicidal patients. *Arch Gen Psychiatry* 1974;30:625–633.

Maltsberger JT, Buie DH Jr. The devices of suicide. *Int Rev Psychoanal* 1980;7:61–72.

Maltsberger JT, Buie DH Jr. Common errors in the management of suicidal patients. In DG Jacobs, HN Brown (eds), *Suicide: Understanding and responding.* Madison CT: International Universities Press 1989.

Maltsberger JT, Buie DH Jr. The psychotherapist as an accomplice in suicide. *Ital J Suicidology* 1994;4:75–81.

Manchon M, Kopp N, Rouzioux JJ, et al. Benzodiazepine receptor and neurotransmitter studies in the brain of suicides. *Life Sci* 1987;41:2623–2630.

Mann JJ. Violence and aggression. In FE Bloom, DJ Kupfer (eds), *Psychopharmacology: The fourth generation of progress.* New York: Raven Press 1995.

Mann JJ. Serotonin marker of suicide risk. *Nature Med* 1997:4(7):25–30.

Mann JJ, Arango V, Marzuk PM, et al. Evidence for the 5-HT hypothesis of suicide: A review of post mortem studies. *Br J Psychiatry* 1989a;155(suppl 8):7–14.

Mann JJ, Henteleff RA, Lagattuta TF, et al. Lower ^{3}H-paroxetine binding in cerebral cortex of suicide victims is partly due to fewer high-affinity, non-transporter sites. *J Neural Transm* 1996a;103:1337–1350.

Mann JJ, Kapur S. The emergence of suicidal ideation and behavior during antidepressant pharmacotherapy. *Arch Gen Psychiatry* 1991;48:1027–1033.

Mann JJ, Malone KM. Cerebrospinal fluid amines and higher lethality suicide attempts in depressed inpatients. *Biol Psychiatry* 1997;41:162–171.

Mann JJ, Malone KM, Sweeney JA, et al. Attempted suicide characteristics and cerebrospinal fluid amine metabolites in depressed inpatients. *Neuropsychopharmacology* 1996b;15:576–586.

Mann JJ, Marzuk PM, Arango V, et al. Neurochemical studies of violent and non-violent suicide. *Psychopharmacol Bull* 1989b;25:407–413.

Mann JJ, McBride PA, Brown RP, et al. Relationship between central and peripheral serotonin indexes in depressed and suicidal psychiatric inpatients. *Arch Gen Psychiatry* 1992;49:442–446.

Mann JJ, McBride PA, Malone KM, et al. Blunted serotonergic responsivity in depressed patients. *Neuropsychopharmacology* 1995;13:53–64.

Mann JJ, Stanley M. Psychobiology of suicidal behavior. *Ann NY Acad Sci* 1986;487:1–356.

Mann JJ, Stanley M, McBride PA, McEwen BS. Increased serotonin-2 and ß-adrenergic receptor binding in the frontal cortices of suicide victims. *Arch Gen Psychiatry* 1986;43:954–959.

Mann JJ, Underwood MD, Arango V. Postmortem studies of suicide victims. In SJ Watson (ed), *Biology of schizophrenia and affective disease.* Association for Research in Nervous and Mental Disease Series, Vol. 73. Washington DC: American Psychiatric Press 1996c:197–221.

Mann JJ, Waternaux C, Haas GL, Malone KM. Toward a clinical model of suicidal behavior in psychiatric patients. *Am J Psychiatry* (in press).

Mannuzza S. Panic disorders in suicide attempts. *J Anx Disord* 1992;6:261–274.

Marcikic M, Mandic N, Homicide-suicide by stabbing. *Am J Forensic Med Path* 1990;11:312–315.

Maris RW. Sociology. In S Perlin (ed), *A handbook for the study of suicide*. New York: Oxford University Press 1975.

Maris RW. *Pathways to suicide: A survey of self-destructive behaviors*. Baltimore: Johns Hopkins University Press 1981.

Maris RW. The relationship of nonfatal suicide attempts to completed suicides. In RW Maris, AL Berman, JT Maltsberger, RI Yufit (eds), *Assessment and prediction of suicide*. New York: Guilford Press 1992:362–380.

Maris RW, Berman AL, Maltsberger JT, Yufit RI (eds). *Assessment and prediction of suicide*. New York: Guilford Press 1992.

Marks M, Lovestone S. The role of the father in parental postnatal mental health. *Br J Med Psychol* 1995;68:157–168.

Marks MN, Kumar R. Infanticide in Scotland. *Med Sci Law* 1995;36:299–305.

Martin RL, Cloninger CR, Guze SB. Alcohol misuse and depression in women criminals. *J Stud Alcohol* 1985;46:65–71.

Martin RL, Cloninger CR, Guze SB, Clayton PJ. Mortality in a follow-up of 500 psychiatric outpatients: I. Total mortality. *Archives of General Psychiatry* 1985a;42:47–54.

Martin RL, Cloninger CR, Guze SB, Clayton PJ. Mortality in a follow-up of 500 psychiatric outpatients: II. Cause-specific mortality. *Arch Gen Psychiatry* 1985b;42:58–66.

Marttunen MJ, Aro MH, Henriksson MM, et al. Mental disorders in adolescent suicide. *Arch Gen Psychiatry* 1991;48:834–839.

Marttunen MJ, Aro HM, Lönnqvist JK. Precipitant stressors in adolescent suicide. *J Am Acad Child Adolesc Psychiatry* 1993;32:1178–1183.

Marzuk PM. Suicide and terminal illness. *Death Stud* 1994;18:497–512.

Marzuk PM. Violence and suicidal behavior: What is the link? In K Tardiff (ed), *Violence: Causes and medical management*. New York: Dekker 1998.

Marzuk PM, Leon AC, Tardiff K, et al. The effect of access to lethal methods of injury on suicide rates. *Arch Gen Psychiatry* 1992a;49:451–458.

Marzuk PM, Mann JJ. Suicide and substance abuse. *Psychiatr Ann* 1988;18:639–645.

Marzuk PM, Tardiff K, Hirsch CS. The epidemiology of murder-suicide. *JAMA* 1992b; 267:3179–3183.

Marzuk PM, Tardiff K, Leon AC, et al. Prevalence of cocaine use among residents of New York City who committed suicide during a one-year period. *Am J Psychiatry* 1992c:149:371–375.

Marzuk PM, Tardiff K, Leon AC, et al. Use of prescription psychotropic drugs among suicide victims in New York City. *Am J Psychiatry* 1995;152:1520–1522.

Marzuk PM, Tardiff K, Leon AC, et al. HIV seroprevalence among suicide victims in New York City, 1991–1993. *Am J Psychiatry* 1997;154:1720–1725.

Marzuk PM, Tardiff K, Leon AC, et al. Dr. Marzuk and colleagues reply (letter). *Am J Psychiatry* 1996;153:1659.

Marzuk PM, Tierney H, Tardiff K, et al. Increased risk of suicide in persons with AIDS. *JAMA* 1988;259:1333–1337.

Mason BJ, Kocsis JH, Rivito EC, Cutler RB. A double-blind, placebo-controlled trial of desipramine for primary alcohol dependence stratified on the presence or absence of major depression. *JAMA* 1996;275:761–767.

Massand P, Dewan M. Suicidality and fluoxetine revisited (letter). *J Clin Psychiatry* 1992;53:102–103.

Masterson J. *Treatment of the borderline adolescent: A developmental approach.* New York: Wiley 1972.

Masterson J. *Psychotherapy of the borderline adult.* New York: Brunner/Mazel 1976.

Masterson J, Rinsley D. The borderline syndrome: The role of the mother in the genesis and psychic structure of the borderline personality. *Int J Psychoanal* 1975;56: 163–177.

Matsubara S, Arora RC, Meltzer HY. Serotonergic measures in suicide brain: 5-HT$_{1A}$ binding sites in frontal cortex of suicide victims. *J Neural Transm* 1991;85:181–194.

Matthews K, Milre S, Ashcroft GW. Role of doctors in the prevention of suicide: The final consultation. *Br J Gen Pract* 1994;44:345–348.

Mayfield DG, Montgomery D. Alcoholism, alcohol intoxication, and suicide attempts. *Arch Gen Psychiatry* 1972;27:349–353.

McAnarney ER. Adolescent and young suicide in the United States: A reflection of social unrest. *Adolescence* 1979;14:765–774.

McArthur JH, Moore D. The two cultures and the health care revolution: Commerce and professionalism in medical care. *JAMA* 1997;277:985–989.

McCombs JS, Nichol MB, Stimmel GL, et al. Cost of antidepressant drug therapy failure: A study of antidepressant use patterns in a Medicaid population. *J Clin Psychiatry* 1990;51(suppl 6):60–69.

McCue JD. The naturalness of dying. *JAMA* 1995;273:1039–1043.

McGlashan TH. Chestnut Lodge follow-up study: II. Long-term outcome of schizophrenia and affective disorders. *Arch Gen Psychiatry* 1984;41:586–601.

McGlashan TH. The Chestnut Lodge follow-up study: III. Long-term outcome of borderline personalities. *Arch Gen Psychiatry* 1986;43:20–30.

McGrath PJ, Nunes EV, Stewart JW, et al. Imipramine treatment of alcoholics with primary depression. *Arch Gen Psychiatry* 1996;53:232–240.

McIntosh JL. Suicide prevention in the elderly (age 65–99). *Suicide Life-Threat Behav* 1995;25:180–192.

McKay M, Fanning P. *Self-esteem.* Oakland CA: New Harbinger Press 1987.

McKegney FP, Ma OD. Suicidality and HIV status. *Am J Psychiatry* 1992;149:396–398.

McLeary R, Chew KSY, Hellsten JJ, Flynn-Bransford M. Age- and sex-specific cycles in United States suicides, 1973 to 1985. *Am J Public Health* 1991;81:1494–1497.

Meana JJ, García-Sevilla JA. Increased a$_2$-adrenoceptor density in the frontal cortex of depressed suicide victims. *J Neural Transm* 1987;70:377–381.

Meehan PJ, Lamb JA, Saltzman LE, et al. Attempted suicide among young adults: Progress toward a meaningful estimate of prevalence. *Am J Psychiatry* 1992;149:41–44.

Meehan PJ, Saltzman LE, Sattin RW. Suicides among older United States residents: Epidemiologic characteristics and trends. *Am J Public Health* 1991;81:1198–1200.

Meier D et al. A national survey of physician-assisted suicide and euthanasia in the United States. *N Engl J Med* 1998;338:1193–1201.

Meiselman K. *Incest.* San Francisco: Jossey-Bass 1978.

Meissner WW. *Internalization in psychoanalysis.* Madison CT: International Universities Press 1981.

Meltzer HY. Reduction of suicidality during clozapine treatment of neuroleptic-resistant schizophrenia: Impact on risk-benefit assessment. *Am J Psychiatry* 1995;152:183–190.

Meltzer HY, Maes M. Effects of buspirone on plasma prolactin and cortisol levels in major depressed and normal subjects. *Biol Psychiatry* 1994;35:316–323.

Meltzer HY, Okayli G. Reduction of suicidality during clozapine treatment of neuroleptic-resistant schizophrenia: Impact on risk-benefit assessment. *Am J Psychiatry* 1995; 152:183–190.

Meltzer HY, Perline R, Tricou BJ, et al. Effect of 5-hydroxytryptophan on serum cortisol levels in major affective disorders: II. Relation to suicide, psychosis and depressive symptoms. *Arch Gen Psychiatry* 1984;41:379–387.

Melville H. *Mardi; and a voyage thither.* London: Richard Bentley 1849.

Melville H. *The confidence man: His masquerade.* New York: Dix, Edwards & Co. 1857.

Mendels J. Electroconvulsive therapy and depression: I. The prognostic significance of clinical factors. *Br J Psychiatry* 1965;111:675–681.

Menninger KA. *Man against himself.* Orlando FL: Harcourt 1938.

Mercy JA, Saltzman LE. Fatal violence among spouses in the United States, 1976–1985. *Am J Public Health* 1989;79:595–599.

Merrill J, Owens J. Age and attempted suicide. *Acta Psychiatr Scand* 1990;82:385–388.

Metzger D, Woody G, De Philippis D, et al. Risk factors for needle sharing among methadone-treated patients. *Am J Psychiatry* 1991;148:636–640.

Meyendorff E, Jain A, Träskman-Bendz L, et al. The effects of fenfluramine on suicidal behavior. *Psychopharmacol Bull* 1986;22:155–159.

Meyerson LR, Wennogle LP, Abel MS, et al. Human brain receptor alterations in suicide victims. *Pharmacol Biochem Behav* 1982;17:159–163.

Miklowitz DJ, Goldstein MJ, Neuchterlein KH, et al. Family factors and the course of bipolar affective disorder. *Arch Gen Psychiatry* 1988;45:225–231.

Miles CP. Conditions predisposing to suicide: A review. *J Nerv Ment Dis* 1977;164: 231–246.

Miller F, Bashkin E. Depersonalization and self-mutilation. *Psychoanal Q* 1974;43: 638–649.

Miller FG, Quill TE, Brody H, et al. Regulating physician-assisted death. *N Engl J Med* 1994;331:119–122.

Miller MC, Jacobs DG, Gutheil TG. Talisman or taboo? The controversy of the suicide prevention contract. *Harvard Rev Psychiatry* 1998;6:78–87.

Milroy CM. The epidemiology of homicide-suicide (dyadic death). *Forensic Sci Int* 1995a;71:117–122.

Milroy CM. Reasons for homicide and suicide in episodes of dyadic death in Yorkshire and Humberside. *Med Sci Law* 1995b;35:213–217.

Mintz HA, Cornett FW. When your patient is a batterer. *Postgrad Med* 1997;101:219–228.

Mintz IL. Autocannibalism. *Am J Psychiatry* 1964;120:1017.

Missel JL. Suicide risk in the medical rehabilitation setting. *Arch Phys Med Rehab* 1978;59:371–376.

Mitchell P, Smythe G. Hormonal responses to fenfluramine in depressed and control subjects. *J Affective Disord* 1990;19:43–51.

Mitchell P, Smythe G, Parker G, et al. Growth hormone and other hormonal responses to clonidine in melancholic and nonmelancholic depressed subjects and controls. *Psychiatry Res* 1990;37:179–193.

Modell AH. Primitive object relationships and the predisposition to schizophrenia. *Int J Psychoanal* 1963;44:282–292.

Modestin J, Schwartzenbach F. Effect of psychopharmacotherapy on suicide risk in discharged psychiatric inpatients. *Acta Psychiatr Scand* 1992a;85:173–175.

Modestin J, Zarro I, Waldvogel D. A study of suicide in schizophrenic inpatients. *Br J Psychiatry* 1992b;160:398–401.

Molcho A, Stanley M. Antidepressants and suicide risk: Issues of chemical and behavioral toxicity. *J Clin Psychopharmacol* 1992;12:13S–18S.

Money J, Jobsris R, Furth G. Apotemnophilia: Two cases of a self-demand amputation as a paraphilia. *J Sex Res* 1977;13:115–125.

Monk M. Epidemiology of suicide. *Epidemiol Rev* 1987;9:51–69.

Montgomery SA. Pharmacokinetics of antidepressants and death from overdoses. *Int Clin Psychopharmacol* 1990;5(suppl 3):67–76.

Montgomery SA, Montgomery DB. Pharmacological prevention of suicidal behavior. *J Affective Dis* 1982;4:291–298.

Montgomery SA, Montgomery DB. The prevention of suicidal acts in high risk patients. In E Usdin (ed), *Frontiers in biochemical and pharmacological research in depression.* New York: Raven Press 1984.

Montgomery SA, Montgomery DB, Green M, et al. Pharmacotherapy in the prevention of suicidal behavior. *J Clin Psychopharmacol* 1992;12:27S–31S.

Moody HR. "Rational suicide" on grounds of old age? *J Geriatr Soc* 1991;24:261.

Morano CD, Cisler RA, Lemerond J. Risk factors for adolescent suicidal behavior. *Adolescence* 1993;28:851–865.

Morgan HG. *Death wishes? The assessment and management of deliberate self-harm.* New York: Wiley 1979.

Morgan HG, Priest P. Suicide and other unexpected deaths among psychiatric inpatients. *Br J Psychiatry* 1991;158:368–374.

Morgan HG, Stanton R. Suicide among psychiatric inpatients in a changing clinical scene. *Br J Psychiatry* 1997;171:561–563.

Morrison J. Childhood sexual histories of women with somatization disorder. *Am J Psychiatry* 1989;146:239–241.

Morrison JR. The family histories of manic-depressive patients with and without alcoholism. *J Nerv Ment Dis* 1975;160:227–229.

Morrison JR. Suicide in psychiatric practice population. *J Clin Psychiatry* 1982;43:348–352.

Morton A. *Diana: Her true story.* New York: Simon & Schuster 1993.

Mościcki EK. Epidemiologic surveys as tools for studying suicidal behavior: A review. *Suicide Life-Threat Behav* 1989;19:131–146.

Mościcki EK. Gender differences in completed and attempted suicides. *Ann Epidemiol* 1994;4:152–158.

Mościcki EK. Epidemiology of suicidal behavior. *Suicide Life-Threat Behav* 1995a;25: 22–34.

Mościcki EK. Epidemiology of suicide. *Int Psychogeriatr* 1995b;7:137–148.

Mościcki EK. Identification of suicide risk factors using epidemiologic studies. *Psychiatr Clin North Am* 1997;20:499–517.

Mościcki EK, O'Carroll P, Lock BZ, et al. Suicidal ideation and attempts: The Epidemiologic Catchment Area Study. In U.S. Department of Health and Human Services; Alcohol, Drug Abuse, and Mental Health Administration, *Report of the Secretary's Task Force on Youth Suicide: Vol 4. Strategies for the prevention of youth suicide.* DHHS Publication No. (ADM)89–1624. Washington DC: U.S. Government Printing Office 1989.

Mościcki EK, O'Carroll P, Regier DA, et al. Suicide attempts in the Epidemiologic Catchment Area Study. *Yale J Biol Med* 1988;61:259–268.

Moser C, Lee J, Christensen P. Nipple piercing. *J Psychol Human Sexuality* 1993;62: 51–61.

Motto JA. Refinement of variables in assessing suicide risk. In AT Beck, HLP Resnik, D Lettieri (eds), *The prediction of suicide.* Bowie MD: Charles Press 1974.

Motto JA. The recognition and management of the suicidal patient. In FF Flach, SC Draghi (eds), *The nature and treatment of depression.* New York: Wiley 1975:229–254.

Motto JA. Guidelines for the management of the suicidal patient. *Weekly Psychiatry Update Series: Lesson 20* 1979;3:3–7.

Motto JA. Suicide risk factors in alcohol abuse. *Suicide Life-Threat Behav* 1980;10: 230–238.

Motto JA. Paradoxes of suicide risk assessment. *Hillside J Clin Psychiatry* 1985;7:109–119.

Muehrer PM. Suicide and sexual orientation: A critical summary of recent research and directions for future research. *Suicide Life-Threat Beh* 1995;25(suppl):72–81.

Mueller SA. Trichotillomania. *J Am Acad Dermatol* 1990;23:56–62.

Mueller TL, Lavori PW, Keller MB, et al. Prognostic effect of the variable course of alcoholism on the 10-year course of depression. *Am J Psychiatry* 1994;151:701–706.

Muhlbauer HD, Müller-Oerlinghausen B. Fenfluramine stimulation of serum cortisol in patients with major affective disorders and healthy controls: Further evidence for a central serotonergic action of lithium in man. *J Neural Transm* 1985;61:81–94.

Mulder AM, Methorst GJ, Diekstra RFW. Prevention of suicidal behavior in adolescents: The role of training of teachers. *Crisis* 1989;10:36–51.

Muldoon MF et al. Lowering cholesterol concentrations and mortality: A quantitative review of primary prevention trials. *Br Med J* 1990;301:309–313.

Muldoon MF et al. Effects of a low-fat diet on brain serotonergic responsivity in cynomolgus monkeys. *Biol Psychiatry* 1992;31:739–742.

Muldoon MF et al. Low or lowered cholesterol and risk of death from suicide and trauma. *Metabolism* 1993;42(9, suppl 1):45–56.

Müller-Oerlinghausen B. Die "IGSLI" Studie zur Mortalität Lithium behandelter Patienten mit affektiven Psychosen. In B Müller-Oerlinghausen, A Berghöfer (eds), *Ziele und Ergebnisse der Medikamentosen Prophylaxe Affektiver Psychosen.* Stuttgart: Thieme Verlag 1994:35–39.

Müller-Oerlinghausen B, Müser-Causemann B, Volk J. Suicides and parasuicides in a high-risk patient group on and off lithium long-term medication. *J Affective Disord* 1992;25:261–270.

Müller-Oerlinghausen B et al. The effect of long-term lithium treatment on the mortality of patients with manic-depressive and schizoaffective illness. *Acta Psychiatr Scand* 1992;86:218–222.

Murphy E, Smith R, Lindesay J, Slattery J. Increased mortality rates in late-life depression. *Br J Psychiatry* 1988;152:347–353.

Murphy GE. The physician's responsibility for suicide: (1) An error of commission and (2) errors of omission. *Ann Intern Med* 1975;82:301–309.

Murphy GE. The prediction of suicide: Why is it so difficult? *Am J Psychother* 1984;38: 341–349.

Murphy GE. Suicide and attempted suicide. In G Winokur, P Clayton (eds), *The medical basis of psychiatry.* Philadelphia: Saunders 1986:562–579.

Murphy GE. Multiple risk factors predict suicide in alcoholism. *Arch Gen Psychiatry* 1992;49:459–463.

Murphy GE, Armstrong JW Jr, Hermele SL, et al. Suicide and alcoholism: Interpersonal loss confirmed as a predictor. *Arch Gen Psychiatry* 1979;36:65–69.

Murphy GE, Robins E. Social factors in suicide. *JAMA* 1967;199:303–308.

Murphy GE, Wetzel RD. The lifetime risk of suicide in alcoholism. *Arch Gen Psychiatry* 1990;47:383–392.

Murphy GE, Wetzel RD, Robins E, McEvoy L. Multiple risk factors predict suicide in alcoholism. *Arch Gen Psychiatry* 1992;49:459–463.

Murphy GE, Woodruff RA, Herjanic M, Super G. Variability of the clinical course of primary affective disorder. *Arch Gen Psychiatry* 1974;30:757–761.

Murphy JM, Monson RR, Olivier DC, et al. Affective disorders and mortality: A general population study. *Arch Gen Psychiatry* 1987;44:473–480.

Murray HA. *Explorations in personality.* New York: Oxford University Press 1938.

Murray HA. *Thematic Apperception Test—Manual.* Cambridge MA: President and Fellows of Harvard College 1943.

Myers DH, Neal CD. Suicide in psychiatric patients. *Br J Psychiatry* 1978;133:38–44.

Myers SA. Maternal filicide. *Am J Dis Child* 1970;120:534–536.

Nace EP, Saxon JJ Jr, Shore N. A comparison of borderline and nonborderline alcoholic patients. *Arch Gen Psychiatry* 1983;40:54–56.

Nagy LM, Morgan CA, Southwick SM, Charney DS. Open prospective trial of fluoxetine for posttraumatic stress disorder. *J Clin Psychopharmacol* 1993;13:107–114.

National Center for Health Statistics. Death rates for 282 selected causes by 5-year age groups, race, and sex: United States, 1979–95, Table GMWK292A. Unpublished data, http://www.cdc.gov/nchswww/datawh/statab/unpubd/mortabs/gmwk292a.htm, 1998.

National Institutes of Health. Consensus conference: Electroconvulsive therapy. *JAMA* 1985;254:2103–2108.

National Victim Center, Crime Victims Research and Treatment Center. *Rape in America: A report to the nation.* Arlington VA: National Victim Center 1992.

Nelson VL, Nielsen EC, Checketts KT. Interpersonal attitudes of suicidal individuals. *Psychol Rep* 1977;40:983–989.

Nemeroff CB, Owens MJ, Bissette G, et al. Reduced corticotropin releasing factor binding sites in the frontal cortex of suicide victims. *Arch Gen Psychiatry* 1988;45:577–579.

Nesse RE, Finlayson RE. Management of depression in patients with coexisting medical illness. *Am Fam Physician* 1996;54:468.

Neuringer C. Dichotomous evaluations in suicidal individuals. *J Consult Clin Psychol* 1961;25:445–449.

Neuringer C. Rigid thinking in suicidal individuals. *J Consult Clin Psychol* 1964;28:54–58.

Neville D, Barnes S. The suicidal phone call. *J Psychosoc Nurs Ment Health Services* 1985;23:14–18.

Newman SC, Bland RC. Suicide risk varies by subtype of affective disorder. *Acta Psychiatr Scand* 1991;83:420–426.

Nielson AS, Stenager E, Brahe UB. Attempted suicide, suicidal intent, and alcohol. *Crisis* 1993;14:32–38.

Nilsson A. Mortality in recurrent mood disorders during periods on and off lithium: A complete population study in 362 patients. *Pharmacopsychiatry* 1995;28:8–13.

Nilsson A, Axelsson R. Lithium discontinuers: Clinical characteristics and outcome. *Acta Psychiatr Scand* 1990;82:433–438.

Nordin C. Relationships between clinical symptoms and monoamine metabolite concentrations in biochemically defined subgroups of depressed patients. *Acta Psychiatr Scand* 1988;78:720–729.

Nordström P, Samuelsson M, Åsberg M. Survival analysis of suicide risk after attempted suicide. *Acta Psychiatr Scand* 1995a;91:336–340.

Nordström P, Samuelsson M, Åsberg M, et al. CSF 5-HIAA predicts suicide risk after attempted suicide. *Suicide Life-Threat Behav* 1994;24:1–9.

Nordström P, Schalling D, Åsberg M. Temperamental vulnerability in attempted suicide. *Acta Psychiatr Scand* 1995b;92:155–160.

Noreik K. Attempted suicide and suicide in functional psychoses. *Acta Psychiatr Scand* 1975;52:81–106.

Norton B, Whalley LJ. Mortality of a lithium treatment population. *Br J Psychiatry* 1984;145:277–282.

Nowak G, Ordway GA, Paul IA. Alterations in the *N*-methyl-D-aspartate (NMDA) receptor complex in the frontal cortex of suicide victims. *Brain Res* 1995;675: 157–164.

Noyes R Jr. Suicide and panic disorder: A review. *J Affective Disord* 1991;22:1–11.

Nyman AK, Jonsson H. Patterns of self-destructive behaviour in schizophrenia. *Acta Psychiatr Scand* 1986;73:252–262.

Nyström S. Depressions: Factors related to 10-year prognosis. *Acta Psychiatr Scand* 1979;60:225–238.

O'Carroll PW. A consideration of the validity and reliability of suicide mortality data. *Suicide Life-Threat Behav* 1989;19:1–16.

O'Carroll PW, Berman AL, Maris RW, et al. Beyond the Tower of Babel: A nomenclature for suicidology. *Suicide Life-Threat Behav* 1996;26:237–252.

O'Carroll PW et al. Programs for the prevention of suicide among adolescents and young adults: Recommendations and reports. *MMWR* 1994;43:1–7.

O'Farrell TJ, Goodenough DS, Cutter HS. Behavioral contracting for repeated suicide attempts: Issues in the treatment of a hospitalized schizophrenic male. *Behav Modif* 1981;5:255–272.

Offord DR, Boyle MH, Szartmari P. Ontario's Child Health Study: II. Six-month prevalence of disorder and rates of service utilization. *Arch Gen Psychiatry* 1987;44: 832–836.

Ogata SN, Silk KR, Goodrich S, et al. Childhood sexual and physical abuse in adult patients with borderline personality disorder. *Am J Psychiatry* 1990;147:1008–1013.

Ohberg A, Lönnqvist JK, Sarna S, et al. Trends and availability of suicide methods in Finland: Proposals for restrictive measures. *Br J Psychiatry* 1995;166:35–43.

Ohmori T, Arora RC, Meltzer HY. Serotonergic measures in suicide brain: The concentration of 5-HIAA, HVA, and tryptophan in frontal cortex of suicide victims. *Biol Psychiatry* 1992;32:57–71.

O'Keane V, Dinan TG. Prolactin and cortisol responses to *d*-fenfluramine in major depression: Evidence for diminished responsivity of central serotonergic function. *Am J Psychiatry* 1991;148:1009–1015.

O'Keane V, Moloney E, O'Neill H, et al. Blunted prolactin responses to d-fenfluramine in sociopathy: Evidence for subsensitivity of central serotonergic function. *Br J Psychiatry* 1992;160:643–646.

Okuma T, Kishimoto A, Inoue K, et al. Antimanic and prophylactic effects of carba-mazepine (Tegretol) on manic-depressive psychosis: A preliminary report. *Folia Psychiatr Neurol Jpn* 1973;27:283–297.

Olin HS. Psychotherapy of the chronically suicidal patient. *Am J Psychother* 1976;30: 570–575.

Oltman JE, Friedman S. Life cycles in patients with manic-depressive psychosis. *Am J Psychiatry* 1962;119:174–176.

Orbach I, Rosenheim E, Hary E. Some aspects of cognitive functioning in suicidal children. *J Am Acad Child Adolesc Psychiatry* 1987;26:181–185.

Ordway GA, Smith KS, Haycock JW. Elevated tyrosine hydroxylase in the locus ceruleus of suicide victims. *J Neurochem* 1994;62:680–685.

Ordway GA, Widdowson PS, Smith KS, Halaris A. Agonist binding to a_2-adrenoceptors is elevated in the locus ceruleus from victims of suicide. *J Neurochem* 1994;63: 617–624.

Orgel S. Fusion with the victim and suicide. *Int J Psychoanal* 1974;55:531–538.

Osgood NJ. Suicide in the elderly: Etiology and assessment. *Int Rev Psychiatry* 1992; 4:217–223.

Ostergard N. CRICO's managed care claims. *Forum* 1997;18(3):9–10.

Ostow M. *Drugs in psychoanalysis and psychotherapy.* New York: Basic Books 1962.

Owen F, Chambers DR, Cooper SJ, et al. Serotonergic mechanisms in brains of suicide victims. *Brain Res* 1986;362:185–188.

Owen F, Cross AJ, Crow TJ, et al. Brain 5-HT$_2$ receptors and suicide. *Lancet* 1983;2: 1256.

Pabis R, Mirla MA, Tozmans S. A case study of autocastration. *Am J Psychiatry* 1980;137:626–627.

Pacheco MA, Stockmeier CA, Meltzer HY, et al. Alterations in phosphoinositide sig-naling and G-protein levels in depressed suicide brain. *Brain Res* 1996;723:37–45.

Pages KP, Russo JE, Roy-Byrne PP, et al. Determinants of suicidal ideation: The role of substance use disorders. *J Clin Psychiatry* 1997;58:510–515.

Palaniappan V, Ramachandran V, Somasundaram O. Suicidal ideation and biogenic amines in depression. *Indian J Psychiatry* 1983;25:286–292.

Palermo GB. Murder-suicide: An extended suicide. *Int J Offender Ther* 1994;38:205–216.

Palmer AM, Burns MA, Arango V, Mann JJ. Similar effects of glycine, zinc and an oxi-dizing agent on dizocilpine binding to the N-methyl-D-aspartate receptor in neo-cortical tissue derived from suicide victims and controls. *J Neural Transm* 1994; 96:1–8.

Palmer S, Humphrey JA. Offender-victim relationships in criminal homicide followed by offender's suicide, North Carolina, 1972–1977. *Suicide Life-Threat Behav* 1980; 10:106–118.

Pampel FC. Cohort size and age-specific suicide rates: A contingent relationship. *De-mography* 1996;33:341–355.

Pandey GN, Dwivedi Y, Pandey SC, et al. Protein kinase C in the postmortem brain of teenage suicide victims. *Neurosci Lett* 1997;228:111–114.

Pappas DM. Recent historical perspectives regarding medical euthanasia and physician-assisted suicide. *Br Med Bull* 1996;52:386–393.

Paré CMB, Yeung DPH, Price K, Stacey RS. 5-Hydroxytryptamine, noradrenaline, and dopamine in brainstem, hypothalamus, and caudate nucleus of controls and of patients committing suicide by coal-gas poisoning. *Lancet* 1969;2:133–135.

Paris J, Brown R, Newlis D. Long-term follow-up of borderline patients in a general hospital. *Compr Psychiatry* 1987;28:530–535.

Paris J, Nowlis D, Brown R. Developmental factors in the outcome of borderline personality disorder. *Compr Psychiatry* 1988;29:147–150.

Paris J, Nowlis D, Brown R. Predictors of suicide in borderline personality disorder. *Can J Psychiatry* 1989;34:8–9.

Parker N. Murderers: A personal series. *Med J Aust* 1979;1:36–39.

Patsiokas A, Clum G, Luscumb R. Cognitive characteristics in suicide attempters. *J Consult Clin Psychology* 1979;47:478–484.

Pattison EM, Kahan J. The deliberate self-harm syndrome. *Am J Psychiatry* 1983;140:867–872.

Paul SM, Rehavi M, Skolnick P, Goodwin FK. High affinity binding of antidepressants to a biogenic amine transport site in human brain and platelet: Studies in depression. In RM Post, CJ Bellinger (eds), *Neurobiology of mood disorders.* Baltimore: Williams & Wilkins 1984:846–853.

Paulsen RH. Psychiatry and primary care as neighbors: From the Promethean primary care physician to multidisciplinary clinic. *Int J Psychiatry Med* 1996;26:115–127.

Pawlicki CM, Gaumer C. Nursing care of the self-mutilating patient. *Bull Menninger Clin* 1993;57:380–389.

Paykel ES, Dienelt MN. Suicide attempts following acute depression. *J Nerv Ment Disord* 1971;153:234–243.

Paykel ES, Myers JK, Lindenthal JJ, et al. Suicidal feelings in the general population: A prevalence study. *Br J Psychiatry* 1974;124:460–469.

Peabody CA, Faull KF, King RJ, et al. CSF amine metabolites and depression. *Psychiatry Res* 1987;21:1–7.

Pearlman LA, Saakvitne KW. Psychoanalytic theory and psychological trauma: History and critical review. In LA Pearlman, KW Saakvitne (eds), *Trauma and the therapist: Countertransference and vicarious traumatization in psychotherapy with incest survivors.* New York: Norton 1995:35–54.

Pederson AM, Barry JD, Babigian HM. Epidemiological considerations of psychotic depression. *Arch Gen Psychiatry* 1972;27:193–197.

Pedinielli JL, Delahousse J, Chabaud B. La "léthalité" des tentatives de suicide. *Ann Med Psychol (Paris)* 1989;147:535–550.

Perr IN. Liability of the hospital and the psychiatrist in suicide. *Am J Psychiatry* 1965;122:631–638.

Perris C, d'Elia G. A study of bipolar (manic-depressive) and unipolar recurrent depressive psychoses: X. Mortality, suicide, and life-cycles. *Acta Psychiatr Scand* 1966;194(suppl):172–183.

Perry JC. Personality disorders, suicide, and self-destructive behavior. In DG Jacobs (ed), *Suicide: Understanding and responding.* Madison CT: International Universities Press 1989:157–169.

Perry PJ. Clinical use of the newer antipsychotic drugs. *Am J Health Syst Pharm* 1995;1(52, suppl):S9–S14.

Perry S, Cooper AM, Michels R. The psychodynamic formulation: Its purpose, structure, and clinical application. *Am J Psychiatry* 1987;144:5.

Perry S, Jacobsberg L, Fishman B. Suicidal ideation and HIV testing. *JAMA* 1990;263: 679–682.

Petronis KR, Samuels JF, Moscicki EK, et al. An epidemiologic investigation of potential risk factors for suicide attempts. *Soc Psychiatry Psychiatr Epidemiol* 1990;35:193–199.

Petterson U. Manic-depressive illness: A clinical, social and genetic study. *Acta Psychiatr Scand* 1977;269(suppl):1–93.

Pfeffer CR. *The suicidal child.* New York: Guilford Press 1986.

Pfeffer CR. Childhood suicidal behavior: A developmental perspective. *Psychiatr Clin North Am* 1997;20:551–562.

Pfeffer CR, Martins P, Mann J. Child survivors of suicide: Psychosocial characteristics. *J Am Acad Child Adolesc Psychiatry* 1997;36:65–74.

Pfeffer CR, Peskin MA, Siefker MA. Suicidal children grow up: Psychiatric treatment during follow-up period. *J Am Acad Child Adolesc Psychiatry* 1992;31:679–685.

Pfohl B, Winokur G. The micropsychopathology of hebephrenic/catatonic schizophrenia. *J Nerv Ment Dis* 1983;171:296–300.

Pickar D, Roy A, Breier A, et al. Suicide and aggression in schizophrenia neurobiologic correlates. *Ann NY Acad Sci* 1986;487:189–196.

Pitchot W, Ansseau M, Moreno AG, et al. The flesinoxan 5-HT1A receptor challenge in major depression and suicidal behavior. *Pharmacopsychiatry* 1995;28:91–92.

Pitman RK. Self-mutilation in combat related post-traumatic stress disorder. *Am J Psychiatry* 1990;147:123–124.

Pitts FN, Winokur G. Affective disorder: III. Diagnostic correlates and incidence of suicide. *J Nerv Ment Dis* 1964;139:176–181.

Planansky K, Johnston R. The occurrence and characteristics of suicidal preoccupation and acts in schizophrenia. *Acta Psychiatr Scand* 1971;47:473–483.

Plutchik R, van Praag HM. Psychosocial correlates of suicide and violence risk. In HM van Praag (ed), *Violence and suicidality.* New York: Brunner/Mazel 1990.

Pokorny AD. Suicide rates in various psychiatric disorders. *J Nerv Ment Dis* 1964;139: 499–506.

Pokorny AD. A follow-up study of 618 suicidal patients. *Am J Psychiatry* 1966;122: 1109–1116.

Pokorny AD. Prediction of suicide in psychiatric patients: Report of a prospective study. *Arch Gen Psychiatry* 1983;40:249–257.

Pokorny AD. Suicide prediction revisited. *Suicide Life-Threat Behav* 1993;23:1–10.

Poole AJ, James HD, Hughes WC. Treatment experiences in the lithium clinic at St. Thomas' Hospital. *J R Soc Med* 1978;71:890–894.

Pope HG Jr, Jonas JM, Hudson JI, et al. The validity of DSM-III borderline personality disorder: A phenomenologic, family history, treatment response, and long-term follow up study. *Arch Gen Psychiatry* 1983;40:23–30.

Porrino LJ, Goldman-Rakic PS. Brainstem innervation of prefrontal and anterior cingulate cortex in the rhesus monkey revealed by retrograde transport of HRP. *J Comp Neurol* 1982;205:63–76.

Portenoy RK, Coyle N, Kash KM, et al. Determinants of the willingness to endorse assisted suicide: A survey of physicians, nurses, and social workers. *Psychosomatics* 1997;38:277–287.

Pratt CC, Schmall VL, Wilson W, Benthin A. A model community education program on depression and suicide in later life. *Gerontologist* 1991;31:692–695.

Pribor EF, Dinwiddie SH. Psychiatric correlates of incest in childhood. *Am J Psychiatry* 1992;149:53–56.

Pribor EF, Yutzy SH, Dean T, Wetzel RD. Briquet's syndrome, dissociation, and abuse. *Am J Psychiatry* 1993;150:1507–1511.

Price JH, Everett SA, Bedell AW, Telljohann SK. Reduction of firearm-related violence through firearm safety counseling: The role of family physicians. *Arch Fam Med* 1997;6:79–83.

Price LH, Charney DS, Delgado PL, Heninger GR. Serotonin function and depression: Neuroendocrine and mood responses to intravenous L-tryptophan in depressed patients and healthy comparison subjects. *Am J Psychiatry* 1991;148:1518–1525.

Prien RF, Klett CJ, Caffey CM. Lithium prophylaxis in recurrent affective illness. *Am J Psychiatry* 1974;131:198–203.

Pritchard C. New patterns of suicide by age and gender in the United Kingdom and the Western World, 1974–1992: An indicator of social change? *Soc Psychiatry Psychiatr Epidemiol* 1996a;31:227–234.

Pritchard C. Suicide in the People's Republic of China categorized by age and gender: Evidence of the influence of culture on suicide. *Acta Psychiatr Scand* 1996b;93: 362–367.

Prudic J, Haskett RF, Mulsant B, et al. Resistance to antidepressant medications and short-term clinical response to ECT. *Am J Psychiatry* 1996;153:985–992.

Prudic J, et al. Relative response of endogenous and non-endogenous symptoms to electroconvulsive therapy. *J Affective Disord* 1989;16:59–64.

Putnam FW. *The diagnosis and treatment of multiple personality disorder.* New York: Guilford Press 1989.

Putnam FW, Guroff JJ, Silberman EK, et al. The clinical phenomenology of multiple personality disorder: A review of 100 cases. *J Clin Psychiatry* 1986;47:258–293.

Quill TE. *Death and dignity: Making choices and taking charge.* New York: Norton 1993.

Quill TE, Brody RV. "You promised me I wouldn't die like this!": A bad death, a medical emergency. *Arch Intern Med* 1995;155:1250–1254.

Quill TE, Cassel CK, Meier DE. Care of the hopelessly ill: Potential clinical criteria for physician-assisted suicide. *N Eng J Med* 1992;327:1380–1384.

Rado S. The psychoanalysis of pharmacothymia (drug addiction). *Psychoanal Q* 1933; 2:1–23.

Ragain RD, Anson JE. The control of self-mutilative behavior with positive reinforcement. *Ment Retard* 1976;14:22–25.

Rajathurai A, Chazan BI, Jeans JE. Self-mutilation as a feature of Addison's disease. *Br Med J* 1983;287:1027.

Ramsay R, Bagley C. The prevalence of suicidal behaviors, attitudes, and associated social experiences in an urban population. *Suicide Life-Threat Behav* 1985;15:151–167.

Range LM, Stringer TA. Reasons for living and coping abilities among older adults. *Int J Aging Hum Dev* 1996;43:1–5.

Rao R, Dening T, Brayne C, Huppert FA. Suicidal thinking in community residents over eighty. *Int J Geriatr Psychiatry* 1997;12:337–343.

Regier DA, Boyd JH, Burke JD, et al. One-month prevalence of mental disorders in the United States: Based on five Epidemiological Catchment Area sites. *Arch Gen Psychiatry* 1988a;45:977–986.

Regier DA, Farmer ME, Locke BZ, et al. Comorbidity of mental disorders with alcohol and other drug abuse: Results from the Epidemiologic Catchment Area (ECA) study. *JAMA* 1990;264:2511–2518.

Regier DA, Goldberg ID, Taube CA. The de facto U.S. mental health services system: A public health perspective. *Arch Gen Psychiatry* 1978;35:685–693.

Regier DA, Hirschfeld RMA, Goodwin FK, et al. The NIMH depression awareness, recognition, and treatment program: Structure, aims, and scientific basis. *Am J Psychiatry* 1988b;145:1351–1357.

Regional variations in suicide rates: United States, 1990–1994. *MMWR* 1997;46:789–793.

Reich P, Kelly MJ. Suicide attempts by hospitalized medical and surgical patients. *N Eng J Med* 1976;294:298–301.

Reinherz HZ, Giacojnia RM, et al. Early psychosocial risks for adolescent suicidal ideation and attempts. *J Am Acad Child Adolesc Psychiatry* 1995;34:599–611.

Reist C, Kaufmann CD, Haier RJ, et al. A controlled trial of desipramine in 18 men with posttraumatic stress disorder. *Am J Psychiatry* 1989;149:513–516.

Remafedi G, Farrow JA, Deisher RW. Risk factors for attempted suicide in gay and bisexual youth. *Pediatrics* 1991;87:869–875.

Remafedi G, Farrow JA, Deisher RW. Risk factors in attempted suicide in gay and bisexual youth. In LD Garnets, DC Kemmel (eds), *Psychological perspectives on lesbian and gay studies.* New York: Columbia University Press 1993:486–499.

Repp AC, Deitz SM. Reducing aggressive and self-injurious behavior of institutionalized retarded children through reinforcement of other behavior. J *Appl Behav Anal* 1974;7:313–325.

Resnick HS, Kilpatrick DG, Dansky BS, et al. Prevalence of civilian trauma and post-traumatic stress disorder in a representative national sample of women. *J Consult Clin Psychology* 1993;61:984–991.

Resnick PJ. Child murder by parents: A psychiatric review of filicide. *Am J Psychiatry* 1969;126:325–334.

Resnick PJ. Murder of the newborn: A psychiatric review of neonaticide. *Am J Psychiatry* 1970;126:1414–1420.

Resnik HLP, Hawthorne BC (eds). *Suicide prevention in the '70s.* DHEW Publication No. HSM 72–9054. Washington DC: U.S. Department of Health, Education and Welfare 1972.

Rich CL, Fowler RC, Fogarty LA, Young D. San Diego Suicide Study: III. Relationships between diagnoses and stressors. *Arch Gen Psychiatry* 1988a;45:589–592.

Rich CL, Fowler RC, Young D, et al. San Diego Suicide Study: Comparison of gay to straight males. *Suicide Life-Threat Behav* 1986a;16:448–457.

Rich CL, Ricketts JE, Fowler RC, Young D. Some differences between men and women who commit suicide. *Am J Psychiatry* 1988b;145:718–722.

Rich CL, Runeson BS. Similarities in diagnostic comorbidity between suicide among young people in Sweden and the United States. *Acta Psychiatr Scand* 1992;86:335–339.

Rich CL, Spiker DG, Jewell SW, Neil JF. Response of energy and suicidal ideation to ECT. *J Clin Psychiatry* 1986b;47:31–32.

Rich CL, Warsradt GM, Nemiroff RA, et al. Suicide, stressors and the life cycle. *Am J Psychiatry* 1991;148:524–527.

Rich CL, Young D, Fowler RC: San Diego Suicide Study: I. Young vs old subjects. *Arch Gen Psychiatry* 1986c;43:577–582.

Rich CL, Young JG, Fowler RC, et al. Guns and suicide: Possible effects of some specific legislation. *Am J Psychiatry* 1990;147:342–346.

Richman J. *Family therapy for suicidal people.* New York: Springer 1986.

Richman J, Charles E. Patient dissatisfaction and attempted suicide. *Community Ment Health J* 1976;12:301–305.

Richman J, Rosenbaum M. A clinical study of the role of hostility and death wishes by the family and society in suicidal attempts. *Isr Ann Psychiatry Rel Disc* 1970;8:213–231.

Rifai AH, George CJ, Seack JA, et al. Hopelessness in suicide attempters after acute treatment of major depression in late life. *Am J Psychiatry* 1994;151:1687–1690.

Rihmer Z, Barsi J, Arato M, Demeter E. Suicide in subtypes of primary major depression. *J Affective Disord* 1990a;18:221–225.

Rihmer Z, Barsi J, Veg K, Katona CLE. Suicide rates in Hungary correlate negatively with reported rates of depression. *J Affective Disord* 1990b;20:87–91.

Rihmer Z, Rutz W, Pihlgren H. Depression and suicide on Götland: An intensive study of all suicides before and after depression-training program for general practitioners. *J Affective Disord* 1995;35:147–152.

Rihmer Z, Szanto K, Barsi J. Suicide prevention: Fact or fiction? *Br J Psychiatry* 1993; 162:130–131.

Roberts JM. Prognostic factors in the electroshock treatment of depressive states: Clinical features from testing and examination. *J Ment Sci* 1959;105:693–713.

Roberts RE et al. Does growing old increase the risk of depression? *Am J Psychiatry* 1997;154:1384–1390.

Robertson MM, Trimbale MR, Lees AL. Self-injurious behavior and the Giles de la Tourette syndrome. *Psychol Med* 1989;19:611–625.

Robins E. *The final months.* New York: Oxford University Press 1981.

Robins E. Psychosis and suicide. *Biol Psychiatry* 1986;21:665–672.

Robins E, Gassner S, Kayes J, et al. The communication of suicidal intent: A study of 134 consecutive cases of successful (completed) suicide. *Am J Psychiatry* 1959a; 115:724–733.

Robins E, Murphy GE, Wilkinson RH, et al. Some clinical considerations in the prevention of suicide based on a study of 134 successful suicides. *Am J Public Health* 1959b;49:888–899.

Rockett IR, Smith GS. Covert suicide among elderly Japanese females: Questioning unintentional drownings. *Soc Sci Med* 1993;36:1467–1472.

Rockland LH. A supportive approach: Psychodynamically oriented therapy-treatment of borderline patients who self-mutilate. *J Personality Disord* 1987;1:350–355.

Rodenburg M. Child murder by depressed parents. *Can Psychiatric Assoc J* 1971;16: 41–48.

Roose SP, Glassman AH, Walsh BT. Depression, delusions, and suicide. *Am J Psychiatry* 1983;140:1159–1162.

Rose RM, Burt RA, Clayton PJ, et al. Consensus Development Conference statement: Electroconvulsive therapy. *JAMA* 1985;254:2103–2108.

Rosel P, Arranz B, Vallejo J, et al. High affinity imipramine and paroxetine binding sites in suicide brains. *J Neural Transm* 1997;104:921–929.

Rosen BK. Suicide pacts: A review. *Psychol Med* 1981;11:525–533.

Rosen DH. Focal suicide. *Am J Psychiatry* 1972;128:1009–1011.

Rosenbaum ML. Crime and punishment: The suicide pact. *Arch Gen Psychiatry* 1983;40:979–982.

Rosenbaum ML. The role of depression in couples involved in murder-suicide and homicide. *Am J Psychiatry* 1990;147:1036–1039.

Rosenberg [Zetzel] E. Anxiety and the capacity to bear it. *Int J Psychoanal* 1949;30:1–12.

Rosenberg HM, Ventura SJ, Maurer JD, et al. Births and deaths: United States, 1995. *Monthly Vital Statistics Report,*1996;4 (3, suppl 2).

Rosenberg ML, Davidson LE, Smith JC, et al. Operational criteria for the determination of suicide. *J Forensic Sci* 1988;33:1445–1456.

Ross CA. *Multiple personality disorder: Diagnosis, clinical features, and treatment.* New York: Wiley 1989.

Ross CA, Anderson G, Fleisher WP, Norton GR. The frequency of multiple personality disorder among psychiatric inpatients. *Am J Psychiatry* 1991;148:1717–1720.

Roswell VA. Professional liability: Issues for behavior therapists in the 1980s and 1990s. *Behav Therapist* 1988;11:163–171.

Roth LH, Meisel A, Lidz CW. Tests of competency to consent to treatment. *Am J Psychiatry* 1977;134:279–284.

Rotheram MJ. Evaluation of imminent danger for suicide among youth. *Am J Orthopsychiatry* 1987;57:102–110.

Rothschild AJ, Locke CA. Reexposure to fluoxetine after serious suicide attempts by three patients: The role of akathisia. *J Clin Psychiatry* 1991;52:491–493.

Rounsaville BJ, Anton SF, Carroll K, et al. Psychiatric diagnoses of treatment-seeking cocaine abusers. *Arch Gen Psychiatry* 1991;48:43–51.

Roy A. Risk factors for suicide in psychiatric patients. *Arch Gen Psychiatry* 1982a;39:1089–1095.

Roy A. Suicide in chronic schizophrenia. *Br J Psychiatry* 1982b;141:171–177.

Roy A. Family history of suicide. *Arch Gen Psychiatry* 1983;40:971–974.

Roy A. Suicide in recurrent affective disorder patients. *Can J Psychiatry* 1984;29:319–322.

Roy A. Suicide in schizophrenia. In A Roy (ed), *Suicide.* Baltimore: Williams & Wilkins 1986:97–112.

Roy A. Genetics and suicidal behavior. In U.S. Department of Health and Human Services; Alcohol, Drug Abuse, and Mental Health Administration, *Report of the Secretary's Task Force on Youth Suicide: Vol 2. Risk factors for youth suicide.* DHHS Publication No (ADM)89–1622. Washington DC: U.S. Department of Health and Human Services 1989a:247–262.

Roy A. Suicide. In HI Kaplan, BJ Sadock (eds), *Comprehensive textbook of psychiatry,* 5th ed. Baltimore: Williams & Wilkins 1989b:1414–1427.

Roy A, Chir B. Suicide. In L Grunhaus, JF Greden (eds), *Severe depressive disorders. Progress in psychiatry.* Washington DC: American Psychiatric Press 1994:223–241.

Roy A, Draper R. Suicide among psychiatric hospital inpatients. *Psychol Med* 1995;25:199–202.

Roy A, Lamparski D, De Jong J, et al. Cerebrospinal fluid monoamine metabolites in alcoholic patients who attempt suicide. *Acta Psychiatr Scand* 1990;81:58–61.

Roy A, Mazonson A, Pickar D. Attempted suicide in chronic schizophrenia. *Br J Psychiatry* 1984;144:303–306.

Roy A, Ninan PT, Mazonson A, et al. CSF monoamine metabolites in chronic schizophrenic patients who attempt suicide. *Psychol Med* 1985;15:335–340.

Roy A, Pickar D, De Jong J, et al. Suicidal behavior in depression: Relationship to noradrenergic function. *Biol Psychiatry* 1989;25:341–350.

Roy A, Rylander G, Sarchiapone M. Genetics of suicide: Family studies and molecular genetics. *Ann NY Acad Sci* 1997a;836:135–157.

Roy A, Rylander G, Sarchiapone M. Genetic studies of suicidal behavior. *Psychiatr Clin North Am* 1997b;20:595–611.

Roy A, Segal NL, Centerwall BS, Robinette D. Suicide in twins. *Arch Gen Psychiatry* 1991;48:29–32.

Roy A, Segal NL, Sarchiapone M. Attempted suicide among living co-twins and twin suicide victims. *Am J Psychiatry* 1995;152:1075–1076.

Royal Dutch Medical Association. *Guidelines on assisted suicide and euthanasia.* Utrecht, Netherlands: Royal Dutch Medical Association 1995.

Roy-Byrne PP, Post RM, Hambrick DD, et al. Suicide and course of illness in major affective disorder. *J Affective Disord* 1988;15:1–8.

Roy-Byrne PP, Post RM, Rubinow DR, et al. CSF 5HIAA and personal and family history of suicide in affectively ill patients: A negative study. *Psychiatry Res* 1983; 10:263–274.

Roy-Byrne PP, Post RM, Uhde TW, et al. The longitudinal course of recurrent affective illness: Life chart data from research patients at NIMH. *Acta Psychiatr Scand* 1985;71(suppl 317):1–34.

Rudd MD, Joiner TE Jr, Rajav MH. Help negation after acute suicidal crisis. *J Consult Clin Psychol* 1995;63:499–503.

Rudorfer MV, Risby ED, Osman OT, et al. Hypothalamic-pituitary-adrenal axis and monoamine transmitter activity in depression: A pilot study of central and peripheral effects of electroconvulsive therapy. *Biol Psychiatry* 1991;29:253–264.

Runeson BS. Mental disorder in youth suicide: DSM-III-R axes I and II. *Acta Psychiatr Scand* 1989;79:490–497.

Runeson BS, Beskow J, Waern M. The suicidal process in suicides among young people. *Acta Psychiatr Scand* 1996;93:35–42.

Rush J, Beck AT, Kovacs M, et al. Comparison of the effects of cognitive therapy and pharmacotherapy on hopelessness and self-concept. *Am J Psychiatry* 1982;139: 862–866.

Russell DEH. *The secret trauma: Incest in the lives of girls and women.* New York: Basic Books 1986.

Rutz W, von Knorring L, Pihlgren H, et al. Prevention of male suicide: Lessons from Götland study. *Lancet* 1995;345(8948):524.

Rynn KO, Graf SE, Palovcek PF. Selective prescribing in suicidal patients. *Ann Pharmacother* 1997;31:924–925.

Sabbath JC. The suicidal adolescent: The expendable child. *J Am Acad Child Adolesc Psychiatry* 1969;8:272–279.

Sabo A, Gunderson J, Najavits L, et al. Changes in self-destructiveness of borderline patients in psychotherapy. *J Nerv Ment Dis* 1995;183:370–376.

Sacchetti E, Vita A, Guarneri L, et al. The effectiveness of fluoxetine, clomipramine, nortriptyline and desipramine in major depressives with suicidal behavior: Preliminary findings. In GB Cassano, HS Akiskal (eds), *Serotonin-related psychiatric syndromes: Clinical and therapeutic links.* London: Royal Society of Medicine Services 1991:47–53.

Sachs G. Adolescent mania: Underdiagnosed and undertreated. Presented at the 150th annual meeting of the American Psychiatric Association, May 1997.

Sachs GA, Ahronheim JC, Rhymes JA, et al. Good care of dying patients: The alternative to physician-assisted suicide and euthanasia. *J Am Geriatr Soc* 1995;43:553–562.

Sackeim HA, Devanand DP, Nobler MS. Electroconvulsive therapy. In FE Bloom, DJ Kupfer (eds), *Psychopharmacology: The fourth generation of progress.* New York: Raven Press 1995:1123–1141.

Sainsbury P, Jenkins JS. The accuracy of officially reported suicide statistics for purposes of epidemiological research. *J Epidemiol Community Health* 1982;36:43–48.

Sakuta T. A study of murder followed by suicide. *Med Law* 1995;14:141–153.

Salib E. Elderly suicide and weather conditions: Is there a link? *Int J Geriatr Psychiatry* 1997;12:937–941.

Salloum IM, Daley DC, Cornelius JR, et al. Disproportionate lethality in psychiatric patients with concurrent alcohol and cocaine abuse. *Am J Psychiatry* 1996;153:953–955.

Salzman C. ECT, research, and professional ambivalence. *Am J Psychiatry* 1998;155:1–2.

Salzman C, Wolfson AN, Schatzberg A, et al. Effect of fluoxetine on anger in symptomatic volunteers with borderline personality disorder. *J Clin Psychopharmacol* 1995;15:23–29.

Saporta JA, Case J. The role of medication in treating adult survivors of incest. In P Paddison (ed), *Treating adult survivors of incest.* Washington DC: American Psychiatric Press 1984:101–134.

Sartorius N. Mental health policies and programmes for the twenty-first century: A personal view. In *The European handbook of psychiatry and mental health,* vol 2. Barcelona: Anthropos Editorial 1991.

Saunders B, Giolas MH. Dissociation and childhood trauma in psychologically disturbed adolescents. *Am J Psychiatry* 1991;148:50–54.

Saxe GN, van der Kolk BA, Berkowitz R, et al. Dissociative disorders in psychiatric inpatients. *Am J Psychiatry* 1993;150:1037–1042.

Schaefer HH. Self-injurious behavior. *J Appl Behav Anal* 1970;3:111–116.

Schafer R. The loving and beloved superego in Freud's structural theory. *Psychoanal Study Child* 1960;15:163–188.

Schifano F, De Leo D. Can pharmacological intervention aid in the prevention of suicidal behavior? *Pharmacopsychiatry* 1991;24:113–117.

Schmidtke A, Bille-Brahe U, De Leo D, et al. Attempted suicide in Europe: Rates, trends and sociodemographic characteristics of suicide attempters during the period 1989–1992. Results of the WHO/EURO Multicentre Study on Parasuicide. *Acta Psychiatr Scand* 1996;93:327–338.

Schmidtke A, Hafner H. The Werther effect after television films: New evidence for an old hypothesis. *Psychol Med* 1988;18:665–676.

Schoenfield M, Myers RH, Cupples LA, et al. Increased rate of suicide among patients with Huntington's disease. *J Neurol Neurosurg Psychiatry* 1984;47:1283–1287.

Schotte DE, Clum GA. Suicide ideation in a college population: A test of a model. *J Consult Clin Psychol* 1982;50:690–696.

Schou M, Weeke A. Did manic-depressive patients who committed suicide receive prophylactic or continuation treatment at the time? *Br J Psychiatry* 1988;153:324–327.

Schulberg HC, Burns BJ. Mental disorders in primary care: Epidemiologic, diagnostic, and treatment research directions. *Gen Hosp Psychiatry* 1988;10:79–87.

Schulsinger F, Kety SS, Rosenthal D, Wender PH. A family study of suicide. In M Schou, E Strömgren (eds), *Origin, prevention, and treatment of affective disorders.* Orlando FL: Academic Press 1979:277–287.

Schultz JM. *Manual of psychiatric nursing care plans.* New York: Little, Brown 1982.

Schulz B. Sterblichkeit endogen Geisteskranker und ihrer Eltern. *Z Mensch Vererb* 1948;29:338–367.

Schwab JJ, Warheit GJ, Holzer CE. Suicide ideation and behavior in a general population. *Dis Nerv Syst* 1972;33:745–748.

Schwartz DA. The suicidal character. *Psychiatr Q* 1979;5:64–70.

Schweizer E, Dever A, Clary C. Suicide upon recovery from depression: A clinical note. *J Nerv Ment Dis* 1988;176:633–636.

Seager CP. A comparison between the results of unmodified and modified electroplexy. *J Ment Sci* 1958;104:206–220.

Seager CP. Controlled trial of straight and modified electroplexy. *J Ment Sci* 1959;105: 1022–1028.

Secunda SK, Cross CK, Koslow S, et al. Biochemistry and suicidal behavior in depressed patients. *Biol Psychiatry* 1986;21:756–767.

Segal P, Mizyglod S. Self-inflicted eye injuries. *Am J Ophthalmol* 1963;53:349–362.

Seidlitz L, Duberstein PR, Cox C, Conwell Y. Attitudes of older people toward suicide and assisted suicide: An analysis of Gallup poll findings. *J Am Geriatr Soc* 1995; 43:993–998.

Selkin J. Rescue fantasies in homicide-suicide. *Suicide Life-Threat Behav* 1976;6:79–85.

Sendbuehler JM, Goldstein S. Attempted suicide among the aged. *J Am Geriatr Soc* 1977;25:245–248.

Shaffer DA. The epidemiology of teen suicide: An examination of risk factors. *J Clin Psychiatry* 1988;49:36–41.

Shaffer DA. Suicide: Risk factors and the public health. *Am J Public Health* 1993;83: 171–172.

Shaffer DA, Fisher P. The epidemiology of suicide in children and young adolescents. *J Am Acad Child Adolesc Psychiatry* 1981;20:545–565.

Shaffer DA, Fisher P, Hicks RH, et al. Sexual orientation in adolescents who commit suicide. *Suicide Life-Threat Behav* 1995;25:64–71.

Shaffer DA, Garland A, Gould MS, et al. Preventing teenage suicide: A critical review. *J Am Acad Child Adol Psychiatry* 1988;27:675–687.

Shaffer DA, Gould MS, Fisher P, et al. Psychiatric diagnosis in child and adolescent suicide. *Arch Gen Psychiatry* 1996;53:339–348.

Shaffer DA, Gould MS, Hicks RC. Worsening suicide rate in black teenagers. *Am J Psychiatry* 1994;151:1810–1812.

Shaffer J, Perlin S, Schmidt C, et al. The prediction of suicide in schizophrenia. *J Nerv Ment Dis* 1974;159:349–355.

Shafii M, Carrigan S, Whittinghill JR, Derrick AM. Psychological autopsy of completed suicide in children and adolescents. *Am J Psychiatry* 1985;142:1061–1064.

Shafii M, Steltz-Lenarsky J, Derrick AM, et al. Comorbidity of mental disorders in the postmortem diagnosis of completed suicide in children and adolescents. *J Affective Disord* 1988;15:227–233.

Shapira B, Lerer B, Kindler S, et al. Enhanced serotonergic responsivity following electroconvulsive therapy in patients with major depression. *Br J Psychiatry* 1992;160:223–229.

Shapiro S. Self-mutilation and self-blame in incest victims. *Am J Psychother* 1987;41:46–54.

Shaunesey K, Cohen JL, Plummer B, Berman A. Suicidality and hospitalized adolescents: Relationship to prior abuse. *Am J Orthopsychiatry* 1993;63:113–119.

Shaw DM, Camps FE, Eccleston EG. 5-Hydroxytryptamine in the hindbrain of depressive suicides. *Br J Psychiatry* 1967;113:1407–1411.

Sheftner WA, Young MA, Endicott J, et al. Family history and five-year suicide risk. *Br J Psychiatry* 1988;153:805–809.

Shengold L. *Soul murder.* New Haven CT: Yale University Press 1989.

Shepherd M. Morbid jealousy: Some clinical and social aspects of a psychiatric syndrome. *J Ment Sci* 1961;107:687–753.

Shneidman ES. *Thematic test analysis.* Philadelphia: Grune & Stratton 1951.

Shneidman ES. Sleep and self-destruction: A phenomenonological study. In ES Shneidman (ed), *Essays in self-destruction.* New York: Science House 1967:510–539.

Shneidman ES. Suicide, lethality, and the psychological autopsy. *Int Psychiatr Clin* 1969;6:225–250.

Shneidman ES. Perturbation and lethality as precursors of suicide in a gifted group. *Suicide Life-Threat Behav* 1971;1:23–45.

Shneidman ES. Suicide notes reconsidered. *Psychiatry* 1973;36:379–395.

Shneidman ES. *Definition of suicide.* New York: Wiley 1985.

Shneidman ES. A psychological approach to suicide. In GR vander Bos, BK Bryant (eds), *Cataclysms, crises, and catastrophes: Psychology in action.* Washington DC: American Psychological Association 1987:147–183.

Shneidman ES. Overview: A multidimensional approach to suicide. In DG Jacobs, HN Brown (eds), *Suicide: Understanding and responding.* Madison CT: International Universities Press 1989:1–30.

Shneidman ES. A conspectus for conceptualizing the suicidal scenario. In RW Maris, AL Berman, JT Maltsberger, RY Yufit (eds), *Assessment and prediction of suicide.* New York: Guilford Press 1992.

Shneidman ES. Commentary: Suicide as psychache. *J Nerv Ment Dis* 1993;181: 147–149.

Shneidman ES. Clues to suicide reconsidered. *Suicide Life-Threat Behav* 1994;24: 395–397.

Shneidman ES. *The suicidal mind.* New York: Oxford University Press 1996.

Shneidman ES, Farberow NL. *Clues to suicide.* New York: McGraw-Hill 1957.

Shobe FO, Brion P. Long-term prognosis in manic-depressive illness. *Arch Gen Psychiatry* 1971;24:334–337.

Shore JH, Vollmer WM, Tatum EI. Community patterns of posttraumatic stress disorder. *J Nerv Ment Dis* 1989;177:681–685.

Siever LJ, Murphy DL, Slater S, et al. Plasma prolactin changes following fenfluramine in depressed patients compared to controls: An evaluation of central serotonergic responsivity in depression. *Life Sci* 1984;34:1029–1039.

Sifneos P. Manipulative suicide. *Psychiatr Q* 1966;40:525–537.

Silberman EK, Sullivan JL. Atypical depression. *Psychiatr Clin North Am* 1984;7: 535–547.

Simon RI. Silent suicide in the elderly. *Bull Am Acad Psychiatry Law* 1989;17:83–95.

Simon RI. The suicide prevention pact: Clinical and legal considerations. In RI Simon (ed), *Review of clinical psychiatry and the law,* vol 2. Washington DC: American Psychiatric Press 1991:441–451.

Simon RI (ed). *Clinical psychiatry and the law,* 2d ed. Washington DC: American Psychiatric Press 1992a.

Simon RI. Clinical risk management of suicidal patients: Assessing the unpredictable. In RI Simon (ed), *Review of clinical psychiatry and the law,* vol 3. Washington DC: American Psychiatric Press 1992b:3–63.

Skodol AE, Karasu TB. Emergency psychiatry and the assaultive patient. *Am J Psychiatry* 1978;135:202–205.

Skoog I, Aevarsson O, Beskow J, et al. Suicidal feelings in a population sample of non-demented 85-year-olds. *Am J Psychiatry* 1996;153:1015–1020.

Slater E. Zur Erbpathologie des manisch-depressiven Irreseins: Die Eltern und Kinder von Manisch-Depressiven. *Z Gesamte Neurol Psychiatr* 1938;163:1–47.

Sletten IW, Brown ML, Evenson RC, et al. Suicide in mental hospital patients. *Dis Nerv Sys* 1972;33:328–334.

Sloan JH, Rivara FP, Reay DT, et al. Firearm regulations and rates of suicide: A comparison of two metropolitan areas. *N Engl J Med* 1990;322(6):368–373.

Smialek JE, Spitz WU. Death behind bars. *JAMA* 1978;240:2563–2564.

Smith BD, Salzman C. Do benzodiazepines cause depression? *Hosp Community Psychiatry* 1991;42:1101–1102.

Smith JC, Mercy JA, Conn JM. Marital status and the risk of suicide. *Am J Pub Health* 1988;78:78–80.

Smith MD, Parker RN. Type of homicide and variation in regional rates. *Soc Forces* 1980;59:136–147.

Smith RM. Biological therapies of PTSD: An overview. Presented at the 149th annual meeting of the American Psychiatric Association, May 1996.

Soloff PH. Pharmacological therapies in borderline personality disorder. In J Paris (ed), *Borderline personality disorder.* Washington DC: American Psychiatric Press 1993: 319–348.

Soloff PH. Risk factors for suicidal behavior in borderline personality disorder. *Am J Psychiatry* 1994;151:1316–1323.

Soloff PH, George A, Nathan RS. et al. Paradoxical effects of amitriptyline on borderline patients. *Am J Psychiatry* 1986a;143:1603–1605.

Soloff PH, George A, Nathan RS, et al. Progress in pharmacotherapy of borderline disorders: A double blind study of amitriptyline, haloperidol, and placebo. *Arch Gen Psychiatry* 1986b;43:691–697.

Soloff PH, George A, Nathan RS, et al. Behavioral dyscontrol in borderline patients treated with amitriptyline. *Psychopharmacol Bull* 1987;23:177–181.

Soloff PH, Lis JA, Kelly T, et al. Risk factors for suicidal behavior in borderline personality disorder. *Am J Psychiatry* 1994a;151:1316–1323.

Soloff PH, Lis JA, Kelly T, et al. Self-mutilation and suicidal behavior in borderline personality disorder. *J Pers Disord* 1994b;8:257–267.

Somander LK, Rammer LM. Intra- and extra-familial child homicide in Sweden, 1971–1980. *Child Abuse Negl* 1991;15:45–55.

Sorenson SB. Suicide among the elderly: Issues facing public health. *Am J Public Health* 1991;81:1109–1110.

Southwick SM, Bremnor D, Krystal JH, Charney DS. Psychobiologic research in posttraumatic stress disorder. *Psychiatr Clin North Am* 1994;17:251–264.

Spiker DG, Hanin I, Cofsky JE, et al. Pharmacological treatment of delusional depressives. *Psychopharmacol Bull* 1981;17:201–202.

Spirito A, Williams CA, Stark LJ, Hart KJ. The hopelessness scale for children: Psychometric properties with normal and emotionally disturbed adolescents. *J Abnorm Child Psychol* 1988;16:445–458.

Spitzer RL, Endicott J. *Schedule for affective disorders and schizophrenia.* New York: Biometrics Research, Evaluation Section, New York State Psychiatric Institute 1978.

Stallone F, Dunner DL, Ahearn J, Fieve RR. Statistical predictions of suicide in depressives. *Compr Psychiatry* 1980;21:381–387.

Stanley M. Cholinergic receptor binding in the frontal cortex of suicide victims. *Am J Psychiatry* 1984;141:1432–1436.

Stanley M, Mann JJ. Increased serotonin-2 binding sites in frontal cortex of suicide victims. *Lancet* 1983;1:214–216.

Stanley M, Stanley B. Biochemical studies in suicide victims: Current findings and future implications. *Suicide Life-Threat Behav* 1989;19:30–42.

Stanley M, Stanley B. Postmortem evidence for serotonin's role in suicide. *J Clin Psychiatry* 1990;51(suppl):22–30.

Stanley M, Virgilio J, Gershon S. Tritiated imipramine binding sites are decreased in the frontal cortex of suicides. *Science* 1982;216:1337–1339.

Stawar TL. Suicidal and homicidal risk for respondents, petitioners, and family members in an injunction program for domestic violence. *Psychol Rep* 1996;79: 553–554.

Steffens DC, Hays JC, George LK, et al. Sociodemographic and clinical correlates of number of previous depressive episodes in the depressed elderly. *J Affective Disord* 1996;39:99–106.

Stenager E, Stenager E. Suicide and patients with neurologic diseases. *Arch Neurol* 1992;49:1296–1303.

Stengel E. *Suicide and attempted suicide.* New York: Penguin 1964.

Stenstedt A. A study in manic-depressive psychosis. *Acta Psychiatr Neurol Scand* 1952;79(suppl):1–111.

Stevenson RL. *The lantern-bearers.* New York: Farrar Strauss Giroux 1988.

Stockmeier CA, Dilley GE, Shapiro LA, et al. Serotonin receptors in suicide victims with major depression. *Neuropsychopharmacology* 1997;16:162–173.

Stockmeier CA, Meltzer HY. b-Adrenergic receptor binding in frontal cortex of suicide victims. *Biol Psychiatry* 1991;29:183–191.

Stoff DM, Mann JJ. Suicide research. In DM Stoff, JJ Mann (eds), *The neurobiology of suicide: From the bench to the clinic.* New York: New York Academy of Sciences 1997:1–11.

Stone MH. The course of borderline personality disorder. In A Tasman, RE Hales, A Frances (eds), *American Psychiatric Press review of psychiatry.* Washington DC: American Psychiatric Press 1987:103–122.

Stone MH. Long-term follow-up of narcissistic/borderline patients. *Psychiatr Clin North Am* 1989;12:621–641.

Stone MH. Suicide and suicidal behavior. In *The fate of borderline patients: Successful outcome and psychiatric practice.* New York: Guilford Press 1990.

Stone MH. Paradoxes in the management of suicidality in borderline patients. *Am J Psychotherapy* 1993a;47:255–272.

Stone MH. Suicide and the borderline patient. *Psychiatric Times* Jul 1993b:26.

Stone MH, Hunt S, Stone D. The PI 500 long-term follow-up of borderline inpatients meeting DSM-III criteria: I. Global outcome. *J Pers Disord* 1987;1:291–298.

Stone MH, Stone D, Hurst S. Natural history of borderline patients treated by intensive hospitalization. *Psychiatr Clin North Am* 1987;10:185–206.

Storm HH, Christiensen N, Jemsen OM. Suicides among Danish patients with cancer, 1971 to 1986. *Cancer* 1992;69:1507–1512.

Styron W. Depression. HBO documentary. Aired Jan. 5, 1998.

Suicide among older persons: United States, 1980–1992. *MMWR* 1996;45:3–6.

Summit R. The child sexual abuse accommodation syndrome. *Child Abuse Negl* 1983; 7:177–193.

Suokas J, Lönnqvist JK. Suicide attempts in which alcohol is involved: A special group in general hospital emergency rooms. *Acta Psychiatr Scand* 1995;91:36–40.

Suominen K, Henriksson MM, Suokas J, et al. Mental disorders and comorbidity in attempted suicide. *Acta Psychiatr Scand* 1996;94:234–240.

Suppes T, Baldessarini RJ, Faedda GL, Tohen M. Risk of recurrence following discontinuation of lithium treatment in bipolar disorder. *Arch Gen Psychiatry* 1991;48: 1082–1088.

Suppes T, Baldessarini RJ, Faedda GL, et al. Discontinuing maintenance treatment in bipolar manic-depression: Risks and implications. *Harvard Rev Psychiatry* 1993; 1:131–144.

Surgenor SD, Travis KS, Ravaris CL. Slow awakening after electroconvulsive therapy due to unrecognized attempted suicide. *Anesth Analg* 1996;82:1105–1106.

Swann A. Mixed or dysphoric manic states: Psychopathology and treatment. *J Clin Psychiatry* 1995;56:6–10.

Swanson L, Biaggo MK. Therapeutic perspectives on father-daughter incest. *Am J Psychiatry* 1985;142:667–674.

Sweeney S, Zamecnik K. Predictors of self-mutilation with schizophrenia. *Am J Psychiatry* 1981;138:1086–1089.

Szanto K, Prigerson H, Houck P, et al. Suicidal ideation in elderly bereaved: The role of complicated grief. *Suicide Life-Threat Behav* 1997;27:194–207.

Tanney BL. Electroconvulsive therapy and suicide. *Suicide Life-Threat Behav* 1986;16: 198–221.

Tanney BL. Mental disorders, psychiatric patients, and suicide. In RW Maris, AL Berman, JT Maltsberger, RY Yufit (eds), *Assessment and prediction of suicide.* New York: Guilford Press 1992:277–320.

Tantam D, Whittaker J. Personality disorder and self-wounding. *Br J Psychiatry* 1992; 161:451–464.

Tarasoff v *Regents of the University of California.* 17 Cal 3d 425, 131 Cal Rptr 14, 551 P2d 334 (1976).

Tardiff K. The current state of psychiatry in the treatment of violent patients. *Arch Gen Psychiatry* 1992;49:493–499.

Tardiff K. *Assessment and management of violent patients,* 2d ed. Washington DC: American Psychiatric Press 1996.

Targum SD. Differential responses to anxiogenic challenge studies in patients with major depressive disorder and panic disorder. *Biol Psychiatry* 1990;28:21–34.

Tarrance Group. *A survey of voter attitudes in the United States.* Houston: Tarrance Group 1994.

Taschev T. The course and prognosis of depression on the basis of 652 patients deceased. In J Angst (ed), *Classification and prediction of outcome of depression.* Stuttgart: Schattauer 1973:157–172.

Taschev T, Roglev M. Das Schicksal der Melancholiker im fortgeschrittenen Alter. *Arch Psychiatr Nervenkr* 1973;217:377–386.

Taube CA, Barrett SA (eds). *Mental health: United States.* NIMH Publication No AOM-85–1378. Bethesda MD: National Institutes of Mental Health 1985.

Tausk V. On the origins of the "influencing machine" in schizophrenia. *Psychoanal Q* 1933;2:519–530.

Taylor M, Ryan H. Fanaticism, political suicide, and terrorism. *Terrorism* 1988;11:91–111.

Teicher MH, Glod C, Cole JO. Emergence of intense suicidal preoccupation during fluoxetine treatment. *Am J Psychiatry* 1990;147:207–210.

Teicher MH, Glod CA, Cole JO. Antidepressant drugs and the emergence of suicidal tendencies. *Drug Safety* 1993;3:186–212.

Temoche A, Pugh T, MacMahon B. Suicide rates among current and former mental institution patients. *J Nerv Ment Dis* 1964;138:124–130.

Teoh JI. The changing psychopathology of amok. *Psychiatry* 1972;35:345–351.

Thies-Flechtner K, Müller-Oerlinghausen B, Seibert W, et al. Effect of prophylactic treatment on suicide risk in patients with major affective disorders. *Pharmacopsychiatry* 1996;29:103–107.

Thomas L. Dying as failure? *Am J Pol Sci* 1984;444:1.

Toch H. *Men in crisis.* Hawthorne NY: Aldine de Gruyter 1975.

Tollefson GD, Beasley CM Jr, Tran PV, et al. Olazepine vs haloperidol in the treatment of schizophrenia, schizoaffective, and schizophreniform disorders. *Am J Psychiatry* 1997;154:457–465.

Tollefson GD, Rampey AH, Beasley CM, et al. Absence of a relationship between adverse events and suicidality during pharmacotherapy for depression. *J Clin Psychopharmacol* 1994;14:163–169.

Tondo L, Baldessarini RJ, Floris G, et al. Lithium maintenance treatment reduces risk of suicidal behavior in bipolar disorder patients. In VS Gallicchio, NJ Birch (eds), *Lithium: Biochemical and clinical advances.* Cheshire CT: Weidner 1996:161–171.

Tondo L, Baldessarini RJ, Floris G, et al. Lithium treatment reduces risk of suicidal behavior in bipolar disorder patients. *J Clin Psychiatry* 1998a.

Tondo L, Baldessarini RJ, Hennen J, Floris G. Lithium maintenance treatment: Depression and mania in bipolar I and II disorders. *Am J Psychiatry* 1998b;155:638–645.

Tondo L, Jamison KR, Baldessarini RJ. Effect of lithium maintenance on suicidal behavior in major mood disorders. *AM NY Acad Sci* 1997;836:339–357.

Toynbee A. *Man's concern with death.* New York: McGraw-Hill 1969.

Träskman L, Åsberg M, Bertilsson L, Sjöstrand L. Monoamine metabolites in CSF and suicidal behavior. *Arch Gen Psychiatry* 1981;38:631–636.

Tsuang MT. Genetic factors in suicide. *Dis Nerv Sys* 1977;38:498–501.

Tsuang MT. Suicide in schizophrenics, maniacs, depressives, and surgical controls: A comparison with general population suicide mortality. *Arch Gen Psychiatry* 1978;35:153–155.

Tsuang MT. Risk of suicide in the relatives of schizophrenics, maniacs, depressives, and controls. *J Clin Psychiatry* 1983;44:396–400.

Tsuang MT, Simpson JC, Fleming JA. Epidemiology of suicide. *Int Rev Psychiatry* 1992;4:117–129.

Tsuang MT, Woolson RF, Fleming JA. Causes of death in schizophrenia and manic-depression. *Br J Psychiatry* 1980a;136:239–242.

Tsuang MT, Woolson RF, Fleming JA. Premature deaths in schizophrenia and affective disorders: An analysis of survival curves and variables affecting shortened survival. *Arch Gen Psychiatry* 1980b;37:979–983.

Tuckman J, Youngman WFA. A scale for assessing suicidal risk of attempted suicide. *J Clin Psychology* 1968;24:17–19.

Twiname G. No-suicide contract for nurses. *J Psychosoc Nurs Ment Health Services* 1981;19:11–12.

Twycross R. A view from the hospice. In L Keown (ed), *Euthanasia examined.* Cambridge: Cambridge University Press 1995.

Ulman RB. *Brothers D: The shattered self.* Hillsdale NJ: Analytic Press 1988.

Upadhyaya AK, Pennell I, Cowen PJ, Deakin JFW. Blunted growth hormone and prolactin responses to L-tryptophan in depression: A state-dependent abnormality. *J Affective Disord* 1991;21:213–218.

U.S. Department of Health and Human Services. *Healthy people 2000: National health promotion and disease prevention objectives.* DHHS Publication No (PHS) 91–50212. Washington DC: U.S. Government Printing Office 1990.

U.S. Department of Health and Human Services, Administration for Children and Families, National Center on Child Abuse and Neglect. *The third national incidence study of child abuse and neglect (1993).* Washington DC: U.S. Government Printing Office 1996.

Vaillant GE. *The natural history of alcoholism revisited.* Cambridge MA: Harvard University Press 1995.

van der Kolk BA, Dreyfuss D, Michaels M, et al. Fluoxetine in posttraumatic stress disorder. *J Clin Psychiatry* 1994;55:517–522.

van der Kolk BA, Perry JC, Herman JL. Childhood origins of self-destructive behavior. *Am J Psychiatry* 1991;148:1665–1671.

Van der Maas PJ, Van Delden JJM, Pijnenborg L. *Euthanasia and other medical decisions concerning the end of life.* New York: Elsevier 1992.

Van der Maas PJ, Van der Wal G, Haverkate I, et al. Euthansia, physician-assisted suicide, and other medical practices involving the end of life in the Netherlands, 1990–1995. *N Engl J Med* 1996;335:1699–1705.

Van der Wal G, Van der Maas PJ, Bosma JM, et al. Evaluation of the notification procedure for physician-assisted death in the Netherlands. *N Engl J Med* 1996;335: 1706–1711.

Van Heeringen C, Jannes S, Buylaert W, et al. The management of non-compliance with referral to outpatient aftercare among attempted suicide patients: A controlled intervention study. *Psychol Med* 1995;25:963–970.

van Praag HM. CSF 5-HIAA and suicide in nondepressed schizophrenics. *Lancet* 1983;2:977–978.

van Praag HM. Indoleamines in depression and suicide. *Prog Brain Res* 1986;65:59–71.

van Praag HM, Plutchik R. Increased suicidality in depression: Group or subgroup characteristic? *Psychiatry Res* 1988;26:273–277.

van Praag HM, Plutchik R, Apter A. *Violence and suicidality: Perspective in clinical and psychobiological research.* New York: Brunner/Mazel 1990.

Vassilas C, Morgan HG. General practitioners' contact with victims of suicide. *Br Med J* 1993;307:300–301.

Venkoba-Rao A, Hariharasubramanian N, Parvathi-Devi S, et al. Lithium prophylaxis in affective disorder. *Indian Psychiatry* 1983;23:22–30.

Vestergaard P, Aagaard J. Five-year mortality in lithium-treated manic-depressive patients. *J Affective Disord* 1991;21:33–38.

Vestergaard P, Sorensen T, Hoppe E, et al. Biogenic amine metabolites in cerebrospinal fluid of patients with affective disorders. *Acta Psychiatr Scand* 1978;58:88–96.

Vieland V, Whittle B, Garland A, et al. The impact of curriculum-based suicide prevention programs for teenagers: An 18-month follow-up. *J Am Acad Child Adolesc Psychiatry* 1991;30:811–815.

Viguera AC, Baldessarini RJ, Friedberg J. Discontinuing antidepressant treatment in major depression. *Harvard Rev Psychiatry* 1998;5:293–306.

Viguera AC, Baldessarini RJ, Hegarty JM, et al. Risk of discontinuing maintenance medication in schizophrenia. *Arch Gen Psychiatry* 1997;54:49–55.

Vinoda KS. Personality characteristics of attempted suicides. *Br J Psychiatry* 1966;112:1143–1150.

Virkkunen M. Suicides in schizophrenia and paranoid psychoses. *Acta Psychiatr Scand* 1974;250;1–305.

Virkkunen M. Attitude to psychiatric treatment before suicide in schizophrenia and paranoid psychosis. *Br J Psychiatry* 1976a;128:47–49.

Virkkunen M. Self-mutilation in antisocial personality disorder. *Acta Psychiatrica Scand* 1976b;54:347–352.

Virkkunen M, De Jong J, Bartko J, Linnoila M. Psychobiological concomitants of history of suicide attempts among violent offenders and impulsive fire setters. *Arch Gen Psychiatry* 1989a;46:604–606.

Virkkunen M, De Jong J, Bartko J, et al. Relationship of psychobiological variables to recidivism in violent offenders and impulsive fire setters: A follow-up study. *Arch Gen Psychiatry* 1989b;46:600–603.

Virkkunen M, Nuutila A, Goodwin FK, Linnoila M. Cerebrospinal fluid monoamine metabolite levels in male arsonists. *Arch Gen Psychiatry* 1987;44:241–247.

Wagg AS, Aylwin SJB. Catalytic converter and suicide risk. *Lancet* 1993;342(8882):1295.

Wagner AW, Linehan MM. Relationship between childhood sexual abuse and topography of parasuicide among women with borderline personality disorder. *J Pers Disord* 1994;8:1–9.

Wagner AW, Linehan MM. A biosocial perspective on the relationship of childhood sexual abuse, suicidal behavior, and borderline personality disorder. In MC Zanarini (ed), *Role of sexual abuse in the etiology of borderline personality disorder.* Progress in Psychiatry; no. 49. Washington DC: American Psychiatric Press 1997:203–223.

Wagner BM. Family risk factors for child and adolescent suicidal behavior. *Psychol Bull* 1997;121:246–298.

Wallace A. *Homicide: The social reality.* Sydney: New South Wales Bureau of Crime Statistics and Research 1986.

Walsh BW, Rosen P. *Self-mutilation: Theory, research, and treatment.* New York: Guilford Press 1988.

Wang TH, Katzev RD. Group commitment and resource conservation: Two field experiments on promoting recycling. *J Appl Psychol* 1990;20:265–275.

Warnes H. Suicide in schizophrenics *Dis Nerv Sys (Suppl)* 1968;29:35–40.

Wasserman D. Passive euthanasia in response to attempted suicide: One form of aggression by relatives. *Acta Psychiatr Scand* 1989;79:460–467.

Watts CAH. The incidence and prognosis of endogenous depression. *Br Med J* 1956;1:1392–1397.

Weeke AL. Causes of death in manic-depressives. In M Schou. E Strömgren (eds), *Origin, prevention, and treatment of affective disorders.* Orlando FL: Academic Press 1979:289–299.

Weeke A, Vaeth M. Excess mortality of bipolar and unipolar manic-depressive patients. *J Affective Disord* 1986;11:227–234.

Weil JG, Hawker JI. Positive findings of mammography may lead to suicide. *Br Med J* 1997;314:754–755.

Weishaar ME, Beck AT. Clinical and cognitive predictors of suicide. In RW Maris, AL Berman, JT Maltsberger, RY Yufit (eds), *Assessment and prediction of suicide.* New York: Guilford Press 1992:467–573.

Weisman AD, Worden JW. Risk rescue rating in suicide assessment. *Arch Gen Psychiatry* 1972;26:553–560.

Weiss RD, Griffin ML, Mirin SM. Drug abuse as self-medication for depression: An empirical study. *Am J Drug Alcohol Abuse* 1992;18:121–129.

Weiss RD, Mirin SM, Griffin ML, Michael JL. Psychopathology in cocaine abusers: Changing trends. *J Nerv Ment Dis* 1988;176:719–725.

Weiss RD, Mirin SM, Michael JL, Sollogub AC. Psychopathology in chronic cocaine abusers. *Am J Drug Alcohol Abuse* 1986;12:17–29.

Weiss RD, Najavits LM. Overview of treatment modalities for dual diagnosis patients: Pharmacotherapy, psychotherapy, and 12-step programs. In HR Kranzler, BJ Rounsaville (eds), *Dual diagnosis and treatment: Substance abuse and comorbid medical and psychiatric disorders.* New York: Dekker 1998:87–105.

Weiss RD, Najavits LM, Mirin SM. Substance abuse and psychiatric disorders. In RJ Frances, SI Miller (eds), *Clinical textbook of addictive disorders,* 2d ed. New York: Guilford Press 1998.

Weissman MM. The epidemiology of suicide attempts, 1960 to 1971. *Arch Gen Psychiatry* 1974;30:737–746.

Weissman MM, Fox K, Klerman GL. Hostility and depression associated with suicide attempts. *Am J Psychiatry* 1973;130:450–455.

Weissman MM, Klerman GL, Johnson J. Panic disorder and suicidal ideation. *Am J Psychiatry* 1992;149:1411–1412.

Weissman MM, Klerman GL, Markowitz JS, et al. Suicidal ideation and suicide attempts in panic disorder and attacks. *N Engl J Med* 1989;321:1209–1214.

Weizman A, Mark M, Gil-Ad I, et al. Plasma cortisol, prolactin, growth hormone, and immunoreactive beta-endorphin response to fenfluramine challenge in depressed patients. *Clin Neuropharmacol* 1988;11:250–256.

Welch SL, Fairburn CG. Histories of childhood trauma in bulimia nervosa: Three integrated case controls. *Am J Psychiatry* 1994;151:402–407.

Wender PH et al. Psychiatric disorders in the biological and adoptive families of adopted individuals with affective disorders. *Arch Gen Psychiatry* 1986;43:923–929.

West DJ. *Murder followed by suicide.* Cambridge MA: Harvard University Press 1967.

Westen D, Ludolph P, Misle B, et al. Physical and sexual abuse in adolescent girls with borderline personality disorder. *Am J Orthopsychiatry* 1990;60:55–66.

Westenberg HG, Verhoeven WM. CSF monoamine metabolites in patients and controls: Support for a bimodal distribution in major affective disorders. *Acta Psychiatr Scand* 1988;78:541–549.

Westermeyer JF, Harrow M, Marengo JT. Risk of suicide in schizophrenia and other psychotic and nonpsychotic disorders. *J Nerv Ment Dis* 1991;175:259–266.

Whitters AC, Cadoret RJ, Widmer RB. Factors associated with suicide attempts in alcohol abusers. *J Affective Disord* 1985;9:19–23.

Wickham EA, Reed FV. Lithium for the control of aggressive and self-mutilating behavior. *Int Clin Psychopharmacol* 1977;2:181–190.

Widdowson PS, Ordway GA, Halaris AE. Reduced neuropeptide Y concentrations in suicide brain. *J Neurochem* 1992;59:73–80.

Wilbanks W. The female homicide offender in Dade County, Florida. *Crim Justice Rev* 1983;8:9.

Wilkey I, Pearn J, Petric G, Nixon J. Neonaticide, infanticide, and child homicide. *Med Sci Law* 1982;22:31–34.

Williams JMG. Autobiographical memory and emotional disorders. In SA Christianson (ed), *Handbook of emotion and memory.* Hillsdale NJ: Erlbaum 1992:451–477.

Wilson WA. Oedipism. *Am J Ophthalmol* 1955;40:563–567.

Winchel RM. Trichotillomania: Presentation and treatment. *Psychiatric Ann* 1992;22: 84–89.

Winchel RM, Stanley M. Self-injurious behavior: A review of the behavior and biology of self-mutilation. *Am J Psychiatry* 1991;148:306–317.

Winnicott D. Hate in the countertransference? *Int J Psychoanal* 1949;30:69–74.

Winnicott D. Transitional objects and transitional phenomena. *Int J Psychoanal* 1953; 34:89–97.

Winokur G, Clayton PJ, Reich T. *Manic-depressive illness.* St. Louis: Mosby 1969.

Winokur G, Tsuang MT. The Iowa 500: Suicide in mania, depression, and schizophrenia. *Am J Psychiatry* 1975;132:650–651.

Wirshing C, Van Putten T, Rosenberg J, et al. Fluoxetine, akathisia, and suicidality: Is there a causal connection? (letter). *Arch Gen Psychiatry* 1992;49:581–582.

Wise ML. Adult self-injury as a survival response in victim-survivors of childhood abuse. *J Chem Depend Treat* 1989;3:185–201.

Wolf ME, Alavi A, Mosnaim AD. Posttraumatic stress disorder in Vietnam veterans: Clinical and EEG findings. *Biol Psychiatry* 1988;23:642–644.

Wolfgang ME. An analysis of homicide-suicide. *Clin Exp Psychopathol* 1958a;19: 208–218.

Wolfgang ME. *Patterns in criminal homicide.* Oxford: Oxford University Press 1958b.

Working Groups, Workshop on Suicide and Sexual Orientation. Recommendations for a research agenda on suicide and sexual orientation. *Suicide Life-Threat Behav (Suppl)* 1995;25:82–88.

World Health Organization. *Manual of the international statistical classification of diseases, injuries, and causes of death, based on recommendations of the Ninth Revision Conference, 1975.* Geneva: World Health Organization 1977.

Wright JH, Thace ME, Beck AT, Ludgate JW (eds), *Cognitive therapy with inpatients.* New York: Guilford Press 1993:91–120.

Wyatt RJ, Henter I. An economic evaluation of manic-depressive illness. *Soc Psychiatry Psychiatr Epidemiol* 1995;30:213–219.

Yalom ID. *Existential psychotherapy.* New York: Basic Books 1980.

Yap PM. Mental diseases peculiar to certain cultures: A survey of comparative psychiatry. *J Ment Sci* 1951;97:313–327.

Yarden PE. Observations on suicide in chronic schizophrenics. *Compr Psychiatry* 1974;15:325–333.

Yates M, Leake A, Candy JM, et al. 5-HT$_2$ receptor changes in major depression. *Biol Psychiatry* 1990;27:489–496.

Yeomans F, Hull J, Clarkin J. Risk factors for self-damaging acts in a borderline population. *J Pers Disord* 1994;8:10–16.

Young MA, Fogg LF, Scheftner WA, Fawcett JA. Interactions of risk factors in predicting suicide. *Am J Psychiatry* 1994;151:434–435.

Young MA, Fogg LF, Scheftner WA, et al. Stable trait components of hopelessness: Baseline and sensitivity to depression. *J Abnorm Psychol* 1996;105:155–165.

Younger SC, Clark DC, Oemig-Lindroth R, Stein RJ. Availability of knowledgeable informants for a psychological autopsy study of suicides committed by elderly people. *J Am Geriatr Soc* 1990;38:1169–1175.

Yuen N, Andrade N, Nahulu L, et al. The rate and characteristics of suicide attempters in the native Hawaiian adolescent population. *Suicide Life-Threat Behav* 1996;26:27–36.

Zanarini MC, Gunderson JG, Marino MF. Childhood experiences of borderline patients. *Comp Psychiatry* 1987;30:18–25.

Zetzel E. Depression and the incapacity to bear it. In M Schur (ed), *Drives, affects, and behavior,* vol. 2. Madison CT: International Universities Press 1965:243–274.

Ziegler LH, Heersema PH. A follow-up of one hundred and eleven nonhospitalized depressed patients after fourteen years. *Am J Psychiatry* 1942;99:813–817.

Zimmerman M, Coryell W, Stangl D, Pfohl B. An American validation of the Newcastle scale: III. Course during index hospitalization and six-month prospective follow-up. *Acta Psychiatr Scand* 1986;73:412–415.

Ziskind E, Somerfeld-Ziskind E, Ziskind L. Metrazol and electric convulsive therapy of the affective psychoses: A controlled series of observations covering a period of five years. *Arch Neurol Psychiatry* 1945;53:212–217.

Zisook S, Byrd D, Kuck J, Jeste DV. Command hallucinations in outpatients with schizophrenia. *J Clin Psychiatry* 1995;56:462–465.

Zisook S, Goff A, Sledge P, Schuchter S. Reported suicidal behavior and current suicidal ideation in a psychiatric outpatient clinic. *Ann Clin Psychiatry* 1994;6:27–31.

Zornberg GL, Pope HG Jr. Treatment of depression in bipolar disorder: New directions for research. *J Clin Psychopharmacol* 1993;13:397–408.

Zweig RA, Hinrichsen GA. Factors associated with suicide attempts by depressed older adults: A perspective study. *Am J Psychiatry* 1993;2:150:1687.

ABOUT THE AUTHORS

Douglas G. Jacobs, M.D., is a nationally recognized expert on suicide and depression. He has authored numerous papers on depression, depression screening, and suicide and helps train psychiatric residents in the identification and management of suicidal patients. He is an associate clinical professor at Harvard Medical School and the founder and executive director of the nonprofit National Mental Illness Screening Project (NMISP), which is the parent organization for National Depression Screening Day and several other national mental health screening programs. Most recently, he established NMISP's Suicide Education and Research Division in order to educate academic and clinical professionals about suicide and related issues. Dr. Jacobs has had a continued interest in professional psychiatric education; he founded the Harvard Medical School Suicide Symposia, which he directed seven years in a row. Dr. Jacobs maintains an active clinical private practice and is regularly asked to serve as a consultant in medical-legal matters. He has testified before Congress, serving as a consultant to the House Armed Services Committee. He received his undergraduate degree from Trinity College in 1967, received his medical degree from the University of Pennsylvania, School of Medicine, in 1971, and did his postdoctoral training at Harvard Medical School. He has two daughters and lives with his wife, Mary, in Waban, Massachusetts.

Victoria Arango, Ph.D., was born in Colombia, South America. She received her Ph.D. in neuroscience in 1982 from the Department of Anatomy and Cell Biology at the State University of New York, Downstate Medical Center. In 1985, Dr. Arango joined the Departments of Neurology and Psychiatry at Cornell University Medical College, where she pioneered anatomical and receptor-binding studies in the brains of suicide victims. From 1969 to 1994, Dr. Arango continued her research at Western Psychiatric Institute and Clinic, University of Pittsburgh. In 1994 she moved to the Department of Psychiatry (New York State Psychiatric Institute) at Columbia University as an associate professor, where she codirects the Division of Neuropathology in the Department of Neuroscience. Dr. Arango's research focuses on examining brain receptor changes in adolescent and adult suicide victims and the effect of alcohol dependence on these receptor systems. Her biochemical studies are complemented by molecular biology and neuro-anatomical morphometric studies. Dr. Arango has published extensively in respected national and international journals.

Ross J. Baldessarini, M.D., D.Sc. (hon.), an internationally known neuroscientist and research psychopharmacologist, has authored more than one thousand publications and is active in the education of basic and clinical researchers, as well as medical trainees and psychiatrists, in psychopharmacology and other biological areas of psychiatry. He is a professor of psychiatry (neuroscience) at Harvard Medical School; a senior consulting psychiatrist at Massachusetts General and McLean Hospitals; and the director of the Laboratories for Psychiatric Research, the Bipolar and Psychotic Disorders Program, and the Psychopharmacology Program at McLean Hospital. Dr. Baldessarini received his undergraduate degree in chemistry from Williams College in 1959, completed medical school at Johns Hopkins University in 1963, and trained at the National Institute of Mental Health (NIMH) from 1964 to 1966. He then returned to Johns Hopkins Hospital for training in psychiatry and was chief resident psychiatrist of the Henry Phipps Psychiatric Clinic. In 1969, Dr. Baldessarini moved to Massachusetts General Hospital, where he helped establish the Laboratories for Psychiatric Research, which he has directed since 1983. Dr. Baldessarini is a career investigator of NIMH. In 1995, he founded the International Consortium for Bipolar Disorder Research with colleagues from the United States, Canada, and Europe. He and his wife, Frances, have two children and live in Waban, Massachusetts.

William R. Beardslee, M.D., is the physician-in-chief and chairman of the Department of Psychiatry at Children's Hospital in Boston. He is also Gardner Monks Professor of Child Psychiatry at Harvard Medical School. He received his bachelor's degree from Haverford College and his medical degree from Case Western Reserve University. He trained in general psychiatry at Massachusetts General Hospital and in child psychiatry and psychiatric research at Children's Hospital in Boston. He has a long-standing research interest in the development of children who are at risk because of severe parental mental illness. He has been especially interested in the protective effects of self-understanding in enabling youngsters and adults to cope with adversity, and he has studied self-understanding in civil rights workers, survivors of cancer, and children of parents with affective disorders. He has received the Blanche F. Ittleson Award of the American Psychiatric Association for outstanding published research contributing to the mental health of children and has been a faculty scholar of the William T. Grant Foundation. Currently, he directs the preventive Intervention Project, an NIMH-funded study to explore the effects of a clinician-facilitated, family-based preventive intervention designed to enhance resilience and family understanding for children of parents with affective disorder. He is married and has four children.

Dan G. Blazer, M.D., Ph.D., is J.P. Gibbons Professor of Psychiatry and dean of medical education at Duke University School of Medicine. He is also professor of community and family medicine and adjunct professor of epidemiology at the School of Public Health, University of North Carolina, Chapel Hill. He is the author of more than two hundred peer-reviewed scientific articles and more than 140 book chapters and has authored or edited twenty-one books. His work has focused primarily on the epidemiology of psychiatric disorders, late-life depression, suicide in late life, and the health status of the elderly. He has led three large community-based studies at Duke, including the ECA study, the EPESEs study, and the MacArthur Field Studies of Successful Aging. Dr. Blazer has received numerous awards and honors, including presidency of the Psychiatric Research Society and the American Geriatrics Society, election to the Institute of Medicine of the National Academy of Sciences, the Jack Weinberg Award from the American Psychiatric Association, and the Milo Leavitt Award from the American Geriatrics Society.

Margaret Brewer, R.N., M.B.A., is a psychiatric nurse consultant who reviews and analyzes risk management and psychiatric malpractice issues. She specialized in clinical and administrative nursing at McLean Hospital for almost a decade and then attended the Simmons College Graduate School of Management. After completing her M.B.A. (1983), she returned to McLean in the quality assurance department where her position included utilization review, quality assurance, and risk management. Since 1990, she has worked with Dr. Douglas Jacobs reviewing psychiatric malpractice cases, researching medical literature, writing suicide assessments guidelines and protocols, and planning medical education seminars.

Pamela Cantor, Ph.D., is a lecturer in psychology in the Department of Psychiatry at the Cambridge Hospital, Harvard Medical School. Dr. Cantor was associate professor at Boston University, taught at the Radcliffe Institute of Harvard

University, was appointed by the governor of Massachusetts to the statewide advisory board for the Office for Children and the Massachusetts Committee for Children and Youth, and was a syndicated columnist for the *Los Angeles Times* for fifteen years. A Ph.D. graduate of Columbia University, she was a National Institute of Mental Health fellow in psychiatry at Johns Hopkins University Medical School and Phipps Psychiatric Clinic and a fellow in psychology at the Judge Baker Guidance Center and Children's Hospital Medical Center of Harvard University.

Dr. Cantor is considered one of the United States' leading authorities on teenage suicide. She has been a member of the Presidents Task Force on Youth Suicide Prevention, chair of the National Committee on Youth Suicide Prevention, and president of the American Association of Suicidology. In her effort to impart mental health knowledge to teenagers and the people who work with or parent them, she has appeared on hundreds of television and radio shows; she also wrote and narrated the award-winning documentary film *Young People in Crisis: How You Can Help.*

Dr. Cantor is in private practice in Needham, Massachusetts, where she specializes in treatment of youngsters with mood disorders, eating disorders, or other self-destructive behaviors. She lectures extensively, addressing academic, public service, professional, and business groups.

James A. Chu, M.D., is widely known for his clinical work, teaching, and research concerning the post-traumatic effects of childhood trauma. He is an assistant professor of psychiatry at Harvard Medical School, the clinical director of the Trauma and Dissociative Disorders Program, and the director of ambulatory services at McLean Hospital, where he has established innovative clinical programs for the treatment of adults with trauma-related disorders. As a teacher, Dr. Chu is known for his empathic and pragmatic approach to understanding and treating survivors of childhood abuse. His publications in the psychiatric literature include both basic research on the effects of childhood abuse and discussions of the nature and techniques of treating abuse survivors. Dr. Chu is a fellow of the American Psychiatric Association and a fellow and past president of the International Society for the Study of Dissociation. He received that organization's Cornelia B. Wilbur Award and Distinguished Achievement Awards for outstanding contributions in the field of dissociative disorders.

David C. Clark, Ph.D., is a clinical psychologist who received his Ph.D. in psychology from the University of Chicago. He is currently the Stanley G. Harris Family Professor of Psychiatry at Rush Medical College. There, he is also professor of psychology and preventive medicine, director of research for the Rush Institute of Mental Well-Being, and director of the Center for Suicide Research and Prevention. In 1989, he was awarded the AAS Shneidman Award for outstanding contributions in suicidology research. Dr. Clark's suicide research includes clinical profile studies, clinical trials, and psychological autopsy studies with young, middle-aged, and elderly suicidal persons. He is currently associate editor of the journal *Suicide and Life-Threatening Behavior* and senior editor of *Crisis,* the official journal of the International Association for Suicide Prevention. He has served as President of the American Association of Suicidology (1991–1992), is a member of the International Academy for Suicide Research, and is currently secretary-general of the International Association for Suicide Prevention.

Joseph T. Coyle, M.D., is the Eben S. Draper Professor of Psychiatry and Neuroscience and chairman of Harvard Medical School's Consolidated Department of Psychiatry, which includes the nine hospital programs of psychiatry affiliated with the medical school. After graduating from Holy Cross College, he received his medical degree from Johns Hopkins School of Medicine in 1969. Following an internship in pediatrics, he spent three years at the National Institutes of Health as a research fellow in the laboratory of Nobel Prize winner Julius Axelrod, Ph.D. He returned to Hopkins in 1973 to complete his residency in psychiatry, in which he is board certified, and joined the faculty. In 1980, he was promoted to professor of neuroscience and psychiatry. In 1982, he assumed the directorship of the Division of Child and Adolescent Psychiatry, being named the Distinguished Service Professor in 1985.

Dr. Coyle's research interests include developmental neurobiology, mechanisms of neuronal vulnerability, and psychopharmacology. He has published more than four hundred scientific articles. In recognition of his research contributions, he has received the John Jacob Abel Award from the American Society for Pharmacology and Experimental Therapeutics, the Gold Medal Award from the Society for Biological Psychiatry, the Foundation Fund Research Award from the American Psychiatric Association, the McAlpin Award from the National Mental Health Association, the Salmon Award from the New York Academy of Medicine, and the Pasarow Foundation Award for Neuroscience.

Dr. Coyle is a member of the Institute of Medicine of the National Academy of Sciences, a member of the American Academy of Arts and Sciences, a fellow of the American Psychiatric Association, and a fellow of the American College of Psychiatry. He served on the National Advisory Mental Health Council for NIMH and is a past president of the Society for Neuroscience.

Timothy Davis, M.D., received his undergraduate degree in biology from Harvard College in 1986 and graduated from Baylor College of Medicine in 1991. He performed his residency training in psychiatry at McLean Hospital, where he gained expertise in the treatment of personality disorders. Following completion of his residency in 1995, Dr. Davis remained at McLean Hospital. There, he helped to establish the Ambulatory Personality Disorder Clinic and served as psychiatrist-in-charge of the Women's Treatment Program, a partial-hospital program specializing in the treatment of trauma-related illnesses. He has written and spoken on the treatment of borderline personality disorder and has been active in instructing and supervising Harvard medical students and residents. Currently, Dr. Davis is in private practice in Westwood, Massachusetts, and is an attending psychiatrist at Westwood Lodge Hospital.

Robert A. Dorwart, M.D., M.P.H., is a psychiatrist, researcher, and clinical administrator in mental health care. He is professor of psychiatry and of social medicine at Harvard Medical School, as well as a professor at the Harvard School of Public Health and at the John F. Kennedy School of Government. He graduated from the Tulane University School of Medicine and received his master's degree in health policy and management from the Harvard School of Public Health, where he was a Kellogg Foundation Fellow. He is currently chairman of the Mental Health Policy Research group at Harvard University and the John F. Kennedy School of Government and chairman and chief of the Department of Psychiatry at the Cambridge Hospital.

Dr. Dorwart has directed several studies of the organizing and financing of mental health care, including an NIMH-funded national survey of psychiatric hospitals, community mental health centers, substance abuse programs, and psychiatrists. He currently serves as a consultant to several national advisory and professional committees and organizations, including the APA, SAMHSA, and NIMH. Dr. Dorwart served on the Service Systems Research Panel of the NIMH National Plan for Research to Improve the Care of the Severely Mentally Ill. He also holds a Research Scientist Award by NIMH to study the economics of mental health provider behavior and the impact of health care reform.

In journals such as the *New England Journal of Medicine* and the *American Journal of Psychiatry,* he has published more than seventy scientific works, including original articles, chapters, reviews, and books on issues in public health and the economics of mental health care. His most recent book is *Privatization of Mental Health Care: A Fragile Balance.*

Armando R. Favazza, M.D., M.P.H., received his undergraduate degree from Columbia University in 1962, his medical degree from the University of Virginia in 1966, and his master's in public health in community psychiatry from the University of Michigan, where he also completed his psychiatric residency in 1971. In 1973, he joined the faculty of the University of Missouri-Columbia, where he is a professor in the Department of Psychiatry and Neurology. He is cofounder of the Society for the Study of Psychiatry and Culture and has written many books, chapters, and articles about cultural psychiatry. He has been researching self-mutilation since the early 1980s, and his *Bodies Under Siege* (first edition, 1987), which is the only book on self-mutilation written by a psychiatrist, complements his numerous publications on the topic. He is an editorial referee for ten journals and is a past president of the Missouri State Psychiatric Association. He and his wife, Dr. Christine Favazza, reside in Columbia, Missouri.

Jan Fawcett, M.D., is chairman of the Department of Psychiatry and the Stanley G. Harris, Sr., Professor of Psychiatry at Rush-Presbyterian–St. Luke's Medical Center. He is also the Grainger Director of the Rush Institute for Mental Well-Being. He serves as principal investigator of the NIMH Psychobiology of Depression Collaborative Study. A frequent contributor to scientific journals, Dr. Fawcett is the editor of *Psychiatric Annals* and past president of both the Psychiatric Research Society and the American Suicide Foundation. Following his graduation from Yale University School of Medicine, Dr. Fawcett received his psychiatric training at Langley Porter Neuropsychiatric Institute and the University of Rochester Medical Center. His research career began at the Clinical Center of NIMH, where he became involved in research concerning the biomedical aspects of depression and suicide. In 1966, he established the Depression Research Unit at the Illinois State Psychiatric Institute to study the pharmacology and biochemistry of depression, as well as the prediction and prevention of suicide. In 1989, Dr. Fawcett received the NDMDA's Dr. Jan Fawcett Humanitarian Award, named in his honor. He received the American Association of Suicidology's Dublin Research Award in 1991 and the American Suicide Foundation Research Award in 1993. He is currently pursuing studies in the areas of depression, suicide, and alcoholism.

Jerome A. Fleming, M.S., is principal associate in the Harvard Medical School Department of Psychiatry, Massachusetts Mental Health Center. He is also health statistician at the Brockton/West Roxbury VA Medical Center. He received his bachelor's degree in biophysics from Iowa State University and his master's degree in biostatistics/epidemiology from the University of Iowa College of Medicine. From 1975 to 1982, he was a research associate at the University of Iowa College of Medicine. In 1982, Mr. Fleming took a position as a research administrator at the Brown University School of Medicine, and since 1985 he has worked for the Harvard Department of Psychiatry, Harvard Medical School. Mr. Fleming has worked for more than twenty years as a researcher and administrator in mental health and has a number of scientific publications in the areas of epidemiology, psychiatry, and suicidality. In addition, he is responsible for helping to coordinate a number of NIMH-funded research projects concerning mental health, epidemiology, and genetics.

Ann E. Goebel-Fabbri, Ph.D., received her doctorate in clinical psychology from Boston University. She is currently working as a postdoctoral fellow at Beth Israel Deaconess Medical Center, Harvard Medical School, after completing an internship there. Dr. Goebel-Fabbri's research has focused on eating disorders, adolescent suicide, adolescent aggressive behavior, and the lifetime impact of family and community exposure to violence. Prior to her graduate training, Dr. Goebel-Fabbri was a research coordinator on a psychological autopsy study of adolescent suicides with Dr. David C. Clark at Rush-Presbyterian–St. Luke's Medical Center in Chicago.

Stuart Goldman, M.D., is the director of psychiatric education and codirector of the Mood Disorders Program at the Children's Hospital in Boston. He is an assistant professor of psychiatry at Harvard Medical School. Dr. Goldman received his undergraduate degree at the Massachusetts Institute of Technology in 1973 and completed medical school at Tufts University in 1997. He did his general and child psychiatric training at the New England Medical Center. After completing his training, he joined the staff at Children's Hospital in 1982. He was the director of diagnostic services in psychiatry from 1982 to 1997, when he and Dr. William Beardslee established the Mood Disorders Program. Dr. Goldman has directed child and adolescent training since 1986. He and his wife, Christine, have three daughters and live in West Newton, Massachusetts.

John G. Gunderson, M.D., is professor of psychiatry at Harvard Medical School and functions as the director of psychotherapy and the Outpatient Personality Disorder Service at McLean Hospital. He is internationally recognized for having conducted a controlled outcome study on psychoanalytic therapy for schizophrenic patients, but he is most associated with his seminal studies on the diagnosis, etiology, and treatment of borderline patients. He authored the most widely used book on borderline personality disorder and is currently writing an updated text on modern standards for its treatment. He is the principal investigator on projects studying the longitudinal course of and response to the psycho-educational family therapy of these patients.

Thomas G. Gutheil, M.D., is a graduate of Harvard College and Harvard Medical School and received his psychiatric training at the Massachusetts Mental Health Center, where he has been on staff for a third of a century. He is co-director of the Program in Psychiatry and the Law, Massachusetts Mental Health Center, and director of the Charles C. Gaughan Fellowship in Forensic and Correctional Psychiatry, Bridgewater State Hospital. Dr. Gutheil is also professor of psychiatry, Harvard Medical School; former visiting lecturer, Harvard Law School; and a fellow of the American Psychiatric Association. He is the first professor of psychiatry in the history of Harvard Medical School to be board certified in both general and forensic psychiatry. He has been author or coauthor of nearly two hundred articles, book chapters, and books and has shared in the three Manfred S. Guttmacher Awards for an outstanding contribution to the forensic psychiatric literature. He has received several teaching awards, including "Teacher of the Year" in 1995 from the *Psychiatric Times*, the Seymour Pollack Award for teaching forensic psychiatry from the American Academy of Psychiatry and the Law, and the Prix Phillippe Pinel for contributions to teaching and research in forensic psychiatry from the International Academy of Law and Mental Health. He was listed under forensic psychiatrists in the 1994 edition of *Best Doctors in America*. Dr. Gutheil lives and works in the Boston area, is married, and has four children.

Leston L. Havens, M.D., is professor of psychiatry at Harvard Medical School and codirector of education in the psychiatry department at the Cambridge Hospital. Dr. Havens received his undergraduate degree at Williams College in 1947, completed medical school at Cornell University in 1952, and did his residency and chief residency at Massachusetts Mental Health Center (MMHC) from 1954 to 1958. He started the psychopharmacology unit at MMHC, did research on catecholamines and ECT there, and was responsible for medical student teaching from 1964 to 1980. He has written six books and ninety papers. He was responsible for the residency program from 1987 to 1996 at the Cambridge Hospital, having been there since 1981. He has four children and lives in Cambridge, Massachusetts, with his wife, Susan Miller-Havens.

Herbert Hendin, M.D., medical director of the American Foundation for Suicide Prevention and professor of psychiatry at New York Medical College, is an internationally known authority on suicide. More than fifty of his professional articles and four of his books—*Suicide and Scandinavia, Black Suicide, Wounds of War*, and *Suicide in America*—have dealt with suicide.

He has won numerous prizes and awards for his work, including a special award from the American Scandinavian Foundation for his study of suicide in Scandinavian countries and the Louis I. Dublin Award of the American Association of Suicidology for "distinguished contributions to our understanding of suicide." Most recently, he received a Rockefeller Scholar in Residence Award for his studies of assisted suicide and euthanasia in this country and the Netherlands.

Dr. Hendin has published twenty articles on assisted suicide and euthanasia and a book, *Seduced by Death: Doctors, Patients, and Assisted Suicide*. His work was cited several times by the U.S. Supreme Court in its 1997 landmark decision on physician-assisted suicide.

Michael R. Hufford, Ph.D., received his undergraduate degree from Purdue University and completed his graduate training at the University of Pittsburgh. He completed his clinical psychology internship at the McLean Hospital, where he was a clinical fellow in the Department of Psychiatry at Harvard Medical School. Dr. Hufford is currently an assistant professor in the Department of Psychology at the University of Montana and has a clinical practice in Missoula, Montana.

His research interests include understanding the relapse process in addictive behaviors with an emphasis on real-time monitoring methodologies. He and his wife, Suzette, have one son and live in Lolo, Montana.

Gary Jacobson, M.D., is a graduate of the Yale University School of Medicine. He has been on the faculty of Harvard Medical School and on the staff of Massachusetts General Hospital since 1969, as well as on the faculty of Boston University School of Medicine since 1984. He is a diplomat of the American Board of Psychiatry and Neurology and has served as an examiner for that board. Dr. Jacobson founded the Westwood Pembroke Health System, a private psychiatric care system in Massachusetts, and currently serves as clinical director of two of its hospitals, Westwood Lodge and Pembroke Hospital. He has been a research associate at NIMH in Bethesda, Maryland, and a lieutenant commander in the U.S. Public Health Service. He has served as an elected member of the Health Planning Council for Greater Boston and as an elected representative to the National Assembly of the American Psychiatric Association. He is a fellow of that association and a past president of its district branch, the Massachusetts Psychiatric Society. He practices general psychiatry with specific interests in risk management, innovative program development, couple therapy, and conflict resolution. From 1989 to 1992, he was on the International Board of Advisors of Harvard's John F. Kennedy School of Government, Institute for Social and Economic Policy in the Middle East, and served as chair of its fellowship committee. He lives in Massachusetts with his wife, who is an attorney, and has three children.

Kay Redfield Jamison, Ph.D., is coauthor of the standard text on manic-depressive illness and author of *Touched with Fire: Manic-Depressive Illness and the Artistic Temperament* and *An Unquiet Mind: A Memoir of Moods and Madness.* The recipient of numerous national and international scientific awards, she also holds an honorary professorship in English studies at the University of St. Andrews in Scotland. Currently, Dr. Jamison is professor of psychiatry at the Johns Hopkins University School of Medicine.

Martin J. Kelly, M.D., an avid boatsman, lives in Newton or Westport, Massachusetts (depending on the season), with his tolerant wife Judy. They have two sons, Matthew, a fly-fishing charter captain, and Daniel, a college student. Dr. Kelly has been on staff at the Brigham and Women's Hospital (née Peter Bent Brigham Hospital) since 1970. He has served as the associate director of psychiatry from the early 1970s to 1989 and as acting director of psychiatry from 1989 to 1990. Throughout his career, Dr. Kelly has been very active in the education of medical students, nonpsychiatric physicians, psychiatric residents, colleagues, and fellows in psychosomatic medicine, consultation/liaison psychiatry and, more recently, forensic psychiatry. He has authored several chapters and articles in medical psychiatry, including a frequently cited 1976 article with

Dr. Peter Reich on suicide attempts in the medical setting. Dr. Kelly values his medical education at Tufts University and particularly his undergraduate experiences at Boston College. He is associate professor of psychiatry at Harvard Medical School.

Marci Klein-Benheim, Ph.D., received a master's degree in education at Harvard University in 1986. She received her doctorate in clinical psychology at the University of Michigan in 1993. She is currently a clinical psychologist in Fairfax, Virginia. Her interests include depression, suicide, homelessness, and social policy issues.

Marsha M. Linehan, Ph.D., is professor of psychology and of psychiatry and behavioral sciences at the University of Washington in Seattle. She is also director of the Behavioral Research and Therapy Clinics, which are federally funded research projects evaluating the efficacy of treatments for suicidal behavior, substance abuse, and borderline personality disorder. She received her Ph.D. in 1971 from Loyola University of Chicago. She then completed a clinical internship at the Suicide Prevention and Crisis Clinic in Buffalo, New York, and a postdoctoral fellowship in behavioral modification at the State University of New York, Stony Brook. She was on the faculty at the Catholic University, Washington, D.C., before going to the University of Washington. She has been on the board of directors of the Association for the Advancement of Behavior Therapy; has been on the editorial boards of several journals; and has published numerous articles on suicidal behaviors, drug abuse, behavior therapy, and behavioral assessment. She has written two books on the treatment of borderline personality disorder: *Cognitive-Behavioral Treatment for Borderline Personality Disorder* (1993) and *Skills Training Manual for Treating Borderline Personality Disorder* (1993). She can be contacted at the Department of Psychology, Box 351525, University of Washington, Seattle, WA 98195–1525.

John T. Maltsberger, M.D., graduated from Princeton University in 1955 and studied medicine at Harvard Medical School. His adult and child psychiatric training were both at the Massachusetts Mental Health Center, Boston, where he was a student of the late Elvin Semrad.
Since he graduated from the Boston Psychoanalytic Society and Institute, his career has been a clinical one. Over the years, he has been associated with a number of Harvard hospitals, including the Cambridge Hospital, Massachusetts General Hospital, and McLean Hospital. He has taught residents and medical students continuously since 1962.

He has long had a special interest in suicide, a topic about which he has written widely. He was instrumental in establishing the New England Division of the American Foundation for Suicide Prevention and is past president of the American Association of Suicidology.

J. John Mann, M.D., was born in Australia and trained there in psychiatry and internal medicine. He also obtained a doctorate in neurochemistry, which equipped him to research the chemical abnormalities of the brain that are responsible for major psychiatric disorders. In 1976, he immigrated to the United States, where he has become one of the country's leading experts in the biochemistry of depression and the biochemical factors that place people at risk for suicidal behavior. He heads the Department of Neuroscience at the New York State Psychiatric Institute and is professor of psychiatry at Columbia University. His research employs the latest techniques in functional brain imaging, neurochemistry, and molecular genetics to probe the causes of depression, suicide, and the mechanisms and actions of antidepressants.

Peter M. Marzuk, M.D., is currently associate professor of psychiatry at Cornell University Medical College, associate attending psychiatrist at the New York Hospital, and associate editor of the *Archives of General Psychiatry*. Dr. Marzuk received his undergraduate degree in chemistry from Brown University in 1978 and his medical degree from Columbia University in 1982. He was a resident in internal medicine at the Hospital of the University of Pennsylvania and completed his psychiatry training at the Payne Whitney Clinic of the New York Hospital–Cornell Medical College in 1987. He has served in many capacities in the department of psychiatry at Cornell, including director of the Psychopharmacology Clinic, associate unit chief of the Mood Disorders Service, and director of medical student education. Dr. Marzuk has studied suicide and violence for most of his career. He has been particularly interested in identifying risk factors for suicidal behavior; understanding the link between suicide, violence, and substance abuse; and researching the neurobiological underpinnings of self-destructiveness and violence.

Eran D. Metzger, M.D., is associate director of geropsychiatry at Hebrew Rehabilitation Center for Aged (HRCA) in Boston, as well as an instructor in psychiatry at Harvard Medical School. Dr. Metzger received a bachelor's degree from Haverford College and a medical degree from the Pennsylvania State University in 1987. He joined the medical staff of Beth Israel Hospital in Boston after completing his psychiatry residency there in 1991. He served as director of ECT Services at Beth Israel from 1991 to 1996 and was appointed medical director of inpatient psychiatry in 1996. He served as medical director until he joined HRCA in 1998. He and his wife, Patricia, live with their twins in Brookline, Massachusetts.

Michael Craig Miller, M.D., is the director of forensic psychiatry at Beth Israel Deaconess Medical Center in Boston and an assistant professor of clinical psychiatry at Harvard Medical School. He also is a teacher and supervisor of residents in the Harvard Longwood Psychiatry Residency Training Program.

Dr. Miller received his undergraduate and medical degrees from Tufts University and Tufts Medical School and did his medical internship, psychiatry residency, and chief residency at Beth Israel Hospital in Boston. At Beth Israel Hospital, he directed the Psychiatric Emergency Service for three years and the Inpatient Psychiatry Service for seven, becoming interested in the problems of suicide assessment and standards of care for managing suicide risk. Dr. Miller currently has a clinical and forensic practice at Beth Israel Deaconess Medical Center.

Eve K. Mościcki, Sc.D., M.P.H., is an epidemiologist and associate director for preventive intervention research in the Division of Services and Intervention Research at NIMH. She is the founding chair of the NIMH Suicide Research Consortium and former cochair of the NIMH Prevention Research Consortium. She has authored numerous publications and presentations on the epidemiology of suicide and suicidal behaviors, based on original research as well as data from the landmark NIMH Epidemiologic Catchment Area Program. Her epidemiologic work has been widely recognized. She has also made contributions in the health policy arena, including *Healthy People 2000* and the National Agenda for Injury Control. She is on the editorial boards of the *American Journal of Epidemiology* and *Suicide and Life-Threatening Behavior* and is listed in *Who's Who in Science and Engineering* and *American Men and Women of Science.*

Jerome A. Motto, M.D., is professor of psychiatry emeritus at the University of California, San Francisco, School of Medicine. He received his medical degree from that institution in 1951 and has served on its faculty in the Department of Psychiatry since 1956. He is a past president of the American Association of Suicidology and past secretary-general of the International Association for Suicide Prevention.

Michael J. Mufson, M.D., is assistant clinical professor of psychiatry at Harvard Medical School. He is director of psychiatry at the West-Roxbury VA Hospital and has been staff psychiatrist at the Brigham and Women's Hospital since 1983. Dr. Mufson is active in the education of Harvard medical students and is co-director of an integrated neuropsychiatry course for medical students. He is also actively involved in the education of psychiatric residents in the Harvard Longwood program, with a special interest in diagnostic teaching and psychopathology.

He received his undergraduate degree with honors from the City University of New York, completed medical school at Tufts University in 1976, and did his psychiatric residency at the Yale University School of Medicine from 1976 to 1980. He served as chief psychiatric resident at the Brigham and Women's Hospital in 1980 and then received a Dupont-Warren Fellowship at Harvard Medical School. His current clinical focus includes treating and evaluating patients with chronic pain, sleep disorders, and comorbid medical and psychiatric disorders.

Melissa Myers, M.D., attended medical school at Jefferson Medical College, then worked in psychiatric crisis intervention, substance abuse treatment, and treatment and case management with psychiatrically ill substance-abusing adults. She is now a third-year psychiatry resident at McLean Hospital, where she is affiliated with the Outpatient Personality Disorders Service and where she will be the outpatient chief resident. After training, she plans to continue her involvement in public mental health and work in community psychiatry.

Matthew K. Nock received his bachelor's degree in psychology from Boston University in 1995. Since that time, he has been working in the area of suicide, violence, and substance abuse in the Department of Psychiatry at Cornell University Medical College. He is also the research coordinator of the American Foundation for Suicide Prevention. Mr. Nock has coauthored numerous articles and has presented lectures on suicide and related topics. He is entering the doctoral program in clinical psychology at Yale University in fall 1998.

Michael J. Ostacher, M.D., M.P.H., is currently an associate chief in the Department of Psychiatry of the Cambridge Health Alliance and the Cambridge and Somerville Hospitals and is the acting director and medical director for addictions in the same department. An instructor in psychiatry at the Harvard Medical School, he received his medical degree from Vanderbilt University and a master's in public health from the Harvard School of Public Health, completing residency training in psychiatry at the Cambridge Hospital and Harvard Medical School. He is fellowship trained in public psychiatry and geriatric psychiatry and is active in residency and medical school education in addictions, geriatric psychiatry, and health care policy. He has written about health care policy and the financing of care for mental illness. He is married to Laurie Ketter and lives in Cambridge, Massachusetts.

Randall Howard Paulsen, M.D., is a general psychiatrist and psychoanalyst, as well as the director of primary care psychiatry in Healthcare Association (a large, multidisciplinary primary care teaching practice) at Beth Israel Deaconess Medical Center. He is a graduate of Yale College (1971), the University of Utah Medical School (1976), the Tufts New England Medical Center Residency in Adult Psychiatry (1980), and the Boston Psychoanalytic Institute (1987). He is an assistant professor of clinical psychiatry at Harvard Medical School and is on the faculty of the Boston Psychoanalytic Society and Institute. He lives with his wife, Sally Bowie, and their two sons, Dolph and Jesse, in Lexington, Massachusetts.

Malcolm P. Rogers, M.D., is a consultation-liaison psychiatrist with an active outpatient psychiatric practice. He is an associate professor of psychiatry at Harvard Medical School and an attending psychiatrist at the Brigham and Women's

Hospital. He has a special interest in psychiatric aspects of medical illness and has published widely in this area. Dr. Rogers received a bachelor's degree from Yale University in 1965, a BMS from Dartmouth Medical School in 1967, and a medical degree from Harvard University in 1969. He completed his residency in psychiatry at the Massachusetts Mental Health Center from 1970 to 1972 and the Peter Bent Brigham Hospital from 1972 to 1973. He and his wife, Susan, have two children and live in Cambridge, Massachusetts.

Carl Salzman, M.D., is a national and internationally known psychopharmacologist and psychiatric educator. He has written more than three hundred publications, including the seminal textbook *Clinical Geriatric Psychopharmacology,* which is now in its third edition. He is a professor of psychiatry at Harvard Medical School and is director of psychopharmacology as well as director of psychiatric education at the Massachusetts Mental Health Center. Dr. Salzman received his undergraduate degree from Union College in 1959, completed medical school at State University of New York Upstate Medical Center in 1963, and received his psychiatric training at the Massachusetts Mental Health Center from 1964 to 1967. Following two years at NIMH, he returned to the Massachusetts Mental Health Center, where he has remained on the faculty. Dr. Salzman has a particular interest in geriatric psychopharmacology, as well as the treatment of anxiety and depressive disorders. He chaired the APA Task Force on Benzodiazepines and wrote its report. He is known for his skills as a psychiatric educator and clinician and for his ability to synthesize the biological and psychologic factors associated with mental disorders. Dr. Salzman has won numerous awards for his teaching and research and serves on many editorial boards, including that of the *American Journal of Psychiatry.*

Edwin Shneidman, Ph.D., is professor of thanatology emeritus in the Department of Psychiatry and Biobehavioral Sciences at the University of California, Los Angeles (UCLA). Dr. Shneidman, who was born in 1918, received his bachelor's degree from UCLA in 1938 and his doctorate in 1948 at the University of Southern California. In the 1950s, he was cofounder of the Los Angeles Suicide Prevention Center, and in the 1960s he was chief of the Center for the Study of Suicide Prevention at NIMH. He has been visiting professor at Harvard and at the Ben Gurion University in Beersheva; research associate at the Karolinska Hospital in Stockholm; and fellow at the Center for the Advanced Study of the Behavioral Sciences at Palo Alto. In 1968, he founded the American Association of Suicidology. From 1970 to 1988, he was a professor at UCLA. He is the author of *Deaths of Man* (nominated for a National Book Award in science), *Voices of Death, Definition of Suicide, The Suicidal Mind,* and numerous chapters and articles. He has been married since 1944 and has four children and six grandchildren.

John C. Simpson, Ph.D., is instructor in the Harvard Medical School Department of Psychiatry, Brockton/West Roxbury VA Medical Center, where he is coordinator of Community Support Services. He received his undergraduate degree in psychology from Macalester College and completed graduate degrees in applied statistics (M.S.) and general experimental psychology (M.A., Ph.D.) at the University of Iowa. Following an NIMH fellowship in statistics and psychology, he was assistant research scientist at the University of Iowa College of Medicine and honorary research fellow at the University of Oxford Unit of Clinical Epidemiology from 1981 to 1982. In 1982, Dr. Simpson was named assistant professor (research) at Brown University, and in 1985, he assumed his current position at the Brockton/West Roxbury VA Medical Center. He is active in psychiatric epidemiology and in clinical research concerned with the treatment and outcome of schizophrenia and other chronic mental illnesses.

David C. Steffens, M.D., is an assistant professor of psychiatry and behavioral sciences at Duke University Medical Center. He is director of clinical services for the Geriatric Affective Disorders Program at Duke University and a consulting geriatric psychiatrist at Duke University's Neurological Disorders Clinic. Dr. Steffens is active in the education of medical students, psychiatrists, and geriatric fellows in affective disorders and geriatric psychiatry. He is the recipient of a Geriatric Clinical Mental Health Academic Award from NIMH. His research interests include the biological underpinnings of geriatric depression and cognitive function in late-life depression. Dr. Steffens graduated from Rice University in 1984 with degrees in biochemistry and Spanish, completed medical school at the University of Texas Health Science Center at Houston in 1988, and received training in psychiatry at Duke University Medical Center, where he served as executive chief resident in 1992. He worked as a full-time clinician in the Affective Disorders Program at Duke from 1992 to 1994, at which time he embarked on a research career in geriatric affective disorders. Dr. Steffens resides in Durham, North Carolina, with his wife, Lori, and their two daughters.

Steve Stelovich, M.D., is the associate medical director for mental health at Harvard Pilgrim Health Care, Massachusetts region. Dr. Stelovich trained at Harvard Medical School, the Massachusetts Mental Health Center, and the Cambridge Hospital. He has been active in medical student and residency teaching at Harvard Medical School and was a member of the planning committee for the Longwood Psychiatric Residency Program, in which he served as an associate training director for two years. Dr. Stelovich has established regular suicide review committees at Harvard Pilgrim Health Care and has developed programs for the early detection and treatment of depression in primary care settings.

Leonardo Tondo, M.D., completed his medical education at the University of Rome, graduating summa cum laude in 1974. He began training in psychiatry with Dr. Anthanasio Koukopoulos in 1974–1975 and has been involved in research on mood disorders since then. In 1977, he became the founding director of the Centro Lucio Bini in Cagliari, and in 1980, he received a permanent appointment as assistant professor at the University of Cagliari Institute of Psychiatry. In 1980, Dr. Tondo was a visiting scientist at the Psychohormonal Unit at Johns Hopkins Hospital with Dr. John Money. In 1983, Dr. Tondo was lecturer in neuropsychopharmacology at the University of Pennsylvania with Dr. Alan Frazer. In 1986, he was assistant researcher in psychobiology at the University of California at Los Angeles with Dr. Russell Poland. Since 1995, he has been research associate in the Department of Psychiatry at Harvard University and the McLean Division of Massachusetts General Hospital with Dr. Ross Baldessarini, with whom he organized the *International Consortium for Bipolar Disorder Research.*

Dr. Tondo is widely known for his research on the course of bipolar disorders. In collaboration with Dr. Baldessarini and other international colleagues, he has made important contributions to quantifying the effects of discontinuing maintenance treatment in bipolar disorders and on the protective effects of lithium treatment on suicidal behavior in such patients. This research has been supported by research awards from NARSAD (1995–1996) and grants from the Theodore and Vada Stanley Foundation (1996–1997). Dr. Tondo is the author of more than one hundred publications and is chief editor of the *Italian Journal of Addictions.* He is also vice president of the *Aretæus Association,* an international organization that encourages research on mood and anxiety disorders. He is also a consultant to the *Italian National Press* and contributes to newspaper and radio programs on mental health matters.

Ming T. Tsuang, M.D., Ph.D., D.Sc., is Stanley Cobb Professor of Psychiatry; director, Harvard Institute of Psychiatric Epidemiology and Genetics; and superintendent and head, Harvard Department of Psychiatry at Massachusetts Mental Health Center. He received his medical degree at the College of Medicine, National Taiwan University, and his doctorate at the Institute of Psychiatry, Faculty of Medicine, University of London. Throughout his career, he has worked as a clinician, teacher, researcher, and administrator in a variety of private, state, federal, and international mental health settings. Dr. Tsuang has received national and international recognition for his research in schizophrenia and other major psychiatric disorders, including manic-depressive illness and drug abuse. One of his interests is in the rapidly developing area concerning mental disorders and their interactions with genetic and environmental factors. He has also published papers on clinical and epidemiological factors as they relate to suicide. He currently has more than 350 publications. Dr. Tsuang has been named to the membership of the Institute of Medicine, National Academy of Sciences, and that of the Academia Sinica, Taiwan. Recently, he received the Lifetime Achievements Award from the International Society of Psychiatric Genetics.

Roger D. Weiss, M.D., is associate professor of psychiatry at Harvard Medical School and clinical director of the Alcohol and Drug Abuse Program, McLean Hospital, Belmont, Massachusetts. He has lectured and consulted nationally and internationally on the treatment of patients with alcohol and drug abuse problems. He has written more than 120 articles and book chapters on the subject.

NAME INDEX

SUBJECT INDEX

U.S. epidemiological trends, 271, 273
substance abuse
  acute intoxication, effects of, 302–303
  age as risk factor, 306
  antisocial personality disorder and, 304
  assessment, 307–308, 310
  in attempted/completed suicide, 46
  clinical management, 308–309, 310
  communication of suicidal ideation, 306
  depression and, 303–304, 305–306
  lethality of attempts in, 389
  lifestyle issues, 307–308
  in murder-suicide, 28, 200–202, 205
  paradoxical effects of alcohol, 227
  precipitants, 305
  psychiatric history, 306–307
  screening for in primary care settings, 527
  self-mutilation in, 135
  studies on rates of suicide, 301–302
substances implicated in depression, 535
"successful" suicide. See completed suicides
sufficient conditions. See potentiating factors
suicidal behaviors, categories of, 26, 317
suicidal drama, 83, 87
suicidal threshold, 13
suicidality
  acute versus chronic, 445, 572–574
  as criterion in borderline personality disorder, 311
  definition, 86
  detecting, 581
  fluctuations in, 400
  identifying, 385–386
suicide. See also attempted suicide; completed
  suicides
  categorizing, 89–90
  classification of types, 40–41
  clinical understanding of, 421–428
  goal of, 87
  justifiable, 540
  neurobiology of, 104
  as problem-solving behavior, 149
  purpose of, 85
  religious prohibitions on, 190
  "ten commonalities of," 318
  uniqueness of each event, 226–227
Suicide Assessment Protocols, 6, 244–246
suicide notes, 387–388
suicide pacts, 195, 393–394
"suicide perspective," 317–318
suicide precautions, 395–397, 498–512
suicide-prevention contracts. See safety contracts
suicide review. See completed suicides,
  reviewing

suicide-vulnerable persons, 81
suicide watch/sitters, 514
suicidology, 84–85, 85–86, 521–522
suisad, 243
superego, 73, 75, 76
superficial-to-moderate self-mutilation,
  132–138, 141
supervision strategy (in DBT), 153
support systems, 173–174, 208
surprise, 567
survivor issues, 439–440, 458, 565–568
symbolic significance, 128, 129
symptoms
  depression, 530
  improvement of, 257–258
  increase of in borderline personality disorder, 379
  schizophrenia, 292, 293, 299
systemic lupus erythematosus, 507
systems perspective, 151. See also dialectical
  behavior therapy (DBT)

T
tactile hallucinations, 132
Tarasoff v. Regents of California, 28. See also
  duty to warn; legal issues
tardive diskinesia, 352. See also involuntary
  movement disorders
Terman Study of the Gifted, 86
termination, 154, 346, 577
terminology. See nomenclature
terrorism, 199
test data, 93–94
Thematic Apperception Test (TAT), 93
therapeutic alliance. See also clinicians
  around safety issues, 339
  assessing the, 31–32, 391–392, 470
  in borderline personality disorder, 323–324
  breach of by patient, 346
  building of, inpatient, 398
  with children/adolescents, 436, 442
  importance of in DBT, 168
  inpatient level of precaution based on, 396
  lack of, 479
  of physicians in medical settings, 519
  safety contracts, 33, 238, 392, 456–457, 470,
    573–574
  with self-mutilators, 142
therapeutic contract, 465–466. See also safety
  contracts
therapeutic levels of antidepressants, 381
therapists. See clinicians
thoughts leading to self-mutilation, categories
  of, 142